PROGRAMMING MICROSOFT
VISUAL BASIC® .NET
FOR MICROSOFT
ACCESS DATABASES

Microsoft®
.net™

Rick Dobson

Microsoft®

PUBLISHED BY
Microsoft Press
A Division of Microsoft Corporation
One Microsoft Way
Redmond, Washington 98052-6399

Library of Congress Cataloging-in-Publication Data
Dobson, Rick, 1944-
    Programming Microsoft Visual Basic .NET for Microsoft Access Databases
       p. cm.
    Includes index.
    ISBN 0-7356-1819-4
    1. Microsoft Access.   2. Microsoft .NET.   3. Microsoft Visual BASIC.
    I. Title.

    QA76.73.B3 D635   2003
    005.2'768--dc21   2002038685

Printed and bound in the United States of America.

1 2 3 4 5 6 7 8 9   QWT   8 7 6 5 4 3

Distributed in Canada by H.B. Fenn and Company Ltd.

A CIP catalogue record for this book is available from the British Library.

Microsoft Press books are available through booksellers and distributors worldwide. For further information about international editions, contact your local Microsoft Corporation office or contact Microsoft Press International directly at fax (425) 936-7329. Visit our Web site at www.microsoft.com/mspress. Send comments to: *mspinput@microsoft.com*.

Acquisitions Editor: Anne Hamilton
Project Editor: Barbara Moreland
Technical Editor: Jean Ross

Body Part No. X08-92511

Table of Contents

Acknowledgments

Authors have the opportunity in their acknowledgment section to praise the kindness afforded them by the folks they believe made a book possible. It would be very difficult for me to give due recognition to all who helped on this particular book. So many persons did huge favors—both for this book and for earlier books leading to this one.

I am going to start by thanking the one person who is closest to me in the whole world—my wife, Mary Virginia Dobson. She vigorously encouraged me to write my first book for Microsoft Press back in 1998. In the years since then, she and I have grown professionally as well as personally closer to one another. She reviewed nearly every chapter in this book twice—once before submittal to Microsoft Press and a second time in the galley proof phase. It is my sincere hope that her proofing added to my efforts and combined with the editorial work by persons at Microsoft Press ensures a quality book that is clear and as error-free as humanly possible.

Next, I want to thank Microsoft Press. I have worked with three other book-publishing organizations as well as numerous computer magazines. Microsoft Press exhibits a degree of care for the author and the technical accuracy of content that exceeds any other organization with which I have prepared published material. I count it an honor to be a Microsoft Press author.

An organization, such as Microsoft Press, is composed of people who reflect that firm's culture. For this book, I have the privilege of mentioning Anne Hamilton, Barbara Moreland, Jean Ross, and Michelle Goodman as significant individuals with whom I interacted. There were others who contributed meaningfully to the book, such as the book indexer, the proof editor, and various marketing persons. I want to say thank you to each of these individuals for their excellent efforts.

The content of this book spans two divisions within Microsoft—the Visual Studio team and the Microsoft Office team. Therefore, I recruited representatives from each one. Sean Draine, from the Visual Studio team, constantly urged me to add content that reflected the new and innovative features of Visual Basic .NET. Paul Cornell encouraged me to add content and orient the book so that it served the needs of practicing Access developers. Both Paul and Sean acted as sounding boards for my own ideas both before the start of writing and into the actual authoring of the book. In spite of their heavy professional obligations at Microsoft, each of them took the time to make valuable contributions.

It is my tradition that with each new book I give thanks to my Lord and Savior, Jesus Christ. I believe that He ordered my steps to get to this point as an author. He is my Chief Technical Officer, and He is my authoring mentor. It is my prayer that you derive blessings from the wisdom that He shared with me.

Introduction

Anyone who buys a book—or considers buying it—wants to know who the book is for, what sets it apart from others like it, and how the book is organized. This introduction answers these three questions, as well as covering sample files, support, and systems requirements.

This is my second book on Microsoft .NET technology. The first was directed to programmers learning to use Microsoft SQL Server 2000 with Microsoft Visual Basic .NET. This second book also targets developers creating solutions using Visual Basic .NET. However, the books differ in several ways.

First, the focus here is almost entirely on Microsoft Access databases. This approach is unusual for .NET database books, which tend to emphasize SQL Server databases. Second, this book addresses a mix of topics that are especially relevant to Access developers, such as using the ADO.NET type libraries in .NET solutions. Third, I cover Visual Basic .NET and related .NET topics in much more depth than in my earlier book. I believe that if you are truly comfortable using either classic Visual Basic or Visual Basic for Applications (VBA) with Microsoft Access databases, you should feel right at home with the samples in this book. Furthermore, after working through the samples, you should be able to create any kind of solution that you care to with Visual Basic .NET and Access databases.

Who Should Read This Book

This book targets developers and computer fans who use Access databases and want to get a firm grasp of the Microsoft .NET Framework. These two defining elements (Access and the .NET Framework) define the book's scope and its treatment of topics. While other types of databases can be used to create solutions with .NET, this book deals almost exclusively with Access databases. The book demonstrates Visual Basic .NET programming techniques instead of addressing a broad range of languages compatible with the .NET Framework because developers creating solutions with Access and Microsoft Office are likely to have experience programming with VBA. Beyond that, many classic Visual Basic developers have substantial experience with Access databases even if they currently work primarily with another database type, such as SQL Server.

You don't need to be familiar with the .NET Framework to learn from this book. However, you will definitely benefit from a working knowledge of how to program solutions with either Visual Basic 6 or VBA in Access. The book uses this knowledge as a springboard for learning how to use Visual Basic .NET to program solutions for Access databases. While this book provides a firm foundation in how to create solutions for Windows applications running on LANs, you will also gain exposure to Web development techniques, including ASP.NET and Web services.

The book also contains instruction in ADO.NET. You can use your ADO.NET skills for crafting solutions operating in either Windows or Web environments. Developers with hard-earned ActiveX Data Objects (ADO) skills will be pleased to learn that they can still use familiar development techniques in the .NET Framework through the application of the COM Interop feature to the ADO type libraries.

> **Note** You can acquire a background suitable for this book from one of my previous books, *Programming Microsoft Access Version 2002* (Microsoft Press, 2001). This earlier book includes numerous code samples illustrating the application of VBA to the creation of solutions with Access databases.

Another audience for this book includes .NET developers who want to enhance their ability to create solutions specifically for Access databases. This community of developers consists of those who have not found the specific information they need in other, more general Visual Basic .NET or ADO.NET books. All the database samples in this book (except one) are for Access databases. Therefore, you are likely to encounter a wide variety of techniques that you will find applicable to creating solutions for Access databases. In particular, the book systematically reviews the use of several OLE DB data provider classes with Access databases. The samples reinforce your general understanding of Windows and Web forms as they illustrate how to leverage that knowledge for performing data access, data manipulation, and even data definition tasks.

Organization of the Book

This book presents practical development techniques, and, therefore, most chapters are rich in code samples. My experience with conducting seminars tells me that developers like to see things work. While I cannot actually run the samples for you, the book includes a rich collection of code samples that demonstrate how to perform typical database tasks as they highlight selected features and Visual Basic .NET capabilities. The book's initial chapter and portions of other chapters set a context for the code samples by discussing conceptual issues.

The book's first and last chapters each treat a distinct topic—namely, an overview of the .NET Framework in the first chapter and a review of security techniques in the last. In between, the book has four groups of chapters that treat major topics from multiple perspectives: Visual Basic .NET, Windows Forms, ADO.NET, and Web development. The book's appendix examines techniques and uses for XML when creating .NET solutions for Access databases.

Overview of the .NET Framework

Chapter 1 presents an introduction to the .NET Framework that is customized to address the specific concerns of Access developers. The overall goal of the book is to equip developers to create .NET solutions for Access databases. The role of Chapter 1 is to present concisely those core concepts that will motivate Access developers to learn the .NET Framework and Visual Basic .NET.

Visual Basic .NET

Chapters 2 through 4 examine Visual Basic .NET. Chapter 2 concludes with a Jump Start sample that illustrates the application of concepts presented in Chapter 1. The sample shows how to populate a DataGrid control on a Windows Forms class instance with the contents of the Shippers table from the Northwind database that ships with Access. The step-by-step instructions for implementing the sample include the addition of just a single line of custom code. The other steps for implementing the sample draw exclusively on graphical techniques.

Chapter 3 shifts the focus to coding techniques. The chapter begins by contrasting Visual Basic data types with Visual Basic .NET data types. The chapter's initial section also clarifies the distinction between value types and reference types and equips developers to deal with the object orientation of Visual Basic .NET. The next three sections deal with traditional coding topics, including procedures, looping, and arrays. Going through the samples in these sections will reinforce your grasp of these topics and highlight selected differences between Visual Basic and Visual Basic .NET. This chapter closes with a review of core concepts on class development techniques and a collection of samples that illustrate the application of the concepts. Since classes are so important in the .NET Framework, an understanding of the material in this concluding section is critical.

Chapter 4 moves on to a mix of four topics that are more advanced and innovative than those covered in Chapter 3. For example, Chapter 4 introduces classes that facilitate file processing while concurrently covering practical topics, such as reading and writing binary and text files. Because of the greater emphasis on classes with Visual Basic .NET, event handling is more important than ever, and the chapter's second section reviews statements and syntax for handling class events. The discussion then moves to class inheritance. Visual Basic .NET is the first version of Visual Basic to enable developers to create custom classes that inherit properties and methods from other custom classes. The sample for this part of the chapter demonstrates how to put class inheritance to work in your applications.

One of the most highly touted innovations in Visual Basic .NET is its structured exception handling. This new feature eliminates the need for the *On Error GoTo* statement that turns your procedures into spaghetti code. The *Try...Catch...Finally* statement implements the new error handling functionality, and Chapter 4 concludes with several samples that demonstrate various approaches to using this new statement.

Windows Forms

Visual Basic .NET introduces a new type of form class for LANs available from the Windows Forms class library. While this form—which is based on the *System. Windows.Forms.Form* class—has a different architecture from Access forms or classic Visual Basic forms, you still populate *Form* class instances with controls via traditional drag-and-drop techniques. Basic techniques for working with the *Form* class received attention in Chapters 2 through 4. Chapter 5 takes a more systematic look at the *Form* class and shows you how to put it to use in an application. In particular, you learn ways of having Visual Studio .NET create codes samples for you.

Next we carefully illustrate some typical kinds of applications for text box controls and present a sample that demonstrates how to present an image on a Windows *Form* class instance based on a selection from a ComboBox control. The chapter closes with samples for working with multiple forms, such as navigating sequentially from one form to another, passing data between parent and child forms, and creating a switchboard form to navigate an application's flow to two or more forms from a central form that serves as a switchboard.

Chapter 6 drills down more deeply into Windows Forms, but it examines only three topics. The first topic concerns navigation between forms and data source assignment to form controls. As explained in Chapter 5, the tie between form controls and data sources occurs through ADO (or more specifically the ADODB and ADOX type libraries) and the .NET Framework's COM Interop feature. Since ADO is a collection of COM objects corresponding to its type libraries, the .NET Framework's COM Interop feature enables the use of ADO from within Visual Basic .NET applications.

The Data Form Wizard, which is the chapter's second major topic, should be particularly attractive to Access developers initially learning Visual Basic

.NET because it offers a graphical user interface for tying Windows Forms to data from an Access database via ADO.NET. The section presents samples particularly familiar to Access developers, including samples demonstrating data access and manipulation via TextBox controls and a main/sub form. The last section in Chapter 6 reviews selected DataGrid control properties. This control is a particularly flexible control for data display and manipulation. The samples in the concluding sections of Chapter 6 extend your grasp of the DataGrid control's functionality from samples that appear in prior chapters.

> **Note**   Selected COM objects, such the Office XP object models, require middleware between the COM Interop feature and the native type library for a COM object. In my testing, the ADODB and ADOX type libraries worked properly without any middleware. However, Microsoft issued special middleware, Office XP Primary Interop Assemblies, for selected Office XP object models, such as those for Access 2002 and Excel 2002. Microsoft published an article online illustrating the use of this middleware for Office XP object models and the COM Interop feature (*http://msdn.microsoft.com/library/ default.asp?url=/library/en-us/dnoxpta/html/odc_oxppias.asp*). At the time that I write this Introduction, there are no special Primary Interop Assemblies for the ADODB and ADOX object models.

ADO.NET

Chapters 7 through 9 equip you to perform ADO.NET development with Access databases. ADO.NET, in contrast to ADO, is the native data component for the .NET Framework. As a consequence, ADO.NET is faster and more flexible than ADO in .NET solutions. Chapter 7 focuses on platform requirements and architectural issues for ADO.NET. The goal of this chapter is to educate you about the main components of the ADO.NET object model. You learn what objects are available as well as how to put them to use. Code samples help to grow your understanding of the ADO.NET objects.

Chapter 8 shifts the focus from learning about ADO.NET objects to applying them. There are numerous samples in this chapter that demonstrate typical kinds of tasks that take advantage of alternative features. For example, you will discover samples showing how to perform dynamic data access with either SQL strings or parameters. One especially informative sample in this chapter illustrates how to handle concurrency violations. A .NET application can generate a concurrency violation when two users attempt to change the same row in a data source. Your application designs should account for the possibility of concurrency violations.

Chapter 9 probes selected advanced ADO.NET topics such as the distinctions between two different types of dataset objects and how to create and apply each kind of dataset. The chapter concludes with the presentation of a case study sample that illustrates typical data access and data manipulation chores with a Windows Forms class instance.

Web Development

The coverage of Web development issues extends across three chapters. Chapters 10 and 11 combine to give coverage of an ASP.NET solution, the type of Web development that creates a Web page for clients to view in a browser. Chapter 10 introduces basic Web design issues and contrasts them with more familiar Windows application development paradigms. You will learn how to collect data from and write content to a Web page during the round trip of a Web page from a browser to a Web server and back to the browser. Chapter 11 moves the focus from design and architecture issues to database tasks. ASP.NET operates with the same kinds of tools, such as the Data Form Wizard and ADO.NET, as applications using Windows Forms. However, the Web environment imposes a special kind of discipline because pages must regularly go back and forth between a browser and a Web server. This chapter illustrates three different approaches to data processing in Web environments. First, you learn how to use the Data Form Wizard for Web development. Next, step-by-step instructions and a short code sample show how to create ADO.NET objects graphically for use with a Web page. The chapter closes with a code sample that demonstrates how to programmatically manage inserts, updates, and deletes in an Access database from a Web page.

Chapter 12 is all about creating, invoking, and deploying XML Web services solutions. A Web service is an application that runs on one computer that a second computer can invoke remotely; the Web services architecture includes all the infrastructure for interfacing the two computers. This built-in infrastructure dramatically simplifies the task of having two computers participate in a peer-to-peer relationship in which one computer hosts the Web service and the other computer hosts the client application. You learn how to build client applications as Windows or Web applications. The chapter concludes with a sample demonstrating how to build a Web service on one computer that returns a dataset based on an Access database to another computer.

Security

Properly securing an application is more important than ever before. Actually, securing a database application includes a mix of technologies—those for the development environment, such as the .NET Framework, and those for the database, such as user-level security in Access. Chapter 13 starts with a broad over-view of .NET Framework security technologies and then demonstrates how to set up and apply Access user-level security in a .NET application. The closing sample illustrates how to apply a .NET Framework Web technique for securing an application that relies on an Access database.

XML

XML is the darling technology of tools developers, but many application devel-opers have limited experience with XML documents and their uses. Tools developers are still in the process of creating a rich set of tools that will enable application developers to accomplish tasks using XML that they now handle via more traditional means. As the application developers become familiar with the technology, they will undoubtedly discover new capabilities that are uniquely available through XML.

The title of the book's appendix succinctly describes its role in the book: "XML for Visual Studio .NET Access Developers." While XML is not essential for database chores with the .NET Framework, a working knowledge of XML serves two purposes. First, it can help you to grasp the mechanics of underlying .NET Framework technologies, such as SOAP for Web services. Second, by learning the basics of XML now, you ready yourself for the oncoming tidal wave of emerging technologies that will expose XML in meaningful ways to application developers.

Installing and Using the Samples and Demo Files

You can download the sample files from the book's Companion Content page on the Web by connecting to

http://www.microsoft.com/mspress/books/6370.asp

To access the sample files and the links to other resources we've provided, click Companion Content in the More Information menu box on the right side of the page. This will load the Companion Content Web page, which includes links for downloading the sample files and connecting to Microsoft Press Sup-port. The download link opens a Web package executable file containing a license agreement. To copy the sample files onto your hard disk, click the link to run the executable and then accept the license agreement that is presented. The sample files will be copied by default to the C:\Microsoft Press Books\Prog VB for Access folder. (During the installation process, you'll be given the option of changing that destination folder.)

Support Information

Every effort has been made to ensure the accuracy of this book and the companion content. Microsoft Press provides corrections for books through the World Wide Web at

http://www.microsoft.com/mspress/support/

To connect directly to the Microsoft Press Knowledge Base and enter a query regarding a question or an issue that you may have, go to

http://www.microsoft.com/mspress/support/search.asp

If you have comments, questions, or ideas regarding the book or its companion content, please send them to Microsoft Press via e-mail to:

MSPInput@microsoft.com

or via postal mail to:

Microsoft Press
Attn: *Programming Microsoft Visual Basic .NET for Microsoft Access Databases* Editor
One Microsoft Way
Redmond, WA 98052-6399

Please note that product support is not offered through the preceding addresses.

System Requirements

This book requires Microsoft Visual Studio .NET Version 2002. I developed the samples with the Enterprise Developer edition, but the samples are designed to run with the Professional edition as well. Installing Visual Studio .NET Version 2002 automatically installs a version of the .NET Framework compatible with the samples in this book. All the Windows applications can run on a single workstation running Windows 98 or any more recent version of Windows. Any of the Web applications, either ASP.NET or XML Web services, requires a version of Windows that supports IIS, such as Windows 2000 or Windows XP. I used an Internet Explorer browser on the client workstations for the ASP.NET Web solutions.

All the database samples, except one, work with a Microsoft Access 2002 database. Because the default file format for Access 2002 is the same as Access 2000, you can also use Microsoft Access 2000. Earlier versions of Access will work as well insofar as they are compatible with Microsoft Access 2000. The one SQL Server sample in this book uses Microsoft SQL Server 2000. Since the SQL Server 2000 file format is incompatible with that for earlier versions, you must have SQL Server 2000 to run this one sample.

1

Introduction to the .NET Framework

Many authors and speakers refer to the .NET Framework and its related technologies—particularly XML and XML Web services—as a revolution in computing practices and note Microsoft's total commitment to the .NET Framework. When I think about the possibilities, I am amazed at the opportunities that the .NET Framework brings to Microsoft Access developers. Yet, in spite of this consensus, Access developers will find a paucity of books that specifically target their special interests and requirements.

This book is for them: developers who create applications for Access (Jet) databases using classic Microsoft Visual Basic and Microsoft Visual Basic for Applications (VBA). If you don't want to be left behind, this is your chance to learn the .NET Framework with databases and coding samples that relate to your experience. While I promise to make this book relevant to the needs of Access developers, I believe the best way to learn a new technology is to use it—to focus on how to exploit the new technology. This book is designed to help you do just that.

The first chapter starts with an overview of the .NET Framework and then drills down in longer sections about why Access developers should learn Microsoft Visual Basic .NET. It introduces selected .NET Framework architecture and programming elements and .NET Framework data processing capabilities. Many of the topics covered in this chapter are presented in more detail later in the book. Practically every database sample application in the book illustrates how to apply the .NET Framework to Access databases. Along with the emphasis on Access databases is a corresponding focus on Visual Basic .NET. My goal is to equip you with concepts and techniques so that you can become productive at coding solutions for your Access databases with Visual Basic .NET. This chapter presents the concepts, and later chapters will illustrate the techniques. Furthermore, this chapter's presentation regularly points out the significance of .NET Framework innovations for Access developers. In addition, I occasionally comment on Access technologies, such as data access pages, when they offer parallel features to .NET Framework technologies, such as ASP.NET.

Many Access developers are creating solutions for Microsoft SQL Server databases. However, this book uses Access and Jet interchangeably. Therefore, I devote little attention to programming SQL Server databases with Visual Basic .NET. For those who want more content on that topic, consult my other book: *Programming Microsoft SQL Server 2000 with Microsoft Visual Basic .NET* (Microsoft Press, 2002).

What Is the .NET Framework?

This section answers the question, "What is the .NET Framework?" in a way that addresses the special needs of Visual Basic and VBA developers who create applications with Access databases. To you, the .NET Framework offers a new way of working that can vastly increase the uses of your Access database applications. I will cover the special benefits the .NET Framework offers for Access developers in the next section. This section aims to give an overview of the .NET Framework that will equip you for the journey through the rest of this chapter.

The .NET Framework is a software development environment that embraces Access databases and other kinds of databases. Rather than working directly with the .NET Framework, developers use their favorite programming language. For Visual Basic and VBA programmers, Visual Basic .NET is a natural choice. This programming language works much like Microsoft Visual Basic 6.0, but it contains special features, many of which let you take advantage of the .NET Framework.

The .NET Framework through Microsoft Visual Studio .NET makes available several templates for starting different kinds of solutions. Access developers regularly create solutions for a local area network (LAN) or even a single workstation. The Windows Application template serves this kind of solution especially well. After opening the template, you will feel right at home with a toolbox that lets you drag controls onto a form that opens for you automatically. The form is an instance of the Windows *Form* class. While the form is tailored for the .NET Framework, it works very much like Visual Basic or Access forms. For example, you can still use the familiar code-behind form development model that you already know and love. The Windows Application template is the one to use when your solution can benefit from exploiting fully the Microsoft Windows operating system's rich user interface features.

In creating applications with Visual Basic .NET or any .NET programming language, Access database developers will need a component to connect to their data. While you are currently programming either ActiveX Data Objects (ADO) or Data Access Objects (DAO) with Visual Basic or VBA to connect with Access databases, the .NET Framework offers ADO.NET for this purpose. ADO and ADO.NET share few specific features. In fact, the new capabilities of ADO.NET enable you to expand the maximum number of concurrent users of your Access databases. (I will explain why later in this chapter when I focus specifically on ADO.NET.)

Another advantage to the .NET Framework is the ease with which you can permit users to tap into your databases via the Web, such as with ASP.NET or with XML Web services. Just as ADO.NET is the component that handles data, ASP.NET is the component that handles interacting with an intranet, an extranet, or the Internet. You can think of ASP.NET as your Web development tool since ASP.NET is easier and more powerful than its predecessor—ASP (Active Server Pages). Access developers will appreciate the many new controls for binding to data. Even more important is the capability to code Web applications with a code-behind page model. This ASP.NET feature works just like the code-behind form feature in Visual Basic and VBA. It isolates control layout issues from code that controls user interactivity. The new capability relieves developers of having to write VBScript and HTML code on the same Web page.

ASP.NET also offers the capability to create XML Web services based on Access databases. An XML Web service lets two computers exchange data even if they are running different operating systems; clients running applications on UNIX can now connect to your Access applications running on Windows. This communication goes both ways. In addition, Access developers can extend the life of existing Access applications by making their contents available as an XML Web service. Access developers can tap the benefits of these and other XML Web services with the ASP.NET component of the .NET Framework. ASP.NET manages all the plumbing for implementing an XML Web service. After you learn a few simple concepts, XML Web services are a snap to program with Visual Basic .NET.

Note   Some readers may be wondering what happened to data access pages. Microsoft introduced this technology as a way of simplifying the creation of Web applications for Access developers. With data access pages, developers can graphically arrange data-bound controls on a Web page. The programming interface for data access pages is similar to Visual InterDev. Microsoft replaced the programming interface with the release of the .NET Framework. This traditional Web development environment requires you to program user interactivity by mixing a scripting language such as VBScript and HTML on the same page. ASP.NET lets you code Web applications with Visual Basic .NET, not some derivative language such as VBScript, and it does not force you to intermingle Visual Basic .NET and HTML on the same page.

Why Should Access Developers Learn Visual Basic .NET?

There are four major reasons for Access developers to learn Visual Basic .NET. This section explains each of them.

Catching the Next Generation Wave

Practicing developers need to decide whether any given innovation is a fad or a long-term trend. Learning fad technologies wastes your time and does not help you grow professionally; you spend time learning about a technology which rapidly becomes obsolete and does not prepare for the next technology. On the other hand, catching a long-term technology early in its development cycle has several benefits. First, clients will recognize you as a serious professional because you stay current with the latest technology. Second, you can undertake more challenging assignments because Microsoft simplifies the implementation of high-end capabilities, such as XML Web services, in its strategic products.

Developers familiar with early releases of Access will remember macros. When Microsoft introduced Access, macros were a popular way of automating applications. Macros offered a graphical approach to adding user interactivity to Access forms. Then came Access Basic, which offered a programmatic means of enabling user interactivity on Access forms. Many Access developers hesitated in migrating to Access Basic because developers could achieve some of the

Access Basic benefits with macros. As a result, they felt justified in avoiding the bother of learning Access Basic. Access Basic was a precursor of VBA, which proved to be one of the important tools available to modern Access developers. Those developers who delayed learning Access Basic fell behind the curve and missed an opportunity to get in on the ground floor of a revolution in desktop database development.

Visual Basic .NET represents an opportunity for Visual Basic and VBA Access developers that parallels the migration from macros to VBA. Developers can create Web applications for their Access databases much more easily with Visual Basic .NET (and ASP.NET) than with the tools available for Visual Basic and VBA. That's true because Visual Basic .NET offers a template for creating XML Web services as well as special constructs, such as Web references, for consuming XML Web services. Once you learn these and related tools for your Access databases, the same approach applies to other databases.

Learning Consistent Tools

Developers are always challenged to do the most with the smallest possible set of tools. Reusing a set of tools in multiple contexts leverages your knowledge of those tools as you learn how to implement new kinds of applications. No matter how expert you are as a developer, there is always a limit to the number of tools with which you can be proficient. Visual Basic .NET allows you to create Windows applications for the Access databases that you currently have. In addition, the .NET Framework allows functionality that is not available with earlier development environments. For example, ASP.NET enables the creation of data-based Web pages. While it is true that data access pages offer some of the same functionality, data access pages rely on an obsolete technology (as noted earlier).

Programming applications with Visual Basic .NET equips you for the next generation in Microsoft development tools by taking advantage of the .NET Framework. Visual Basic .NET drastically simplifies the creation and consumption of XML Web services.

Another important .NET Framework innovation is the interoperability of ADO.NET with XML. Visual Basic .NET developers have powerful techniques for interacting with XML. Furthermore, the same basic approaches that work for Access databases apply equally well to other databases.

Yet another advantage is the interoperability of applications created using Visual Basic .NET with those of languages compatible with .NET, such as C# or Visual C++. Because of subtle incompatibilities in how languages not compatible with .NET implement Windows functionality, it is difficult to have applications developed by Visual Basic developers used by C++ developers. All languages that support .NET draw on the same set of base classes. This means that the subtle incompatibilities between how languages implement Windows functionality is gone because all languages supported by .NET draw on the exact same set of classes. In addition, all languages compatible with .NET compile code for the common language runtime (CLR), which actually executes the code on an operating system. (See more about the CLR later in this chapter.) Languages compatible with .NET can still express some individuality by exposing different subsets of classes for use by the CLR. The consistency between languages supported by .NET enables organizations to achieve better efficiency from their programming professionals because Visual Basic .NET developers and Visual C++ developers can create classes that interoperate with one another.

> **Note**   The .NET Framework includes built-in support for the following programming languages: Visual Basic .NET, C#, Visual C++, and JScript .NET. However, many third-party firms offer .NET compilers for other languages, such as COBOL, FORTRAN, RPG, and Perl. Navigate to *http://msdn.microsoft.com/vstudio/partners/language/* for a list of the current .NET compilers registered with Microsoft.

Exposing Access Databases Over the Web

By using ADO.NET and ASP.NET together, you can expose Access databases over the Web with Visual Basic .NET. Notice that I said Visual Basic .NET and not VScript.NET (or some other Visual Basic variation). The same Visual Basic .NET that you use for creating forms in Windows applications also works for creating forms in Web applications. Not only that, but Visual Studio .NET, which includes Visual Basic .NET, provides a consistent development environment for creating Windows, Web, and other kinds of applications, such as XML Web services and Windows services, not formerly available to Visual Basic developers. The wide range of application topics that you can tackle with Visual Basic .NET means that you can use the same IDE for creating Windows and Web applications as well as other kinds of applications.

Creating applications with ASP.NET is exciting for several reasons. ASP.NET pages are compiled instead of interpreted. (ASP pages are interpreted.) This means ASP.NET pages will run many times faster than comparable ASP pages. Second, ASP.NET Web pages rely on a new *Page* class. Instances of this class can split the design of a Web page into layout and programming across two separate but related files. It is this innovation (the *Page* class and code-behind page) that allows a developer to avoid intermingling Visual Basic .NET with HTML. Third, ASP.NET offers a broad mix of controls that you can use to populate Web pages. Nearly all controls can render in HTML 3.2 exclusively on the server, making it possible to design pages that work in nearly any browser. However, even with this conscious attempt on the part of Microsoft to accommodate browsers other than Internet Explorer, you will still have easier and richer capabilities for creating Web pages for Internet Explorer browsers.

Exposing Access Databases via XML Web Services

Typical ASP.NET applications work from a browser. However, you may also care to expose database application functionality from a Windows application via the Internet. With this approach, users enjoy the benefit of using a traditional Windows form, but they have access to an Access database on a remote computer. This kind of capability is one of the main benefits of an XML Web service for Access developers.

I will drill down into the underlying technologies and give you several examples of XML Web services in Chapter 12. The important point here is that switching to Visual Basic .NET makes it relatively easy to implement an XML Web service based on an Access database.

Getting the .NET Framework

To create applications with Visual Basic .NET, you need to meet minimum hardware and software requirements for the .NET Framework. One easy way to update your computer to meet the software requirements and to get the .NET Framework on your computer is to install Visual Studio .NET. This package includes a Windows Update Component CD that refreshes your system with the appropriate updates for the .NET Framework. In addition to the .NET Framework, you also gain the availability of the Visual Studio .NET IDE as well as other useful development aids. I suggest you put aside several hours for a full installation of the Windows Update, including the .NET Framework, and Visual Studio .NET.

Visual Studio .NET comes in three editions: Professional, Enterprise Developer, and Enterprise Architect. Within the Visual Studio .NET site, there is a page for helping you decide which edition of Visual Studio .NET

(continued)

best meets your requirements (*http://msdn.microsoft.com/vstudio/howto-buy/choosing.asp*). Because this book targets professional Access database developers, I tested sample applications with the Enterprise Developer edition running on two computers with Windows 2000. One computer ran the Windows 2000 Professional edition, and the other computer ran the Windows 2000 Server edition.

You can also download and install the .NET Framework without Visual Studio .NET. The MSDN site offers a Microsoft .NET Framework section (*http://msdn.microsoft.com/netframework/*). This section at the MSDN site permits you to examine hardware and software system requirements and download the .NET Framework as well as any service pack updates. In addition, you can purchase Visual Basic .NET Standard edition as a stand-alone unit that is not a part of Visual Studio .NET (*http://msdn.microsoft.com/vbasic/howtobuy/choosing.asp*). While Visual Basic .NET Standard edition does install basic .NET Framework components, it does not include tools that many professional developers will consider important, such as the templates for creating reusable components as well as custom controls for Windows and Web applications.

Elements of the .NET Framework

Your grasp of the suitability of the .NET Framework and Visual Basic .NET to tackle problems within your business or those of your clients can depend on how well you understand major elements of the .NET Framework. A full discussion of these elements is well beyond the scope of this book. Nevertheless, this section presents selected background on three helpful elements of the .NET Framework: the common language runtime (CLR), preparations to run source code, and assemblies.

For those with a desire to learn more about the .NET Framework architecture, I recommend *Introducing Microsoft .NET, Second Edition* by David S. Platt (Microsoft Press, 2002). Another resource is available to those with Visual Studio .NET installed on their machine. After you install Visual Studio .NET, you can open the .NET documentation from the Start menu by selecting All Programs, Microsoft Visual Studio .NET, and then choosing Microsoft Visual Studio .NET Documentation. While this documentation includes some material that overlaps with the Help files from within Visual Studio .NET, the documentation also contains background material that enriches your understanding of a topic instead of just explaining how to perform a task.

Common Language Runtime

The common language runtime, or CLR, is a run-time engine for all languages that are compatible with .NET. This runtime interprets code and enables it to run on an operating system, much like the Access run-time engine or VBRUN does. The notion of a runtime engine for compiling or interpreting code is common among current languages. In fact, the Java language gains a substantial degree of its notoriety because of its run-time engine.

The CLR for the .NET Framework is a run-time engine for all languages compatible with .NET. The CLR and its components implement the compiled source code that you write in Visual Basic .NET. Not all languages have to expose the same set of features from the CLR, but any capabilities that languages supported by .NET expose must first be available in the CLR. For this reason, applications created with different languages supported by .NET are fully interoperable.

Because the CLR delivers programming functionality to all languages, it can deliver traditional as well as some nontraditional services. One of the most popular nontraditional services is *garbage collection*. The CLR automatically disposes of memory references when they are no longer needed. Through its automatic garbage ("unused references") collection feature, the CLR helps to eliminate memory leaks, which is a particularly common problem with applications that enable the instantiation of the same object by many users or repeated instantiation of the same object by a single user. Garbage collection makes obsolete the practice of removing an object from memory by setting its reference to *Nothing*. The automatic aspect of garbage collection frees the CLR to pick a time for removing unused references that has minimal impact on your application's performance.

> **Note**   Garbage collection is all about memory management. While you do not need to set reference variables pointing at objects to *Nothing*, your code should still release other system resources such as files and database connections when they are no longer needed.

The programming capabilities available through the CLR derive from its base class library. Earlier in this chapter, I mentioned that Visual Basic .NET developers can program data tasks with ADO.NET and Web tasks with

ASP.NET. Both ADO.NET and ASP.NET correspond to components within the base class library that implement specialized functionality. The .NET Framework represents these components in the class library with one or more namespaces. For example, the *System.Web* namespace supports ASP.NET functionality.

A namespace can contain a set of related types. Types are entities that you can use in your programs, such as classes, delegates, enumerations, interfaces, and structures. Classes are designs for objects that have properties, methods, and events as type members. (Other members of this group include fields and nested types.) Within Visual Basic .NET, delegates facilitate event processing by helping to manage communication between event senders and event receivers. An enumeration is a related set of constant values defined by an *Enum* statement. Interfaces are a contract. An interface specifies members that are fulfilled by another entity, such as a class instance. A structure is a user-defined value type.

Table 1-1 describes selected data and XML namespaces that you are likely to use as an Access database developer. These namespaces generally expose types that you can use to implement the features of ADO.NET for Access databases. The descriptions for the *System.Data* and *System.Data.OleDb* namespaces highlight their applicability to Access database files. However, these namespaces can work with data from data sources other than Access database files. Depending on the data source, you may find other namespaces appropriate for your needs.

Table 1-1 Selected Data and XML Namespaces

Namespace Name	Description
System.Data.OleDb	Namespace for the OLE DB .NET data provider; permits connecting to, reading data from, and executing commands against Access database files
System.Data	Enables disconnected data representations (datasets) from multiple database files by representing data types, relations, and constraints; facilitates data manipulation tasks between disconnected datasets and original Access database files
System.Xml	Enables persisting, reading, and processing XML documents based on datasets and other data sources

The three namespaces in Table 1-1 point to different ways in which you are likely to interact with data in the .NET Framework. First, use the *System.Data.OleDb* namespace to connect to a data source, such as an Access database file. The conceptual pipe connecting your application to a data source can function like a firehose that supports forward-only, read-only data access, or it can enable disconnected data access. The local copy of data from one or more data sources is a dataset.

Second, your application can make changes to a dataset and then subsequently attempt to synchronize local changes with the corresponding data in the original data source. Access developers know this style of data processing as optimistic locking. The *System.Data* namespace in coordination with the *System.Data.OleDb* namespace facilitates this second group of activities.

Third, you can process XML documents with the *System.Xml* namespace. The architecture for datasets permits them to expose their contents as linked tables—such as you may view in the Access Relationships window—and as hierarchical XML documents. See Chapter Appendix for an introduction to XML documents and processing issues.

Running Source Code

Now you know that the CLR ultimately runs your source code. However, the CLR does not read source code, such as Visual Basic .NET. The code that you write in Visual Basic .NET goes through two rounds of compilations before the CLR executes it. These compilations are an integral part of how the .NET Framework delivers its cross-language benefits.

The .NET Framework documentation describes the execution of source code in four steps. The first step is to pick a language compatible with .NET. Just because the .NET Framework exists on your computer doesn't mean you are required to program the computer using .NET. You can still use Visual Basic or VBA to code applications. Code developed with a language that is not compatible with .NET is called *unmanaged code*, and it does not enjoy the benefits of execution by the CLR. If you use Visual Basic .NET or one of the many other languages supported by .NET, you create *managed code*, and this code does enjoy the benefits delivered by the .NET Framework. One of these benefits is that your Visual Basic .NET classes can interoperate freely with classes created by developers using other languages, such as C#.

The second step explains why classes coded with Visual Basic .NET can interoperate freely with classes coded with other languages supported by .NET. In the second step, a source code compiler translates the source code to Microsoft Intermediate Language (MSIL). All language compilers in the .NET Framework perform this translation from your source code. The format of MSIL is the same for any language supported by .NET. After conversion to MSIL, all these languages represent applications with the same format.

As a source language compiler creates MSIL, it saves the MSIL in a portable executable file (with either an .exe or a .dll extension). While creating the

MSIL for an application, the source language compiler also creates metadata describing the application, and the compilation process stores the metadata in the portable executable file. Every type member in an application is described by the metadata. Therefore, the metadata fully describes the structure of an application. It is this self-description that eliminates the need for type library files.

Metadata supports three important benefits for .NET solutions. First, metadata self-describes files. The storing of metadata with MSIL permits the .NET Framework to use a single file for both definition and implementation. If you were creating solutions with COM, metadata would eliminate the need for Interface Description Language (IDL) files. Second, metadata contains the necessary information for the compiled source code in a portable executable file developed initially with one source language to be inherited by a compiled solution developed with a different source language. (A more precise definition for inheritance appears later in this chapter, but the general notion of inheritance is sufficient here.) No custom programming or any other special steps are necessary to facilitate inheritance of compiled classes across languages. Third, the .NET Framework allows you to annotate your source code with attributes that extend the basic description of an application. In fact, the .NET Framework uses this attribute capability as it defines an XML Web service and the individual methods that an XML Web service exposes (as well as in many other contexts).

The third step in preparing to run source code is the compilation of the MSIL and metadata to native code, which is processor-specific machine code. A second compiler performs this task. The .NET Framework will typically perform this second execution with a just-in-time (JIT) compiler. Because the JIT compiler returns native code, it varies by operating system and CPU architecture. For example, it will differ from 64-bit systems to 32-bit systems. During this second compilation, the JIT compiler checks to make sure an invoked element is type safe. This check verifies that code will not override unauthorized memory locations and maintains isolation from other applications at run time. Unless an administrator explicitly overrides the type safety requirement, the .NET Framework will not run code unless it is type safe.

The just-in-time (JIT) name for the second compiler derives from the fact that the .NET Framework does not compile the MSIL code for the whole application at once. Instead, it compiles a type's member only as a user invokes the member's functionality, allowing the .NET Framework to deliver performance to a user as she calls for it. Members that are not invoked by a user do not require compilation by the JIT compiler. After the JIT compiler operates on the code for a type member, the .NET Framework can store the code for the member in a cache for faster reference the next time a user invokes it. Both JIT compilation and caching compiled native code speed performance.

After JIT compilation, the code is ready to be run by the CLR in the fourth and final step for running source code. By this time, the initial source code has undergone two compilations. This managed code receives special benefits, such as memory management, security, interoperability with unmanaged code, and debugging support. All of these benefits and more derive from the capabilities of the CLR and the JIT compilation of the MSIL code, which is, in turn, based on the source code.

Assemblies

Assemblies are the basic deployment unit for applications and custom classes within the .NET Framework. An individual assembly will typically include one or more modules plus an assembly manifest. A module is a portable executable file. The assembly manifest is metadata for an assembly. For example, an assembly manifest enumerates the files in an application, which can include multiple modules, graphic files, XML documents, Access database files, or other kinds of files. Because the assembly manifest knows about the files within an assembly, the assembly manifest maps requests for type members to individual files within the assembly. In addition, the assembly manifest enumerates other assemblies on which its assembly depends.

> **Note**   Assemblies can be static or dynamic. Static assemblies, which this section explains, refer to saved assembly files. Dynamic assemblies are created on the fly and used from memory. You can save a dynamic assembly after its use.

When you are working with Visual Studio .NET, it will automatically create a file directory folder for your Windows application projects. This folder is the assembly for the project. If you have a simple Windows application, your file can have one Windows form. A project's folder can also contain an Access database. By copying the folder to another computer in the exact same location, your application can work on the second computer without any adjustment. If you must copy the folder to a new location on the second computer, you may need to respecify the connection string for linking to the Access database on the second computer.

As the preceding description demonstrates, you can deploy a Visual Basic .NET Windows application to another computer as easily as copying a folder (say, with XCOPY). There is no need to set a reference to a type library or make changes to the registry on the computer receiving the deployed application. For this approach to work, you have to be willing to run the application from the .exe file in the project's solution. If you create multiple versions of a project, you can deploy each version to a different folder or copy over existing folders when they become obsolete. This approach to deployment eliminates "DLL hell" because everything for an application is contained in a single folder from which your clients run the application.

The assembly construct in the .NET Framework is rich enough to support another deployment model. This second approach takes advantage of a global assembly cache (GAC) for storing assemblies that you must share with two or more other assemblies. When you install the .NET Framework on a computer, the installation process automatically creates a GAC in the assembly folder of the Windows directory. On a Windows 2000 computer, the path to the GAC is \Winnt\assembly. While you cannot use XCOPY to move an assembly to the GAC, you can drag and drop the folder for an assembly into the GAC from Windows Explorer. In addition, the global assembly cache tool (gacutil.exe) that ships with the .NET Framework SDK (and installs with Visual Studio .NET) allows you to view and manipulate the contents of the GAC on a computer. Of course, you must have permission to work with the Windows directory.

Shared assemblies require a *strong name* before you can store them in the GAC. A strong name uniquely identifies an assembly. You can generate a strong name for an assembly with the strong name tool (sn.exe), which ships with the .NET Framework SDK. After developing a strong name, you must sign an assembly with the strong name for the name to uniquely identify the assembly. You can use the Assembly Linker (al.exe), another .NET Framework SDK tool, to sign an assembly with the key pair generated by the strong name tool.

The .NET Framework uses the terms *shared assembly* and *private assembly* to refer to the two types of assemblies. An assembly that operates from its own private folder is called a private assembly. An assembly that other assemblies reference from the GAC is called a shared assembly. You can run different versions of an assembly in side-by-side fashion. Build a new assembly that references a version of an assembly in the GAC, and the new assembly will automatically use the correct version for as long as it is available in the GAC. If you build a second new assembly that references a different version of an assembly in the GAC, this second new assembly will automatically use its version of the supporting assembly for as long as its version is in the GAC.

The .NET Framework documentation recommends against using shared assemblies as a general practice because private assemblies are easier to administer. For example, there is no need to make strong names for private assemblies, and it is easier to copy private assemblies. (You can use XCOPY for private but not shared assemblies.) Shared assemblies must reside in the Windows folder on a computer—for example, the Winnt folder on a Windows 2000 computer. Administrators often restrict access to the files in the Windows folder to protect its contents. However, this practice can restrict the ability to administer shared assemblies in the GAC.

Selected .NET Programming Innovations

This section presents short summaries of three selected innovations that will impact the way developers create solutions with Visual Basic .NET. While the subject is programming innovations, I specifically avoid presenting code samples to expose you to concepts. You will find this background valuable when we turn to code samples and step-by-step techniques for creating solutions.

Namespaces

A namespace is a way of organizing and exposing functionality in .NET Framework solutions. The .NET Framework types enable all .NET applications, and the way to tap .NET Framework types is through namespaces. (Selected namespaces for supporting Web and data functionality in the .NET Framework were discussed earlier.)

Your applications can reference .NET Framework types by following a two-part naming convention for denoting types. The first denotes the namespace. The second part denotes the type within a namespace. The names for .NET Framework type namespaces have a hierarchical structure that typically starts with *System*. Visual Basic .NET has additional namespaces: these start with *Microsoft.VisualBasic*. You will likely use namespaces starting with *System* most often, other times use *Microsoft.VisualBasic*. You can also create your own custom namespaces. When used like this, namespaces offer a familiar means for organizing the objects within an assembly.

A useful way for understanding namespaces is to examine specific instances of them. The "Introduction to the .NET Framework Class Library in Visual Studio" topic in the Microsoft Visual Studio .NET documentation includes an overview of the namespaces for the .NET Framework base class library along with links for drilling down further on namespaces for individual parts of the base class library. The *System.Windows.Forms* namespace facilitates the management of Windows applications containing forms with controls on them. Nested within this namespace is the *System.Window.Forms.Form* namespace, which points at the Windows *Form* class. The class name corresponds to the namespace for the class. When you start a Windows application within Visual Studio .NET, the code for the Windows Form Designer automatically inherits from the *System.Window.Forms.Form* class. This class exposes properties, methods, and events for controlling your application. When a Windows application initializes, the caption for the default form is Form1. You can use the form's load event procedure to reset the caption by assigning a new value to the form's *Text* property.

Object Orientation

The .NET Framework is object-oriented, and since Visual Basic .NET is a language supported by .NET, it is object-oriented. One interesting indication of the switch is that the *Set* statement for assigning object references to variables representing object instances is gone. What's the reason? All assignment statements are for objects—even assignments to a data type. For example, the Visual Basic .NET *Integer* data type is derived from the *System.Int32* type in the .NET Framework base class library. Since the *System.Int32* type offers a collection of properties and methods, so does the corresponding *Integer* data type in Visual Basic .NET. Visual Basic .NET permits you to convert an *Integer* to a *String* with the *ToString* method. You can code *int1.ToString* instead of *CStr(int1)*. Since *ToString* is a method, IntelliSense reminds you of its availability as soon as you click . after the integer's name.

Visual Basic .NET offers three standard object-oriented features—encapsulation, inheritance, and polymorphism. Encapsulation embodies the core notion of a class: that you can group properties, methods, and other members together and treat them as a single unit, such as a residence. Inheritance allows the creation of new classes—such as single-family homes, condominiums, and cooperatives—based on a previously existing class, such as a residence. The new class is called a *derived class*, and the existing class is called a *base class*. For example, the *System.Object* class is the base class in the .NET Framework. All other classes inherit originally from this class. When a derived class inherits a base class, it can add new members, change the definition of some inherited members, and hide other inherited members. Polymorphism refers to the capability to define an identically named member differently in both the base class and the derived class.

As you begin to investigate the object orientation of Visual Basic .NET, you are likely to encounter terms such as overloading, overriding, and shadowing. *Overloading* refers to the practice of defining multiple procedures with the same name but different argument lists. Developers can use overloading to define methods in classes that accept different arguments. Without this feature, you would have to define a separate method for each type of argument or include elaborate code in a single procedure to analyze the arguments for acting appropriately from a single procedure. Both *overriding* and *shadowing* offer different approaches for redefining members in a derived class. Either of these approaches enables polymorphism.

Exception Handling

An exception is a fault that occurs while a program is executing. Exceptions "throw" an instance of the *Exception* class. The CLR can throw an *Exception* class instance when a fault occurs during the execution of an application. One way to bullet-proof your applications from these *Exception* instances is to raise exceptions while you are testing your applications before their production deployment. If an exception goes unhandled by your program's code, your application crashes and your program ends abruptly with a system error message.

The whole purpose of exception handling is to avoid abrupt ends. With exception handling, your program can diagnose the cause of a fault and pass back guidance to the user on how to correct the fault. This kind of solution is particularly appropriate when the error causing an exception results from wrong user input. In other situations, the user cannot remedy a problem (for example, if a database file was moved or deleted). In the second situation, your exception handling can provide feedback on the cause of the error and return control to an application's form so that your user can try another task until the problem generating the error is resolved.

One exciting innovation of Visual Basic .NET is the introduction of structured exception handling. With this new technique for processing errors, you can avoid the "spaghetti logic" associated with unstructured exception handling. Recall that unstructured exception handling used the *On Error* statement with a *GoTo* clause. The *On Error* condition could trap only whether an exception occurred. You then had to work with error codes from different systems, such as Visual Basic, ADO, or DAO.

Structured exception handling removes the introduction of spaghetti code based on a *GoTo* clause in an *On Error* statement by allowing you to test for the validity of code in its normal flow. Open a *Try...Catch...Finally* statement to start structured exception handling. Insert the *Try* keyword just before the block of code that you want to test. At the end of a code block you want to test for run-time errors, open one or more successive *Catch* clauses. You can use multiple *Catch* clauses with a *Try* clause to trap different types of exceptions in a code block. By knowing the exception thrown by the CLR, you can develop the most constructive feedback to a user. This may allow the remedy of a fault by the user without any input from the program's designer.

Your sequence of *Catch* clauses should generally close with a trap for any error not detected by a specific filter for a previous *Catch* clause. After the last *Catch* clause in a structured error-handling statement, you can optionally include a *Finally* clause. If present, this clause will always execute. You can use it for actions such as releasing a database connection or closing a file. Whether or not your structured exception-handling statement includes a *Finally* clause, the *Try...Catch...Finally* statement must end with the *End Try* keyword phrase. The following layout is a template that illustrates the general design of a *Try...Catch...Finally* statement:

```
Try    ' Code block to test goes here.
Catch [optional filters]
    ' Code to process a filtered exception goes here.
[Additional Catch blocks]
Finally
    ' This code always runs immediately before
    ' the Try statement exits.
End Try
```

The *Try...Catch...Finally* statement represents a new syntax for exception handling by Visual Basic developers. To use this new syntax effectively, you will have to develop an understanding of the kinds of exceptions that can occur and the range of remedial actions appropriate for different kinds of errors. Chapter 4 will illustrate typical scenarios for using structured exceptions with different kinds of errors.

Visual Basic .NET Data Processing Capabilities

As an Access database developer, you will probably spend an exceptional amount of time working with ADO.NET—the .NET Framework data component. This section gives special focus to this topic from an introductory perspective. As with other sections of this chapter, attention is drawn to features that have special importance for Access developers. Chapters 7 through 9 will explore ADO.NET in much more depth. However, this section should prepare you for those chapters as well as for the Jump Start example application that closes Chapter 2.

Why Move to ADO.NET?

ADO.NET is, loosely speaking, an extension of the ADO technology introduced slightly before Access 2000. Since ADO is actually a new data model relative to the earlier Remote Data Objects (RDO) and DAO technologies, you may be wondering why we need yet another set of objects for accessing and manipulating data.

There are a couple of legitimate answers to the question, why move to ADO.NET? First, the .NET Framework is built from the ground up to be an integrated cross-language development platform that uses a common run-time engine for all languages supported by .NET. The former data object models (DAO, ADO, and RDO) were designed before the introduction of the .NET Framework. ADO.NET retains selected ADO concepts, but ADO.NET integrates tightly with the .NET Framework in a way that ADO cannot without breaking its backward compatibility. Second, ADO.NET was designed with the Web in mind, particularly for its disconnected data management capabilities. ADO.NET supports only disconnected data manipulation (namely, tasks such as updates, inserts, and deletes). Scalability increases dramatically with disconnected data access and data manipulation and is particularly beneficial for Web applications where the number of users can grow rapidly from an already large base.

If you previously made the move from DAO to ADO, you will have a running start on learning ADO.NET. ADO was a strategic database technology because it offered integrated programming for Access, other databases, and Web applications. ADO.NET maintains those benefits while adding significantly to performance and scalability. By not requiring, or even allowing, a constant connection for datasets, ADO.NET enables a database to serve many more users. In addition, ADO.NET works with data in memory, which can dramatically speed performance.

Another important reason for using ADO.NET is that it is smart about XML. You can readily persist ADO.NET data as XML documents and later read the persisted data to repopulate ADO.NET data structures. In addition, ADO.NET integrates tightly with XML Web services—a powerful technology for sharing data over a Web in XML format.

ADO.NET Data Providers

In order to begin an ADO.NET application, you must pick an appropriate data provider for the data source with which you want to work. The .NET Framework installs with two .NET data providers—OLE DB .NET and SQL Server—and a third is available from the Microsoft downloads site—ODBC .NET. At the time this chapter was written, the ODBC .NET Data Provider was available from the following URL:

http://msdn.microsoft.com/downloads/default.asp?URL=/downloads/ sample.asp?url=/MSDN-FILES/027/001/668/msdncompositedoc.xml

When you are connecting to an Access 2000 or Access 2002 database, you should use the OLE DB .NET Data Provider. As the data provider's name implies, it actually works with the native OLE DB Data Provider. (You may recall using this provider with ADO.) In fact, the OLE DB .NET Data Provider runs the native OLE DB Data Provider through the COM Interop assembly. In addition to Access databases, you can link to Oracle and SQL Server data sources with the OLE DB .NET Data Provider. You should not use the OLE DB .NET Data Provider for any other data sources.

> **Note** COM was the development technology for exposing functionality and hosting applications. The .NET Framework will eventually supplant COM. In the interim, it will be necessary to run COM applications, such as the OLE DB Data Provider, with .NET applications. The COM Interop assembly facilitates this objective by mapping COM object members to equivalent members in the .NET Framework.

Since SQL Server is Microsoft's enterprise database, the .NET Framework ships with the SQL Server .NET Data Provider that is especially optimized for use with SQL Server 7 and later. This data provider does not invoke a COM Interop assembly because it communicates directly with SQL Server data sources. If your application uses a version prior to SQL Server 7, you should use the OLE DB .NET Data Provider instead of the SQL Server .NET Data Provider.

The ODBC .NET Data Provider is the third .NET data provider. After the download, the data provider becomes an add-on component to the .NET Framework SDK. Your applications can use this data provider with any ODBC data source. Microsoft Knowledge Base article Q310985 provides insight on the use of this data provider, including sample code demonstrating its use with Visual Basic .NET.

ADO.NET Architecture

There are two main elements to the ADO.NET architecture. First, the .NET data provider implements classes for connecting to and querying a database. Second, the .NET data providers transfer data to and from a database and a local *DataSet* object. The users of your ADO.NET application will typically interact with the local dataset object. When appropriate, your application can convey inserts, updates, and deletes performed against the local dataset to the data source to which your .NET data provider connects.

The four classes that a .NET data provider implements are the *Connection, Command, DataReader,* and *DataAdapter* classes. The names for the classes change slightly from one provider to the next. There are also minor differences in how the classes offered by different providers perform their functionality, but all .NET data providers make available substantially the same four classes.

The name of the *Connection* class implemented by the OLE DB .NET Data Provider is *OleDbConnection*. This class resides in the *System.Data.OleDb* namespace. In fact, all the classes implemented by the OLE DB .NET Data Provider reside in this namespace. To open a connection to an Access database file, you need a connection string designating the OLE DB provider and pointing at the database file. It is good practice to declare and instantiate the connection object with a single statement using the *New* keyword. The following statement demonstrates the syntax for declaring and instantiating a new *Connection* object (*cnn1*) based on the *OleDbConnection* class; the sample also opens the connection.

```
Dim cnn1 As System.Data.OleDb.OleDbConnection = New _
    System.Data.OleDb.OleDbConnection _
    ("Provider=Microsoft.Jet.OLEDB.4.0;" & _
    "Data Source=C:\myDB.mdb;")
cnn1.Open()
```

If you program ADO, you will notice the striking similarity to ADO syntax. In spite of garbage collection, you should close the connection object as soon as you no longer need it. Invoke the object's *Close* or *Dispose* method to achieve this result.

After you create a connection to a database, you can execute commands against the database to perform data access, data manipulation, and data definition tasks. The name of the *Command* class implemented by the OLE DB .NET Data Provider is *OleDbCommand*. It resides in the same namespace as the *OleDbConnection* class. Use parameters to permit run-time specification of how a command operates. *Command* objects can pass data to other objects, such as DataReaders and DataAdapters.

The OLE DB .NET Data Provider implements the *DataReader* object with the *OleDbDataReader* class in the *System.Data.OleDb* namespace. Instances of this class provide read-only, forward-only access to a data source specified by a *Connection* object and a *Command* object. When all you need to do is pass through some data, such as instructions to populate a list box, instances of the *DataReader* class provide high performance. One reason for the high performance of *DataReader* objects is that they maintain an open connection to a data source. You should close the *DataReader* and its associated connection as soon as your application no longer needs them. This frees the database to accommodate more requests from other users.

The *DataAdapter* class acts as a bridge between an Access database or other external data source providing data to an ADO.NET application and a local *DataSet* object. Users of a form in a Windows application do not interact directly with the connected data source as is common with ADO applications coded with Visual Basic or VBA. Instead, the form in a Windows application points at the local *DataSet* object. This object is disconnected from the data source until a *DataAdapter* object either fills the local dataset or updates the data source based on inserts, updates, and deletes to a local dataset. The name of the *DataAdapter* class from the OLE DB .NET Data Provider is *OleDbDataAdapter*; it resides in the *System.Data.OleDb* namespace.

The *DataSet* class is in the *System.Data* namespace. You can think of *DataSet* objects as in-memory databases that contain one or more tables. When a dataset has more than one table, you can specify relationships between tables. You can also designate foreign key constraints in a table that point at another table to define the column(s) linking two tables. You can populate and pass revisions from the tables in a dataset to the tables in a database via a *DataAdapter* object based on the *DataAdapter* class from any of the three .NET data providers.

The *DataSet* class is an exceptionally rich class that offers advantages for many data processing scenarios. Because a dataset can represent a whole database structure in memory, you can denote a data structure such as the Northwind database with multiple tables and many relationships. Within the *DataSet* class are collections for the tables and relationships in a dataset instance. Any individual table within a dataset can have a data row collection for representing values in the table and a data column collection for representing structure.

Perhaps the most important aspect of a dataset is that it is disconnected from its source. This feature increases the ability of the database source for a dataset to serve more users. That's because the ADO.NET architecture causes users to connect to a database only for a brief moment to either populate the dataset from the database source or to update the database source based on changes made to the dataset. Since Access databases tend to be bound by the number of concurrent users, this ADO.NET disconnected dataset feature can help to extend the life of Access databases that are currently experiencing performance degradation because of too many concurrent users.

Summary

This chapter aims to orient you to the .NET Framework. It starts with a brief introduction to the .NET Framework and progressively selects different aspects to highlight. Another major objective of the chapter, and indeed the whole book, is to show the relevance of the .NET Framework and Visual Basic .NET to Access database development. One section in the chapter tackles this topic from four different perspectives. The chapter closes with a brief introduction to ADO.NET—the .NET Framework data processing tool. As you create native .NET Framework solutions for your Access databases, you will find a working knowledge of ADO.NET essential.

2

Using Visual Basic .NET with Visual Studio .NET

This chapter will get you started with Microsoft Visual Basic .NET in Microsoft Visual Studio .NET. Microsoft Access developers creating solutions with Visual Basic .NET will find Visual Studio .NET a convenient and powerful IDE. This chapter presents a progression of topics designed to make Access developers productive with Visual Basic .NET as soon as possible. The first section introduces Visual Studio .NET. After describing how to configure Visual Studio .NET for Visual Basic .NET and presenting a brief introduction to the IDE, the chapter switches its focus to template types for building projects. While the chapter gives an overview of all 11 Visual Basic .NET project templates for starting a project, it provides demonstrations only for Windows Application and Class Library projects. Windows Application projects will be important for most Access developers because this type is most similar to the ones Access developers commonly build with Microsoft Visual Basic and VBA. The Class Library project is important because Visual Basic .NET is so object oriented.

The chapter's next-to-last section selectively addresses what's new and different about Visual Basic .NET vs. Visual Basic and VBA. In spite of the complaints of some developers, I found the differences well worth the effort of learning because of the increased capabilities available from Visual Basic .NET and the .NET Framework. You'll have to make the decision for yourself about learning Visual Basic .NET, but the coverage of what's new and different will help you to make an informed decision. Chapters 3 and 4 convey a sense of Visual Basic .NET programming techniques while drilling down more thoroughly on what's new and different about Visual Basic .NET.

This chapter closes with an example, named Jump Start, of creating a Visual Basic .NET solution for the Shippers table in the Northwind database. The sample pulls together conceptual ADO.NET elements from Chapter 1 with the hands-on demonstrations of initiating and populating a Windows Application project with Visual Studio .NET from this chapter. One interesting feature of the example is that it takes just one line of code to build the application. The Jump Start example, along with the other projects mentioned throughout the chapter, are available in folders for running from Visual Studio .NET.

My goal in this chapter, as with the whole book, is to prepare you to create database solutions for Access data files (mdb) with Visual Basic .NET. I'll begin by discussing the relationships between the two technologies.

> **Note** You can view and run the samples described throughout this book by looking at the solutions included with this book's sample files. In most cases, simply open the .sln file in the root directory within each folder to load the corresponding project into Visual Studio .NET. For the sample projects in this chapter, you may find it more instructive to create the projects from scratch than to load the folders from the .sln file because one of the major goals of the chapter is to get you comfortable creating Visual Basic .NET projects. Whether you use the sample projects available for this chapter or re-create your own versions of them, you can run the projects by invoking the .exe file in the bin subdirectory of a project's folder. If a project has a .dll file instead of an .exe file in its bin subdirectory, invoke the .exe file from the folder of a project that references the project with the .dll file.

Getting Started with Visual Studio .NET

Getting started with Visual Studio .NET is not difficult. This section highlights some critical steps along the way. First, I describe how to configure Visual Studio .NET for Visual Basic .NET. Second, you get an introduction on how to make new projects and open existing Visual Basic .NET projects from the Start Page in Visual Studio .NET. This section closes with a review of some important IDE windows. Like many sections throughout this book, our goal is not to cover any of these topics exhaustively. Instead, the aim is to expose you to selected issues and equip you to discover whatever else you need on your own.

Configuring Visual Studio .NET for Visual Basic .NET

As indicated in Chapter 1, Visual Studio .NET and the .NET Framework support multiple programming languages. Therefore, you will probably want to configure Visual Studio .NET for whatever languages you are using. In this case, the language is Visual Basic .NET. You can perform the configuration at any time after installation by opening Visual Studio to its Start Page.

Begin to open the Start Page by launching Visual Studio .NET immediately after installation. You can do this from the Start menu by pointing to All Programs, Microsoft Visual Studio .NET, and choosing Microsoft Visual Studio .NET. At a minimum, the menu exposes items for the documentation (Microsoft Visual Studio .NET Documentation) and the Visual Studio .NET application (Microsoft Visual Studio .NET). Choosing the item for the Visual Studio .NET application opens the Start Page with its default configuration. This configuration is not optimized for Visual Basic .NET.

> **Note**   After the initial launch of the Visual Studio .NET program, the Start Page need not show when you open the application. However, you can always show the Start Page by choosing Help, Show Start Page.

Select My Profile from the left border of the Start Page to configure the Visual Studio .NET IDE. This allows you to choose individual settings for the Keyboard Scheme, Window Layout, and Help Filter drop-down boxes. You can do this independently for each box, or you can make a selection from the Profile box above these three configuration boxes. As a Visual Basic .NET developer, you will probably find the Visual Basic Developer selection from the Profile box most suited to your needs. This will automatically set the first two boxes below it to Visual Basic 6 and the third box below it to Visual Basic. The setting for the first two boxes will give you a familiar Visual Basic–style layout for your IDE. Figure 2-1 illustrates the My Profile tab for the Start Page with the Visual Basic Developer selection for the Profile drop-down box.

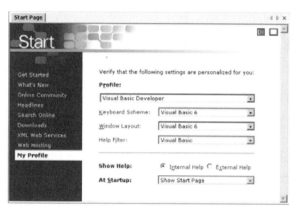

Figure 2-1   My Profile selections for starting Visual Studio .NET for a Visual Basic .NET developer

A Profile setting of Visual Basic Developer returns pages relevant exclusively to Visual Basic developers when you choose any item that opens a Help window, such as Contents, Index, or Search on the Help menu. However, developers with a general curiosity about the .NET Framework may prefer a "(No Filter)" setting for the Help Filter box. This setting will return information relevant for all possible audiences in response to a Help menu selection. If you find yourself with a heavy load of Web work, the Internet Development filter may be especially beneficial. Visual Studio .NET has an automation object model that is convenient for creating macros that run repetitive tasks in the IDE or extending the IDE for special kinds of tasks. Select Visual Studio Macros as the Help Filter setting to restrict Help screens to content for those using the Visual Studio .NET automation model. Several additional filters exist which you may find it useful to experiment with. In addition, you can manually alter the Help filter in the Visual Studio .NET documentation even after you configure Visual Studio .NET to open with any specific Help filter selection.

The Show Help option group offers two radio buttons. The default Internal Help selection presents Help within a window in the IDE. If you click

External Help, choosing any of the Help menu items, such as Contents, Index, or Search, opens a new window or uses an existing Help window outside the Visual Studio IDE.

The last drop-down box on the My Profile tab for the Start Page lets you configure how Visual Studio .NET starts the next time that it opens. Use this drop-down box to have Visual Studio .NET open to another window besides the Start Page, such as the last project loaded or the New Project dialog box (which, not surprisingly, helps you to start a new project).

Using the Start Page

After closing and reopening Visual Studio .NET, you commit your profile changes so that the application starts according to your settings. Selecting Get Started on the Start Page offers you two buttons—one for opening an existing project and a second for starting a new project. Links for your four most recent projects will appear in a table above the buttons. Clicking the link for the project automatically opens that project in Visual Studio .NET.

Click the New Project button to start a new project. This opens the New Project dialog box with a selection of templates for launching new projects. (The project types are summarized in the next section.) As an Access developer, you are likely to be interested in the Windows Application template. This template facilitates creating Access database solutions on a LAN. Just as with your current solutions created with Access forms or Visual Basic forms, solutions started with this template can take advantage of the rich graphics capability of a local Windows workstation. The Windows Application template opens a project with a new blank instance of the Windows *Form* class in the .NET Framework. In building Visual Basic .NET LAN–based solutions for your Access databases, you will use this new type of form rather than Access forms or Visual Basic forms.

Figure 2-2 shows the New Project dialog box with the Windows Application template selected. By default, Visual Studio .NET names the project WindowsApplication1 (or some other number if this is not your first Windows Application project in a directory). Unless you change the default, the dialog box will create a folder for the project in the path specified by the Location box. The name of the folder corresponds to the name of the project. This folder is the physical representation of the assembly for your project. You can deploy a solution by copying this folder to another computer on a LAN or even by copying the folder over the Internet. For example, I regularly use WinZip to package folders with the sample solutions for a chapter and send them via e-mail to my project editor at Microsoft Press. After unzipping the folder, a technical editor working with the project editor can run my solutions to verify that they work as described in the text for a chapter.

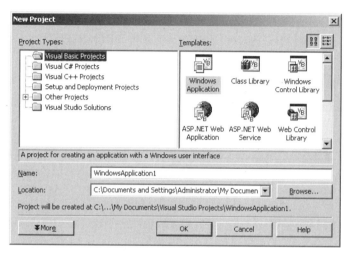

Figure 2-2   The New Project dialog box with the selection for starting your first Windows application using the Windows Application template

Clicking the Open Project button on the Start Page opens a dialog box that lets you navigate to any folder to open a project in the Visual Studio .NET IDE. Navigate to the project folder by using the dialog box, and open the file with the project's name and an .sln extension. For example, if you had previously created a WindowsApplication1 project, navigate to its folder and open WindowsApplication1.sln.

Introducing Three Important IDE Windows

As an experienced Access developer, you are probably used to thinking of the IDE as your personal playground. When moving to Visual Studio .NET, you get a new, bigger yard to play in. Figure 2-3 shows the layout of the IDE with a form named *Form1*; the form resides in the test05153 project. (See the resource files for this chapter.) The IDE shows three of the more important windows that you are likely to use when creating Visual Basic .NET solutions for your Access databases.

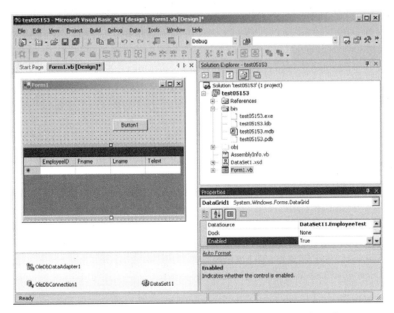

Figure 2-3   The Visual Studio .NET IDE for the test05153 project

The window on the left shows a Windows *Form* class instance with a Data Grid Control and a button control on it. The three icons in the tray below the form denote design-time specifications for *OleDbConnection*, *OleDbDataAdapter*, and *DataSet* objects. The tab name for the view showing these controls is Form1.vb[Design]. An asterisk (*) after the tab name denotes that the form has changes that are not saved. You cannot just make a change and run the code as you would in the VBA IDE in Access. All changes must be compiled before you can run them. Notice the Start Page is also a tab that you can select from the window on the left. You can have multiple selectable views that you can display in the left window, such as the code-behind *Form1*. The tab name for the code window will be Form1.vb.

The top window on the right is Solution Explorer. The assembly name for the project appears right after Solution Explorer in the window's title. I clicked the Show All Files control on the Solution Explorer toolbar, and I expanded the bin subdirectory within the test05153 assembly. As you know, you can discover the name for any Windows control by placing the mouse over it. Notice that the bin subdirectory contains an Access database file named test05153.mdb. The DataGrid control in the form on the left actually displays the contents of a table from the database when you open the form.

A full description of the process for binding a DataGrid control to a table in an Access database is beyond the scope of this section. However, a discussion of the Properties window below Solution Explorer gives us some insight into the process. Notice that the Form1.vb[Design] view shows the DataGrid control selected. A currently selected entity, such as the DataGrid, has its properties shown in the Properties window. The name for the currently selected item, *DataGrid1*, appears at the top of the Properties window.

Notice that the *DataSource* property for *DataGrid1* is *DataSet11.Employ-eeTest*. This specification designates the EmployeeTest table in the local *DataSet11* object that shows in the tray below the form. You can set the *Data-Source* property with a drop-down box that lists the available options. When a user runs the application with *Form1*, *DataGrid1* displays data from the EmployeeTest table in the test05153.mdb file. This display occurs so long as a form load event procedure behind *Form1* populates, or fills, the EmployeeTest table in *DataSet11* with the EmployeeTest table from the Access database file. The important point here is that you can graphically bind *DataGrid1* to a table in a local dataset.

Overview of Project Types and Project Folders

By introducing a wide variety of project types, Visual Basic .NET aims to make life easier as you tackle traditional and new development topics. The project types come with built-in design setups that simplify performing a task. For example, Windows Application projects include references to multiple .NET Framework namespaces, including the critical *System.Windows.Forms* namespace. The best thing about these project types is that you do not need to know what's in them to benefit from them. All you need to know is what types of projects there are.

This section gives you a summary of the types of projects that you can create with the Visual Basic .NET project templates. Don't get overwhelmed by the fact that there are 11 project types. You can readily start with just one or two and then get familiar with others as you need them.

For example, this section examines the Windows Application and Class Library templates. The Windows Application template will create the typical kind of client/server application that many Access developers routinely build on LANs. Visual Basic .NET is more object-oriented than Visual Basic and VBA. The Class Library project is one way to construct classes that you can instantiate as objects in your applications. Therefore, this section introduces you to Class Library projects. Both of these topics get substantial attention at many other points throughout the book.

Summary of Project Types

When you launch a new project with the Professional edition or higher of Visual Studio .NET, the New Project dialog box offers 11 Visual Basic .NET templates that you can use to start a new project. These templates automatically configure the IDE to handle a selected type of project. For example, one template starts a blank form, and another creates an empty class definition. Table 2-1 includes a list with each type of template and a brief description of the kind of projects you can start with each template.

Table 2-1   Visual Studio .NET Project Templates

Project Template Name	Description of Project Created
Windows Application	This project type automatically opens a project with a blank form inherited from the *Form* class in the *System .Windows.Forms* namespace. Windows applications can perform data access and manipulation tasks via ADO.NET against an Access database on the local computer or LAN. Additionally, you can use a Windows Application project as the client for an XML Web service that exposes an Access database via the Internet.
Class Library	A class library project is for the creation of components that other projects will reference and use. To use the reusable class or component, you need another project that references the stand-alone class library. The components can do anything an application needs, such as perform sophisticated calculations with the result set from a query.
Windows Control Library	Use this type of project to create your own custom, reusable controls for use on forms in Windows applications.
ASP.NET Web Application	Just as Windows applications are built around Windows Forms, ASP.NET Web applications are built around Web Forms (.aspx files). Web Forms can be designed for use by any browser compatible with HTML 3.2, but the use of Microsoft Internet Explorer 5 or later provides enhanced application capabilities and easier design—especially for developers familiar with Visual Basic or Access forms. You can invoke ADO.NET on a Web Forms page to work with an Access database just as you can on a Windows form. To create Web Forms applications, a workstation must have access to a computer with Microsoft Internet Information Services (IIS) running and the .NET Framework installed.

(continued)

Table 2-1 **Visual Studio .NET Project Templates** *(continued)*

Project Template Name	Description of Project Created
ASP.NET Web Service	Just as ASP.NET Web applications enable an end user to interact with an application over the Web, ASP.NET Web Service applications enable peer-to-peer computing between any pair of computers. One computer can invoke procedures, or exposed methods, on another computer. For example, a Web service can return tax rates or shipping costs that another computer uses to compute the final cost of an order. An ASP.NET Web Service project does not use Web Forms, but it relies on an .asmx file that provides addressable points for another computer to reference the methods exposed by a Web service.
Web Control Library	This project type parallels the functionality of a Windows Control Library project for Web Forms in ASP.NET Web applications.
Console Application	A console application runs from the command prompt in a command window. This type of project is useful for testing programming techniques without the overhead of designing and managing a graphical user interface.
Windows Service	Use this template to create a Windows Service application, which runs on a server in a session of its own. This project type is for advanced developers creating custom Windows Service applications that get called by other projects.
New Project In Existing Folder	This type of project facilitates the adding of files from a previously existing application into a new blank project. If your development workstation is running IIS, you can copy files from a previously existing Web folder for an ASP.NET Web application to a new blank project.
Empty Project	This project type creates a new blank project in a new folder. Developers must add their references, files, and components manually.
Empty Web Project	This project type creates a new blank project in a Web folder on a computer running IIS. The developer must add references for Web Forms and classes needed for the project.

Access developers are likely to spend most of their time with Windows Application projects when they first start using Visual Basic .NET; that's because this type of project is closest to the ones that most Access developers build already. I think that Web applications and Web services are important growth opportunities for any Access developer switching from Visual Basic or VBA to Visual Basic .NET. Chapters 10 through 12 address these project types in more detail. Class library applications are likely to be important to your work whether or not you take my advice about diving into Web applications and XML Web services. The other kinds of application are more specialized, and you can add them to your repertoire as the demands of your project mix dictate.

Starting a Windows Application

The next example illustrates the process for starting a Windows application and reviews the resulting folder structure. As mentioned earlier, a Windows application features a form based on the .NET Framework *Form* class in the *System.Windows.Forms* namespace. This new type of form offers the same kind of functionality available from traditional Visual Basic and Access forms, but it also offers some new capabilities.

To start a new Windows application, launch Visual Studio .NET and click New Project on the Start Page. Figure 2-2 on page 30 shows the selection of the Windows Application template. The Location box on the New Project dialog box displays the last path used for a new project (or the default location for Visual Studio .NET projects immediately after setup). You can specify a new path by typing a string in the Location box that designates the new path. This path need not already exist.

Figure 2-4 shows the New Project dialog box for creating a project named WindowsApplication1 in the pawvbnet path of the C drive on a computer. Clicking OK will open the IDE with a blank form named *Form1*, and it will add a new directory within the pawvbnet path on the computer. The new directory has the name WindowsApplication1. The directory contains several starter files reflecting the initial setup of the Windows application and a couple of subdirectories named bin and obj. The bin subdirectory normally contains an .exe file named after the project (WindowsApplication1.exe); Visual Studio .NET does not populate this directory with the file until after the first compilation.

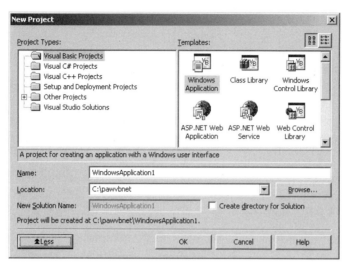

Figure 2-4   The New Project dialog box with the selection for starting your first Windows application in the C:\pawvbnet directory

Note   Visual Studio .NET adds an .sln file to the root folder of the project's folder. Use the .sln file named after a project to open the project within the IDE. You can select the .sln file from the Open Project dialog box as described previously, or you can double-click the .sln file directly from Windows Explorer.

Figure 2-4 also shows the Create Directory For Solution check box. Selecting this check box and clicking OK creates the directory for the project in the pawvbnet\WindowsApplication1 path on the C drive. Selecting the Create Directory For Solution check box enables the New Solution Name box and automatically populates the box with the contents of the Name box. You can override the entry in the New Solution Name box to specify a new subdirectory name for your project's folder. For example, if the New Solution Name box contained MyWindowsApplication1, the folder changes to the pawvbnet\ MyWindowsApplication1 path.

No matter where you position the folder for a project, you can force a compilation and open *Form1* for the WindowsApplication1 project by pressing the F5 function key in the IDE. The IDE allows only one instance of the form to be open at a time; this capability is helpful for debugging your applications. Double-clicking the WindowsApplication1.exe file from Windows Explorer will also open *Form1*. From Windows Explorer, you can open multiple instances of *Form1* by repeatedly double-clicking the WindowsApplication1.exe file. In addition, you can open the WindowsApplication1.exe file on this computer from any other computer with the .NET Framework installed.

Adding a Message Box to a Windows Application

Message boxes have many uses in Windows programming. As you know from your VBA and Visual Basic work, a message box is a modal form that displays a message and contains one or more buttons. Visual Basic and VBA provide the *MsgBox* function for displaying message boxes and optionally capturing which button a user clicked on a message box.

The .NET Framework supports the old *MsgBox* function, but it adds a *MessageBox* class. The *Show* method, which is safe for multithreaded operation, displays a message box. This method can take parameters for the message to show, the caption for the message box, the buttons and icons to show, as well as selected other features offered through the class. You do not need to instantiate an instance of the *MessageBox* class before invoking the *Show* method to display a message. When a method is safe for multithreaded operation, you can invoke the members in multiple, concurrently running threads.

> **Note** The *Show* method for the *MessageBox* class is overloaded to facilitate its invocation with different series of arguments. See the *MessageBox.Show* Method topic in the Visual Studio .NET documentation for details on the different overloaded specifications. Invoke the Help, Index command from the documentation window. Then enter the topic name in the Look For box.

The following Visual Basic .NET event procedure fires before *Form1* loads. You can open a shell for a form load event procedure by double-clicking the blank form. Do this for *Form1* in the WindowsApplication1 project. The *Form1_Load* event procedure shell appears because the *Form_Load* event is the default event for a Windows form. Next, insert the indicated code within the shell for the event procedure. The procedure causes four message boxes to appear before conditionally opening *Form1*. The condition for opening *Form1* depends on which button a user clicks on the third message box. The sample also demonstrates the syntax for assigning a string constant to a string object. (Data types are objects in Visual Basic .NET.) The *Dim* statements at the top of the procedure point the *str1*, *str2*, and *str3* variables at the string objects. The variables *str1*, *str2*, and *str3* specify arguments for the message boxes.

```
Private Sub Form1_Load(ByVal sender As System.Object, _
    ByVal e As System.EventArgs) Handles MyBase.Load

    Dim str1 As String = "Hello, from WindowsApplication1"
    Dim str2 As String = "Show form?"
    Dim str3 As String = "Show Form Message Box"

    'Old style for presenting message box still works.
    MsgBox(str1)

    'A new style is available.
    MessageBox.Show(str1)

    'Conditionally process return from a message box.
    If MsgBoxResult.No = _
        System.Windows.Forms.MessageBox.Show(str2, str3, _
        MessageBoxButtons.YesNoCancel) Then
        MsgBox("Click 'OK' to exit.")
        Me.Close()
    Else
        MsgBox("Click 'OK' to show form.")
    End If

End Sub
```

After the form load event procedure is added, pressing F5 from the IDE or double-clicking WindowsApplication1.exe from Windows Explorer does not automatically present *Form1*. Instead, a message box initially appears with a greeting. The procedure uses the traditional *MsgBox* function to present this initial message box. After a user clicks OK, a second message box appears with the same greeting. This second message box results from the invocation of the *Show* method for the *MessageBox* class. Although the first and second message boxes display the same message, they are subtly different. The second message box has a blank caption, and the first one has the project's name as a caption, which results from a default setting for the *MsgBox* function. You can readily assign a caption to the second message box by specifying a string value for the *Show* method's second argument. In fact, IntelliSense prompts for the input, but its designation is optional.

The third and fourth message boxes appear in a coordinated fashion. The message for the third message box is a question asking whether to show the form. This third message box contains three buttons labeled Yes, No, and Cancel. Its caption has the value of the *str3* object. The procedure uses the *MsgBoxResult* enumeration in an *If...Then* statement to verify whether the user clicked the button labeled No. You can use the *MsgBoxResult* enumeration with Visual Basic .NET instead of the *vb* intrinsic constants, such as *vbYes*, *vbNo*, and *vbCancel,* popular in VBA and Visual Basic solutions. The sample code presents one of two different message boxes as its fourth message box, depending on the button clicked by a user on the third message box. If the user clicks the No button, the procedure additionally invokes the *Close* method for the *Me* object, which is *Form1*, after control returns from the fourth message box. Otherwise, the *Form1_Load* event procedure ends and opens *Form1*.

Creating and Consuming a Class Library Project

A Class Library project is a component. It is similar to a Windows form, but it has no visual interface. One or more classes in a class library can expose methods and properties. You do not run Class Library projects directly. Instead, you run a project that makes an instance of a class in the class library; you can then work with properties and methods of the class.

Creating a Class Library Project

You can create a class library with the Class Library template. After clicking New Project from the Start Page, select the Class Library template in the New Project dialog box. If this is your first class library created in the path named in the Location box, Visual Studio .NET automatically enters ClassLibrary1 in the Name box. For those continuing from the previous sample, the Location box points at the pawvbnet path on the C drive. You can type over the entries in either box to change the class library's name or its destination, but this example accepts the defaults. When you click OK, Visual Studio .NET opens the IDE with the shell and settings for a class library project. In addition, Visual Studio .NET adds a folder to the file system named after the Class Library project in the path specified in the Location box.

A class library project opens to a code module with the shell for one class already defined. The default name for the class is *Class1*. The class declaration includes the *Public* keyword so that other projects that reference the class can access its properties, methods, and events. Your code for the class can restrict access to selected class entities (for example, by using the *Private* keyword in their declaration). You can create properties for classes with property functions and fields. Implement class methods with *Sub* or *Function* procedures. Use the *Events* keyword to declare events. Classes will be discussed in greater detail later in this chapter, and Chapter 3 includes a whole section on them. Chapter 4 includes a section demonstrating event-handling techniques.

Figure 2-5 shows the definition of an *About* method for *Class1* in the ClassLibrary1 project. This function procedure returns a string. This kind of method enables another project with an instance of the class to get information about the class. In this case, the information denotes the name of the class library as well as two sentences describing it. (This is my story. This is my song.) The procedure uses the *vbCr* constant to format the return string with carriage returns. The procedure also illustrates the syntax for the *StrDup* function. This function duplicates a string value a fixed number of times. The *StrDup* function performs similarly to the *String* function in VBA. In the *About* function procedure, the *StrDup* function inserts two carriage returns into the return string (*str1*).

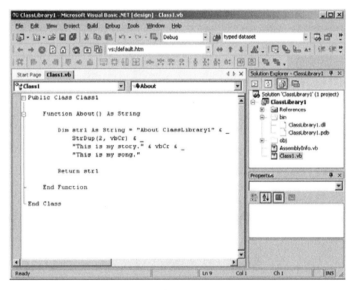

Figure 2-5 The IDE for the ClassLibrary1 project after the compilation of the solution, with the .dll file in the bin folder within the solution

> **Note**   The *vbCr* constant represents one of the printing and display intrinsic constants. The *vbCr* constant name represents the code for a carriage return, *Chr(13)*. View the "Print and Display Constants" topic in Visual Studio .NET documentation for more intrinsic constant names along with their function and value.

After entering your code, such as in Figure 2-5, you can compile it by choosing Build, Build Solution from the IDE menu bar. This creates the .dll file for the ClassLibrary1 project. This file has the name of the project (ClassLibrary1) in the bin subdirectory within the class library's project folder. As you can see from Solution Explorer in Figure 2-5, the file's full name is ClassLibrary1.dll. When another project references the class library, it must reference this .dll file.

Consuming a Class Library Project

You need a second project to take advantage of the functionality exposed by a class library project. A Windows application can serve this role by referencing a class library. In the current case, all we need is a Windows application with a button on a form. The button can invoke the *About* method implemented by the function procedure in the *Class1* class of the ClassLibrary1 project. The Windows application will manage the reference to the *Class1* class so that clicking the button allows the invocation of the *About* method.

Create a Windows application with a name of InvokeAboutInClass-Library1. You can position the project folder in the same directory as the prior samples, pawvbnet. The first step in preparing the project is to have it reference the ClassLibrary1.dll. From the IDE menu, choose Project, Add Reference. Then, click Browse in the Add Reference dialog box. In the Select Component dialog box, navigate to the .dll file you want to reference. Click Open to close the Select Component dialog box, and then click OK to confirm your reference selection and close the Add Reference dialog box. These steps update the items in the References folder within Solution Explorer for the InvokeAboutInClassLibrary1 project. The collection of references now includes ClassLibrary1 along with other built-in references for a Windows Application project, such as *System.Windows.Forms*.

The next step is to add a button to *Form1*. The button will eventually get a click event procedure that invokes the *About* method in *Class1* and displays its return string value. Choose View, Toolbox to open the Toolbox. From the Windows Forms tab in Toolbox, drag a Button control to *Form1*. Figure 2-6 shows the IDE after the addition of the button to *Form1*. The Toolbox appears on the left. Notice that it is tabbed to organize similar sets of controls. The example makes a selection from the Windows Forms tab because that's where many of the common controls are for Windows forms. The Data tab includes controls for ADO.NET objects, such as *Connection* and *DataAdapter* objects.

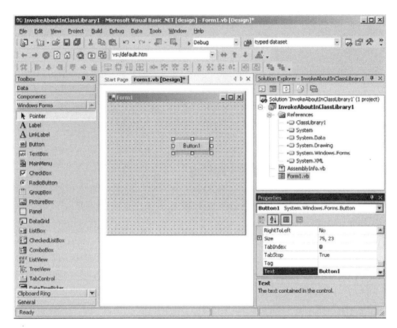

Figure 2-6   The IDE for the InvokeAboutInClassLibrary1 project after the addition of a reference to the ClassLibrary1.dll file and a button to *Form1*

The Properties window below Solution Explorer shows that the name of the button is *Button1*, and the button's *Text* property also has a string value of *Button1*. The *Text* property shows on the button, and the button's *Name* property is how you reference it in code. If this sample was for production instead of tutorial purposes, I might set the *Text* property to *About* and the *Name* property to *cmdAbout* in order to follow traditional naming conventions and to distinguish between the *Name* and *Text* property settings.

Before turning our focus away from Figure 2-6, look at Solution Explorer. The References folder is expanded so that you can see the individual references in the InvokeAboutInClassLibrary1 project. At the top of the list of references is the one added with the Project, Add Reference menu command. All the other references are added automatically by the selection of the Windows Application template at the project's launch.

You can open the code module behind the form by double-clicking Button1. This step adds the shell for a *Click* event procedure for Button1 as it opens the code module. As with the form load event in the preceding sample, the click event in this sample is the default event for the button.

> **Note**   You can add the shell for nondefault events with Visual Basic .NET in the standard way that you do with Visual Basic and VBA. Use the Class box, formerly called the Object box, just above the code module on the left to select a control. Use the Method box, formerly called the Procedure box, to the right of the Class box to specify a type of event.

The click event procedure has just two lines. The first line instantiates a new instance of the *Class1* class in the ClassLibrary1 component. The second line opens a message box with the contents of the return value from the *About* method for *Class1*. The second argument for the *Show* method designates a caption for the message box. Figure 2-7 shows the appearance of the text. You can see the impact of the formatting conducted in the *About* function within *Class1*.

```
Private Sub Button1_Click(ByVal sender As System.Object, _
    ByVal e As System.EventArgs) Handles Button1.Click

    Dim MyClass1 As New ClassLibrary1.Class1()

    MessageBox.Show(MyClass1.About, _
        "Invoke About method for ClassLibrary1")

End Sub
```

Figure 2-7   The message box that displays with a return value from the *About* method in the ClassLibrary1 component

Selected New and Different Visual Basic .NET Topics

Visual Basic .NET is a brave new world for Visual Basic and VBA developers. Understanding this new world can catapult our fortunes far ahead of those who lag behind. However, rising to the top of the developer space is not without its costs. In particular, we have to learn new ways to handle traditional as well as nontraditional topics. There is no better time than right now to learn the concepts discussed in this section because we can expect future versions of Visual Basic .NET to add new functionality at the cost of greater complexity, just as we saw with successive Visual Basic versions. Therefore, learning the basic concepts now will position you to readily digest future advances when they come along.

When I refer to Visual Basic and VBA throughout this section, I am designating the syntax and conventions consistent with Visual Basic 6, which applies to the version of VBA in Microsoft Office 2000 and later editions.

Data Types

As Visual Basic and VBA developers migrate to Visual Basic .NET, it is important to know changes in the names, declaration characters, and recommended usage for 2-byte, 4-byte, and 8-byte signed integer data types. Table 2-2 summarizes the name and declaration type changes for signed integers. Notice that Visual Basic .NET retains the names *Integer* and *Long*, but it uses these names for different data types. Visual Basic and VBA developers migrating to Visual Basic .NET gain a new integer data type for large integer data values. You can now represent 8-byte signed integer values with a *Long* data type.

The 32-bit systems, such as Microsoft Windows 98 and Windows 2000, process Visual Basic .NET integer data types slightly faster than either of the comparable data types in Table 2-2. Therefore, you can improve performance marginally by using 4-byte integers in development contexts where 2-byte integers were recommended to save memory. A more noticeable performance advantage results from replacing a *Decimal* data type with an *Integer* data type, but you must be sure that your range of values does not exceed the *Integer* data type range.

Table 2-2   Changes for 2-Byte, 4-Byte, and 8-Byte Signed Integers

Integer Size	Visual Basic/VBA Name (declaration character)	Visual Basic .NET Name (declaration character)
2 bytes	*Integer* (%)	*Short* (not available)
4 bytes	*Long* (&)	*Integer* (%)
8 bytes	Not available	*Long* (&)

Another important data type change is the dropping of the *Currency* data type. In Visual Basic and VBA, this data type represented signed integer values up to an 8-byte length with integer precision scaled for 4 fixed places after the decimal. Visual Basic .NET offers a better *Decimal* data type than what was available with Visual Basic and VBA. The new *Decimal* data type represents 16-byte signed integer values with a variable scaling factor as a power of 10. Visual Basic and VBA allowed only up to 12-byte signed integer values in a *Decimal* value, and you had to represent the values with the *CDec* function inside a *Variant* data type. As a result of these changes, Visual Basic .NET developers must use their *Decimal* data type in contexts in which Visual Basic and VBA developers used the *Currency* data type. This shift provides greater flexibility in the range and precision of currency values that you can process in Visual Basic .NET vs. Visual Basic/VBA.

The last data type change is the dropping of the *Variant* data type. In Visual Basic and VBA, if you did not explicitly assign a variable to another data type, it was implicitly designated as a *Variant* data type. In addition, a *Variant* data type can hold all other data types. The *Object* data type in Visual Basic .NET plays a similar role to the *Variant* data type in Visual Basic and VBA. (The *Object* data type will be discussed more in Chapter 3.) However, as with the *Variant* data type, recommended practice is to use a more specific data type designation whenever possible.

Arrays

Because ADO.NET introduces the *DataSet* class as an in-memory data store, Access developers will have fewer uses for arrays than in the past. Nevertheless, there will be times when you can represent sets of values in memory outside a dataset, such as when there is no database with which to coordinate a set of values or when your application can benefit from representing data in multiple dimensions and the number of dimensions is greater than two.

If you do use arrays in your application development efforts, there are several changes in the way Visual Basic .NET processes arrays from Visual Basic and VBA. First, Visual Basic .NET permits you to declare an array only with a *Dim* statement. Visual Basic and VBA enabled the declaration of an array with either *Dim* or *ReDim* statements. Second, arrays in Visual Basic .NET always have a lower bound of 0. Visual Basic .NET does not support the *Option Base* statement that enabled Visual Basic and VBA developers to specify a lower bound value of 1 for an array dimension instead of the default value of 0. Third, array sizes are always variable in Visual Basic .NET. You can respecify the size of any array with a *ReDim* statement in a procedure. In Visual Basic and VBA, you could specify fixed-size arrays, which the *ReDim* statement could not change.

New Keyword and *Sub* Procedures

The *New* keyword in a *Dim* statement has taken on new and slightly different functionality. In Visual Basic and VBA, declaring an object reference with *New* allowed you to use the object without an explicit *Set* statement. In Visual Basic .NET, there is no *Set* statement. Therefore, you need to use the *New* keyword in any *Dim* statement declaring an object reference based on a class. Visual Basic .NET adds extra functionality to the *New* keyword by allowing it to specify startup parameters for an object in a *Dim* statement. For example, if you have a *chair* class, you can specify any of multiple arguments for it when you declare a new *chair* instance. You can designate its type (*loveseat, patio, recliner*) or fabric (*cloth, leather, plastic*). The syntax for the *New* keyword in a *Dim* statement is as follows:

```
Dim VariableName As New ClassName(comma separated argument list)
```

The reason you can specify arguments for a class instance is because of a *New Sub* procedure inside the class library for a class. The .NET Framework refers to this procedure as a *class constructor*. The .NET Framework constructs a class instance for a code block that invokes the constructor with the *New* keyword in a *Dim* statement. If you design a class without explicitly creating a *New Sub* procedure, Visual Basic .NET implicitly creates one for the class. With the new overloading feature in Visual Basic .NET, you can specify alternative versions of the *New Sub* procedure—one for each argument list that you want to make available for defining a class instance at startup. Visual Basic .NET is smart enough to invoke the *New Sub* procedure that corresponds to the argument list that you provide.

Opening and Closing Class References

Some readers may recognize the *New Sub* procedure in a class as a substitute for the *Class_Initialize* event procedure, which you could specify with Visual Basic and VBA. Visual Basic .NET no longer supports the *Class_Initialize* event. While there are some differences between *Class_Initialize* event procedures and *New Sub* procedures, both types of procedures serve one central purpose—to get a class instance ready for initial use.

Just as there is no *Class_Initialize* event in Visual Basic .NET, there is no *Class_Terminate* event. Visual Basic and VBA raised the *Class_Terminate* event after an instance of a class was set to *Nothing*. Setting a class to *Nothing* in Visual Basic and VBA removed the reference for a class instance from memory. Your Visual Basic and VBA code can use a procedure associated with the *Class_Terminate* event for a class instance to close resources managed by the class instance, such as a file or a database connection. In Visual Basic .NET, setting an object reference to *Nothing* does not remove a reference to a class instance from memory. Instead, assigning *Nothing* marks the variable for selection in the next garbage collection cycle. At that time, the common language runtime (CLR) engine removes the reference from memory. Even without your setting an object reference to *Nothing*, the .NET Framework can evaluate whether to remove the object. Specifically, the garbage collector automatically determines when a class instance is out of scope (can no longer be referenced).

No matter how the .NET Framework discovers when to remove an object reference, the reference is removed nondeterministically. In other words, you cannot know in advance when the memory for a reference will be reclaimed, only that it will be reclaimed eventually. Since garbage collection cycles depend on the memory available on a system and the system load, the time to reclaim the memory for an unused reference can vary between computers with different amounts of memory, or even over time on the same machine as the load shifts by time of day.

So how do you release extra resources associated with a class instance? These extra resources, such as files and database connections, are not automatically closed when the garbage collector cleans up the memory for unused object references. One approach is to invoke *Sub Finalize*. This is a protected method of the *Object* class from which all components derive. The .NET Framework invokes the *Finalize* method whenever it removes a class instance from memory. You can associate code to dispose of extra resources with this class method. Unfortunately, there are several disadvantages associated with using the *Finalize* method, including a performance penalty, nondeterministic occurrence, and trickier-than-normal rules about when and how to use the method.

A second approach is to close extra resources independently of a class. (For example, invoke the *Close* method for a database connection associated with a class instance in the application invoking the class.) This can deterministically remove resources associated with a class. Of course, programmers sometimes fail to follow good programming habits, such as invoking the *Close* method when a resource is not needed. Therefore, it is possible for a programmer to fail to close a file or database connection associated with a class instance. When you are working on very sophisticated systems, you can use the *Finalize* method to close resources not explicitly closed earlier.

> **Note** Which approach you should use for removing extra resources associated with a class instance depends on the cost of having the resources not closed in your operational context. In my opinion, the easiest way is to dispose explicitly of extra resources associated with a class instance outside the *Finalize* method.

Class Inheritance

Inheritance is one of the most exciting new features available with Visual Basic .NET. With this feature, you can have one class inherit the properties, methods, and events of another class. The class that gets inherited is the *base class*; the class inheriting the base class is called the *derived class*. When a derived class inherits a base class, the derived class can optionally expose properties, methods, and events from the base class. The derived class can also change the definition of properties and methods or add new properties, methods, and events. A derived class can inherit from only one other class directly, but your applications can have multiple levels of inheritance so that class C can inherit from class B, which inherits from class A. As you begin to build inheritance into your solutions, I recommend keeping your inheritance levels shallow.

Use the *Inherits* keyword within a class to derive that class from a base class. When you use the *Inherits* keyword in a derived class, it must be the first line of code in the class. The *Inherits* keyword takes a single argument, which is the name of the base class. As it turns out, all classes in Visual Basic .NET applications are inherited, except for one. This is the *Object* class, which is ultimately the base class for all other classes. If you define a class without the *Inherits* keyword, the class inherits directly from the *Object* class.

A derived class can change base class members via *overriding* or *shadowing*. These two approaches to changing a base class member in a derived class work similarly but not identically. Overriding applies exclusively to *Function, Sub*, and *Property* elements in a base class, and the overriding member in the derived class must have the same type and argument list as the base class. In order to override a base class member in a derived class, the base class member must have the *Overridable* keyword as part of its declaration and the corresponding derived class member must have *Overrides* as part of its declaration.

Any named type in a derived class can shadow a correspondingly named type in a base class. The derived class type hides the shadowed type in the base class. A procedure of a field in a derived class can shadow either a procedure or a field in a base class. There is no requirement that the shadowing type match the shadowed type. While you can include the *Shadows* keyword in the derived type declaration, the use of the *Shadows* keyword is not mandatory. There is no keyword to apply to a base class type declaration that a derived class type shadows.

A derived class may refer to the overridden version of a method or the base class implementation of a method. You can use the *MyBase* and *MyClass* keywords to clarify these references. To designate the base class implementation of an overridden method in a derived class, use *MyBase.Method1*. To specify the overridden derived class implementation of the same method in the base class, use *MyClass.Method1*. If a method is not overridden in a derived class, *MyBase.Method1* and *MyClass.Method1* return the same result. Both *MyBase* and *MyClass* are just keywords, not objects, and are used exclusively with methods.

One of the easiest ways to grasp new programming concepts is to review sample code generated by someone else. Visual Studio .NET puts the *Inherits* statement and the *MyBase* keyword to use as it instantiates the form for a Windows application. This code resides in a region in the code module behind the form. By default, the region is collapsed, but you can expand it to see how Windows handles the job of making a new form. In fact, Visual Studio .NET manages the code in this region as you manually add, edit, and remove controls on the form. By examining the code in this region, you can learn a lot about programming techniques for controlling the layout of controls on a form. The string identifying the region is Windows Form Designer Generated Code.

Note   A *region* is a block of lines within a code module that you can expand and collapse.

Figure 2-8 displays an excerpt from the top of the completed code module behind the form appearing in Figure 2-6. I inserted the code listed in the "Creating and Consuming a Class Library Project" section and compiled the application, so there is no asterisk after Form1.vb on the tab for the view. The code excerpt starts with the declaration of a class named *Form1*. This is the name of the form that appears when you initially open a Windows application. You can see in Figure 2-8 the syntax for the *Inherits* statement. In this case, the Windows form in the InvokeAboutInClassLibrary1 project inherits from the *Form* class in the *System.Windows.Forms* namespace. After inheriting the class, the code invokes the *New* method from the *Form* class. By using the *MyBase* keyword, the automatically generated code refers back to the code in the *Form* class. The Forms Designer uses the call to *InitializeComponent* as a helper routine for the *New Sub* procedure to create the form instance that initially appears in the Windows application as *Form1*.

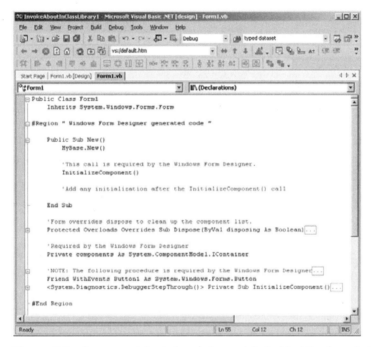

Figure 2-8 An excerpt from the code module behind the form in the InvokeAboutInClassLibrary1 project that illustrates the instantiation of a form

Namespaces

The .NET Framework uses namespaces as a means of organizing the objects in an assembly. The discussion of Figure 2-8 illustrated an application for the *System.Windows.Forms* namespace. The discussion focused on the *Form* class within the namespace. However, there are many other classes in the *System. Windows.Forms* namespace, and adding controls to a form can cause the

Forms Designer to create code illustrating how to use it. By default, each assembly has a namespace associated with it (named after the project). However, you can designate multiple namespaces for a single assembly or define a namespace that spans multiple assemblies.

Use the *Namespace* keyword to define a namespace. Namespaces can contain one or more types, such as classes, and user-defined types known as structures, enumerations, and delegates (which can process events), interfaces, and other namespaces. If you do not explicitly declare a namespace, Visual Basic .NET automatically creates one named after each assembly. Since namespaces are always public, the types within a namespace cannot include any access modifiers, except for *Public* and *Friend*; Chapter 3 defines access modifiers, such as *Public* and *Friend*, for namespaces of other .NET entities.

The names of types within a namespace must be unique. However, the names of types between namespaces can overlap with one another. By placing the namespace name before the type name, you can unambiguously designate a type even if the same name exists in two or more namespaces.

> **Note** It is good to keep life simple. Use just one namespace per assembly unless there are compelling reasons to do otherwise. You can view the default namespace for an assembly based on an .exe file by right-clicking the project file in Solution Explorer and selecting General under Common Properties in the project's Property Pages dialog box. The entry in the Root Namespace box denotes the root namespace for the project. Clearing this box allows you to specify a new root namespace or multiple root namespaces in the same assembly. Otherwise, all namespaces you designate with the *Namespace* keyword will have this name as their root.

The *Imports* keyword enables you to create shortcut names in your applications to refer to namespaces (and even names within them). You must use this keyword at the top of a module directly below any *Option* statements, such as *Option Explicit On*. Recall that the InvokeAboutInClassLibrary1 project added a reference to the ClassLibrary1 project, which made the namespace for the ClassLibrary1 project available in the InvokeAboutInClassLibrary1 project. However, to clarify the reference to the *Class1* class in the *ClassLibrary1* namespace, our preceding sample prefixed the class name with the namespace name. Figure 2-9 shows a modification to the code module behind *Form1* in the InvokeAboutInClassLibrary1 project that demonstrates the use of the *Imports* statement. The sample sets *MyClassLib* as an alias for the *Class1* class in the *ClassLibrary1* namespace. The *Imports* statement at the top of the module shortens the reference to *Class1* from *ClassLibrary1.Class1*. Figure 2-9 shows the syntax for using the *MyClassLib* alias in place of the full namespace name and class name.

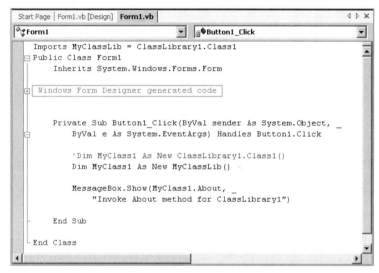

```
Imports MyClassLib = ClassLibrary1.Class1
Public Class Form1
    Inherits System.Windows.Forms.Form

    Windows Form Designer generated code


    Private Sub Button1_Click(ByVal sender As System.Object, _
        ByVal e As System.EventArgs) Handles Button1.Click

        'Dim MyClass1 As New ClassLibrary1.Class1()
        Dim MyClass1 As New MyClassLib()

        MessageBox.Show(MyClass1.About, _
            "Invoke About method for ClassLibrary1")

    End Sub

End Class
```

Figure 2-9 A modification to the InvokeAboutInClassLibrary1 project that illustrates the syntax for and use of the *Imports* keyword

Jump Start: A DataGrid Sample for the Northwind Shippers Table

This section constructs an example that pulls together many of the conceptual points and hands-on demonstrations covered in this chapter and Chapter 1. In addition, this sample works with a database that all experienced Access database developers know about—the sample Northwind database. The presentation of the example reveals how to create a form in a Windows application project that reflects the most recent data in the Shippers table from the Access database file. The directions for constructing the example accomplish nearly everything with graphical techniques, such as dragging controls and making property assignments by choosing an item from a drop-down box. It takes just one line of code to complete this example!

Building the Jump Start Example

To launch this sample, create a new Windows application; this example names the project JumpStart. (One of my favorite mottos is that real programmers do not use spaces.) The folder for the project is stored in the C:\pawvbnet directory. Our first step will be to add the *Connection* and *DataAdapter* objects to our project. There are several approaches to this task. One of the easiest is to drag a table from an Access database to a blank form. After installing Visual Studio .NET, you will automatically have a connection to the Northwind database if you have the database file on your computer in the standard location. In case you need to create a new connection to a database, the steps are shown in the sidebar titled, "Adding a Data Connection to Server Explorer."

Note   When referring to ADO.NET objects, such as *Connection*, I will often use the generic name instead of the name specific to an individual .NET data provider. For example, the *Connection* object has the names *OleDbConnection*, *SqlConnection*, and *OdbcConnection* for the OLE DB, SQL Server, and ODBC .NET data providers, respectively. Using the generic term identifies that we are talking about the same kind of object no matter which data provider an application uses.

You can start to drag a table from the database to *Form1* in the JumpStart project by opening the Server Explorer window; do this by choosing View, Server Explorer. Expand Data Connections in Server Explorer. Then expand the data connection for the Northwind database, and drag its Shippers table to the project's form. This adds two objects to a tray below the form; the object names are *OleDbConnection1* and *OleDbDataAdapter1*. These are the names that Visual Basic .NET automatically assigns to our *Connection* and *DataAdapter* objects.

Adding a Data Connection to Server Explorer

The following directions describe the steps for adding a connection to Server Explorer. The connection points at the Northwind database in its default path for Access 2002. You can adapt the directions for any Access database file name and path. For the example, I deleted the standard connection that Visual Studio .NET routinely sets for the Northwind database so that I could establish them again under manual control.

1. Open Server Explorer if it is not already open; choose View, Server Explorer.

2. Right-click Data Connections in Server Explorer and choose Add Connection.

3. On the Provider tab of the Data Link Properties dialog box, select Microsoft Jet 4.0 OLE DB Provider and click Next.

4. Click the Browse button (…) next to the Select Or Enter A Database Name box.

5. In the Select Access Database dialog box, navigate to the Northwind.mdb file in the \Program Files\Microsoft Office\Office10 \Samples directory.

6. Select the database file, and click Open to return to the Data Link Properties dialog box.

7. Click OK to close the Data Link Properties dialog box and add the connection for the Access Northwind database to Server Explorer.

You are now in a position to preview the data to which the *DataAdapter* connects (the Shippers table in the Northwind database). Select the *DataAdapter* in the tray below *Form1*. If the Properties window is not already open, expose it by choosing View, Properties Window. Next, click the Preview Data link below the list of *DataAdapter* properties in the Properties window. In the Data Adapter Preview dialog box, click Fill Dataset. Figure 2-10 shows the results from clicking the button in the dialog box.

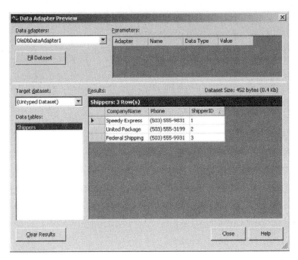

Figure 2-10   The Data Adapter Preview dialog box that lets you preview
the data to which a *DataAdapter* connects without populating a local
dataset for a control on the form

From the name on the button (Fill Dataset) that you clicked, you might be
persuaded to believe that you have filled the dataset on the form. That's wrong!
In fact, the Jump Start example has not added a dataset to the project yet. The
important clues for what's happening are the name of the dialog box (Data
Adapter Preview) and the link to open the dialog box (Preview Data). This process is useful for confirming the data to which a *DataAdapter* connects. Click
Close to close the dialog box and expose the Properties window again.

With the *DataAdapter* still selected, click the Generate Dataset link in the
Properties window. This starts the process of adding a local dataset with the structure from the Shippers table. If this is the first time you are generating a dataset
for the application, Visual Basic .NET will automatically designate DataSet1 as
the name and Shippers as the table to add to the dataset. In addition, the Generate Dataset dialog box appears with the Add This Dataset To The Designer
check box selected. It is this last check box that adds a *DataSet* object to the
tray below *Form1* when you click OK. If you have been following along with
the example, you will see a new object, named *DataSet11*, in the tray below
Form1.

Open Solution Explorer (if it is not already open) by choosing View, Solution Explorer. Notice that Solution Explorer lists a file named DataSet1.xsd. This
is the file that represents the dataset. If you decide to re-create the dataset from

scratch, I recommend that you delete this file from Solution Explorer. The .xsd
extension denotes the file as an XML schema file consistent with World Wide
Web Consortium (W3C) standards; see the Chapter Appendix if you want a
brief introduction to XML. This type of file defines the structure of a data
source. At design time, this dataset in the project contains the structure, but not
the contents, of the Shippers table from the Northwind database file.

Figure 2-11 shows the Form Designer view after the addition of the
dataset. (Server Explorer, which was open previously, has been closed.) The
figure shows the *DataSet11* object in the tray below the form selected because
that was the last object manipulated. You can also see the DataSet1.xsd file in
Solution Explorer. Are you confused by the fact that the file name (DataSet1)
and the object name (*DataSet11*) are not the same? This is not a problem. The
Properties window reveals that the object name and dataset name correspond
to different properties of the same object.

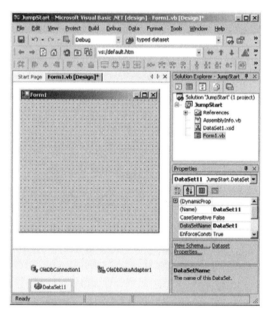

Figure 2-11   The Form Designer view of the Jump Start example after
the addition of a dataset to the project

You are now ready to add a DataGrid control to the form. The *DataSet11*
object can serve as the source for the control. (DataGrid controls will be covered more fully in Chapters 6 and 7. For now, you can think of a DataGrid
control as a control for displaying data with the layout of a datasheet.) Open
the Toolbox by choosing View, Toolbox. Before dragging a control from the

Toolbox, widen the form slightly; a width of 336 pixels should be adequate for the demonstration. Select *Form1* and drag its right border. You can use the *Size* property for *Form1* to see how wide your form is. Then, drag the DataGrid control from the Windows Forms tab in the Toolbox to *Form1*. Drag the DataGrid so that it fills the width of *Form1*.

In the Properties window, you can see that Visual Basic .NET automatically assigns the name *DataGrid1* to the control. You can optionally close the Toolbox to conserve space by clicking Close at the top of the Toolbox window. From the Properties window, click the drop-down control in the DataGrid's *DataSource* property. Select *DataSet11.Shippers*. This selects the local Shippers table from the *DataSet11* object as the source for the DataGrid control.

We need just one line of code to complete the Jump Start example. In the *Form1_Load* event procedure, we need to fill the Shippers data table in the *DataSet11* object with the Shippers table from the Northwind database file. The .NET Framework documentation refers to a table in a *DataSet* object as a *DataTable* object. This *DataTable* object is part of the *DataSet* object model that Chapter 1 covered in its closing section and Chapter 7 examines more fully. Open a shell for the form load event procedure by double-clicking *Form1* in any blank area. Then insert the following line of code:

```
OleDbDataAdapter1.Fill(DataSet11,"Shippers")
```

This statement in the form load event instructs the CLR to populate the local Shippers *DataTable* with the Shippers table from the Northwind database. Each time the form opens, the CLR freshly populates the dataset, which in turn shows in *DataGrid1*. Therefore, if the table changes between two successive openings of the form, the table will show new contents. In the Jump Start example, there is no Refresh button for repopulating *DataGrid1* without reopening the form. In addition, there is no path for data updated in *DataGrid1* to find its way back to the Shippers table in the Northwind database file. Samples in Chapters 7 and 8 will demonstrate this kind of functionality.

Demonstrating the Jump Start Example

After completing the design of the Jump Start example, it's time to see it in action. Choose Debug, Start to open *Form1*. This menu selection generates the same result as pressing F5. Notice *Form1* shows the contents of the Northwind Shippers table in the DataGrid control on the form. You can resize the columns in the DataGrid for the width of the data in the columns. Drag the right edge of a column heading to resize a column. Click the column title to sort the rows in the DataGrid by the values in the column. Clicking the same column title successively toggles the sort order between ascending and descending. Figure 2-12 shows the DataGrid control displaying the rows in alphabetical order by CompanyName; the default order for rows is the primary key, ShipperID, for the Shippers table.

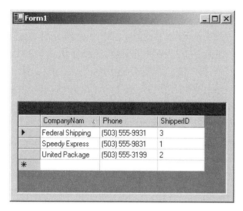

Figure 2-12 The Jump Start example showing the data from the Shippers table from the Northwind database in a DataGrid control sorted in alphabetical order by CompanyName

You can make a change to a value in any cell of the DataGrid. However, if you close and reopen the form, the change disappears. You can close *Form1* by clicking the Close control in its top right corner. When you reopen the form, it shows the current data from the Northwind Shippers table. In fact, if you change the data in the Shippers table from within Access, the DataGrid control reflects the changed data the next time that you open the form. However, the DataGrid does not reflect changes to the Shippers table in the Access database file until you reopen the form.

Summary

Despite its limitations, the Jump Start example pulls together content covered in this chapter and Chapter 1, and it demonstrates new functionality: how to populate a *DataTable* object with a *DataAdapter* object. In addition, you learned how to work with Server Explorer to expeditiously create a *Connection* object and a *DataAdapter* object that tie to an Access database file. Finally, the discussion of the Jump Start example includes step-by-step instructions for creating a new data connection that points at any Access database file in Solution Explorer.

3

Visual Basic .NET Fundamentals

This chapter and Chapter 4 will help Microsoft Access developers achieve the same degree of comfort with Microsoft Visual Basic .NET that they currently enjoy with classic Microsoft Visual Basic—which practicing developers often call VBA and VB, respectively. In both these chapters, I focus on content that has special relevance to Access database developers and that can measurably improve the flexibility of solutions they create. All the database samples in this chapter feature Access databases, and these samples are available either as folders or as code listings from which you can readily create folders.

Access database developers use various types of data to create solutions. If you don't use the right data types, you can force the premature reengineering—or at the very least slow down the operation—of an otherwise well-designed system. This chapter starts by reviewing Visual Basic .NET data types and contrasting them with Access table data types. In particular, you will learn how to map traditional Access data types to those in Visual Basic .NET. The discussion of data types has a couple of goals: introducing data types as objects and contrasting values types with reference types. Understanding these two topics will enable you to use Visual Basic .NET data types more effectively when crafting Access database solutions.

This chapter will also expose you to traditional Visual Basic .NET programming topics, including *Sub* and *Function* procedures, branching and looping, and arrays. The code samples in these sections have two main objectives: to show you how similar Visual Basic .NET is to the classic Visual Basic that you already know and love, and to show you how to take advantage of new functionality as well as drop old programming habits that don't carry over to Visual Basic .NET. Furthermore, I will introduce you to the COM Interop feature of

Visual Basic .NET. Access developers migrating to Visual Basic .NET are likely to find this feature particularly important because it enables them to use Microsoft ActiveX Data Objects (ADO) classes in Visual Basic .NET solutions.

The chapter closes with a review of programming techniques for implementing properties and methods in custom classes. All the samples in this section feature the familiar Northwind database. The focus on objects in Visual Basic .NET makes programming objects more natural than ever before (for example, data types are objects). Regardless of whether you regularly program custom classes with classic Visual Basic, this closing section offers new functionality that you will need to know. The treatment of classes in this chapter lays a foundation for some more advanced topics covered in Chapter 4, such as event processing and class inheritance.

Visual Basic .NET, Access, and System Data Types

As an Access developer, you know the importance of typing data properly. The idea behind using data types is to specify a structure for interpreting a value. Users of your applications can perform different operations on the number *1* than they can on the string "1". Although classic Visual Basic obscured this kind of distinction with the *Variant* data type, good programming practice dictates that you should not use the *Variant* data type unless no alternative exists. Regardless, Visual Basic .NET no longer supports the *Variant* data type. Instead, it offers a new *Object* data type that is even broader in scope than the *Variant* data type. Just as you should avoid using the *Variant* data type in Visual Basic when a more specific type will serve an application, you should avoid using the *Object* data type in Visual Basic .NET when a more specific type will do.

The Visual Basic .NET data types correspond to data types for the .NET Framework's common language runtime (CLR). The CLR data types belong to the *System* namespace. This correspondence between Visual Basic .NET and CLR data types is part of the reason languages are interoperable in the .NET Framework. Chapter 2 highlighted some differences between classic Visual Basic and Visual Basic .NET data types. These differences are most important when you are trying to migrate a classic Visual Basic application to Visual Basic .NET. My recommendation is that you avoid such migrations. Use Visual Basic .NET for your new applications so that they can benefit from all its new features. Leave your old applications in classic Visual Basic so that you can devote your programming resources to new challenges instead of retrofitting new techniques to previously solved tasks.

Visual Basic .NET Data Type Summary

Table 3-1 lists the Visual Basic .NET data types along with their matching CLR *System* names. The third column in the table denotes the memory requirement for each data type, and the fourth column displays the range of values a data type can represent. I would normally refer you to a page in the Visual Studio .NET documentation for content such as this, but data types are so critical to Access database programming that I included portions of this information here. The unedited version of this material is available under the "Data Type Summary" topic of the documentation.

Table 3-1   Visual Basic .NET Data Types

Visual Basic .NET Data Type	CLR DataType	Size in Bytes	Value Range
Byte	System.Byte	1	0 through 255 (unsigned)
Short	System.Int16	2	-32,768 through 32,767
Integer	System.Int32	4	-2,147,483,648 through 2,147,483,647
Long (long integer)	System.Int64	8	-9,223,372,036,854,775,808 through 9,223,372,036,854,775,807
Decimal	System.Decimal	1	0 through +/-79,228,162,514,264,337,593,543,950,335, with no decimal point; 0 through +/-7.9228162514264337593543950335, with 28 places to the right of the decimal; smallest nonzero number is +/-0.0000000000000000000000000001 (+/-1E-28)
Single (single-precision floating-point number)	System.Single	4	-3.4028235E+38 through -1.401298E-45 for negative values; 1.401298E-45 through 3.4028235E+38 for positive values
Double (double-precision floating-point number)	System.Double	8	-1.79769313486231570E+308 through -4.94065645841246544E-324 for negative values; 4.94065645841246544E-324 through 1.79769313486231570E+308 for positive values
Char	System.Char	2	0 through 65,535 (unsigned)
String (variable length)	*System.String* (class)	Depends on implementing platform	0 to approximately 2 billion Unicode characters
Date	System.DateTime	8	0:00:00 on January 1, 0001 through 11:59:59 P.M. on December 31, 9999
Boolean	System.Boolean	2	*True* or *False*
Object	*System.Object* (class)	4	Any type can be stored in a variable of type *Object*.

The *Byte* through *Long* data types represent discrete whole numbers (values with no numbers to the right of the decimal point). When you are programming loops, use the *Integer* data type whenever possible because it speeds performance. Recall from Chapter 2 that the *Integer* data type in Visual Basic .NET refers to a 4-byte value instead of a 2-byte value, as it does in classic Visual Basic.

The *Decimal* data type represents precise values in the same way that *Byte*, *Short*, and *Integer* data types do. However, *Decimal* permits digits after the decimal point, such as the *Single* and *Double* data types. *Decimal* is a good candidate for replacing the *Currency* data type found in classic Visual Basic but missing from Visual Basic .NET. The *Decimal* data type is a full-fledged data type in Visual Basic .NET and not a subdata type of *Variant*. Visual Basic .NET enables you to declare a variable as a *Decimal* data type. (Classic Visual Basic required you to specify a *Variant* data type and allowed the return of the *Decimal* data type value with the *CDec* function.)

The *Char* data type, which complements the *String* data type, is a new one for classic Visual Basic developers. Both the *Char* and *String* data types represent displayable or printable Unicode characters, but the *Char* data type specifies a fixed-length string of exactly one character. With a maximum capacity of 2 ^ 31—about 2 billion—characters, the *String* data type accommodates more characters than most applications will typically need. (It's OK to smile.) Unicode character representations use 2 bytes to represent each character. The full Unicode set of values for characters—which range from 0 through 65,535—is particularly convenient for representing worldwide character sets, and Unicode codes include ASCII character codes as a subset.

A variable declared as a *Boolean* data type can have one of two states. Assign *True* and *False* to set the variable for each state. As with classic Visual Basic, *True* corresponds to a numeric value of -1, and *False* converts to 0. However, it is safest in assignment statements to use the logical values for which the *Boolean* data was designed.

The *Date* data type represents the date and time values in an 8-byte format. The range of date values extends from January 1, 0001 A.D. through December 31, 9999 A.D. As with classic Visual Basic, Visual Basic .NET represents days with integers to the left of the decimal point and fractions of a day with the value to the right of the decimal point. Visual Basic .NET offers a rich array of functions that return dates and times, perform arithmetic with *Date* data type values, and convert between *Date* data type and *String* data type representations for date values. These functions offer most developers a more efficient means of processing date values than direct manipulation of the numeric value underlying a date.

The *Object* data type is the root of all other types in Visual Basic .NET as well as in the whole .NET Framework. A variable with an *Object* data type can hold any other data type value. With the exception of *String* and *Object*, all other data types are value types. The memory for a value type contains the value. The size of the memory allocation for a value type depends on its size in bytes, as shown in Table 3-1. The *Object* data type is a reference data type. In this case, a variable declared as an *Object* data type does not contain a value. Instead, such a variable points at, or references, an object. The object can be very large or very small, but the variable with the *Object* data type will always take only 4 bytes. Of course, the object pointed at will require additional memory. Setting one variable equal to another when both are declared as *Object* data types does not create a copy of the object—it creates only a copy of the pointer in the original variable.

It is sometimes useful to know the default value for data types. For example, knowing the default value can streamline your code. You do not have to set a variable equal to its default value if that is the value you want it to have initially. The default value for all numeric data types such as *Byte* and *Single* is 0. Dates have a default value of the first date and time, namely January 1, 0001 at 12:00:00 A.M. *Boolean* data types are *False* by default. The *Char* data type's default value is *Chr(0)*, which is the nonprintable ASCII code for *Null*. If you declare a *String* variable without explicitly assigning an initial string value to the memory variable, the variable equals a zero-length string (""). In the case of *Object* data types, the default value is *Null*.

Visual Basic .NET Data Types vs. Access Data Types

Now that you know the Visual Basic .NET data types, you have solved half the puzzle of understanding how to use Visual Basic .NET to process data in Access databases. The other half of the puzzle is understanding the relationship between Visual Basic .NET and Access data types for tables. Tables are ultimately where you will collect data from Access for your Visual Basic .NET applications. (Queries, another potential data source, simply select and aggregate data from Access tables.)

Table 3-2 enumerates the 15 kinds of data types that you can create from an Access Design view for a table. Some Access data types such as *Text* and *DateTime* are stand-alone data types that you specify fully in the top grid in the Design view when you are creating or editing a table. Other important Access data types such as *Byte*, *Integer*, and *Long Integer* are actually subtypes of the Access *Number* data type. When specifying one of these other data types for a column in a table, you choose *Number* as the data type in the top grid within the Design view, and then you select the subtype as a Field Size setting in the lower portion of the Design view. For this reason, Table 3-2 uses two columns to denote the Access data types—one for the data type and a second for the *Number* subtype specified in the Field Size setting.

Table 3-2   Visual Basic .NET and Access Data Types

Access Data Type	Number Subtype	Corresponding Visual Basic .NET Data Type
Text	Not applicable	*String*
Memo	Not applicable	*String*
Number	*Byte*	*Byte*
Number	*Integer*	*Short*
Number	*Long Integer*	*Integer*
Number	*Single*	*Single*
Number	*Double*	*Double*
Number	*Replication ID*	Not supported (*System.Guid*)
Number	*Decimal*	*Decimal*
Datetime	Not applicable	*Date*
Currency	Not applicable	Not supported (*System.Decimal*)
Autonumber	Not applicable	*Integer*
Yes/No	Not applicable	*Boolean*
OLE *Object*	Not applicable	Not supported (*Stream* class)
Hyperlink	Not applicable	*String*

The third column in Table 3-2 shows the corresponding Visual Basic .NET data types for the Access table data types. Table 3-2 is constructed from two primary resources. The first resource is the "Comparison of Data Types" section in the Microsoft Office documentation. You can find this page on the MSDN site at the following URL:

http://msdn.microsoft.com/library/default.asp?url=/library/en-us/off2000/html/ acdatComparisonDataTypes.asp

This Web page includes a table containing a pair of columns mapping Access 2000 and Access 2002 data types to Visual Basic 6 data types. The second resource Table 3-2 draws from is the table with information on Visual Basic .NET data types from the Visual Studio .NET documentation. (This is the same material that Table 3-1 was based on.) For example, the Access *Currency* data type maps to the *Currency* data type in Visual Basic 6, but as stated earlier,

Visual Basic .NET dropped support for the *Currency* data type. Instead, the Access *Currency* data type maps to the *Decimal* data type in Visual Basic .NET. Visual Basic .NET also does not support the *Replication ID* subtype for the *Number* data type. A *Replication ID* data type value is a globally unique identifier (GUID), which is a 16-byte hexadecimal number. However, the .NET Framework will translate the Access *Replication ID* subtype of the *Number* type to the *System.Guid* type. The Access OLE *Object* data type corresponds to a binary object, such as a bitmap or a Microsoft Excel spreadsheet. No direct Visual Basic .NET translation for this Access data type exists. The .NET Framework can represent this data as a stream of bytes. Study the *Stream* class to learn how to read and write object instances of this class.

Table 3-2 borrows from the preceding Web page reference the convention of mapping the Access *Hyperlink* data type to the Visual Basic .NET *String* data type. Although this might be technically true in terms of the contents of the *Hyperlink* data type field, you cannot link a field with a *Hyperlink* data type in Visual Basic .NET. The Access *Hyperlink* data type does not follow traditional Web conventions for specifying a link. Instead, Access creates a four-part definition for *Hyperlink* data types. Some parts of this definition are optional. To implement the linking capability, you will need to parse the Access *Hyperlink* value into its parts and then transfer control according to the instructions embedded in the value.

Value Type Objects vs. Reference Type Objects

Visual Basic .NET is object oriented, and Visual Basic .NET data types are no exception. All the data types have properties and methods. In addition, you can create your own objects as either structures or classes. Your custom objects can have properties and methods—just like the native objects available through Visual Basic .NET. The next sample demonstrates this capability while highlighting the distinction between value types, such as *Integer* and *Single*, and reference types, such as *Object* and *String*.

As explained earlier, a value data type saves its value with the memory representing an instance of the data type object. Copying an instance of a value type object copies the value of the data type instance to a new memory location. With a reference type object, the memory management for copying is different: the memory for the reference variable does not contain the object. Instead, the memory for a reference type object contains a pointer to the referenced object. The .NET Framework manages the memory for value and reference types in a list, referred to as the *stack*. Items in the stack have a known number of bytes determined by the type's size in bytes. The memory for items in the stack gets released immediately when an item goes out of scope—for example, when a procedure declaring the value type closes. The objects at which reference types point reside in another area of memory known in the .NET Framework as the *heap*. The heap is managed by garbage collection.

You can specify a custom value type with the *Structure* type in Visual Basic .NET. This type essentially lets you designate a variable for a user-defined data type. The *Structure* type is similar in some ways to the *Class* type. Both let you create objects. When you create an object with the *Class* type, it is always a reference type. Creating your own object with the *Structure* type always yields a value type—even if your user-defined variable contains reference variables that are not value types, such as strings. The same rule applies to objects instantiated with a *Class* type. Namely, the *Class* type always instantiates a reference type—even if your definition for the class exclusively uses value types. The following sample contrasts the behavior of objects based on a *Structure* type with that of objects based on a *Class* type.

Start the construction of the sample by creating a new project based on the Empty Project template. In my sample materials for this chapter, I named the project ReferenceValueComparison. You create a project based on the Empty Project template just as you create a Microsoft Windows application, but you choose the Empty Project template. Because of the template selected, Visual Studio .NET creates a project shell with a matching folder. To make a Code window start a sample, choose Project, Add Module. Accept the default name of Module1.vb by clicking Open (unless you need to change the name before opening the module).

The code sample starts by declaring two types: *NameStructure* and *NameClass*. The *NameStructure* type uses the *Structure* keyword to define the blueprint for an object that will create value types when our application makes instances of the *NameStructure* structure. The *NameClass* type uses the *Class* keyword. The *NameClass* type will create reference types when our application makes instances of it.

Notice that the definitions for the *NameStructure* and *NameClass* types directly parallel one another, except that one is a *Structure* type and the other is a *Class* type. This distinction causes instances based on either definition to behave differently. Either object definition can create an object with two members (properties), *p1* and *p2*. The *p1* property designates the first name of the object instance, and the *p2* property value specifies the last name of the object instance. Because the *NameStructure* type creates value type instances, you can make different changes to the members of different instances. By contrast, the *NameClass* type creates reference type values. Therefore, changing a property for one instance based on the *NameClass* type causes the modification to appear in all instances based on the *NameClass* type.

The *Sub main* procedure is the startup object for the ReferenceValue-Comparison project. This is the default setting for an empty project to which you add a module. When you start the project (for example, by choosing Debug, Start), the CLR runs the project's *Sub main*. This procedure calls two other *Sub* procedures, *democlass* and *demostructure*. The *democlass* and *demostructure Sub* procedures are the same, except for two statements. The first is the *Dim* statement declaring the *a* and *b* instances of a name object. In the *democlass Sub* procedure, the instances are declared on the *NameClass* type so that the *a* and *b* instances point at the same name object. The *demostructure Sub* procedure declares *a* and *b* name instances based on the *NameStructure* type so that the two instances point at different value types, each containing their own values for the members in an instance. The second statement that distinguishes the *Sub* procedures displays the *p1* property values for the *a* and *b* instances of the name object. Each procedure sets the message box title in order to identify which procedure generated the message box.

The type used for specifying *a* and *b* instances is by far the most important distinction between the *democlass* and *demostructure* procedures. Otherwise, the procedures are essentially the same. After the object declarations, the procedures create a new instance: *a*, with the *p1* and *p2* values of *Rick* and *Dobson*. Then the logic copies the *a* instance to a *b* instance. Next the logic assigns a new value to the *p1* property of the *a* instance. The procedures close by invoking the *MsgBox* function to display the *p1* property values for the *a* and *b* instances. Let's take a look at the code now:

```
Module Module1

    'Declare a user-defined data type.
    Public Structure NameStructure
        Dim p1, p2 As String
        Sub New(ByVal Fname As String, ByVal Lname As String)
            Me.p1 = Fname
            Me.p2 = Lname
        End Sub
    End Structure

    'Declare a class.
    Public Class NameClass
        Public p1, p2 As String
        Sub New(ByVal Fname As String, ByVal Lname As String)
            Me.p1 = Fname
            Me.p2 = Lname
        End Sub
    End Class
```

(continued)

```
Sub main()

    'Demo the operation of the class.
    democlass()

    'Demo the operation of the structure.
    demostructure()

End Sub

Sub democlass()

    'Declare two instances of the class.
    Dim a, b As NameClass

    'Assign values to a instance with New method.
    a = New NameClass("Rick", "Dobson")

    'Set b instance equal to a instance.
    b = a

    'Reset p1 member of a instance.
    a.p1 = "Virginia"

    'Display p1 member of a and b instances.
    Dim str1 As String
    str1 = "a.p1 = " & a.p1 & _
        "; b.p1 = " & b.p1
    MsgBox(str1, MsgBoxStyle.Information, _
        "From democlass")

End Sub

Sub demostructure()

    'Declare two instances of the structure.
    Dim a, b As NameStructure

    'Assign values to a instance with New method.
    a = New NameStructure("Rick", "Dobson")

    'Set b instance equal to a instance.
    b = a

    'Reset p1 member of a instance.
    a.p1 = "Virginia"
```

```
'Display p1 member of a and b instances.
Dim str1 As String
str1 = "a.p1 = " & a.p1 & _
    "; b.p1 = " & b.p1
MsgBox(str1, MsgBoxStyle.Information, _
    "From demostructure")

End Sub

End Module
```

Figure 3-1 shows the two messages generated by the *Sub main* calls of the *democlass* and *demostructure* procedures. In the From Democlass message box, a change to the *p1* property for the *a* instance maps to the *b* instance. *Virginia* is the *p1* property for both the *a* and *b* instances. The From Demostructure message box maintains separate property values for the *a* and *b* instances; therefore, a modification of the *a* instance's *p1* value does not revise the *b* instance. In the From Demostructure message box, the *p1* property for *b* is still *Rick*, although the *p1* member for the *a* instance is *Virginia*.

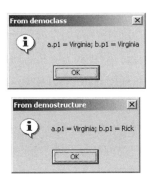

Figure 3-1   The message boxes generated when you run the ReferenceValueComparison project

Sub and *Function* Procedures

Sub and *Function* procedures are workhorses for encapsulating classic Visual Basic code. Although a few new rules about their use exist in the .NET version of Visual Basic, many syntax conventions are exactly the same. This section discusses the important issues of using these two types of procedures. In addition, the section highlights new topics for each procedure type so that you can take advantage of them as appropriate.

Creating Reusable Code Blocks

Classic Visual Basic developers have benefited from the ability to create code blocks that collectively comprise an application. This ability to compartmentalize code and reuse it anticipated the power of object-oriented programming. A code block in a *Sub* procedure or a *Function* procedure performs a set of instructions. You can pass values into either of these two types of *Sub* procedures. The *Function* procedure provides a built-in mechanism for returning an object, such as the outcome of a computation. By calling these procedures at different points from another procedure, you are essentially reusing the code in the procedures.

A *Sub* procedure can perform a task. You can vary the operation of the task performed by the parameters that you pass to the *Sub* procedure. For example, a *Sub* procedure can compute the product of two numbers and display the result. If the two numbers happen to be the same, the product denotes the area of a square. If the two numbers are different, the product can represent the area of a rectangle. By internally checking the values of passed parameters, the *Sub* procedure can indicate whether the product represents the area of a square or a rectangle.

Passing Values

Sub procedures in Visual Basic .NET work similarly to *Sub* procedures in classic Visual Basic. However, in this section, we will discuss a couple of enhancements to .NET *Sub* procedures.

You likely will notice the *ByValue* and *ByRef* keywords before passed arguments. By default, classic Visual Basic passes arguments to procedures by reference. When a *Sub* procedure accepts an argument this way, the *Sub* procedure can update the original value in the calling procedure. This feature introduces a potential source of error—or, at the very least, lack of isolation—between the code blocks in a solution. With Visual Basic .NET, the default technique to pass an argument is by using the *ByVal* keyword. The *ByVal* keyword specifies the acceptance of a copy of the argument value from the calling procedure. This enables the *Sub* procedure to manipulate the value of a passed argument without updating the corresponding argument value in the calling procedure. If you want your *Sub* procedure to recompute one or more values in its calling procedure, use the *ByRef* keyword before those arguments in the *Sub* statement.

The sample presented at the end of the preceding section demonstrates the syntax for calling *Sub* procedures with and without passing arguments. The *main* procedure called two *Sub* procedures—*democlass* and *demostructure*.

The editor in Visual Studio .NET automatically inserts the closing parentheses, which are mandatory even when a *Sub* procedure requires no arguments. The *New* procedure in the *NameClass* class illustrates the syntax for the *ByVal* keyword. To accept values by reference instead of by value, replace each *ByVal* keyword in the *Sub* statement with the *ByRef*. The *democlass* procedure demonstrates the syntax for invoking the *New* method implemented by the *Sub* procedure with that name in the *NameClass* class. Although the *ByVal* keyword prohibits updating the *p1* and *p2* members by using the *New* method, the declaration of these members enables updating with a simple assignment statement. *Dim* statements for variables implicitly denote a *Public* access modifier. (We will discuss using access modifiers a bit later in the section.)

Function procedures are designed to pass back a value. In fact, a *Function* procedure will frequently appear in an expression in the calling procedure so that it supplies a value for the computation of a result. By using an *As* keyword in the *Function* procedure declaration, you can specify the data type for the returned object from the function. Although you can return a value by setting the function name equal to the value, a new *Return* keyword offers an alternative means of designating a function's return value.

The following *main* procedure invokes a *Function* procedure named *MySquare*. The script is available in the materials posted for this chapter as MySquarer.txt; you can copy the script into an empty project shell to test its performance. The *Function* procedure takes a single argument by value and returns the square of the input argument. The *Function* procedure contains a single line of code that illustrates the syntax for the *Return* keyword. Both the input and output from the *Function* procedure have a *Double* data type.

The *main* procedure performs three steps. First, it collects the number to square. An *InputBox* function gets the input as a string, and a *CDbl* function converts the string to a *Double* data type, which a *Dim* statement stores in *MyNumb*. Second, the *main* procedure computes a string for display in a message box function. The expression for computing the string invokes the *MySquare* procedure to compute the square of the value collected in the first step. The second step explicitly converts the return value to a string for its use in the string expression. The final step invokes the *MsgBox* function to display the string computed in the second step. This last step shows the result evaluated by the *MySquare* procedure.

```
Sub main()
    'Get input.
    Dim MyNumb As Double = _
        CDbl(InputBox("Enter a number", "Number to square"))
```

(continued)

```
'Compute output.
Dim str1 As String = "The square of " & MyNumb.ToString & _
    " is " & CStr(MySquare(MyNumb)) & "."

'Display result.
MsgBox(str1, MsgBoxStyle.Information, "Your result")

End Sub

Function MySquare(ByVal MyNumb As Double) As Double

'Compute and return value for function.
Return (MyNumb ^ 2)

End Function
```

Using *Option Strict*

The *Option Strict* statement is a statement introduced with Visual Basic .NET. As with the *Option Explicit* statement available with classic Visual Basic, you must specify this directive as the first line of any code module. You can turn the *Option Strict* on or off by following the statement with the *On* or *Off* keyword. This statement is turned off by default.

Although you can still use *Option Explicit* to require the explicit declaration of variable data types, the new *Option Strict* directive implies *Option Explicit*. In addition, the *Option Strict* directive governs how you can specify the input and output values from procedures. In the preceding *MySquare* procedure, the input argument (*MyNumb*) and the output argument (the function name) have data type assignments via the *As* keyword. Without the *Option Strict On* directive at the top of a code module, you can remove either or both *As* clauses and the project will still compile properly. But once you designate the *Option Strict On* directive, the project will not compile without both *As* clauses. The use of the *Option Explicit* directive does not result in sensitivity to explicit type declarations for input and output arguments for procedures.

More generally, the *Option Strict On* directive allows only *widening* data type conversions—conversions that will surely succeed. For example, you can always convert a variable declared as a *Byte* data type to an *Integer* data type. This is a widening conversion because no data loss can occur. On the other hand, transforming a variable declared as an *Integer* type to another variable declared as a *Byte* data type is a *narrowing* conversion. Because the *Integer* data type range extends well above and below the range of legitimate values for a *Byte* data type, it is possible—but not necessary—for the conversion of the *Integer* data type to the *Byte* data type to throw a run-time error, which is known in the .NET Framework as an *Exception* object. (See Chapter 4 for more details on run-time error processing and *Exception* objects.)

Using Access Modifiers

Access modifiers control access to entities within class and structure instances. You can use access modifier keywords when declaring entities such as variables and procedures within classes and structures. Understanding access modifiers will reinforce your understanding of Visual Basic .NET types and how you can use those types. This section briefly summarizes selected access modifier keywords to help you determine which access modifiers to use in various contexts.

Table 3-3 includes a summary of the most common access modifiers. Even if you do not specify an access modifier when declaring an entity, the .NET Framework will infer some level of accessibility for an entity. For example, the default level of accessibility for a class is *Public*. Even if you declare a class as having *Public* access, its members can have narrower access, such as *Private* access. In fact, this specific use of access modifiers is typical. You often will want to define local variables within a class that are accessible only from the same class. This practice allows you to tightly restrict access to selected class members.

Table 3-3   Access Modifiers for Procedures and Variables

Access Modifier	Description
Public	Provides unrestricted access to an entity.
Protected	Provides access within a class or any derived classes based on a class.
Friend	Limits access to other elements within an assembly.
Protected Friend	Permits accessibility by union of *Protected* and *Friend* so that access is possible from within the same assembly and derived classes. The combination of these terms applies exclusively to class members.
Private	Enables access only from within a declaration context, such as a class, enumeration, or procedure.
Shared	Specifies access exclusively for members of a class or a structure. Shared members are available without instantiating an instance of a class.
Static	No longer applies to procedures but is still available for use with individual variables. Static variables retain their values between calls to a procedure.

A couple of modifier keywords in Table 3-3 apply to special situations. The *Static* keyword maintains variable values between calls to a procedure. In contrast to its use in classic Visual Basic, the *Static* keyword does not apply to *Sub* and *Function* procedures. With Visual Basic .NET, you must apply the *Static* keyword to the variables within a procedure to which it applies. The *Shared* keyword is another special member modifier. Members declared with *Shared* are not associated with any particular instance of a class. You can reference shared members even without creating an instance of a class, and shared members such as properties will have the same value across all instances of a class. If you change a *Shared* variable in one instance, all instances will have access to the revised value.

Optional Parameters and Parameter Arrays

One of the best ways to make procedures reusable is to make them flexible. Two argument declaration techniques facilitate this goal. The first allows you to designate an optional argument for a procedure. The second allows you to specify a parameter array containing an indefinite number of items. This section will present two samples that demonstrate how to put these techniques to work in an application.

Optional Parameters

The *Optional* keyword in Visual Basic .NET works similarly but not identically to the way it worked in classic Visual Basic. Use *Optional* as the first keyword for any argument declaration that specifies an optional argument. After designating any argument in the list for a procedure as optional, all subsequent arguments for a procedure must be optional. Nevertheless, you must mark each subsequent argument with the *Optional* keyword. Visual Basic .NET adds the requirement that you must designate a default value for an argument to which you apply the *Optional* keyword. With classic Visual Basic, the designation of a default value was not mandatory. You specify the default value for an argument by trailing its declaration with an equal sign (=) and the value to assign to the argument if the calling procedure does not specify a value for the optional argument.

The following code builds on the earlier sample that computed the square for a number. (The text for the earlier sample is available as MySquarer.txt in the materials posted for this chapter.) MySquarer.txt prompted for a number with the *InputBox* function. If a user clicks the Cancel button on the *InputBox* dialog box or clicks OK without inputting a number, the function returns a zero-length string (""). This return value causes the sample in MySquarer.txt to fail because the *CDbl* function cannot convert a zero-length string to the *Double* data type value required by the *MySquare Function* procedure.

The following sample, MySquarer2.txt, remedies the problem created by the built-in *CDbl* function. It does so by replacing the built-in function with a custom *StrToDbl Function* procedure and varying the argument list for the call to the function depending on the return value from the *InputBox* function. The custom *StrToDbl* function accepts a string and returns a *Double*. However, if no string is passed to *StrToDbl*, the function uses a default value of 0. The calling procedure for the *StrToDbl Function* procedure omits the string input argument when the return value from the *InputBox* function is a zero-length string. To make this sample easy to run, we repeat the *MySquare Function* procedure, although the procedure does not change from its earlier incarnation in this section.

All the changes to the *main* procedure occur in its first segment, which gets the input from the user. The *InputBox* function returns its value to a string variable named *str2* instead of serving directly as the argument for the *CDbl* function. Next the *main* procedure tests *str2* to see whether it is a zero-length string. If *str2* is a zero-length string, the procedure calls *StrToDbl* with no arguments. If it is not, the procedure calls *StrToDbl* with *str2* as its argument. The function declaration line for *StrToDbl* shows the syntax for specifying an optional value. The procedure applies the built-in *CDbl* function to the value of its *MyNumb* argument, which equals either the string in *str2* or nothing. If the call to *StrToDbl* does not have an argument for *MyNumb*, the *Optional* argument specification assigns *MyNumb* a value of 0. This returns a double with the value 0.0. The rest of the sample works identically to the earlier version.

```
Sub main()
    Dim MyNumb As Double

    'Get input.
    Dim str2 As String = _
        InputBox("Enter a number", "Number to square")
    If str2 = "" Then
        MyNumb = StrToDbl()
    Else
        MyNumb = StrToDbl(str2)
    End If

    'Compute output.
    Dim str1 As String = "The square of " & MyNumb.ToString & _
        " is " & CStr(MySquare(MyNumb)) & "."

    'Display result.
    MsgBox(str1, MsgBoxStyle.Information, "Your result")

End Sub
```

(continued)

```
Function StrToDbl(Optional ByVal MyNumb As String = "0") _
    As Double

    'Return double.
    Return (CDbl(MyNumb))

End Function

Function MySquare(ByVal MyNumb As Double) As Double

    'Compute and return value for function.
    Return (MyNumb ^ 2)

End Function
```

Parameter Arrays

The next sample shows how to use one procedure to compute the area of a circle, rectangle, or trapezoid. The Visual Basic .NET code is available in the material posted for this chapter as AreaComputer.txt. The formula to compute the area for each type of shape is different. More importantly, each formula requires a different number of arguments. Parameter arrays apply to situations in which you do not know from one invocation to the next how many arguments you will need to pass. Before the introduction of *overloading*—which Chapter 4 demonstrates—parameter arrays were the only way to specify functions that required different numbers of arguments.

The following sample consists of two procedures—a *main* procedure and a *Function* procedure named *ComputeArea*. The *main* procedure calls the *ComputeArea Function* procedure four times. The first three calls are to compute—in order—the area of a circle, rectangle, and trapezoid. The *Compute-Area* procedure has a formula for each of these three shapes. The fourth call to the *ComputeArea* procedure is to compute the area of a triangle, but the *Function* procedure does not have a formula for this shape. The code in *ComputeArea* traps this erroneous input.

The *ComputeArea* procedure takes two types of arguments—a string named *type*, and a parameter array named *Lengths*. The *type* argument is the name of the shape. To familiarize you with *String* functions, this code demonstrates how to process the shape name in uppercase, lowercase, and proper case (which uses uppercase for first letter only). The most important syntax element of the sample is the use of the *ParamArray* keyword to designate the *Lengths* parameter array. You do not have to know in advance the number of arguments you are passing in a parameter array, but you do have to specify a single data type for all the elements. For example, when the *main* procedure calls *ComputeArea* for a circle, the procedure passes a single element for the parameter array to represent the circle's radius. When computing the area for a rectangle, the call statement for *ComputeArea* passes two arguments—one for the rectangle's width and one for its height. The formula for the area of a trapezoid relies on three parameters—the lengths of the two parallel lines and the distance between them. Beyond the number of parameters, the details of these formulas are not important to this sample. However, if you are curious, you can see these formulas at *http://www.aaamath.com/geo.html*.

```
Sub main()
    'Display the area of a circle.
    MsgBox("Radius = 7 " & StrDup(2, vbCr) & _
        ComputeArea("circle", 7).ToString, , "Area of Circle")

    'Display the area of a rectangle.
    MsgBox("Width = 7; Height = 6" & StrDup(2, vbCr) & _
        ComputeArea("rectangle", 7, 6).ToString, , _
        "Area of Rectangle")

    'Display the area of a trapezoid.
    MsgBox("First parallel side = 7; Second parallel side = 3;" & _
        vbCr & "Height = 6" & StrDup(2, vbCr) & _
        ComputeArea("trapezoid", 7, 3, 6), , "Area of Trapezoid")

    'Attempt to display the area of a triangle.
    MsgBox(ComputeArea("triangle", 3, 4), , "Wrong type")

End Sub

Function ComputeArea(ByVal type As String, _
    ByVal ParamArray Lengths() As Single) As Single

    If UCase(type) = "CIRCLE" Then
        Return (3.14159265 * Lengths(0) ^ 2)
    ElseIf LCase(type) = "rectangle" Or type = "Square" Then
        Return (Lengths(0) * Lengths(1))
    ElseIf UCase(Left(type, 1)) & LCase(Mid(type, 2)) = _
        "Trapezoid" Then
        Return (0.5 * (Lengths(0) + Lengths(1)) * Lengths(2))
    Else
        MsgBox("Type not interpretable.  Enter circle, " & _
            "rectangle, or trapezoid.")
        Exit Function
    End If

End Function
```

Branching and Looping

Branching and looping statements help you control the flow of the active statement within your applications. It is difficult to write even a simple application without using a branching statement, such as *If...Then* or *If...Then...Else*. Several code samples shown earlier in this chapter demonstrated these two types of branching statements. This section takes a more focused look at branching and looping statements by using samples that demonstrate how to use the COM Interop feature in the .NET Framework. With COM Interop capability, you can set a reference in a Visual Basic .NET procedure to type libraries, such as those used in the *References* collection with classic Visual Basic.

With...End With Statements

Perhaps the most basic statement for controlling the flow within a code block is *With...End With*. Nothing about using this statement in Visual Basic .NET has changed from its use in classic Visual Basic. This type of statement delimits a code block. Because the *With...End With* statement is inline code, a single pass through the code block is unconditional. A common use for a *With...End With* statement is to assign values to multiple properties for a single object instance. The main benefit of this statement is that within its code block, you do not have to name the object instance for each statement assigning a property value. Instead, you can represent the object instance by using a period (.) inside the *With...End With* statement.

Branching Statements

The *If...Then* and *If...Then...Else* statements support branching. Another branching statement type is the *Select...Case* statement. As with the *With...End With* statement, no changes in the syntax for these statements have occurred in their .NET incarnations. The basic *If...Then* statement allows you to execute a block of code based on the value of an expression that represents a condition. The expression should evaluate to *True* or *False*. The *If...Then...Else* statement extends this capability by letting you conditionally execute either of two code blocks. By adding *ElseIf* clauses after the *Then* clause, you can specify the conditional execution of more than two code blocks. Another option for conditionally executing multiple code blocks is to use the *Select...Case* statement. The *Select...Case* statement applies to situations in which you want to execute code blocks dependent on the value of a variable or expression. Although you can check for different values in each *Case* clause within a *Select...Case* statement, each *Case* clause must apply to the same variable or expression. The

If...Then...Else statement can accommodate different expressions in each *ElseIf* clause.

When using branching statements, it is good programming practice to have a catchall clause for variable or expression values that do not match any other clause that you specify. Use the *Else* clause as the last clause in an *If...Then...Else* statement with multiple *ElseIf* clauses to catch a condition not represented by the expression for any *If* or *ElseIf* clause. With the *Select...Case* statement, use the *Case Else* clause as the last clause to catch variable or expression values not specified in preceding *Case* clauses. The use of the *Else* and *Case Else* clauses is optional.

A new type of branching statement is the *Try...Catch...Finally* statement. This statement introduces a new style of processing for run-time errors that relieves the need for the *On Error GoTo* statement that has been available to programmers since the inception of classic Visual Basic. Chapter 4 includes a section that drills down on the syntax for the *Try...Catch...Finally* statement as well as its new style of error processing based on exceptions. This new statement type is a radical innovation because it eliminates the need for *GoTo* statements for error processing in your applications. Use of the *GoTo* statement introduces the possibility of code that is hard to follow and debug. (Developers sometimes refer to code with *GoTo* statements as *spaghetti code*.) Visual Basic .NET relentlessly aims to avoid spaghetti code by dropping the *GoSub*, *On...GoSub*, and *On...GoTo* statements.

Looping Statements

Looping statements allow you to iterate through a code block multiple times. The condition for looping through the code block depends on the type of looping statement. The looping statement types are *While...End While*, *Do...Loop*, *For...Next*, and *For Each...Next*. As with the branching statements, the basic syntax and operation of these Visual Basic .NET statements mirror their counterparts in classic Visual Basic. The sole syntax change was made to the former *While...Wend* statement, which has been updated to *While...End While*.

Both the *Do...Loop* and *While...End While* statements permit looping as long as a condition is *True*. In addition, the *Do...Loop* statement allows a code block to execute until a condition becomes *True*. You can pass control to the first statement following either type of looping statement by using either an *Exit While* or *Exit Do* statement.

The *For...Next* statement allows you to pass through code for a fixed number of iterations based on your arguments for the statement. You can specify a value that increases or decreases by a fixed numeric increment up to or down to a limit. When the value passes the limit, control transfers to the first statement after the *For...Next* loop.

The *For Each...Next* statement has a statement name similar to the *For...Next* statement, but its operation differs significantly. The *For Each...Next* statement lets you pass through the elements in a set, such as an array or a collection. The key point is that the loop passes through the individual elements—not the indexes for the elements—in a set. When you are working with the members of a set, the *For Each...Next* syntax will often be simpler than the *For...Next* syntax. However, when you are not iterating over the members of a set, it is helpful to have the *For...Next* statement available.

Both types of *For* loops provide support for common looping features. For example, you can invoke an *Exit For* statement to exit a loop before reaching its end. You can nest *For* loops within one another. It is common to have an inner loop pass through the columns on a row while an outer loop designates a succession of rows.

COM Interop

COM Interop is not a branching or looping topic, but we will discuss this feature briefly here because subsequent looping samples will apply it. The COM Interop feature in the .NET Framework permits the invoking of a COM object from Visual Basic .NET. Because almost all recent Microsoft software preceding the release of the .NET Framework is based on COM objects, you likely will need the COM Interop feature as you migrate from traditional Microsoft applications to .NET applications. For example, ADO is available as several COM objects for Access. Therefore, invoking the COM Interop feature with one or more of these COM objects enables you to tap your ADO programming skills as you first migrate to Visual Basic .NET.

The COM Interop feature essentially puts a wrapper around a COM object so that you can use it from within Visual Basic .NET. The process of invoking the COM Interop feature is similar to setting a reference to a type library in classic Visual Basic. In fact, you add a reference to your Visual Basic .NET project that points to the type library for the COM object that you want to use. After setting a reference for a type library, you can optionally use an *Imports* statement to create a shortcut for the reference. (Chapter 2 initially presented the *Imports* statement.)

Begin the demonstration of the COM Interop feature by starting a new Windows application. (The project in the sample materials for this chapter has the name MetaDataLooping.) After the project opens, add a reference to a COM object by choosing Project, Add Reference. In the Add Reference dialog box, select the COM tab. This reveals the list of all registered COM objects on a workstation. This example will add two references—one for the ADO object library that supports data access (including making a connection), and a second reference for the ADO Extensions for DDL and Security (*ADOX*) object library that permits the examination of metadata for an Access database file (.mdb).

From the COM tab of the Add Reference dialog box, scroll down to the name of the version of ADO that you are using. Figure 3-2 shows the 2.5 version of the library selected. This version is common in many environments running Access 2002. You need some version of this library to make a connection to an Access database file with ADO. In addition, the looping samples with the COM Interop feature from the MetaDataLooping project work with metadata. Therefore, the MetaDataLooping project can benefit from another reference to the *ADOX* library. Figure 3-2 shows the Add Reference dialog box just before the selection of the Microsoft ADO Ext. 2.5 For DDL And Security 2.5. Clicking Select will add the second reference name to the Selected Components list box. Then clicking OK will commit the selected items.

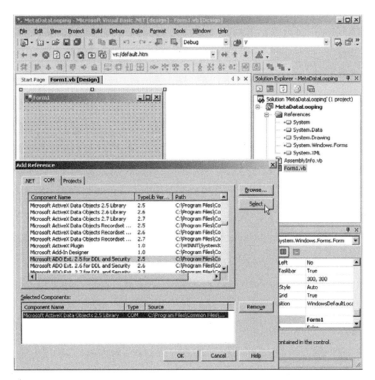

Figure 3-2   Open the Add Reference dialog box to add references to a project for COM objects.

After closing the Add Reference dialog box, names for the libraries (*ADODB* and *ADOX*) will be added to the References folder in the Solution Explorer for the project. Access developers experienced with ADO will recognize *ADODB* and *ADOX* as the names used to reference the ADO data access and the ADO data definition language and security libraries. Therefore, after you make the connection, you should feel right at home programming ADO inside a Visual Basic .NET project. The balance of this chapter contains samples illustrating various approaches for using ADO within Visual Basic .NET.

> **Note** This discussion assumes you are familiar with ADO programming. Readers without ADO experience might want to simply skim the samples to get a feel for the looping syntax, which is basically the same as for classic Visual Basic. ADO has been available for Access developers since the release of Access 2000. For in-depth ADO coverage that targets Access developers, see my book *Programming Microsoft Access Version 2002* (Microsoft Press, 2002). In addition, the Microsoft Data Access Objects (DAO) 3.51 Object Library and the Microsoft DAO 3.6 Object Library offer COM references that you can add to your projects.

Iterating Through Tables in a Database

The first sample using looping and the COM Interop feature in the Northwind database displays the names of user-defined tables in a message box—for example, Shippers and Categories. The approach to this task relies on the *ADODB* and *ADOX* references added to the MetaDataLooping project shown earlier in this section. Before starting the sample, add a button to *Form1* in the Windows application; its name will be *Button1* unless you override the default assignment to the button's *Name* property. You can drag the button from the Toolbox. Use the Properties window to change the button's *Text* property from Button1 to List Tables.

After adding the button to the form in Design view, show the code behind the form by right-clicking a blank area on the form and choosing View Code from the shortcut menu. Just below the Windows Form Designer Generated Code region, enter the following Visual Basic .NET code. (The completed sample is available in the materials posted for this chapter in the MetaDataLooping project in the folder with the same name.)

The sample code begins by declaring a module-level variable (*cat1*) for an *ADOX Catalog* object. The declaration is at the module level because several procedures will reference it. This sample code references the declaration from two procedures, but a subsequent piece of sample code references it from a third procedure. (See the "Iterating Through Columns in a Table" discussion.) A *Catalog* object stores the metadata for a connection to an Access database. The *Form1_Load* event procedure instantiates an *ADODB Connection* object named *cnn1* and uses *cnn1* to open a connection to the Northwind database. Notice that the connection string is identical to the ADO connection string. That's because we are using ADO. The point is that you are using coding techniques that developers have had available to them since the release of Access 2000. The *Form1_Load* event procedure concludes by assigning the *Connection* object named *cnn1* to the *ActiveConnection* property of the *Catalog* object named *cat1*. Therefore, *cat1* can expose metadata about the Northwind database.

> **Note**   The following sample code specifies the user ID and password. However, they are optional when no security exists on a database file (as is true for the sample Northwind database). Chapter 13, "Securing .NET Applications with Access Database," drills down on security topics.

The *Button1_Click* event procedure puts *cat1* to work by listing the user-defined tables in the Northwind database within a message box. The procedure begins by declaring a string variable and assigning a value to it for the header within the message box. This single string will eventually populate the whole message box. Next the procedure uses a *For Each...Next* loop to pass through the tables within the Northwind database. Besides user-defined tables, several types of table objects exist within a database, such as the Customers and Orders tables. However, all user-defined tables have a *Type* property of TABLE. This sample code takes advantage of the *Type* property by filtering with an *If...Then* statement for tables with a *Type* property of TABLE. When the *If...Then* statement discovers a table with a *Type* property of TABLE, the code block within the *If...Then* statement appends the table's name to the *str1* variable initially declared at the start of the event procedure.

After passing through all the tables in the Northwind database, the sample displays the value of *str1* in a message box by invoking the *Show* method for the *MessageBox* class. As you saw in Chapter 2, you can invoke the *Show* method without first invoking an instance of the *MessageBox* class. The message box should show the tables appearing in the Database container window with Tables selected in the Objects bar. The default filtering (not showing *Hidden* and *System* objects) should also be selected.

```
'Declare a reference to an ADOX Catalog object.
Dim cat1 As New ADOX.Catalog()

Private Sub Form1_Load(ByVal sender As System.Object, _
    ByVal e As System.EventArgs) Handles MyBase.Load

    'Declare a new ADO Connection object.
    Dim cnn1 As New ADODB.Connection()

    'Open an ADO Connection object.
    cnn1.Open("Provider=Microsoft.Jet.OLEDB.4.0;" & _
        "Data Source=C:\Program Files\" & _
        "Microsoft Office\Office10\Samples\Northwind.mdb;", _
        "Admin", "")

    'Assign the connection to the catalog.
    cat1.ActiveConnection = cnn1

End Sub

Private Sub Button1_Click(ByVal sender As System.Object, _
    ByVal e As System.EventArgs) Handles Button1.Click

    'Declare a string to head the table names.
    Dim str1 As String = _
        "The user-defined table names are:" & StrDup(2, vbCr)

    'Loop through the tables in the catalog defined in
    'the Form1_Load event procedure.
    Dim tbl1 As ADOX.Table
    For Each tbl1 In cat1.Tables
        If tbl1.Type = "TABLE" Then
            str1 = str1 & tbl1.Name & vbCr
        End If
    Next

    'Display the results in a message box.
    MessageBox.Show(str1, "From Chapter 3", _
        MessageBoxButtons.OK)

End Sub
```

Iterating Through Columns in a Table

Among the most common kinds of metadata are the data types for the columns in a table. You can report the data types for the columns in a table by designating a particular table in a catalog and then iterating through the elements of the *Columns* collection in that table. By displaying the *Name* and *Type* property for each column, you can derive the data type for each column. The next piece of sample code demonstrates this approach for the Categories table, which has just four columns, each one containing a different data type.

Start the sample by adding a second button to *Form1* in the MetaData-Looping project. The button's default name will be *Button2*. Change its *Text* property to *List Data Types*. Drag the right edge of the button to show the whole *Text* property setting.

This sample code illustrates one approach to printing the column names and their data type codes in the Debug panel of the Output window. After the declarations for the *Button2_Click* event procedure, the sample points the *tbl1* variable to the Categories table in the Northwind database. Then a *For Each…Next* statement loops through the columns in the Categories table. The code block within the loop assigns a value to a string (*str1*) with the column's *Name* and *Type* properties for each successive column. Next the sample invokes the *WriteLine* method for the *Debug* class to print the string to the Output window.

```
Private Sub Button2_Click(ByVal sender As System.Object, _
    ByVal e As System.EventArgs) Handles Button2.Click

    'Declare objects for procedure.
    Dim tbl1 As ADOX.Table
    Dim col1 As ADOX.Column
    Dim str1 As String

    'Loop through columns in the Categories table from the
    'Northwind database, and write results to the Output window.
    tbl1 = cat1.Tables("Categories")
    For Each col1 In tbl1.Columns
        str1 = col1.Name & "; " & col1.Type & vbCr
        Debug.WriteLine(str1)
    Next

End Sub
```

Figure 3-3 shows an excerpt from the Output window for the preceding sample code. (The figure clips the right edge of selected lines.) You have to close *Form1* and end the running application to return to the IDE so that you can view the contents of the Output window. If the Output window is not already in view, choose View, Other Windows, Output. The window starts by listing various assemblies loaded to support the project. Then the window displays the four column names in the Categories table along with the *DataType-Enum* value for the data type of each column. The *Type* property does not return the member name of the *DataTypeEnum* for a column's type; instead, it returns the numeric code for the column's data type. You can look up these *DataTypeEnum* values in the Object Browser in a code window for your favorite version of Access or classic Visual Basic. The *DateTypeEnum* is a class in both the *ADODB* and *ADOX* libraries. Next we will discuss a *Function* procedure that automates the return of the *DateTypeEnum* member name corresponding to a data type code.

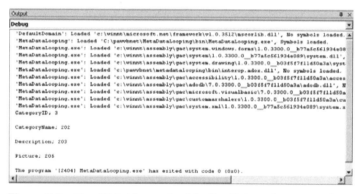

Figure 3-3   The *WriteLine* method for the *Debug* class can write strings to the Output window.

Translating Access Data Types

The preceding sample represented the *DataTypeEnum* values for the columns in the Categories table of the Northwind database. As mentioned, having the *DataTypeEnum* names would be more helpful. Decoding a number to a corresponding name is a task that lends itself well to using a *Select...Case* statement inside a *Function* procedure. The procedure can accept a number as an input parameter and return a string. The input parameter number can correspond to the *DataTypeEnum* value, and the return string can be its matching *DataType-Enum* name. This section will demonstrate the construction of a sample to implement this task. This sample will also contrast the performance of the ADO features through the COM Interop feature with the native Visual Basic .NET procedures for translating Access data types.

The output for the preceding sample shows a *DataTypeEnum* value of 3 for the CategoryID column in the Categories table. (See Figure 3-3.) Whether you look up the *DataTypeEnum* name for the value 3 manually or programmatically, the result will be *adInteger*. Because *adInteger* does not correspond to an Access data type, some Access developers might wonder what data type they are actually using (regardless of whether they see the *DataTypeEnum* value or name). The following sample tackles this issue by constructing a table named DataTypes with all 15 Access data types shown in Table 3-2. The column name for each table corresponds to a recognizable Access data type name. Figure 3-4 shows the Design view from Access for the DataTypes table. The Description column specifies the Field Size setting for the *Number* data types that have subtypes.

Figure 3-4   The DataTypes table in the dbDataTypes Access database file has all 15 Access data types.

I constructed the DataTypes table in the dbDataTypes database file, and I saved the database file in the bin subdirectory within the MetaDataLooping folder. Therefore, you get the database with its table automatically when you download the MetaDataLooping folder with the sample materials for this chapter. Storing an Access database in the folder for a solution is a convenient way of deploying an Access database file with a Visual Basic .NET solution. Just copy the solution's folder to another computer, and the database file appears in a known location. If you use the same name for the folder on both computers, you will not need to manually edit the code for the location of the database file. If copying the folder to another machine is not feasible, you can create a simple setup procedure that copies the name of the new directory for the folder containing a solution (and its associated database).

To start implementing this sample, add another button to *Form1* in the MetaDataLooping project. Set the button's *Text* property to *List Data Type Names*. The button's default *Name* property is *Button3*. Then insert the following code for an event procedure for the button and a *Function* procedure that translates the *DataTypeEnum* values to names.

The *Button3_Click* event procedure actually translates the Access data types for the columns of the DataTypes table into both ADO and .NET Framework data types. The preceding sample code demonstrates how to programmatically create an ADO connection to a database. However, this section's sample needs an ADO.NET *Connection* object pointing at the dbDataTypes database and an *OleDbDataAdapter* referencing the DataTypes table in the database. In addition, you need a *DataSet* object, which the sample refers to as *DsDataTypes1*, to hold a local version of the contents in the DataTypes table within the dbDataTypes database file. See the Jump Start sample at the end of Chapter 2 for a model of how to construct these objects. Figure 3-5 shows the Design view for *Form1* after the addition of the *OleDbConnection1*, *OleDbDataAdapter1*, and the *DsDataTypes1* objects. I started the process of creating the objects by dragging the DataTypes table from Server Explorer to *Form1*. The Properties window shows that *DsDataTypes1* is a *DataSet* object that points at the *DsDataTypes* dataset. (See the *DataSetName* property setting.)

The code within the *Button3_Click* event procedure starts by making an ADO connection to the dbDataTypes database. Then the code assigns the connection to the *ActiveConnection* property for the *cat2 Catalog* object. The event procedure next loops through the columns of the DataTypes table in the dbDataTypes database. So far, this code sample follows the general design of the preceding sample. But here the approach changes. Instead of returning the raw *Type* property value for the columns in the table, the sample passes the *Type* property value as an argument to the *ADODataType Function* procedure, and the procedure returns the corresponding *DataTypeEnum* name. Therefore, the display in the Output window from the *Debug.Writeline* statement contains the Access column name, which is based on its Access data type name, and the matching ADO data type name. The *ADODataType Function* demonstrates the syntax for applying the *Select...Case* statement to decode a number to its matching string value.

Figure 3-5   The Design view for *Form1* in the MetaDataLooping project with the ADO.NET connection, data adapter, and dataset objects for the *Button3_Click* event procedure

The remainder of the *Button3_Click* event procedure demonstrates how to translate the Access data types to their matching .NET Framework data types. First, the code fills the DataTypes *DataTable* in the *DsDataTypes1 DataSet* with the contents of the DataTypes table from the dbDataTypes database. This process implicitly converts Access data types to .NET Framework data types. Then the sample loops through the columns of the local DataTypes *DataTable*. Although the concept is the same as in the preceding code that uses ADO, the actual objects are different because the block of code within the click event procedure deals with ADO.NET objects instead of ADO ones. The *Column-Name* property contains the name of a column in the local datatable, and the *DataType* property returns the data type value. By applying the *ToString* method, the procedure converts the value for display in the Output window by using the *Writeline* method for the *Debug* class.

```
Private Sub Button3_Click(ByVal sender As System.Object, _
    ByVal e As System.EventArgs) Handles Button3.Click

    'Declare objects.
    Dim cnn1 As New ADODB.Connection()
    Dim cat2 As New ADOX.Catalog()
    Dim tbl1 As ADOX.Table
    Dim col1 As ADOX.Column
    Dim str1 As String

    'Open ADO connection to database.
    cnn1.Open("Provider=Microsoft.Jet.OLEDB.4.0;" & _
        "Data Source=C:\pawvbnet\" & _
        "MetaDataLooping\bin\dbDataTypes.mdb;", _
        "Admin", "")

    'Assign connection to catalog and open
    'a table in the catalog.
    cat2.ActiveConnection = cnn1
    tbl1 = cat2.Tables("DataTypes")

    'Iterate through the columns in the table
    'and decode ADO type numbers to ADO type names.
    For Each col1 In tbl1.Columns
        str1 = col1.Name & "; " & ADODataType(col1.Type)
        Debug.WriteLine(str1)
    Next

    'Fill a local dataset with a table from
    'an Access database.
    OleDbDataAdapter1.Fill(DsDataTypes1, "DataTypes")
    Dim dt1 As DataTable
    Dim dtcol As DataColumn

    'Iterate through the columns in the dataset's
    'table based on the original in the Access database.
    For Each dtcol In DsDataTypes1.Tables("DataTypes").Columns
        str1 = dtcol.ColumnName & ", " & dtcol.DataType.ToString
        Debug.WriteLine(str1)
    Next

End Sub

Function ADODataType(ByVal intType As String) _
    As String
```

```
'Decode ADO type number to ADO type name.
Select Case intType
    Case 2
        Return "adSmallint"
    Case 3
        Return "adInteger"
    Case 4
        Return "adSingle"
    Case 5
        Return "adDouble"
    Case 6
        Return "adCurrency"
    Case 7
        Return "adDate"
    Case 11
        Return "adBoolean"
    Case 17
        Return "adUnsignedTinyInt"
    Case 72
        Return "adGuid"
    Case 130
        Return "adWChar"
    Case 131
        Return "adNumeric"
    Case 202
        Return "adVarWChar"
    Case 203
        Return "adLongVarWChar"
    Case 205
        Return "adLongVarBinary"
    Case Else
        Return "Unspecified ADO type number"
End Select

End Function
```

Figure 3-6 displays an excerpt from the Output window from the *Button3_Click* event procedure. The top set of column and data type names show the DataTypes column names with their matching ADO data type names. The bottom set of column names and data types show comparable results for .NET Framework data types. (These data types appear with a *System* prefix.) Notice that Visual Basic .NET displays *System* data type names even for Access data types that it does not support directly. For example, Visual Basic .NET offers no data type for processing GUIDs. However, the procedure seamlessly inserts the name of a *System* data type (*System.Guid*) from the .NET Framework.

Figure 3-6   The Output window results generated by the *Button3_Click* event procedure from the MetaDataLooping project

Arrays

Real programmers don't use internal spaces in object names, and real programmers use arrays as elements in their solution toolkit. Arrays are a lightweight, in-memory data store. Once you know a few of the basics, arrays are easy to program. For example, your knowledge of *For* loops will come in very handy. This section reviews traditional array topics for classic Visual Basic developers while presenting some new information on array processing with Visual Basic .NET. The section closes with a sample that illustrates how to use arrays to consolidate data from different sources and display that data in a unified way.

Overview of Array Design

Arrays are collections of values that you can refer to with a single variable name. Just as a memory variable refers to a single value in memory, an array variable designates a collection of values in memory. Because an array is based on memory, data access and data manipulation can be very fast. In addition, arrays are lightweight. Although an array offers less functionality than a *Data-Table* object from ADO.NET, an array has less overhead. For example, a datatable offers built-in constraints, such as primary keys. Arrays do not use primary keys, but you can add and edit values in an array. (In addition, arrays offer other features, such as sorts.)

The values, or elements, within an array can have up to 32 dimensions. An array's *Rank* property reflects the number of dimensions in an array. The first dimension represents rows, the second represents columns, the third represents sets of rows and columns, and so on. The dimensions within an array have a length property that reflects the number of items along a dimension. All the elements in an array typically have the same value type, such as an *Integer* or a *Single* data type designation. The type specification in an array's declaration restricts the array values. When an array must store values with different data types, you can declare the array with an *Object* data type. The *Object* data type designation permits an array to contain values with different subtypes in its elements, such as *Strings* and *Integers*.

> **Note**   It is good programming practice to keep the number of array dimensions low, say at one or two dimensions. As the rank (number of dimensions) of an array grows, the array's memory requirements can increase drastically. For example, an array with two dimensions with a length of 2 on each dimension and a *Byte* data type requires 4 bytes of memory. If the array's length stays at 2 per dimension but its rank increases to 32, the array will require 4 MB of memory!

Visual Basic .NET permits your applications to refer to the individual values, or elements, within an array by using zero-based index numbers. With classic Visual Basic, developers could select either a one-based or a zero-based index for array dimensions. You can return the maximum index value along a dimension by using the *GetUpperBound* method. Use a zero-based number as an argument for the *GetUpperBound* method to indicate the dimension for which you seek the highest index value. Because arrays in Visual Basic .NET always have a lower bound of zero, the maximum index value of an array's dimension will be 1 less than the length of that dimension. You can also use the *GetLength* method to return the number of items along a dimension. The *GetLength* method takes the same kind of argument as the *GetUpperBound* method.

You declare a variable referencing an array in a way that's similar to how you declare a variable for a memory variable. Use the *Dim* statement or an access modifier such as *Private* to declare an array variable. Include parentheses after the variable name to indicate that the variable represents an array of values instead of a scalar value (that is, a single value in memory). When a variable denotes an array with more than one dimension, within the parentheses, add a comma followed by a blank character for each additional dimension. Within the parentheses, following a variable name, you can optionally designate the upper index value as a zero-based number for each dimension. The following example declares an array with two dimensions and a length of 2 for each dimension. This array has a *Byte* data type. All four values in the array will initially equal 0 because the declaration does not assign values to the array elements. (The default value for a *Byte* data type is 0.)

```
Dim MyArray (1, 1) as Byte
```

The length of each dimension for all arrays in Visual Basic .NET is variable. You can use the *ReDim* statement to vary the length of an array in any dimension in the array after its initial declaration. As with classic Visual Basic, you can use the *Preserve* keyword to retain the values in an array when you resize. Using the *Preserve* keyword restricts upper-limit specifications to the last dimension. The *ReDim* statement is useful for reducing the memory requirements of a large array that you do not need for the lifetime of the array variable's declaration.

> **Note** The *ReDim* statement applies only to arrays declared at the procedure level. Arrays declared for a whole module or class cannot have their dimension length respecified.

Arrays are objects in the .NET Framework, and an array variable can point at more than one array object over its lifetime. You can use the *Erase* statement to remove from memory the object at which an array variable points. Then you can use the *ReDim* statement to reassign the array variable to a new array object. You can use the *ReDim* and *Erase* statements at the procedure level only. These statements do not operate at the class or module level.

Processing a One-Dimensional Array

The first sample we will look at in this section demonstrates how to declare and manipulate a one-dimensional array. This sample will also reinforce your understanding of data types. The code consists of a couple of *Sub* procedures in a project started from the Empty Project template. The project's name is ArrayDemos. The first procedure has the name *main*, which is the default startup object for a module in an empty project. This procedure contains two *Sub* procedure calls, but only one lacks a comment marker—the second *Sub* procedure, *OneDArrayDemo*.

The *OneDArrayDemo* procedure starts with the declaration of an array, *ary_int1*. The parentheses after the array's name mark *ary_int1* as pointing at a one-dimensional array of values. Notice that no commas separating values in the parentheses exist. The data type of values in the *ary_int1* array must be *Integer*. The procedure's first line declares the array and instantiates its elements. The *New* keyword to the right of the equal sign (=), followed by the *Integer* keyword and parentheses, instantiate an array with a length of 2. The two members in the array have index values of 0 and 1. The array values (9 and 99) are delimited by commas within curly braces (*{}*).

After declaring and instantiating the *ary_int1* array, the procedure displays two message boxes—one with the type for the overall array and the other with the type for the second element in the array. A separate message box displays the data type value for each array element. When you run the procedure, the first message box shows *System.Int32[]*. The square brackets denote a sequence of values, and *System.Int32* indicates the type of values in the sequence. This system data type corresponds to the Visual Basic .NET *Integer* data type. (See Table 3-1.) The second message box shows *System.Int32* without any trailing brackets. This is because this message box reports the data type for a single value, the one corresponding to the second element in the *ary_int1* array.

The final segment of the *OneDArrayDemo* procedure displays the contents of the *ary_int1* array. One of the strengths of arrays is the ease with which you can process them with *For* loops. This final segment loops through the elements within the *ary_int1* array with a single *For* loop. The loop starts at 0, which is always the first index value in a dimension in a Visual Basic .NET array. The loop continues until reaching the uppermost index value, 1, which the *GetUpperBound* method returns. The code within the loop builds a string value for display in a message box function. The code invokes the *ToString* method to convert the integer values within the array to strings for display in the message box. Visual Basic .NET automatically converts from an *Integer* data type to a *String* data type, but explicitly indicating the conversion saves the operating system work. In addition, if your code operates in a module with an *Option Strict On* statement, Visual Basic .NET raises a compile error unless you convert explicitly from *Integer* to *String*. The third message box presented by the *OneDArrayDemo* procedure shows the values 9 and 99 on separate lines.

```
Sub main()
    OneDArrayDemo()
    'TwoDArrayDemo()

End Sub

Sub OneDArrayDemo()

    'Declare a one-dimensional Integer array of length 2
    'and populate it with 9 and 99.
    Dim ary_int1() As Integer = New Integer(1) {9, 99}

    'Display type for the array followed by
    'an individual element within the array.
    MsgBox(ary_int1.GetType.ToString)
    MsgBox(ary_int1(1).GetType.ToString)

    'Display array elements.
    Dim int1 As Integer
    Dim str1 As String
    For int1 = 0 To ary_int1.GetUpperBound(0)
        str1 = str1 & ary_int1(int1).ToString & vbCr
    Next
    MsgBox(str1)

End Sub
```

Processing a Two-Dimensional Array

An array with two dimensions represents a table with rows and columns. The first dimension corresponds to rows, and the second dimension points to columns in the table specified by an array. The following code sample adds two procedures to the ArrayDemos project created for the preceding sample. The first procedure, *TwoDArrayDemo*, illustrates various processing techniques for manipulating a two-dimensional array. In particular, the sample demonstrates how to initialize a two-dimensional array, how to resize its length, and how to add new values to an array after you resize it. The second procedure, *DisplayTwoDArray*, displays a two-dimensional array. This procedure accepts any array as an argument and prints the first two dimensions. Because you pass the array to this procedure as an object, you can reuse it with a two-dimensional array of any data type. You can start this second array processing sample from the *main* procedure. To do so, place a comment marker in front of the call to the *OneDArrayDemo* procedure, and remove the comment marker from the call to the *TwoDArrayDemo* procedure.

The *TwoDArrayDemo* procedure commences by initializing the *ary_sng1* array. The initialization process in this sample differs from the preceding sample in two respects. First, the data type is *Single* in this case. (The data type was *Integer* in the preceding sample.) The *Single* data type in this sample allows the representation and computation of numbers with values to the right of a decimal point. Second, the array in this sample has two dimensions, instead of just one, as in the preceding sample. The *Dim* statement declaring the array uses a *New* constructor with nested curly braces. The outside set of curly braces applies to the overall array. The three sets of curly braces within the outside curly braces apply to each of the three rows within the two-dimensional array.

After initializing the array, the *TwoDArrayDemo* procedure starts to process the array. This procedure begins by calling the *DisplayTwoDArray* procedure. This call displays the initial values for the array in a message box. We will examine the *DisplayTwoDArray* procedure and its output after discussing the entire *TwoDArrayDemo* procedure. The remainder of the *TwoDArrayDemo* procedure manipulates the *ary_sng1* array and displays various results. For example, the code block you are about to see shows the length of the first and second dimensions before and after the code modifies the length of the second dimension with a *ReDim* statement. The *ReDim* statement adds a new column to the array and preserves the initial values. This statement converts the table in the array from one with three rows and two columns to a table with three rows and three columns. The last three code blocks in the procedure display the array elements before and after the code populates the last column in the array. The procedure populates the last column by using a *For* loop to loop down the rows in the third column. In each pass through the loop, the code computes a new *Single* value for a row in the third column.

The *DisplayTwoDArray* procedure accepts an array as an argument. The procedure uses nested *For* loops to pass through the column values for successive rows in the array. As the procedure passes through the columns, it constructs a string value (*str1*) with the column index and value for each column on a row. A comma and a space (", ") delimits the column index and value for the columns within a row. After finishing the processing for a row, the procedure removes the trailing command and space delimiter with the *Mid* function and appends a *vbCr* constant to separate the rows with a carriage return. Figure 3-7 contrasts the first message box for this sample with its three-by-two table, and the last message box with its three-by-three table.

Figure 3-7 With the *ReDim* statement, you can add a new column of values to an existing array while retaining the original values.

```
Sub TwoDArrayDemo()
    'Declare a two-dimensional Integer array with
    'lengths of 3 and 2; populate with three two-tuples.
    Dim ary_sng1(,) As Single = _
        New Single(2, 1) {{1.1, 2.2}, {3.3, 4.4}, {5.5, 6.6}}

    'Display array elements.
    DisplayTwoDArray(ary_sng1)

    'Display length of array dimensions before and after
    'increasing the length of the last dimension; this adds
    'a third column to the ary_sng1 array.
    MsgBox(ary_sng1.GetLength(0).ToString & ", " & _
        ary_sng1.GetLength(1).ToString)
    ReDim Preserve ary_sng1(2, 2)
    MsgBox(ary_sng1.GetLength(0).ToString & ", " & _
        ary_sng1.GetLength(1).ToString)

    'Now, display the array elements again.
    DisplayTwoDArray(ary_sng1)

    'Populate third column in the array.
    Dim int1 As Integer
```

```
    For int1 = 0 To ary_sng1.GetUpperBound(0)
        ary_sng1(int1, 2) = 10 + ((int1 + 1) / 100)
    Next
    'Display array elements with the new values.
    DisplayTwoDArray(ary_sng1)

End Sub

Sub DisplayTwoDArray(ByVal ary_int As Array)

    'Declare objects.
    Dim str1 As String
    Dim int1 As Integer
    Dim int2 As Integer

    'Display data elements by looping through the second
    'dimension elements for each first dimension element.
    For int1 = 0 To ary_int.GetUpperBound(0)
        For int2 = 0 To ary_int.GetUpperBound(1)
            str1 = str1 & _
                "Column(" & int2.ToString & "): " & _
                CStr(ary_int(int1, int2)) & ", "
        Next
        str1 = Mid(str1, 1, str1.Length - 2) & vbCr
    Next int1
    MsgBox(str1)

End Sub
```

Consolidating Metadata with an Array

The last sample for processing an array that we will look at extends an earlier sample from the MetaDataLooping project. The closing demonstration from the "Translating Access Data Types" section contrasted Access table data types with ADO data types, and in a second listing, the sample contrasted Access table data types with Visual Basic .NET data types. The listings from that earlier sample appeared in the Output window, one after the other. But what if you want to create a single listing with Access table data types and their corresponding ADO and Visual Basic .NET data types side by side? The following sample shows how to achieve this with array processing.

This sample adds a new button (*Button4*) to *Form1* in the MetaDataLooping project. I updated the default *Text* property for the button to Show Data Type Comparison. The *Button4_Click* event procedure has the main part of the logic for the sample, but the event procedure calls the *DisplayTwoDArray* procedure that initially appeared in the ArrayDemos project. One simple approach to making the *DisplayTwoDArray* procedure available in the MetaDataLooping project is to copy from one procedure and paste the code into the other procedure. The following code listing shows only the *Button4_Click* event procedure because the *DisplayTwoDArray* procedure is not edited in any way. The *Button4_Click* event procedure additionally calls the *ADODataType* procedure, summarized earlier in the "Translating Access Data Types" section. Because this procedure does not change for its use here, it does not appear in the following code listing. Also, you do not need to copy the procedure into the project because I initially developed it for the project.

Much of the code in the *Button4_Click* event procedure is a direct copy of the material from the *Button3_Click* event procedure discussed in the previous section. To help you identify the fresh content for array processing, the new code appears in boldface. Starting with the declaration area, the sample will use two *Integer* variables, *int1* and *int2*, to assist with array processing. Of course, we need to declare an array to have one available for processing. The declaration of *ary_str1* specifies an array containing 15 rows and 3 columns that hold string data.

After the declarations, the sample procedure makes a connection to the dbDataTypes Access database and points a *Catalog* variable (*cat2*) at the database. Then the procedure points an *ADOX.Table* object (*tbl1*) at the DataTypes table in the database. Recall that these steps require references to COM objects. The next segment of code in boldface illustrates how to loop through the columns of *tbl1* and preserve in the *ary_str1* array the column name and the ADO *DataTypeEnum* name matching the Access table data type. The *For* loop populates the first two columns of the array for each of the 15 columns in the *tbl1* object. Then the procedure copies the DataTypes table from the dbDataTypes database to the DataTypes in the *dsDateTypes1* object within the MetaData-Looping project. During the copying process, Visual Basic .NET automatically converts from Access data types to .NET Framework data types.

A second loop (also in bold) iterates through the local datatable and extracts the .NET Framework name for the data type of each column. The loop saves these .NET Framework names in the third column of the *ary_str1* array. After looping completes, control passes to the *DisplayTwoDArray* procedure, which displays a message box with three columns. (See Figure 3-8.) As you can see, this message box shows the column names from the table in the Access database, along with their corresponding ADO and .NET Framework data types as the second and third column values.

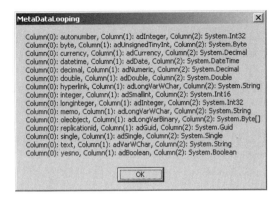

MetaDataLooping

```
Column(0): autonumber, Column(1): adInteger, Column(2): System.Int32
Column(0): byte, Column(1): adUnsignedTinyInt, Column(2): System.Byte
Column(0): currency, Column(1): adCurrency, Column(2): System.Decimal
Column(0): datetime, Column(1): adDate, Column(2): System.DateTime
Column(0): decimal, Column(1): adNumeric, Column(2): System.Decimal
Column(0): double, Column(1): adDouble, Column(2): System.Double
Column(0): hyperlink, Column(1): adLongVarWChar, Column(2): System.String
Column(0): integer, Column(1): adSmallint, Column(2): System.Int16
Column(0): longinteger, Column(1): adInteger, Column(2): System.Int32
Column(0): memo, Column(1): adLongVarWChar, Column(2): System.String
Column(0): oleobject, Column(1): adLongVarBinary, Column(2): System.Byte[]
Column(0): replicationid, Column(1): adGuid, Column(2): System.Guid
Column(0): single, Column(1): adSingle, Column(2): System.Single
Column(0): text, Column(1): adVarWChar, Column(2): System.String
Column(0): yesno, Column(1): adBoolean, Column(2): System.Boolean
```

OK

Figure 3-8   You can use arrays to consolidate multiple types of data because this output contrasts ADO and .NET Framework data types corresponding to Access data types.

> **Note**   The *Button4_Click* event procedure demonstrates the use of the += operator. Visual Basic .NET introduces this operator to classic Visual Basic developers. This operator enables you to add a constant to a memory variable. In the sample, += adds the value 1 to the *int1* memory variable.

```
Private Sub Button4_Click(ByVal sender As System.Object, _
    ByVal e As System.EventArgs) Handles Button4.Click

    'Declare objects.
    Dim cnn1 As New ADODB.Connection()
    Dim cat2 As New ADOX.Catalog()
    Dim tbl1 As ADOX.Table
    Dim col1 As ADOX.Column
    Dim int1, int2 As Integer
    Dim ary_str1(14, 2) As String

    'Open ADO connection to database.
    cnn1.Open("Provider=Microsoft.Jet.OLEDB.4.0;" & _
        "Data Source=C:\pawvbnet\" & _
        "MetaDataLooping\bin\dbDataTypes.mdb;", _
        "Admin", "")
```

(continued)

```
'Assign connection to catalog and open
'a table in the catalog.
cat2.ActiveConnection = cnn1
tbl1 = cat2.Tables("DataTypes")

'Iterate through the columns in the table
'and decode ADO type numbers to ADO type name;
'save the column name and ADO data type in the
'first two columns of the ary_str1 array.
For Each col1 In tbl1.Columns
    ary_str1(int1, int2) = col1.Name
    ary_str1(int1, int2 + 1) = ADODataType(col1.Type)
    int1 += 1
Next

'Fill a local dataset with a table from
'an Access database.
OleDbDataAdapter1.Fill(DsDataTypes1, "DataTypes")
Dim dt1 As DataTable
Dim dtcol As DataColumn

'Begin by resetting int1 to its default value.
'Then, iterate through the columns in the dataset's
'table based on the original in the Access database;
'save the string representation of the .NET data type
'in the third column of the ary_str1 array.
int1 = 0
For Each dtcol In DsDataTypes1.Tables("DataTypes").Columns
    ary_str1(int1, 2) = dtcol.DataType.ToString
    int1 += 1
Next

'Display array elements.
DisplayTwoDArray(ary_str1)

End Sub
```

Classes

One of the major thrusts of Visual Basic .NET is its enhanced emphasis of object-oriented programming capabilities. Classes are the main type for building custom components. This section presents a brief overview of class design and processing issues; it serves as a prelude to two additional sections that demonstrate programming techniques for creating and using class properties and class methods. Chapter 4 extends this introduction to class programming by providing more in-depth coverage of techniques such as event processing and inheritance.

Overview

Classes are your tools for building custom components. A class is the model for an object. Consider a cookie class. A cookie eater can remove a cookie from its jar to make a cookie instance available for eating. In addition, a cookie eater can remove multiple cookies (instances) from the jar at the same time. The multiple instances for a class can expose properties with different values. For example, one cookie can have a hard-texture property while another cookie can have a soft-texture property. Cookies can have methods as well, such as *start_eating* and *stop_eating*. After launching the *start_eating* method for a cookie, you can invoke its *stop_eating* method any time before its *percent_consumed* property equals 100. When the *percent_consumed* property reaches 100, the cookie can raise an *all_gone* event. The cookie eater is the consumer of a cookie instance.

In our analogy, the cookie eater corresponds to a Windows application project or any other project that can make a reference to a class, such as the cookie class. If the cookie eater has an event handler for the *all_gone* event, the cookie eater can respond to the event (for example, by making a new cookie instance). When the cookie eater is finished, he or she can leave the room with the cookie jar (go out of scope) or put the cover back on the jar (assign *Nothing* to the cookie class). Eventually, the .NET garbage collector will remove the cookie jar instance from the kitchen counter (memory) when it determines that no more active references to the class exist.

In fact, you can have multiple classes that inherit from one another. Consider a base cookie class. It can have methods such as *start_eating* and *stop_eating*, a *percent_consumed* property, and an *all_gone* event. All cookies must have these properties. Different derived cookie classes will have the properties and methods for the base class as well as additional properties, methods, and events. A chocolate chip cookie class and a wafer cookie class can both derive from the base cookie class. This inheritance feature permits a chocolate chip cookie to possess all the properties, methods, and events of the base cookie class. The same goes for the wafer cookie class. However, the wafer class can have a flavor property with settings of vanilla, strawberry, and chocolate that is not available for the chocolate chip class. Likewise, the chocolate chip class might have a *with_nuts* property with settings of *True* or *False* that is not present in the wafer cookie class.

Creating and Using Class Properties

There are two main ways to implement properties with classes—with public fields and with property procedures. Property procedures offer more flexibility, but they also require more programming. These two approaches for implementing properties in Visual Basic .NET parallel those for classic Visual Basic, but property procedures have minor syntax differences. In addition, Visual Basic .NET introduces the notion of a *shared member*, which can apply equally well to a property or a method. You reference shared members directly from a class instead of from a class instance. Rather than dwell on the differences in class processing techniques between classic Visual Basic and Visual Basic .NET, this presentation of property processing techniques explains how to implement properties and manipulate them with Visual Basic .NET.

The demonstrations for class properties rely on two projects. The first project, PropertiesDemoLibrary, is a Class Library project. This project contains three classes that implement properties differently. All three classes use the COM Interop feature to reference the *ADODB* COM object. The code for each class extracts values from a column in any table from the Northwind database and persists them within the class in a one-dimensional array. The properties exposed by each class are for the array with the data from the Access database. The three properties for each class include the length of the array, the first value in the array, and the last value in the array.

I created the second project from the Empty Project template. This second project, PropertiesDemoLibUser, consumes objects based on the classes in the first project. For this second project to interoperate with the first project, you must create a reference in the second project that points at the .dll file for the first project. (See the "Consuming a Class Library Project" section in Chapter 2 for detailed instructions on referencing a class library .dll file.) In a sense, you can think of the first project as the cookie jar and the second project as the cookie eater. The second project extracts an object from the first project by invoking the *New* method for a class, and it specifies the type of cookie, or object, that it wants to extract by specifying a table name and column number. You can use the second project to extract a cookie, or object, based on any of the tables in the Northwind database. For example, an object instance based on the first column in the Shippers table will have different properties for its length (*MyArrayLength*), first value (*MyArrayFirst*), and last value (*MyArrayLast*) than for an object based on the second column in the Customers table.

Class Listing

The listing for the PropertiesDemoLibrary appears next. The overall listing is lengthy, but it divides well into three parts—one part for each class declaration within the class library. Each class exposes its properties differently. Therefore, the code for each class is presented separately. The *MyArrayField Properties* class implements its properties via fields with a *Public* access modifier. When using this approach to implement a property, your properties are always read/ write. That is, a client implementing an instance of the class can read the class property and write to it. In addition, you cannot put any code behind the property, such as validation code to make sure it meets certain requirements (for example, a birthday being on or after today).

The *MyArrayField Properties* class has a single procedure named *New*. This *Sub* procedure is the constructor for the class. The procedure takes two arguments, which designate the table name and column to extract from the Northwind database and store in a local array, *ary_obj1*. The procedure uses the COM Interop feature with the *ADODB* library to extract the values from the Northwind database. The code specifies a connection for the Northwind database in its default location. The sample then proceeds to use the connection to open a recordset on the table designated by the first argument for the *New* method. Next the sample declares the *ary_obj1* array. The array's upper index value is computed from the *RecordCount* property of the *Recordset* object. The code declares the array to have an *Object* type so that it can accommodate a column with any type from the Northwind database. After making the recordset and the array available, the constructor loops through the recordset rows and copies values from the designated table column to the *ary_obj1* array. The constructor concludes by setting properties declared at the top of the procedure. These property value settings depend on the array populated by passing through the preceding loop.

```
Public Class MyArrayFieldProperties
    Private My_int1 As Integer

    'Declare properties as fields with
    'Public access modifier.
    Public MyArrayLength As Integer
    Public MyArrayFirst As Object
    Public MyArrayLast As Object

    'Class constructor
    Sub New(ByVal TblName As String, _
        ByVal ColNumber As Integer)

        'Declare and instantiate ADODB objects;
        'add references through COM Interop to
        'to class library project.
```

(continued)

```
Dim cnn1 As New ADODB.Connection()
Dim rst1 As New ADODB.Recordset()

'Open an ADO Connection object.
cnn1.Open("Provider=Microsoft.Jet.OLEDB.4.0;" & _
    "Data Source=C:\Program Files\" & _
    "Microsoft Office\Office10\Samples\Northwind.mdb;", _
    "Admin", "")

'Open a recordset on a table.
With rst1
    .ActiveConnection = cnn1
    .Open(TblName, , _
        ADODB.CursorTypeEnum.adOpenKeyset, _
        ADODB.LockTypeEnum.adLockOptimistic)
End With

'Declare the array with an upper bound.
Dim ary_obj1(rst1.RecordCount - 1) As Object

'Loop through the ADO recordset and assign column
'values to the array.
Do Until rst1.EOF
    ary_obj1(My_int1) = rst1(ColNumber).Value
    My_int1 += 1
    rst1.MoveNext()
Loop

'After initializing array, assign class properties.
MyArrayLength = ary_obj1.GetLength(0)
MyArrayFirst = ary_obj1(0)
MyArrayLast = ary_obj1(ary_obj1.GetUpperBound(0))

    End Sub

End Class
```

The second class, *MyArrayPropertyProcedures*, extends the preceding class by implementing the three properties with property procedures. Because some code is borrowed from the preceding class, the listing shows the new code in boldface. No field declarations appear at the beginning of this class because the class implements properties with procedures. However, it is necessary to declare the *ary_obj1* array with a *Private* access modifier. The array was implicitly private in the preceding class definition because the code for that class defined the array within the *New* procedure. However, for this class, several procedures must have access to the array. Declaring the array at the top of the class makes the array available to all procedures within the class. Three property procedures for the length, first, and last property values appear after the close of the code for the *New Sub* procedure. The first value property, *MyArrayFirst*, is a read/write property. Although the *MyArrayFirst* property is for the first procedure, it actually appears second among the property procedures. The *MyArrayLength* and *MyArrayLast* properties are both read-only. As you can see, the only difference between these two types of properties is that the read-only properties omit the *Set* clause. This clause permits your application to copy a value into a property, and you can insert validation logic if you want. The *Get* clause returns a property value to an instance of the class.

```
Public Class MyArrayPropertyProcedures
    'Declare with Private access modifier for exclusive
    'access from within objects based on the class.
    Private ary_obj1() As Object

    'Declare private Integer variable used in the class.
    Private My_int1 As Integer

    'Class constructor
    Sub New(ByVal TblName As String, ByVal ColNumber As Integer)

        'Declare and instantiate ADODB objects.
        Dim cnn1 As New ADODB.Connection()
        Dim rst1 As New ADODB.Recordset()

        'Open an ADO Connection object.
        cnn1.Open("Provider=Microsoft.Jet.OLEDB.4.0;" & _
            "Data Source=C:\Program Files\" & _
            "Microsoft Office\Office10\Samples\Northwind.mdb;", _
            "Admin", "")

        'Open a recordset on a table.
        With rst1
            .ActiveConnection = cnn1
            .Open(TblName, , _
                ADODB.CursorTypeEnum.adOpenKeyset, _
                ADODB.LockTypeEnum.adLockOptimistic)
        End With

        'Declare the array with an upper bound.
        'Dim ary_obj1(rst1.RecordCount - 1) As Object
        ReDim ary_obj1(rst1.RecordCount - 1)
```

(continued)

```
                    'Loop through the ADO recordset and assign column
                    'values to the array.
                    Do Until rst1.EOF
                        ary_obj1(My_int1) = rst1(ColNumber).Value
                        My_int1 += 1
                        rst1.MoveNext()
                    Loop

                End Sub

                'MyArrayLength property is read-only.
                Public ReadOnly Property MyArrayLength() As Integer
                    Get
                        Return ary_obj1.GetLength(0)
                    End Get
                End Property

                'MyArrayFirst property is read/write.
                Public Property MyArrayFirst() As Object
                    Get
                        Return ary_obj1(0)
                    End Get
                    Set(ByVal Value As Object)
                        ary_obj1(0) = Value
                    End Set
                End Property

                'MyArrayLast property is read-only.
                Public ReadOnly Property MyArrayLast() As Object
                    Get
                        Return ary_obj1(ary_obj1.GetUpperBound(0))
                    End Get
                End Property

            End Class
```

The third class in the PropertiesDemoLibrary project has the name *MyArraySharedPropertyProcedures*. Because the code for this class again borrows from the preceding two classes, the new code is highlighted in bold. This class demonstrates the use of the *Shared* modifier for a property. Shared modifiers enable the user of a class to reference the class member—either a property or a method—before instantiating an object based on the class.

As is common practice for classes based on variables, the MyArrayShared-PropertyProcedures code declares the m_TblName and m_ColName fields with a Private modifier for use within the class. The TblName and ColName properties are shared outside the class. Users can specify these properties even before instantiating the object. Then all subsequent instances based on the class will use those property settings until the user application changes the shared property values. Shared property values go with the class rather than the specific class instances, so changing them for the class changes them for all instances of the class. Property values declared without the Shared modifier have specific values for each instance.

```
Public Class MyArraySharedPropertyProcedures

    'Declare private member of class used
    'in computations to return read-only properties.
    Private ary_obj1() As Object
    Private Shared m_TblName As String
    Private Shared m_ColNumber As Integer

    'Declare private Integer variable used in the class.
    Private My_int1 As Integer

    'Class constructor
    Sub New()

        'Declare and instantiate ADODB objects.
        Dim cnn1 As New ADODB.Connection()
        Dim rst1 As New ADODB.Recordset()

        'Open an ADO Connection object.
        cnn1.Open("Provider=Microsoft.Jet.OLEDB.4.0;" & _
            "Data Source=C:\Program Files\" & _
            "Microsoft Office\Office10\Samples\Northwind.mdb;", _
            "Admin", "")

        'Open a recordset on a table.
        With rst1
            .ActiveConnection = cnn1
            .Open(m_TblName, , _
                ADODB.CursorTypeEnum.adOpenKeyset, _
                ADODB.LockTypeEnum.adLockOptimistic)
        End With

        'Declare the array with an upper bound.
        'Dim ary_obj1(rst1.RecordCount - 1) As Object
        ReDim ary_obj1(rst1.RecordCount - 1)
```

(continued)

```vb
    'Loop through the ADO recordset and assign column
    'values to the array.
    Do Until rst1.EOF
        ary_obj1(My_int1) = rst1(m_ColNumber).Value
        My_int1 += 1
        rst1.MoveNext()
    Loop

End Sub

'TblName property is Shared.
Shared Property TblName() As String
    Get
        Return m_TblName
    End Get
    Set(ByVal Value As String)
        m_TblName = Value
    End Set
End Property

'ColName property is Shared.
Shared Property ColNumber() As Integer
    Get
        Return m_ColNumber
    End Get
    Set(ByVal Value As Integer)
        m_ColNumber = Value
    End Set
End Property

'MyArrayLength property is read-only.
Public ReadOnly Property MyArrayLength() As Integer
    Get
        Return ary_obj1.GetLength(0)
    End Get
End Property

'MyArrayFirst property is read/write.
Public Property MyArrayFirst() As Object
    Get
        Return ary_obj1(0)
    End Get
    Set(ByVal Value As Object)
        ary_obj1(0) = Value
```

```
        End Set
    End Property

    'MyArrayLength property is read-only.
    Public ReadOnly Property MyArrayLast() As Object
        Get
            Return ary_obj1(ary_obj1.GetUpperBound(0))
        End Get
    End Property

End Class
```

Demonstrations for Invoking Classes

A single client project can demonstrate various features of the preceding three classes. The PropertiesDemoLibUser project includes a main procedure that can call any of the other four procedures in the project. Run the four successive demonstrations one at a time by removing the comment marker from a procedure name in the *main* procedure. Three *Imports* statements precede any of the procedures. These statements create shortcuts for each of the three classes in the PropertiesDemoLibrary project.

The *CreateFieldPropertyInstance* procedure invokes the *MyArrayField-Properties* class within the PropertiesDemoLibrary project. First, the procedure instantiates an instance of the class. Then it displays the length (*MyArray-Length*), first (*MyArrayFirst*), and last (*MyArrayLast*) property values. These values derive from the constructor within the class for the table name and column number passed to the constructor when instantiating an object. The column number is zero-based, meaning that a column number of 1 denotes the second column. Next the procedure updates the first value property. This changes the value in the object instance; it does not update the record source, which is Shippers in the sample, for the underlying Northwind database. To demonstrate the change to the property value, the procedure presents two message boxes—one containing the property value before the change, and a second containing the property value after the change. Figure 3-9 shows the three message boxes generated by the *CreateFieldPropertyInstance* procedure. If you rerun the procedure, the same three message boxes appear. This is because the change indicated in the third message box is made only to the in-memory object instance, not the underlying data source in the Northwind database file.

Figure 3-9 After instantiating an object, you can access property values of the object—for example, for display in a message box. You can also change property values from their initial values (Speedy Express) to new values (anything).

The message boxes generated by the second and third procedure calls in the *main* procedure are the same as the ones appearing in Figure 3-9. In spite of this similarity in the output, some important differences exist in the behavior of the classes and how you invoke them. For example, all three properties for the object generated by the call to the *CreateFieldPropertyInstance* procedure are updatable. This is because the *CreateFieldPropertyInstance* procedure generates a property based on the *MyArrayFieldProperties* class, and this class implements properties with public fields. However, only the first value property is updatable for objects based on the *MyArrayPropertyProcedures* class. The second procedure call in the *main* procedure, *CreateProcedurePropertyInstance*, creates an object based on the *MyArrayPropertyProcedures* class, which uses property procedures to provide read/write access to only the first value property. The *CreateProcedurePropertyInstance* includes a commented attempt to update the last value property. If you remove the comment marker ('), Visual Studio .NET detects that you are attempting to edit a read-only property and generates a compilation error.

The *CreateSharedProcedurePropertyInstance* procedure illustrates the syntax for using shared properties. Notice that you specify shared properties relative to the name of the underlying class for an object instead of the name for an object instance. In addition, you can designate a value for a shared property value before you instantiate an object. Furthermore, the property values that you designate before instantiating an object (namely, the Shippers table and its second column) can help to specify the object that a class creates.

The primary purpose of the *ProcessTwoObjectInstances* procedure is to demonstrate issues related to opening two instances of a class at the same time. The initial code block starts by defining the *TblName* and *ColName* properties for the class. Then the code invokes the *New* method for the class to create *MyInstance1*. Creating the second instance (*MyInstance2*) is more direct because you do not need to specify the *TblName* and *ColName* shared class property values. After creating two instances of the *MyArraySharedProperty-Procedures* class, the *ProcessTwoObjectInstances* procedure displays in messages the first value property for each instance before and after editing the property. (See Figure 3-10.) The first message box shows the initial value for the property value in each instance. The second message box shows the property values for each instance after editing. Notice that instances preserve their distinct property assignments because we are dealing with two distinct object instances. As noted early in the chapter in the "Value Type Objects vs. Reference Type Objects" section, if two variables point at the same object instance, you cannot control independent values for each variable.

Figure 3-10   When you have multiple instances of a single object class, you can control the property value of individual instances independently of one another.

```
Imports FieldProps = _
    PropertiesDemoLibrary.MyArrayFieldProperties
Imports ProcedureProps = _
    PropertiesDemoLibrary.MyArrayPropertyProcedures
Imports SharedProcedureProps = _
    PropertiesDemoLibrary.MyArraySharedPropertyProcedures


Module Module1
    Sub main()
```

(continued)

```
    'CreateFieldPropertyInstance("Shippers", 1)
    'CreateProcedurePropertyInstance("Shippers", 1)
    'CreateSharedProcedurePropertyInstance("Shippers", 1)
    'ProcessTwoObjectInstances("Shippers", 1)

End Sub

Sub CreateFieldPropertyInstance(ByVal InstanceTable As String, _
    ByVal InstanceColNumber As Integer)

    'Instantiate an object.
    Dim MyInstance As New FieldProps(InstanceTable, _
        InstanceColNumber)

    'Display properties for object.
    Dim str1 As String
    str1 = _
        "MyInstance's length = " & _
            MyInstance.MyArrayLength.ToString & vbCr & _
        "MyInstance's first value = " & _
            MyInstance.MyArrayFirst.ToString & vbCr & _
        "MyInstance's last value = " & _
            MyInstance.MyArrayLast.ToString
    MsgBox(str1)

    'Display an object property before and after altering it.
    MsgBox(MyInstance.MyArrayFirst)
    MyInstance.MyArrayFirst = "anything"
    MsgBox(MyInstance.MyArrayFirst)

End Sub

Sub CreateProcedurePropertyInstance(ByVal InstanceTable As String, _
    ByVal InstanceColNumber As Integer)

    'Instantiate an object.
    Dim MyInstance As New ProcedureProps(InstanceTable, _
        InstanceColNumber)

    'Display properties for object.
    Dim str1 As String
    str1 = _
        "MyInstance's length = " & _
            MyInstance.MyArrayLength.ToString & vbCr & _
        "MyInstance's first value = " & _
            MyInstance.MyArrayFirst.ToString & vbCr & _
```

```
            "MyInstance's last value = " & _
                MyInstance.MyArrayLast.ToString
      MsgBox(str1)

      'Display an object property before and after altering it.
      MsgBox("Before - MyArrayFirst property = " & _
          MyInstance.MyArrayFirst.ToString)
      MyInstance.MyArrayFirst = "anything"
      MsgBox("After - MyArrayFirst property = " & _
          MyInstance.MyArrayFirst.ToString)

      'Removing comment marker generates a compile error
      'because MyArrayLast is read-only.
      'MyInstance.MyArrayLast = "anything"

End Sub

Sub CreateSharedProcedurePropertyInstance(ByVal InstanceTable _
    As String, _
    ByVal InstanceColNumber As Integer)

      'Instantiate an object.
      SharedProcedureProps.TblName = InstanceTable
      SharedProcedureProps.ColNumber = InstanceColNumber
      Dim MyInstance As New SharedProcedureProps()

      'Display properties for object.
      Dim str1 As String
      str1 = _
          "MyInstance's length = " & _
              MyInstance.MyArrayLength.ToString & vbCr & _
          "MyInstance's first value = " & _
              MyInstance.MyArrayFirst.ToString & vbCr & _
          "MyInstance's last value = " & _
              MyInstance.MyArrayLast.ToString
      MsgBox(str1)

      'Display an object property before and after altering it.
      MsgBox("Before - MyArrayFirst property = " & _
          MyInstance.MyArrayFirst.ToString)
      MyInstance.MyArrayFirst = "anything"
      MsgBox("After - MyArrayFirst property = " & _
          MyInstance.MyArrayFirst.ToString)

      'Removing comment marker generates a compile error
      'because MyArrayLast is read-only.
      'MyInstance.MyArrayLast = "anything"
```

(continued)

```
   End Sub

   Sub ProcessTwoObjectInstances(ByVal InstanceTable As String, _
       ByVal InstanceColNumber As Integer)

       'Instantiate a first object instance.
       SharedProcedureProps.TblName = InstanceTable
       SharedProcedureProps.ColNumber = InstanceColNumber
       Dim MyInstance1 As New SharedProcedureProps()

       'Instantiate a second object instance.
       Dim MyInstance2 As New SharedProcedureProps()

       'Display MyArrayFirst property from both instances
       'before editing.
       Dim str1 = "Before" & vbCr & _
           "MyArrayFirst property for MyInstance1 = " & _
           MyInstance1.MyArrayFirst.ToString & vbCr & _
           "MyArrayFirst property for MyInstance2 = " & _
           MyInstance2.MyArrayFirst.ToString
       MsgBox(str1)

       'Edit MyArrayFirst property differently in
       'each instance.
       MyInstance1.MyArrayFirst = "anything"
       MyInstance2.MyArrayFirst = "anything else"

       'Display MyArrayFirst property from both instances
       'before editing.
       Dim str2 = "After" & vbCr & _
           "MyArrayFirst property for MyInstance1 = " & _
           MyInstance1.MyArrayFirst.ToString & vbCr & _
           "MyArrayFirst property for MyInstance2 = " & _
           MyInstance2.MyArrayFirst.ToString
       MsgBox(str2)

   End Sub

End Module
```

Creating and Using Methods

Two main ways to program class methods exist—by using *Sub* procedures or by using *Function* procedures. Methods differ from properties in that methods perform a task while properties either return or save a property setting for the class. Actually, this distinction between methods and properties is only partially true because you can perform tasks inside property procedures. However, the task that a property procedure completes typically relates to the property setting, such as ensuring a new property value is in a proper range before assigning the value to the property.

Both *Sub* and *Function* procedures can perform tasks. As indicated earlier, these procedures typically have a much wider scope than property procedures. For example, you can make a connection to an Access database in a *Sub* procedure or return the result of a computation based on a subset of the rows in an Access table with a *Function* procedure. The *New* method from the property samples presented earlier in the section instantiated *Connection* and *Recordset* objects to help populate an array that, in turn, served as the basis for the properties in a custom class. A *Sub* procedure implements this method. In addition, you can use the *Shared* keyword to modify your declaration of *Sub* and *Function* procedures. As with properties, a shared method is accessible without instantiating an instance of the object. In the discussion in Chapter 2 of the *Show* method for the *MessageBox* class, you learned that you can invoke the method without instantiating an object based on the *MessageBox* class. This is because the *Show* method is a shared method. You can define shared methods for custom classes that you can use without having to instantiate an object based on the class.

This section relies on two projects. The first project was derived from a Class Library project template. This project, MethodsDemoLibrary, contains a single class that demonstrates how to implement methods with both *Sub* and *Function* procedures. The second project, MethodsDemoLibUser, was created with an Empty Project template. This project demonstrates the syntax for invoking custom methods implemented with either *Sub* or *Function* procedures and shows the differences in invoking a shared method.

Class Listing

The MethodsDemoLibrary project contains a reference to the *ADODB* library. Pick the appropriate library version for your requirements; my sample selected the 2.5 version because so many Access 2002 applications use this version. The project defines a single class named *MyArraySubAndFunctionMethods*. This class is an adaptation of the *MyArrayPropertyProcedures* class from the PropertiesDemoLibrary project reviewed earlier in the section. The fresh code for this application appears in bold. Showing the whole class definition makes it easy to see how the application fits together. The adaptation drops the *MyArrayLength* property but retains the *MyArrayFirst* and *MyArrayLast* properties. One of the retained properties is applied in the review of method coding techniques, and the potential applicability of the other retained property will be obvious. The reason for the sample is the addition of two procedures. These procedures demonstrate the syntax for programming methods based on *Sub* and *Function* procedures. Both of the new procedures illustrate different techniques for putting an Access database to use with Visual Basic .NET.

The *Sub* procedure implements the *ChangedShippersName* method. The procedure implementing this method makes a connection to the Northwind database. Then the procedure uses the connection to invoke a Jet SQL UPDATE statement for the Shippers table. The *ChangedShippersName* procedure takes two arguments. One argument is a string value for the new CompanyName column value. The second argument is a ShipperID column value for the row in the Shippers table to update. The procedure constructs the UPDATE statement from its two arguments. Because the ShipperID column is a primary key, a value for this column uniquely identifies a row in the Shippers table for which to modify the CompanyName column value. It normally is not a good idea to implement user interface code within a class method. This is because you do not want to pause an application for a user who is away from his or her machine when a prompt occurs or whose incorrect response generates a runtime error. However, in this case, we want the user to confirm the edit before implementing it. The sample uses a *MessageBox* function that shows the UPDATE statement and asks whether the user is sure about making the change. If the user replies Yes, the procedure invokes the *Connection* object's *Execute* method for the SQL string (*str1*) composed earlier in the procedure.

Use a *Function* procedure instead of a *Sub* procedure when your method needs to return a value type or object reference. The *TotalOrder* procedure computes the extended price for all the line items in an order. The procedure takes a single parameter, *OrderID*, to identify the rows to process in the Order Details table from the Northwind database. The *Function* procedure returns a *Decimal* value with the total extended price for the order. The procedure starts by making a connection to the Northwind database. Then the procedure creates a Jet SQL statement to select the rows from the Order Details table that match the *OrderID* value passed as an argument. This SQL string becomes an argument for a recordset's *Open* statement, which designs the recordset to contain the line items in the Order Details table for the designated *OrderID* value. A *Do* loop passes through the rows in the recordset and accumulates the extended price for each line item. When the loop relinquishes control, the *OrderTotal* memory variable contains the total extended price for the order designated by the *OrderID* argument. The *Return* statement at the close of the *TotalOrder* procedure passes this memory variable's value back to the calling procedure.

To keep the focus on the *TotalOrder* procedure's logic and its role in returning a value, I did not comment on the fact that the following listing actually contains two *Function* statements. You should use one of these *Function* declaration statements, but not both. I commented the basic *Function* statement and retained the *Function* statement with the *Shared* keyword because the MethodsDemoLibUser project references the *Shared Function* statement. As mentioned, using the *Shared* keyword before a procedure allows you to invoke a method even if you have no object based on the class. If you know that an application will always use a method with an object instance, you can specify a standard *Function* declaration statement. If it is necessary to invoke a method some or all of the time without an object instance, you must use the *Shared* keyword with your *Function* declaration statement.

```
Public Class MyArraySubAndFunctionMethods
    'Declare with Private access modifier for exclusive
    'access from within objects based on the class.
    Private ary_obj1() As Object

    'Declare private Integer variable used in the class.
    Private My_int1 As Integer

    'Class constructor
    Sub New(ByVal TblName As String, ByVal ColNumber As Integer)

        'Declare and instantiate ADODB objects.
        Dim cnn1 As New ADODB.Connection()
        Dim rst1 As New ADODB.Recordset()

        'Open an ADO Connection object.
        cnn1.Open("Provider=Microsoft.Jet.OLEDB.4.0;" & _
            "Data Source=C:\Program Files\" & _
            "Microsoft Office\Office10\Samples\Northwind.mdb;", _
            "Admin", "")

        'Open a recordset on a table.
        With rst1
            .ActiveConnection = cnn1
            .Open(TblName, , _
                ADODB.CursorTypeEnum.adOpenKeyset, _
                ADODB.LockTypeEnum.adLockOptimistic)
        End With

        'Declare the array with an upper bound.
        'Dim ary_obj1(rst1.RecordCount - 1) As Object
        ReDim ary_obj1(rst1.RecordCount - 1)
```

(continued)

```
        'Loop through the ADO recordset and assign column
        'values to the array.
        Do Until rst1.EOF
            ary_obj1(My_int1) = rst1(ColNumber).Value
            My_int1 += 1
            rst1.MoveNext()
        Loop

    End Sub

    'MyArrayLength property is read-only.
    Public ReadOnly Property MyArrayLength() As Integer
        Get
            Return ary_obj1.GetLength(0)
        End Get
    End Property

    'MyArrayFirst property is read/write.
    Public Property MyArrayFirst() As Object
        Get
            Return ary_obj1(0)
        End Get
        Set(ByVal Value As Object)
            ary_obj1(0) = Value
        End Set
    End Property

    'MyArrayLast property is read-only.
    Public ReadOnly Property MyArrayLast() As Object
        Get
            Return ary_obj1(ary_obj1.GetUpperBound(0))
        End Get
    End Property

    Sub ChangeShippersName(ByVal NewName As String, _
        ByVal TargetID As Integer)

        'Declare and instantiate ADODB objects.
        Dim cnn1 As New ADODB.Connection()

        'Open an ADO Connection object.
        cnn1.Open("Provider=Microsoft.Jet.OLEDB.4.0;" & _
            "Data Source=C:\Program Files\" & _
            "Microsoft Office\Office10\Samples\Northwind.mdb;", _
            "Admin", "")
```

```vb
    'Set up string for update.
    Dim str1 As String = _
        "UPDATE Shippers SET CompanyName = '" & NewName & _
        "' WHERE ShipperID=" & TargetID.ToString

    'Set up string for prompt.
    Dim str2 As String = _
        "Are you sure that you want to execute this?" & _
        vbCr & str1

    'Get confirmation before performing update.
    If MsgBoxResult.Yes = MsgBox(str2, MsgBoxStyle.YesNo) Then
        cnn1.Execute(str1)
    End If
End Sub

Shared Function TotalOrder(ByVal OrderID As Integer) As Decimal
    'Function TotalOrder(ByVal OrderID As Integer) As Decimal

    'Declare and instantiate ADODB objects.
    Dim cnn1 As New ADODB.Connection()
    Dim rst1 As New ADODB.Recordset()

    'Open an ADO Connection object.
    cnn1.Open("Provider=Microsoft.Jet.OLEDB.4.0;" & _
        "Data Source=C:\Program Files\" & _
        "Microsoft Office\Office10\Samples\Northwind.mdb;", _
        "Admin", "")

    'Open recordset for rows from Order Details,
    'matching OrderID.
    Dim str1 As String = _
        "SELECT * FROM [Order Details] " & _
        "WHERE OrderID =" & OrderID.ToString
    'Open a recordset on a table.
    With rst1
        .ActiveConnection = cnn1
        .Open(str1, , _
            ADODB.CursorTypeEnum.adOpenForwardOnly, _
            ADODB.LockTypeEnum.adLockReadOnly)
    End With

    'Loop through the ADO recordset and compute
    'the total for the designated OrderID.
```

(continued)

```
Dim Quantity As Integer
Dim UnitPrice As Decimal
Dim Discount As Decimal
Dim OrderTotal As Decimal
Do Until rst1.EOF
    Quantity = CInt(rst1("Quantity").Value)
    UnitPrice = CDec(rst1("UnitPrice").Value)
    Discount = CDec(rst1("Discount").Value)
    OrderTotal = _
        Quantity * UnitPrice * (1 - Discount) + OrderTotal
    rst1.MoveNext()
Loop

'Return OrderTotal value from TotalOrder method.
Return OrderTotal

End Function

End Class
```

Demonstrations for Invoking Methods

The listing for the MethodsDemoLibUser project appears next. This project contains a *main* procedure with calls to three *Sub* procedures. The listing shows all the *Sub* procedure calls commented. I tested them one at a time by removing the comment marker for a *Sub* procedure call. Before running the samples in the listing, make sure that the MethodsDemoLibUser project has a reference pointing at the MethodsDemoLibrary project. The *Imports* statement is included at the top of the listing as a reminder of the need for the reference. If the MethodsDemoLibUser project had references to two different projects containing classes named *MyArraySubAndFunctionMethods*, the *Imports* statement could give you a shortcut name for each, eliminating the possibility of conflicts between the namespaces of each referenced project.

The call to the *AddxToLastShipperAndRestore* procedure performs two main tasks. First, the procedure appends an *x* to the CompanyName column value for the last row in the Shippers table. Second, the procedure restores the row to its initial value. Typically, you will want to run just the first part of a sample like this. The second part has the virtue of restoring your Shippers table to its initial state. A series of message boxes updates you on what's happening between the occurrence of the first task and the second one.

The *AddxToLastShipperAndRestore* procedure's first task starts by invoking the *New* method for the *MyArraySubAndFunctionMethods* class to create a fresh object based on the class. The object refers to the Shippers table and returns the CompanyName column, which has an index value of 1. The

MyArrayLast property preserves the initial value in *str1*, which the procedure also uses as a basis for computing the new company name (namely, *str1 & "x"*). The *str2* string variable preserves this value. Next the procedure presents in a message box the initial CompanyName column value for the last row in the Shippers table. Then the procedure invokes the *ChangeShippersName* method for the object instance (*MyInstance*) created at the beginning of the procedure. By passing *str2* and 3 as arguments, the procedure directs the method to change the CompanyName column value to the value represented by the *str2* string in the table's row with a ShipperID value of 3.

> **Note**   The *ChangeShippersName* method can update the underlying recordset value for the *MyArrayLast* property. It does not matter that the property is read-only because the method changes the source for the property rather than the actual property value.

After the method completes the update, the CompanyName column value in the Shippers table will have a different value in its last row than the *MyArrayLast* property for the *MyInstance* object. To confirm the update by showing the new value in a message box, the sample needs a new instance of the *MyArraySubAndFunctionMethods* class (*MyInstance2*). However, the Visual Basic .NET code runs ahead of the Access update cycle for making the update available. (Access makes the update, but Visual Basic .NET can check for the changed value before it is available.) Therefore, the procedure introduces a 1-second pause. The code implements the pause with the *DateAdd* function and a *Do* loop. (In Chapter 4, you will see how to pause an application with either of two built-in timer classes.) After the pause, the first task concludes by displaying a message box with the value of the *MyArrayLast* property for the second object instance (*MyInstance2*).

The second task uses the same kind of logic as in the first task to change the CompanyName column value for the row in the Shippers table with a ShipperID value of 3. Because the sample saved the initial value of the CompanyName column value in the *str1* memory variable, the application uses that as one of the arguments for the *ChangeShippersName* method. To view the restored value, the code implementing the procedure's second task must resort to the same techniques for showing the initial change to the CompanyName column value—namely, waiting a second and creating a new object instance based on the *MyArraySubAndFunctionMethods* class. Figure 3-11 presents the series of message boxes that the *AddxToLastShipperAndRestore* procedure presents. In the figure, you can see the message boxes directly programmed by the procedure as well as those indirectly invoked by calls to the *ChangeShippersName* method.

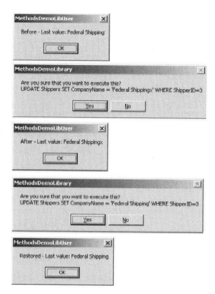

Figure 3-11 The sequence of message boxes generated by running *AddxToLastShipperAndRestore* procedure

The *ComputeOrderTotal* procedure computes the total extended price across all line items for any *OrderID* value designated in its calling routine. The main routine listing that follows designates an *OrderID* value of 10248, but you can specify any valid *OrderID* number from the Northwind database. *OrderID* values appear in both the Orders and Order Details tables within the database.

The *ComputeOrderTotal* procedure starts by instantiating a new object instance based on the *MyArraySubAndFunctionMethods* class. The procedure specifies the Shippers table to populate the private array, *ary_obj1*, used by objects based on the class, but the Shippers table is immaterial to the *TotalOrder* method. That's because the code for the *TotalOrder* method always creates a new connection and recordset based on a subset of the rows from the Order Details table in the Northwind database. The rows comprising the subset are the set whose *OrderID* values match the value passed when invoking the *TotalOrder* method. The method returns a *Decimal* value representing a currency. The procedure displays the currency with a message box. The currency appears with the local Windows currency by using the *Format* function. The *MsgBox* function designates a title for its message that specifies that the value showing in the message box is the total for whatever *OrderID* value is passed to the *ComputeOrderTotal* procedure.

The *ComputeWithSharedTotalOrder* procedure highlights the syntax for using a shared method. You can contrast this procedure with the *Compute-OrderTotal* procedure to reinforce your understanding of how to use standard methods from shared methods. You do not need to instantiate an object for the *MyArraySubAndFunctionMethods* class before invoking the shared method. In fact, you specify the method name relative to the class name instead of the name for an object instance. After the method returns a value, you can process the return the same way that you process a return value from any method—regardless of whether the method is shared.

```
Imports MyArraySubAndFunctionMethods = _
    MethodsDemoLibrary.MyArraySubAndFunctionMethods
Module Module1

    Sub main()

        'AddxToLastShipperAndRestore()

        'ComputeOrderTotal(10248)

        'ComputeWithSharedTotalOrder(10248)
    End Sub

    Sub AddxToLastShipperAndRestore()

        'Instantiate object.
        Dim MyInstance As New _
            MyArraySubAndFunctionMethods("Shippers", 1)

        'Persist original last value property and
        'prepare edited value.
        Dim str1 = MyInstance.MyArrayLast
        Dim str2 = str1 & "x"

        'Display last shipper's name before edit,
        'then invoke ChangeShippersName.
        MsgBox("Before - Last value: " & _
            MyInstance.MyArrayLast)
        MyInstance.ChangeShippersName(str2, 3)
```

(continued)

```
        'Introduce a short pause (1 second) without a timer;
        'allows time for automatic refresh to show edit.
        Dim ASecondLater = _
            DateAdd(DateInterval.Second, 1, Now())
        Do Until Now() > ASecondLater
        Loop

        'Create a new instance so that you can show the change.
        Dim MyInstance2 As New _
            MyArraySubAndFunctionMethods("Shippers", 1)
        MsgBox("After - Last value: " & MyInstance2.MyArrayLast)

        'Restore original value.
        MyInstance.ChangeShippersName(str1, 3)

        'Introduce a short pause without a timer.
        ASecondLater = DateAdd(DateInterval.Second, 1, Now())
        Do Until Now() > ASecondLater
        Loop

        'Create a new instance so that you can show the change.
        Dim MyInstance3 As New _
            MyArraySubAndFunctionMethods("Shippers", 1)
        MsgBox("Restored - Last value: " & MyInstance3.MyArrayLast)

    End Sub

    Sub ComputeOrderTotal(ByVal OrderID As Integer)

        'Instantiate object.
        Dim MyInstance As New MyArraySubAndFunctionMethods("Shippers", 1)

        'Compute with TotalOrder method for instance.
        Dim OrderTotal As Decimal = MyInstance.TotalOrder(OrderID)

        'Display results formatted as currency.
        MsgBox(Format(OrderTotal, "C"), _
            MsgBoxStyle.Information, _
            "Total for Order " & OrderID.ToString)

    End Sub

    Sub ComputeWithSharedTotalOrder(ByVal OrderID As Integer)

        'Compute with TotalOrder method without an instance.
        Dim OrderTotal As Decimal = _
            MyArraySubAndFunctionMethods.TotalOrder(OrderID)
```

```
        'Display results formatted as currency.
        MsgBox(Format(OrderTotal, "C"), _
            MsgBoxStyle.Information, _
            "Total for Order " & OrderID.ToString)

    End Sub

End Module
```

Summary

This chapter presents a variety of traditional programming topics that can have a material impact on the operation of Visual Basic .NET solutions created by Access developers. For example, the chapter begins with a review of Visual Basic .NET data types, highlighting issues and techniques for mapping Access data types to Visual Basic .NET data types. Several additional sections drill down on traditional programming topics, including the creation and usage of procedures, branching and looping techniques, and array processing guidelines. The chapter closes with an introduction to classes and demonstrates how to use them with Access databases in Visual Basic .NET. Sample code throughout the chapter illustrates how to process Access databases with the familiar *ADODB* library by using the Visual Basic .NET COM Interop feature.

4

Selected Visual Basic .NET Advanced Topics

Chapter 3 introduced selected core Microsoft Visual Basic .NET programming issues. Most of those issues are traditional ones that have a strong relationship with similar topics in classic Visual Basic. This chapter considers four additional Visual Basic .NET topics. However, these features of the programming environment are either brand new or substantially changed from Visual Basic's previous incarnation. My goal in this chapter is to arouse your curiosity about the new programming topics and to present code samples that will empower you to exploit the new techniques as you create your own custom solutions.

My objective for Chapter 3 and this chapter is to convey a good working knowledge of many core Visual Basic .NET programming topics that target the skill sets that Microsoft Access developers will likely find useful. In several cases, I explicitly use Microsoft Access databases to make it easy for you to see the relevance of these techniques to your particular kind of programming tasks. In other cases, I present the core topics without a database reference to present the programming concept cleanly and simply.

The four areas covered in this chapter are file processing, event processing, class inheritance, and a new style of run-time error processing. The *System.IO* namespace introduces a set of new classes for manipulating files. In particular, you will learn about the *StreamWriter* and *StreamReader* objects for processing text files, but you will also learn how to programmatically manipulate binary files such as the image files associated with the Northwind database. Furthermore, you will learn about new ways of handling events and will see samples demonstrating the raising of events from classes that expose Access database objects. In addition, you will learn how to work with inheritance, a powerful concept that facilitates code reuse by letting one class inherit members, such as properties and methods, from another. Again, you will see inheritance in action with Access database objects. The chapter closes with a discussion of structured exception handling (SEH)—a new and improved means of processing run-time errors. I'll explain why SEH is superior to the unstructured run-time error processing in classic Visual Basic. As with most of the topics covered throughout the book, the SEH focus is on the presentation of code samples that will empower you.

File Processing Techniques

Although the .NET Framework offers traditional file-processing tools, such as the *FileSystemObject*, there is a new way of performing file processing that draws on the capabilities introduced with the .NET Framework. The classes for these new capabilities reside in the *System.IO* namespace. This section introduces these new capabilities, while demonstrating how to perform typical kinds of file-processing tasks.

System.IO Objects for File Processing

The *System.IO* namespace exposes a collection of classes to facilitate the access and manipulation of directories and individual files within a directory. The classes in the *System.IO* namespace expose methods, properties, and events to enable you to find, copy, delete, and write files. You can use these classes to process string or binary data. For example, you can copy a subset of the contents from a database on another computer to a file on a local computer. Later, you can read the file and process the data. When working with objects based on the classes in the *System.IO* namespace, you must add a reference to the namespace and use an *Imports* statement or just prefix the class name with *System.IO* when instantiating objects.

The *System.IO* namespace offers shared and instance-based classes for processing directories and files. As you've learned, you can invoke shared classes without an instance of the object. The *Directory* class exposes shared methods for creating, moving, and enumerating the contents of directories. Use the *GetFiles* method for returning the names of files in a specified directory. You can also set the current directory, get the names of the subdirectories within a directory, or create a new directory with the *SetCurrentDirectory*, *GetDirectories*, and *CreateDirectory* methods. See the "Directory Class" topic in the Visual Studio .NET documentation for the complete list of methods for the *Directory* class, along with links for further details on each method. You can open the documentation from the Windows Start button. (Go to Programs, Microsoft Visual Studio .NET, and choose Microsoft Visual Studio .NET Documentation.)

> **Note**   In the Visual Studio .NET documentation, you will notice the *Directory* class referred to as a class with static methods. *Static* is a synonym for *shared* in Visual Basic .NET. The *Show* method of the *MessageBox* class is a shared method—that is, you can invoke the method without creating an instance of the object.

The *File* class is another class exposing shared methods. This class offers methods for creating, copying, moving, and opening files. You can also use the *File* class to assist in the creation of *FileStream* objects. A *FileStream* object is a sequence of bytes representing the contents of a file. You can use *File* class methods to read and write to the *FileStream* object representing the contents of a file. You can use *File* class methods such as *Create*, *CreateText*, and *Append-Text* to create and populate files. Invoke the *Delete* method to remove a file that an application no longer needs. Other methods support the reading and manipulation of file attributes. Invoke the *SetCreationTime* method to set the date and time for the creation of a file or the *SetLastWriteTime* method to designate the last time that a file was modified.

The *DirectoryInfo* and *FileInfo* classes are instance-based classes that correspond to the *Directory* and *File* classes with their static methods. These two sets of classes perform comparable functions. However, the *DirectoryInfo* and *FileInfo* classes require you to create an instance of the class before you can refer to or manipulate a directory or a file. If an application repeatedly refers to the same file, the instance-based classes provide faster performance. This occurs because instance-based methods do not require a security check before invoking a method, such as *Delete*, each time you designate the same file. The security check is necessary only for the first use of a method for an instance. Classes with static methods, such as *File*, do require security checks each time you invoke a method. A static method does not know from one invocation to the next whether it is dealing with the same file or a different one.

The *StreamWriter* and *StreamReader* classes explicitly target writing to and reading from a file containing characters (the elements of a string). The bytes represent characters in a specific encoding; the default encoding is UTF-8 encoding. The UTF-8 encoding is for representing Unicode characters with a variable number of bytes, but it is optimized for the lower 127 ASCII characters—

American ASCII. Visual Basic .NET also offers the *BinaryWriter* and *Binary-Reader* classes for reading and writing .NET Framework data types to a file. You can use the *BinaryWriter* and *BinaryReader* classes to process binary data files with streams of bytes representing objects, such as an image or a spreadsheet.

Listing Files in a Folder

This section demonstrates how to use the *DirectoryInfo* and *Directory* classes to enumerate the files in a directory. All the code samples illustrating file-processing techniques reside in the FileProcessingSamples project, which is a Microsoft Windows application. This makes it easy to launch procedures by clicking a button. One sample also demonstrates the use of the PictureBox control on a Windows form to display the contents of a file with a binary representation for an image.

Enumerating Files with the *DirectoryInfo* Class

Access 2002 ships the Northwind database with the employee images as stand-alone files instead of integrated into the database, as with previous versions of the Northwind.mdb file. Images, even relatively small ones such as those for the employees in the Northwind database, are relatively large in comparison to data type values normally stored in databases. Each employee image is around 40 KB. However, the ReportsTo column values, which have a *Long Integer* data type, each require just 4 bytes. This size difference can degrade database performance. Storing the files externally to the database and retaining just the path to the file in the database can speed performance. However, maintaining files outside the database requires procedures for managing the files.

The first file-processing sample illustrates how to iterate through all the .eps files in the Samples folder within the \Program Files\Microsoft Office\Office10 path. These .eps files are the image files for the employees in the Northwind database. There are nine .eps files—one for each employee. The filenames are EMPID*x*, where *x* represents a number corresponding to the EmployeeID column value for an employee in the Employees table of the Northwind database.

Add a button (*Button1*) to *Form1* in the FileProcessingSamples project. In the button's event procedure, you can specify the path to process. A second procedure, *BmpReporter*, can accept the path and demonstrate the use of the *DirectoryInfo* class for iterating through the .eps files in the target path. In the sample, the *BmpReporter* procedure concludes by presenting a message box with some feedback on its search. The following listing illustrates one approach to this task.

The *BmpReporter* procedure begins by declaring objects that it will use. Critically, this procedure instantiates an instance of the *DirectoryInfo* class as *dir1*. The constructor for this class takes an argument, *strPath*, that designates the folder to process. The declaration for *fil1* does not instantiate an object, but it declares a variable based on the *FileInfo* class. As you know, both the *Directory-Info* and *FileInfo* classes work with specific instances of a directory and a file.

The procedure then illustrates the syntax for looping through a subset of the files in the target path with .eps file extensions. These files contain the employee pictures. Within the loop, the sample saves the full name of each successive image file with its path in the *str1* string variable, and it adds 1 to the *int1* variable. After the last pass through the loop, *str1* contains the name of the last .eps file in the target path, and *int1* equals the number of .eps files in the path for *dir1*. The *BmpReport* procedure concludes by presenting one of two message boxes based on the value of *int1*. With a default installation of Access 2002, the procedure returns a message box with three lines—one each for the name of the target folder, the number of .eps files in the folder, and the full name of the last .eps file in the target folder. (See Figure 4-1.)

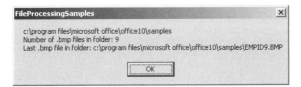

Figure 4-1   The message box generated when you run the
Button1_Click event procedure in the FileProcessingSamples project

```
Private Sub Button1_Click(ByVal sender As System.Object, _
    ByVal e As System.EventArgs) Handles Button1.Click
    'If user has permission, this code works on a workstation.
    Dim strFolder = _
        "c:\program files\microsoft office\" & _
        "office10\samples\"
    BmpReporter(strFolder)

End Sub

Sub BmpReporter(ByVal strPath As String)

    Dim dir1 As New System.IO.DirectoryInfo(strPath)
    Dim fil1 As System.IO.FileInfo
    Dim str1 As String
    Dim int1 As Integer
```

(continued)

```
'For…Each loop to iterate through .eps files
'in the strPath path.
For Each fil1 In dir1.GetFiles("*.eps")
    str1 = fil1.FullName
    int1 += 1
Next fil1

'Return path name, number of .eps files, name
'of last .eps file (include path) in strPath.
Dim str2 As String
If int1 > 0 Then
    str2 = dir1.FullName & vbCr & _
    "Number of .eps files in folder: " & _
    int1.ToString & vbCr & _
    "Last .eps file in folder: " & str1
Else
    str2 = "No .eps files found."
End If
MsgBox(str2)

End Sub
```

The next procedure listing, which is for the *Click* event for *Button2* on *Form1*, illustrates the use of UNC notation for specifying the path to a target folder. The *Click* event procedure directs the *BmpReporter* procedure to search one of two paths in the c share on another computer named cablat. Depending on the response to a message box, the procedure assigns a string for the Access 2002 Samples folder or the Access 2000 Samples folder. The cablat has both versions of Access installed, but only the Access 2002 Samples folder has the .eps files in its Samples folder. The Access 2000 version shipped with the employee image representations inside the database instead of as stand-alone files. Therefore, when I run this *Button2 Click* event procedure, the message box from *BmpReporter* reads, "No .eps files found." You can achieve the same outcome by designating any target path that does not contain .eps files.

```
Private Sub Button2_Click(ByVal sender As System.Object, _
    ByVal e As System.EventArgs) Handles Button2.Click

    'Declare a string for the target folder.
    Dim strFolder As String

    'Instantiate a string for the prompt in a message box.
    Dim str1 = "Click Yes to search the Access 2002 " & _
        "Samples folder or No to search the Access " & _
        "2000 Samples folder."
```

```
'Set the target folder to search the Samples folder for
'either Access 2002 (Office 10) or Access 2000 (Office).
If MsgBox(str1, MsgBoxStyle.YesNo) = MsgBoxResult.Yes Then
    strFolder = _
        "\\cablat\c\program files\microsoft office\" & _
        "office10\samples\"
Else
    strFolder = _
        "\\cablat\c\program files\microsoft office\" & _
        "office\samples\"
End If

'Pass the path to BmpReporter.
BmpReporter(strFolder)

End Sub
```

Enumerating Files with the *Directory* Class

When using the *Directory* class to enumerate the files within a folder, the process changes. For example, you do not instantiate an object pointing at a directory. Although the *Directory* and *DirectoryInfo* classes both have a *GetFiles* method, the input and return from the method is different for each class. In the case of the *Directory* class, you have to designate a path whenever you invoke a method. This is not necessary for the *DirectoryInfo* class. Once you instantiate a *DirectoryInfo* object for a path, you can reuse different methods for that instance of the *DirectoryInfo* class. The *GetFiles* method for both classes can take a string indicating which subset of files to search for within a directory, but with the *Directory* class, this method must always precede this optional string with a string indicating the target folder to search. The *DirectoryInfo* class returns *FileInfo* instances from its *GetFiles* method, but the *Directory* class returns strings representing the name of the files returned by the method.

The following two procedures illustrate how to use the *Directory* class to search for all .eps files in the Access 2002 Samples folder. The *Click* event procedure for *Button3* specifies the path to search and passes the string with that information to the *BmpReporter2* procedure. The syntax in the *For…Each* statement shows the arguments to search for only .eps files in the target path. You can omit the second argument for the *GetFiles* method if you want to search for all files within a directory.

Both the *BmpReporter* and *BmpReporter2* procedures use a variable named *fil1* to enumerate the members of the return set from the *GetFiles* method. However, *BmpReport2* declares *fil1* as a string, while *BmpReporter* declares *fil1* as a *FileInfo* object. This is because the *GetFiles* method for the *Directory* class returns the names of files, while the *DirectoryInfo* class returns

FileInfo objects with its *GetFiles* methods. Although the *BmpReporter* procedure does initially capture a *FileInfo* object, it does save a string by storing the *FullName* property value for the *FileInfo* object in the *str1* string. In the *BmpReporter2* procedure, the *fil1* variable is already a string value. The *BmpReporter2* procedure extends the *BmpReporter* procedure by stripping the path from before the filename. This path is not necessary in the message box showing the result because the path already shows on the first line of the message box prompt. The *Mid* function extracts only the portion of the string returned by the *GetFiles* method after the last "\" in the name. The *InStrRev* function returns the position of this target string. The *Length* property for a string is the total number of characters in the string.

```
Private Sub Button3_Click(ByVal sender As System.Object, _
    ByVal e As System.EventArgs) Handles Button3.Click

    'Declare a string variable with the target folder to
    'search and pass the string to BmpReporter2.
    Dim strFolder = _
        "c:\program files\microsoft office\" & _
        "office10\samples\"
    BmpReporter2(strFolder)

End Sub

Sub BmpReporter2(ByVal strPath As String)

    Dim fil1 As String
    Dim str1 As String
    Dim int1 As Integer

    'For...Each loop to iterate through all files
    'in the strPath path, but select just .eps files;
    'strip filename from path for selected files.
    For Each fil1 In System.IO.Directory.GetFiles(strPath, "*.eps")
        str1 = Mid(fil1, (InStrRev(fil1, "\") + 1), _
            (fil1.Length - InStrRev(fil1, "\")))
            int1 += 1
    Next fil1

    'Return path name, number of .eps files,
    'name of last .eps file in strPath.
    Dim str2 As String
    If int1 > 0 Then
        str2 = strPath & vbCr & _
        "Number of .eps files in folder: " & _
```

```
        int1.ToString & vbCr & _
        "Last .eps file in folder: " & str1
    Else
        str2 = strPath & vbCr & _
        "Number of .eps files in folder: " & _
        int1.ToString
    End If
    MsgBox(str2)

End Sub
```

Selecting and Showing Binary Files

Now that you know how to iterate through the image files in a folder and find out information about them, such as their name, it is natural to want to display the images in the files. The .eps files for employees in the Access 2002 Samples folder are binary files because they are meant for any application that can run .eps files. You can't view the image by opening the file in a text reader such as the Windows Notepad utility. Therefore, we need a control in Visual Basic .NET that can decipher the byte stream in a .eps file in order to display the image. Visual Basic and Visual Basic for Applications (VBA) developers are familiar with the Image control for displaying the image corresponding to a binary image file, but this control is not available in Visual Basic .NET. However, the PictureBox control serves a similar role. The PictureBox control works differently from the Image control in that the PictureBox control actually displays the binary image that you assign to its *Image* property.

> **Note**   This section uses a control, the PictureBox, for a form in a Windows application. The sample discussion mentions manually setting control properties, such as *Width* and *Height*. Chapter 2 introduces form design in Windows applications, and Chapters 5 and 6 explore forms and controls for Windows applications in much more depth.

You can drag a PictureBox control from the Toolbox to *Form1* in the FileProcessingSamples project. This creates an instance, PictureBox1, of the control on the form. Select the instance and then set its *Width* and *Height* properties in the Properties window to 188 and 217 pixels; these settings appear nested within the *Size* property for the PictureBox1 control. The dimensions are appropriate for the employee image files within the Access 2002 Samples folder.

The sample for showing an image file uses two event procedures. The *Form1_Load* procedure hides the PictureBox1 control. It achieves this result by setting the control's *Visible* property to *False*, which hides the control when it has no image to display. The second procedure will make the control visible after a user selects an employee for which to show a picture.

The second procedure, *Button4_Click*, performs multiple tasks. First, the event procedure makes a connection to the Northwind database to generate a recordset with fields identifying each employee in the Employees table. Second, it presents an input box with information for a subset of the employees from the Employees table. This second step also captures the response to the user's selection of an employee from the list showing in the input box. Third, the procedure creates a setting for the *Image* property of *PictureBox1* that corresponds to the selected employee. The setting for the *Image* property contains the bytes from one of the .eps files in the Access 2002 Samples folder (the one corresponding to the selected employee).

The second procedure uses the *ADODB* library to open a connection to the Northwind database and creates a recordset based on selected columns from the Employees table. Chapter 3 gives instructions for using the COM Interop feature to create a reference to the *ADODB* library from a Visual Basic .NET project. The declaration area of the *Button4_Click* procedure declares and instantiates *ADODB* connection objects. After that, a block of standard ActiveX Data Objects (ADO) code inside the Visual Basic .NET procedure makes the connection and recordset objects. The *Select* statement for the recordset designates the EmployeeID, FirstName, LastName, and Photo columns as fields in the recordset.

The second task starts by extracting fields for the first five employees from the recordset. A *Do* loop with a nested *If...Then* statement implements this part of the task. The code inside the loop constructs a string with a separate line for each of the first five employees. Saving the recordset values to variables declared as Visual Basic .NET *Strings* converts the recordset values from *ADODB* data types to Visual Basic .NET data types. This is necessary to display the values in an input box. The sample uses the *Chr* function with an argument of *10* to force a linefeed character at the end of each line within the *str1* variable. After looping through the required rows from the recordset to create *str1*, the procedure closes the recordset and its connection to the Northwind database. The second task concludes by invoking the *InputBox* function with *str1* as the argument for the input box's prompt. Visual Basic .NET offers more robust tools for diplaying data than the *InputBox* function, but the sample purposefully takes a minimalist approach here to highlight the use of the binary file in a PictureBox control.

The third task begins by taking the user's response to the input box and preparing a setting for the *Image* property of *PictureBox1*. This property points at the file that the PictureBox control is to show. The setting for the property must include the full path to the image file, which is one of the nine employee image files in the Access 2002 Samples folder. If your image files are in another location, either move them to the designated folder or update the expression setting the path to the image for the selected employee. The assignment of the *Image* property for the PictureBox1 control depends on the shared *FromFile* method for the *Image* class. The *Image* class method creates an image object from the path to a binary image file. The third task ends by setting the *Visible* property for the *PictureBox1* control to *True*. This makes the image container, along with its image, visible on the form.

```
Private Sub Form1_Load(ByVal sender As System.Object, _
    ByVal e As System.EventArgs) Handles MyBase.Load

    'Hide Picture box conrol when form opens.
    PictureBox1.Visible = False

End Sub

Private Sub Button4_Click(ByVal sender As System.Object, _
    ByVal e As System.EventArgs) Handles Button4.Click

    Dim cnn1 As New ADODB.Connection()
    Dim rst1 As New ADODB.Recordset()
    Dim str2 As String
    Dim int1 As Integer

    'Make a connection to the Northwind database
    'and open a recordset based on selected columns
    'from the Employees table.
    cnn1.Open("Provider=Microsoft.Jet.OLEDB.4.0;" & _
        "Data Source=C:\Program Files\" & _
        "Microsoft Office\Office10\" & _
        "Samples\Northwind.mdb")
    Dim str1 As String = "SELECT EmployeeID, " & _
        "FirstName, LastName, Photo " & _
        "FROM Employees"
    With rst1
        .ActiveConnection = cnn1
        .Open(str1, , _
        ADODB.CursorTypeEnum.adOpenForwardOnly, _
```

(continued)

```
            ADODB.LockTypeEnum.adLockPessimistic)
End With

'Loop through the recordset to extract information
'for the first five employees.
str1 = ""
int1 = 1
Do Until rst1.EOF
    If rst1("EmployeeID").Value <= 5 Then
        Dim strID As String = _
            CStr(rst1("EmployeeID").Value)
        Dim strFname As String = _
            rst1("FirstName").Value
        Dim strLname As String = _
            rst1("LastName").Value
        Dim strPhoto As String = _
            rst1("Photo").Value
        str1 += strID & _
            ", " & strFname & _
            ", " & strLname & _
            ", " & strPhoto & Chr(10)
        rst1.MoveNext()
    Else
        Exit Do
    End If
Loop

'Close the connection and recordset objects
'now that you no longer need them.
rst1.Close()
rst1 = Nothing
cnn1.Close()
cnn1 = Nothing

'Present an input box requesting a selection
'about which employee picture to show.
str2 = InputBox(str1, _
    "Show picture for one of 1st 5 employees", _
    "1")

'Specify the path to the image file for
'the selected employee and assign the picture
'file in the path to the Image property of
'a PictureBox control.
str2 = "C:\Program Files\Microsoft Office\" & _
    "Office10\Samples\EmpID" & str2 & ".eps"
```

```
'Show the binary image file for the
'selected employee.
Me.PictureBox1.Image = Image.FromFile(str2)
Me.PictureBox1.Visible = True
```

End Sub

Figure 4-2 shows the application that lets a user select an employee and then displays the corresponding image file. The top window shows *Button4* on *Form1* just before a user clicks it. After clicking the button, the input box opens; the caption for the box is Show Picture For One Of 1st Five Employees. The default reply is 1, but Figure 4-2 shows an override of the default value to a new value of 5. The bottom window in Figure 4-2 displays the image of Steven Buchanan, whose EmployeeID value is 5, inside the form's PictureBox1 control. The control also was present in the top window in Figure 4-2, but the control's *Visible* property was set to *False*.

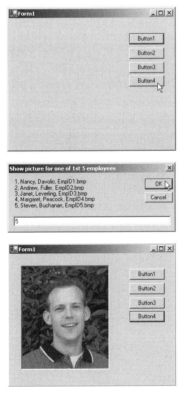

Figure 4-2   The sequence of windows presented by an application that lets a user pick an employee whose picture will show on *Form1*

Writing Access Database Contents to Files

The preceding application is interesting because it displays a binary image file. However, it does very little file processing. (Mostly, it forms an expression for the path to a file and then passes the image in the file to a control on a form in a Windows application.) The file processing developers traditionally think of has more to do with writing or reading values in memory to a file. This section presents a sample that illustrates how to write data values as string values to a file. The next section demonstrates how to read the file that this sample creates. The combined capability to write database contents to a local file and then subsequently read database values from the file is particularly useful whenever the connection to a database is not persistent—for example, because of travel away from headquarters or an unreliable connection to a computer storing a database file.

The *StreamWriter* class is one easy tool for writing memory values to a file. Construct a *StreamWriter* object instance to which you can write memory values. These should be string values because the *StreamWriter* is for writing a text stream to a file. After invoking the *Write* method for the object instance as many times as necessary, invoke the *Close* method. This method ensures that all data is flushed from *StreamWriter* buffers to the file and calls the *Dispose* method for the object instance so that the garbage collector can remove the *StreamWriter* instance from memory on the next collection cycle.

You can invoke the sample by clicking Button5. This sample commences by creating a recordset object, *rst1*, based on the Employees table in the Northwind database. The code to perform this task is identical to that in the preceding sample. Because the FileProcessingSamples project already has a reference to the *ADODB* library, you do not need to invoke the COM Interop feature a second time to create a new reference. After making the recordset, the sample loops through its records and creates a string with a separate line for each employee. The code sample uses the *vbLf* constant to delimit lines because the output is not constrained by the limitations of the *InputBox* function, which does not process the constant but instead requires the *Chr* function with a value of 10. In this case, you can just as easily use the *vbCr* constant or the *vbCrLf* constant; either of these intrinsic constants generates a new line. As in the preceding sample, this sample closes the recordset and connection after composing the string based on the Employees table.

The code to this point in the sample prepares a string for saving as a disk file. This code appears in boldface so that you know it is original, rather than recycled from earlier material in the chapter. The filename and extension will be Employees.txt. The *str2* string stores the filename and extension as well as its path. The "..\" points to the root folder in the directory for the current project.

The program running this code has the filename FileProcessingSamples.exe, and it resides in the bin subdirectory of the folder for the project. By using the *"..\"* notation, the code points to the folder one up from the bin subdirectory— the root folder for the FileProcessingSamples project.

When the sample invokes the *New* method for the *StreamWriter* class to create a new instance of a file stream, it specifies two arguments. One argument is the name of the path to the file corresponding to the file stream. The second argument is a Boolean variable that designates whether to write over existing data in the file or append new data to the existing data. The value of *True* in the sample indicates the *Write* method should append to existing data. Next, the *Write* method for the *StreamWriter* instance copies the string with employee data (*str1*) to the *StreamWriter* object. Finally, the *Close* method flushes the *Stream-Writer* of any data not committed to the physical file and marks the *StreamWriter* object instance for removal from memory by the garbage collector. The last line of the procedure confirms that the attempt to write to disk is completed.

```
Private Sub Button5_Click(ByVal sender As System.Object, _
    ByVal e As System.EventArgs) Handles Button5.Click

    Dim cnn1 As New ADODB.Connection()
    Dim rst1 As New ADODB.Recordset()
    Dim str1 As String
    Dim int1 As Integer

    'Make a connection to the Northwind database
    'and open a recordset based on selected columns
    'from the Employees table.
    cnn1.Open("Provider=Microsoft.Jet.OLEDB.4.0;" & _
        "Data Source=C:\Program Files\" & _
        "Microsoft Office\Office10\" & _
        "Samples\Northwind.mdb")
    str1 = "SELECT EmployeeID, " & _
        "FirstName, LastName, Photo " & _
        "FROM Employees"
    With rst1
        .ActiveConnection = cnn1
        .Open(str1, , _
        ADODB.CursorTypeEnum.adOpenForwardOnly, _
        ADODB.LockTypeEnum.adLockPessimistic)
    End With

    'Loop through the recordset to extract information
    'for all employees.
    str1 = ""
```

(continued)

```
int1 = 1
Do Until rst1.EOF
    Dim strID As String = _
        CStr(rst1("EmployeeID").Value)
    Dim strFname As String = _
        rst1("FirstName").Value
    Dim strLname As String = _
        rst1("LastName").Value
    Dim strPhoto As String = _
        rst1("Photo").Value
    str1 += strID & _
        ", " & strFname & _
        ", " & strLname & _
        ", " & strPhoto & vbLf
    rst1.MoveNext()
Loop
'Close the connection and recordset objects
'now that you no longer need them.
rst1.Close()
rst1 = Nothing
cnn1.Close()
cnn1 = Nothing

'Declare a StreamWriter to build the text
'filename Employees.txt in the root folder
'for the current project.
Dim str2 As String = "..\Employees.txt"
Dim fsw1 As New System.IO.StreamWriter(str2, True)

'Write the string of employee data.
fsw1.Write(str1)

'Close the file.
fsw1.Close()

MsgBox("File closed.")

End Sub
```

After running the *Button5_Click* procedure, you will have added a new file to the project's assembly. You can verify the existence of this file from Solution Explorer. Depending on your existing settings for Solution Explorer, you might need to click the Show All Files and Refresh controls on the toolbar within Solution Explorer. You can always discern the purpose of a Windows tool by placing your mouse over it. Double-clicking the Employees.txt file in Solution Explorer opens the file's contents inside the IDE. Figure 4-3 shows the

Employees.txt file contents in the IDE after a double-click of Employees.txt in Solution Explorer.

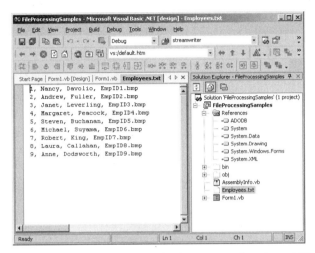

Figure 4-3   Using Solution Explorer to confirm the addition of files to a project and preview their contents

Reading and Managing Text Files

Although being able to view a saved file in the IDE is nice, one major reason for saving a file is to read it programmatically later. The final sample of this section illustrates how to do this. After reading a file, you might want to remove it from disk storage. Therefore, this sample also illustrates how to delete a file. By combining this sample with the earlier samples that show how to create files, add text to files, and search for files, you can create powerful file-processing solutions that enrich your Access database solutions.

The sample in this section reads the file prepared by the preceding sample and gives the user an opportunity to delete the file after reading it. You can read a text file with an instance of the *StreamReader* class. To open a *StreamReader* object instance that points at a file, invoke the *New* method with an argument. The argument should point at the path to the file that you want to open. Immediately after opening a text file with a *StreamReader* object, you can use the *ReadToEnd* method to transfer the contents of the whole file to a memory variable. The sample illustrates the syntax to accomplish this. Other *StreamReader* methods enable your applications to read parts of a text file.

After reading the whole text file into memory, the procedure prompts the user about whether to delete the Employees.txt file. If the user clicks the Yes button on the message box, the application instantiates a *FileInfo* object (*fin1*) pointing at the Employees.txt file in the project's root folder. Then, the sample code invokes the *Delete* method for the *FileInfo* object. This removes the file from the project's folder. You can use the code from the preceding sample to reconstruct the Employees.txt file if you need it.

```
Private Sub Button6_Click(ByVal sender As System.Object, _
    ByVal e As System.EventArgs) Handles Button6.Click

    'Instantiate StreamReader pointing at
    'Employees.txt in root folder of current project.
    Dim str1 As String = "..\Employees.txt"
    Dim fsr1 As New System.IO.StreamReader(str1)

    'Read Employees.txt and display contents in
    'a message box.
    Dim str2 As String = fsr1.ReadToEnd
    MsgBox(str2)
    fsr1.Close()

    'Remove file if user says to.
    If MsgBox("Delete Employees.txt?", _
        MsgBoxStyle.YesNo) = MsgBoxResult.Yes Then
        Dim fin1 As New System.IO.FileInfo(str1)
        fin1.Delete()
    End If

End Sub
```

Event Handlers and Custom Events

Windows programming with Visual Basic has always been special because of how events and event procedures simplify application development. This section explores the creation of event handlers and the propagation of custom events from your own classes. By running and understanding the samples in this section, you will learn robust ways to take advantage of the built-in events for the .NET Framework classes as well as how to propagate events from your own custom classes.

Overview of Event Processing

In real life, events happen. For example, your telephone rings. You have the option to pick up the phone and respond to the event. If two or more phones are conveniently available, you can respond to the telephone ring (event) from any of the (multiple) phones. In your programming applications, you can elect to respond or ignore events. Normally, you respond to events with an event procedure, but an application can elect to ignore events by not specifying a procedure to handle an event. Although you can have multiple procedures to handle events, it is often best to keep things simple and have just one handler for each type of event.

Events can remind you of something just by their name, but often they can also return information that helps your application respond properly to them. When events return information, such as the identity of their sender, your event handler must know how to receive the information the event conveys. Events return information as values in a way that parallels the way you pass information to a procedure. Both the calling routine and the called routine must have the same list of arguments. Visual Basic .NET refers to the name of an event and its argument list as an *event signature*. To process an event, you must specify its signature properly.

Many beginning Visual Basic developers do not pay much attention to the structure of event handlers. These developers generate the shell for an event just by double-clicking an object, such as a button on a form. Double-clicking an object creates the shell for an object's default event in the code behind a form. The IDE responds by creating a shell that automatically specifies the event signature. Then, the developer enters his code into the shell. Unfortunately, all events do not come with automatically generated shells. This is especially true for custom events from the classes that you create for an application. (This would be a great time to review the "Classes" section in Chapter 3.) By learning how to raise events from custom classes and developing standards for responding to them appropriately, your organization can dramatically reduce the programming effort associated with projects or accomplish tasks not otherwise possible.

Custom classes require an *Event* keyword to declare each event emanating from them. When you declare an event, you give it a name and specify its signature. Although you must declare an event in order for it to occur, the mere declaration of an event is not sufficient to make it occur. You must also specify when an event will happen. Use the *RaiseEvent* keyword to trigger an event from your custom classes. By specifying argument values in a *RaiseEvent* statement, you can properly specify the signature for an event and pass information to an event handler. For example, an event handler for credit checks might receive information such as the amount of an order or the customer ID.

Visual Basic .NET assigns the term *delegate* to a procedure handling an event. This is because the application responding to an event delegates the handling of the event to the event-handling procedure. The procedure handling an event does the work of acknowledging the event for an application. By the way, this notion of delegates is part of what makes events so powerful. Your main procedure does not have to do everything. It delegates work to other procedures. This simplifies and segments your code development process. The other element that makes events so valuable is that event procedures do not have to be invoked (and therefore compiled). This can make your application start and run faster by requiring only the compilation of code that users actually invoke.

There are two ways to designate a procedure as a handler for a specific event. The *Handles* clause in a procedure declaration can specify the object and event that a procedure handles. To use the *Handles* clause, you must declare the object in the application by using the *WithEvents* keyword. This keyword is one way to let events propagate from one code block (such as a class) to another (such as a project referencing the class). When you drag controls from the Toolbox, Visual Studio .NET automatically declares the object instance for a control or a component by using the *WithEvents* keyword. This declaration appears in the code behind a form within the region named Windows Form Designer Generated Code. By double-clicking a control, you cause the IDE to create an event procedure shell with a *Handles* clause.

The second way to designate a procedure as an event handler is by using the *AddHandler* statement. The *AddHandler* statement allows you to declare an event handler. This statement has two clauses. The first clause starts with the *AddHandler* keyword. Follow this keyword with the name of the event. An event name has two parts: the object name and the name of the event within the object. Delimit the two parts with a period. The second clause starts with the *AddressOf* keyword. Follow this keyword with the name of the procedure that you are delegating as the processor for the event named in the *AddHandler* clause. You can—but do not have to—use the convention of naming an event procedure with the name of the object separated from the event name by an underscore (for example, *MyClass1_MyEvent*). Delimit the two clauses in the *AddHandler* statement from one another with a comma and a space. Visual Studio .NET simplifies the task of designating the arguments for the *AddHandler* and *AddressOf* clauses by displaying a list of appropriate replies. For example, after you enter the *AddHandler* keyword, IntelliSense offers a menu of available objects to select. Then, when you highlight an object and press the period key, IntelliSense returns with a list of events for the selected object.

The *AddHandler* statement is more flexible than the *Handles* clause for delegating event processing to a procedure. First, you do not have to declare a class by using the *WithEvents* keyword to process events from the class. Second, the *AddHandler* event allows for the dynamic management of events at run time. When you designate the handling of an event by using an *AddHandler* statement, you can halt processing of the event by invoking the *RemoveHandler* statement for the same event. You can even change the event handler for an event at run time. This kind of dynamic control of event processing is not possible when you specify an event handler with the *Handles* clause.

Form *Load* Event Basics

If you double-click a form in a Windows application project, Visual Studio .NET creates the shell for a form *Load* event procedure. For example, if you double-click in a blank area on *Form1*, Visual Studio .NET creates the *Form1_Load* event procedure shell in the current project. To demonstrate this basic event procedure and selected other event procedures that have more substance, I created a Windows application project named EventSamples. Within the shell that Visual Studio .NET creates, you can place any code you want. This basic sample merely echoes information about the event arguments.

Figure 4-4 shows a message box populated by an event procedure in the Visual Studio .NET IDE behind it. As with classic Visual Basic, the form *Load* event procedure in Visual Basic .NET fires before the form opens. Chapter 5 will show you how to take advantage of this feature to format a form before it opens. Notice that the form *Load* event procedure includes a *Handles* clause that refers to the *Load* event for the form's base class. The *Inherits* statement at the top of a module window specifies this class as the *Form* class in the *System.Windows.Forms* namespace.

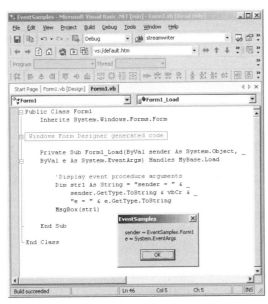

Figure 4-4   The Visual Studio .NET IDE in the background with a form *Load* event procedure behind a message box under the control of the event procedure

The *Form1_Load* event procedure has two arguments: *sender* and *e*. Both of these values are passed by value from the base class to the form, which is itself a class named *Form1*. (See the declaration at the top of the module in Figure 4-4.) The *sender* argument has a type of *Object*, the generic base class for all other objects in the .NET Framework. In the sample, the message box portrays the *sender* argument as coming from *Form1* within the EventSamples project. The *e* argument has a type of *EventArgs*. The *EventArgs* type is a base class for other classes that can pass information to an event handler. In particular, the .NET Framework uses derived classes based on the *EventArgs* type to pass state information to an event handler. This argument plays no role in Windows applications. The message box merely reflects the type for the *e* argument, and that type gives no indication of its function because it is a base class. Base classes have meaning only to derived classes that are based on them. A later section, "Class Inheritance," more fully explores the relationship between base and derived classes.

Working with Windows and System Timers

Visual Basic .NET offers three timer classes. This section compares and contrasts two of these classes while demonstrating event-processing techniques. These two timer classes are interesting for event processing because they share a common purpose—to raise an event at fixed intervals. The two timer classes examined are the Windows form timer from the *System.Windows.Forms* namespace and the System timer from the *System.Timers* namespace. Both of these timer classes are available as components on the Toolbox in a Windows application. Therefore, you can drag instances of them into a Windows application at design time.

> **Note**   The third timer class comes from the *System.Threading* namespace. It executes a method at fixed intervals. The timer has two intervals associated with it. One is for the wait to the first invocation of a method, and the second is the period between successive invocations of a method after the initial wait.

The Windows timer and the System timer can behave similarly within a form in a Windows application, but the timers offer different features that optimize them for different contexts. One timer class is the traditional Windows timer available with classic Visual Basic. It is popular for purposes such as presenting a splash screen at the start of an application for a fixed duration or repeatedly querying a database to get the most recently entered data in a database file. Instances of this timer class are designed for exclusive use on a form in a Windows application. This timer is a single-threaded timer. Therefore, other activities associated with a form in a Windows timer (such as computing loops) can interfere with the accuracy of the timed intervals.

The System timer is new with the .NET Framework. This timer is for use within a multithreaded environment. The System timer is not constrained to using the thread for a Windows form, so it can be more accurate in circumstances where a form has other activities that can consume thread resources when a timer class needs them. In addition, the System timer does not require a Windows form in order to operate as does the Windows timer. In fact, the System timer is often referred to as the *Server timer* because you can use it to monitor server operations for which no user interface is available. On the other hand, the System timer's ability to operate on any of multiple threads can cause the thread associated with a Windows form to miss its events. When you drag a System timer to a form in a Windows application, Visual Studio .NET automatically sets the timer's *SychronizingObject* property to the form. This ensures the timer events will not go unrecognized by an associated form.

Using the Windows Timer
You can locate the Windows Timer on the Windows Forms tab of the Toolbox. Drag the Timer component from the Toolbox to the body of a form, such as *Form1* in the EventSamples project. Visual Studio .NET responds by opening a tray below the form if one does not exist already, and it places an icon representing the timer in the tray. If this is the first Windows timer that you drag to the form, the timer's name will be *Timer1*. In setting up this demonstration for the Windows timer, I renamed the timer object to *MyWindowsTimer* by using the *Name* property in the Properties window. Figure 4-5 shows the IDE immediately after the specification of a new *Name* property for the timer component. You can see the Timer component class icon on the Toolbox in the lower portion of the Windows Forms tab. The Timer component is selected so that the Properties window displays the properties for the component. The new timer *Name* property setting appears in the Properties window with the *Name* property selected.

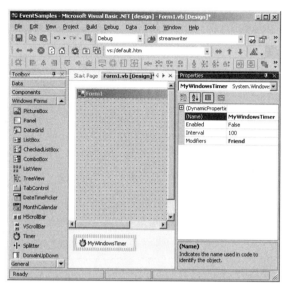

Figure 4-5 Dragging a Windows Timer component from the Toolbox's Windows Forms tab to a form and then manually changing its properties in the Properties window

This sample launches the timer object from the *Click* event procedure for a button. Therefore, you need to add a button to the form. In doing so, you can accept the default name of *Button1*. The event procedure sets a property for and launches the timer. The Windows timer has an *Interval* property greater than 0, namely 9000. When a timer's *Enabled* property is *True* and its *Interval* property is greater than 0, a Windows timer object instance continues to measure time. At the end of a duration equal to the timer's *Interval* property setting, the timer raises a *Tick* event. The sample indicates how you can respond to this *Tick* event with a user interface.

> **Note** Before launching this sample, place a comment marker (') in front of the *MsgBox* function within the *Form1 Load* event procedure. This will stop you from having to click OK to see *Form1* open.

From the preceding description of the sample's operation, you can tell that the sample has two event procedures. One of these is for the *Click* event for *Button1*. This event procedure sets up the timer. The second event procedure is for the *Tick* event from the *MyWindowsTimer* object instance. This event procedure manages the timer, provides feedback about the *Tick* event, and allows a user to continue the timer for another interval or to stop the timer at the end of the current interval.

The *Button1_Click* event procedure contains three statements. The first statement assigns a delegate to handle the *Tick* events raised by the *MyWindowsTimer* object. This statement demonstrates the syntax for *AddHandler*. The second statement sets the *Interval* property for the Windows timer to 9000 milliseconds. This causes the timer to raise a *Tick* event every 9 seconds after you enable it. The timer's *Enabled* property is initially *False*. You can change the setting to *True* by directly assigning a value of *True* to the *Enabled* property or by invoking the timer's *Start* method. The third statement takes the second route to starting the timer. Nine seconds after the *Click* event procedure's last statement executes, control passes to *MyWindowsTimer_Tick*, which is the event procedure for *Tick* events from the *MyWindowsTimer* object.

You can create the shell for the *Tick* event procedure in the normal way by double-clicking the *MyWindowsTimer* object in the Design view of *Form1*. As mentioned earlier, this approach generates a shell with the proper signature for the *Tick* event that includes a *Handles* clause. However, because a button's *Click* event procedure specifies an event handler with the *AddHandler* statement, you will process each *Tick* event twice unless you comment out the *AddHandler* statement or remove the *Handles* clause from the automatically generated shell for the *Tick* event procedure. The sample takes the latter approach, but comments remind you how to use the *Handles* clause.

The *Tick* event procedure starts by setting the timer's *Enabled* property to *False*. This stops the timer while the procedure processes the timer event. If the procedure did not set the *Enabled* property to *False*, the timer would continue running to the next *Tick* event, even while your application processes the current *Tick* event. This is not a good idea because the time between *Tick* events will then depend on how long it takes to process an event, which can vary. After halting the timer, the procedure presents a message box announcing the type of event; consider this a variation of the "Hello world" sample from an event procedure. The event procedure concludes by giving the user a chance to restart the timer and cause another *Tick* event. If the user elects to restart the timer, the procedure sets the timer's *Enabled* property to *True* and exits. This causes the *Tick* event procedure to start again in 9 seconds. If a user declines to repeat the cycle, the procedure exits normally with the *Enabled* property set to *False*. Therefore, the timer remains inoperative until a user clicks *Button1* again.

> **Note**   Some readers might find it curious that I refer to the Windows timer with the name *MyWindowsTimer* in the button *Click* event procedure but use the term *Me.MyWindowsTimer* in the *Tick* event procedure. Both designations are equivalent in the context of this sample. The fact that I use two different names to refer to the same object confirms this.

```
Private Sub Button1_Click(ByVal sender As System.Object, _
    ByVal e As System.EventArgs) Handles Button1.Click

    'Delegate MyWindowsTimer_Tick as the event procedure
    'for the Tick event of the MyWindowsTimer object;
    'use this statement or a Handles clause, but not both.
    AddHandler MyWindowsTimer.Tick, _
        AddressOf MyWindowsTimer_Tick

    'Set an interval between tick events.
    'When process depends on user input, use long intervals.
    MyWindowsTimer.Interval = 9000

    'Start the timer.
    MyWindowsTimer.Start()

End Sub

'If you use an AddHandler statement, choose the
'Sub declaration without the Handles clause.
'    Private Sub _
'        MyWindowsTimer_Tick(ByVal sender As System.Object, _
'        ByVal e As System.EventArgs) _
'        Handles MyWindowsTimer.Tick
Private Sub MyWindowsTimer_Tick(ByVal sender As System.Object, _
        ByVal e As System.EventArgs)
```

```
'Stop timer.
Me.MyWindowsTimer.Enabled = False

'Process Tick event.
MsgBox("Windows Timer Tick Event")

'Prompt about restarting the timer.
If MsgBox("Do it again?", MsgBoxStyle.YesNo, _
    "Repeat?") = MsgBoxResult.Yes Then
    Me.MyWindowsTimer.Enabled = True

End If

End Sub
```

Using the System Timer

You can add a System timer to a Windows application similarly to the way you add a Windows timer. Open the Toolbox. Instead of using the Windows Forms tab, select the Components tab. Then, drag the Timer component to a form. Unless a timer with a *Name* property of *Timer1* already exists, Visual Studio .NET assigns this name to the timer. This sample assigns *MySystemTimer* as the *Name* property for the System timer. When comparing the Properties window for Windows and System timers, you will notice a couple of differences. First, the System timer has a *SynchronizingObject* property not present for the Windows timer. In the sample application, this property has the setting *Form1* because the System timer resides on *Form1*. Second, the *Enabled* property is *True* by default, instead of *False* as it is for a Windows timer. Therefore, the System timer will start as soon as you assign a value to the timer's *Interval* property. To make the operation of the two timers more compatible, the sample sets the *Enabled* property to *False* in the Properties window.

The goal of the sample for the System timer is to have it operate the same way as the Windows timer. To achieve this, we need to add another button (*Button2*) to *Form1* to launch an event procedure that sets up and starts the System timer. Then, we need a second event procedure to handle the event signaling the end of an interval. A couple of features of this event are noteworthy. First, the event has a different name than the comparable event for a Windows timer. The Windows timer raises the *Tick* event at the end of an interval, but the System timer raises an *Elapsed* event. Second, the signature for the *Elapsed* event is different than that for the *Tick* event. Therefore, you can't just copy the shell and modify the event name from the *Tick* event for the *Elapsed* event (because the two events have different signatures).

The listing for the use of the System timer appears next. Aside from the differences just noted, its syntax is nearly identical to that of the application for the Windows timer. I dropped the *Me* qualifier from the name for the timer in the *Elapsed* event procedure, although it appears in the comparable *Tick* event procedure for the Windows timer sample. I generated the shell for the *Elapsed* event by double-clicking *MySystemTimer* in Design view. Then, I edited out the *Handles* clause. Following this process automatically creates the proper signature for any built-in event. Because the System timer event has a different signature than the Windows timer and other common events, such as the form *Load* event and the button *Click* event, we need to focus on getting the signature right for the System timer.

```
Private Sub Button2_Click(ByVal sender As System.Object, _
    ByVal e As System.EventArgs) Handles Button2.Click

    'Delegate MySystemTimer_Elapsed as the event procedure
    'for the Elapsed event of the MyWindowsTimer object.
    AddHandler MySystemTimer.Elapsed, _
        AddressOf MySystemTimer_Elapsed

    'Set timer interval between Elasped events.
    MySystemTimer.Interval = 9000

    'Launch timer by setting Enabled to True.
    MySystemTimer.Start()

End Sub

'Notice the signature for the Elapsed event procedure of a
'SystemTimer is different than that of the Tick event for
'a WindowsTimer.
Private Sub _
    MySystemTimer_Elapsed(ByVal sender As System.Object, _
    ByVal e As System.Timers.ElapsedEventArgs)

    'Stop timer.
    MySystemTimer.Enabled = False

    'Process Elapsed event.
    MsgBox("System Timer Elapsed Event")

    'Prompt about restarting the timer.
    If MsgBox("Do it again?", MsgBoxStyle.YesNo, _
```

```
            "Repeat?") = MsgBoxResult.Yes Then
            MySystemTimer.Enabled = True
        End If

    End Sub
```

Raising Events from Custom Classes

The final event sample illustrates how to raise an event from a class library and process that event in a Windows application project. The class library project, EventDemoLib, contains a single class named *LookAtHighDiscounts*. A class method uses the COM Interop feature to make a connection to the Northwind database and compute a recordset for the rows from the Order Details table that match an *OrderID* value passed to the class method when you invoke it. The *Function* procedure implementing the method computes and returns the extended price of the line items for the order designated by the *OrderID* value passed to the function.

Although you have seen this part of the sample before, it's relisted here for a couple of reasons. First, we want to extend the sample to raise an event for any line item in an order with a Discount column value greater than or equal to 20 percent (.2). Second, I want to demonstrate the process for raising an event in the context of a sample that includes database processing. It is possible to fine-tune the design of this sample in several areas, but the point is to reuse familiar code so that you can readily focus on how to expand the functionality available from a class via event programming.

To construct the sample, create a new Class Library project named Event-DemoLib. Add a reference, as described in Chapter 3, via the COM Interop feature to the *ADODB* library. Then, insert the code that follows. As with most of the samples throughout this book, project folders are available with the code already inserted. You might recognize a high degree of overlap in the design of this *TotalOrder* function from this sample with the *TotalOrder* function in the *MyArraySubAndFunctionMethods* class from the MethodsDemoLibrary project. The listing that follows uses boldface for the lines of code that are new.

The first line within the class uses the *Event* keyword to declare the *High-Discount* event. The signature for this event indicates that the event returns two column values, an *OrderID* and a *ProductID*. Both of these column values return to the event handler for the *HighDiscount* event as *Integer* data types. The *TotalOrder* function composes a recordset from the Order Details table for a specific order—the one matching the *OrderID* passed to the *HighDiscount* function. The new version of the *TotalOrder* function converts the *ADODB* column values for *OrderID* and *ProductID* to Visual Basic .NET data types. The *HighDiscount* event returns these column values to its event handler when the *Discount* column value is greater than or equal to .2. The procedure adds an *If...Then* statement to assess when to raise the *HighDiscount* event. Recordset rows with a *Discount* column value qualifying to trigger the event cause the execution of the single line of code within the *If...Then* statement. The *RaiseEvent* statement within the *If...Then* statement shows how simple it is to return values with an event from a class. The *ReturnOrderID* and *ProductID* values are arguments that match the *Event* declaration at the class's declaration area. After composing the class, choose Build, Build Solution to create the .dll file for the class library.

```
Public Class LookAtHighDiscounts
Public Event HighDiscount(ByVal ReturnOrderID As Integer, _
    ByVal ProductID As Integer)
    Function TotalOrder(ByVal OrderID As Integer) As Decimal

        'Declare and instantiate ADODB objects.
        Dim cnn1 As New ADODB.Connection()
        Dim rst1 As New ADODB.Recordset()

        'Open an ADO Connection object.
        cnn1.Open("Provider=Microsoft.Jet.OLEDB.4.0;" & _
            "Data Source=C:\Program Files\" & _
            "Microsoft Office\Office10\Samples\Northwind.mdb;", _
            "Admin", "")

        'Open recordset for rows from Order Details,
        'matching OrderID.
        Dim str1 As String = _
            "SELECT * FROM [Order Details] " & _
            "WHERE OrderID =" & OrderID.ToString
        'Open a recordset on a table.
        With rst1
            .ActiveConnection = cnn1
            .Open(str1, , _
                ADODB.CursorTypeEnum.adOpenForwardOnly, _
                ADODB.LockTypeEnum.adLockReadOnly)
        End With

        'Loop through the ADO recordset and compute
        'the total for the designated OrderID.
        Dim ReturnOrderID As Integer
```

```
            Dim ProductID As Integer
            Dim Quantity As Integer
            Dim UnitPrice As Decimal
            Dim Discount As Decimal
            Dim OrderTotal As Decimal
            Do Until rst1.EOF
                ReturnOrderID = CInt(rst1("OrderID").Value)
                ProductID = CInt(rst1("ProductID").Value)
                Quantity = CInt(rst1("Quantity").Value)
                UnitPrice = CDec(rst1("UnitPrice").Value)
                Discount = CDec(rst1("Discount").Value)
                'If condition for raising the HighDiscount event
                If Discount >= 0.2 Then
                    RaiseEvent HighDiscount(ReturnOrderID, ProductID)
                End If
                OrderTotal = _
                    Quantity * UnitPrice * (1 - Discount) + OrderTotal
                rst1.MoveNext()
            Loop

            'Return OrderTotal value from TotalOrder method.
            Return OrderTotal
        End Function

End Class
```

After creating the .dll for the class library, return to the EventSamples project. Then, update the EventSamples project to work with EventDemoLib.dll. First, create a reference to the .dll file. Choose Project, Add Reference. Select the Projects tab in the Add Reference dialog box. Click the Browse button, and navigate to EventDemoLib.dll. Double-click the filename so that it appears in the Selected Components list box in the Add Reference dialog box. Then, click OK to commit the reference to the external class library.

The next major change is to update the form to interact with the newly referenced class library. The sample application will pass through a series of orders to compute the total extended price for each order. The *Click* event procedure launching the sample will save the computed extended price to the Output window with a *Debug.Writeline* statement. In addition, an event procedure will save to a disk file the *OrderID* and *ProductID* for any line items with a *Discount* value greater than .2. The form modifications include the addition of a new button (*Button3*) to launch the sample and the addition of three text boxes. The first and second text boxes (*TextBox1* and *TextBox2*) are for input. A user will input the first and last *OrderID* values over which the application will compute results. The third text box (*TextBox3*) is for feedback. It shows the current order being processed. Figure 4-6 shows the completed version of the form in action.

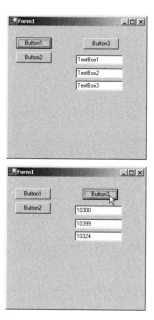

Figure 4-6 Two screens from a Windows application with a class library. The class library performs the processing, with the results appearing on the Windows form.

The listings for the *Button3_Click* event procedure and the event handler for the event raised from the *LookAtHighDiscounts* class in the Event-DemoLib.dll appears next. For the purposes of this sample, the most important tasks performed by the *Button3_Click* procedure are to instantiate an object based on the *LookAtHighDiscounts* class and to designate a delegate for handling the *HighDiscount* event when the class raises it. A simple *Dim* statement suffices to declare the *MyInstance* variable based on the class. Next, an *AddHandler* statement designates the *LookAtHighDiscounts_HighDiscount* procedure in the EventSamples project as the event handler for the *HighDiscount* event. The balance of the procedure is a loop that repeatedly invokes the *TotalOrder* method for the *MyInstance* object based on the *LookAtHighDiscounts* class. The loop starts with the *OrderID* value in *TextBox1* and continues through the *OrderID* value in *TextBox2*. *TextBox3* reflects the current *OrderID* being processed. When the value in *TextBox3* matches the value in *TextBox2*, the application is finished.

The *LookAtHighDiscounts_HighDiscount* procedure starts by creating or opening a *StreamWriter* class instance pointing at the HighDiscountLog.txt file in the bin subdirectory for the current project's folder. By setting a Boolean argument for the *StreamWriter's* constructor to *True*, the procedure will append values to an existing file or create a new file if one does not exist already. Next, the sample computes a string and writes it as a line in the text file. The event procedure concludes by closing the *StreamWriter* class instance.

```
Private Sub Button3_Click(ByVal sender As System.Object, _
    ByVal e As System.EventArgs) Handles Button3.Click

    'Instantiate object.
    Dim MyInstance As _
        New EventDemoLib.LookAtHighDiscounts()

    'Delegate LookAtHighDiscounts_HighDiscount as the
    'event procedure for the Elapsed event of the
    'MySystemTimer2 object.
    AddHandler MyInstance.HighDiscount, _
        AddressOf LookAtHighDiscounts_HighDiscount

    'Loop through Orders from TextBox2 value
    'to TextBox3 value and print to Output window
    'OrderID and OrderTotal.
    Dim int1 As Integer
    For int1 = CInt(TextBox1.Text) To CInt(TextBox2.Text)
        TextBox3.Text = int1.ToString
        TextBox3.Refresh()
        Dim OrderTotal As Decimal = _
            MyInstance.TotalOrder(int1)
        Dim str1 As String = int1.ToString & _
            ", " & CStr(OrderTotal)
        Debug.WriteLine(str1)
    Next
End Sub

Sub LookAtHighDiscounts_HighDiscount( _
    ByVal OrderID As Integer, _
    ByVal ProductID As Integer)

    'Declare a StreamWriter to build a text
    'filename HighDiscountLog.txt in the bin
    'folder for the current project.
    Dim str1 As String = "HighDiscountLog.txt"
    Dim fsw1 As New System.IO.StreamWriter(str1, True)
```

(continued)

```
'Prepare a string with discount exception info
'and write the info to HighDiscountLog.txt.
Dim str2 As String = Now().ToString & ", " & _
    OrderID.ToString & ", " & _
    ProductID.ToString
fsw1.WriteLine(str2)
fsw1.Close()
```

End Sub

Figure 4-6 shows the sample application, which handles events from a class library in a Windows application project. The top screen shows how *Form1* looks before a user inputs the first and last *OrderID* values for processing. The form shows the default name for the text boxes as values within the text boxes; this is the default setting for text boxes. The bottom screen in Figure 4-6 shows the application in process. The application is processing a block of orders from *OrderID* 10300 through *OrderID* 10399. The current order being processed is 10324.

Class Inheritance

Class inheritance might be the single most exciting innovation introduced for Visual Basic and VBA developers with Visual Basic .NET. Authors performing comparative language reviews were quick to point out that classic Visual Basic did not support class inheritance. Visual Basic .NET corrects that deficiency. Class inheritance is an important capability because it provides a means for adapting and extending code in previously created class libraries. With class inheritance, a new class can build on the code in an old class while concurrently adding new functionality and redefining the way old class members work. In short, you can think of class inheritance as a tool for creating classier classes.

Now that we have class inheritance, our challenge as Access database developers is to find practical ways of putting it to use in our applications. Before diving into this section, you need a good grasp of how to use classes. The overview in the "Classes" section in Chapter 3 presents basic coding techniques for class libraries that you will find useful to know as you read this section. The introduction to that section in Chapter 3 succinctly describes how class inheritance helps you to get more value out of your classes. So if you're feeling a little hazy on classes, now would be a good time to revisit that discussion.

This section has a couple of practical objectives. First, it briefly reviews key class concepts as a prelude to reviewing keywords that help you implement class inheritance with Visual Basic .NET. Second, the section demonstrates the use of these keywords with samples that work with Access databases.

Overview of Concepts and Keywords

Classes deliver benefits in three main areas. First, classes facilitate encapsulation. This benefit allows you to use a class and take advantage of its functionality without needing to know the inner workings of how that class exposes methods and properties as well as propagates events. Second, classes can enable inheritance. This section focuses on showing you how to take advantage of this benefit. You can inherit one class, known as a *base class*, into another class, known as a *derived class*. The derived class can make available all the members (properties, methods, and events) of the base class. This feature takes advantage of the encapsulation benefit, but a derived class does not have to create an instance of the base class to tap the members of its base class. In addition, derived classes can supplement base class members with new members. When applications instantiate objects based on a derived class, the instantiated object can expose members for both the base class and the derived class. The third main benefit of classes is polymorphism. This capability allows derived classes to expose members that work differently in the derived class than they do in the base class. Polymorphism enables you to change the definition of a base class in a derived class. In addition, an application instantiating an object for the derived class can access the original members of the base class or the modified members of the derived class.

The single most important concept of class inheritance to grasp is the *Inherits* keyword. This keyword permits a derived class to inherit the members of a base class. *Inherits* must appear in the first line of code in any derived class. Its syntax is very straightforward. The keyword takes one argument—the name of the base class. In addition, your derived class must have a reference to the class library project serving as the base class. The *Inherits* statement in the derived class will not function unless this project reference exists for the base class.

The matter of references is important when working with derived classes. Any application instantiating objects based on a derived class must have a reference to the derived class as well as to the base class for the derived class. For example, if projectA instantiates objects based on a derived classB in projectB and the base class for classB is classC in projectC, then projectA must have references to both projectB and projectC.

You will likely use a couple of keywords in a derived class—especially when you are redefining the operation of members. These keywords point at either the base class (*MyBase*) or the derived class (*MyClass*). By using the keywords as qualifiers for member names, you can clearly distinguish in a derived class among references to base class members and derived class members. In the following samples, you will discover that the base class and the derived class define the *TotalOrder* method differently. By using *MyBase.TotalOrder*, your code can refer unambiguously to the base class implementation of the method. Similarly, *MyClass.TotalOrder* designates the derived class implementation of the method.

Three additional keywords help you take advantage of the polymorphism benefit. When you plan to change a member in a derived class with the same signature (name, type, and arguments) as a member in a base class, you can use the *Overridable* and *Overrides* keywords. Mark the base class member with the *Overridable* keyword, and apply the *Overrides* keyword to the corresponding derived class member. To change the implementation of a member with the *Overrides* keyword, you must anticipate the need in your base class by applying the *Overridable* keyword to a member. If you decide to change a base class to add the *Overridable* keyword after it is compiled, you must recompile the base class and refresh the reference of the derived class for the base class. The *Shadows* keyword allows you to more flexibly redefine base class members in a derived class. When a derived class member shadows a base class member, the base class member does not require any special keyword. In addition, the signature for base class members and derived class members can differ. Therefore, you can use a property member in a derived class to redefine a member initially defined as a method in the base class.

Overloads is another keyword that implements a style of shadowing within a class. .NET Framework classes commonly offer overloaded constructors. An overloaded constructor is actually a set of *New* methods within a class. Each *New* method has the same name, but the list of arguments for each constructor is different. For example, an object offering database functionality can use a default record source. Therefore, its default constructor will not need an argument designating a record source. On the other hand, you can obtain more functionality from the class by letting a user specify his own record source for the class when constructing a new instance. By overloading the default constructor with a different *New* method that takes an argument for the record source, you can accommodate this expanded functionality for the class. The great thing about overloaded constructors is that Visual Basic .NET figures out what constructor to use based on the arguments you provide! With constructors, you do not actually use the *Overloads* keyword, although the .NET Framework implements overloaded constructors through its overloading capability.

You can also use the *Overloads* keyword with functions implementing methods in a class. For example, you can have a class with different functions for computing the areas of geometric shapes, such as squares, triangles, and trapezoids. A piece of sample code in the "Parameter Arrays" section in Chapter 3 showed how to implement this task with a single function procedure that takes a parameter array. Those familiar with class programming methods will probably find using a single class with an overloaded *Area* method simpler to code. By applying the *Overloads* keyword to three different *Area* methods, you can specify area expressions for each shape. Because each shape requires a different number of arguments, the signature for the method corresponding to each shape will be distinct. Again, the beauty of overloading is that Visual Basic .NET will automatically figure out which function to use for implementing the *Area* method based on the number and type of arguments passed when invoking the method.

Setting Up for Class Inheritance Demonstrations

When you run applications using class inheritance, you will typically have at least three projects to manage. First, you will need a project for your base class. You should make this a class library project. The project can contain as many different base classes as you need. Second, you will need another project for your derived class. This project must include a reference to the project containing the base class. Third, you need a project for the application that creates one or more instances of derived classes in the second project. This project must contain references to the .dll files for the projects containing the base class and the derived class.

> **Note**   You can include a class within another project for demonstration and quick reference, but this has limited utility because multiple other projects will not be able to reference the class. When working with class inheritance, it is even more useful to isolate classes in their own projects.

Base Class Features

The base class, *MyAnalyzer*, resides in the ADODBOrderDetailAnalyzer project. This is a class library project. As with all Visual Basic projects, this project has its own folder named after it. Within the bin subdirectory of that folder is the .dll file for the class library. Therefore, the ADODBOrderDetailAnalyzer.dll file resides in the bin folder of the ADODBOrderDetailAnalyzer folder. This .dll file contains the compiled code for the *MyAnalyzer* class.

The *MyAnalyzer* class implements a method named *TotalOrder* and a read-only property named *OrderLineItems*. You should be familiar with the techniques for implementing both the method and the property by now because they borrow from previous samples in this chapter as well as Chapter 3. The *TotalOrder* method computes the total extended price for an *OrderID* value passed as a value when invoking the method, and the property returns the number of line items in the order passed to the method.

The listing that follows highlights in boldface the code lines that are special to this class in one way or another. For example, notice the *Overridable* keyword appearing in the declaration of the *TotalOrder* function for the method by the same name. Using this keyword in the function declaration enables a derived class to override the implementation for the *TotalOrder* method in the base class. The property returning the number of line items is initially computed as the value for a private field, *m_count*. The sample uses a *Byte* data type for the *OrderLineItems* property because the number of line items is expected to be less than 256 but always positive. The *OrderLineItems* property procedure exposes the *m_count* field value as a read-only property.

```
Public Class MyAnalyzer
    Private m_count As Byte
    Overridable Function TotalOrder(ByVal OrderID As Integer) As Decimal

        'Declare and instantiate ADODB objects.
        Dim cnn1 As New ADODB.Connection()
        Dim rst1 As New ADODB.Recordset()

        'Open an ADO Connection object.
        cnn1.Open("Provider=Microsoft.Jet.OLEDB.4.0;" & _
            "Data Source=C:\Program Files\" & _
            "Microsoft Office\Office10\Samples\Northwind.mdb;", _
            "Admin", "")

        'Open recordset for rows from Order Details,
        'matching OrderID.
        Dim str1 As String = _
            "SELECT * FROM [Order Details] " & _
            "WHERE OrderID =" & OrderID.ToString
        'Open a recordset on a table.
        With rst1
            .ActiveConnection = cnn1
            .Open(str1, , _
```

```
                    ADODB.CursorTypeEnum.adOpenForwardOnly, _
                    ADODB.LockTypeEnum.adLockReadOnly)
        End With

        'Loop through the ADO recordset and compute
        'the total for the designated OrderID.
        Dim Quantity As Integer
        Dim UnitPrice As Decimal
        Dim Discount As Decimal
        Dim OrderTotal As Decimal
        Dim byt1 As Byte
        Do Until rst1.EOF
            Quantity = CInt(rst1("Quantity").Value)
            UnitPrice = CDec(rst1("UnitPrice").Value)
            Discount = CDec(rst1("Discount").Value)
            OrderTotal = _
                Quantity * UnitPrice * (1 - Discount) + OrderTotal
            byt1 += 1
            rst1.MoveNext()
        Loop

        'Count of line items in order
        m_count = byt1

        'Return OrderTotal value from TotalOrder method.
        Return OrderTotal

    End Function

    ReadOnly Property OrderLineItems() As Byte
        Get
            Return m_count
        End Get
    End Property

End Class
```

Derived Class Features

The derived class, *MyADODBNorthwind*, resides in the ADODBNorthwind project. The project actually contains two classes. The second class, *Rows*, is not a derived class. The *Rows* class demonstrates how to implement overloaded constructors.

Notice that the first line in the *MyADODBNorthwind* class is the *Inherits* keyword. This keyword points back to the *MyAnalyzer* class in the ADODB-OrderDetailAnalyzer project. For the *Inherits* statement to function properly, the ADODBNorthwind project requires a reference to the ADODBOrderDetail-Analyzer.dll file. You can achieve this by opening the Add Reference dialog box, selecting the Projects tab, navigating to the .dll file, and closing the Add Reference dialog box to confirm your selection.

The first function, *MyTotalOrder*, actually exposes the implementation for the *TotalOrder* method in the base class. The use of the *MyClass* keyword passes a reference back to the base class.

The second function, *TotalOrder*, overrides the implementation of the *Total-Order* method by the function with that name in the base class. The *MyADODB-Northwind* class uses the *TotalOrder* function to return the number of line items as a *Decimal* data type. The function uses the *Decimal* data type for the return value to keep the signature for the function the same as in the base class. Failing to maintain the data type as *Decimal* for the return value from the function causes a compilation error.

The third function is a new method, *MyPercentIncrease*, which is added by the derived class. This method is not available in the base class. The method takes two arguments. One specifies the *OrderID* for an order. The second argument, *Percent*, indicates how much to increase the total extended price for an order on a percentage basis. Specifying a *Percent* argument value of 1.1 increases the total extended price for the order matching the *OrderID* value by 10 percent. Although this method requires the value returned by the *TotalOrder* method from the base class, it requires just one line. The expression *Me.MyTotalOrder* refers to a function in the current class that, in turn, refers back to the *TotalOrder* method in the base class. In this way, the *MyPercent-Increase* method uses the *TotalOrder* base class method to create a new class.

The *InheritedLineItems* property procedure directly passes back the *OrderLineItems* property from the base class. This approach is desirable when you shadow a base class property with another property or method but still want to retain access to the original property in the base class. The *MyADODB-Northwind* class concludes with an example of how to shadow a base class property with a derived class method. The old definition of the *OrderLineItems* property in the base class returns the number of line items for the order designated in the base class implementation of the *TotalOrder* method. The new definition of the *OrderLineItems* method in the derived class is the total number of line items for a range of orders, from a beginning *OrderID* through an ending *OrderID*.

The *Rows* class that appears after the *MyADODBNorthwind* class demonstrates the syntax for overloading a constructor. This class creates a recordset with one of two constructors. If the user does not specify a record source argument for the *Rows* class, the recordset automatically points at the Shippers table from the Northwind database. If the user designates a record source by using the second constructor, the function uses the table or row-returning query from the Northwind database designated by the string argument. The recordset is private to the *Rows* class, but two properties expose the *Source* property for the recordset as well as the number of rows in the recordset. The *Source* property for a recordset based on a Jet database is a SQL string designating the source specified by the *ActiveConnection* property for the recordset.

```
Public Class MyADODBNorthwind
    Inherits ADODBOrderDetailAnalyzer.MyAnalyzer

    Function MyTotalOrder(ByVal OrderID As Integer) As Decimal

        Return (MyBase.TotalOrder(OrderID))

    End Function

    Overrides Function TotalOrder(ByVal OrderID As Integer) _
        As Decimal

        'Declare and instantiate ADODB objects.
        Dim cnn1 As New ADODB.Connection()
        Dim rst1 As New ADODB.Recordset()

        'Open an ADO Connection object.
        cnn1.Open("Provider=Microsoft.Jet.OLEDB.4.0;" & _
            "Data Source=C:\Program Files\" & _
            "Microsoft Office\Office10\Samples\" & _
            "Northwind.mdb;", _
            "Admin", "")

        'Open recordset for rows from Order Details,
        'matching OrderID.
        Dim str1 As String = _
            "SELECT * FROM [Order Details] " & _
            "WHERE OrderID =" & OrderID.ToString
        'Open a recordset on a table.
        With rst1
            .ActiveConnection = cnn1
            .Open(str1, , _
                ADODB.CursorTypeEnum.adOpenForwardOnly, _
                ADODB.LockTypeEnum.adLockReadOnly)
        End With

        'Loop through the ADO recordset and compute
        'the total for the designated OrderID.
        Dim Quantity As Integer
```

(continued)

```
        Dim UnitPrice As Decimal
        Dim Discount As Decimal
        Dim OrderTotal As Decimal
        Dim int1 As Integer
        Do Until rst1.EOF

            'Convert ADODB recordset line items to
            'Visual Basic .NET data types.
            Quantity = CInt(rst1("Quantity").Value)
            UnitPrice = CDec(rst1("UnitPrice").Value)
            Discount = CDec(rst1("Discount").Value)

            'Compute total for order.
            OrderTotal = _
                Quantity * UnitPrice * (1 - Discount) + OrderTotal
            int1 += 1

            rst1.MoveNext()
        Loop

        'Return OrderTotal value from TotalOrder method as
        'a count of the number of line items.
        Return CDec(int1)

    End Function

    Function MyPercentIncrease(ByVal OrderID As Integer, _
        ByVal Percent As Double) As Decimal

        Return Me.MyTotalOrder(OrderID) * Percent

    End Function

    ReadOnly Property InheritedLineItems()
        Get
            Return MyBase.OrderLineItems()
        End Get
    End Property

    Shadows Function OrderLineItems( _
        ByVal FirstOrderID As Integer, _
        ByVal SecondOrderID As Integer) As Integer

        'Declare and instantiate ADODB objects.
        Dim cnn1 As New ADODB.Connection()
        Dim rst1 As New ADODB.Recordset()
```

```vb
'Open an ADO Connection object.
cnn1.Open("Provider=Microsoft.Jet.OLEDB.4.0;" & _
    "Data Source=C:\Program Files\" & _
    "Microsoft Office\Office10\Samples\Northwind.mdb;", _
    "Admin", "")

'Open recordset for rows from Order Details,
'matching OrderID.
Dim str1 As String = _
    "SELECT * FROM [Order Details] " & _
    "WHERE OrderID >=" & FirstOrderID.ToString & _
    " AND OrderID <=" & SecondOrderID.ToString
'Open a recordset on a table.
With rst1
    .ActiveConnection = cnn1
    .Open(str1, , _
        ADODB.CursorTypeEnum.adOpenKeyset, _
        ADODB.LockTypeEnum.adLockOptimistic)
End With

Return rst1.RecordCount

End Function

End Class

Public Class Rows

Private rst1 As New ADODB.Recordset()

Sub New()

    'Declare and instantiate ADODB objects.
    Dim cnn1 As New ADODB.Connection()

    'Open an ADO Connection object.
    cnn1.Open("Provider=Microsoft.Jet.OLEDB.4.0;" & _
        "Data Source=C:\Program Files\" & _
        "Microsoft Office\Office10\Samples\Northwind.mdb;", _
        "Admin", "")

    'Open recordset for rows from Shippers table.
    Dim str1 As String = _
        "SELECT * FROM Shippers"
```

(continued)

```
        'Open a recordset on a table.
        With rst1
            .ActiveConnection = cnn1
            .Open(str1, , _
                ADODB.CursorTypeEnum.adOpenKeyset, _
                ADODB.LockTypeEnum.adLockOptimistic)
        End With

    End Sub

    Sub New(ByVal RecordSourceName As String)

        'Declare and instantiate ADODB objects.
        Dim cnn1 As New ADODB.Connection()

        'Open an ADO Connection object.
        cnn1.Open("Provider=Microsoft.Jet.OLEDB.4.0;" & _
            "Data Source=C:\Program Files\" & _
            "Microsoft Office\Office10\Samples\Northwind.mdb;", _
            "Admin", "")

        'Open recordset for rows from Shippers table.
        Dim str1 As String = _
            "SELECT * FROM " & RecordSourceName
        'Open a recordset on a table.
        With rst1
            .ActiveConnection = cnn1
            .Open(str1, , _
                ADODB.CursorTypeEnum.adOpenKeyset, _
                ADODB.LockTypeEnum.adLockOptimistic)
        End With

    End Sub

    ReadOnly Property RowCount() As Integer
        Get
            Return rst1.RecordCount
        End Get
    End Property

    ReadOnly Property RowSource() As String
        Get
            Return rst1.Source
        End Get
    End Property

End Class
```

Application Project Features

To make the process for invoking the classes as obvious as possible, the sample uses a project based on the Empty Project template. This type of project has no customization or built-in references to assist or interfere with the invoking of class methods and properties. The project in the sample has the name ADODB-NorthwindLibUser. This project demonstrates the syntax for using the classes defined in the ADODBNorthwind project.

The project has a single module, *Module1*, with a main procedure and a series of *Sub* procedures. Each *Sub* procedure invocation illustrates a different aspect of working with class inheritance or overloading. These *Sub* procedures, in turn, invoke properties and methods in the derived class, *MyADODBNorthwind*, or the *Rows* class that demonstrates overloading syntax for a *New* method serving as a constructor.

The names of all the *Sub* procedure calls are commented out in the main procedure. I tested the *Sub* procedure calls by removing the comments for each *Sub* procedure one at a time. You can interpret the outcome of each *Sub* procedure because they each present one or more message boxes to display values returned by methods and properties from the classes in the ADODBNorthwind.dll.

For the code in the ADODBNorthwindLibUser project to compile correctly, you must add references to the MyADODBNorthwind.dll file and the ADODB-OrderDetailAnalyzer.dll file. To do so, verify that the projects for the .dll files are on a workstation and are compiled. You generate the .dll file for a project when you invoke the Build, Build Solution command or Build, Rebuild Solution command. You add the .dll for a referenced component with the Project, Add Reference command. Your application depends on the application project folder and its related component project folders. Therefore, you can ship a solution that invokes classes just by shipping the application's project folder and its related component project folders. You do not need any special installation program that makes registry entries. In this sample, just copy the three folders for the ADODBOrderDetailAnalyzer, ADODBNorthwind, and ADODBNorthwindLibUser projects to a directory on any computer with the .NET Framework installed, the Northwind.mdb file in its default location for Access 2002, and the 2.5 version of the *ADODB* library installed on the computer. This library installs automatically with Access 2002.

```
Module Module1
    Sub main()

        Dim OrderID As Integer = 10248
```

(continued)

```
        Dim PercentGrowth As Double = 1.1

        'BaseMethod(OrderID)
        'BaseMethodandProperty(OrderID)
        'DerivedMethod(OrderID, PercentGrowth)
        'OverriddenBaseMethod(OrderID)

        Dim SecondOrderID As Integer = 10250
        'MethodShadowsProperty(OrderID, SecondOrderID)

        'OverloadedConstructor("Categories")

    End Sub

    Sub BaseMethod(ByVal OrderID As Integer)

        'Instantiate object based on MyADODBNorthwind
        'class.
        Dim MyInstance As _
            New ADODBNorthwind.MyADODBNorthwind()

        'Invoke base class implementation of
        'TotalOrder method through derived class,
        'MyTotalOrder method.
        Dim dec1 As Decimal = _
            MyInstance.MyTotalOrder(OrderID)

        'Display return from base class method.
        MsgBox(dec1.ToString, , _
            "From BaseMethod")

    End Sub

    Sub BaseMethodandProperty(ByVal OrderID As Integer)

        'Instantiate object based on MyADODBNorthwind
        'class.
        Dim MyInstance As _
            New ADODBNorthwind.MyADODBNorthwind()

        'Invoke derived class method and property that
        'are mapped to base class method and property.
        Dim dec1 As Decimal = _
            MyInstance.MyTotalOrder(OrderID)
        Dim dec2 As Decimal = _
            MyInstance.InheritedLineItems()

        'Display return from base class method and
        'property.
```

```
        MsgBox(dec1.ToString & ", " & dec2.ToString, , _
            "From BaseMethodandProperty")

End Sub

Sub DerivedMethod(ByVal OrderID As Integer, _
    ByVal PercentGrowth As Double)

        'Instantiate object based on MyADODBNorthwind
        'class.
        Dim MyInstance As _
            New ADODBNorthwind.MyADODBNorthwind()

        'Invoke new derived class method.
        Dim dec1 As Decimal = _
            MyInstance.MyPercentIncrease(OrderID, _
            PercentGrowth)

        'Display return from derived class.
        MsgBox(dec1.ToString, , _
            "From DerivedMethod")

End Sub

Sub OverriddenBaseMethod(ByVal OrderID As Integer)

        'Instantiate object based on MyADODBNorthwind
        'class.
        Dim MyInstance As _
            New ADODBNorthwind.MyADODBNorthwind()

        'Invoke derived class method overridding
        'base class method.
        Dim dec1 As Decimal = _
            MyInstance.TotalOrder(OrderID)

        'Display return from derived class
        'overriding method.
        MsgBox(dec1.ToString, , _
                "From OverriddenBaseMethod")

End Sub

Sub MethodShadowsProperty( _
    ByVal FirstOrderID As Integer, _
    ByVal SecondOrderID As Integer)
```

(continued)

```
        'Instantiate object based on MyADODBNorthwind
        'class.
        Dim MyInstance As _
            New ADODBNorthwind.MyADODBNorthwind()

        'Invoke derived class method shadowing
        'base class property.
        Dim int1 As Integer = _
            MyInstance.OrderLineItems(FirstOrderID, _
            SecondOrderID)

        'Display return from derived class
        'shadowing method.
        MsgBox(int1.ToString, , _
            "MethodShadowsProperty")

    End Sub

    Sub OverloadedConstructor(ByVal TableName As String)

        'Instantiate object based on Rows class
        'with default constructor not specifying
        'a record source.
        Dim MyInstance As _
            New ADODBNorthwind.Rows()

        'Display return from RowSource and
        'RowCount properties based on default
        'constructor.
        MsgBox(MyInstance.RowSource & ", " & _
            MyInstance.RowCount.ToString, , _
            "OverloadedConstructor")

        'Instantiate object based on Rows class
        'with constructor allowing specification
        'of a record source.
        Dim MyInstance2 As _
            New ADODBNorthwind.Rows(TableName)

        'Display return from RowSource and
        'RowCount properties based on constructor
        'allowing specification of a record source.
        MsgBox(MyInstance2.RowSource & ", " & _
            MyInstance2.RowCount.ToString, , _
            "OverloadedConstructor")

    End Sub

End Module
```

Running the Application Project

Because each *Sub* procedure called by the main procedure in the ADODB-NorthwindLibUser project displays at least one message box, the samples are self-explanatory. The main routine contains six *Sub* procedure calls. This section gives you a feel for how to explore this sample application by reviewing the operation of the second, fifth, and sixth procedure calls.

The second *Sub* procedure has the name *BaseMethodandProperty*. This procedure ultimately invokes the *TotalOrder* method and returns a value from the *OrderLineItem* property from the *MyAnalyzer* class in the ADODBOrderDetailAnalyzer project. However, the *BaseMethodandProperty* procedure invokes the base class method and property by invoking a derived class method and property that, in turn, references the base class method and property. This approach enables you to expose base class methods and procedures even when you directly reference a derived class.

The *BaseMethodandProperty* procedure takes an *OrderID* argument defined in the main routine as 10248 in a *Dim* statement. The procedure then references the *MyADODBNorthwind* class with the *MyInstance* variable. Next, the procedure saves the return value from the *MyTotalOrder* method in the *dec1* variable. The return value is the total extended price based on the *TotalOrder* method in the *MyAnalyzer* class of the ADODBOrderDetailAnalyzer project. You can confirm this by referring to the listing for the *MyTotalOrder* method in the ADODBNorthwind project, which references the base class method with the expression *MyBase.TotalOrder(OrderID)*. The *BaseMethodandProperty* procedure then references the *InheritedLineItems* property in the derived class. However, the property procedure for the *InheritedLineItems* property references the base class implementation of the *OrderLineItems* property with the expression *MyBase.OrderLineItems*.

Figure 4-7 shows the results of running the *BaseMethodandProperty* procedure. Its message box contains two numbers. The first one is 440, which is the total extended price for the order with an *OrderID* of 10248. The second number is 3, which is the number of line items in the order.

Figure 4-7   A message box showing results from a base class method and property obtained by invoking a derived class method and returning a value from a derived class property

To run the fifth procedure, *MethodShadowsProperty*, you must remove the comment marker from the procedure call in the main routine. This procedure requires two arguments—one for a beginning *OrderID* value and a second for an ending *OrderID* value. The value of *OrderID* should be less than or equal to the value of *SecondOrderID*. I report results for the *OrderID* and *SecondOrderID* values that appear in the main procedure listing just shown. The *Sub* procedure invokes the *OrderLineItems* method in the derived class. This method shadows, or obscures, the visibility of the base class property by the same name. Shadowing is one of the most powerful inheritance techniques for supporting polymorphism because any derived class member can shadow any base class method—even if they are of different types, as in this case, where the base class member is a property and the derived class member is a method.

Figure 4-8 shows the results of running the *MethodShadowsProperty* procedure. The message box shows a value of 8. By reviewing the code for the *OrderLineItems* method in the derived class, you can see this method returns the total number of line items for a range of orders, from the beginning order to the ending one. The *OrderID* and *SecondOrderID* values in the previous sample listing specify the return of the sum of the line items for the orders with *OrderID* values of 10248 through 10250. You can readily confirm that 8 is a valid return from the Order Details table in the Northwind database.

Figure 4-8 The *MethodShadowsProperty* procedure, which returns the value 8 in its message box when run with default beginning and ending *OrderID* and *SecondOrderID* values of 10248 and 10250

The *OverloadedConstructor* procedure is the only one in the sample application to instantiate an object based on the *Rows* class in the ADODBNorthwind project. The *New* method for the *Rows* class is overloaded. That is, it contains two or more different versions of the *New* function—each with a different argument list. In this case, only two versions exist. The default version with no argument creates an object instance based on the Shippers table from the Northwind database; as mentioned, this table initially ships with three rows. However, you can specify any other table or row-returning query from the Northwind database when you instantiate an instance of the *Rows* class. If you name a table or query, you automatically invoke the second version of the *New* method.

The *OverloadedConstructor* procedure instantiates two objects, *MyInstance* and *MyInstance2*, based on the *Rows* class. Each object is based on a different version of the *New* method. Both *New* method versions create a recordset based on either the Shippers table in the first instance or the Categories table in the second instance. The procedure also displays a message box after instantiating an object that returns the *RowSource* and *RecordCount* properties for the recordset underlying the instantiated object.

Figure 4-9 shows the result from running the *OverloadedConstructor* procedure. When creating instances based on a class with overloaded methods, you can obtain different outcomes just by using different arguments. The top message box shows the result of running the default version of the *New* method for the *Rows* class. As you've learned, this method constructs an object based on the Shippers table. The *RecordSource* property, which is a simple SELECT statement for all the rows and columns from the Shippers table, appears first. The second item shows the number of rows in the Shippers table. The second message box displays the outcome from using the second version of the *New* method with an argument of *Categories*.

Figure 4-9   Two message boxes resulting from two different invocations of the *New* method for the *Rows* class

Structured Exception Handling

Structured exception handling, or SEH, is the new kid on the block for run-time error processing. Although using SEH requires you to learn a new style of error processing, it offers several advantages. My personal favorite is that it gets you away from using the *On Error GoTo* statement, which leads to spaghetti code that can be difficult to debug. Many developers prefer not to dwell on run-time error processing, but the reality is that any professional program is likely to require competent processing of run-time errors. SEH is now the best way to do this.

Overview

Exceptions are the Visual Basic .NET way of referring to run-time errors. Because run-time errors frequently stem from faulty user input or other kinds of environmental errors, all applications are likely to have them. This is simply because you cannot force users of your applications to do the "right" thing. Therefore, you just have to live with the possibility of run-time errors occurring in your applications.

Living with exceptions is not the same as ignoring them. An unhandled exception can cause your application to relinquish control to the common language runtime (CLR). To recover from exceptions and still retain control so that users can continue using your application without having to restart it, you need to intercept exceptions before the CLR starts to process them. Visual Basic .NET offers two approaches for handling errors: unstructured exception handling and structured exception handling. Unstructured exception handling is based on the familiar *On Error GoTo* statement. Until now, Visual Basic and VBA developers knew this approach as their only option for processing run-time errors. As mentioned a moment ago, the second approach to handling exceptions—SEH—is new with Visual Basic .NET.

SEH initially gained popularity with C++ and Java, but Microsoft further enhanced this style of error processing with the introduction of the .NET Framework. All managed code has a uniform error-reporting format. This is because all run-time errors for managed code have to emanate from .NET Framework classes and the CLR. (That's why we call it *managed code.*) In earlier versions of Visual Basic and VBA, the style for reporting an error could vary by the source (such as Visual Basic), the data access tool used (Data Access Objects, Remote Data Objects, or ActiveX Data Objects), and the database engine. In the .NET Framework, exceptions are classes. A base class exception exists, and you can inherit it and build your own custom exceptions. You can throw your own run-time errors as easily as instantiating a new instance of the *Exception* class.

SEH offers a strategic advantage over unstructured exception handling. As mentioned, SEH avoids the introduction of spaghetti code associated with the *On Error GoTo* statement used with unstructured exception handling. A *Try* block (*Try...End Try*) marks a block of code for exception handling with SEH. Every *Try* block must contain at least one *Catch* clause or a *Finally* clause. The *Catch* clause allows you to catch a type of error. You can specify particular types of exceptions to catch a narrow range of run-time errors, or you can use the *System.Exception* class to catch any type of run-time error.

In addition, an optional *When* clause is available to further refine the criteria for invoking the code for a *Catch* clause. You can include multiple *Catch* clauses within a single *Try* block. As soon as the .NET Framework detects an error matching a *Catch* clause, the code for that clause executes. In this way, *Catch* clauses are similar to *Case* clauses in a *Select...Case* statement. The syntax for *Try* blocks even allows you to nest blocks within one another, but you might want to use single-level blocks as you introduce *Try* blocks into your coding tools. The optional *Finally* clause for each *Try* block executes whether or not an error occurs in the block. This clause can be especially useful for closing resources, such as database connections or files.

The general syntax for a *Try* block follows. The design shows a single-level *Try* block with two *Catch* clauses. The second clause illustrates the use of the optional *When* clause to further refine the criteria for selecting an individual *Catch* clause. You can have, at most, one *Finally* clause per *Try* block. The code in the *Finally* clause executes for every pass through a *Try* block.

```
Try
    'Code to do something for which you want to check for
    'exceptions
Catch expression1
    'Code to handle the first type of exception
Catch expression2 When other_expression2
    'Code to handle the second type of exception
Finally
    'Code to execute whether or not an exception occurs
End Try
```

Setting Up the SEH Sample

The form for all the SEH samples appears in Figure 4-10. Because user input is a common source of exceptions, this SEH sample includes three text boxes for collecting user input to the application's code. The figure displays the form immediately after launching the sample. The text boxes have *Name* properties of *TextBox1*, *TextBox2*, and *TextBox3*, from top to bottom. The buttons follow the same convention, from *Button1* through *Button5*. This form resides in the SEHSamples project and has five buttons for launching different approaches to programming SEH.

The text boxes on the form allow the run-time specification of the beginning, ending, and step values for a *For...Next* loop. The sample uses this loop as a source for exceptions. To cut down on your needs for inputting values to the text boxes, the *Form1_Load* event procedure primes the text boxes with some values. The following listing shows the values. Notice that the ending value is set to the maximum integer value with the *MaxValue* method for the *Integer* class. (Isn't it cool that data types are classes?) Visual Basic .NET automatically converts this to a string for the *Text* property of *TextBox2*. The beginning value is just one less than the ending value.

Figure 4-10   The SEH sample, which includes three text boxes for collecting user input to the application's code

```
Private Sub Form1_Load(ByVal sender As System.Object, _
    ByVal e As System.EventArgs) Handles MyBase.Load

    'Initialize For...Next loop parameters.
    TextBox1.Text = Integer.MaxValue - 1
    TextBox2.Text = Integer.MaxValue
    TextBox3.Text = 1

End Sub
```

SEH Programming vs. Programming Without Error Trapping

This section contrasts running an application with a basic form of SEH programming with running an application that has no exception handling. You can use this sample as a springboard for understanding subsequent samples that are more complex as well as a basis for appreciating what value SEH programming can add to an application.

Demonstrating an Exception Without a Catch

The purpose of the samples in this section is to demonstrate the generation (and handling) of exceptions. To that end, the *Click* event procedure for *Button1* shows a *For...Next* loop that ends in an overflow error, which is a *System.OverflowException* object in Visual Basic .NET. When you run this procedure with the default values in the text boxes that the *Form1_Load* event places in the boxes, the code generates an error at the beginning of the third pass through the loop. The procedure will not normally make a third pass through the loop, but the code must add 1 to the *int1* value when *int1* is already at the maximum *Integer* value (2147483647). The procedure does this to determine whether to make a third pass through the loop. In adding 1 to the maximum *Integer* value, the procedure generates an overflow.

Because no catch for an exception within the procedure exists, the CLR handles the exception at run time. When the CLR catches the exception, it presents a dialog box describing that it detected an unhandled exception. A user can click one of three buttons to close the dialog box. One of these buttons allows a user to return to the application at a point before the onset of the error. Note that your application loses control of the session when the CLR presents the dialog box for an unhandled exception. In addition to returning to the application from the unhandled exception dialog box, the user can click a button to get more information about the error or even quit so that control does not return to the program.

```
Private Sub Button1_Click(ByVal sender As System.Object, _
    ByVal e As System.EventArgs) Handles Button1.Click

    'When there is no exception handling,
    'exceptions pass control to the CLR.

    Dim intBegin As Integer = CInt(TextBox1.Text)
    Dim intEnd As Integer = CInt(TextBox2.Text)
    Dim intStep As Integer = CInt(TextBox3.Text)
    Dim int1 As Integer

    'Try to perform a For...Next loop based
    'on values in text boxes.
    For int1 = intBegin To intEnd Step intStep
        Debug.WriteLine(int1.ToString)
    Next

End Sub
```

To run the SEHSamples project and demonstrate the error as it appears normally, you need to start the program outside the Visual Studio .NET debugger. (Errors found with the debugger do not present the same unhandled exception dialog box as those found without the debugger.) You can do this by choosing the Windows Start button and then clicking Run. In the Run dialog box, you can type or navigate to the path and program executable for starting the project, such as C:\pawvbnet\SEHSamples\bin\SEHSamples.exe. Then, click OK on the Run dialog box. This opens the project outside of the debugger. Click Button1 to generate the dialog box reporting the unhandled exception. (See Figure 4-11.)

Figure 4-11 Dialog box for unhandled exceptions presented by the CLR for a *System.OverflowException* object

Catching an Exception

The event procedure for *Button2* demonstrates the syntax for a very simple *Try* block that allows the application to retain control of the user's environment even after the exception. The *Try* block starts just before the beginning of the *For...Next* loop, and the block ends after the *Catch* clause inside the block. The block contains only one *Catch* clause, and it starts immediately after the *For...Next* loop. This arrangement tests the *For...Next* loop for exceptions and offers one remedy for any kind of error. The remedy is the presentation of a message box that denotes the type of message and description (or message) for the exception.

```
Private Sub Button2_Click(ByVal sender As System.Object, _
    ByVal e As System.EventArgs) Handles Button2.Click

    'Exception handling returns built-in type and
    'message; catch just one type of error.

    Dim intBegin As Integer = CInt(TextBox1.Text)
    Dim intEnd As Integer = CInt(TextBox2.Text)
    Dim intStep As Integer = CInt(TextBox3.Text)
    Dim int1 As Integer

    Try
        'Try to perform a For...Next loop based
        'on values in text boxes.
        For int1 = intBegin To intEnd Step intStep
            Debug.WriteLine(int1.ToString)
        Next
    Catch er As System.Exception
        MessageBox.Show( _
        "Type = " & _
            er.GetType.ToString() & vbCr & _
        "Message = " & _
            er.Message)
    End Try

End Sub
```

As an Access database developer creating a solution for a client, it is good practice to prepare custom messages for exceptions that provide the maximum amount of helpful information to users. Microsoft has to write generic messages because its software will be used in a wide variety of situations. However, you can prepare custom messages that add value to a solution by helping users to rectify a problem.

You will notice that I did not add any special message in this situation. That's because the sample code for the *Button2 Click* event procedure has another point. When you catch an exception, the code in the *Catch* clause runs instead of the CLR code for presenting a dialog box in response to an unhandled exception. This means your application retains control of the user's environment when an exception occurs. In this sample, by clicking OK in the message box presented from the *Catch* clause (shown in Figure 4-12), the user can return to the application to change the values in the text boxes or to click another button. By handling the exception with a *Try* block, your application never relinquishes control of the user's environment. This is not true for an unhandled exception.

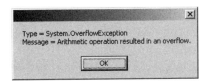

Figure 4-12   Handled exceptions enable your application to remain in control and determine user feedback.

Catching Multiple Exceptions in a *Try* Block

The *Click* event for *Button3* demonstrates how to catch different kinds of errors. In addition, this event shows an example of a helpful message that suggests a remedy to the user. The preceding sample merely echoed the built-in error type and message. This sample divides errors into two types: those that fit a suggested remedy and those that do not. The procedure checks for these two types of errors with two *Catch* clauses inside the *Try* block.

The first *Catch* clause tests whether to suggest the remedy. The remedy is to reduce the ending value for the *For...Next* loop by one step value. This remedy applies when an overflow exists and the *int1* value in the loop is already at the maximum *Integer* value. The first *Catch* clause demonstrates the syntax for using the *When* clause inside a *Catch* clause. The first part of the *Catch* expression checks for a *System.OverflowException* object. If that's the kind of exception object that occurs, the first *Catch* clause uses the *When* clause to determine whether *int1* equals the maximum *Integer* value. If both conditions are *True*, the first *Catch* clause suggests the remedy in a message box.

Any other kind of error invokes the second *Catch* clause. Without this general type of *Catch* clause, you can have a *Try* block that lets unhandled exceptions bubble up from the code in the *Try* block. Always place this kind of *Catch* clause as the last one in a *Try* block. This clause tests for any kind of *Exception* object and prints out a general message about it. Notice that the *Err* object that you used in classic Visual Basic is still available in Visual Basic .NET.

```
Private Sub Button3_Click(ByVal sender As System.Object, _
    ByVal e As System.EventArgs) Handles Button3.Click

    'Exception handling returns custom error message and
    'demonstrates an "all else" exception catch.

    Dim intBegin As Integer = CInt(TextBox1.Text)
    Dim intEnd As Integer = CInt(TextBox2.Text)
    Dim intStep As Integer = CInt(TextBox3.Text)
    Dim int1 As Integer

    Try
        'Try to perform a For...Next loop based
        'on values in text boxes.
        For int1 = intBegin To intEnd Step intStep
            Debug.WriteLine(int1.ToString)
        Next
    Catch er As System.OverflowException _
        When int1 = Integer.MaxValue
        MessageBox.Show _
            ("Upper bound exceeds maximum Integer " & _
            "value. Reduce the Ending value by " & _
            intStep.ToString & ".")
    Catch er As System.Exception
        MessageBox.Show("Time for a call to your system " & _
        "pro." & vbCr & "Error description: " & _
        Err.Description & vbCr & _
        "Source for error: " & er.Source & ".")
    End Try

End Sub
```

You can demonstrate the operation of the *Button3_Click* event procedure by opening a fresh instance of the application. Clicking F5 in Visual Studio .NET is sufficient in this case. Change the beginning value to 2147483643 (which merely involves updating the last digit to 3) and the step value to 2. Clicking Button3 with these text box values causes a message box to appear, similar to the one in Figure 4-13. This message states the remedy—namely, reduce the ending value by 2. Make the change recommended in the message to confirm that the procedure comes to a normal end (no error message exists) with the recommended text box value settings.

Figure 4-13   Displaying in your application dynamic exception messages that tell the user exactly what to do

Now, modify the step value from 2 to 5 and click Button3. This causes the overflow to occur. The value for *int1* is less than the maximum *Integer* value, so the first *Catch* clause does not apply. Therefore, the second *Catch* clause handles the exception.

Using the *Finally* Clause

The discussion of the preceding samples on exception processing dwelled on exceptions. However, with any luck at all, your programs will come to a normal end most of the time. It would be helpful if we received a final message that told us the outcome. (For example, "The program came to a normal end.") The preceding samples gave you feedback only if something went wrong. You can use the *Finally* clause in a *Try* block to provide feedback for any kind of outcome.

The next sample, *Button4_Click*, illustrates the use of the *Finally* clause to provide one of three types of feedback. As you know, the *Finally* clause executes whether or not the *Try* block detects an exception. First, the *Finally* clause can confirm that the program runs to its normal end. Second, the *Finally* clause can confirm that an error happened but that the application tried to fix it automatically. Third, the application can confirm that an error happened but that the procedure didn't attempt to fix the exception automatically.

This sample includes three *Catch* clauses. The first detects overflows where the step value is 1. In this case, the loop values are legitimate. However, a test exists for a loop that will not execute. This test generates an overflow. Therefore, the application automatically fixes this exception by passing beginning, ending, and step values to another procedure that performs the loop by using *Decimal* instead of *Integer* data types. The sample does not print an error message in this path unless the attempt to fix the problem fails. The second *Catch* clause catches any overflow associated with the *For...Next* loop for any other purpose, such as for a loop with beginning, ending, and step values of 2147483643, 2147483646, and 5, respectively. With these values, the first attempt to pass through the *For...Next* loop generates a *System.OverflowException* object. The third *Catch* clause collects any other exception that the *Try* block detects.

A couple of Boolean variables help the *Finally* clause determine which of its three closing messages to display. First, if the *bolNoException* variable is *True*, the *Finally* clause confirms a normal end. If the *bolNoException* variable is *False* and the *bolFixup* variable is *True*, the *Finally* clause confirms an automatic fixup attempt. If an error occurs during the attempt, a separate message box conveys that result. If the *bolNoException* variable and the *bolFixup* variable are both *False*, the *Finally* clause presents a message that an exception occurred but that no action was taken to fix the exception automatically. Again, a separate message box from a *Catch* clause provides more specific feedback.

```
Private Sub Button4_Click(ByVal sender As System.Object, _
    ByVal e As System.EventArgs) Handles Button4.Click

    'Exception handling for multiple error types
    'with automatic fixup try; demonstrates Finally
    'clause syntax.
    Dim intBegin As Integer = CInt(TextBox1.Text)
    Dim intEnd As Integer = CInt(TextBox2.Text)
    Dim intStep As Integer = CInt(TextBox3.Text)
    Dim int1 As Integer
    Dim bolNoException As Boolean
    Dim bolFixup As Boolean

    Try
        'Try to perform a For...Next loop based
        'on values in text boxes.
        For int1 = intBegin To intEnd Step intStep
            Debug.WriteLine(int1.ToString)
        Next
        bolNoException = True
    Catch er As System.OverflowException When intStep = 1
        IntToDecFixUP(int1, intBegin, intEnd, intStep)
        bolFixup = True
    Catch er As System.OverflowException When intStep > 1
        Dim int2 As Integer = _
            CDec(int1) + CDec(intStep) - Integer.MaxValue
        MessageBox.Show("Last iteration exceeds maximum " & _
            "Integer value by " & int2.ToString & " with " & _
            "a step value of " & intStep.ToString & ".  " & _
            "Reset beginning, ending, or step value to " & _
            "avoid this result.")
    Catch er As System.Exception
```

```
            MessageBox.Show("Time for a call to your system " & _
            "pro." & vbCr & "Error description: " & _
            Err.Description & vbCr & _
            "Source for error: " & er.Source & ".")
        Finally
            If bolNoException Then
                MessageBox.Show("Program ran to normal end.")
            ElseIf bolFixup Then
                MessageBox.Show("Exception happened, " & _
                    "but fix up tried.")
            Else
                MessageBox.Show("Exception happened, " & _
                    "but no fix up tried.")
            End If
        End Try

End Sub

Sub IntToDecFixUP(ByVal int1 As Integer, _
    ByVal intBegin As Integer, _
    ByVal IntEnd As Integer, _
    ByVal IntStep As Integer)

    'Automatic fixup routine

    Dim Myint1 As Decimal = CDec(int1)

    Myint1 = intBegin
    Try
        Do While Myint1 <= IntEnd
            Debug.WriteLine(Myint1.ToString)
            Myint1 += IntStep
        Loop
    Catch er As System.Exception
        MessageBox.Show("Automatic fixup failed")
    End Try

End Sub
```

You can generate the three different messages from the sample by performing the following steps. Start the application (for example, by pressing F5). With the default text box values, click Button4 on Form1. This generates the message about the automatic fixup. No intermediate messages appear on the way to this message from the *Finally* clause. Next, set the beginning and ending values in the text boxes to 2147483643 and 2147483646; you can change only the last digit of the default values to set these values. Clicking Button4 with these values causes the *Finally* clause to display a message box confirming that a normal end occurred. Then, change the value in the step value text box to 5. (Leave the other two text boxes with the values that generated the message about a normal end.) Clicking Button4 generates a message about an error but says that no automatic fixup was tried. Before this message appears from the *Finally* clause, another message appears from the *Catch* clause with instructions on how to alter the text box values to remove the exception.

Throwing Your Own Exceptions

Developers might find it convenient to set traps for errors at run time that are awkward or difficult to generate manually. Throwing exceptions programmatically is an efficient way to test the *Catch* clauses in a *Try* block. The *Click* event for *Button5* that follows illustrates how to throw exceptions programmatically. *Button5_Click* is an adaptation of *Button3_Click*, which we discussed earlier. *Button3_Click* was the first sample to demonstrate the syntax for two *Catch* clauses in a single *Try* block. The expression for the first *Catch* clause is purposefully narrow to make it easy to demonstrate the applicability of the second *Catch* clause. However, it might be difficult to create an error condition for a clause. (This is especially true when you are working with a general exception and are not certain what might throw it, which is different than saying you do not believe the exception will be thrown in the production version of an application.)

You need to understand that exceptions are objects. The following sample throws a general exception (*Exception* object). This is the base class for all the more specific exceptions in the .NET Framework. You can make available the full list of *Exception* classes from the Debug, Exceptions menu command in the IDE. The resulting Exceptions dialog box presents a TreeView control that lets you browse for *Exception* classes, similar to the way that you can browse for files in Windows Explorer. To find the *System.OverflowException* class, open the Exceptions dialog box with the Debug, Exceptions command. Then, open the Common Language Runtime Exceptions and System branches of the TreeView control. Next, scroll down within the System branch to the System.OverflowException node. You can use this dialog box to view any exception. Once you have the name of the exception, you can create an instance of it.

The *Button5_Click* procedure is a replica of the *Button3_Click* procedure, except for the addition of a statement that throws the *Exception* class to create an instance of it. The statement appears after the *For...Next* loop and before the first *Catch* clause. Therefore, the *Catch* clauses can detect the thrown exception. The first *Catch* clause ignores the exception because this clause filters exclusively for *System.OverflowException* object instances. However, the second *Catch* clause can detect an *Exception* class instance thrown by the statement after the

For...Next loop. Because the sample creates an instance of the class whenever the *For...Next* loop executes normally, all you have to do to throw the exception is set the text box values so that the *For...Next* loop terminates successfully.

```
Private Sub Button5_Click(ByVal sender As System.Object, _
    ByVal e As System.EventArgs) Handles Button5.Click

    'Throwing your own exception

    Dim intBegin As Integer = CInt(TextBox1.Text)
    Dim intEnd As Integer = CInt(TextBox2.Text)
    Dim intStep As Integer = CInt(TextBox3.Text)
    Dim int1 As Integer

    Try
        'Try to perform a For...Next loop based
        'on values in text boxes.
        For int1 = intBegin To intEnd Step intStep
            Debug.WriteLine(int1.ToString)
        Next

        'Throwing my test error
        Throw New Exception("My Unresolved test error.")

    Catch er As System.OverflowException _
        When int1 = Integer.MaxValue
        MessageBox.Show _
            ("Upper bound exceeds maximum Integer " & _
            "value. Reduce the Ending value by " & _
            intStep.ToString & ".")
    Catch er As System.Exception
        MessageBox.Show("Time for a call to to system " & _
        "pro." & vbCr & "Error description: " & _
        Err.Description & vbCr & _
        "Source for error: " & er.Source & ".")
    End Try

End Sub
```

To test the procedure, open the application by pressing F5. Then, change the last digit for the ending value so that it is one number less than its default value. Next, click Button5. This causes the *For...Next* loop to terminate normally. After the loop completes, control transfers to the *Throw* statement. This statement creates an *Exception* class object. The statement provides a message for the new *Exception* instance ("My Unresolved test error"). The second *Catch*

statement detects this exception and displays the *Message* property as
Err.Description. (See Figure 4-14.)

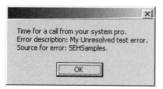

Figure 4-14   Creating an *Exception* instance and then catching it with a
Catch clause in a *Try* block

Summary

This chapter and Chapter 3 give Access database developers like you a summary of core Visual Basic .NET programming topics that you are likely to use in
your applications. While Chapter 3 presents traditional topics, this chapter
focuses on topics that are new or substantially revised in the .NET Framework.
Developers have long requested the class inheritance feature because of its
ability to facilitate code reuse. If you understood the class programming topics
that Chapter 3 covers, you should have little difficulty appreciating how useful
this concept will be in your Visual Basic .NET applications. To help you understand the value of class inheritance, this chapter presents class inheritance samples that use the Northwind database. Other concepts discussed in this chapter
include file processing, event handling, and structured exception handling—a
new style of run-time error processing.

5

Fundamentals of Programming Windows Forms and Controls

Chapter 2 gives you step-by-step instructions for starting a Microsoft Windows application project. This type of project initially opens to a Windows form. Chapters 3 and 4 demonstrate how to add controls from the Toolbox in the IDE to a Windows form. Previous examples using Windows Forms emphasize graphical approaches and stress the comparability of forms in a Windows application project with forms in a classic Microsoft Visual Basic or Microsoft Access project.

This chapter takes a more systematic approach to introducing forms and controls in a Windows application project. In three major sections, you will gain a solid foundation in programming Windows Forms and controls with Visual Basic .NET. The first section presents several samples that illustrate the kind of functionality you can manage with code behind a form. This section takes a close look at code generated by the Windows Form Designer before launching into a series of samples that extends and complements this automatically generated code. You also learn where to look to discover programming syntax tips from the Windows Form Designer.

The second section in this chapter examines programming issues associated with using more than one form in an application. You will learn two styles for opening one form from another, as well as techniques for sharing data among the code modules of each form in an application.

The chapter closes with an in-depth look at coding techniques for managing traditional controls, such as text boxes, combo boxes, and list boxes. You will also see sample code that deals with new types of controls introduced with Visual Basic .NET, such as the PictureBox control and the LinkLabel control. The control sample code demonstrates traditional Access database programming chores, such as working with ActiveX Data Objects (ADO) data access.

Programming Code-Behind Forms

Adding code to the modules behind forms is how you make them smart and interactive. This section introduces the topic, but it keeps the focus on forms rather than the controls in forms. The section starts by drilling down into the Windows Form Designer code automatically generated behind a form and contrasts it with code that you can place in form event procedures. The section then demonstrates how to add code to the form *Load* and *Closing* events. You also learn how to abort an attempt to close a form—for example, if your application's logic prevents a form from closing when a user clicks the Close control. This section also shows how to persist a value to a disk file when a form closes and how to reuse the value the next time that form opens.

Windows Form Designer Generated Code Region

When you start a Windows application project, the Windows Form Designer creates a blank form (*Form1*) based on the *Form* class in the *System.Windows.Forms* namespace. For this reason, the first statement in the code module behind *Form 1* is an *Inherits* statement. Directly below the *Inherits* statement is a region created by the Windows Forms Designer. This region, which is collapsed by default, includes automatically generated code; you can expand the region to view its code. When you first start a Windows application project, the Form Designer puts some code in this region to instantiate the form, initialize it, and prepare for its removal from memory when your application no longer needs it. As you manually add controls or manipulate the form in other ways, the Form Designer will create new code to reflect the changes you've made to the form.

You typically should not place code in the Windows Form Designer region, but knowing what's in this region will help you to write better code to manage your forms. The following listing from the CodeBehindFormSamples project is the code for *Form1* in the Windows Form Designer region for a new Windows application project. You can create this code by creating a project with the Windows Application template. (See Chapter 2 for specific instructions on doing so.) Open the code module behind *Form1* by right-clicking Form1 and choosing View Code. Then, click the + icon next to the label marking the *Windows Form Designer generated code* region. This expands the region so that you can view the code.

> **Note**   The code listing for the Windows Form Designer region in *Form1* for the CodeBehindFormSamples project contains a couple of additional lines that are not referenced in the next section. These lines are for a subsequent sample.

As you can see, the Form Designer region initially contains three procedures. The *New* procedure instantiates a form instance based on the *Form* class. As you've learned, the *MyBase* keyword refers to the class named in the *Inherits* statement. Although the *New* procedure has a comment inviting you to place initialization code after it, you can perform any necessary customization code with the *Form1_Load* event procedure. It is good practice not to populate this region with custom code. The next procedure has the name *Dispose*. The code in this procedure sets up the form instance for removal from memory by the .NET Framework garbage collector. When you need to program an action to occur immediately before or after closing a form, use the *Closing* or *Closed* events instead of placing custom code in the *Dispose* procedure.

The third procedure in the Form Designer generated code region has the name *InitializeComponent*. A *Private* declaration for components, *System.ComponentModel.IContainer*, appears just before the procedure declaration. The Form Designer actively manages both of these code blocks. Placing custom code in either of these areas makes it highly vulnerable to being overridden by the Form Designer. I like to manage the layout of my forms programmatically rather than use the visual layout techniques. In my opinion, programmatically managing the form layout makes it easy to read and maintain because you do not have to go through the Properties window for every change to an object. The program documents the layout, and the program makes it easy to change the layout by changing one or two lines of code. You can place this code in the *Load* event procedure for a form. However, if you are stumped on how to program some layout feature for a form or a control on a form, you can make the change visually and then view the *InitializeComponent* procedure to see how to make a property assignment. For example, the listing that follows shows how to set the caption for a form as its *Text* property. (See *Me.Text = "Form1".*)

```
#Region " Windows Form Designer generated code "
    Public Sub New()
        MyBase.New()

        'This call is required by the Windows Form Designer.
        InitializeComponent()

        'Add any initialization after the InitializeComponent call.

    End Sub

    'Form overrides Dispose to clean up the component list.
    Protected Overloads Overrides Sub Dispose(ByVal disposing As Boolean)
        If disposing Then
            If Not (components Is Nothing) Then
                components.Dispose()
            End If
        End If
        MyBase.Dispose(disposing)
    End Sub

    'Required by the Windows Form Designer.
    Private components As System.ComponentModel.IContainer

    'NOTE: The following procedure is required by the Windows Form Designer.
    'It can be modified using the Windows Form Designer.
    'Do not modify it using the code editor.
    <System.Diagnostics.DebuggerStepThrough()>
    Private Sub InitializeComponent()
        components = New System.ComponentModel.Container()
        Me.Text = "Form1"
    End Sub

#End Region
```

Adding Custom Code to the Module Behind a Form

It is often useful to program actions around the initialization and the termination of a form. Program a *Load* event procedure for actions that need to take place before a form opens. You can program data access or handle layout issues in a form *Load* event procedure. Visual Basic .NET raises the *Load* event for a form after instantiating the form with the *New* procedure from the Windows Form

Designer region. Instances of the Windows *Form* class offer a couple of events for helping to manage actions around the closing of a form; both of these events occur before the invocation of the *Dispose* procedure in the Windows Form Designer region. Use the *Closing* event to program actions that should take place before a form closes. Program a *Closed* event procedure for actions that should take place after a form closes.

To demonstrate when events occur relative to the built-in procedures within the Windows Form Designer region, you can modify the preceding listing to insert two *Debug.WriteLine* statements. As you can tell from the syntax, the statement specifies the *WriteLine* method for the *Debug* object. With the *Debug.WriteLine* statement, you can write a line of text to the console. The console for output in a Windows application is the Output window in Visual Studio .NET. Therefore, you can view your output lines along with standard output from the .NET Framework about the loading of assemblies and completion of programs. Place the first *Debug.WriteLine* statement, which follows, immediately after the comment in the *New* procedure inviting the addition of custom code:

```
Debug.WriteLine ("from Sub New")
```

Place the second *Debug.WriteLine* statement just before the *End Sub* statement in the *Dispose* procedure. This line reads as follows:

```
Debug.WriteLine ("from Sub Dispose")
```

Below the Windows Form Designer region in the *Form1* code module, you can enter three event procedures for the *Load*, *Closing*, and *Closed* events. Chapter 2 mentioned that you can create a shell for the default event for an object by double-clicking the object in Design view. However, you sometimes need to work with an event besides the default one for an object. In these cases, you can select the object, such as *Button1*, from the Class Name drop-down box in the Code window (on the top left) and choose an event for the class from the Method Name drop-down box in the Code window (on the top right).

When working with events for a form, as opposed to the controls on a form, the process is slightly different. From the Class Name drop-down box, select Base Class Events instead of the object name. Figure 5-1 shows the process for generating the *Form1_Load* event procedure shell with the Class Name and Method Name boxes; the name *Form1_Load* is the default name for the *Load* event procedure for *Form1*. Insert the following line of code within the event procedure:

```
Debug.WriteLine ("from Form1 Load event")
```

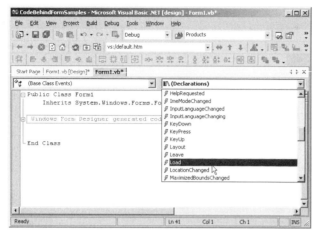

Figure 5-1   The process for creating a *Load* event procedure shell for
a form

You can add *Closing* and *Closed* event procedure shells with the same process. Insert a *WriteLine* statement within each of these other two procedures
specifying the name of the event. The application allows you to trace in the
Output window the order of the three event procedures relative to the invocation of the *New* and *Dispose* procedures in the Windows Form Designer region.
The *Debug.WriteLine* statements leave footprints in the Output window about
when a procedure runs relative to other procedures.

The following listing shows the three event procedures. Notice that the
Closing event procedure has one argument (*e*) with a different type than the other
two event procedures. You can use this argument to manage how and when an
application permits the closing of a form. A subsequent sample will illustrate
the syntax for managing this process.

```
Private Sub Form1_Load(ByVal sender As Object, _
        ByVal e As System.EventArgs) Handles MyBase.Load

        Debug.WriteLine("from Form1 Load event")

    End Sub

    Private Sub Form1_Closing(ByVal sender As Object, _
        ByVal e As System.ComponentModel.CancelEventArgs) _
        Handles MyBase.Closing
```

```
    Debug.WriteLine("from Form1 Closing event")

End Sub

Private Sub Form1_Closed(ByVal sender As Object, _
    ByVal e As System.EventArgs) _
    Handles MyBase.Closed

    Debug.WriteLine("from Form1 Closed event")

End Sub
```

Figure 5-2 shows an excerpt from the Output window for the Code-BehindFormSamples project from opening and closing *Form1*. Open the form by simply pressing the F5 function key. Close *Form1* by clicking the X control in the control box that appears in its top right corner. The application's output lines appear interspersed with messages from the .NET Framework. The first output line is from the *New* procedure, and the last one is from the *Dispose* procedure. Between these two markers are three additional output lines from the three event procedures. From this output, you can confirm that the *Load*, *Closing*, and *Closed* events occur in order between the invocation of the *New* and *Dispose* procedures.

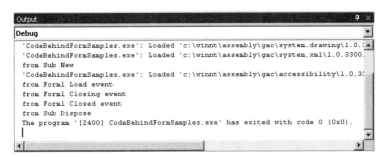

Figure 5-2   Output window tracking the *Load*, *Closing*, and *Closed* events relative to one another and the *New* and *Dispose* procedures

Manipulating a Form with Event Procedures

Manipulating a form in a program can serve multiple purposes in typical application development environments. For example, specifying a form's parameters in a *Load* event procedure can make it easy to see all the specifications for a form in one easy-to-read script. Second, when you have to copy all or part of the specifications from one form to another, having the specifications as code reduces setting the second form's parameters to a copy-and-paste operation (for the code). Third, you might want to specify the start location of a form so that the form does not obscure another form that you want a user to view at the same time. You can manipulate the position of several forms to make them appear in an order that emphasizes a point that you want to make. Fourth, you might find it convenient to revamp the look of a form drastically so that one form can serve two purposes in your application. The next code sample illustrates only the basics of manipulating a form with event procedures, but several other samples in this chapter demonstrate typical applications of the techniques presented here.

You can add a second form to any Windows application by choosing Project, Add Windows Form. This opens the Add New Item dialog box with a suggested name for the form, such as Form2.vb. This name applies to a form's Design tab as well as the tab for the code module behind a form. You can accept the default name or specify another that suits the needs of your application by changing the entry in the Name box on the dialog box. Clicking Open creates a new blank form in your application named after whatever entry appears in the Name box.

To start the project with the new form, *Form2*, instead of with the original form, you need to specify *Form2* as the startup object. *Form1* is the default startup object for a Windows application project. You can change the startup object for a project by selecting the project in Solution Explorer. The project item is the second item from the top that has the name of the project. Then, right-click the project name and choose General under Common Properties in the project's Property Pages dialog box. Next, use the drop-down box labeled Startup Object to select *Form2* (or any other form you want to start up when your project opens). Finally, commit your change by clicking OK. The next time you press F5, the project starts with the new form that you designated as the startup object.

Add six buttons to the new form that you added to the project. The sample uses these buttons to enable a user to manipulate the size and position of a form on her desktop screen. Figure 5-3 shows the arrangement of buttons on the form in Design view. Notice that the buttons appear with the default *Text* property assignments as captions—namely, *Button1*, *Button2*, and so on. The *Form2_Load* procedure assigns new names to each button that reflect their roles.

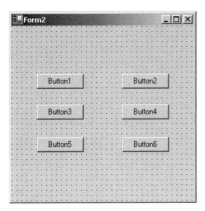

Figure 5-3   The Design view layout of a form before the run-time assignment of *Text* property settings for the form's buttons

The next listing is for all the event procedures behind *Form2*. The form's *Load* event procedure performs two types of tasks. First, it assigns captions to the buttons by setting their *Text* property. The buttons perform three kinds of tasks, with one button performing a task one way and its matching button on a row performing the same kind of task in the opposite direction. The buttons on a row essentially undo the actions of one another. For example, *Button1* adds 50 pixels to the height of *Form 2*, but *Button2* decreases the height of *Form2* by 50 pixels. *Button3* and *Button4* complement each other in the same way for the width of *Form2*, and *Button5* and *Button6* move *Form2* left or right by 50 pixels. The *Form2_Load* event procedure assigns *Text* property settings, such as *"+Height"* and *"-Height"*, which reflect the outcome of the event procedures behind the buttons. After assigning the *Text* property values, the *Load* event procedure centers the form on the user's screen. This is desirable in the current application because the default start location can end up in the top left corner of the desktop, which can cause a form to move partially off the screen at the first click to *Button5*.

Notice that the base *Form* class members (such as *CenterToScreen*) and added controls (such as *Button1*) are both class members of *Form2* (*Me*). The designation of a *Text* property depends on both the form (*Form2* denoted as *Me*) and the button. When developing code for multiple forms, you can have two members in different forms with the same name. As long as you designate the form before the member, you can specify the member unambiguously. Subsequent samples will show techniques for assigning values to members in other forms by using this and other design principles.

Windows forms specify their height and width with a scalar value representing the *Height* and *Width* properties. The value denotes a number of pixels. The default width and height for a Windows form is 300 pixels. You can change either of these property settings at design time or run time. When you use the Properties window, you are changing the setting at design time—that is, before the application runs. When you use an event procedure to alter the *Height* and *Width* property settings for a procedure, you are updating the property at run time. In general, run-time assignments offer more flexibility because you can accommodate user input and change the value from time to time depending on how an application uses a form.

The *Click* event procedures for *Button1* and *Button2* demonstrate the syntax for growing and shrinking the height of *Form2* by 50 pixels. The expression for adding 50 pixels uses the += operator. Similarly, the expression for shrinking the height by 50 pixels relies on the -= operator. The *Click* event procedures for *Button3* and *Button4* work identically to those for *Button1* and *Button2*, except that *Button3* and *Button4* manipulate the form's *Width* property instead of its *Height* property.

The *Text* property settings for *Button5* and *Button6* are *+Left* and *+Right*, which respectively signify a movement of the form to the left or away from the left (that is, to the right). There are at least two tricks to understanding the positioning of a form on a screen. First, the *Left* and *Top* property settings are offsets from the left and top edges of a screen. Therefore, decreasing the *Left* property for a form actually moves the form toward the left, but adding 50 to the *Left* property moves the form to the right by 50 pixels. The second trick relates to how you actually change the position of a form. Although you can increase and decrease the *Left* property of a form, doing so does not move a form or persist the property change. You must use a *Point* structure of a left offset and a top offset and assign this structure to a form property capable of accepting both offsets at once. A form's *DesktopLocation* property is one of the properties that can accept a point structure value. You can assign a value to the *DesktopLocation* property with the *Point* class in the *System.Drawing* namespace. The *Point* merely represents a position in a two-dimensional plane based on an ordered pair of integer values.

Because a Windows application has an automatic reference to the *System.Drawing* namespace, you can optionally represent the namespace when using a *Point* class instance. The event procedure for *Button5* shows the syntax without the namespace designation, and *Button6* shows the syntax with the namespace designation. Using the namespace designation is a lengthier approach, but it reminds you about the source for the *Point* class.

```
Private Sub Form2_Load(ByVal sender As System.Object, _
    ByVal e As System.EventArgs) Handles MyBase.Load

    'Assign captions to buttons.
    Me.Button1.Text = "+ Height"
    Me.Button2.Text = "- Height"
    Me.Button3.Text = "+ Width"
    Me.Button4.Text = "- Width"
    Me.Button5.Text = "+ Left"
    Me.Button6.Text = "+ Right"

    'Designate start location for form.
    Me.CenterToScreen()

End Sub

Private Sub Button1_Click(ByVal sender As System.Object, _
    ByVal e As System.EventArgs) Handles Button1.Click

    Me.Height += 50

End Sub

Private Sub Button2_Click(ByVal sender As System.Object, _
    ByVal e As System.EventArgs) Handles Button2.Click

    Me.Height -= 50

End Sub

Private Sub Button3_Click(ByVal sender As System.Object, _
    ByVal e As System.EventArgs) Handles Button3.Click

    Me.Width += 50

End Sub

Private Sub Button4_Click(ByVal sender As System.Object, _
    ByVal e As System.EventArgs) Handles Button4.Click

    Me.Width -= 50

End Sub

Private Sub Button5_Click(ByVal sender As System.Object, _
    ByVal e As System.EventArgs) Handles Button5.Click
```

(continued)

```
        'Decrease the form's Left property by 50.
        Me.Left -= 50

        'Assign a new position to the form based on
        'the updated Left property setting.
        Me.DesktopLocation = New Point(Me.Left, Me.Top)

    End Sub

    Private Sub Button6_Click(ByVal sender As System.Object, _
        ByVal e As System.EventArgs) Handles Button6.Click

        'Increase the form's Left property by 50.
        Me.Left += 50

        'Assign a new position to the form based on
        'the updated Left property setting.
        Me.DesktopLocation = _
            New System.Drawing.Point(Me.Left, Me.Top)

    End Sub
```

Disabling the Close Control in the Control Box

You can disable the Close control in a form's control box by using the *e* argument for a form's *Closing* event. In the discussion of the code behind *Form1* in the CodeBehindSamples project, you saw that the type for the *e* argument of the *Closing* event is *System.ComponentModel.CancelEventArgs*. The *Cancel* property for this type lets an application get or set whether the event should be cancelled. The *Cancel* property is a Boolean variable that is *False* by default. When the *Cancel* property is *False*, the attempt to close the form succeeds. Assigning a value of *True* to the *Cancel* property for the *e* object causes the attempt to close the form to fail. No run-time error or exception occurs—the form just doesn't close when the *Cancel* property is *True*.

The following code sample for *Form3* demonstrates how to use the *e* object argument for the *Closing* event to disable the Close control in a form's control box. As mentioned, the control box is the set of three controls in the top right corner of a default Windows form; the control with an X on it is the Close control. The form, *Form3*, contains a button, *Button1*, with a run-time assigned *Text* property of *Close*. The application lets a user close the form only by clicking *Button1*, not by clicking the Close control in the control box. This is trickier than it sounds because the Close button in the control box and *Button1* both raise the *Closing* event. (The .NET Framework always raises the *Closing* event in response to an attempt to close a form.) Therefore, the application's code for the form's *Closing* event procedure must distinguish between a user clicking the Close control in the control box or in *Button1*.

The code in the following sample demonstrates another interesting capability: it toggles the visibility of the control box. When *Form3* initially opens, its control box shows. However, because the control box doesn't function or because its Close control fails, you might reasonably decide to suppress the visibility of the control box. The second time that a user opens the form, the control box is not visible. In fact, the application toggles the visibility of the control box on alternate form openings. The application manages the toggling by reading and writing a Boolean value from a disk file. In between the reading and writing of the value, the code toggles the value so that the application saves *True* if it reads *False*, and vice versa. This capability to persist one or a few values to a disk file and then reread the values the next time that an application opens is handy in many circumstances. Access database developers might be inclined to use a table with a single row and one or more columns for as many variables that need to be saved and reread. However, using a local disk file can yield superior performance and consume fewer resources. You are especially likely to obtain superior performance when the Access database file is available only via a network connection or the Internet.

If you are creating this sample along with this discussion, create a new form and let the form have the name Form3.vb in the Add New Item dialog box. Open the Toolbox with the View, Toolbox command and drag a button to *Form3*. Accept the default *Text* property of *Button1*. Then close the Toolbox.

Right-click a blank area in the form, and choose View Code from the shortcut menu to open the code module behind *Form3*. The code sample relies on four procedures that use two module-level Boolean variables. The sample also requires a file, SavedbolShowControlBox.scb, with a single Boolean value whose initial value is *True*. The file must reside in the project's root folder. The easiest way to populate the code module is to copy the completed sample from the CodeBehindFormSamples project. The file is also available for copying from the root folder for the completed project to your project folder. The *bolDisableClose* variable tracks whether to abort the attempt to close the form. The *bolShowControlBox* variable detects whether to show the control box for a form instance. Before attempting to test your code, remember to make *Form3* the project's startup object. (You do this from the Property Pages dialog box.)

The *Form3_Load* event procedure performs three tasks. First, it assigns a caption to *Button1* by setting its *Text* property. Next, the procedure reads the SavedbolShowControlBox.scb file in the root folder for the project to set the value of *bolShowControlBox*. The value of *bolShowControlBox* determines whether the application will display the control box on a form. After closing the

Filestream and *BinaryReader* objects for reading the persisted value of *bolShowControlBox* in the SavedbolShowControlBox.scb file, the procedure sets the value of the form's *ControlBox* property to either *True* or *False*. A value of *True* shows the control box in the form instance.

The second procedure, *Button1_Click*, has just two lines. Clicking this button is the only way to close the form. The procedure begins by setting the *bolDisableClose* variable to *False*. Notice that the module-level declaration for this variable assigns it a default value of *True*. The only way for this variable to be *False* in the *Closing* event procedure is for the user to click *Button1*. Clicking the Close button in the control box does not affect the variable's value. After assigning a new value to the variable, the procedure invokes the form's *Close* method (*Me.Close*). This statement raises the *Closing* event. Clicking the Close button in the control box has the same effect.

The *Form3_Closing* event procedure works in tandem with the fourth procedure, *ToggleControlBox*. The *Closing* event procedure might or might not close the form, depending on the value of *bolDisableClose*. This value will be *True* until a user clicks *Button1*. A value of *True* for *bolDisableClose* causes the *Closing* event procedure to disable the attempt to close the form by setting the *Cancel* property for the *e* object to *True*. The procedure also displays an explanatory message, in this case, explaining how to close the form. If the *bolDisable-Close* variable equals *False*, the procedure leaves *e.Cancel* at its default value of *False* so that the attempt to close the form succeeds when the event procedure relinquishes control. Before closing the form normally, the procedure displays a confirmation message.

In addition to closing the form when the *bolDisableClose* variable equals *False*, the *Form3_Closing* event procedure invokes the *ToggleControlBox* procedure, which toggles the setting for the Boolean variable persisted in the SavedbolShowControlBox.scb file. As mentioned, the variable in this file determines whether to show the form's control box. The process for toggling the variable value starts by wiping out the old file that persisted the value. The procedure demonstrates the syntax for checking for the existence of a file before attempting to delete it. However, the sample's code requires the file to exist. (For example, you cannot read from the file unless it already exists.) Next, the code instantiates a *FileStream* object that points at the new version of the file and instantiates a *BinaryWriter* object for writing a value to the file. After preparing the file, the procedure toggles the current value of the *bolShowControl-Box* variable before writing the variable's value to the file with the *BinaryWriter*'s *Write* method. The procedure ends by closing the *BinaryWriter* and *FileStream* objects.

```vb
'Boolean variables for disabling the Close
    'control and showing the form's control box
    Dim bolDisableClose As Boolean = True
    Dim bolShowControlBox

    Private Sub Form3_Load(ByVal sender As System.Object, _
        ByVal e As System.EventArgs) Handles MyBase.Load

        'Assign label to button.
        Button1.Text = "My Close"

        'Use FileStream and BinaryReader objects to get
        'value written last time form closed.
        Dim str1 As String = "..\SavedbolShowControlBox.scb"
        Dim fst1 As New System.IO.FileStream(str1, _
            System.IO.FileMode.Open, _
            System.IO.FileAccess.Read)
        Dim bnr1 As New System.IO.BinaryReader(fst1)

        bolShowControlBox = bnr1.ReadBoolean

        bnr1.Close()
        fst1.Close()

        'Set ControlBox property.
        If bolShowControlBox = True Then
            Me.ControlBox = True
        Else
            Me.ControlBox = False
        End If

    End Sub

    Private Sub Button1_Click(ByVal sender As System.Object, _
        ByVal e As System.EventArgs) Handles Button1.Click

        'If user clicks button, set bolDisableClose so that
        'form's Close method succeeds.
        bolDisableClose = False
        Me.Close()

    End Sub

    Private Sub Form3_Closing(ByVal sender As Object, _
        ByVal e As System.ComponentModel.CancelEventArgs) _
        Handles MyBase.Closing
```

(continued)

```
    'Toggle form's ControlBox property and save the
    'property's value to a file.
    ToggleControlBox()

    'Disable attempt to close
    'if the user attempts to use the Close button
    'in the control box.
    If bolDisableClose = True Then
        e.Cancel = True
        MsgBox("Use My Close button to close form.")
    Else
        MsgBox("See you next time.")
    End If

End Sub

Sub ToggleControlBox()

    'Specify file for persisting ControlBox property.
    Dim str1 As String = _
        "..\SavedbolShowControlBox.scb"

    'Delete file if it already exists.
    If System.IO.File.Exists(str1) Then
        System.IO.File.Delete(str1)
    End If

    'Use FileStream and BinaryWriter to Save toggled
    'value of ControlBox property.
    Dim fst1 As New System.IO.FileStream(str1, _
            System.IO.FileMode.CreateNew)
    Dim bnw1 As New System.IO.BinaryWriter(fst1)

    If bolShowControlBox = True Then
        bolShowControlBox = False
    Else
        bolShowControlBox = True
    End If

    bnw1.Write(bolShowControlBox)

    'Close BinaryWriter and FileStream objects.
    bnw1.Close()
    fst1.Close()

End Sub
```

Figure 5-4 shows the application in operation. The version of *Form3* in the top left corner shows the form when the application initially opens. Notice the control box in its top right corner. If a user clicks the Close control (X) from the control box, the application responds with a reminder that the way to close the form is by clicking the button labeled My Close. If the user clicks the My Close button, the application displays a message confirming the successful close. The next time that a user starts the application, *Form3* opens without a control box. (See the second version of *Form 3* in Figure 5-4.) In a sense, the application remembers its state from the previous time the form was open and toggles to an alternate state. When a user starts the application again, it starts over with the top version of *Form3*, even if the computer powers down and boots up again. The capability to remember state derives from a small disk file (SavedbolShowControlBox.scb) that holds a single Boolean variable.

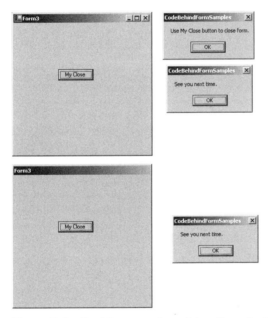

Figure 5-4   *Form3* opens alternately with and without its control box.

Working with Multiple Forms

Processing multiple forms in a single application is a common requirement. This section introduces the basics of the task and demonstrates some techniques for passing values between forms that might not be obvious from the standard Visual Studio .NET documentation. The background and special techniques conveyed by this section can equip you with the knowledge to build powerful form solutions with Visual Basic .NET.

Modal vs. Modeless Forms

You can open one form from another in two ways. If you open a second form as a *modal* form, you cannot change the focus from the second form until you close it. A message box represents this kind of a form. This behavior is convenient for applications that require a response to the second form before actions on other forms make sense. Another way in which you can open one form from another is *nonmodally*. In this second style, a user can switch back and forth between the forms without closing the second form before returning to the first form. The spreadsheet windows in a Microsoft Excel workbook file demonstrate this kind of behavior. Opening forms nonmodally is suitable for applications in which users need the freedom to browse two or more forms in any order.

Visual Basic .NET offers different methods for opening one form from another based on whether you open a second form modally or nonmodally. Use the *Show* method to open a form nonmodally so that users can browse freely between a child form and the parent form used to open the child form. Invoke the *ShowDialog* method when a parent form needs to open a child form as a modal form. The method name, *ShowDialog*, connotes the type of form you are opening. In a dialog box, you normally complete an action before returning to the normal flow of an application.

Before you can open a second form, you must instantiate an instance of the second *Form* class that you want to open. Do this in a *Dim* statement with the *New* keyword. The *New* method requires an existing *Form* class on which to base its new form instance. You can add a *Form* class to your project with the Project, Add Windows Form command. This second *Form* class will not be the basis for a startup object because you want to open an instance based on this *Form* class from a form instance based on another *Form* class. In the most straightforward example, you can have two form instances—one based on a *Form1* class and the other based on a *Form2* class. You can open an instance of the *Form2* class with the *Show* method or the *ShowDialog* method from an instance of the *Form1* class.

The next sample demonstrates the basics of modal and modeless forms with *Form1* and *Form2* in the MultipleFormSamples project. The startup object is set to *Form1*, which means that the application opens to an automatically opened form instance based on the *Form1* class. This form instance contains a couple of buttons. Clicking *Button1* opens via the *Show* method a form instance based on the *Form2* class. Clicking *Button2* opens another form instance based on the *Form2* class; this instance opens by means of the *ShowDialog* method. The *Form2* class has code in its module that detects whether its instances open modally or nonmodally. The application positions modal and modeless instances of *Form2* in different locations so that you can readily contrast the behavior of the two instances.

The code behind the *Form1* class consists of three event procedures. The *Form1_Load* procedure commences by positioning the form instance in the top left corner of the screen. Next, the procedure assigns *Text* property settings to *Button1* and *Button2*. The *Text* property setting for *Button1* designates the modeless opening of *Form2* instances, and the *Text* property setting for *Button2* specifies the modal opening of *Form2* instances.

In addition, this procedure sets the width of the two buttons to 150 pixels so that each button can display its full *Text* property setting. The *Click* event procedure for *Button1* begins by instantiating *Form2* and representing the form instance with the *frmNonModal* variable. Next, the procedure assigns a *Text* property value for the form instance, reminding the user that it is OK to switch back to *Form1* while *Form2* is open. The procedure concludes by invoking the *Show* method for the *frmNonModal* variable. The *Click* event procedure for *Button2* parallels that for *Button1*, but it has some important deviations. The most significant of these is the use of the *ShowDialog* method for opening an instance of *Form2*. You will also note that the caption for the form changes to reflect the fact that you must close this instance of *Form2* before you can switch the focus back to the *Form1* instance.

```
Private Sub Form1_Load(ByVal sender As System.Object, _
    ByVal e As System.EventArgs) Handles MyBase.Load

    'Position Form1 in top left corner of desktop.
    Me.DesktopLocation = New Point(0, 0)

    'Assign Text property for buttons.
    Button1.Text = "Open Modeless Form2"
    Button2.Text = "Open Modal Form2"

    'Set width to show Text property setting.
    Button1.Width = 150
    Button2.Width = 150

End Sub

Private Sub Button1_Click(ByVal sender As System.Object, _
    ByVal e As System.EventArgs) Handles Button1.Click
```

(continued)

```
      Dim frmNonModal As New Form2()

      'Open Form2 in modeless version.
      frmNonModal.Text = "Form2 - Use Form1 while I am open"
      frmNonModal.Show()

End Sub

Private Sub Button2_Click(ByVal sender As System.Object, _
    ByVal e As System.EventArgs) Handles Button2.Click

      Dim frmModal As New Form2()

      'Open Form2 in modal version.
      frmModal.Text = "Form2 - Close Me before using Form1"
      frmModal.ShowDialog()

End Sub
```

This application is interesting because it instantiates two different instances of the same form class (*Form2*) that exhibit distinct capabilities. As mentioned earlier, modeless instances of *Form2* let a user switch the focus back to *Form1* without requiring the closing of *Form2*. In fact, users can switch back and forth as often as necessary. Users can change the focus to a form by clicking any blank area on it. When a click to *Button2* opens *Form2* modally, users cannot change the focus back to *Form1* until *Form2* closes. To contrast the behavior of the two form instances, you will want to have them occupy different screen areas, which will make it easier for users to confirm how the form instances behave differently. Therefore, the code behind the *Form2* class positions form instances on the screen in different desktop locations, depending on whether the form instance is modal or modeless.

The code behind the *Form2* class consists of a pair of event procedures. The *Form2_Load* procedure checks the *Modal* property of the *Form2* instance that is about to open. This property is *True* whenever a form instance is invoked with the *ShowDialog* method, but it is *False* otherwise. When the property is *False*, the code positions the *Form2* instance 15 pixels to the right of the *Form1* instance. This procedure assumes that the size for *Form1* remains at its default setting of 300 by 300 pixels. If the *Modal* property is *True*, it means the user clicked *Button2* on the *Form1* instance to open *Form2* modally. In this case, the *Form2_Load* event procedure positions the *Form2* instance 15 pixels to the right and 15 pixels below the lower edge of the *Form1* instance. The

Click event procedure for *Button1* on *Form2* closes the current form instance. Users can also use the Close control in the form's control box.

```
Private Sub Form2_Load(ByVal sender As System.Object, _
    ByVal e As System.EventArgs) Handles MyBase.Load

    'Position modeless version of Form2 to the
    'right of Form1 and above modal version of Form2.
    If Me.Modal = False Then
        DesktopLocation = New Point(315, 0)
    Else
        DesktopLocation = New Point(315, 315)
    End If

    'Label button.
    Me.Button1.Text = "Close"

End Sub

Private Sub Button1_Click(ByVal sender As System.Object, _
    ByVal e As System.EventArgs) Handles Button1.Click

    Me.Close()

End Sub
```

Figure 5-5 shows the arrangement of the forms for this application. An instance of *Form1* appears in the top left corner. If the user clicks the top button that opens an instance of *Form2* nonmodally, the form to its right appears. At this point, a user can click back and forth freely between the two form instances. In fact, users can repeatedly click the top button in the *Form1* instance and generate multiple modeless instances of *Form2*. These instances stack on top of one another, but you can drag copies off the stack to show the underlying instances. In addition, you can shift the focus to any modeless instance of *Form2* or back to the *Form1* instance. Clicking the bottom button in *Form1* creates a modal instance of *Form2*. When this happens, the focus shifts to that instance of *Form2*, and the user cannot change the focus to another form instance by clicking a blank area on that instance. The only option is to close the modal *Form2* instance, which transfers control back to its parent *Form1* instance. At that point, the user can shift the focus to any open form instances or open one or more modeless *Form2* instances.

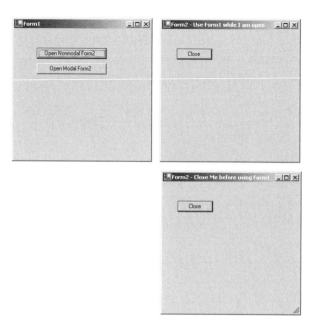

Figure 5-5 Modeless and modal instances of *Form2*

Returning a Result from a Child Form

The ease of manipulating forms and the fact that the same *Form* class can appear in multiple instances within a single application creates some interesting possibilities. The sample code in this section demonstrates the use of a *Form* class for a startup form in two different ways: as a main form and as a message box. The second instance is not strictly a message box instance, but it simulates some of the behavior of a message box—particularly when combined with the first instance based on the class for the startup form. The application shows both instances on the screen at the same time. The contents of the message in the second instance of the startup *Form* class derives from a child form. This child form is a modal form opened from the first instance of the startup *Form* class.

Demonstrating the Sample Application

This sample is the kind of application that greatly benefits from a demonstration before reviewing the code underlying it. When a user starts the application from the MultipleFormSamples project, *Form3* appears by itself with two buttons. One of these buttons has a *Text* property assignment of *Compute*. Clicking this button pops up a second modal form to its right, *Form4*, which contains two text boxes and a button. The *Text* property for the button on the modal form is *Return Sum*. The purpose of the modal form is for the user to input numeric values in *TextBox1* and *TextBox2* before clicking the button on the form. Figure 5-6 shows the startup instance of *Form3* and the *Form4* instance. I entered values into the text boxes on *Form4*, and the right window depicts the *Form4* instance just before a click to the form's button.

> **Note**   The application uses *Form3* as the startup object. Therefore, you will need to make sure that *Form3* is set as the startup object for the project. One way to do so is to open the Property Pages dialog box for the project and select *Form3* as the startup object.

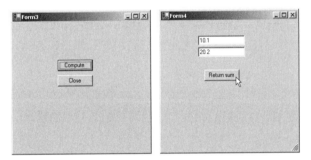

Figure 5-6   Clicking Compute in the startup instance of *Form3* opens an instance of *Form4* that is ready to accept quantities to sum.

Clicking the Return Sum button in *Form4* creates a new instance of *Form3* below the instance of *Form3* to the left of *Form4* and closes *Form4*. (See Figure 5-7.) The new instance of *Form3* has a look entirely different from its predecessor. First, it contains a label showing the text box values and their sum. Second, the new instance of *Form3* shows no buttons—not even a control box. Third, the size of the second *Form3* instance is different from that for the first instance. Finally, when a user clicks the Close button in the first instance of *Form3*, it closes both instances of *Form3*.

Figure 5-7   After clicking the Return Sum button in Figure 5-6, the screen reconfigures to appear like this.

The Code Behind the Application

You can start creating your version of this application by adding *Form3* and *Form4* to your project. *Form4* looks like the form on the right in Figure 5-6; it is more difficult to discern what the *Form3* class looks like because it appears in Figure 5-7 in two radically different layouts. The best way to understand the layout for *Form3* is probably with a picture of it in Design view. (See Figure 5-8.) As you can see, the *Form3* class has a couple of buttons, a label, and a control box. In addition, the form has a standard shape and size of 300 by 300 pixels. The code behind the form causes *Form3* to appear in such different instances in Figure 5-7.

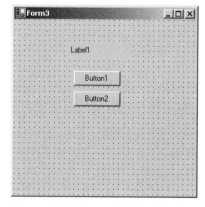

Figure 5-8   The underlying Design view of the *Form3* class that appears in two different layouts in the top and bottom forms in Figure 5-7

After adding controls so that your version of *Form3* matches the layout shown in Figure 5-8, you can add code to the module behind *Form3*. As you can see, the code consists of three short procedures. The *Form3_Load* event procedure includes just four simple layout statements. First, the event procedure positions the form in the screen's top left corner. Then it assigns *Text* property settings to *Button1* and *Button2*. Next the procedure makes the label invisible so that the two buttons appear to be the only controls on the form. The *Button1_Click* procedure instantiates *Form4* and uses *frm1* as a variable pointing at the *Form4* instance. Then, the procedure opens the form instance by invoking the *ShowDialog* method; this opens *Form4* as a modal form. The *Button2_Click* procedure closes *Form3* and any child (or grandchild) form instances.

As it turns out, the second form in Figure 5-7 is a grandchild of the top form in Figure 5-7. This is because the top instance in the figure instantiates *Form4* (shown in Figure 5-6), which, in turn, instantiates the bottom form. Therefore, the *Form4* instance in Figure 5-6 is the child of the startup instance of *Form3*. However, this *Form4* instance instantiates a second instance of *Form3* that appears as the bottom form in Figure 5-7. When you close a startup form instance such as the one in the top window of Figure 5-7, Visual Basic .NET closes all forms in a project and exits the application.

```
Private Sub Form3_Load(ByVal sender As System.Object, _
    ByVal e As System.EventArgs) Handles MyBase.Load
    'Format Form3 for main form.
    DesktopLocation = New Point(0, 0)
    Button1.Text = "Compute"
    Button2.Text = "Close"
    Label1.Visible = False

End Sub


Private Sub Button1_Click(ByVal sender As System.Object, _
    ByVal e As System.EventArgs) Handles Button1.Click

    'Instantiate Form4.
    Dim frm1 As New Form4()

    'Open Form4 modally.
    frm1.ShowDialog()

End Sub
```

(continued)

```
Private Sub Button2_Click(ByVal sender As System.Object, _
    ByVal e As System.EventArgs) Handles Button2.Click

    'Closing this instance of Form3 also closes the
    'message from the computation window instance of Form3.
    Me.Close()

End Sub
```

The code behind *Form4* contains just two procedures. The *Form4_Load* procedure positions the form instance to the right of the startup instance of *Form3*. The *Load* event procedure also assigns a *Text* property value, *Return Sum*, to the button on the form.

After a user enters values in the two text boxes on *Form4*, clicking *Button1* opens a new instance of *Form3* below the startup version that appears to the left of *Form4*. The *Button1_Click* procedure in the module behind *Form4* starts by adding the numbers represented by the *Text* property settings of *TextBox1* and *TextBox2* and then saves the result in a variable, *sum*, which has a *Double* data type. Next, the procedure instantiates a new instance of *Form3* and assigns it to the *frm1* variable in the procedure. Then the procedure computes a string based on the *Text* property settings for *TextBox1* and *TextBox2* as well as the *sum* variable, and it saves the string in the *Text* property setting for the Label1 control on the new instance of *Form3*.

The new instance of *Form3* is now almost ready to show its result, but the form will look odd containing only a couple of buttons that exist for the sole purpose of displaying a result. Therefore, we need to make the buttons invisible; to do so, make their *Visible* property settings *False*. You can follow the same approach for making the control box on the form instance invisible. In addition, shorten the height of the new *Form3* instance to make the message stand out more in a smaller form instance. In fact, you will need to change the *Visible* property setting for Label1 so that it is not visible at all. You can also add a *Text* property setting to the form to explain that it is just a message, and you can position the new instance of *Form3* below the startup instance of *Form3*. Finally, you can position the new instance of *Form3* so that it appears right below the startup instance of *Form3*. Several of these formatting assignments require a form instance to show before they can apply to a form instance. Therefore, the procedure invokes the *Show* method for *frm1* before making any property assignments for the new form instance.

The *Button1_Click* procedure concludes by invoking the *Close* method for the open instance of *Form4*. This leaves just two instances of *Form3* open—the two that appear in Figure 5-7. When the user clicks the Close button in the startup instance of *Form3*, the application closes both instances of *Form3*.

```
Private Sub Form4_Load(ByVal sender As System.Object, _
    ByVal e As System.EventArgs) Handles MyBase.Load

    'Position Form4 to right of Form3.
    DesktopLocation = New Point(315, 0)

    Button1.Text = "Return sum"

End Sub

Private Sub Button1_Click(ByVal sender As System.Object, _
    ByVal e As System.EventArgs) Handles Button1.Click

    'Perform computation.
    Dim sum As Double
    sum = CDbl(TextBox1.Text) + CDbl(TextBox2.Text)

    'Instantiate new instance of Form3.
    Dim frm1 As New Form3()

    'Prepare label text for new Form3.
    frm1.Label1.Text = _
        TextBox1.Text & _
        " + " & _
        TextBox2.Text & _
        " = " & _
        sum.ToString

    'Show Form3.
    frm1.Show()

    'Then, reformat Form3 instance for showing
    'a message.
    frm1.Button1.Visible = False
    frm1.Button2.Visible = False
    frm1.ControlBox = False
    frm1.Height = 150
    frm1.Label1.Visible = True
    frm1.Text = "Message from Computation Window"
    frm1.DesktopLocation = New Point(0, 315)

    'Close Form4.
    Me.Close()

End Sub
```

Passing Values Both Ways Between Forms

The preceding sample displays a message on a child form, but the parent of the form with the message is itself a child of another form that remains open until a user clicks its Close button to remove the startup object for the project. Although the preceding sample returns from a child form a result on a separate form instance for display along with its parent form, the sample does not pass a value back to the parent form. In addition, no communication of values from the parent form to the child form occurs. However, you will commonly need to share data between parent and child form instances. The next pair of forms, *Form5* and *Form6* in the MultipleFormSamples project, illustrates a couple of ways to exchange data between a parent form and its child. Exchanging values between two forms is more complicated than it might seem at first because no built-in collection of open forms exists (as exists in classic Visual Basic). Although you can create your own custom collection of form instances, many developers might prefer this alternative approach, which depends on public variables and shared variables.

Passing data values from a parent form to a child form is relatively straightforward. Declare one or more public variables in the child form. Then when a parent form creates an instance of the child form, the parent form can assign values to the child form as property values for the class instance. Creating a reference from the child form to its parent form is more challenging. You can readily create a new instance of the parent form class from the child form instance, but this new parent form instance will not be the same instance as the one used to create the child form. However, by declaring a public, shared variable in the parent form class, any child instance can update the shared variable in the original parent instance. You do not need to create a new instance of the parent form. When the child form relinquishes control to its original parent form instance, the newly updated shared value will be available to the parent form instance.

After adding *Form5* and *Form6* to your project, designate *Form5* as the startup object for the project. *Form5* has two buttons on it. *Button1* instantiates *Form6* and passes a pair of values to the *Form6* instance in the process. *Button2* displays the value of the shared variable in a message box. *Form6* has an even simpler design than *Form5*: *Form6* contains no controls. The *Load* event procedure does all the work for the form, including displaying a message box with the passed values. This *Load* event procedure also sets the shared public value in its parent form (*Form5*).

The following code listing shows the custom code behind *Form5*. Critically, the listing commences with a shared public variable named *input1*. This is the variable to which the child form instance (*Form6*) assigns a value. After the variable declaration, the listing contains three short event procedures. The *Load* event procedure merely formats the two buttons on *Form5*. The *Click* event procedure for *Button1* demonstrates the syntax for passing values from a parent form to a child form. First, you instantiate an instance of the child form (*Form6*). The sample assigns this instance to the *frm1* variable. Second, you assign values to the public variables for the child form. The public variables in *Form6* have the names *input1* and *input2*. Third, you invoke the *Show* (or *ShowDialog*) method for the variable representing the child form to display the child form for this parent form instance. The third event procedure, *Button2_Click*, merely presents in a message box the value of the parent form's shared public variable (*input1* in *Form5*). This value is initially 0, but the child form assigns a new value to the variable.

> **Note**   The sample uses the variable name, *input1*, in both *Form5* and *Form6*. However, Visual Basic .NET is smart enough to track separate values for both variables and avoid any name conflicts between the two.

```
'Expose input1 in Form5 as a public,
'shared field.
Public Shared input1 As Double

Private Sub Form5_Load(ByVal sender As System.Object, _
    ByVal e As System.EventArgs) Handles MyBase.Load

    'Format buttons on form.
    Button1.Text = "Pass values to second form"
    Button1.Width = 175

    Button2.Text = "Displayed Shared input1 value"
    Button2.Width = 175

End Sub

Private Sub Button1_Click(ByVal sender As System.Object, _
    ByVal e As System.EventArgs) Handles Button1.Click

    'Instantiate an instance of Form6.
    Dim frm1 As New Form6()

    'Assign value to public fields in the form.
```

(continued)

```
        frm1.input1 = 10
        frm1.input2 = 20

        'Open the form.
        frm1.Show()

End Sub

Private Sub Button2_Click(ByVal sender As System.Object, _
    ByVal e As System.EventArgs) Handles Button2.Click

        'Display current value of input1 on Form5.
        MsgBox(input1.ToString)

End Sub
```

The code behind *Form6* is even more basic. Its listing includes a couple of public variable declarations followed by a single event procedure. The public variable declarations correspond to the variables getting assignments in the code behind *Form5*. This correspondence is the trick that enables a parent form to pass values to a child form. The form's *Load* event procedure performs three tasks. First, it opens a message box to display the passed values, which allows you to confirm the success of the operation. Second, the procedure assigns a value to the shared public variable in the parent form by creating a new instance of the parent form (*frm2*) and assigning a value to the shared variable (*frm2.input1*). Because *Form5* assigns the value 10 to *input1* in *Form6*, the expression in *Form6* for *frm2.input1* assigns the value 10.5 to *input1* in *Form5*. Notice that the code never creates an instance of *Form5*; this is not necessary because *Form5* exposes its *input1* field as a shared, public variable. Third, the event procedure closes the child form. This operation returns control to the parent form instance (*Form5*). After control returns to the parent form, you can click *Button2* to display the value returned from the child form to the parent form.

```
'Declare input1 and input2 as public fields
'from Form6.
Public input1 As Double
Public input2 As Double

Private Sub Form6_Load(ByVal sender As System.Object, _
    ByVal e As System.EventArgs) Handles MyBase.Load

        'Display passed values for input1 and input2
        'in a comma-delimited format.
        MsgBox(input1.ToString & ", " & input2.ToString)

        'Reference Form5 to make its shared, public variable
```

```
'available and assign a value to it.
Dim frm2 As Form5
frm2.input1 = input1 + 0.5

'Close the form instance after you no longer
'need it.
frm2.Close()

'Close this form to return focus to its
'parent form.
Me.Close()
```

End Sub

Figure 5-9 shows the sample application in operation. The top version of *Form5* shows the form instance just after the application starts. A click to *Button1* causes the display of the message box to its right. The message box actually results from the *Load* event procedure for *Form6*. Initially clicking *Button2* before clicking *Button1* presents a message box with a value of 0. This value reflects the current value for the shared, public variable: *input1* from *Form5*. However, the second display of *Form5* shows the result of clicking *Button2* after clicking *Button1*. At this point, *Form6* updated the default value of 0 for *input1* to 10.5. This value appears in a message box to the right of *Form5* just after a click to *Button2*.

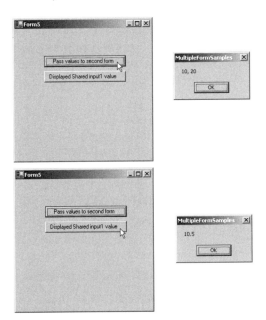

Figure 5-9   The application for *Form5* and *Form6* demonstrates approaches to passing values between parent and child form instances.

Programming Controls with the Northwind Database

This section builds on the general background for Windows forms created in the previous two sections to highlight several kinds of chores that Access database developers are likely to perform with Windows forms. Because many readers will already have a working knowledge of ADO, the data samples use the COM Interop feature to reference the *ADODB* library for data access tasks. Chapter 7 and Chapter 9 focus on ADO.NET development techniques. In addition, Chapter 7 builds on the Jump Start sample from Chapter 2 to examine the use of ADO.NET techniques with Windows forms. However, learning to use the *ADODB* library via the COM Interop will give many Access developers a fast path to creating solutions with Visual Basic .NET and their existing Access databases.

Validating a Password with a TextBox Control

One common database programming chore is to validate a user. For example, an application can require the input of user ID and password data into a couple of TextBox controls. In forms processing, the password must not show as a user enters it. Common practice is to show an asterisk (*) for each typed character in the text box. After the form accepts the user ID and password data, one typical use for the data is to look up the entries in a database table to confirm the validity of the user ID and password.

The sample for this section demonstrates how to implement this kind of task with the CompanyName and CustomerID column values from the Customers table in the Northwind database serving as the user IDs and passwords. Because the application uses the Access Northwind database file, you need a way of connecting to it. The sample uses the *ADODB* library through the COM Interop feature. To use the *ADODB* library this way, you need to add a reference to your project to the *ADODB* library. (See Chapter 3 for a description of how to do this.) This sample uses *Form1* in the FormControlSamples project. You can follow the next set of instructions for building the sample or go directly to that form in the sample materials for this chapter.

Figure 5-10 shows the layout for the form in the password application. The figure contains a couple of TextBox controls for the user ID and password fields and a button for submitting the user-supplied data for a validation check. Label controls identify the type of data for each text box. The *PasswordChar* property for a TextBox control allows you to designate any text character to appear instead of the typed input. You can set this property in the Properties window at design time, or you can assign the property at run time (for example, in a *Load* event procedure). You can optionally specify a maximum length for the text box holding a password, allowing your application to automatically invalidate entries that are longer than the maximum length. You can use the *MaxLength* property for a TextBox control to designate the maximum number of characters it will accept.

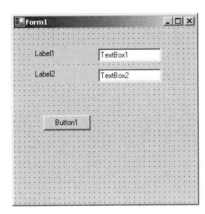

Figure 5-10   The form layout for the user ID and password validation sample

The code behind the form has three procedures. The *Form1_Load* procedure performs typical property assignment functions for the controls on the form. However, in this application, two of these assignments are critical because they designate how *TextBox2* acts as a control for a password. By assigning a string character value to the *PasswordChar* property, you designate that character to appear in lieu of typed input to the control. The *Load* event procedure assigns an asterisk. The *MaxLength* property setting for *TextBox2* is 5 because all the CustomerID column values in the Customers table are exactly five characters in length.

The *Button1_Click* procedure works in tandem with the *IsCustomerID-Valid* function procedure. The function procedure does the work of connecting to the Northwind database, creating a recordset based on the Customers table and the CompanyName and CustomerID values passed to it. The function procedure returns a value of *True* or *False*, depending on whether the CompanyName and CustomerID values exist in the Customers table. The *Button1_Click* procedure merely passes the TextBox values to the function procedure for the CompanyName and CustomerID arguments and displays a message box with the return value from the function.

```
Private Sub Form1_Load(ByVal sender As System.Object, _
    ByVal e As System.EventArgs) Handles MyBase.Load

    'Set TextBox properties.
    TextBox1.Text = ""
    TextBox2.PasswordChar = "*"
    TextBox2.MaxLength = 5

    'Set other control properties.
    Label1.Text = "Company Name"
    Label2.Text = "CustomerID"
    Button1.Text = "Lookup"

End Sub

Private Sub Button1_Click(ByVal sender As System.Object, _
    ByVal e As System.EventArgs) Handles Button1.Click

    Dim Cname As String = TextBox1.Text
    Dim CustID As String = TextBox2.Text

    MsgBox(IsCustomerIDValid(Cname, CustID).ToString)

End Sub

Function IsCustomerIDValid( _
    ByVal CName As String, _
    ByVal CustID As String) As Boolean

    'Declare and instantiate ADODB objects.
    Dim cnn1 As New ADODB.Connection()
    Dim rst1 As New ADODB.Recordset()

    'Open an ADO Connection object.
    cnn1.Open("Provider=Microsoft.Jet.OLEDB.4.0;" & _
        "Data Source=C:\Program Files\" & _
        "Microsoft Office\Office10\Samples\Northwind.mdb;", _
        "Admin", "")

    'Define SQL string for lookup.
    Dim str1 As String = "SELECT CustomerID " & _
        "FROM Customers " & _
        "WHERE CustomerID = '" & CustID & "' and " & _
        "CompanyName = '" & CName & "'"

    'Perform lookup.
    With rst1
        .ActiveConnection = cnn1
```

```
    .Open(str1, , _
        ADODB.CursorTypeEnum.adOpenKeyset, _
        ADODB.LockTypeEnum.adLockOptimistic)
End With

'Return True or False based on whether a
'match is found.
If rst1.RecordCount > 0 Then
    Return True
Else
    Return False
End If
```

```
End Function
```

Figure 5-11 shows the user ID and password form with an entry of Around The Horn for the Company Name box that serves as the user ID in this sample. The CustomerID field serving as the password is filled with asterisks—one for each of the five typed characters. A value of AROUP, which is incorrect, causes a click to the Lookup button to present a message box that reads False. Changing the CustomerID value to AROUT, which happens to be valid, returns a message box containing True.

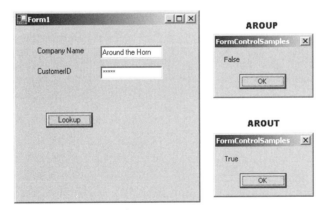

Figure 5-11   The user ID and password validation sample in action

Browsing the Shippers Table with TextBox Controls

Browsing data records with a form is a common database development application. You can optionally enable data manipulation (updates, inserts, and deletes) as well as data access. You need some type of control, such as a text box, to show field values from a record source. A browsing application typically has at least four controls for enabling the browsing function. These controls let users move to the first, previous, next, and last record in a record source. This record source supplies data to the controls on the form that show data.

Figure 5-12 shows the sample form for data browsing in the FormControl-Samples project. The sample is on *Form2* in the project. You will need to make *Form2* the startup object for the project. In addition, you need a reference to the *ADODB* library in the project. If you successfully completed the prior sample, this reference already exists. The form contains three TextBox controls, three label controls to describe the TextBox controls, and four buttons for navigating through the form's record source. *Button1* through *Button4* enable browsing to the first, previous, next, and last record in the record source, which is the Shippers table in the Northwind database. However, you can readily modify the sample to work with any other table, query, or even a more complex Jet SQL SELECT statement, such as one that joined two or more tables and performed some aggregation. The code behind the form performs *Text* property assignments for the label and button controls as well as managing the values that the TextBox controls display.

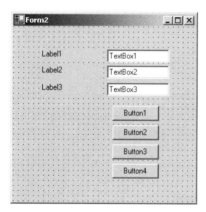

Figure 5-12   A Design view of the form for the data browsing sample

The code behind the form in Figure 5-12 includes six procedures and one module-level object declaration. The module-level declaration is for an ADO recordset object that points at the record source for the form. You must declare this object outside any one procedure because all the procedures have a need for it. The *Form2_Load* procedure starts with two related tasks. First, it instantiates and opens an ADO *Connection* object pointing at the Northwind database. Second, it opens a recordset for the Shippers table in the Northwind database. In database applications, it is common to specify the data source for a form in the *Load* event procedure. The third task is the formatting of the controls contained in *Form2*. In this case, the formatting involves assigning strings to the *Text* property for the form's controls.

Each button control has a short *Click* event procedure that works directly with the *AssignCurrentRecord* procedure. The button *Click* event procedures contain just two lines. The first of these lines invokes a navigation method for the recordset object, such as *MoveFirst* or *MovePrevious*. The second line calls the *AssignCurrentRecord* procedure. The *AssignCurrentRecord* procedure performs two kinds of tasks. First, the procedure checks whether the navigation move is beyond the first record or the last record. If the procedure discovers that the user made either kind of move, the procedure displays a message box informing the user of the problem. In addition, the procedure moves the record to the first or last position, whichever is nearest. If the navigation is to a valid record, the procedure reads the data from the current record in the recordset and populates the *Text* property settings for the TextBox controls with the field values from the record.

```
'Module-level declaration and instantiation
'for a recordset object
Dim rst1 As New ADODB.Recordset()

Private Sub Form2_Load(ByVal sender As Object, _
    ByVal e As System.EventArgs) Handles MyBase.Load

    'Open an ADO Connection object to Northwind database.
    Dim cnn1 As New ADODB.Connection()
    cnn1.Open("Provider=Microsoft.Jet.OLEDB.4.0;" & _
             "Data Source=C:\Program Files\" & _
             "Microsoft Office\Office10\" & _
             "Samples\Northwind.mdb;", _
             "Admin", "")

    'Open recordset for Shippers table based on
    'module-level declaration.
    Dim str1 As String = "SELECT * FROM Shippers"
    With rst1
        .ActiveConnection = cnn1
        .Open(str1, , _
            ADODB.CursorTypeEnum.adOpenKeyset, _
            ADODB.LockTypeEnum.adLockOptimistic)
    End With

    'Initialize Form controls.
    TextBox1.Text = ""
    TextBox2.Text = ""
    TextBox3.Text = ""
    Label1.Text = "ShipperID"
    Label2.Text = "Company Name"
    Label3.Text = "Phone"
```

(continued)

```
        Button1.Text = "First"
        Button2.Text = "Previous"
        Button3.Text = "Next"
        Button4.Text = "Last"

    End Sub

    Private Sub Button1_Click(ByVal sender As System.Object, _
        ByVal e As System.EventArgs) Handles Button1.Click

        'Display first record.
        rst1.MoveFirst()
        AssignCurrentRecord()

    End Sub

    Private Sub Button2_Click(ByVal sender As System.Object, _
        ByVal e As System.EventArgs) Handles Button2.Click

        'Display previous record.
        rst1.MovePrevious()
        AssignCurrentRecord()

    End Sub

    Private Sub Button3_Click(ByVal sender As Object, _
        ByVal e As System.EventArgs) Handles Button3.Click

        'Display next record.
        rst1.MoveNext()
        AssignCurrentRecord()

    End Sub

    Private Sub Button4_Click(ByVal sender As System.Object, _
        ByVal e As System.EventArgs) Handles Button4.Click

        'Display last record.
        rst1.MoveLast()
        AssignCurrentRecord()

    End Sub

    Sub AssignCurrentRecord()

        'Check for BOF or EOF before assigning
        'current record to text boxes.
        If rst1.BOF Then
```

```
        MsgBox("Already at first record.")
        rst1.MoveNext()
    ElseIf rst1.EOF Then
        MsgBox("Already at last record.")
        rst1.MovePrevious()
    Else
        TextBox1.Text = CStr(rst1("ShipperID").Value)
        TextBox2.Text = CStr(rst1("CompanyName").Value)
        TextBox3.Text = CStr(rst1("Phone").Value)
    End If

End Sub
```

When *Form2* opens, its TextBox controls are empty. You can optionally program it to open the form so that the first record shows. In any event, a user can display the first record by clicking the First button. (See the top left form window in Figure 5-13.) Clicking the Previous button at this point generates the error message that appears to the right of the top form in Figure 5-13. However, clicking the Next button repopulates the TextBox controls with field values for the Shipper whose ShipperID value equals 2. (See the bottom left form window in Figure 5-13.) The Next and Last buttons work similarly to the Previous and First buttons.

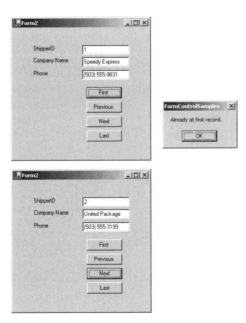

Figure 5-13   An operational view of the data browsing sample for a move outside the recordset and a normal move to the next record

Navigating with a ComboBox and Showing Pictures

The previous sample browses through a record source along a sequential path with the Previous and Next buttons, but it allows users to jump to the first and the last record. Using a ComboBox control, you can let a user browse to any record in a record source. The next sample shows how to use a ComboBox control with category names as a basis for navigating to rows in the Categories table from the Northwind database. In addition, the sample uses a PictureBox control to display category pictures on the sample form, *Form3* in the Form-ControlSamples project. Make *Form3* the startup object for your current project, and then copy the controls from the sample form to your version of *Form3* and copy the code behind the sample form to the module behind your sample form.

Adding Pictures to the Project Folder

You need to complete one more step before you can run the sample. This sample requires the .eps files for the category pictures in the root folder for your project folder. Within the Northwind database, the bitmap image representations reside in the Picture column of the Categories table. Although storing images in a database can be convenient, it can also slow down the performance of a database. Another approach that can make your application run faster is to store the images in your file system. As we've discussed earlier, the Access 2002 version of the Northwind database follows this approach for its employee pictures. Therefore, this sample depends on the category image files residing in files within the root project folder.

You can copy the image representations from the Picture column in the Categories table to the root folder of your current project folder by performing the following steps:

1. Select the Bitmap Image for the first row in the Categories table.

2. Right-click the image and choose Bitmap Image Object, Open; this opens the image in Microsoft Paint or your default processor for .eps files.

3. Save the image in the root folder for the current project directory with the filename catimp1.eps. For example, on the computer that I used for this sample, the path and filename is c:\pawvbnet\Form-ControlSamples\catimp1.eps.

4. Close the bitmap reader to return to the Categories table.

5. Repeat the process for the second and subsequent rows in the Categories tables while successively naming the file for each new image catimp2.eps, catimp3.eps, and so on.

Chapter 5   Fundamentals of Programming Windows Forms and Controls   **233**

6. Close the Categories table when you no longer need it open for copying image files.

The Design View of *Form3*

After completing the previous steps, you will be ready to demonstrate the application. However, before running the sample, I want to preview *Form3* in Design view as a point of reference for the form in operation because the code behind the form edits the layout in interesting ways. Figure 5-14 shows *Form3* in Design view with the PictureBox1 control selected. You can see from its Properties window that the size of PictureBox1 is 100 by 50 pixels. This is the default size of a PictureBox control dragged from the Toolbox to a form. However, this size will clip the category images because they have pixel width and height dimensions of 172 by 120. Although it is possible to alter the size at design time in the Properties window, this sample demonstrates the technique of using the code behind a form. This latter approach enables your applications to change a PictureBox size dynamically when the sizes of different images become available along with the image. Also note that *Form3* contains a couple of TextBox controls of default size. Regardless of whether it is obvious that the TextBox controls are of default size, the controls are clearly of the same size. Finally, *Form3* is a form of default dimensions (300 by 300 pixels).

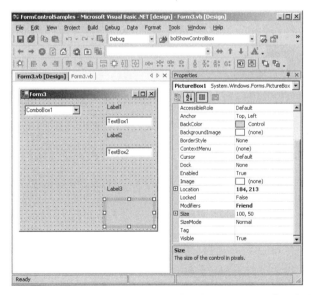

Figure 5-14   The Design view for *Form3* with a ComboBox control to specify the display contents for a couple of TextBox controls and a Picture-Box control

How *Form3* Operates

When *Form3* opens, it automatically shows the Category name for CategoryID equal to 1 in the ComboBox control because the code behind the form designates an initial selection for the ComboBox control. The two text boxes display the CategoryID value and the category description. (See Figure 5-15.) These text box values are also dependent on the specification of an initial selection for the ComboBox control because an event procedure for the ComboBox control determines *Text* property assignments for the TextBox controls. To display the full category description, you need to enlarge the size of *TextBox2*. In addition, the PictureBox control enlarges in the operational view of *Form3* as opposed to the Design view. The code behind *Form3* grows the PictureBox size dimensions to 172 by 120 pixels, the size of the category images. For the PictureBox to fit on *Form3* without clipping, its dimensions must grow as well. In this case, the code behind the form grows *Form3*'s dimensions to 375 by 375 pixels from the default size of 300 by 300 pixels.

Figure 5-15   An operational view of *Form3* after it initially opens with a resized form as well as PictureBox and TextBox controls

The point of this application is to enable a user to change the values displaying in the CategoryID and Description text boxes as well as the image showing in the PictureBox control. By clicking the down arrow in the combo box, a user can see the names of categories in a drop-down list. Selecting any name from the drop-down list updates the display in the TextBox and PictureBox controls to reflect the selected item.

The Code Behind *Form3*

The code behind *Form3* consists of a module-level declaration for an array object and two procedures. The array object, *ary_Cats*, stores the Categories table column values. This design feature allows the application to release its connection to the Northwind database after populating the array with Categories table column values. The application declares the array at the module level because the array gets used by both procedures in the application.

The *Form3_Load* procedure begins by making a connection to the Northwind database and creating a recordset based on the Categories table. If you have run either of the two preceding samples in this section, your project already has a reference to the *ADODB* library. If not, you might need to create a reference to the *ADODB* library. Next, the procedure iterates with a *For...Next* loop through the records of the recordset and copies their contents to the *ary_Cats* array declared at the module level. On each iteration through the loop, the code also uses the *Add* method for the *Items* collection of the ComboBox object (*ComboBox1*) to add category names to the combo box. This step enables the drop-down box in the combo box to show the category names. After the loop relinquishes control, the procedure closes and marks for removal the *Recordset* and *Connection* objects.

The remaining lines in the *Form3_Load* procedure format the form. These lines start by assigning *Text* property values for the label controls on *Form3*. Next, the code sets the *SelectedItem* property for *ComboBox1* to 0. This step (in coordination with the *ComboBox1_SelectedIndexChanged* procedure) causes the form to open, showing the data for the first category. *SelectedItem* index values are zero-based so that for a set of eight items, such as that in the Categories table, the index values range from 0 to 7.

Next the *Load* event procedure sets three properties for *TextBox2* so that it can display multiple lines and wrap the text. To display more than one line, the event procedure's *MultiLine* property must be *True* and its height (the second *Size* argument) must be greater than the default value of 20 pixels. A height setting of 50 pixels is sufficient for displaying three lines of text, which accommodate all the descriptions in the Categories table. When setting the height property of a TextBox control and selected other items, such as a PictureBox and a *Form* object, you need to designate the height setting along with the width setting as part of a *Size* specification. The next two lines show the same syntax for enlarging *PictureBox1* and *Form3* (*Me*). The specification for *Form3* shows the full name for the *Size* class. Because a Windows application already has a reference to the *System.Drawing* namespace, the full name for the *Size* class is not strictly necessary. However, some developers might prefer to designate it for the sake of clarity.

The second procedure, *ComboBox1_SelectedIndexChanged*, runs whenever the *SelectedIndex* value for *ComboBox1* changes. This happens whenever a user makes a selection or the program explicitly assigns a value to the *SelectedIndex* property for *ComboBox1*. The procedure uses the *SelectedIndex* value to designate items from the *ary_Cats* array to display in the two text boxes on *Form3*. The procedure also designates a filename that points at one of the image files, which in turn designates the image to display in *PictureBox1*.

```
'Dim statement for array
Dim ary_Cats(7, 3) As System.Object

Private Sub Form3_Load( _
    ByVal sender As System.Object, _
    ByVal e As System.EventArgs) _
    Handles MyBase.Load

    'Dim statement for database
    Dim cnn1 As New ADODB.Connection()
    Dim rst1 As New ADODB.Recordset()

    'Make connection to Northwind database.
    cnn1.Open("Provider=Microsoft.Jet.OLEDB.4.0;" & _
            "Data Source=C:\Program Files\" & _
            "Microsoft Office\Office10\" & _
            "Samples\Northwind.mdb;", _
            "Admin", "")

    'Open recordset for Categories table.
    Dim str1 As String = "SELECT * FROM Categories"
    With rst1
        .ActiveConnection = cnn1
        .Open(str1, , _
            ADODB.CursorTypeEnum.adOpenKeyset, _
            ADODB.LockTypeEnum.adLockOptimistic)
    End With

    'Declare array for Categories column
    'values and For...Next loop.
    Dim int1 As Integer

    'Populate ary_Cats array and ComboBox1.
    For int1 = 0 To rst1.RecordCount - 1
        ary_Cats(int1, 0) = CInt(rst1(0).Value)
        ary_Cats(int1, 1) = CStr(rst1(1).Value)
        ComboBox1.Items.Add(ary_Cats(int1, 1))
        ary_Cats(int1, 2) = CStr(rst1(2).Value)
        rst1.MoveNext()
    Next
```

```
        'Get rid of objects.
        rst1.Close()
        rst1 = Nothing
        cnn1.Close()
        cnn1 = Nothing

        'Assign label text property values.
        Label1.Text = "CategoryID"
        Label2.Text = "Description"
        Label3.Text = "Picture"

        'Initialize ComboBox1 to show first
        'category item.
        ComboBox1.SelectedIndex = 0

        'Set TextBox2 to show category description.
        TextBox2.Multiline = True
        TextBox2.WordWrap = True
        TextBox2.Size = New System.Drawing.Size(100, 50)

        'Size PictureBox control for category pictures; use
        'the full name for Size, including its namespace.
        PictureBox1.Size = New System.Drawing.Size(172, 120)

        'Resize form for PictureBox control.
        Me.Size = New Size(375, 375)

End Sub

Private Sub ComboBox1_SelectedIndexChanged( _
    ByVal sender As System.Object, _
    ByVal e As System.EventArgs) _
    Handles ComboBox1.SelectedIndexChanged

        'Assign array values matching selected
        'combo box item to text boxes.
        TextBox1.Text = _
            ary_Cats(ComboBox1.SelectedIndex, 0).ToString
        TextBox2.Text = _
            CStr(ary_Cats(ComboBox1.SelectedIndex, 2))

        'Compute address for category picture matching
        'selected combo box item and assign the picture
        'to the Image property for the PictureBox control.
        Dim str1 As String = _
            "..\catimp" & _
            ((ComboBox1.SelectedIndex) + 1).ToString & _
            ".eps"
        PictureBox1.Image = Image.FromFile(str1)

End Sub
```

Using One Form to Designate Data for a Second

All the database form samples to this point in the chapter involve a single form, but it is common to use multiple forms in database applications. For example, many database samples have what I refer to as a *pick-one form*, which allows a user to specify a value and then open a second form that lets him perform some task with the selected item, such as viewing detailed information about it on the preceding form, selecting from a subset according to the choice made on the first form, or changing some data for the selected item.

The sample in this section gives you a chance to see yet another control in operation. The pick-one form in this sample is *Form4* in the FormControlSamples project. This form contains a single combo box that lets a user pick a category by name. After the selection, *Form4* opens an instance of *Form5* and passes the *SelectedIndex* value for the category a user chose in the combo box. *Form5* shows a ListBox control populated exclusively with product names that belong to the category selected from *Form4*. When a user picks one of the products in the list box, the application uses three text boxes to show a subset of items from the Products table for that product.

Before attempting to run the sample, follow the standard steps described for the preceding samples. If you are running the application from the Form-ControlSamples project, remember to designate *Form4* as the startup object and make sure the project has a reference to the *ADODB* library on the computer used to run the application. If you are creating the sample from scratch, one easy approach is to use the Project, Add Windows Form command to add *Form4* and *Form5* to your project. Then, copy the controls from the versions of *Form4* and *Form5* in the FormControlSamples project to your project. Next, copy the code behind each form in the FormControlSamples project to the code modules in your project for the corresponding forms.

Figure 5-16 shows *Form4* as the left window after the selection of the Condiments category. This selection from the combo box automatically opens *Form5*, which will have its list box populated with products from the Condiments category. The right window in Figure 5-16 illustrates the TextBox control *Text* property settings after the selection of a product from the list box. You can open the Products table in the Northwind database to confirm that the three text boxes show the UnitsInStock, UnitsOnOrder, and ReorderLevel column values for the row with a ProductName column value equal to Grandma's Boysenberry Spread. Notice that the full name for the product does not display in the ListBox control. However, an optional horizontal scroll bar allows a user to scroll right to view the end of a product name. Two conditions need to be met for the horizontal scroll bar to appear. First, you have to set the *Horizontal-*

Scrollbar property for the ListBox control to *True*. Second, an item in the list box has to exceed the maximum width of the list box.

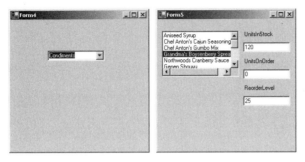

Figure 5-16   *Form4* and *Form5* work together in a single application within the FormControlSamples project so that a selection on *Form4* determines the entries in the list box on *Form5*.

The Code Behind the First Form

The code behind *Form4* is generally similar to that behind *Form3*, but the behavior of *Form4* is distinctive from that of *Form3* in several areas. For example, this code module uses a Boolean variable, *bolFirstTime*, to track whether this is the first time the form opened in a session. This is because the first time that the *ComboBox1_SelectedIndexChanged* procedure fires, this application needs to exit the procedure without executing all its code. However, on all subsequent invocations of the *ComboBox1_SelectedIndexChanged* procedure, the application needs to execute all the code in the procedure. In addition, an array does not need to store column values from the Categories table. In this application, only a single column of values is needed, and it is convenient to store these as items in the ComboBox control.

Under normal circumstances, the *ComboBox1_SelectedIndexChanged* procedure has two special roles that were not required in the application for *Form3*. First, the procedure passes the *SelectedIndex* property value from the ComboBox control to a field on *Form5*. Second, the procedure opens a form instance based on the *Form5* class.

```
'Declare a variable monitoring whether this is the
'first time the form opens in a session.
Dim bolFirstTime As Boolean = True

Private Sub Form4_Load(ByVal sender As System.Object, _
    ByVal e As System.EventArgs) Handles MyBase.Load
    'Dim statement for database
    Dim cnn1 As New ADODB.Connection()
```

(continued)

```
    Dim rst1 As New ADODB.Recordset()

    'Make connection to Northwind database.
    cnn1.Open("Provider=Microsoft.Jet.OLEDB.4.0;" & _
              "Data Source=C:\Program Files\" & _
              "Microsoft Office\Office10\" & _
              "Samples\Northwind.mdb;", _
              "Admin", "")

    'Open recordset for Categories table.
    Dim str1 As String = "SELECT CategoryName " & _
        "FROM Categories"
    With rst1
        .ActiveConnection = cnn1
        .Open(str1, , _
            ADODB.CursorTypeEnum.adOpenKeyset, _
            ADODB.LockTypeEnum.adLockOptimistic)
    End With

    'Declare array for Categories column
    'values and For...Next loop.
    Dim int1 As Integer

    'Populate ary_Cats array and ComboBox1.
    For int1 = 0 To rst1.RecordCount - 1
        ComboBox1.Items.Add( _
            CStr(rst1("CategoryName").Value))
        rst1.MoveNext()
    Next

    'Get rid of objects.
    rst1.Close()
    rst1 = Nothing
    cnn1.Close()
    cnn1 = Nothing

    'Initialize ComboBox1 to show first.
    'category item
    ComboBox1.SelectedIndex = 0

End Sub

Private Sub ComboBox1_SelectedIndexChanged( _
    ByVal sender As System.Object, _
    ByVal e As System.EventArgs) _
    Handles ComboBox1.SelectedIndexChanged

    'If this is the first time the procedure
```

```
'opens, toggle bolFirstTime and exit.
If bolFirstTime = True Then
    bolFirstTime = False
    Exit Sub
End If

'Open an instance of Form5 and pass the combo
'box SelectedIndex value from this form instance.
Dim frm1 As New Form5()
frm1.MainSelected = ComboBox1.SelectedIndex
frm1.Show()

End Sub
```

The Code Behind the Second Form

The code behind *Form5* in this application is again similar to the code behind *Form3*, but distinct differences also exist. For example, this form must accept a value from *Form4* and properly use it. *Form5* accepts a value from *Form4* by declaring a public variable, *MainSelected*, which *Form4* sets before showing *Form5*. *Form5* uses an array to store selected column values from the Products table, but *Form5* initially declares the array, *ary_Products*, without designating a specific number of rows and columns for the size of the array. This is because the application can specify only the number of rows in the array after populating a recordset based on the passed value to *Form5* from *Form4* and counting the rows in the recordset. A *ReDim* statement dynamically assigns the size of the *ary_Products* array when the information is available to accomplish the task.

Just one more distinctive feature of the code behind *Form5* exists, and it has to do with form layout issues as opposed to data issues. The ListBox control has a couple of lines specifying its properties. One of these is a statement assigning a width to the control. You want to use a wider setting than the default *Width* property value for the ListBox control to reduce as much as possible the need to scroll to view the end of product names. You do not need a *Size* setting when changing the width of a ListBox control. You can directly assign a scalar value representing the number of pixels over which you want the ListBox control's width to extend. The *HorizontalScrollbar* property takes a Boolean variable value to specify whether to show an optional horizontal scroll bar when at least one item in the list box exceeds the *Width* property setting for the list box.

Aside from these differences, *Form5* operates similarly to *Form3*. Instead of using a combo box to let a user make a selection, *Form5* offers a selection through a list box. However, the ListBox and ComboBox controls both have a *SelectedIndex* property value that operates the same way. Therefore, the application uses this property value to designate values to display from the array object in the text boxes on the form. In addition, both the ComboBox and ListBox controls share a *SelectedIndexChanged* event that can be used to determine when to revise the values showing in the text boxes.

```vb
Public MainSelected As Integer
Dim ary_Products(,) As System.Object

Private Sub Form5_Load(ByVal sender As System.Object, _
    ByVal e As System.EventArgs) Handles MyBase.Load

    'Dim statement for database
    Dim cnn1 As New ADODB.Connection()
    Dim rst1 As New ADODB.Recordset()

    'Make connection to Northwind database.
    cnn1.Open("Provider=Microsoft.Jet.OLEDB.4.0;" & _
              "Data Source=C:\Program Files\" & _
              "Microsoft Office\Office10\" & _
              "Samples\Northwind.mdb;", _
              "Admin", "")

    'Open recordset for subset of Products table.
    Dim str1 As String = "SELECT ProductName, " & _
        "UnitsInStock, UnitsOnOrder, " & _
        "ReorderLevel " & _
        "FROM Products " & _
        "WHERE CategoryID = " & _
        (MainSelected + 1).ToString

    With (rst1)
        .ActiveConnection = cnn1
        .Open(str1, , _
            ADODB.CursorTypeEnum.adOpenKeyset, _
            ADODB.LockTypeEnum.adLockOptimistic)
    End With

    'Iterate through selected recordset and assign
    'values to array; also, add Product names
    'to the list box.
    Dim int1 As Integer
    ReDim ary_Products(rst1.RecordCount - 1, 3)

    For int1 = 1 To rst1.RecordCount
        ary_Products(int1 - 1, 0) = _
            CStr(rst1("ProductName").Value)
```

```
            ListBox1.Items.Add( _
            ary_Products(int1 - 1, 0))
            ary_Products(int1 - 1, 1) = _
                CStr(rst1("UnitsInStock").Value)
            ary_Products(int1 - 1, 2) = _
                CStr(rst1("UnitsOnOrder").Value)
            ary_Products(int1 - 1, 3) = _
                CStr(rst1("ReorderLevel").Value)
            rst1.MoveNext()
        Next

        'Get rid of objects.
        rst1.Close()
        rst1 = Nothing
        cnn1.Close()
        cnn1 = Nothing

        'Set width and optional horizontal
        'scroll bar for the list box.
        ListBox1.Width = 165
        ListBox1.HorizontalScrollbar = True

        'Initialize text boxes and labels.
        TextBox1.Text = ""
        TextBox2.Text = ""
        TextBox3.Text = ""
        Label1.Text = "UnitsInStock"
        Label2.Text = "UnitsOnOrder"
        Label3.Text = "ReorderLevel"

End Sub

Private Sub ListBox1_SelectedIndexChanged( _
    ByVal sender As System.Object, _
    ByVal e As System.EventArgs) _
    Handles ListBox1.SelectedIndexChanged

    'Assign array values to text boxes.
    TextBox1.Text = _
        ary_Products(ListBox1.SelectedIndex, 1)
    TextBox2.Text = _
        ary_Products(ListBox1.SelectedIndex, 2)
    TextBox3.Text = _
        ary_Products(ListBox1.SelectedIndex, 3)

End Sub
```

Building a Switchboard Form with the LinkLabel Control

A switchboard form is a common type of application many Access database developers use. This form contains no database connections; instead, it passes control (or focus) to other forms in an application. This type of form acts as a switchboard to which applications can return control after completing a task so that users can switch to another task. Visual Basic .NET introduces a new type of control, a LinkLabel, that is particularly well suited for switchboard forms.

The LinkLabel control acts similarly to a hyperlink on a Web page, but you can use it to pass control to other forms within an application. Therefore, a collection of LinkLabel controls on a form can enable a form to serve as a switchboard form. A LinkLabel control can also start up the default browser on a computer and open a designated Web page with the browser. This feature enables Access application developers to readily incorporate Web pages on an intranet or the Internet directly into their application.

This next sample demonstrates how to use several LinkLabel control properties and one type of event to build a switchboard application. As you lay out a switchboard form, you must position and size the LinkLabel controls so that their *Text* property displays properly on the form. The *Text* property of a LinkLabel control (or a subset of characters within the *Text* property) offers a link for transferring control to another form or Web page. The *Text* property often describes why users should click the control. You can use the *Width* property of a LinkLabel control to designate the horizontal extent in pixels for displaying the *Text* property of a control on a form. The *Left* property for a LinkLabel control is an offset for designating the number of pixels between the left edge of the LinkLabel control and the left edge of the form in which the control resides. Failing to position LinkLabel controls with relatively long *Text* and *Width* property values far enough to the left can result in a form clipping the *Text* property when displaying the LinkLabel control.

The *LinkVisited* property is another interesting property. Setting this property to *True* causes the LinkLabel control to change color after a user initially clicks the control after the form opens. The transition in color occurs only once, the first time the LinkLabel control is clicked.

Note   The *LinkVisited* property for a LinkLabel control is *False* by default. You can use the *VisitedLinkColor* property to explicitly specify the color to which a link changes after a click. The default setting for the *VisitedLinkColor* property is different from the default color for a LinkLabel control.

Windows forms detect when a user clicks a LinkLabel control through the *LinkClicked* event. Because this is the default event for a LinkLabel control, double-clicking the control in Design view causes Visual Studio .NET to automatically build a *LinkClicked* event procedure shell.

The following switchboard sample relies on the availability of completed versions of the preceding four samples. If you do not have these samples conveniently available, you can demonstrate the operation of the sample by opening *Form6* in the FormControlSamples project. This code is available in the sample materials for this chapter. Make sure that *Form6* is the startup application for your project. *Form6* contains LinkLabel controls for switching the focus to the other four samples. In addition, a fifth LinkLabel control opens an Internet page describing my favorite seminar tour. Because the page resides on the Internet, your application needs an open connection to the Internet for the LinkLabel control to work. By contrasting the processing for this fifth LinkLabel control with the preceding four, you can see what special steps are necessary for working with a URL.

Figure 5-17 shows the switchboard form in Design view. As you can see, it consists of five evenly spaced LinkLabel controls placed down the center of the form. You can drag a LinkLabel control to a form from the Windows tab of the Toolbox just as you can with a Label control or a TextBox control. Visual Studio .NET numbers the LinkLabel controls by default in a sequential pattern just as it does with buttons. As with buttons and other types of controls, you can override the default *Name* property value. When you arrange controls on a form, you will often find the Layout toolbar in the IDE convenient. This toolbar contains many controls to make quick work of manually sizing, aligning, and spacing controls. For example, the toolbar has controls for increasing and decreasing the spacing between a set of controls as well as making the spacing between controls even. This toolbar's operation is highly intuitive. This book does not spend much time discussing the use of graphical layout aids such as the Layout toolbar because our focus is on programming techniques.

The following code listing shows the code behind the form appearing in Figure 5-17. The module behind the form contains a *Load* event procedure to reformat the LinkLabel controls from their default properties that show in Figure 5-17. The reformatting adds custom *Text* property settings to each LinkLabel control, and it sets the *Width* and *Left* properties of the controls to manage how the controls display on the form. Because the *Text* property settings are long, the *Width* setting is expanded from its default property. In addition, the *Left* property offset value is reduced so the LinkLabel controls are closer to the form's left edge than normal.

Figure 5-17 A Design view of a form with multiple LinkLabel controls that can serve as a switchboard form

One particularly interesting feature of the *Load* event procedure is the way it uses a *For...Each* loop to pass through the LinkLabel controls on the form. Because the loop passes through all controls on the form (*Me.Controls*), you need to filter only for LinkLabel controls. The procedure uses an *If...Then* statement with a condition based on the default name for the control type. A *Select...Case* statement within the loop assigns a custom *Text* property setting based on the sequential default names from *LinkLabel1* through *LinkLabel5*.

The code listing includes a separate *LinkClicked* event procedure for each of the five LinkLabel controls, but the first four of these (for LinkLabel1 through LinkLabel4) pass control to the *HandleLocalForms* procedure to complete the processing of the event. Before invoking the *HandleLocalForms* procedure, each of the four *LinkClicked* event procedures instantiates a local form instance, such as *Form1*. These form instances refer to *Form1* through *Form4* in the preceding four samples. The event procedures then pass the form instance along with the LinkLabel control to the *HandleLocalForms* procedure. This procedure opens the passed form and sets the *LinkVisited* property for the passed LinkLabel control to *True*, which changes the color for the link during a session.

The *LinkClicked* event procedure for *LinkLabel5* is slightly different from the other four LinkLabel controls because this LinkLabel control must open the default browser to point at a URL. Use the *Start* method of the *System.Diagnostic .Process* class to launch the default browser as a process. Passing a URL as the argument specifies the opening of the default browser. The second line in this *LinkClicked* event procedure marks the link as visited after the first click to the LinkLabel control in a session.

```
Private Sub Form6_Load(ByVal sender As System.Object, _
    ByVal e As System.EventArgs) Handles MyBase.Load

    'Loop through LinkLabel controls to reposition
    'and resize each control, and assign a custom
    'Text property value.
    Dim mylinklabel As LinkLabel
    Dim ctl1 As Control
    For Each ctl1 In Me.Controls
        If Mid(ctl1.Text, 1, 9) = "LinkLabel" Then
            mylinklabel = ctl1
            mylinklabel.Left = 50
            mylinklabel.Width = 225
            Select Case mylinklabel.Text
                Case "LinkLabel1"
                    LinkLabel1.Text = _
                        "TextBox Password Sample"
                Case "LinkLabel2"
                    LinkLabel2.Text = _
                        "TextBox Browsing Sample"
                Case "LinkLabel3"
                    LinkLabel3.Text = _
                        "ComboBox To Other Controls Sample"
                Case "LinkLabel4"
                    LinkLabel4.Text = _
                        "ComboBox To Other Form Sample"
                Case "LinkLabel5"
                    LinkLabel5.Text = _
                        "My Favorite Seminar Tour"
            End Select
        End If
    Next
End Sub

Private Sub LinkLabel1_LinkClicked( _
    ByVal sender As System.Object, _
    ByVal e As _
    System.Windows.Forms.LinkLabelLinkClickedEventArgs) _
    Handles LinkLabel1.LinkClicked

    'Instantiate new instance of Form1 from data samples
    'and pass form instance and LinkLabel control to
    'HandleLocalForms.
    Dim frm1 As New Form1()
    HandleLocalForms(frm1, LinkLabel1)

End Sub
```

(continued)

```
Private Sub LinkLabel2_LinkClicked( _
    ByVal sender As System.Object, _
    ByVal e As _
    System.Windows.Forms.LinkLabelLinkClickedEventArgs) _
    Handles LinkLabel2.LinkClicked

    'Instantiate new instance of Form2 from data samples
    'and pass form instance and LinkLabel control to
    'HandleLocalForms.
    Dim frm1 As New Form2()
    HandleLocalForms(frm1, LinkLabel2)

End Sub

Private Sub LinkLabel3_LinkClicked( _
    ByVal sender As System.Object, _
    ByVal e As _
    System.Windows.Forms.LinkLabelLinkClickedEventArgs) _
    Handles LinkLabel3.LinkClicked

    'Instantiate new instance of Form3 from data samples
    'and pass form instance and LinkLabel control to
    'HandleLocalForms.
    Dim frm1 As New Form3()
    HandleLocalForms(frm1, LinkLabel3)

End Sub

Private Sub LinkLabel4_LinkClicked( _
    ByVal sender As System.Object, _
    ByVal e As _
    System.Windows.Forms.LinkLabelLinkClickedEventArgs) _
    Handles LinkLabel4.LinkClicked

    'Instantiate new instance of Form4 from data samples
    'and pass form instance and LinkLabel control to
    'HandleLocalForms.
    Dim frm1 As New Form4()
    HandleLocalForms(frm1, LinkLabel4)

End Sub

Sub HandleLocalForms(ByVal frm As Form, _
    ByVal mylink As LinkLabel)
```

```
'Show passed form instance and mark
'link visited.
frm.Show()
mylink.LinkVisited = True

End Sub

Private Sub LinkLabel5_LinkClicked( _
    ByVal sender As System.Object, _
    ByVal e As _
    System.Windows.Forms.LinkLabelLinkClickedEventArgs) _
    Handles LinkLabel5.LinkClicked

    'Open the default browser for a designated URL and
    'mark link visited.
    System.Diagnostics.Process.Start( _
        "http://www.programmingmsaccess.com/seminar2002/")
    LinkLabel5.LinkVisited = True

End Sub
```

Figure 5-18 shows the switchboard application in operation. The form on the left depicts how the switchboard form looks just after a user clicks LinkLabel3. You'll notice when you run this program that the color of this link changes relative to the color of the other LinkLabel controls on the form that have not been clicked yet. The form to the right shows the *Form3* sample after it has just opened. This is the form to which LinkLabel3 passes control.

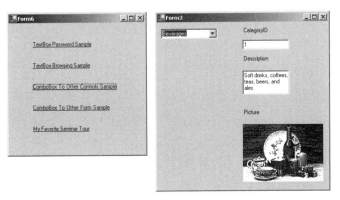

Figure 5-18   The LinkLabel switchboard sample in operation after a click to LinkLabel3

Summary

This chapter introduces the basics of using Windows Forms in Visual Basic .NET applications. In particular, it highlights using code-behind forms. One piece of sample code in the initial section illustrates how to persist the state of a form between sessions. You also learn how to open one form from another and coordinate the operation of the two forms by exchanging data between two form instances. Many Access developers will consider the most important feature of this chapter its demonstration of techniques for using Access databases with Windows Forms controls. The chapter demonstrates techniques for password validation, data browsing, combo box navigation within and between forms, and image file processing. It also presents a classic switchboard processing sample implemented with the Visual Basic .NET LinkLabel control.

6

Programming Windows Forms: Building on Fundamentals

This chapter builds on the introduction to Microsoft Windows forms and controls presented in Chapter 5 by focusing on how to populate controls with Microsoft Access database information using graphical ADO.NET development techniques. The programming samples in this chapter emphasize how to make form controls interact with ADO.NET components that you drag to your form either from Server Explorer or the Data tab of the Toolbox. The sample code also highlights techniques for making form controls interactive by managing their property settings and handling their events. In addition, you will learn how to process the data behind your controls on Windows forms.

A significant portion of the chapter demonstrates several ways to work with an Access database by using the Data Form Wizard. This powerful wizard enables you to graphically create data-bound forms. With the wizard, you can generate forms with two types of data-bound controls in various configurations that draw on both tables and queries from Access databases. In addition, you can create a main/sub form. One of the major advantages of using the Data

Form Wizard is that you do not have to write code for forms, data access, or data manipulation. However, the wizard generates Windows forms that enable the display and manipulation of data via standard Microsoft Visual Basic .NET and ADO.NET programming techniques. Therefore, by examining the code behind the forms that the wizard generates, you can see programming samples of data access and manipulation as well as form layout. Access developers can tap these samples as a helpful starting point for developing their own custom solutions.

Navigation and Data Source Assignment Issues

Forms are the windows into your Access database applications. Users interact with forms to view data and change it. Chapter 5 introduced techniques based on the *ADODB library* and the COM Interop feature for working with data through forms. This section shows you another way—one based on ADO.NET—to enable your forms to perform data access tasks. Although the samples in this section do use code, the easiest approach to creating ADO.NET objects is almost exclusively graphical. Visual Basic .NET merely manages the controls on a form and determines how those controls interact with ADO.NET objects.

Switchboard Form for Samples

One way to appreciate the scope of this section and to reinforce skills introduced in Chapter 5 is to start by reviewing the switchboard form for the five samples in this section. All the projects in the section reside in the NavigationandAssignment project. Figure 6-1 shows *Form1*, the project's startup object. As you can see, the application opens to a series of LinkLabel controls on the startup switchboard form. The form includes links to five other forms that demonstrate selected data source navigation and assignment issues. The switchboard form in Figure 6-1 enables a user to open each sample form as a dialog box. When the user clicks a link on the switchboard to open a sample form, the switchboard form hides and the sample form replaces it on the user's desktop. Then, when the user closes a sample form, the switchboard form is displayed again and the selected link for the previously opened sample form has the appearance of a visited link.

Figure 6-1   The switchboard form for the NavigationandAssignment project

This switchboard application differs slightly from the sample at the close of Chapter 5. (See *Form6* in the FormControlSamples project.) In that chapter's switchboard sample, the switchboard form did not become invisible when a sample opened. Neither switchboard design—the one in this chapter and the one in Chapter 5—is "right." The two switchboard samples merely illustrate different ways of tackling the same problem. The design in this chapter forces the focus on one sample at a time by using the *ShowDialog* method to open a sample form. The design in Chapter 5 used the *Show* method for opening a sample form. Using the *ShowDialog* method in combination with hiding the switchboard form draws attention to a sample form. This coding technique makes the sample form the only form to appear on the desktop. No other form can have focus until the user closes the sample form.

The full listing makes it easy for you to see the steps for designing this kind of application in context. Because this sample borrows many design guidelines from the switchboard sample in Chapter 5, the listing that follows uses boldface to highlight two special sections of the code. First, the *Text* property assignments for the LinkLabel controls succinctly remind you of the topics that the remaining samples in this section tackle. The form in Figure 6-1 reflects these assignments. Second, the *PassandRecoverControl* procedure in this sample replaces the *HandleLocalForms* procedure from the corresponding sample at the close of Chapter 5. The *PassandRecoverControl* procedure manages the appearance of forms for the NavigationandAssignment project.

```
Private Sub Form1_Load(ByVal sender As System.Object, _
    ByVal e As System.EventArgs) Handles MyBase.Load
    'Loop through LinkLabel controls to reposition
    'and resize each control, and assign a custom
    'Text property value.
    Dim mylinklabel As LinkLabel
    Dim ctl1 As Control
    For Each ctl1 In Me.Controls
        If Mid(ctl1.Text, 1, 9) = "LinkLabel" Then
            mylinklabel = ctl1
            mylinklabel.Left = 50
            mylinklabel.Width = 225
            Select Case mylinklabel.Text
                Case "LinkLabel1"
                    LinkLabel1.Text = _
                        "TextBox Navigation"
                Case "LinkLabel2"
                    LinkLabel2.Text = _
                        "TextBox Navigation and Formatting"
                Case "LinkLabel3"
                    LinkLabel3.Text = _
                        "ComboBox Navigation"
                Case "LinkLabel4"
                    LinkLabel4.Text = _
                        "Add 1 Data Source to DataGrid"
                Case "LinkLabel5"
                    LinkLabel5.Text = _
                        "Add 1 of 3 Data Sources to DataGrid"
            End Select
        End If
    Next

End Sub

Private Sub LinkLabel1_LinkClicked( _
    ByVal sender As System.Object, _
    ByVal e As _
    System.Windows.Forms.LinkLabelLinkClickedEventArgs) _
    Handles LinkLabel1.LinkClicked

    Dim frm1 As New Form2()
    PassandRecoverControl(frm1, LinkLabel1)

End Sub

Private Sub LinkLabel2_LinkClicked( _
    ByVal sender As System.Object, _
```

```
    ByVal e As _
    System.Windows.Forms.LinkLabelLinkClickedEventArgs) _
    Handles LinkLabel2.LinkClicked

    Dim frm1 As New Form3()
    PassandRecoverControl(frm1, LinkLabel2)

End Sub

Private Sub LinkLabel3_LinkClicked( _
    ByVal sender As System.Object, _
    ByVal e As _
    System.Windows.Forms.LinkLabelLinkClickedEventArgs) _
    Handles LinkLabel3.LinkClicked

    Dim frm1 As New Form4()
    PassandRecoverControl(frm1, LinkLabel3)

End Sub

Private Sub LinkLabel4_LinkClicked( _
    ByVal sender As System.Object, _
    ByVal e As _
    System.Windows.Forms.LinkLabelLinkClickedEventArgs) _
    Handles LinkLabel4.LinkClicked

    Dim frm1 As New Form5()
    PassandRecoverControl(frm1, LinkLabel4)

End Sub

Private Sub LinkLabel5_LinkClicked( _
    ByVal sender As System.Object, _
    ByVal e As _
    System.Windows.Forms.LinkLabelLinkClickedEventArgs) _
    Handles LinkLabel5.LinkClicked

    Dim frm1 As New Form6()
    PassandRecoverControl(frm1, LinkLabel5)

End Sub

Sub PassandRecoverControl(ByVal frm1 As Form, _
    ByVal mylinklabel As LinkLabel)

    Me.Hide()
    frm1.ShowDialog()
    Me.Visible = True
    mylinklabel.LinkVisited = True

End Sub
```

Navigation with Text Boxes

The sample in this section demonstrates how to navigate through a table in an ADO.NET dataset with text boxes and four buttons for moving to the first, previous, next, or last row. The focus is on the form design and application management issues as opposed to the database issues. This is because the book reserves an in-depth look at ADO.NET until Chapters 7 through 9. To make the discussion of forms and their controls as relevant as possible to Access developers, I cover the topic relative to the familiar Northwind Access database.

Chapter 5 presented a sample form (Form1 in the FormControlSamples project) for navigating through data with text boxes, but this sample form deviates from that chapter's sample in a couple of ways. The first—and by far the most important—way this sample differs from the one in the previous chapter is in the style of connecting to a data source. The sample in Chapter 5 uses the ADODB library through the COM Interop feature. Therefore, it connects to the Northwind database via an ActiveX Data Objects (ADO) Connection object and pulls data from an ADO Recordset object. The corresponding sample in this chapter binds the form to the Northwind database via OleDbConnection and OleDbDataAdapter objects. The OleDbConnection object links the form to the Northwind database. The OleDbDataAdapter object can transfer data back and forth between the remote database file and a local DataSet object. You can optionally program an OleDbDataAdapter instance to serve as a one-way or a two-way link between a database file and your form. Actually, the form does not bind to a data source within an Access database file. Instead, the form binds to a local DataSet object populated by the OleDbDataAdapter object.

The second way that this sample differs from its Chapter 5 counterpart is by using a different data source within the Northwind database. The data source for this sample is the Orders table, while the sample in the previous chapter used the Shippers table. By performing data access with various objects, you reinforce and grow your mastery of Visual Basic .NET data processing techniques.

ADO.NET features two approaches to binding a data source to the controls on a Windows form: *simple binding* and *complex binding*. With simple binding, a property for a control binds to an element in a dataset, such as a column of values in a table. With complex binding, you can link multiple elements from a dataset to a control, such as a DataGrid control. Unlike simple binding, complex binding allows you to link more than one *DataSet* element with a control.

The Design View of the Sample Application

The sample in this section demonstrates simple binding. A Windows form (*Form2*) with two text boxes, corresponding labels, and four buttons enables basic navigation features, such as moving to the next row. See the Design view of the form in Figure 6-2. I will describe later other windows appearing in the figure besides the one containing *Form2*. Two text boxes, one for OrderID and a second for freight charges, can show values from *DataSet* elements bound to them. Nothing in the Design view of the form indicates what values a text box shows. The management of the form controls occurs in the code behind the form.

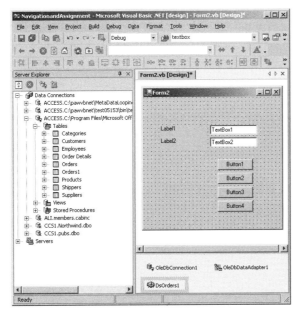

Figure 6-2   The Design view of a form for basic navigation through *DataSet* elements bound to the *Text* property of each TextBox control

Although you can manually edit a form in Design view (as you can see by looking at Server Explorer and the ADO.NET objects in the tray below the form), performing the tasks with code offers important advantages. Using the code behind the form allows you to document design features in an easy-to-read format that travels with the form. In addition, using code is more flexible than manually editing because you can dynamically change the *DataSet* element at run time to which a control links.

> **Note** To link a control such as *TextBox1* to a *DataSet* element at design time, you need to know the name of the dataset and the table within it containing the column that you want to link to the control. For example, you might want to link the OrderID column from the Orders table in a dataset named *DsOrders1*. Select a text box such as *TextBox1* to make its properties available through the Properties window. Then, expand the *DataBindings* property, and click the down arrow across from the control's *Text* property. Click OrderID from the Orders branch of the *DsOrders1* root. This enters *DsOrders1 – Orders.OrderID* as the *DataBinding* expression for the *Text* property of *TextBox1*. The default *DataBinding* property for the *Text* property of a TextBox control is *(None)*.

The code in this sample depends on three ADO.NET objects that you create graphically in the *Form2* Design view. These objects are instances of the *OleDbConnection*, *OleDbDataAdapter*, and *DataSet* classes. You can add *OleDbConnection* and *OleDbDataAdapter* instances by dragging a table or view from Server Explorer to your form. Choose View, Server Explorer to open Server Explorer. For this sample application, select the Orders table in the connection for the Northwind database. If you do not already have a connection to the Northwind database, see the "Adding a Data Connection to Server Explorer" sidebar in Chapter 2 for step-by-step instructions on how to create a new connection for an Access database file. After selecting the table in the Server Explorer window, drag the table and drop it in *Form2*. This adds *OleDbConnection* and *OleDbDataAdapter* instances to a tray below your form. If these steps create the first instance for each object, they will have the names *OleDbConnection1* and *OleDbDataAdapter1*.

You can create a *DataSet* object instance by right-clicking *OleDbDataAdapter1* and choosing Generate Dataset. In the text box next to the radio button with a label of New, enter **DsOrders** and click OK. This adds the *DsOrders1* object variable to the tray below *Form2*, and it adds a *DataSet* object named *DsOrders* to Class view in Solution Explorer. The *DsOrders1* object in the tray points at the dataset depicted in Solution Explorer. Figure 6-2 shows the Server Explorer window to the left of the Design view for *Form2* immediately after the addition of the *DsOrders1* object variable to *Form2*.

The Code View of the Sample Application

The code module behind the form appearing in Figure 6-2 includes five event procedures: one for each of the navigation buttons below the two text boxes, and a form load event procedure that sets up the application. The form load event procedure performs two kinds of tasks. First, it makes the data available for the application. Second, the procedure assigns *Text* property settings to the buttons and labels on the form.

You should be familiar with the process for making *Text* property assignments by now, but the process of linking form controls to a data source is relatively new at this point in the book. Before I describe the code, note that you need to have the *OleDbConnection1*, *OleDbDataAdapter1*, and *DsOrders1* objects created by a process similar to the one just described . You'll learn how to create these objects programmatically in Chapter 7.

With any ADO.NET application using a disconnected dataset, such as the one that the *DsOrders1* variable points at, you need to start by populating the dataset. Use the *Fill* method for the data adapter that services the dataset. In this case, the *OleDbDataAdapter1* object provides data to the *DsOrders* dataset. The *Fill* method creates a table named Orders in the dataset with the same column values as the Orders table in the Northwind database file. The dataset contains a snapshot of the Orders table from the database file taken at the time that your application invokes the *Fill* method.

> **Note**   ADO.NET features disconnected datasets to improve scalability. The disconnected aspect of a dataset has several important implications for how you use it, which Chapter 7 discusses more completely. For now, just realize that this application sets up a local dataset containing a copy of the Orders table from the Northwind database file.

After creating a local version of the Orders table, the application needs to link form controls to the OrderID and Freight columns in the table. You can accomplish this task with the *Add* method for the *ControlBindingsCollection* class, which is accessible through a control's *DataBindings* property. Each data binding element specifies the link between a form control and a data source element. Data binding elements hierarchically relate to form controls, such as text boxes. By invoking the *Add* method for the *DataBindings* collection property, the procedure specifies a new data binding element for a control. In the case of *TextBox1*, the procedure links the OrderID column in the local Orders table to the *Text* property value. The procedure also links the *Text* property for *TextBox2* to the Freight column.

The *BindingContext* class applies to a control container, such as a Windows *Form* instance. Although you apply a data binding element to an individual property for a control, the *BindingContext* class can refer to the whole form—not the individual controls on the form. Any one form can have multiple *BindingContext* class instances; the .NET documentation refers to these individual instances as *BindingManagerBase* objects. The *BindingContext* property for a control, such as *Me.BindingContext*, returns a *BindingManagerBase* object. This sample uses a single *BindingContext* instance based on the Orders table in the dataset at which the *DsOrders1* variable points. The sample code uses the *Position* property of the *BindingManagerBase* object representing the *BindingContext* instance to specify navigation for the values that appear in the TextBox controls on the form. *Position* property values extend from 0 through 1 minus the *Count* property value for a *BindingManagerBase* object. Therefore, assigning a value of 0 to the *Position* property moves the current object to the first row in the Orders table. Similarly, setting the *Position* property to the *Count* property value of the *BindingContext* instance minus 1 moves the current object to the last row in the Orders table. Adding or subtracting 1 to or from the *Position* value moves the current object forward or backward one row in the Orders table.

Note   When writing expressions for ADO.NET navigation, you do not need an out-of-bounds trap as you do with the ADO *Recordset* objects.

```
Private Sub Form2_Load( _
    ByVal sender As Object, _
    ByVal e As System.EventArgs) _
    Handles MyBase.Load

    'Fill DsOrders1 dataset.
    OleDbDataAdapter1.Fill(DsOrders1)

    'Add data binds to Text property of each text box.
    TextBox1.DataBindings.Add( _
        "Text", DsOrders1, "Orders.OrderID")
```

```vb
    TextBox2.DataBindings.Add( _
        "Text", DsOrders1, "Orders.Freight")

    'Assign Text property values to buttons.
    Button1.Text = "First"
    Button2.Text = "Previous"
    Button3.Text = "Next"
    Button4.Text = "Last"

    'Assign Text property values to labels.
    Label1.Text = "OrderID"
    Label2.Text = "Freight"

End Sub

Private Sub Button1_Click(ByVal sender As Object, _
    ByVal e As EventArgs) Handles Button1.Click

    'Move to first position.
    Me.BindingContext(DsOrders1, "Orders").Position _
        = 0

End Sub

Private Sub Button2_Click(ByVal sender As Object, _
    ByVal e As EventArgs) Handles Button2.Click

    'Move to previous position.
    Me.BindingContext(DsOrders1, "Orders").Position _
        -= 1

End Sub

Private Sub Button3_Click(ByVal sender As System.Object, _
    ByVal e As System.EventArgs) Handles Button3.Click

    'Move to next position.
    Me.BindingContext(DsOrders1, "Orders").Position _
        += 1

End Sub

Private Sub Button4_Click(ByVal sender As System.Object, _
    ByVal e As System.EventArgs) Handles Button4.Click

    'Move to last position.
    Me.BindingContext(DsOrders1, "Orders").Position = _
        Me.BindingContext(DsOrders1, "orders").Count - 1

End Sub
```

The Solution in Action

You can launch the navigation application in *Form2* by running the NavigationandAssignment project. This automatically starts the switchboard form shown in Figure 6-1. Click the first hyperlink to start the text box navigation sample in *Form2*. The window on the left in Figure 6-3 shows how the sample opens. It displays the OrderID and Freight column values in the first row of the Orders table. Clicking the Next button navigates to the second row. From that point, a click to the Last button moves the current object for the *BindingContext* class instance to the final row in the Orders table.

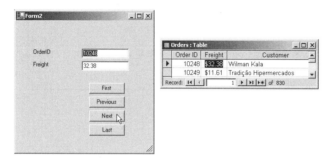

Figure 6-3 The text box navigation sample based on a dataset in operation with comparison values from the Northwind database

The window on the right in Figure 6-3 displays the first pair of rows in the OrderID and Freight columns from the Orders table in the Northwind database. This Datasheet view from Access should help you recognize the OrderID and Freight values in *Form2*. Unless these values or those in the dataset get modified after the sample application populates the Orders table in the dataset, the Orders column values in both sources will be identical. Because this sample makes no changes, you can confirm the form values by checking them against the values from the Orders table datasheet in the Northwind database.

Adding Formatting to TextBox Navigation

The preceding sample demonstrates the basics of navigation through a dataset, but most applications require more than that sample delivers. The next sample refines the preceding one in a couple of ways. First, it formats the content of both text boxes so that they appear right justified. Second, the application presents the contents of the text box showing Freight column values formatted based on the Currency specification in the Regional Options or Regional Settings dialog box of your Windows installation. Understanding the code behind these two simple design enhancements will provide you with the foundation you need to begin making a broader range of adjustments to your form applications.

> **Note**   You can modify the currency format for the Freight column values by altering settings of the Regional Settings in Control Panel for a Windows installation. If you have an international application, you need to account for the likelihood that these regional settings will vary by country.

The form design for this application is identical to the one in the preceding sample. The difference is in how the data looks on the form; this is because of the code behind the form. Figure 6-4 shows the refined application as it opens. Notice this application resides on *Form3*. You can launch it from the second option on the switchboard application on *Form1* in the Navigationand-Assignment project. Contrast the window in Figure 6-4 with the top left one in Figure 6-3. The right justification and the currency formatting are typical of a normal database development project.

Figure 6-4   The text box navigation sample enhanced with right justification and currency formatting

Before you can run the code, you must add the connection, data adapter, and *DataSet* object variables to the form. If you already created these objects for *Form2*, you can select them on that form and paste them into *Form3*. This opens a tray below *Form3* for the three ADO.NET objects. The *DsOrders1* object variable in *Form3* points at the same *DsOrders DataSet* object as the one in *Form2*. You can share a *DataSet* object across multiple forms throughout a project.

The following listing shows the code behind *Form3*. The refinements to the code behind *Form2* appear in boldface. The two formatting refinements have different points of application. You implement justification via a TextBox control property. Specifically, you assign a value to the *TextAlign* property for a TextBox control. Use the *HorizontalAlignment* enumeration to designate that text alignment at the left, center, or right of a TextBox control. Once you set the alignment for a text box, the setting remains until you designate a new one. Both the list of properties for a control and the range of enumeration values available for setting a property pop up automatically in a code window because of IntelliSense. Look up the *TextBox* class in the Microsoft Visual Studio .NET documentation for summaries of all its class members. Links let you drill down and get more detailed information, which occasionally includes code samples.

The sample application makes the *HorizontalAlignment.Right* assignment in the form load event. This position for the alignment assignment allows the setting to persist throughout the lifetime of the form instance or until another assignment statement resets the *TextAlign* property. The *Format* function in the form load event procedure serves a slightly different purpose. This function applies to the current *Text* property setting of a text box. When the application assigns a new value to the *Text* property setting, you need to reassign the *Format* function if you want the result to appear with the regional currency settings. Therefore, the *Format* function appears in the form load event to assign currency formatting to the value appearing in *TextBox2* when *Form3* initially opens. In addition, the *Format* function appears in the click event procedure for each button on the form. This assigns currency formatting to the new value appearing in *TextBox2* after the *BindingContext* instance repopulates the text box with a new row from the Orders table within the dataset that the *DsOrders1* variable points at.

```
Private Sub Form3_Load( _
    ByVal sender As Object, _
    ByVal e As System.EventArgs) _
    Handles MyBase.Load

    'Fill DsOrders1 dataset.
    OleDbDataAdapter1.Fill(DsOrders1)

    'Add data binds to Text property of each text box.
    TextBox1.DataBindings.Add( _
        "Text", DsOrders1, "Orders.OrderID")
    TextBox2.DataBindings.Add( _
        "Text", DsOrders1, "Orders.Freight")

    'Format text boxes.
```

```vb
    TextBox1.TextAlign = HorizontalAlignment.Right
    TextBox2.TextAlign = HorizontalAlignment.Right
    TextBox2.Text = Format(TextBox2.Text, "Currency")

    'Assign Text property values to buttons.
    Button1.Text = "First"
    Button2.Text = "Previous"
    Button3.Text = "Next"
    Button4.Text = "Last"

    'Assign Text property values to labels.
    Label1.Text = "OrderID"
    Label2.Text = "Freight"

End Sub

Private Sub Button1_Click(ByVal sender As Object, _
    ByVal e As EventArgs) Handles Button1.Click

    'Move to first position and format for currency.
    Me.BindingContext(DsOrders1, "Orders").Position _
        = 0
    TextBox2.Text = Format(TextBox2.Text, "Currency")

End Sub

Private Sub Button2_Click(ByVal sender As Object, _
    ByVal e As EventArgs) Handles Button2.Click

    'Move to previous position and format for currency.
    Me.BindingContext(DsOrders1, "Orders").Position _
        -= 1
    TextBox2.Text = Format(TextBox2.Text, "Currency")

End Sub

Private Sub Button3_Click(ByVal sender As System.Object, _
    ByVal e As System.EventArgs) Handles Button3.Click

    'Move to next position and format for currency.
    Me.BindingContext(DsOrders1, "Orders").Position _
        += 1
    TextBox2.Text = Format(TextBox2.Text, "Currency")

End Sub
```

(continued)

```
Private Sub Button4_Click(ByVal sender As System.Object, _
    ByVal e As System.EventArgs) Handles Button4.Click

    'Move to last position and format for currency.
    Me.BindingContext(DsOrders1, "Orders").Position = _
        Me.BindingContext(DsOrders1, "orders").Count - 1
    TextBox2.Text = Format(TextBox2.Text, "Currency")

End Sub
```

ComboBox Navigation

A common means of navigating through the rows in a data source is by using a combo box. Users can make a selection from a combo box. Then, the form populates text boxes with values that correspond to the selected value from the combo box. The sample in this section lets a user pick an OrderID value from a combo box. The code behind the form automatically populates the text boxes with the ShipCountry and Freight column values from the Orders table for the row with the selected OrderID value. The form initially opens with the combo box displaying the OrderID for the first row in the Orders table and the text boxes displaying the ShipCountry and Freight column values from that row. Figure 6-5 shows *Form4* in the NavigationandAssignment project displaying values from the first row in the Orders table with a selection for the third row in process. After the selection, the combo box will display 10250, and the text boxes will show ShipCountry and Freight column values from the third row in the Orders table.

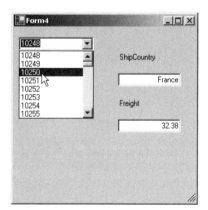

Figure 6-5 Enabling navigation with a combo box can provide your Visual Basic .NET applications with a popular feature.

The Design view for the application includes form controls in a layout corresponding to the arrangement in Figure 6-5. You can drag the controls from the Windows Forms tab of the Toolbox to the form. In addition, you need ADO.NET connection, data adapter, and *DataSet* objects on the form. You can copy these objects from either of the preceding two sample applications or create the objects from scratch if this is the first sample you are implementing. See the discussion of the immediately preceding sample for directions on copying the objects and the discussion of the earlier sample for directions on creating the object references from scratch.

The ComboBox control has a different form of data binding than the TextBox control. With a ComboBox control, you implement complex binding. Despite its name, complex binding is easy to program. All you have to do is set the *DataSource* property for the control equal to the table in the local dataset that you want to use as the source of data for a form. You must additionally specify which column from a data source the combo box should display when a user expands that combo box. Use a ComboBox control's *DisplayMember* property to specify a display column from the data source for a combo box.

After you initialize a combo box, the .NET Framework offers many members that help you control and monitor the performance of a combo box on a Windows form. One of the most important of these is the *SelectedIndex* property. This zero-based value reflects the row corresponding to the currently selected item. When you open a new instance of *Form4*, as in Figure 6-5, the *SelectedIndex* property value is 0. After completing the selection depicted in the figure, the *SelectedIndex* property changes to 2. Once a user makes a selection from a combo box, the ComboBox raises the *SelectedIndexChanged* event. You can use this event to program actions that must take place after a selection is made from the combo box, such as the repopulating of the text boxes for ShipCountry and Freight.

The following listing shows the code behind *Form4* to implement the features of the application. As is typical of ADO.NET applications, this application's code starts by invoking the *Fill* method for a data adapter. The *OleDbDataAdapter1* object in the sample populates the Orders table in the dataset at which the *DsOrders1* variable points. The *OleDbConnection1* object (not visible in this code listing—see the sample file for this setting) designates the Access database file that serves as the source for the local table.

> **Note** All the graphical samples for specifying data adapters in this book use Server Explorer. You can also drag onto a form an unconfigured data adapter from the Toolbox. The Visual Studio .NET IDE includes a built-in Data Adapter Configuration Wizard for customizing the configuration of a data adapter from either source. Although this wizard works properly in certain circumstances, it fails reliably in others for Access databases. For example, you cannot create an inner join for three tables directly from the Data Adapter Configuration Wizard. (By the way, this problem does not exist for Microsoft SQL Server databases.) Therefore, you should consider building your queries within Access and then dragging them from Server Explorer. You can also create your queries with ADO (or the *ADODB* library) directly with Jet SQL.

After populating the local Orders table in the form load event procedure, the code assigns the table to the *DataSource* property for *ComboBox1*. To make the combo box function properly, you must designate a *DisplayMember* property value. The code uses the OrderID column values for this purpose. The syntax for the statement reveals that the *Columns* collection depends on the *Tables* collection within a *DataSet* object. (The *DataSet* object is part of the ADO.NET object model, which Chapter 7 explores much more thoroughly, but I'll briefly explain a few ADO.NET features used in this chapter as we go.

The form load event procedure invokes the *PopulateTextBoxes* procedure immediately after setting *DataSource* and *DisplayMember* property values for *ComboBox1*. This procedure sets the two text boxes on *Form4*. The procedure selects a row from the Orders table in the dataset at which the *DsOrders1* variable points. The selection process involves saving a row from the Orders table in an ADO.NET *DataRow* object. By passing a value of 0 in the form load event procedure, the sample code assigns values for the first row in the Orders table. The *ComboBox1_SelectedIndexChanged* event procedure also invokes the *PopulateTextBoxes* procedure. In this second case, the event procedure passes the recently updated *SelectedIndex* property value for *ComboBox1*. This single line of code in the event procedure synchronizes the text boxes with the combo box whenever a user makes a selection from the combo box.

```
Private Sub Form4_Load(ByVal sender As System.Object, _
    ByVal e As System.EventArgs) Handles MyBase.Load
```

```vb
    'Fill DsOrders1 dataset.
    OleDbDataAdapter1.Fill(DsOrders1, "Orders")

    'Bind ComboBox1 and display first member.
    ComboBox1.DataSource = DsOrders1.Tables("Orders")
    ComboBox1.DisplayMember = _
        DsOrders1.Tables("Orders").Columns("OrderID").ToString

    'Populate text boxes with matching values.
    PopulateTextBoxes(0)

    'Format text boxes.
    TextBox1.TextAlign = HorizontalAlignment.Right
    TextBox2.TextAlign = HorizontalAlignment.Right
    TextBox2.Text = Format(TextBox2.Text, "Currency")

    'Assign Text property for labels.
    Label1.Text = "ShipCountry"
    Label2.Text = "Freight"

End Sub

Private Sub ComboBox1_SelectedIndexChanged( _
    ByVal sender As System.Object, _
    ByVal e As System.EventArgs) _
    Handles ComboBox1.SelectedIndexChanged

    'Populate text boxes with matching values.
    PopulateTextBoxes(ComboBox1.SelectedIndex)

End Sub

Sub PopulateTextBoxes(ByVal RowID As Integer)

    'Assign Text property values for text boxes based on
    'RowID value for a row in the Orders table within the
    'dataset at which the DsOrders1 variable points.
    Dim drw1 As DataRow = _
        DsOrders1.Tables("Orders").Rows(RowID)
    TextBox1.Text = drw1("ShipCountry")
    TextBox2.Text = drw1("Freight")

End Sub
```

Dynamically Formatting a DataGrid Control

The DataGrid control offers many options for formatting its contents and display. The Visual Basic .NET DataGrid control behaves somewhat similarly to the

Datasheet view for a table or query in Access and the DataGrid control from classic Visual Basic. However, both of these have important distinctions from the .NET DataGrid control. The "DataGrid Control Changes in Visual Basic .NET" topic in the Microsoft Visual Studio .NET documentation details a long list of specific changes. My recommendation is to approach the Visual Basic .NET DataGrid control as a new control with functionality you're already familiar with. Accept the fact that you have to learn how to use the control through its properties, methods, and events just as you would for any object. The next two samples will introduce you to some typical uses and techniques for manipulating the control.

The sample for this section opens a form without automatically populating any controls on the form with data. The form, *Form5*, includes four controls—a button, a pair of radio buttons, and a data grid. Clicking the button loads data into the grid. In fact, whenever you click the button, the application automatically refreshes the contents of the DataGrid control with the most current data from the Access database file supplying the control with data through a local dataset. Although the Button control lets a user modify the contents of the DataGrid control, the RadioButton controls enable a user to alter the look of the data in the DataGrid control by adding or removing a background color to every other row.

Figure 6-6 shows *Form5* when the sample application for this section opens. Notice that the data grid below the Button control and the two RadioButton controls is not populated. The DataGrid control fills when the user clicks the Load Grid button. This window also has its RadioButton controls disabled. Because you can't modify the appearance of the data in the grid until after the data appears, it makes sense to disable a set of controls that modify the look of the application.

Figure 6-6 The DataGrid is initially empty to show that you can dynamically populate and modify the formatting for a DataGrid control on a form with code behind other controls on a form.

After a user clicks the Load Grid button, *Form5* looks like the top window in Figure 6-7. Notice that the grid dynamically expands to show all the columns in its data source and that the form is widened to avoid cropping the grid control. Initially, the grid formats without an alternating background. Therefore, *Form5* opens with the No Alternating Background radio button selected. This radio button and the one immediately above it work together to control the *AlternatingBackColor* property for the DataGrid control. Clicking the Alternating Background radio button selects it and deselects the No Alternating Background radio button. (See the bottom window in Figure 6-7.) Equally important, clicking the top radio button changes every other row in the grid from the default background color to cyan. Clicking the No Alternating Background radio button toggles the look of the form so that all rows appear again in the default background color. In summary, these are the two main features of this application:

- Dynamically populates a DataGrid control with data on the user's command

- Alters the formatting of a DataGrid control

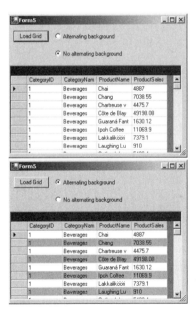

Figure 6-7   You can dynamically change the appearance of a DataGrid control.

The code behind *Form5* consists of three event procedures and a module-level variable. The module-level variable, *mycolor*, tracks the default background color for *DataGrid1*. Notice that the .NET Framework has a *Color* type. The type is actually a structure. The *Color* structure features shared members. These members include a long list of specific color names as well as operators for determining whether two colors are equal or unequal. You cannot use standard equality (=) or inequality (<>) operators for determining whether two colors are the same. The initial declaration of *mycolor* sets it equal to an empty color. When a user clicks the Load Grid button (*Button1*), the click event procedure for the button checks to see whether *mycolor* is still empty. If so, the procedure assigns the current alternating background color to *mycolor*.

If the color is not empty, a *Color* value was previously assigned to the *mycolor* variable. The *mycolor* variable is empty just once within a session—before the procedure assigns a *Color* value to it. Later, when a user clicks either of the RadioButton controls, Visual Basic .NET raises the *CheckedChanged* event for *RadioButton1*. The *RadioButton1_CheckedChanged* procedure, which handles this event, toggles the *AlternatingBackColor* property for *DataGrid1* between the value of *mycolor* and *Color.Cyan*.

The load event procedure for *Form5* is simple but nevertheless important. It starts with a few *Text* property assignments for *Button1* and the two RadioButton controls. Next, the load event procedure disables both radio buttons. Because of the design of this program, we need to take this precaution to prevent a user from undermining the ability of the application to toggle the color of alternating background rows in the grid. The closing statement of the load event procedure assigns *RadioButton2*'s *Checked* property a value of *True*. This selects the control when the form opens (although it is disabled so that a user cannot change the selection). Then, when the user clicks *Button1* for the first time, the correct radio button will already be selected.

Notice that I have made no explicit mention of populating the DataGrid control so far. This is because this function is now an interactive feature that the user can control while the form is open, instead of being tied to the opening of the form. The *Button1* click event procedure starts by filling the Sales By Category table in the *DsSalesbyCategory* dataset. (The *DsSalesbyCategory1* variable points at the dataset.) The next step is to assign the dataset's Sales By Category table to the *DataSource* property of *DataGrid1*. Because a DataGrid control can display multiple columns, you do not need to designate an individual column for a *DisplayMember* property.

Next, the click event procedure widens the DataGrid control to accommodate the display of all the columns in the Sales By Category table and widens the form to accommodate the DataGrid control. Then, the procedure moves on to assigning a value to the *mycolor* variable if it has not already set the variable's value in the current session. Finally, the event procedure enables both radio buttons. These last assignments permit users to toggle the color of alternating rows in the DataGrid control.

```
Dim mycolor As Color = Color.Empty
Private Sub Form5_Load(ByVal sender As System.Object, _
    ByVal e As System.EventArgs) Handles MyBase.Load

    'Set Text property values.
    Button1.Text = "Load Grid"
    RadioButton1.Text = "Alternating background"
    RadioButton2.Text = "No alternating background"

    'Disable radio buttons to preserve setting of
    'mycolor until the user initially populates
    'DataGrid1 with values.
    RadioButton1.Enabled = False
    RadioButton2.Enabled = False

    'Check RadioButton2.
    RadioButton2.Checked = True

End Sub

Private Sub Button1_Click(ByVal sender As System.Object, _
    ByVal e As System.EventArgs) Handles Button1.Click

    'Populate DataGrid1 with Sales by Category query.
    OleDbDataAdapter1.Fill _
        (DsSalesbyCategory1, "Sales by Category")
    DataGrid1.DataSource = _
        DsSalesbyCategory1.Tables("Sales by Category")

    'Resize form and grid to accommodate sales data.
    DataGrid1.Size = _
        New System.Drawing.Size(368, 184)
    Me.Size = _
        New System.Drawing.Size(384, 300)

    'Save color of default background for grid.
    If Color.op_Equality(mycolor, Color.Empty) Then
        mycolor = DataGrid1.AlternatingBackColor
    End If
```

(continued)

```
        'Enable buttons for toggling alternating
        'background color for grid.
        RadioButton1.Enabled = True
        RadioButton2.Enabled = True

    End Sub

    Private Sub RadioButton1_CheckedChanged( _
        ByVal sender As System.Object, _
        ByVal e As System.EventArgs) _
        Handles RadioButton1.CheckedChanged

        'Toggle alternating background color for grid.
        If RadioButton1.Checked Then
            DataGrid1.AlternatingBackColor = Color.Cyan
        Else
            DataGrid1.AlternatingBackColor = mycolor
        End If

    End Sub
```

Loading One of Three Data Sources into a DataGrid Control

The preceding sample creates a dataset based on the Sales By Category query in the Northwind database. This query performs an aggregation of the extended prices by product within category for orders in 1997; the expression for extended price is *UnitPrice*Quantity*(1-Discount/100)*100*. Although a query returns a result set without actually holding the values, this makes no difference to Visual Basic .NET. Whether you download a table or a query to populate controls on a form, Visual Basic .NET creates the same end result—a local table with actual values in a dataset.

Using the graphical techniques this chapter highlights, you cannot process an Access parameter query with Visual Basic .NET. (Don't worry, Chapter 8 shows how to process parameter queries with code.) However, we can create multiple queries without parameters within an Access database that are identical except for one element. Then, a Visual Basic .NET application can transfer one of those queries to a local dataset for viewing in the controls on a Windows form. The sample for this section illustrates a three-step approach to performing this task:

1.   Create queries that parallel one another in an Access database. For example, you can create separate Sales By Category queries for 1996, 1997, and 1998 with the data in the Northwind database.

2. Allow a user to designate with a form control which query she wants to download for populating one or more other controls on the form. One way to perform this second step is to let a user enter the name of the query, or a nickname for it, in a text box.

3. After verifying a valid entry for the query, your application can create a local dataset based on the Access data source and populate one or more controls on a Windows form.

Although the second and third steps are logically distinct, you are likely to perform both in a single module behind a Windows form. The first step can take place in any of several locations. However, the graphical query designer in Access is one especially easy place to perform this step.

Creating Three Sales by Category Queries in the Northwind Database

Because you already know how to process sales by category, it is an especially convenient place to start building three separate, parallel queries. The Northwind built-in Sales By Category query returns extended price results by product within category for one year: 1997. Therefore, it is relatively easy to modify this base query to create three more queries named Sales By Category 1996, Sales By Category 1997, and Sales By Category 1998. Figure 6-8 shows the SQL view for the Sales By Category 1996 query. This query is identical to the built-in query for Sales By Category, except for replacing the year 1997 with the year 1996. This replacement is necessary twice on the third line from the bottom in Figure 6-8. After making the update, save the query with the name Sales By Category 1996.

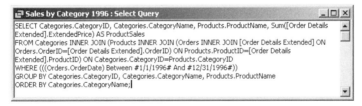

Figure 6-8 A SQL view of one of three parallel queries created for the Northwind database

You can create the Sales By Category 1998 query in a nearly identical fashion to the technique used for creating the Sales By Category 1996 query. In short, replace "1997" in the original Sales By Category query with "1998" and save the edited query with the name Sales By Category 1998.

Creating the Sales By Category 1997 query is the easiest of all. Open the original Sales By Category query. Then, use the File, Save As command to save the query with the name Sales By Category 1997. This process preserves the original query and makes another just like it with a new name.

Creating a Form for the Sample

You are likely to perform the second and third steps on page 275 together when selecting one of many parallel queries in an Access database. Both of these steps require a form. The second step requires a form to accept a value from a user designating which query to process into a local table within a dataset on a Windows workstation. The third step requires a form with one or more controls for displaying the dataset that corresponds to the query that a user designates in the second step.

When dragging queries from the *Views* collection of an Access database in Server Explorer, you will end up with one *OleDbConnection* object but three data adapters. Each data adapter manages one local dataset holding a table based on one of the three queries created in the first step listed on page 274. The same connection to the Northwind database can service each of the three data adapters. Visual Studio .NET presents a Data Adapter Configuration Error dialog box about not creating *Update* and *Delete* statements. These statements are inconsequential for this sample and earlier samples in this chapter because the forms are meant for viewing data, not updating it.

The next subsection presents a graphical form design technique that creates forms capable of editing data, and Chapter 8 and Chapter 9 present code-based approaches to data manipulation with ADO.NET and Visual Basic .NET. Right-click each data adapter and choose Generate Dataset to create a matching dataset. Name the datasets *DsSalesbyCategory1996*, *DsSalesbyCategory1997*, and *DsSalesbyCategory1998*. Visual Studio .NET responds by adding object variables to a tray below the form with the same names as the datasets (except for an appended *1*).

Figure 6-9 shows the Design view for *Form6* in the NavigationandAssignment project. The form includes a Button control to enable users to specify when to start populating a local dataset from the Access database. A TextBox control with a corresponding Label control allows a user to designate a nickname that specifies which query to use for populating a local dataset. The populated dataset serves as the *DataSource* property for the form's DataGrid control. Below the form in a tray are the ADO.NET object variables: *OleDbConnection1* points at the Northwind database. *OleDbDataAdapter1* through *OleDbDataAdapter3* point at the three queries added to the Northwind database. These variables represent data adapters as well as point at local datasets. The variables *DsSalesbyCategory19961* through *DsSalesbyCategory19981* point at local datasets. The Solution Explorer in Figure 6-9 depicts the *DsSalesbyCategory1998* dataset highlighted.

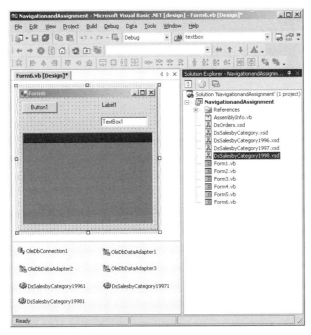

Figure 6-9 A Windows form that lets a user populate a DataGrid with one of three different datasets based on various queries in the Northwind database

Code Behind the Form

The following listing shows the code behind *Form6*. The listing consists of just two event procedures. The load event procedure for *Form6* performs the typical functions of assigning *Text* property values for controls and related setup activities. Comments describe the role of each block of code within the load event procedure. In this case, the third block of code is particularly interesting because it dynamically sizes and positions the Label control relative to the TextBox control. First, the code assigns the *Width* property setting from the TextBox control to the Label control. (TextBox controls are narrower by default.) Second, the code positions the Label control so that it is left aligned with the TextBox control and its bottom edge is 3 pixels above the top edge of the TextBox control.

The click event procedure for *Button1* manages the data for the application. With a *Select...Case* statement, the code runs one of four blocks of code depending on the *Text* property value for *TextBox1*. The legitimate values for *TextBox1* are 1996, 1997, or 1998. Any other value generates a reminder to the user to enter one of these three values, and the label above the text box indicates the need to enter one of the three legitimate values. The code for each year has the same form, but each draws on a different query and local dataset. For example, a value of 1996 fills the dataset at which the *OleDbDataAdapter1* points from the Sales By Category 1996 query in the Northwind database. After filling the dataset, the procedure assigns the dataset to the *DataSource* property for *DataGrid1*.

```
Private Sub Form6_Load(ByVal sender As System.Object, _
    ByVal e As System.EventArgs) Handles MyBase.Load

    'Set Text property values for button and
    'text box.
    Button1.Text = "Load Grid"
    TextBox1.Text = ""

    'Set Text property and alignment for label.
    Label1.Text = "Enter 1996, 1997, or 1998"
    Label1.TextAlign = ContentAlignment.MiddleRight

    'Position and size label so that it:
    ' has the same Width property as the text box,
    ' has the same Left property as the text box, and
    ' is three pixels above the text box.
    Label1.Size = _
        New System.Drawing.Size( _
        TextBox1.Width, Label1.Height)
    Label1.Left = TextBox1.Left
    Label1.Top = TextBox1.Top - Label1.Height - 3

    'Resize form and grid to accommodate sales data.
    DataGrid1.Size = _
        New System.Drawing.Size(368, 184)
    Me.Size = _
        New System.Drawing.Size(384, 300)

End Sub
```

```
Private Sub Button1_Click(ByVal sender As System.Object, _
    ByVal e As System.EventArgs) Handles Button1.Click

    'Before running this procedure, you need to create
    'three queries in the Northwind database based on
    'the Sales by Category query for product-within-category
    'sales by year (1996, 1997, and 1998).

    'Set the DataSource property for DataGrid1 based on the
    'year entered in the text box.
    Select Case TextBox1.Text
        Case "1996"
            OleDbDataAdapter1.Fill( _
                DsSalesbyCategory19961, "Sales by Category 1996")
            DataGrid1.DataSource = _
                DsSalesbyCategory19961. _
                    Tables("Sales by Category 1996")
        Case "1997"
            OleDbDataAdapter2.Fill( _
                DsSalesbyCategory19971, "Sales by Category 1997")
            DataGrid1.DataSource = _
                DsSalesbyCategory19971. _
                    Tables("Sales by Category 1997")
        Case "1998"
            OleDbDataAdapter3.Fill( _
                DsSalesbyCategory19981, "Sales by Category 1998")
            DataGrid1.DataSource = _
                DsSalesbyCategory19981. _
                    Tables("Sales by Category 1998")
        Case Else
            MsgBox("Please enter 1996, 1997, or 1998 " & _
                "in the text box.", MsgBoxStyle.Exclamation)
    End Select

End Sub
```

You can run this application just as you would any of the other samples in this section. Open *Form1* in the NavigationandAssignment project. Click the bottom link label. This opens *Form6* with empty DataGrid and TextBox controls. Entering a value such as 1996 and clicking the Load Grid button populates the grid with values for the year showing in the text box. Figure 6-10 presents the results for 1996 in the text box.

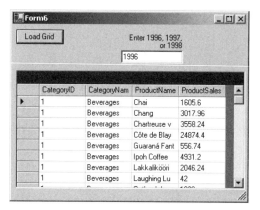

Figure 6-10   Using simple graphical techniques and elementary Visual Basic .NET code, you can dynamically specify at run time the values to populate a control such as a DataGrid on a Windows form.

Using the Data Form Wizard

The Data Form Wizard is a graphical tool for binding form controls to data sources. You can create data-bound controls for Windows and Web applications with the Data Form Wizard. This section examines the use of the wizard with Windows forms. If you are an Access developer learning Visual Basic .NET and ADO.NET, one of the great advantages of using the Data Form Wizard is that you can build form solutions for your Access databases without writing any code. However, the code behind the automatically generated forms is all standard code. Therefore, you can view the code as a learning aid or as a starting point for more customized solutions.

Menu for the Section

You will frequently build switchboard forms toward the end of an application development project. This is because you need to have the forms to which a switchboard directs traffic available for the code behind the switchboard form to compile properly. In spite of this application development requirement, switchboard forms are useful in tutorial presentations at the beginning of a section, such as this presentation. A switchboard form can succinctly summarize the topics a section covers.

Figure 6-11 shows the switchboard form for this section. The form exists as *Form1* in the DataFormWizSamples project. The code behind this form works identically to the code behind the switchboard form in the preceding section, except that this form's code references four samples instead of five. The most significant point of the samples referenced from this switchboard is that the Data Form Wizard generated all their forms. I did not have to code any of them. However, these forms do typical database chores in a database form. The first sample enables data access and manipulation via text boxes. The second sample enables data manipulation via a DataGrid control. The third sample presents two DataGrid controls in a main/sub form configuration. The fourth sample takes this main/sub form to a higher level by showing aggregated data in the sub form.

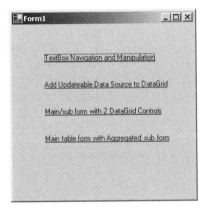

Figure 6-11   The switchboard form for the discussion of the Data Form Wizard

Data Access and Manipulation with TextBox Controls

The first Data Form Wizard demonstration creates a Windows form with three text boxes bound to the Freight, OrderDate, and OrderID columns in the Orders table of the Northwind database. By now, you should understand that a dataset contains a local cache of data that gets filled by a data adapter. As mentioned (but not demonstrated yet), data adapters are two-way pipes between an Access database file and a local dataset. This means that a user can update the local cache of data in the *DataSet* object and then invoke a method for the data adapter that copies changes from the local data cache to the database file. Chapters 7 through 9, which cover ADO.NET, explore conceptual, architectural, and programming aspects of this and related tasks. However, for the purpose of this sample (and this chapter), let's see how simple the Data Form Wizard can make this task.

To invoke the Data Form Wizard, you will need to start from a type of project that supports the wizard. One of these types is the Windows application project that we have repeatedly explored in this chapter and earlier ones.

Starting the Data Form Wizard from a Windows application project creates a Windows form. Successive forms created with the Data Form Wizard have the default names *DataForm1*, *DataForm2*, and so on. This sample is located in the DataFormWizSamples project. It has a *Form1*, formatted to look like Figure 6-11, and four data forms that were created with the Data Form Wizard. If you do not use a switchboard menu in your project, you need another mechanism for transferring control to the form created by the Data Form Wizard. (For example, you could make the form created by the wizard the project's startup object.)

Creating *DataForm1*

You invoke the Data Form Wizard by choosing Project, Add New Item, and selecting Data Form Wizard from the Templates. The wizard suggests a name for the form file, such as DataForm1.vb, which you can override. Click Open to launch the wizard. Because you are working with a wizard, screens will appear successively, offering a range of options for performing a task, which in this case is creating a data-bound form. These are the steps that were used to create the forms in this sample:

1.   Click Next on the wizard's Welcome screen.

2.   Specify the creation of a new dataset by entering **DsOrders** in the text box for naming a new dataset, and then click Next.

3.   Use the drop-down box to select a previously created connection for the Northwind database, or click the New Connection button to create a new connection to the Northwind database. Then click Next.

4.   Highlight Orders from the Tables collection of Available Items, and click the > button so that the table name migrates to the Selected Items box. Then click Next.

5.   Designate the three items to show on your form by clearing the checked status of all check boxes, except for Freight, OrderDate, and OrderID. Then click Next.

6.   Specify a form with text boxes by selecting the radio button with the label Single Record In Individual Controls, and then click Finish.

The Design View of *DataForm1*

Following the preceding steps can add an object named *DataForm1* to your project. As mentioned, this object is really a Windows form that the wizard created for you based on your inputs to the wizard screens. Figure 6-12 shows the Design view for *DataForm1*.

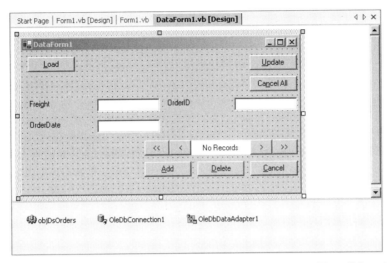

Figure 6-12   Design view of a form created with the Data Form Wizard
that contains text boxes for browsing and manipulating values

This section provides an overview of the design features of *DataForm1*,
and it describes specific features associated with each control. The basic purpose of *DataForm1* is to offer a Windows form that controls data access and
manipulation to the Orders table in the Northwind database. Clicking the Load
button populates the *DsOrders* dataset, which the *objDsOrders* variable points
at. After downloading a snapshot of the Orders table from the Northwind database to the Orders table in the *DsOrders* dataset, users can browse through the
rows of the local Orders table with the <<, <, >, and >> buttons. The label
between the < and > buttons displays the ordinal position of the current row
among all rows in the data source for the form (namely, the Orders table in the
DsOrders dataset).

In addition to browsing through rows, users can perform updates, inserts,
and deletes. Making an update is as simple as editing a column value appearing
in a text box and navigating off a row. Clicking the Cancel button below the >
and >> buttons restores the current row in the local dataset to the value it had
before any changes were made to its column values. Clicking the Delete button
marks the current row showing in the text boxes for deletion. Clicking the Add
button creates a form with all fields blank except for OrderID, which shows the
next unused autonumber value from the Access data source to the data adapter
for the local dataset.

All the changes to the local dataset persist for the current session. However, if you close the form without first clicking the Update button, any changes you made to the local dataset do not propagate to the database serving as the source for the local dataset. Therefore, the next time the form opens, it will be as though no updates, inserts, or deletes ever happened. Furthermore, clicking the Cancel All button below the Update button restores the Orders table in the *DsOrders* dataset to the state it was in immediately after you clicked the Load button. The only way to persist the changes to the local dataset to the database is to click the Update button. After updating an Access database file from the form, you can capture any changes entered by other users since your last load by clicking the Load button. This repopulates the local dataset showing in the form with the most recent version of the Access database object—namely, a table or a query—underlying the local dataset.

> **Note**   Rows marked for deletion in the local dataset are not physically removed from the local dataset until after a user clicks the Update button. However, rows marked for deletion do not display when a user browses the local dataset.

DataForm1 in Action

The original Freight column values for rows with OrderID values of 10248, 10249, and 10250 are 32.38, 11.61, and 65.83, respectively. You need to understand that a disconnected dataset maintains a local data cache that is separate and distinct from the database version of the same data. Therefore, you can have independent updates in both versions. When performing any kind of data manipulation with a *Form* object created by the Data Form Wizard, you should always include the primary key column(s) in the local dataset. Thus, when you attempt to propagate a change to a local dataset back to its database source, your application can identify the specific rows to edit or delete.

Figure 6-13 shows a progression of screens from the Access Datasheet view for the Orders table and the Windows form managed by the *DataForm1* object. I moved the Freight column values so that they appear to the immediate right of the OrderID column values in the Datasheet view. The top window shows the original OrderID and Freight values in the Datasheet view. The center window shows *DataForm1* after an edit of the Freight column value for OrderID 10248 from 32.38 to 32.3. After clicking the Update button on *DataForm1*, the Datasheet view in Access looks like the bottom window; you might have to refresh or reopen the Orders table Datasheet view to actually see the change.

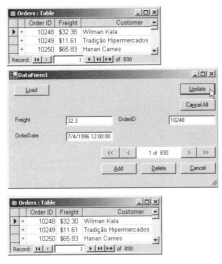

Figure 6-13   Making a change in a *DataForm* object can update the corresponding record in a table in an Access database after you click the form's Update button.

Changes can also go the other way—namely, from the Datasheet view of a table in Access to the *DataForm*. However, clicking the Update button does not transfer data from Access to the *DataForm*. A user needs to click the Load button to see updates to the database in *DataForm1*. This repopulates the dataset behind the text boxes on the form. For a data source the size of the Orders table, which has 830 rows, this repopulation process occurs very quickly. Figure 6-14 tracks *DataForm1* before and after the modification of the Freight value for OrderID 10250 from 65.83 to 65.80. The top left window shows *DataForm1* before the change in the Datasheet view. The top right window shows the Freight value (65.80) after the change. The bottom window displays

DataForm1 after a click to the Load button. Because this button refreshes and moves the current row to the first row in the Orders table for the local dataset, I need to move the row pointer to 3 of 830 with the > navigation button.

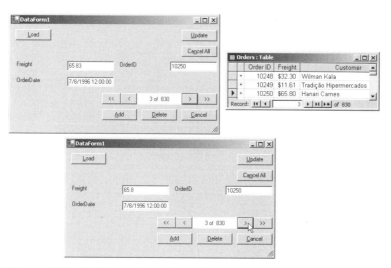

Figure 6-14   Making a change in an Access Datasheet view propagates to a *DataForm* object after a user clicks the Load button.

Add an Updateable Data Source to a DataGrid Control

Some applications work better with a DataGrid control, which lets users see multiple rows at once and navigate rapidly with a vertical scroll bar. For this reason, the Data Form Wizard enables the creation of forms with DataGrid controls. In fact, the Data Form Wizard creates forms only with a DataGrid design when you use it to develop a Web solution, but developers creating solutions within a Windows application project can choose between DataGrid and text box designs. Both designs can enable the same range of functions, but the two designs enable the manipulation of those functions via different techniques.

Creating *DataForm2*

The steps presented next show how to create a *Form* object containing a DataGrid control with the Data Form Wizard. To make this sample application comparable to the preceding one, it uses the same local dataset, *DsOrders*. Because the second application reuses the dataset created in the first application, the steps for creating the DataGrid sample illustrate how to reuse a dataset. Open the Data Form Wizard by choosing Project, Add New Item. Then, highlight Data Form Wizard in the Templates collection, and click Open to start the wizard's process for creating a *Form* object named *DataForm2*. Click Next on the Welcome screen to advance to the first wizard screen, from which you can make a choice. Then, follow these steps:

1.   Instead of attempting to create a new dataset, indicate that you want to reuse an existing dataset by accepting the selection to use the *DataFormWizSamples.DsOrders* dataset. Then click Next.

2.   Choose *FillDataSet* from *DataFormWizSamples.DataForm1* in the top drop-down box as the method to fill the dataset, click the Include An Update check box, and choose *UpdateDataSource* from *DataFormWizSamples.DataForm1* as the method to update the dataset. Then click Next.

3.   Designate the three items to show on your form by clearing the checked status of all check boxes, except those for Freight, Order-Date, and OrderID. Then click Next.

4.   Accept the default selection to display all records in a grid, and click Finish.

The Design View of *DataForm2*

DataForm2 contains just four controls (see Figure 6-15), but it supports the same range of data access and manipulation functions offered by *DataForm1*, which contained many more controls. A Load button populates (or repopulates) the DataGrid control that appears below it. When a user opens *DataForm2* to browse and manipulate data, the Orders table from the *DsOrders* dataset appears with a vertical scroll bar for moving forward and backward through the data. This feature enables users to quickly browse through the rows in the Orders table. The *objDsOrders* variable shown in the tray below the form in Figure 6-15 points at the *DsOrders* dataset. You can confirm this for yourself by selecting the object in the tray and viewing its *DatasetName* property (which is *DsOrders*).

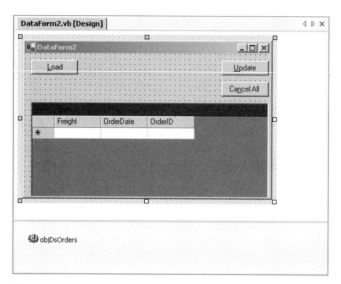

Figure 6-15 Design view of a form created with the Data Form Wizard that contains a DataGrid control for browsing and manipulating values

Users can edit the value in any DataGrid cell. These edits automatically persist in the local dataset for the current session, but they do not automatically propagate to the Access database file that you use as a data source for the local dataset. To pass changes from the local dataset to an Access database (or any other kind of database), click the Update button. The Cancel All button in this application works like the button with the same label in the preceding sample application. Clicking this button before clicking Update undoes any changes made since the last time the Update button was clicked.

You can also click the Update button to remove rows from a database based on deleted rows in a local dataset or to add rows to a database based on rows inserted into a local dataset. This might seem confusing at first because no Add and Delete buttons exist on *DataForm2*. You can add a new row to a table in a local dataset by scrolling to the last row, which has an asterisk (*) in its row selector. Then, enter new values in the row, and move off the row. To mark a row for deletion, select the row. Then, press the Delete key on the keyboard.

DataForm2 in Action

Making an edit to a DataGrid cell is straightforward. Double-click a cell, and then edit the value. Figure 6-16 shows *DataForm2* after double-clicking the DataGrid control's top left cell. An edit is in process for the first row, as evidenced by the symbol in the selector for that row; the edit is to change the default value of 32.38 to 32.3. Clicking Update will commit the edit in the local dataset and propagate the revised Freight column value to the Orders table of the Northwind database. Clicking the Cancel All button instead of the Update button clears the modification and restores the original value, 32.38, in place of the edited value, 32.3. Just as with the preceding form sample application containing text boxes, clicking the Load button after users make their edits updates the local dataset to reflect those changes. If you want to persist any uncommitted changes to the database, you must click Update before clicking Load.

Note   Just as with a form containing text boxes, clicking the Update button on a form containing a DataGrid control commits all changes not yet propagated to the database source from a local dataset—not just a pending change for a single row.

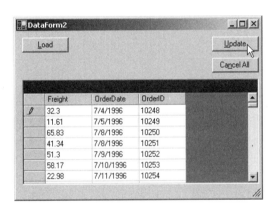

Figure 6-16   Committing an edit from the DataGrid control is as easy as clicking the Update button.

Moving to the last row in a DataGrid control enables you to add a new row to a local dataset. Figure 6-17 shows the Freight column value open for the addition of a new row. Just type the new values into the columns for the row. If you are using an autonumber column value, as with the OrderID column in Figure 6-17, the form shows the next autonumber as 1 plus the last value for the autonumber column in the DataGrid. Because Access can discard autonumbers for uncommitted rows or deleted rows, it is possible for the appropriate autonumber to be different than the DataGrid control shows. When you click

Update, Access automatically corrects an invalid autonumber and replaces it with a valid one. The next time a user repopulates the DataGrid control by clicking the Load button, the control reflects the valid autonumber set by the Jet database engine.

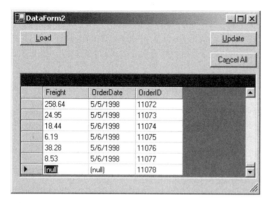

Figure 6-17 When adding a new row through a DataGrid control, the .NET Framework assigns an autonumber for the row based on the last autonumber column value in the DataGrid control.

Main/sub Forms

You can use the Data Form Wizard to create classic main/sub forms in Visual Basic .NET similar to those that Access makes easy to create. A main/sub form is a single form that contains two nested forms—a main form and a sub form. Each form has its own data source. The sub form is synchronized with the main form to show the subset of rows from its data source that match the currently selected row in the main form. For the process to work, your application needs to know about the relationship between the data sources for the main and sub forms.

To implement a main/sub form with the Data Form Wizard, you need to specify at least two data sources for the form. One data source is for the main form, and the second is for the sub form. You can choose any table or view (row-returning query without parameters) in an Access database as the data source for a form. In addition, you must specify in the Data Form Wizard screens the relationship between the two data sources.

Creating *DataForm3*

The sample demonstrating the process for creating main/sub forms uses the Orders and Order Details tables from the Northwind database as the sources for the main form and sub form, respectively. The two tables serving as data sources relate to one another via their OrderID columns values. Start to create this main/sub form by invoking the Project, Add New Item command. If you have been following along, the default *DataForm* filename will be DataForm3.vb. Accept this name by clicking Open. Then, click Next to advance to the first Data Form Wizard screen from which you can make a selection. From there, follow these instructions:

1. Select the radio button for creating a new dataset, enter the name **DsOrdersOrderDetails** in the text box below the button, and then click Next.

2. Use the drop-down box to select a previously created connection for the Northwind database, or click the New Connection button to create a new connection to the Northwind database. Then click Next.

3. From the Available Items box, click the Orders table followed by the > button before clicking the Order Details table followed by the > button so that the Orders and Order Details tables appear in the Selected Item(s) box. Then click Next.

4. On the Create A Relationship Between Tables dialog box, specify a relationship name, parent and child table names, and keys for linking the parent and child tables as shown in Figure 6-18 before clicking the > button to save your specification for the relationship between the two data sources. Then click Next.

5. Designate three items to show on your master form by clearing the checked status of all check boxes, except for Freight, OrderDate, and OrderID, and clear the OrderID check box for the detail table to show all other columns from its data source. Then click Next.

6. Accept the default selection to display all rows in a grid, and click Finish.

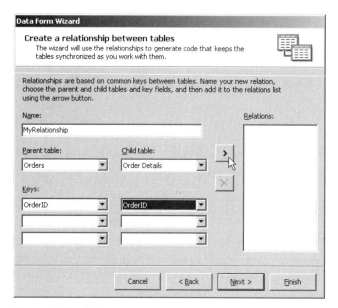

Figure 6-18   When you designate two separate data sources in the Data Form Wizard, you can designate a relationship between them to create a main/sub form.

The Design View of *DataForm3*

Figure 6-19 shows the main/sub form in Design view created by following the instructions given a moment ago. You can see all of the DataGrid control for the main form with column values of Freight, OrderDate, and OrderID. Below the main form, you can see the top of the DataGrid control for the sub form. Notice that the sub form does not show a column for OrderID.

The display columns in the grids do not tell the whole story about what's available as a data source behind these two forms. Both forms have all the columns available from their respective data sources. This facilitates the coding for data manipulation tasks. Happily, all these details are managed by the Data Form Wizard. For those who want to dig deeper, you can examine the Data Adapter Configuration Wizard screens for the *OleDbDataAdapter1* and *OleDbDataAdapter2* object variables in the tray below the form. You can start the wizard by right-clicking either object and choosing Configure Data Adapter. Do not edit any settings; looking at how the wizard makes settings can give you a starting point when you begin creating your own custom solutions without the wizard.

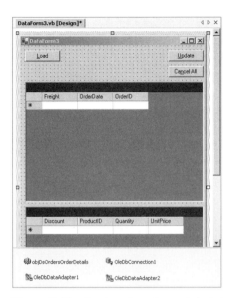

Figure 6-19   Design view of a main/sub form created with the Data Form Wizard

DataForm3 in Action

After opening *DataForm3*, you can populate the DataGrid controls for the main and sub forms by clicking Load. Initially, the main form selects the first row in the Orders table with an OrderID column value of 10248. The sub form shows the three rows in the Order Details table that match the selected row in the Orders table from the main form. After selecting the second row in the main form (for OrderID 10249), the sub form changes to reflect rows for OrderID 10249. The left and right windows in Figure 6-20 portray these two views of data that characterize the operation of a main/sub form.

Because the data sources for the main and sub forms are both tables, you can perform data manipulation tasks such as inserts, updates, and deletes in the same way that you would for a form with a single DataGrid control connected to a single table. You can also perform data manipulation for a query serving as a data source as long as the Jet engine permits updates to the query. For example, you cannot edit rows in a query that aggregates rows because the column values appearing in a grid do not physically exist; the column values in an aggregate query are computed just for the query.

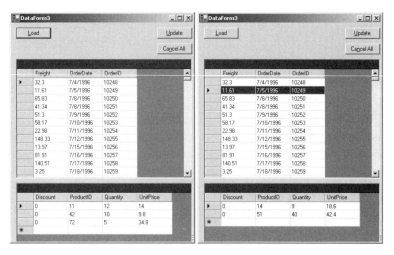

Figure 6-20   A main/sub form when it initially opens (on left) and after the selection of a row in the main form (on right)

Main Table with Aggregated Sub Form

The discussion of the preceding sample's output revealed that you cannot perform updates to column values on a sub form when it contains aggregate values. Figure 6-20 shows another outcome that Access database developers might find interesting: the ProductID column values displayed as a number. Often, Access automatically looks up and displays the matching name for a column value, such as ProductName from the Products table, instead of presenting the less meaningful column value as a ProductID number. Visual Basic .NET follows the tradition of SQL Server development: it is common for the developer to program the lookup. After all, this merely involves linking a table with columns for both the numeric codes (such as ProductID) and their names (such as ProductName) as column values.

The final Data Form Wizard sample application generates a main/sub form with a table, Categories, as the source for the main form and an aggregated query as a data source for the sub form. The aggregated query, ExtendedPricesSummedbyProduct, computes extended price by product within CategoryID. This custom query returns three columns: CategoryID, ProductName, and the sum of extended prices. The custom query is an aggregation of the Order Details Extended built-in query for the Northwind database, which computes extended price for individual line items within Orders. The SQL statement for the ExtendedPricesSummedbyProduct query joins the aggregation with the Products table by ProductID to add CategoryID column values to the result set from the query. The following SQL expression defines the custom query:

```
SELECT Products.CategoryID, Products.ProductName,
 Sum([Order Details Extended].ExtendedPrice) AS SumOfExtendedPrice
 FROM Products INNER JOIN [Order Details Extended] ON
Products.ProductID = [Order Details Extended].ProductID
GROUP BY Products.CategoryID, Products.ProductName
```

The CategoryID column values in the result set from the query enable joining the aggregated query with the Categories table. Through a relationship based on this join, the main/sub form can show category names in the rows of its grid on its main form. The sub form shows the names of products in its grid along with the summed extended prices for each product within a category. By changing the selected category in the main form, you cause the sub form to display different sets of products. Figure 6-21 shows the main/sub form in action—immediately after opening and then selecting the last row in the main form.

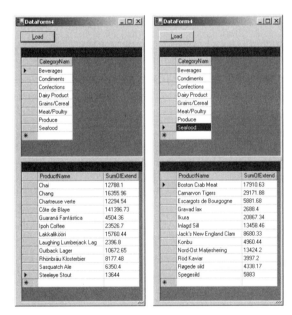

Figure 6-21   You can customize the look of a DataForm by dropping and resizing controls.

Some custom editing went into the form in Figure 6-21, but the steps for creating the main/sub form in the figure generally mirror those of the preceding main/sub form sample. Of course, you need to select the Categories table and the ExtendedPricesSummedbyProduct query as the data sources for the main and sub forms. The DataFormWizSamples project available for this chapter named the dataset with both data sources as *DsCategoriesExtendedPricesby-Product*. On the last Data Form Wizard screen, clear the Cancel All check box to remove the button by this name from the form. In Design view, you can remove the Update button because the form is strictly for reporting editing, not enabling it. The form instances in Figure 6-21 show additional editing to resize the form and grids for easier viewing. You can accomplish this resizing by selecting the control or form and dragging the selected item to a new size.

Managing DataGrid Properties

As mentioned previously, the DataGrid control is likely to be a popular tool for displaying data in your database applications. This is because it is a very rich control with lots of flexibility. For example, an earlier sample (*Form5* in the NavigationandAssignment project) showed how to dynamically populate the control and toggle the display of alternating background colors. This section demonstrates how to program four more DataGrid control properties in two sample applications. This section also demonstrates how to process the *CurrentCell-Changed* event for the DataGrid control. The two samples in this section aim to familiarize you with programming the DataGrid control on a Windows form. However, the second sample illustrates how to combine a series of basic features that are highly useful for reading values from a grid to perform computations and facilitate user navigation around the grid cells.

> **Note**   If after finishing these samples you want more advanced coverage of programming DataGrid controls, I urge you to use the Data Form Wizard to create forms with one to two DataGrid controls. Then, view the code behind the form. Take special note of the code in the Windows Form Designer region.

The *ReadOnly* and *AllowSorting* Properties

This section describes a sample that demonstrates how to dynamically manipulate the *ReadOnly* and the *AllowSorting* properties for a DataGrid control. The *ReadOnly* property for a DataGrid control determines whether a user can edit the values in the cells of a DataGrid control. By default, users can edit the content of cells. However, you can dynamically change this property's setting at run time—for example, after a user clicks a button—to protect the values in a DataGrid control.

Although the *ReadOnly* property enables and disables the editing of individual cells, you manipulate the *ReadOnly* property for all the cells in a DataGrid control at once. The *AllowSorting* property determines whether you can click a column header in a DataGrid control to sort the rows by that column. The *AllowSorting* property is *True* by default. Unless the *AllowSorting* property is *False*, users can toggle the sort order of the rows in a DataGrid control by clicking a column header successively. The first click sorts in ascending order, and the second click reverses the order. After that, successive clicks continue to toggle the sort order between the two directions.

> **Note** If the DataGrid control cells point back at a table in a local dataset, changes to those cells persist for the current session—namely, the lifetime of the form with the DataGrid control. You can persist the DataGrid cell values beyond the lifetime of the form that contains a DataGrid control by storing the cells in a nonvolatile medium, such as an Access database file.

Figure 6-22 presents a design view of the sample form for this application, *Form2* in the ManagingGrids project. *Form1* in the project is a switchboard form that lets a user move to either of the two forms in this section. The tray below *Form2* indicates the ADO.NET variables for making a connection to the Ten Most Expensive Products query in the Northwind database. You can create these ADO.NET variables with the help of Server Explorer and by generating a dataset from the resulting data adapter.

Three buttons along the top of the form allow users to manipulate and examine properties for the DataGrid control that appears below them. *Button1* opens a message box that reports the current value of the *ReadOnly* property for the DataGrid control. This property setting is initially *False*, but users can toggle it with *Button2*. *Button3* allows you to set the *AllowSorting* property to *True*. When a *DataGrid* initially opens, the *AllowSorting* property is *True* by default, but the *Form2_Load* procedure sets the *AllowSorting* property to *False*. *Button3* does not enable toggling. Therefore, once a user switches sorting on with *Button3*, the form continues to support dynamic sorting by the user for its lifetime. Closing and reopening the form disables sorting again until a user clicks *Button3*.

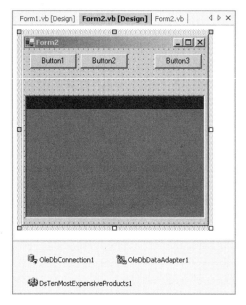

Figure 6-22 The Design view of a form with three buttons to control and monitor the formatting of a DataGrid control

The code behind *Form2* includes four event procedures: one for each button, plus a form load event procedure. The form's load event procedure performs four kinds of tasks. These start by setting the first table in the local dataset—*Tables (0)*—to the *DataSource* property for *DataGrid1*. The application initially disables sorting. Therefore, the second block sets the DataGrid control's *AllowSorting* property to *False*. Next, the code assigns *Text* property settings to the buttons. The event procedure sets the *Text* property for *Button2* to *True*. The *Text* property for this button indicates what the *ReadOnly* property will be after a click to the button. Because the *ReadOnly* property is *False* by default, the initial setting of the button is *True*. Clicking the button switches the *Text* property's setting to *False*. The last block of code in the load event procedure lengthens the form and DataGrid control to display all 10 products without the need for a vertical scroll bar.

The *Button1* click event procedure might be the most straightforward of the three procedures, but all the button click event procedures are easy to follow. The event procedure for *Button1* presents a message box displaying the *ReadOnly* property setting for *DataGrid1* as a string value.

The *Button2* click event procedure works in coordination with the *Button1_Click* procedure. The event procedure for *Button2* toggles the *ReadOnly* property for *DataGrid1* and the *Text* property for *Button2*. As mentioned, the *ReadOnly* property is initially *False*. If the user clicks *Button2* immediately after opening the form, the DataGrid control on the form becomes *ReadOnly*. (The *ReadOnly* property setting becomes *True*.) At this point, a user cannot edit the values in any grid cell. However, clicking *Button2* again restores the ability to edit cell values in a DataGrid control. Successive clicks to *Button2* toggle between these two states. By clicking *Button1*, a user can verify the *ReadOnly* status of the form's DataGrid control.

The *Button3_Click* event procedure prompts the user with a message box asking whether to enable sorting. As you have learned, the form's load event procedure disables the capability. If the user replies Yes to the prompt in the message box, the procedure sets the *AllowSorting* property for *DataGrid1* to *True*. After that, sorting is available for columns in the grid control until a user closes the session.

```
Private Sub Form2_Load(ByVal sender As Object, _
    ByVal e As System.EventArgs) Handles MyBase.Load

    'Populate DataGrid1.
    OleDbDataAdapter1.Fill(DsTenMostExpensiveProducts1, _
        "Ten Most Expensive Products")
    DataGrid1.DataSource = _
        DsTenMostExpensiveProducts1.Tables(0)

    'Disable ability to sort columns.
    DataGrid1.AllowSorting = False

    'Assign Text property values to buttons.
    Button1.Text = "ReadOnly?"
    Button2.Text = "True"
    Button3.Text = "Sorting OK?"

    'Adjust form and control height to
    'display 10 items without scrolling.
    Me.Height += 40
    DataGrid1.Height += 40

End Sub

Private Sub Button1_Click(ByVal sender As System.Object, _
    ByVal e As System.EventArgs) Handles Button1.Click

    'Display ReadOnly property value for DataGrid1.
    MsgBox(DataGrid1.ReadOnly.ToString)
```

(continued)

```
End Sub

Private Sub Button2_Click(ByVal sender As System.Object, _
    ByVal e As System.EventArgs) Handles Button2.Click

    'Toggle the Text property of Button2 and ReadOnly
    'property value for DataGrid1.
    If Button2.Text = "True" Then
        DataGrid1.ReadOnly = True
        Button2.Text = "False"
    Else
        DataGrid1.ReadOnly = False
        Button2.Text = "True"
    End If

End Sub

Private Sub Button3_Click(ByVal sender As System.Object, _
    ByVal e As System.EventArgs) Handles Button3.Click

    'Enable sorting only if user is sure it is OK.
    If MsgBox("Are you sure?", _
        MsgBoxStyle.Exclamation + MsgBoxStyle.YesNo) = _
        MsgBoxResult.Yes Then
        DataGrid1.AllowSorting = True
    End If

End Sub
```

The *CurrentCell* and *CurrentRowIndex* Properties

The previous sample has no screens illustrating its performance because its purpose was to demonstrate programming techniques, such as initializing properties for the DataGrid control on a Windows form. The DataGrid control for a Windows form has an extensive collection of properties. For example, a sample in the "Navigation and Data Source Assignment Issues" section earlier in this chapter demonstrated how to program the *AlternatingBackColor* property.

This section will illustrate how to manage navigation across a grid and read values from the grid with the *CurrentCell* and *CurrentRowIndex* properties. You can view the full list of DataGrid control properties for Windows forms in the Microsoft Visual Studio .NET documentation. Use the guidelines for programming control properties in this chapter as you start to program other DataGrid control properties and even properties for other controls.

> **Note**   When you have a specific topic to look up in the Visual Studio .NET documentation, it can be helpful to use the Index tab. If this tab is not open in the documentation window, choose Help, Index. Then, type the specific term you seek in the Look For box and press Enter. For example, if you type **DataGrid**, you will see many help topics, but one of them will be "DataGrid class (System.Windows.Forms)". Nested within that topic will be several subtopics, including one named "properties". Clicking this topic will open a Help page with an exhaustive list of *DataGrid* class properties for Windows forms.

The sample application for this section programs the *CurrentCell* and *CurrentRowIndex* properties to facilitate two types of functions for a grid on a Windows form. The first type of function facilitates navigation between rows. Although it is relatively easy to move around a DataGrid control on a form by clicking a cell in one row or another, the ease of this approach diminishes as the number of rows increases. For example, scrolling to the last row in a grid with thousands of rows can be tedious. The second type of function demonstrates how to extract values from any subset of cells on the current row in a grid. The sample application computes the extended price for a row from a DataGrid control with a *DataSource* property set to a table in a dataset initially populated from the Order Details table in the Northwind database.

The Design View of *Form3*

Figure 6-23 shows the form for the application, which is *Form3* in the Managing-Grids project. Five Button controls and a TextBox control at the top of the form help to manage navigation across the rows in the DataGrid control at the bottom of the form. A text box between the second and third buttons in the top row of controls provides feedback on the current row in the total set of rows for the DataGrid control. Users can also use the text box along with the far right button to navigate to a new row.

To give you a feel for working with a dataset that is not tiny, the DataGrid control's data source is the Order Details table, which contains 2155 rows. The *DsOrderDetails1* variable points at the *DsOrderDetails* dataset containing the Order Details table that a data adapter populates from the Northwind database. Between the navigation controls and the DataGrid control are a pair of text boxes with corresponding labels above them. The role of *TextBox2* is to display the OrderID for the current row, and *TextBox3* displays the extended price for the selected row in the DataGrid control. As mentioned earlier, extended price is the product of Quantity, UnitPrice, and 1 minus Discount.

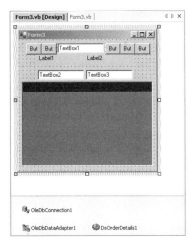

Figure 6-23   The Design view of a form for controlling navigation and reading grid cell values via the programming of the *CurrentCell* and *CurrentRowIndex* properties

Form3 in Action

The sample application supports three styles of navigation. Figure 6-24 reveals two screens from the application in operation. The top window depicts *Form3* when the application opens but with the mouse pointer positioned over row 7 to click the OrderID column. Notice that the form initially opens *Form3* with the OrderID column value selected on the first row. The bottom window shows *Form3* after the click to the OrderID column in row 7. Notice the text box between the navigation buttons at the top of the form refreshes its contents from 1 of 2155 to 7 of 2155. In addition, the OrderID and Price boxes just above the grid change their values to reflect the current row.

> **Note**   By contrasting Figure 6-24 with Figure 6-23, you can see that the application formats the labels that tag *TextBox2* and *TextBox3*. The application resizes and repositions the labels relative to the text boxes and changes the text alignment for the labels. In addition, the contents of the two text boxes has formatting for alignment, and the box showing extended price applies a currency format to its contents.

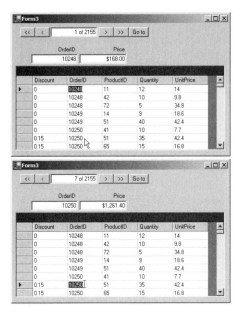

Figure 6-24   The sample illustrating the use of the *CurrentCell* and *CurrentRowIndex* properties permits navigation via three techniques, including simply clicking a cell.

Figure 6-25 illustrates another means of navigating around the contents of the grid. The top window shows *Form3* after a click to the >> button, but just before a click to the < button. The >> button navigates to the last row in the grid. The < button navigates to the previous row. Notice that no particular cell is selected. Instead, the top and bottom windows mark the selected item in the row selector on the left edge of the grid control.

A third way to navigate to a row is by typing a row number into the text box between the < and > buttons. Figure 6-26 shows the next to the last row selected. However, the text box between the navigation buttons has the value 8 in it. (See the top window.) After clicking the Go To button, which is the far right navigation button, the current row transfers to row 8. Because of the direction of navigation, this row appears at the top of the grid. (See the bottom window.) However, you can confirm that it is the eighth row by comparing the column values for the top row in the bottom window of Figure 6-26 with the column values for the last row in the top window from Figure 6-24. The top window from Figure 6-24 shows the first eight rows in the grid, and its last row of column values matches the column values of the row navigated to by clicking the Go To button in the bottom window of Figure 6-26.

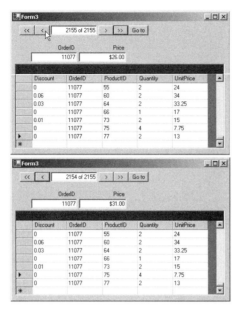

Figure 6-25 The *CurrentCell* and *CurrentRowIndex* property sample enables navigation via buttons at the top of *Form3*.

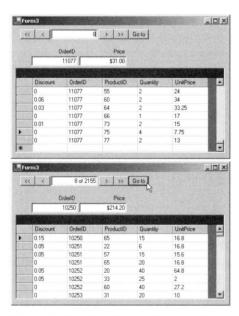

Figure 6-26 The *CurrentCell* and *CurrentRowIndex* property sample enables navigation when the user enters a row number in a text box and clicks a button.

Let's look at another interesting operational feature of the sample application. Clicking the very bottom row (which has an asterisk in the row selector) generates an error when the code behind the form attempts to compute extended price for the Price text box. This is because the inputs to the expression for extended price are *Null* for the very last row in the DataGrid control. The program intercepts the exception resulting from a computation on *Null* values and rolls the current row back to the last valid row. However, the program moves the selected column cell to the column selected in the very bottom row of the grid. Figure 6-27 illustrates this behavior. The top window shows the OrderID cell selected on row 2150. In addition, you can see the mouse pointer in the Quantity column of the very bottom row. Clicking at that point generates the exception that the code traps and repositions the currently selected cell to the Quantity column of row 2150. (See the bottom window.)

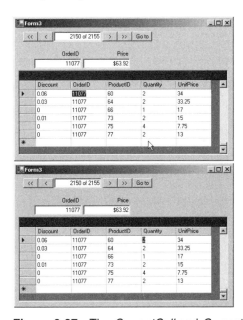

Figure 6-27   The *CurrentCell* and *CurrentRowIndex* property sample traps invalid navigation to the blank row at the bottom of the grid and repositions the currently selected cell.

The Code Behind *Form3*

The code behind the form contains three parts. The form load event is the first part. It sets up the form with data and navigates to the initial cell position. The second part handles navigating by clicking to a cell. This part can also process a click out of bounds to the very bottom row in the grid. The third part is a set of event procedures for using the navigation bar at the top of the form. In addition to these distinct parts, a module-level variable tracks the last legitimate row for recovering from an out-of-bounds move.

The *intOldRow* variable is the module-level variable that tracks the last legitimate row position. The variable is set initially in the load event procedure for *Form3*. The first setting will be legitimate. Then, the application resets *intOldRow* after each successful move. When the .NET Framework throws an error for the computation of extended price because of an attempt to move out of bounds (the empty row at the very bottom of the grid), the event procedure handling a changed current cell recovers by using the last legitimate value in *intOldRow* to move to a valid row.

The form load event procedure starts by populating the grid with the Order Details table from the Northwind database. Then, the procedure sets the focus to the second column in the first row by setting the DataGrid control's *CurrentCell* property. The procedure instantiates a *DataGridCell* structure value pointing at the starting location for the cursor when the form opens. Next, the procedure saves the *CurrentRowIndex* property value in the *intOldRow* variable. The next task for the load event procedure is the resizing of the DataGrid control and the form. The code for this resizing effort precedes another block of code making *Text* and *Height* property assignments for the navigation buttons. The assignments for *Button5* (the Go To button) are slightly different because this button needs a wider face than the other buttons. The *Height* settings make the buttons the same height as *TextBox1*, which gives an even appearance to the navigation bar at the top of the form. The last segment of code in the form load event procedure manages the appearance of the labels for the TextBox controls holding the OrderID and Price for the currently selected row.

One of the most pivotal procedures in the code behind the form is the *DataGrid1_CurrentCellChanged* procedure. The .NET Framework raises the *CurrentCellChanged* event whenever the *CurrentCell* property for *DataGrid1* changes. Users can change the current cell by clicking another cell or using one of the navigation buttons. In fact, initializing the *CurrentCell* property in the form load event procedure raises the *CurrentCellChanged* event. This procedure populates *TextBox1*, *TextBox2*, and *TextBox3*. The procedure updates *TextBox1* with the value of the current position through a call to the *UpdatePositionIndicator* procedure. The expression for *TextBox3* can raise an exception because of *Null* values. Therefore, the *DataGrid1_CurrentCellChanged* procedure uses a *Try...Catch...Finally* statement to trap errors that result from the computation. *Null* values throw an *InvalidCastException* object. If the *Try...Catch...Finally* statement detects this object, it means the user clicked the empty cell at the bottom of the grid. Therefore, the procedure recovers in the *Catch* clause. The recovery technique sets the *CurrentCell* property for *DataGrid1*. This action transfers control to the start of the *DataGrid1_CurrentCellChanged* procedure. A *Catch* clause for a *SystemException* object detects any other kind of error and exits the *Try...Catch...Finally* statement so that the user can recover manually. The *Finally* clause handles any legitimate move by resetting the value of the *intOldRow* variable.

The *UpdatePositionIndicator* procedure is short, but it is interesting for a couple of reasons. The position indicator for the current row is the *Text* property for *TextBox1*. This text box shows two values—one for the current row and the other for the total number of rows in the table behind *DataGrid1*. The procedure uses the *RowNumber* property of the *CurrentCell* member of the grid to return the current row. Because *RowNumber* property values are zero-based but the row indicator in *TextBox1* is one-based, the expression for the row number adds 1 to the *RowNumber* property. To compute the total number of rows in the grid, the procedure invokes the *Count* method for the *Rows* collection of the Order Details table in the local dataset. (The *DsOrderDetails1* variable points at the dataset.)

All the remaining procedures in the application handle the navigation buttons. *Button1* through *Button4* correspond to the << through >> buttons. For example, the *Button1_Click* procedure moves to the first row by setting the *CurrentRowIndex* property to 0, which ultimately invokes the *UpdatePosition-Indicator* procedure. The *Button4_Click* procedure is very similar, except that it sets the *CurrentRowIndex* property to the last row value, which is 1 less than the count of rows in the Order Details table. The *Button2_Click* and *Button3_Click* procedures also have a symmetry because they move the current row in opposite directions by a single row. These two procedures merely add or subtract 1 from the *CurrentRowIndex* property.

The *Button5_Click* procedure works in tandem with the current *Text* property for *TextBox1*. If the *Button5_Click* procedure discovers that the return value for the *CInt* function called on the *Text* property is in the range of valid rows for the DataGrid control, the procedure assigns the valid row number to the *CurrentRowIndex* property and resets the position indicator to reflect the current row position in the DataGrid control. If the *Text* property for *TextBox1* does not point at a valid row number, the procedure reverts to resetting the

CurrentRowIndex property to the last legitimate position. Before closing, the procedure updates the display in *TextBox1*.

```
Dim intOldRow As Integer
Private Sub Form3_Load(ByVal sender As System.Object, _
    ByVal e As System.EventArgs) Handles MyBase.Load

    'Populate DataGrid1.
    OleDbDataAdapter1.Fill(DsOrderDetails1, _
        "Order Details")
    DataGrid1.DataSource = _
        DsOrderDetails1.Tables("Order Details")

    'Position current cell in OrderID column
    'of the first row and save row position.
    DataGrid1.CurrentCell = New DataGridCell(0, 1)
    intOldRow = DataGrid1.CurrentRowIndex

    'Reset grid size to show data without horizontal
    'scrolling and update form size for grid.
    DataGrid1.Size = _
        New System.Drawing.Size(448, DataGrid1.Height)
    Me.Size = New System.Drawing.Size(470, 300)

    'Set properties for navigation buttons.
    Button1.Height = TextBox1.Height
    Button2.Height = TextBox1.Height
    Button3.Height = TextBox1.Height
    Button4.Height = TextBox1.Height
    Button1.Text = "<<"
    Button2.Text = "<"
    Button3.Text = ">"
    Button4.Text = ">>"

    'Set properties for Go To record button.
    Button5.Text = "Go to"
    Button5.Size = _
        New System.Drawing.Size(42, TextBox1.Height)

    'Text and TextAlign property settings for labels
    Label1.Text = "OrderID"
    Label2.Text = "Price"
    Label1.TextAlign = ContentAlignment.MiddleRight
    Label2.TextAlign = ContentAlignment.MiddleRight
```

```vb
        'Position labels relative to corresponding
        'text boxes.
        Label1.Height = TextBox2.Height
        Label1.Top = TextBox2.Top - Label1.Height
        Label2.Height = TextBox3.Height
        Label2.Top = TextBox3.Top - Label1.Height

End Sub

Private Sub DataGrid1_CurrentCellChanged( _
    ByVal sender As Object, _
    ByVal e As System.EventArgs) _
    Handles DataGrid1.CurrentCellChanged

        'Create a pointer for the DataGrid control.
        Dim dg As DataGrid
        dg = DataGrid1

        'Compute text box display showing current row
        'relative to total number of rows.
        UpdatePositionIndicator(dg)

        'Display the OrderID for the current row.
        TextBox2.Text = _
            dg(dg.CurrentCell.RowNumber, 1).ToString
        TextBox2.TextAlign = HorizontalAlignment.Right

        'Computation throws error if selection is
        'out of bounds.
        Try
            'Compute and display extended price for
            'the current row.
            TextBox3.Text = _
                Format( _
                dg(dg.CurrentCell.RowNumber, 3) * _
                dg(dg.CurrentCell.RowNumber, 4) * _
                (1 - dg(dg.CurrentCell.RowNumber, 0)) _
                , "C").ToString
            TextBox3.TextAlign = HorizontalAlignment.Right
            'If error is InvalidCastException, reset position
            'to last valid row; otherwise, display error.
        Catch er As System.InvalidCastException
            dg.CurrentCell = _
                New DataGridCell(intOldRow, _
```

(continued)

```
                dg.CurrentCell.ColumnNumber)
        Catch er As System.Exception
            MsgBox(er.Message & vbCr & er.ToString & _
                vbCr & "Reset row application manually.")
            Exit Try
        Finally
            'In any event, save row position.
            intOldRow = dg.CurrentRowIndex
        End Try

End Sub

Sub UpdatePositionIndicator(ByVal dg As DataGrid)

    'Update position display in TextBox1.
    TextBox1.Text = _
        (dg.CurrentCell.RowNumber + 1).ToString & _
        " of " & DsOrderDetails1. _
        Tables("Order Details").Rows.Count
    TextBox1.TextAlign = HorizontalAlignment.Right

End Sub

Private Sub Button1_Click(ByVal sender As System.Object, _
    ByVal e As System.EventArgs) Handles Button1.Click

    'Move to first row and save row position.
    DataGrid1.CurrentRowIndex = 0
    intOldRow = DataGrid1.CurrentRowIndex

End Sub

Private Sub Button2_Click(ByVal sender As System.Object, _
    ByVal e As System.EventArgs) Handles Button2.Click

    'Move backward one row if not already at
    'first row, and save row position.
    If DataGrid1.CurrentRowIndex > 0 Then
        DataGrid1.CurrentRowIndex -= 1
        intOldRow = DataGrid1.CurrentRowIndex
    End If

End Sub
```

```vb
Private Sub Button3_Click(ByVal sender As System.Object, _
    ByVal e As System.EventArgs) Handles Button3.Click

    'Move forward one row if not already at
    'last row, and save row position.
    If DataGrid1.CurrentRowIndex < DsOrderDetails1. _
        Tables("Order Details").Rows.Count - 1 Then
        DataGrid1.CurrentRowIndex += 1
        intOldRow = DataGrid1.CurrentRowIndex
    End If

End Sub

Private Sub Button4_Click(ByVal sender As System.Object, _
    ByVal e As System.EventArgs) Handles Button4.Click

    'Move to last row and save row position.
    DataGrid1.CurrentRowIndex = DsOrderDetails1. _
        Tables("Order Details").Rows.Count - 1
    intOldRow = DataGrid1.CurrentRowIndex

End Sub

Private Sub Button5_Click(ByVal sender As System.Object, _
    ByVal e As System.EventArgs) Handles Button5.Click

    'Set pointer for new row value.
    Dim int1 = CInt(TextBox1.Text) - 1

    'Go to designated row, and save row position or
    'restore old row position.
    If int1 >= 0 And int1 <= DsOrderDetails1. _
        Tables("Order Details").Rows.Count - 1 Then
        DataGrid1.CurrentRowIndex = int1
        intOldRow = DataGrid1.CurrentRowIndex
    Else
        DataGrid1.CurrentRowIndex = intOldRow
    End If

    'Compute text box display showing current row
    'relative to total number of rows.
    UpdatePositionIndicator(DataGrid1)

End Sub
```

Summary

Using Windows Forms to retrieve and manipulate data from Access databases via ADO.NET represents two learning opportunities for most Access developers. First, developers can learn about programming Windows form controls. Second, developers can learn the basics of ADO.NET and interfacing ADO.NET objects with form controls. This chapter addresses both of these issues without jumping deeply into ADO.NET. You primarily learn how to manage ADO.NET objects by dragging them from Server Explorer and creating *DataSet* objects with the Generate Dataset context command for a data adapter.

This chapter's coverage of Windows form controls presents familiar controls such as text boxes, combo boxes, and radio buttons—with one exception: the DataGrid control, a new .NET Framework control that you can program with Visual Basic .NET. This highly flexible control has many properties to help you dynamically populate it with data values and format how those values look as well as how users can interact with them. The chapter also includes extensive coverage of the Data Form Wizard, which can easily generate forms that enable data access and manipulation of Access databases. Several samples illustrate the breadth of functionality available through the wizard.

7

ADO.NET: Concepts and Architecture

This chapter formally introduces ADO.NET, the collection of classes that support data manipulation in the .NET Framework. Chapter 8 and Chapter 9 build on the foundation developed in this chapter. The coverage of ADO.NET in this chapter is distinctive for several reasons. First, this chapter focuses almost exclusively on using ADO.NET with Microsoft Access databases. All the sample code uses the Northwind database. Second, the discussion of ADO.NET selects core concepts that are easy to understand and that reinforce one another. The goal of this coverage is to help you understand why ADO.NET exists in the .NET Framework and how it contrasts with earlier data access technologies—particularly, ActiveX Data Objects (ADO). For example, you'll learn how ADO.NET can substantially improve the scalability of Access databases. Third, this chapter emphasizes conceptual and architectural issues, rather than coding issues. Several pieces of sample code are presented, but their purpose is to reveal interesting design elements about ADO.NET classes. In addition, the sample code demonstrates ways of using ADO.NET class instances to support one another.

This chapter is organized into three sections. The first section starts by discussing platform requirements. Because ADO.NET has different platform requirements than Access, you might want to look this material over as you plan your deployment of ADO.NET solutions for Access databases. This first section dwells on design issues such as the major ADO.NET classes and how they contrast with ADO. The second section systematically examines the core classes for the .NET data provider that you will use with Access databases. This section discusses the important properties and methods for each class and demonstrates how to use a subset of these elements with sample code. The third section dwells on the ADO.NET *DataSet* object model. *DataSet* is a new and distinctive class introduced by ADO.NET. Learning to use this object model will enable you to put ADO.NET to work in your solutions.

ADO.NET Platform and Design Issues

ADO.NET is the set of data components for the .NET Framework. In Chapters 3 through 5 you saw that you can also use the *ADODB* library through the COM Interop feature to perform traditional data access tasks. However, ADO.NET is the preferred route to data in Microsoft Visual Basic .NET applications because it is built into the .NET Framework. The tight integration of ADO.NET means that it offers richer capabilities and faster performance than *ADODB*. To tap these benefits, you have to learn ADO.NET concepts and architecture. This chapter is where you start.

Overview of ADO.NET Platform Issues

ADO.NET platform requirements include specifications for the operating system, Microsoft Data Access Components (MDAC), and the .NET Framework. To run ADO.NET solutions in Microsoft Windows application projects, your operating system must be one of the following: Windows 98, Windows Me, Windows XP, Windows NT (Service Pack 6A required), Windows 2000 (Service Pack 2 recommended), or Windows .NET Server. This chapter focuses on Windows application projects only; the operating system requirements change for ASP.NET and XML Web services solutions. See Chapter 10 for a review of ASP.NET requirements and Chapter 12 for commentary on the XML Web services requirements.

You need MDAC version 2.6 or later on a workstation running ADO.NET. Visit the Microsoft Universal Data Access site (*http://www.microsoft.com/data*) to download the most recent MDAC version free of charge. Because ADO.NET is built into the .NET Framework, a workstation requires the .NET Framework be installed in order to run an ADO.NET solution in a Windows application project. For most developers, the preferred route is to use Microsoft Visual Studio .NET, which includes the .NET Framework, to meet the ADO.NET installation requirements. However, you can also download the .NET Framework in redistributable or SDK versions from *http://msdn.microsoft.com/netframework/downloads/howtoget.asp*. Neither free version includes the graphical development tools or the rich, intuitive debugging tools that ship with Visual Studio .NET.

> **Note**   Because Access 2002 installs MDAC 2.5 by default and Access 2000 installs MDAC 2.1 by default, you need to check workstations with Access installed to make sure their MDAC versions have been upgraded to run an ADO.NET solution.

Like ADO, ADO.NET offers multiple data providers. Two ADO.NET data providers install with the .NET Framework. In addition, Microsoft offers two other ADO.NET data providers, which are available for download from the MSDN Web site. When using an Access database (Jet 4.0), you can use the OLE DB .NET Data Provider, which is one of the two data providers that installs with the .NET Framework. This same data provider is appropriate for Microsoft SQL Server databases earlier than version 7.0 and can also be used with Oracle databases. When you use this data provider, your Visual Basic .NET projects will require a reference that gives access to the *System.Data.OleDb* namespace. Applications processing databases in SQL Server 7.0 or SQL Server 2000 should use the SQL Server .NET Data Provider, the second provider that installs with the .NET Framework. When you use SQL Server .NET Data Provider elements, your projects will require a reference that gives access to the *System.Data.Sql-Client* namespace. Windows application projects make the appropriate namespace references available by default for the OLE DB .NET and SQL Server .NET data providers.

> **Note**   Many Access developers regularly use SQL Server databases. For those seeking more in-depth coverage of programming SQL Server solutions, I recommend another of my books: *Programming Microsoft SQL Server 2000 with Microsoft Visual Basic .NET* (Microsoft Press, 2002). This book presents extensive detail on SQL Server data access issues with T-SQL, Web releases for SQL Server 2000, and special .NET features available for SQL Server databases.

In spite of its name, the OLE DB .NET Data Provider is not generally suitable for working with databases other than Access, Oracle, and versions of SQL Server prior to version 7.0. For example, if you have an application that requires the Microsoft OLE DB Provider for ODBC, MSDASQL, you should not use the

OLE DB .NET driver. You should instead download a third driver, the ODBC .NET Data Provider, from the Microsoft downloads site. The ODBC .NET Data Provider is a .NET Framework add-on component. With this component, your applications can work with the native ODBC driver in the same way that the OLE DB .NET Data Provider permits your applications to work with Access, Oracle, and SQL Server databases prior to version 7.0. A workstation requires MDAC 2.7 or later to work with the ODBC .NET Data Provider. You can download the ODBC .NET Data Provider from this URL:

http://msdn.microsoft.com/downloads/default.asp?url=/downloads/ sample.asp?url=/MSDN-FILES/027/001/668/msdncompositedoc.xml

As with the *OleDb* and *SqlClient* namespaces, the *ODBC* namespace is a simple extension of the *System.Data* namespace after installation. A useful reference with sample code demonstrating how to use the ODBC .NET Data Provider with Visual Basic .NET is available here:

http://support.microsoft.com/default.aspx?scid=kb;en-us;q310985

After the release of Visual Studio .NET, Microsoft made a fourth data provider available for download. This data provider is for developers to use with Oracle databases. You can find information about the .NET Data Provider for Oracle and download the provider from the following URL:

http://msdn.microsoft.com/downloads/default.asp?url=/downloads/ sample.asp?url=/msdn-files/027/001/940/msdncompositedoc.xml

Overview of ADO.NET Design Elements

Because ADO.NET is so critical, you will benefit from reviewing the design features that make ADO.NET particularly valuable for the next generation of computing. ADO.NET maintains backward compatibility while delivering performance enhancements. This combination of benefits permits Access developers to enjoy enhanced performance from their legacy Access databases as they migrate to ADO.NET.

ADO.NET has two major element types: data providers and datasets. Earlier, this section described four Microsoft-supplied .NET data providers and explained when to use each one. The sample code in Chapter 6 and the Jump Start sample in Chapter 2 used the OLE DB .NET Data Provider without discussing it conceptually or architecturally. Together, the data provider and dataset elements provide a wide scope for the applicability of ADO.NET solutions. The Jump Start sample application in Chapter 2 and all the samples in Chapter 6 demonstrate the broad scope of uses that ADO.NET can have in Windows application projects. However, you can also use ADO.NET to access and manipulate data with ASP.NET applications that are tailored for Web solutions (see Chapter 11), or you can use ADO.NET with XML Web services solutions that can access data from another computer over the Internet or an intranet (see Chapter 12). In addition, ADO.NET is suitable in even more exotic environments, such as those used by mobile devices.

You have probably read dozens of articles and possibly a book or two about the .NET Framework and perhaps even ADO.NET. However, you might still be wondering how the ADO.NET design elements interface with relational database objects—especially tables and queries from Access databases. In addition, you might want to know how ADO.NET design elements relate to XML— the emerging lingua franca for data exchange.

Figure 7-1 provides a high-level overview of key linkages and highlights some roles of data providers and datasets. .NET data providers can connect, read, and update database objects. The way that data providers accomplish these tasks varies from one provider to another, but all providers expose the same kind of objects to permit the same general range of functions. One component exposed by the .NET data providers is the *DataAdapter* class. Its role is to serve as a pipe between relational database objects (such as tables in an Access database) and a *DataSet* object. The *DataSet* class is a new data component. A *DataSet* instance can hold one or more tables that are populated by various data adapters. A dataset can represent its data much like a relational database, with relationships among tables or like an XML document. The capability to represent datasets natively as XML documents is important. This is because XML can pass through corporate firewalls, while COM objects such as ADO recordsets cannot pass through firewalls without special settings, which can expose a network to security breaches. See this book's Chapter Appendix for information on some of the important XML features that apply to Access developers creating solutions with Visual Basic .NET.

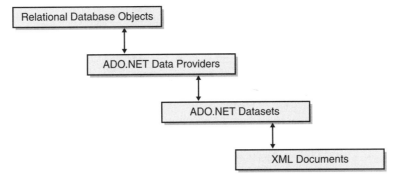

Figure 7-1   The ADO.NET Data Provider and dataset elements relative to relational database objects and XML documents

The .NET data providers expose functionality through four standard classes: *Connection*, *Command*, *DataReader*, and *DataAdapter*. The good news is that the ADO.NET *Connection* class functions similarly to the familiar ADO *Connection* class. In fact, this class's ADO.NET connection strings are remarkably similar to ADO connection strings. ADO.NET *Connection* objects link a .NET application to a database such as Northwind.

You use the *Command* class for executing SQL statements against a database. You can perform data access, data manipulation, and even data definition tasks with *Command* objects. The *data access* capability is a standard query capability, except you will typically need to deliver the result set to an object— a data reader—that can use a result set. *Data manipulation* includes insert, update, and delete tasks. Again, you have to specify the operation in SQL, but you can bypass the use of another object. A *data definition* task refers to the definition of a database object, such as a table or a query, in a database. Using the *Command* object this way requires an understanding of the Jet SQL data definition language (DDL). Unlike queries, Access has no graphical designer for data definition tasks.

The *DataReader* class provides read-only, forward-only access to a data source designated by a SQL SELECT statement for a *Command* object. Therefore, a *DataReader* class instance functions similarly to a read-only, forward-only cursor. A *DataReader* object does one thing: it reads data. The class provides no opportunity to scroll backward and forward through the data returned by a *Command* object. Nor does the *DataReader* class allow you to modify this data.

The *DataAdapter* object serves two main purposes. First, it populates a *DataSet* object from a database. Second, it can convey to a database the result of manipulating a local dataset. You typically associate a different data adapter with each table in a dataset so that a dataset with multiple tables can have multiple data adapters managing the flow of data between itself and a database. *DataAdapter* instances do not require an open connection to a database.

Both the *DataAdapter* and the *DataReader* objects provide access to database information. However, the *DataReader* object achieves superior performance to *DataAdapter* instances populating *DataSet* instances for a couple of reasons. First, no overhead is associated with managing the in-memory data cache for the dataset. Second, a *DataReader* must have a dedicated, open *Connection* object to a data source. As mentioned, the *DataAdapter* object interfaces with a disconnected dataset, meaning you can use the *DataAdapter* object without a dedicated, open connection to a data source. As a result, a *DataAdapter* instance has to manage its connection in a way that a *DataReader* instance does not. However, this same feature supports the scalability improvements of data adapters over data readers. By not requiring an open connection, the *DataAdapter* object permits a database to service more concurrent users. *DataAdapter* objects do not require stand-alone *Command* objects with SQL statements because you can define SQL statements as property settings for a *DataAdapter* object.

Data manipulation is an especially interesting topic because a data adapter performs this kind of task for a dataset that is disconnected from its database source, except during the actual update. In other words, ADO.NET performs data manipulation via dataset objects to a database with *optimistic concurrency*. As long as your application enables only one user at a time to update a row, data manipulation will occur without a hitch. However, if two users in a multiuser application can manipulate the same row at the same time, a concurrency violation is possible.

Imagine a scenario in which user 1 makes a change to a column value in a local dataset. If user 2 makes a change to the same column value and updates the database before user 1, when user 1 attempts to update the column value, a concurrency violation can occur. This occurs because the database is different from when user 1 initially invoked a command to populate its dataset from the database. The .NET Framework offers a couple of strategies for handling such a concurrency violation in your applications. You need to be aware of the potential problem, and you should design your database solutions to prohibit such concurrency violations or to handle them when they occur. See the "Concurrency Violations" section in Chapter 8 for more detailed commentary on concurrency violations along with a sample that demonstrates an approach for handling them if they occur.

> **Note**   The built-in procedures for detecting concurrency violations is at the level of individual rows. If you require more granular concurrency violation checks—for example, for individual column values within a row—the .NET Framework is flexible enough to accommodate your specialized requirements.

Comparison of ADO.NET and ADO Data Access

As you begin creating Access database solutions with Visual Basic .NET, one of your major decisions will be whether to use ADO.NET or ADO. As you know, ADO is available to Visual Basic .NET developers through the COM Interop feature. Although many Access developers are already familiar with the basics of ADO, ADO.NET has important advantages that make it the better choice for any application with a long life expectancy. The lifetime of the application is an important consideration because ADO.NET is at the beginning of its life cycle, while ADO is at the end of its lifetime. ADO.NET already enjoys more innovative design features than ADO, but the ADO.NET advantage naturally will grow over time as ADO.NET adds functionality consistent with the latest advances and standards in data access technology. ADO functionality, on the other hand, will remain fixed. In some ways, Access developers are at a turning point, just as they were when ADO was introduced as an alternative to Data Access Objects (DAO). Most Access developers who switched to ADO enjoyed significant advantages over those who stayed with DAO.

One major shift in ADO.NET is the elimination of the ADO recordset. In some ways, the ADO.NET *DataSet* object replaces the *Recordset* object, but important differences between a recordset and a dataset exist. A recordset is meant primarily for connected data access, but a dataset is a disconnected data cache that can be filled with data from a database file by a data adapter. Although you can program ADO recordsets for disconnected access, this is not their normal function and the disconnected mode does not take advantage of the full feature set built into the *Recordset* object. The dataset is built from the ground up for disconnected data access, and the only way to use the dataset is as a disconnected data store. Disconnected access vastly expands the scalability of a database. Thus, you can service more users of an Access database file with a dataset than you can with a recordset.

As mentioned earlier, ADO.NET also offers the *DataReader* object for forward-only, read-only access to data. Again, this is a pure play. You cannot use a data reader to enable data manipulation some of the time and as a read-only object at other times. The ADO recordset lets you switch between these and other modes based on your cursor settings.

The ADO *Recordset* object allows the representation of data from two or more record sources, but the representation always appears as a flat collection of rows and columns. A recordset displays one, two, three, or more tables and queries as a single collection of rows. The ADO.NET *DataSet* object can represent separate and distinct collections of rows in various tables. In addition, a dataset can designate a relationship between any pair of tables within it. Visual Studio .NET includes graphical tools for creating a *typed dataset* instead of the default, an *untyped dataset*. A typed dataset exposes data similarly to a class instance so that it is easier to program. Recordsets do not offer this functionality.

A dataset is natively an XML document, which offers important benefits for passing through firewalls and representing data types relative to a recordset. Because a saved XML document is a text file with tags, to a firewall an XML document looks just like an HTML document that the firewall allows to pass through. On the other hand, firewalls are designed to block the entry of programs that can perform malicious acts to the network. Because a *Recordset* object is a COM object, firewalls typically block them, even though a recordset contains only data. Furthermore, as a COM object, data in a *Recordset* must conform to one of the predefined COM data types. This typically requires conversion from native database data types to predefined COM data types. XML documents have a broader array of native data types, and XML allows programmers to create custom data types. Therefore, datasets offer more flexible data types than recordsets. Because a dataset is an XML document, it requires no conversion of its data types. Therefore, transfer between computers is faster with a dataset than with a recordset.

ADO.NET Architecture

As the previous section mentioned, the .NET data providers offer four classes for handling data: *Connection, Command, DataReader,* and *DataAdapter*. This section reviews selected properties and methods for each of these classes. In addition, a few pieces of sample code illustrate the basics of using the properties and methods for these classes. The samples in Chapter 8 and Chapter 9 will illustrate more practical ways of using these classes that build on the foundation laid by this chapter's discussion and sample code. You will find all this chapter's forms and sample code in the OleDbObjectSamples project. A switchboard program in *Form1*, the startup object, lets you navigate to each of the other forms.

OleDbConnection

The *OleDbConnection* class is the OLE DB .NET Data Provider class for implementing a connection with a database. You point an *OleDbConnection* object at a database. Other ADO.NET objects can use the contents of the database through an *OleDbConnection* object that points at it.

Selected *OleDbConnection* Properties and Methods

You can use the *New* method of the *OleDbConnection* class to create a fresh connection to a database. The *New* method takes an optional string argument that designates a connection string for the database to which you want to point an *OleDbConnection* instance. If you do not specify an argument for the *New* method, you can assign a connection string to an *OleDbConnection* object through its *ConnectionString* property. These two alternative formulations comprise the set of overloaded constructors for the *OleDbConnection* class. See the "Overview of Concepts and Keywords" and "Derived Class Features" sections in Chapter 4 for background material of the power that overloaded constructors bring to .NET Framework classes.

You can look at the contents of the *ConnectionString* property to verify the arguments for an *OleDbConnection* instance. The *ConnectionString* property reflects the connection properties that you set before you open the database connection. Use the *Open* method to enable a connection to a database and the *Close* method to free a connection to a database. You cannot assign a new *ConnectionString* property value for an *OleDbConnection* object while the object is open, but you can assign a new value to the property after invoking the *Close* method for the *OleDbConnection* instance.

> **Note** To refer to *System.Data.OleDb* namespace members by their name without designating the namespace name as a prefix, the module instantiating a connection object must have an *Imports* statement, such as *Imports System.Data.OleDb*. Without this *Imports* statement, any reference in code to a namespace member must have the namespace as a prefix.

The details of a connection string are specific to the type of database that you are using and the way that you want to use it. To connect to an Access database, you need to specify a *Provider* clause and a *Data Source* clause. Assign a string value to the *Provider* argument that designates the name of the provider. This is the same argument that you used with ADO: *Microsoft.Jet.OLEDB.4.0*. Follow the provider string with a semicolon. Then designate the *Data Source* clause. This is the path and filename to the Access database file. For example, for the Northwind database in Access 2002 at its default location, you can specify c:\Program Files\Microsoft Office\Office10\Samples\Northwind.mdb. You do not have to designate the full path when your database is in the bin subdirectory of the project folder. Instead, you can specify just the filename. Therefore, if you have a copy of the Northwind.mdb file in the bin subdirectory of the project folder, you can designate the *Data Source* argument as Northwind.mdb without any path information.

Sample Code

Figure 7-2 shows *Form2* in the OleDbObjectSamples project. This form has two buttons, each with a click event procedure in the module behind the form. In addition, a connection object from the OLE DB .NET Data Provider appears below the form with the name *OleDbConnection1*. I dragged the whole connection (not any particular database object) from Server Explorer to create the object instance. Because I dragged the connection instead of an object within the database, Visual Studio .NET did not generate a data adapter. In addition, Visual Studio .NET was smart enough to recognize that an Access database needs a connection object from the OLE DB .NET Data Provider. Therefore, the IDE created an instance of the *OleDbConnection* class as opposed to a connection class based on one of the other .NET data providers.

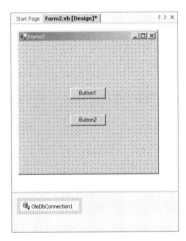

Figure 7-2   A form with a pair of buttons and a connection object created with Visual Studio .NET at design time

The module behind *Form2* processes two connections. First, it works with a connection object instantiated via code at run time, which means you do not need a preexisting connection defined in Server Explorer. You can simply define the two minimum clauses for the connection object's connection string and call the *Open* method on the object to have a live connection to a database. Second, the code behind *Form2* works with the *OleDbConnection1* object that appears below the form in Figure 7-2. *OleDbConnection1* is a design-time instance of an *OleDbConnection* object. By displaying the connection string for *OleDbConnection1*, you can see the special assignments that Windows Form Designer makes as you drag items from Server Explorer to a form.

Deploying a Project with a Connection

In general, you should deploy Windows application projects for running on another computer as the project folder. The "Using the Start Page" section in Chapter 2 briefly describes a couple of approaches for implementing this. For projects that use a database, the connection can point to a database in the project folder, in some standard location for the database on every computer, or in a single standard UNC specification on a LAN from which all workstations access the database.

Although you can sometimes run a project with a database connection residing on another computer, my recommendation is to always deploy the project folder to the computer running the project. This avoids potential problems from cross-computer security settings that can block the execution of the project. Access developers will note that this approach is similar to the requirement for .adp files that work with SQL Server databases or for a front-end/back-end solution for .mdb files. In the latter case, all users have their own front-end project (an .mdb file) that links to a common back-end project (another .mdb file shared by multiple users). Releasing a change to the front-end design involves distributing a new front-end file to each user. Similarly, with Visual Basic .NET projects connecting to an Access project, you should distribute a Visual Basic .NET project to each user.

I will discuss security issues for Access databases in Visual Basic .NET solutions in more detail in Chapter 13. For now, we will focus on the basics of instantiating ADO.NET objects in code and using those objects.

The listing for the code behind *Form2* appears next. The code module for *Form2* contains an *Imports* statement for the *System.Data.OleDb* namespace not shown in the listing.

The click event procedure for *Button1* is the most interesting of the two event procedures. The *Button1_Click* procedure starts by designing a connection string that points at the Northwind database. You can readily adapt this approach to any other database simply by changing the string value in the second assignment to *str1*. After designing the connection string, the procedure puts the string to work by creating an *OleDbConnection* object named *cnn1* and opens the connection. At this point, you can tell whether your settings are correct and the database file is available. After connecting successfully, the procedure displays the *Provider* and *DataSource* properties for the *cnn1* object.

These two properties correspond to the two connection string clauses specified before instantiating the *Connection* object.

In production solutions, you will probably want to place your statements invoking the *Open* method in a *Try...Catch...Finally* statement. The procedure illustrates the syntax for a simple *Try...Catch...Finally* statement that catches an error from an attempt to invoke an invalid call to the *Open* method.

After making one connection with the *cnn1* object, the procedure prepares to reuse the *cnn1* object to connect to a new database. To revise the connection string, the procedure needs to call the *Close* method to close the *cnn1* object. (Microsoft recommends using the *Close* method rather than the more generic *Dispose* method.) The new *Connection* object has an intentional error in its connection string. The string designates a connection to the *Northwinds* database, instead of the Northwind database. My test computers for this book have no Northwinds database, so the procedure fails. The attempt to open the connection for the *cnn1* variable generates an error with a *System.Data.OleDb.OleDbException* object. To keep the code simple, the *Try...Catch...Finally* statement checks for a general system *Exception* object and displays a general message. Even this elementary statement design manages to recover gracefully from the error when it occurs. Notice in the *Finally* clause that the procedure closes the *cnn1* object. The .NET Framework does not throw another exception in this case, even though the *cnn1* object is already closed. Therefore, it is good practice to include a *Close* method for a connection in the *Finally* clause when you embed its *Open* method in the *Try* clause.

```
Private Sub Button1_Click(ByVal sender As System.Object, _
    ByVal e As System.EventArgs) Handles Button1.Click

    'Designate string for connection to Northwind database.
    Dim str1 As String = _
        "Provider = Microsoft.Jet.OLEDB.4.0;"
    str1 += _
        "Data Source = c:\Program Files\" & _
        "Microsoft Office\Office10\Samples\Northwind.mdb"

    'Instantiate and open cnn1 instance of
    'OleDbConnection class.
    Dim cnn1 As OleDbConnection = New OleDbConnection(str1)
    cnn1.Open()

    'Display Provider and Data Source.
    MsgBox("Provider=" & cnn1.Provider & vbCr & _
        "Data Source=" & cnn1.DataSource, _
        MsgBoxStyle.Information, _
```

(continued)

```
            "After initial open")

        'Close connection.
        cnn1.Close()

        'Specify new erroneous connection string to
        'the "Northwinds.mdb" Access database file.
        cnn1.ConnectionString = _
            "Provider = Microsoft.Jet.OLEDB.4.0;"
        cnn1.ConnectionString += _
            "Data Source = c:\Program Files\" & _
            "Microsoft Office\Office10\Samples\" & _
            "Northwinds.mdb"

        'Display Provider and Data Source.
        MsgBox("Provider=" & cnn1.Provider & vbCr & _
            "Data Source=" & cnn1.DataSource, _
            MsgBoxStyle.Information, _
            "After resetting connection string")

        'Attempt to connect with invalid
        'connection string.
        Try         cnn1.Open()
        Catch exc1 As Exception
            MsgBox("Something went wrong.", _
                MsgBoxStyle.Exclamation, _
                "Wrong Connection String")
        Finally
            cnn1.Close        Me.Close()
        End Try

    End Sub

    Private Sub Button2_Click(ByVal sender As System.Object, _
        ByVal e As System.EventArgs) Handles Button2.Click

        Dim str1 As String = OleDbConnection1.ConnectionString

        'Display full list of connection string
        'clauses for a default connection.
        MsgBox(str1)

        'Close the form.
        Me.Close()

    End Sub
```

The second procedure in the preceding listing handles a click to *Button2*. This procedure merely displays the connection string for the *OleDbConnection1* object before closing the form. As mentioned, I created the *OleDbConnection1* object at design time by dragging a connection from Server Explorer to *Form2*. Therefore, Visual Studio .NET constructed the connection string for the application. Figure 7-3 shows the message box opened by a click to *Button2*. Notice that it contains substantially more than the *Provider* and *Data Source* clauses designed in the click event procedure for *Button1*. These additional clauses are specified by the Windows Form Designer. The items in the message box do not represent the total set of *OleDbConnection* object properties. In fact, many of these items are not connection properties but instead are optional settings for the Jet engine. The message box returns these clauses because the Windows Form Designer specifies them. These items suggest that you have some flexibility in creating your connection strings. For example, for database files with user-level security, you will need to specify connection strings with *UserID* and *Password* clauses.

Figure 7-3   A message box showing an expanded range of connection string clauses that are available for your use

OleDbCommand

An *OleDbCommand* object is a wrapper for a SQL statement. With this kind of ADO.NET object, your applications can program any of the three classic SQL language functions of data access, data manipulation, and data definition. The *OleDbCommand* object is capable by itself of returning a scalar value from a database, such as the count or the sum of the values in a column of a table. You can also use the *OleDbCommand* object with either an *OleDbDataReader* or an *OleDbDataAdapter* to process sets of rows from a data source. The SQL statement inside an *OleDbCommand* requires a database context that designates where to invoke that statement. You can assign the database context for the SQL statement by assigning an *OleDbConnection* instance to the *Connection* property for the *OleDbCommand* object.

> **Note** To get the most from the *OleDbCommand* class, you will need valid Jet SQL statements that can accomplish the tasks you want to perform. Access developers can still build a query graphically within Access, then copy and paste the code from the query's SQL view into another location, such as a Visual Basic .NET procedure. The "SQL Reserved Words" Access Help topic under "Microsoft Jet SQL Reference," "Overview," documents Jet SQL statements, but the links from this page do not offer many code samples. My book *Programming Microsoft Access Version 2002* (Microsoft Press, 2001) includes 20 pages that present Jet SQL code samples for most data access tasks and another 10 pages with Jet SQL samples for data definition tasks.

The *CommandText* and *CommandType* properties help you specify the contents of or the source for an *OleDbCommand* instance. By default, the *Command-Type* property equals *Text*. With this default setting, you can assign a string with a SQL statement to the *CommandText* property. You can also specify a name for a query with parameters (a stored procedure) or even a table name. When you use one of these alternative specifications for the *CommandText* property, you must designate either *StoredProcedure* or *TableDirect* for the *Command-Type* property of the *OleDbCommand* object.

Another special feature of commands is their ability to accept parameters. For example, if you have an *OleDbCommand* object to insert a new row in a table, you can use parameters to specify the column values for the new row. This enables the reuse of the same *OleDbCommand* object for the insertion of new rows with different column values (namely, the parameter value assignments).

After specifying the *Connection* and *CommandText* properties along with any other required properties for your implementation of an *OleDbCommand* object, you can execute the command. If you are using the command directly, choose either the *ExecuteScalar* method or the *ExecuteNonQuery* method. The *ExecuteScalar* method returns just the first column value from the first row in the result set for a query. You can assign the return value to a memory variable for use in your program. The *ExecuteNonQuery* method does not provide a result set. This method is suitable when the SQL statement does not return a result set, such as for a data definition statement that adds a new query to a database.

Note   The constructor, which is implemented by the *New* method, for the *OleDbCommand* class is overloaded. Therefore, you can specify a basic instantiation of a new *OleDbCommand* object, or you can use a more elaborate form of the method that designates several property settings that you might need (such as the SQL statement and the connection) with your *OleDbCommand* instantiation statement.

Form3 in the OleDbObjectSamples project illustrates a couple of *OleDb-Command* object application issues. The form's design has the same basic layout as that of *Form2* with two buttons. (See Figure 7-2 on page 323.) The code behind the form extends the coverage of OLE DB .NET Data Provider classes to include both connections and commands. The click event procedure for the first button demonstrates the use of the *ExecuteScalar* method after setting up the *OleDbCommand* object. The second button demonstrates a basic approach to managing the insertion and deletion of rows within a table in a database. You will find the *OleDbDataAdapter* object a more robust tool for data manipulation tasks such as this, but if you have simple application requirements (or very unusual requirements), you might find using a command can keep your overhead lower while still being highly flexible.

The code behind *Form3* includes three procedures—a click event procedure for each button and a *Function* procedure that instantiates and returns an *OleDbConnection*. Because both click event procedures work with the Northwind database, the *Function* procedure enables them to avoid repeating the same code to instantiate a connection to the Northwind database. The sample function, *ConnectToNorthwind*, connects to the Northwind database, but you could easily generalize the function by passing a connection string argument. The code behind *Form3* does not include an *Imports* statement for the *System.Data.OleDb* namespace. Therefore, the code in the module must use the namespace name before each reference to a member in the namespace. This is a mixed blessing. On the one hand, it requires more typing. On the other hand, this code is self-documenting.

The click event procedure for *Button1* starts by declaring and instantiating empty *OleDbConnection* and *OleDbCommand* instances; *cnn1* represents the connection, and *cmd1* denotes the command. Next, the *Button1_Click* procedure invokes the *ConnectToNorthwind* procedure to create a connection to the

Northwind database. After assigning the returned object from the *ConnectTo-Northwind* function to *cnn1*, the procedure opens the connection. Then the click event procedure sets the *Connection* and *CommandText* property values for the *cmd1* object. The SQL statement in the string variable for *CommandText* counts the number of CategoryID values in the Categories table. Because the CategoryID column is the primary key for the table, the count of CategoryID is the number of rows in the Categories table. The *Button1_Click* procedure invokes the *ExecuteScalar* method for *cmd1* to return the count of categories and displays the result in a message box. The event procedure then closes the connection.

The *Button2_Click* procedure begins similarly to the preceding event procedure. The preliminary steps conclude by assigning the opened *cnn1* object to the *Connection* property for *cmd1*. The *Button2_Click* procedure toggles the insertion and deletion of a customer in the Customers table. On the first pass through the procedure, the code inserts a new row with Customer-ID and CompanyName values of *MYCOM* and *ProgrammingMS-Access.com*. Because this row is not initially in the Customers table, the first attempt succeeds in the *Try…Catch…Finally* statement. Clicking *Button2* a second time throws a *System.Data.OleDb.OleDbException* object. The *Try…Catch…Finally* statement catches the exception and deletes the row with a CustomerID column value of *MYCOM*. With just a little editing, you can readily extend the simple logic here to add more column values, automatically copy over a duplicate row or save the values in a duplicate row to a disk file.

```
Private Sub Button1_Click(ByVal sender As System.Object, _
    ByVal e As System.EventArgs) Handles Button1.Click

    'Declare and instantiate Connection and Command objects.
    Dim cnn1 As New System.Data.OleDb.OleDbConnection()
    Dim cmd1 As New System.Data.OleDb.OleDbCommand()

    'Open connection to Northwind database.
    cnn1 = ConnectToNorthwind()
    cnn1.Open()

    'Assign Connection and CommandText property values
    'for the cmd1 OleDbCommand object.
    cmd1.Connection = cnn1
    cmd1.CommandText = _
        "SELECT Count(CategoryID) FROM Categories"

    'Save result set from command in int1 memory variable.
    Dim int1 As Integer = cmd1.ExecuteScalar
```

```
    'Display result from query.
    MsgBox("The number of categories is " & _
        int1.ToString & ".")

    'Close connection.
    cnn1.Close()

End Sub

Private Sub Button2_Click(ByVal sender As System.Object, _
    ByVal e As System.EventArgs) Handles Button2.Click

    'Declare and instantiate Connection and Command objects.
    Dim cnn1 As New System.Data.OleDb.OleDbConnection()
    Dim cmd1 As New System.Data.OleDb.OleDbCommand()

    'Open connection to Northwind database.
    cnn1 = ConnectToNorthwind()
    cnn1.Open()

    'Assign connection.
    cmd1.Connection = cnn1

    'Attempt to insert MYCOM CustomerID; if record is already
    'there, attempt to delete.
    Try
        cmd1.CommandText = _
            "INSERT INTO Customers (CustomerID, CompanyName) " & _
            "Values ('MYCOM', 'ProgrammingMSAccess.com')"
        cmd1.ExecuteNonQuery()
        MsgBox("Inserted Customer with CustomerID of MYCOM", , _
            "Inserted it")
    Catch exc1 As System.Data.OleDb.OleDbException
        cmd1.CommandText = _
            "Delete * FROM Customers WHERE CustomerID = 'MYCOM'"
        cmd1.ExecuteNonQuery()
        MsgBox("Deleted Customer with CustomerID of MYCOM", , _
            "Deleted it")
    Finally
        cnn1.Close()
    End Try

End Sub

Function ConnectToNorthwind() As System.Data.OleDb.OleDbConnection
```

(continued)

```
'Designate string for connection to Northwind database.
Dim str1 As String = _
    "Provider = Microsoft.Jet.OLEDB.4.0;"
str1 += _
    "Data Source = c:\Program Files\" & _
    "Microsoft Office\Office10\Samples\Northwind.mdb"

'Instantiate and assign the connection string
'to the Connection object.
Dim cnn1 As New System.Data.OleDb.OleDbConnection()
cnn1.ConnectionString = str1

'Return the Connection object.
Return cnn1

End Function
```

OleDbDataReader

As mentioned previously, an *OleDbDataReader* object enables a forward-only, read-only pass through the result set returned by an *OleDbCommand* object. Although you must declare a *DataReader* variable to programmatically manipulate one, the *OleDbDataReader* class does not offer a *New* method. The only way to instantiate a data reader is with the *ExecuteReader* method for a *Command* object. The *OleDbDataReader* object requires the exclusive use of the connection associated with its *OleDbCommand* object. When you are finished looping through the rows of a result set, you should close both the data reader and the connection.

After creating an instance of an *OleDbDataReader* class, your initial position within the result set will be just before the first row. To gain access to the first (and subsequent) rows, you can invoke the *Read* method. The *Read* method advances your position one row in a result set each time you invoke it. The column positions within a row are zero-based. You can read the column values for the current row position with a collection of *Get* methods, such as *GetInt32* and *GetString*. Each *System* data type has a *Get* method. (See Chapter 3 for a comparison of .NET Framework *System* data types with Visual Basic .NET data types.) Use the *FieldCount* property to determine the number of columns in a result set. The *FieldCount* property is not dependent on moving to a row with data so that you can invoke it before moving to the first row. After moving to the first row, you can iterate through the columns in the row and report the *System* data type for each column. This information is useful in determining which *Get* method to use to extract data from a column in the current row.

Form4 in the OleDbObjectSamples project illustrates design principles for applying *OleDbDataReader* instances. As with the preceding samples in this chapter, the form has two buttons. The click event for *Button1* presents a couple of message boxes, one after the other. The first message box reports the number of columns in the Shippers table. The second message box reports the data type for each column in the table. You often will know this information when you are the architect of a database or you use the database often. However, database developers and administrators regularly inherit a database from another analyst or as part of an upgrading project from end users. Adaptations of a procedure such as this can be helpful in these cases. The click event procedure for *Button2* iterates through the rows in the Shippers table and displays the column values for each row.

There are four procedures in the module behind *Form4*—one click event procedure each for *Button1* and *Button2*, plus a pair of functions for returning a connection to the Northwind database (*ConnectToNorthwind*) and a data reader with a result set containing the column values for all rows in the Shippers table (*ShippersDataReader*). The event procedures manage a task or two and invoke the *Function* procedures to help achieve their tasks. The *Connect-ToNorthwind* function is identical to the earlier sample; this is a good example of code reuse based on procedures. The *ShippersDataReader* function accepts a connection argument passed to it and returns an *OleDbDataReader* object. The function starts by instantiating an *OleDbCommand* object, *cmd1*. Next, the function defines the *Connection* and *CommandText* property values so that executing the SQL statement in *cmd1* generates a result set with the column values for all rows in the Shippers table of the Northwind database.

You have seen this kind of code before. What's new is the invocation of the *ExecuteReader* method for the *Command* object. This method creates a data reader that can process the result set in *cmd1*. No built-in *OleDbCommand* method exists for processing a result set with multiple rows. The *Shippers-DataReader* function concludes by returning the data reader for its use in the routine calling it. In the current application, this function can be called by the click event procedure for *Button1* or *Button2*.

The *Button1_Click* procedure starts by instantiating and opening an *Ole-DbConnection* object named *cnn1*. Then, the procedure passes *cnn1* to the *ShippersDataReader* function to generate a *DataReader* object (*drd1*) based on the Shippers table. Next, the procedure displays the number of columns in the Shippers table by displaying in a message box the *FieldCount* property for *drd1*. After a user closes the message box, the procedure moves on to read the first row in the result set with the *Read* method for the *OleDbDataReader* object. In a *For...Next* loop, the code iterates through the columns to develop a string that lists the field number, name, and data type for each successive field in the result set.

Notice the syntax distinction in how the procedure references the *Get-Name* method and the *GetType* method. For the *GetName* method, you pass the index for the column as an argument to the method. For the *GetType* method, you apply the method to an indexed column (*drd1(int1)*). The procedure's code delimits the metadata for each field with a carriage return. The procedure concludes by invoking the *Close* method for both the data reader and the connection. This is good Visual Basic .NET coding practice.

> **Note**   You're probably already familiar with the term *metadata*, but just to make sure, it means data about data. For example, the field number, name, and data type are metadata for a result set based on a table.

Figure 7-4 shows the two message boxes generated by the *Button1_Click* procedure. The Shippers table contains the standard number of rows (three) after it is installed. The second message box contains a sentence with the metadata for each column in the result set. The sentence for each column lists the field number and name along with the .NET Framework *System* data type. You can use this information to determine how to read values from the result set.

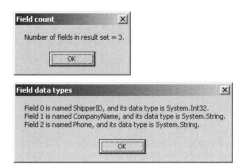

Figure 7-4   The top message box shows metadata about the number of fields in a result set that a data reader points at, and the bottom message box shows more detailed data about each field in the result set.

The *Button2_Click* procedure demonstrates how to iterate through the rows of a data reader and return the column values for each row. The procedure copies these values to a string, but you could just as easily use an array, a disk file, or another database, such as one in the project folder. This click event procedure starts the same way as the *Button1* click procedure. After creating a data reader with the column values for the Shippers table, the code starts a *Do Loop* construct and successively invokes the *Read* method for the data reader. As long as the data reader contains another row, the loop continues to iterate. When no more rows remain unread, the *Do Loop* construct passes control to the statement immediately after the loop. Within the loop, the procedure creates a string with the three column values on each row. The code delimits the values for each row from one another by a carriage return. A message box after the loop displays the string constructed within the loop.

```
Private Sub Button1_Click(ByVal sender As System.Object, _
    ByVal e As System.EventArgs) Handles Button1.Click

    'Open connection to Northwind database.
    Dim cnn1 As _
        System.Data.OleDb.OleDbConnection = _
        ConnectToNorthwind()
    cnn1.Open()

    'Make available a data reader for the Shippers table.
    Dim drd1 As System.Data.OleDb.OleDbDataReader
    drd1 = ShippersDataReader(cnn1)

    'Return the count of fields in the result set.
    MsgBox("Number of fields in result set = " & _
        drd1.FieldCount.ToString & ".", , _
        "Field count")

    'Read the first row in the result set.
    drd1.Read()
    'Report the data types of the fields in the row.
    Dim int1 As Integer
    Dim str1 As String
    For int1 = 0 To drd1.FieldCount - 1
        str1 += "Field " & int1.ToString & _
            " is named " & drd1.GetName(int1) & _
            ", and its data type is " & _
            drd1(int1).GetType.ToString() & "." & vbCr
    Next int1
    MsgBox(str1, , "Field data types")

    'Clean up.
    drd1.Close()
    cnn1.Close()
```

(continued)

```
End Sub

Private Sub Button2_Click(ByVal sender As System.Object, _
    ByVal e As System.EventArgs) Handles Button2.Click

    'Open connection to Northwind database.
    Dim cnn1 As _
        System.Data.OleDb.OleDbConnection = _
        ConnectToNorthwind()
    cnn1.Open()

    'Make available a data reader for the Shippers table.
    Dim drd1 As System.Data.OleDb.OleDbDataReader
    drd1 = ShippersDataReader(cnn1)

    'Iterate through rows of the result set
    'returned by cmd1 and display column values
    'in a message box.
    Dim str1 As String
    Do While drd1.Read
        str1 += drd1.GetInt32(0).ToString & _
            ", " & drd1.GetString(1) & _
            ", " & drd1.GetString(2) & vbCr
    Loop
    MsgBox(str1)

    'Clean up.
    drd1.Close()
    cnn1.Close()

End Sub

Function ShippersDataReader(ByVal cnn1 As _
    System.Data.OleDb.OleDbConnection) As _
    System.Data.OleDb.OleDbDataReader

    'Declare and instantiate Command object.
    Dim cmd1 As New System.Data.OleDb.OleDbCommand()

    'Assign Connection and CommandText property values
    'for the cmd1 OleDbCommand object.
    cmd1.Connection = cnn1
    cmd1.CommandText = _
        "SELECT * FROM Shippers"

    'Create an instance of a data reader for
    'the result set returned by cmd1.
    Dim drd1 As System.Data.OleDb.OleDbDataReader
```

```
        drd1 = cmd1.ExecuteReader

        Return drd1

End Function

Function ConnectToNorthwind() As _
    System.Data.OleDb.OleDbConnection

        'Designate string for connection to Northwind database.
        Dim str1 As String = _
            "Provider = Microsoft.Jet.OLEDB.4.0;"
        str1 += _
            "Data Source = c:\Program Files\" & _
            "Microsoft Office\Office10\Samples\Northwind.mdb"

        'Instantiate and assign the connection string
        'to the Connection object.
        Dim cnn1 As New System.Data.OleDb.OleDbConnection()
        cnn1.ConnectionString = str1

        'Return the Connection object.
        Return cnn1

End Function
```

OleDbDataAdapter

The *OleDbDataAdapter* class has two main roles. First, a class instance can fill a table within a local dataset with the contents of a database object, such as a table or query. Use the *Fill* method to implement this role. Second, a class instance can update the object in the database used to fill the table in the local dataset with any changes made to the local dataset. Apply the *Update* method to carry out this role. The update to the database object reflects any data manipulation tasks performed against the table in the local dataset, including the revision of a column value in an existing row, the deletion of an existing row, and the addition of a new row.

Properties and Methods

The *OleDbDataAdapter* object has four properties that moderate the operation of the *Fill* and *Update* methods. These properties designate the database object in a database to reference and indicate what kind of operation to perform. The four property names are *SelectCommand*, *UpdateCommand*, *InsertCommand*, and *DeleteCommand*. You can assign *OleDbCommand* objects to these properties. The *CommandText* property for the *OleDbCommand* object designates the result set or action associated with the property. The *SelectCommand* property is a specification for the result set from a database that a data adapter makes available to a local dataset. This result set is based on the *CommandText* property for the command object returned by the *SelectCommand* property. The *UpdateCommand*, *InsertCommand*, and *DeleteCommand* properties each designate classic Access action queries for updating an existing row, inserting a new row, or deleting an existing row. After specifying the *SelectCommand* property for a data adapter, you can automatically generate the *UpdateCommand*, *InsertCommand*, and *DeleteCommand* properties with the *OleDbCommand-Builder* class.

Use the *OleDbDataAdapter* object's *Fill* method to populate a table in a local dataset with the result set from the *SelectCommand* property for a data adapter. The *Fill* method will not create a dataset, but it can add a new table to an existing dataset if that table does not already exist in the dataset. Whether or not the method has to create a local table, the *Fill* method populates a local table on its initial use in a session. After the initial invocation of the *Fill* method in a session, subsequent invocations of the method append rows from the result set for the command designated by the *SelectCommand* property to the referenced table in the local dataset. If you want to replace rather than add to the existing data in the local table, you must clear the local table before invoking the *Fill* method. This clear-and-fill technique enables a table in a local dataset to reflect changes made by other users.

The *Update* method conveys changes made to a local table since the last time the local table was populated from a database source. In spite of its name (*Update*), this single method passes back inserts, updates, and deletes from a local table to its source in a database. The *Connection* object for the data adapter specifies the database, and the *InsertCommand*, *UpdateCommand*, and *DeleteCommand* properties designate the operation of the insert, update, and delete operations. If you have multiple users making changes to a database that might conflict with one another, your application must handle concurrency violations. Chapter 8 and Chapter 9 will demonstrate how to do this from different perspectives.

Sample Code

Form5 in the OleDbObjectSamples project contains a collection of sample code that demonstrates syntax for typical tasks, such as populating a DataGrid control and permitting updates from it. An *OleDbDataAdapter* object enables these functions, and the code behind the sample shows you the syntax for managing these kinds of tasks. Unlike earlier samples addressing this topic, these samples programmatically manage the creation of *Connection*, *Command*, *DataAdapter*, *CommandBuilder*, and *DataSet* objects. Knowing how to programmatically manage the creation of these objects enables your applications to create and customize ADO.NET objects as at run time.

Figure 7-5 shows *Form5* in Design view and after it opens. The form contains a DataGrid control (*DataGrid1*) below three buttons. The code behind this form demonstrates syntax conventions for the *OleDbDataAdapter* object. The form load event procedure and some module-level declarations initialize the ADO.NET objects that enable the populating of *DataGrid1*. Users can double-click a grid cell to open the cell for editing. For example, double-clicking the second column of the first row lets you append an *x* to the name *Speedy Express* (so that the CompanyName column value appears as *Speedy Expressx*). This updates the Shippers table in the dataset behind the form. However, just making the change locally does not force the Shippers table in the Northwind database to update accordingly. Therefore, clicking *Button1* to populate the local Shippers table from the Shippers table in the Northwind database obliterates the update and restores the name to *Speedy Express*.

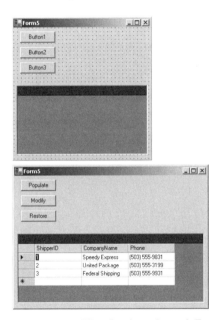

Figure 7-5   The Design view of *Form5* in the OleDbObjectSamples project (on top) and the operational view after the form initially opens

Button2 and *Button3* enable you to copy changes from the Shippers table in the local dataset to the Shippers table in the Northwind database. *Button2* programmatically appends an *x* to the end of the value in the second column of the first row. In addition to changing the value locally, the code updates the value in the Northwind database. Therefore, the next time a user opens the form or clicks *Button1*, the appended *x* remains visible. To make it simple for you to restore the Shippers table in the Northwind database, *Button3* reverses the operation of appending an *x* in the second column of the first row. The code behind this button removes the last character from the column value before invoking the *Update* method to persist the change in the table within the dataset to the table with the same name in the Northwind database.

The code behind *Form5* consists of a load event procedure, a separate click event procedure for each button, and a function to return an *OleDb-Connection* object pointing at the Northwind database. The latter function is the familiar *ConnectToNorthwind Function* procedure.

The *Form5_Load* procedure starts by calling the *ConnectToNorthwind* function to return a connection (*cnn1*) pointing at the Northwind database. Next, the procedure instantiates an *OleDbCommand* object with a result set containing all the column values for all the rows in the Shippers table of the Northwind database. Instead of instantiating an empty command object and assigning its *Connection* and *CommandType* property values, this sample uses an overloaded version of the *OleDbCommand* constructor to simultaneously instantiate the object and sets its property values.

After instantiating the *Connection* and *Command* objects, the procedure assigns a value for the *SelectCommand* property of the *dap1 OleDbDataAdapter*. The *dap1* object is one of two objects declared at the module level because of its use in multiple procedures; the other object declared at the module level is *das1*, the *DataSet* object that the data adapter populates. The code in the form load event procedure assigns the *cmd1* object to the *SelectCommand* property for *dap1*.

The procedure does not explicitly set the *UpdateCommand*, *InsertCommand*, and *DeleteCommand* properties of the *dap1 OleDbDataAdapter*. This is because the procedure designates a *CommandBuilder* object to manage the function of these properties. Whenever the code invokes the *Update* method for the *dap1* object, the *OleDbCommandBuilder* object intercepts the request to perform an update and executes the revision to the database object on behalf of the data adapter.

After setting up the data adapter, the form load event procedure invokes the *Fill* method. This invocation of the *Fill* method adds the Shippers table to the *das1 DataSet* object as it populates the table. Notice that the procedure never explicitly opens the *cnn1* connection object. The *OleDbDataAdapter* object is smart enough to open the *cnn1* connection object only when it needs the connection to perform a task.

The form load event procedure concludes with a mix of cosmetic activities. For example, the code resizes *DataGrid1* and *Form5* to better show the data in the grid and make it easy to see edits. In addition, the setting of a *Preferred-ColumnWidth* property helps to make edits visible. Before closing the *With...End With* statement that groups the assignments involving *DataGrid1*, the procedure sets the *DataSource* property for the grid to the Shippers table in the *das1 DataSet* object. Some *Text* property assignments at the very end of the procedure make the purpose of the buttons more obvious than their default names, such as *Button1*.

The *Button1_Click* procedure has just two lines. The first line clears the Shippers table in the *das1* dataset. Then, the procedure invokes the *Fill* method for the *dap1 OleDbDataAdapter* object. This causes *DataGrid1* to show any changes made by other users since the last time the application invoked the *Fill* method for the *dap1* object.

The *Button2_Click* and *Button3_Click* procedures have a parallel design. The first line in the *Button2_Click* procedure makes a change to the CompanyName column value in the first row. Because row and column numbers are zero-based, the code designates the row as 0 and the column as 1. The &= operator simplifies appending an *x* to the end of the value in the Shippers table cell. Although the change is visible in the grid, it is still not fully committed or accepted. For example, you can uncommit the edit to the CompanyName column value by invoking the *RejectChanges* method for the *DataTable* object showing in *DataGrid1*. (See the next section in the chapter for a review of the *DataSet* object model, including *DataTable* objects.)

The invocation of the *Update* method in the second line propagates the revision from the local Shippers table to the Shippers table in the Northwind database, and the method commits the change locally so that the update cannot be undone, except by a new edit to the local Shippers table. Similarly, the *Button3_Click* procedure makes a change in its first couple of lines and commits the change in its last line as it updates the Shippers table in the Northwind database. The change in this case is the removal of the last character from the second column value for the first row. The *Button3_Click* procedure can undo the edit implemented with a click to *Button2* in both the local dataset and the Northwind database.

```
Dim das1 As New System.Data.DataSet()
Dim dap1 As New _
    System.Data.OleDb.OleDbDataAdapter()

Private Sub Form5_Load(ByVal sender As System.Object, _
    ByVal e As System.EventArgs) Handles MyBase.Load
```

(continued)

```
'Instantiate the cnn1 Connection object based
'on the Northwind database.
Dim cnn1 As _
    System.Data.OleDb.OleDbConnection = _
    ConnectToNorthwind()

'Instantiate the cmd1 OleDbCommand object and
'assign a SQL statement and connection in the
'constructor.
Dim str1 As String = "SELECT * FROM Shippers"
Dim cmd1 As _
    New System.Data.OleDb.OleDbCommand( _
    str1, cnn1)

'Assign a command to the SelectCommand
'property of the dap1 DataAdapter object.
dap1.SelectCommand = cmd1

'Automate the design of the UpdateCommand,
'InsertCommand, and DeleteCommand properties
'for the dap1 DataAdapter object.
Dim cmb1 As New _
    System.Data.OleDb.OleDbCommandBuilder()
cmb1 = _
    New System.Data.OleDb.OleDbCommandBuilder(dap1)

'Fill the Shippers table in the das1 dataset.
dap1.Fill(das1, "Shippers")

'Resize datagrid and form and assign Shippers
'table from das1 to DataSource property for DataGrid1.
With DataGrid1
    .Size = New System.Drawing.Size(400, .Height)
    Me.Size = _
        New System.Drawing.Size(.Width + 20, Me.Height)
    .PreferredColumnWidth = 100
    .DataSource = das1.Tables("Shippers")
End With

'Assign button Text property values.
Button1.Text = "Populate"
Button2.Text = "Modify"
Button3.Text = "Restore"

End Sub

Private Sub Button1_Click(ByVal sender As System.Object, _
    ByVal e As System.EventArgs) Handles Button1.Click

    'Clear dataset contents.
```

```vbnet
        das1.Tables("Shippers").Clear()

        'Fill dataset with most recent data from database.
        dap1.Fill(das1, "Shippers")

End Sub

Private Sub Button2_Click(ByVal sender As System.Object, _
    ByVal e As System.EventArgs) Handles Button2.Click

        'Update second column of first row in Shippers
        'table within das1 with trailing x.
        das1.Tables("Shippers").Rows(0)(1) &= "x"

        'Convey change in das1 to Northwind database.
        dap1.Update(das1, "Shippers")

End Sub

Private Sub Button3_Click(ByVal sender As System.Object, _
    ByVal e As System.EventArgs) Handles Button3.Click

        'Remove last character from second column of
        'first row in Shippers table within das1.
        Dim str1 As String = das1.Tables("Shippers").Rows(0)(1)
        das1.Tables("Shippers").Rows(0)(1) = _
            Mid(str1, 1, Len(str1) - 1)

        'Convey change in das1 to Northwind database.
        dap1.Update(das1, "Shippers")

End Sub

Function ConnectToNorthwind() As System.Data.OleDb.OleDbConnection

        'Designate string for connection to Northwind database.
        Dim str1 As String = _
            "Provider = Microsoft.Jet.OLEDB.4.0;"
        str1 += _
            "Data Source = c:\Program Files\" & _
            "Microsoft Office\Office10\Samples\Northwind.mdb"

        'Instantiate and assign the connection string
        'to the Connection object.
        Dim cnn1 As New System.Data.OleDb.OleDbConnection()
        cnn1.ConnectionString = str1

        'Return the Connection object.
        Return cnn1

End Function
```

DataSet Object Model and Designer

Many ADO.NET applications have one or more dataset objects at their core. This section begins with an overview of the *DataSet* object model. It also includes a short example of how to specify multitable datasets with a graphical designer. The section concludes with a collection of sample code that illustrates the breadth of capabilities the *DataSet* object model provides.

Overview

Datasets are multifaceted data stores that characterize the flexibility and genius of the .NET Framework data access model. You can think of the dataset as a mini-database in memory. A dataset is not just a flat array of joined columns from one or more data sources. A dataset can contain one or more tables. These tables can come from a single database, multiple databases, or even a mixture of sources, such as a saved XML document and a database. You can also programmatically create tables inside a dataset and populate them with data that a user enters from a form or some other source. In addition to containing multiple tables, a dataset can contain objects representing the structure of the data within and between tables, a capability that can be very convenient. For example, the *DataSet* object's *Relations* property offers a built-in way of discovering the tables participating in a relationship. The *Relations* property can point at a relationship between a parent table and a child table. Your applications can use this parent-child relationship to automatically return the rows in a child table that match a row in a parent table, such as the line items belonging to an order or the orders belonging to a customer.

Figure 7-6 presents an overview of the *DataSet* object model. As you can see, a dataset holds two collections—one for tables and one for relationships between tables. The elements in the *Tables* collection property are *DataTable* objects. A *DataTable* object holds a tabular array of data as well as information describing the data, such as data types for the columns in a table. A *DataTable* object can hold all the columns and rows from an Access table or a subset of those columns or rows. You can also use this object to hold the column values in a query. The *DataTable* in a dataset can hold a snapshot of the contents of an Access database object. Use the *OleDbDataAdapter* object to synchronize the contents of the *DataTable* object with its Access database object counterpart.

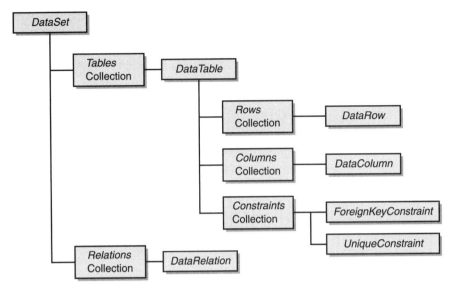

Figure 7-6 The *DataSet* object model

You can access the contents of a *DataTable* object through its *Rows* collection property. The *Rows* collection contains *DataRow* elements. The column values within a row are available as an array. For example, the expression *tbl1.Rows(0)(0)* denotes the first column value in the first row for the *DataTable* that the *tbl1* variable points at. The *Columns* collection property contains *DataColumn* objects. These objects contain metadata about the columns of a *DataTable*, such as the data types for columns, whether a column auto-increments, and whether a column must have unique values. Think of the *Rows* collection as corresponding to the Datasheet view of an Access table and the *Columns* collection as the counterpart to an Access table's Design view. A single table can expose itself from multiple perspectives.

The *Constraints* collection property denotes two types of constraints for a *DataTable* object. The *UniqueConstraint* object indicates that the values in a column of a table must be distinct from one another. You can create an instance of the *UniqueConstraint* object by setting the *Unique* property for a *DataColumn* object to *True*. The *ForeignKeyConstraint* object is the other type of item in the *Constraints* collection of a *DataTable*. This constraint specifies how updates and deletes to one *DataTable* affect another related *DataTable* (for example, whether or not they cascade). You can add a *ForeignKeyConstraint* object directly with its own constructor (*New* method) or indirectly by adding a *DataRelation* object to the *Relations* collection for a *DataSet* object.

The *Relations* collection property for a *DataSet* object contains *DataRelation* objects. This type of object specifies the parent-child relationships between the *DataTable* objects within a dataset. Specifying *DataRelation* objects between tables can speed your access to rows from a child table that match the currently selected row from a parent table.

You can use a graphical designer (the XML Designer) to build datasets in a Visual Studio .NET project based on an Access database. Choose Project, Add New Item. Then, select DataSet from the Templates pane of the Add New Item dialog box. The dialog box automatically names successive datasets: Dataset1.xsd, Dataset2.xsd, and so on. However, you can override this default naming convention with a new entry in the Name box. The XML Designer opens with an empty dataset and displays the dataset name, such as Dataset1.xsd, on its tab. Click the Server Explorer link on the designer if Server Explorer is not already visible. Then, expand the Data Connections folder, and within that folder, expand the connection for the database that you want to serve as the basis for one or more *DataTable* objects in your dataset. Drag over the tables and queries from the connection to the XML Designer. Both tables and queries from a connection pointing at an Access database can serve as the database source for *DataTable* objects within the dataset. The graphical design shows the column names along with their data types in a table headed by the table name.

The first paragraph in this "Overview" section stated that specifying a relationship between two *DataTable* objects allows you to designate a parent-child relationship between a pair of data sources, such as two *DataTable* objects based on the Orders and Order Details tables in the Northwind database. Designating this parent-child relationship graphically is beyond the scope of this chapter because it involves more familiarity with the XML Designer used to create datasets than this chapter assumes. The Chapter Appendix, "XML for Visual Studio .NET Access Developers," reviews the use of the XML Designer in detail, including specifying the *Relations* property for a dataset. I personally find using Visual Basic .NET code a more convenient way to specify and use a parent-child relationship between a pair of *DataTable* objects. The next section, "Demonstrating Code Syntax," includes an introductory sample illustrating coding techniques for creating and processing a parent-child relationship. The "Processing Parent-Child Relationships" section in Chapter 9 fully explores coding issues for creating and using parent-child relationships.

Demonstrating Code Syntax

Form6 in the OleDbObjectSamples projects illustrates various design principles for using datasets with the OLE DB .NET Data Provider. Figure 7-7 shows *Form6* after it initially opens. The *Text* property values for the buttons indicate the order in which to click the buttons. For example, you click the top button first. Then, you click the button immediately below it. Next, go back and click the top button again. In addition, you must click the third button before clicking the last button because the event procedure for the third button creates a *DataTable* object that the event procedure for the last button references.

Figure 7-7   The sample used to demonstrate dataset coding conventions requires that the user click the buttons in the right order.

The module behind *Form6* has six procedures: a form load event procedure, four click event procedures for the buttons, and the familiar *ConnectTo-Northwind* procedure. If you want a form in a Windows application to show data in its controls when the form opens, you must include in the form load event procedure the code to connect to a data source and populate a dataset that is bound to form controls or at least serves as a source for unbound form controls. This form does not show data in a form control. Nevertheless, the form load event procedure illustrates one approach to filling a *DataTable* object in a dataset. The variable pointing at the dataset has the name *das1*, and *Orders* is the name of the *DataTable*. The form load event procedure concludes by formatting the buttons on the form. The click event procedures for *Button1* through *Button4* have the following roles:

■   Display metadata about the table(s) in the *das1* dataset associated with the module behind *Form6* (*Button1*).

■   Add a second *DataTable* object (*OrderDetails*) to the *das1* dataset (*Button2*).

■   Add a *DataRelation* object to the *das1* dataset with the *Orders DataTable* as the parent for the *OrderDetails DataTable* (*Button3*).

■   Calculate the total extended price for the child rows in the *OrderDetails DataTable* that match the currently selected row in the *Orders DataTable* (*Button4*).

> **Note**   This application illustrates the relevance of two of my favorite coding mottos: real programmers don't allow blanks in object names, and real programmers use arrays whenever necessary. Avoiding blanks in object names avoids all the odd programming conventions for dealing with spaces in object names. Arrays make sense in any situation where a process returns more than a single scalar value at a time. That's the case in the click event procedure for *Button4*, which uses the *GetChildRows* method to extract the child rows matching a parent row. Each row can have multiple columns, and a set of child rows can have one or more rows. Using an array is more efficient than creating a new temporary dataset to hold the rows returned by the *GetChildRows* method.

Before the listing for the form load event procedure, you will see two module-level object declarations. One of these is for the *das1* variable, which points at a dataset that holds *DataTable* objects for the application. This variable appears in the form load event procedure as well as all the click event procedures. The *cnn1* variable appears in the form load event procedure and the click event procedure for *Button2* as well as the *ConnectToNorthwind* procedure. Both the form load event procedure and the click event procedure need the *cnn1* object to instantiate *Command* objects for defining result sets that they use to populate *DataTable* objects in the *das1* dataset.

The form load event procedure starts by defining a *Command* object (*cmd1*) that the procedure ultimately assigns to the *SelectCommand* property for the *dap1 OleDbDataAdapter* object. This assignment equips *dap1* to populate a *DataTable* object (*Orders*) in the *das1* dataset. The form load event procedure actually creates the *DataTable* object because the procedure fills the *DataTable* object for the first time. See the "*OleDbDataAdapter*" section earlier in this chapter for sample code and commentary on refilling an existing *Data-Table* object in a dataset. After populating the *das1* dataset, the procedure formats the buttons by specifying *Text* property values and designating *Size* and *Left* property settings.

The *Button1_Click* procedure illustrates how to iterate through the items in the *Tables* collection for a dataset. The *MsgBox* statement inside the loop displays the name, number of columns, and number of rows for each *DataTable* object in the *Tables* collection. If you click *Button1* initially, the button's click event procedure will report metadata for a single table, the *Orders DataTable* object. If you click *Button1* after clicking *Button2*, the *Button1_Click* procedure reports metadata for the *Orders* and *OrderDetails DataTable* objects.

The *Button2_Click* procedure demonstrates an approach to adding a *DataTable* object (*OrderDetails*) to a dataset that already contains a *DataTable* object. The procedure parallels the form load event procedure steps for adding the *Orders DataTable* object. The main point to note is that the *Button2_Click* procedure uses a separate *OleDbDataAdapter* (*dap2*). This is convenient because a *DataAdapter* object can have only a single value for the *SelectCommand* property. This property determines the data source that you use to fill a *DataTable* object. Although it is possible to dynamically assign this property at run time, you reduce the complexity of your code by using a second data adapter. Notice that the *CommandText* property for the *cmd1* object in the procedure encloses the Order Details table name in square brackets ([ ]). The brackets are necessary because the Order Details table in the Access database includes a blank within its name. By naming the local *DataTable OrderDetails*, you avoid the requirement to specify the internal blank with an escape code (_x0020_).

The *Button3_Click* procedure shows you how to add a *DataRelation* object to a dataset. The *DataRelation* object specifies a parent-child relationship between the *Orders DataTable* object and the *OrderDetails DataTable* object, with the *Orders DataTable* object serving as the parent. The column of OrderID values in each *DataTable* object allows the .NET Framework to link the two *DataTable* objects. With a *DataRelation* object, you first define the object, and then you add it to the *Relations* collection for a dataset.

The *Button4_Click* procedure illustrates how to process the rows in a child *DataTable* object that match a current selection in a parent *DataTable* object. This sample selects a row in the *Orders DataTable* object, and the procedure goes on to compute and accumulate the extended price for each line item in the child *DataTable* object that matches the parent *DataTable*. The procedure begins by pointing *tbl1* at the *Orders DataTable* object and *tbl2* at the *OrderDetails DataTable* object. Next, the procedure declares several variables to hold the matching child rows and to loop through them. Then, the procedure invokes the *GetChildRows* method to return an array of *DataRow* objects. The *ary_Rows* variable points at the array. This array contains as many columns as the *SelectCommand* property for *dap1* specifies and a separate row for each line item in the order specified by the currently designated row in the *Orders DataTable* object. The currently designated row is determined by the *Rows* method, and in this case is the second row in the *Orders DataTable* object, which has an index of 1 and corresponds to an OrderID value of 10249. The *For...Next* loop iterates through the line items for this order. The expression within the loop computes the extended price for each matching row and accumulates the values in the *dec1* variable. The procedure concludes by displaying a message box that shows the extended price and the OrderID for the currently selected row in the *Orders DataTable*.

```
Dim das1 As New System.Data.DataSet()
Dim cnn1 As _
    System.Data.OleDb.OleDbConnection = _
    ConnectToNorthwind()

Private Sub Form6_Load(ByVal sender As System.Object, _
    ByVal e As System.EventArgs) Handles MyBase.Load

    'Create a Command object based on the Orders table.
    Dim str1 As String = _
        "SELECT OrderID, OrderDate FROM Orders "
    Dim cmd1 As _
        New System.Data.OleDb.OleDbCommand( _
        str1, cnn1)

    'Instantiate the dap1 DataAdapter object
    'and assign the Command object to the
    'SelectCommand property for the dap1
    'DataAdapter object.
    Dim dap1 As New _
        System.Data.OleDb.OleDbDataAdapter()
    dap1.SelectCommand = cmd1

    'Fill the das1 DataSet object with
    'the Orders table.
    dap1.Fill(das1, "Orders")

    'Set Button Text property values.
    Button1.Text = "Click me first and third"
    Button2.Text = "Click me second"
    Button3.Text = "Click me fourth"
    Button4.Text = "Click me fifth"
```

```
    'Size and position Button1.
    Button1.Size = New System.Drawing.Size(125, Button1.Height)
    Button1.Left = 85

    'Align and size other buttons relative to Button1.
    Button2.Size = _
        New System.Drawing.Size(Button1.Width, Button2.Height)
    Button2.Left = Button1.Left
    Button3.Size = _
        New System.Drawing.Size(Button1.Width, Button3.Height)
    Button3.Left = Button1.Left
    Button4.Size = _
        New System.Drawing.Size(Button1.Width, Button4.Height)
    Button4.Left = Button1.Left

End Sub

Private Sub Button1_Click(ByVal sender As System.Object, _
    ByVal e As System.EventArgs) Handles Button1.Click

    'Declare DataTable variable.
    Dim tbl1 As DataTable

    'Iterate through the tables in das1 dataset.
    For Each tbl1 In das1.Tables
        MsgBox(tbl1.TableName & " has " & _
            tbl1.Columns.Count.ToString & " columns" & _
            " and " & tbl1.Rows.Count & " rows.", , _
            "Metadata in Das1")
    Next

End Sub

Private Sub Button2_Click(ByVal sender As System.Object, _
    ByVal e As System.EventArgs) Handles Button2.Click

    'Instantiate a new DataAdapter object.
    Dim dap2 As New System.Data.OleDb.OleDbDataAdapter()

    'Instantiate cmd1 OleDbCommand object and assign
    'SQL statement and connection in the constructor.
    Dim str1 As String = _
        "SELECT OrderID, ProductID, UnitPrice, " & _
        "Quantity, Discount FROM [Order Details]"
    Dim cmd1 As _
        New System.Data.OleDb.OleDbCommand( _
        str1, cnn1)
```

(continued)

```
        'Assign the Command object to the
        'SelectCommand property for the dap2
        'DataAdapter object.
        dap2.SelectCommand = cmd1

        'Fill the das1 DataSet object with
        'the OrderDetails table.
        dap2.Fill(das1, "OrderDetails")

    End Sub

    Private Sub Button3_Click(ByVal sender As System.Object, _
        ByVal e As System.EventArgs) Handles Button3.Click

        'Define parent and child columns for
        'a DataRelation object.
        Dim parentcol As DataColumn = _
            das1.Tables("Orders").Columns("OrderID")
        Dim childcol As DataColumn = _
            das1.Tables("OrderDetails").Columns("OrderID")

        'Instantiate a new DataRelation object.
        Dim drl1 As DataRelation
        drl1 = New _
            DataRelation("OrdersOrderDetails", _
            parentcol, childcol)

        'Add the DataRelation object to the Relations
        'collection for das1.
        das1.Relations.Add(drl1)

    End Sub

    Private Sub Button4_Click(ByVal sender As System.Object, _
        ByVal e As System.EventArgs) Handles Button4.Click

        'Point DataTable variable at the parent
        'table (Orders).
        Dim tbl1 As DataTable
        Dim drl1 As DataRelation = _
            das1.Relations("OrdersOrderDetails")
        tbl1 = drl1.ParentTable

        'Point another DataTable variable at
        'the child table (Order Details).
        Dim tbl2 As DataTable = drl1.ChildTable

        'Declare variables for looping through child rows.
        Dim drw1 As DataRow
```

```
        Dim ary_Rows() As DataRow
        Dim int1 As Integer
        Dim col1 As DataColumn
        Dim int2 As Integer
        Dim dec1 As Decimal

        'Specify row in Orders table for which to
        'accumulate extended prices for line items.
        drw1 = tbl1.Rows(1)

        'Return array of child rows matching selected parent row.
        ary_Rows = drw1.GetChildRows(tbl1.ChildRelations(0))

        'Loop through child rows to accumulate extended
        'price for line items.
        For int1 = 0 To ary_Rows.GetUpperBound(0)
            dec1 += ary_Rows(int1)(2) * _
                ary_Rows(int1)(3) * (1 - ary_Rows(int1)(4))
        Next

        'Display result.
        int2 = drw1(0)
        MsgBox("Extended Price = " & _
            dec1.ToString & " for Order ID " & _
            int2.ToString & ".", , _
            "Computed value from Child Table")

End Sub

Function ConnectToNorthwind() As System.Data.OleDb.OleDbConnection

        'Designate string for connection to Northwind database.
        Dim str1 As String = _
            "Provider = Microsoft.Jet.OLEDB.4.0;"
        str1 += _
            "Data Source = c:\Program Files\" & _
            "Microsoft Office\Office10\Samples\Northwind.mdb"

        'Instantiate and assign the connection string
        'to the Connection object.
        Dim cnn1 As New System.Data.OleDb.OleDbConnection()
        cnn1.ConnectionString = str1

        'Return the Connection object.
        Return cnn1

End Function
```

Summary

The chapter presents a conceptual and architectural review of ADO.NET concepts. It familiarizes you with .NET data providers and how they complement datasets. In particular, this presentation dwells on the OLE DB .NET Data Provider, which is the one to use with Access databases. Beyond an architectural and conceptual overview, the chapter demonstrates programming techniques for each of the four core ADO.NET classes: *OleDbConnection*, *OleDbCommand*, *OleDbDataReader*, and *OleDbDataAdapter*. The examination of datasets exposes you to the *DataSet* object model and highlights how to programmatically create and use relationships between *DataTable* objects.

8

ADO.NET Coding Techniques

This chapter builds on the introduction to ADO.NET presented in Chapter 7. This chapter's goal is to move beyond architectural and conceptual issues and focus on the typical tasks that you are likely to perform with Microsoft Visual Basic .NET solutions for Microsoft Access databases. At the same time, the chapter focuses on fundamental ADO.NET building blocks, such as the *Connection*, *Command*, *DataAdapter*, and *DataSet* objects. Another major theme of this chapter is enabling dynamic behavior. To that end, the chapter introduces the *Parameters* collection. With this collection, you can dynamically modify the behavior of *Command* objects based on either SQL strings or Access parameter queries. This chapter's primary focus is on data manipulation, which we'll cover from several perspectives, including running action queries in Visual Basic .NET transactions; performing inserts, deletes, and updates via data adapters from a local dataset; and handling concurrency violations.

The chapter has four major sections. The first of these dwells on programming database *Connection* objects. This section carefully reviews all properties and selected methods for the *OleDbConnection* object. The section demonstrates using connection strings for Access and Microsoft SQL Server databases. The second section illustrates dynamic data access techniques via *Command* objects. You will learn how to make a *Command* object dynamic by using SQL strings with variables or parameters. The third section is a case study for performing data manipulation within transactions. You will learn what transactions are and how to use them with Visual Basic .NET and Access databases. This section literally builds the sample. You will also discover how to programmatically create an Access database file and add tables to a database with

Visual Basic .NET. The closing section discusses performing data manipulation via the *DataAdapter* and *DataSet* objects. This is a highly scalable approach to enabling data manipulation with Access databases via Visual Basic .NET. You will learn how to configure datasets programmatically and graphically. Sample code illustrates the fundamentals of inserting, deleting, and updating rows in an Access database based on changes to a local dataset. You will also learn how to handle conflicts when a data adapter tries to update an Access database that has changed since the last data access. This last scenario simulates a multiuser application.

Programming Database Connections

Programming database connections is largely a matter of getting the connection string right and using the proper .NET data provider. The connection string is determined by the demands of the database and the particular way in which your application uses the database. However, the properties for a database connection can indicate settings made in a connection string or help you manage the state of a connection (whether it is open or closed). Chapter 7 already examined roles for the *Provider* and *DataSource* properties. You can also use the *Database* property to report the name of the database for a SQL Server instance and other server-based database managers. Access does not use the *Database* property because it is exclusively used for server-based systems, as opposed to file-based ones. This section introduces you to programming database connections for use with Access and SQL Server databases.

All the samples for this section reside on *Form2* of the ADONETSamples project included with this book's sample files. This project is a Microsoft Windows application with multiple forms. *Form1* is a switchboard menu built with LinkLabel controls for selecting the code samples in the module behind *Form2* and other form modules mentioned throughout this chapter. You can either use *Form1* or make another form the startup object for the project to work with the code samples.

Figure 8-1 shows *Form2* in Design view and immediately after it opens. The form contains three buttons with click event procedures that illustrate different Visual Basic .NET coding techniques for managing connections. *Button1* launches a connection to the Access Northwind database. Its main role is to demonstrate how to monitor the full set of *Connection* properties. *Button2* focuses on making a connection to a SQL Server database. The click event procedure interacts with the RadioButton controls in the GroupBox control to enable the demonstration of connection strings for logins based on either Windows or SQL Server security. *Button3* shows one approach to handling a classic deployment issue dynamically: the developer creates a solution with an Access database in one path, but the deployment of the solution requires a different path to the database file.

> **Note**   The load event procedure for *Form2* includes code for editing the controls to manage their appearance when the form opens. This is true for the other Windows Forms samples in the ADONETSamples project. To keep this chapter's focus on ADO.NET coding techniques, I have not included the control management code in any listings. You can view this code in the ADONETSamples project.

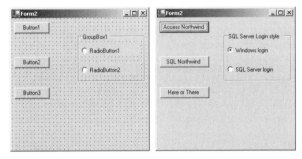

Figure 8-1   A Design view and an initial operational view of *Form2* in the ADONETSamples project

Reporting *Connection* Properties for Microsoft Access

The first piece of sample code in this section is the click event procedure behind *Button1* in *Form2*. The sample code has a couple of objectives, including demonstrating the syntax for all the *OleDbConnection* properties and demonstrating how to use one of the properties to monitor the state of a connection. This sample makes a connection to an Access database. You can contrast its output with that for the second sample, which makes a connection to a SQL Server database. This will clarify the roles of the properties.

This *Button1_Click* procedure has three segments. In the initial segment, the procedure uses the *OleDbConnection* constructor that accepts a connection string. This constructor points an *OleDbConnection* object at an Access database file as it instantiates the object. You can also use a constructor that has no connection string at the time that you instantiate an *OleDbConnection* object and then assign the object's *ConnectionString* property later. You can reuse an existing *OleDbConnection* object for more than one database by closing the connection to a database, making a new *ConnectionString* property assignment that points at another database, and then reopening the *Connection* object.

The second segment of the *Button1_Click* procedure illustrates the syntax for designating each of the *OleDbConnection* object properties. This segment begins with the opening of the *cnn1* object specified in the first segment. Then, it constructs a string variable for a *MsgBox* function that returns the initial value for each *cnn1* object property. Most of the *Connection* object properties are read-only. You can change their setting through the connection string. The only property that is an exception to this general rule is, of course, *Connection-String*. You can use the *ConnectionTimeout* property to determine how long the application will wait for the availability of a database server before returning an error. This feature will come into play when you connect to a non-Access database. The property applies to connections for classic Access ODBC data sources, such as SQL Server and Oracle. Its default value is 15 seconds. If you elect to change it, use a positive integer to designate the number of seconds to wait. Avoid negative values that generate *Exception* objects and values of 0 that can cause indefinite waits for a connection.

The *Provider* and *DataSource* properties are also typical of many *Connection* object properties; you can get their value, but you set them through the connection string. These are particularly important properties for a connection to an Access database because they can completely define the connection. Another potentially interesting *Connection* object property is the *State* property. This property indicates whether a connection is open or closed. The *Database* property applies exclusively to classic Access ODBC data sources. Therefore, this property returns an empty string for connections to Access databases. The *ServerVersion* property returns information about the major and minor version number as well as the build number of a database server product providing a data source through an *OleDbConnection* object. For a connection to an Access database, the *ServerVersion* property returns information about the OLE DB .NET Data Provider version as opposed to the Access database version.

The final code block in the procedure displays the *State* property value after the *Button1_Click* procedure closes the *cnn1* object. Notice that you can apply the *ToString* method to represent the return value from the *State* property in a *MsgBox* function. The *State* property returns a value of *Open* or *Closed* through the *ToString* method to indicate the status of a *Connection* object. This property can prove useful when you allow a user to close a connection either directly or indirectly, or when a connection can be disabled by environmental conditions such as a temporarily disabled network connection.

```
Private Sub Button1_Click(ByVal sender As System.Object, _
    ByVal e As System.EventArgs) Handles Button1.Click

    'Embed a connection string in a constructor
    Dim cnn1 As New OleDb.OleDbConnection( _
        "Provider=Microsoft.Jet.OLEDB.4.0;" & _
        "Data Source=c:\Program Files\" & _
        "Microsoft Office\Office10\Samples\Northwind.mdb")

    'After opening, display OleDbConnection property values;
    'Database property not supported for Access databases
    cnn1.Open()
    Dim str1 As String
    str1 = "ConnectionString = " & _
        cnn1.ConnectionString & vbCr & _
        "ConnectionTimeout = " & _
        cnn1.ConnectionTimeout & vbCr & _
        "Database = " & cnn1.Database() & vbCr & _
        "DataSource = " & cnn1.DataSource & vbCr & _
        "Provider = " & cnn1.Provider & vbCr & _
        "ServerVersion = " & cnn1.ServerVersion & vbCr & _
        "State = " & cnn1.State.ToString()
    MsgBox(str1, , "After Open")

    'Display just state property after closing the
    'OleDbConnection property
    cnn1.Close()
    str1 = "State = " & cnn1.State.ToString()
    MsgBox(str1, , "After Close")

End Sub
```

As a point of reference, Figure 8-2 shows the output from both message boxes generated by the *Button1_Click* procedure. The top message box initially displays the *cnn1* properties after a user clicks *Button1*. Because the code connects to an Access database (Northwind), the *Database* property returns an empty string. The *State* property shows a value of *Open* through the *ToString* method. Clicking the OK button in the top message box advances the procedure to the message box shown at the bottom of Figure 8-2. This second message box displays the value of the *State* property after invoking the *Close* method for the *cnn1* object.

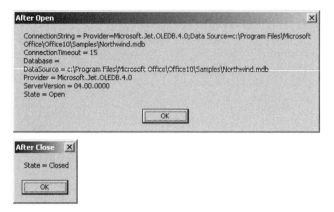

Figure 8-2 Message boxes showing the initial default values for properties after a connection to the Access Northwind database as well as a change in value for the *State* property

Connecting to a SQL Server Database

Some Access developers connect occasionally or often to SQL Server databases too. However, the connection string settings are different for a SQL Server database than for an Access database. In addition, SQL Server databases require that you login via one of two secure routes: SQL Server security or Windows security. From a client application perspective, the main difference between these two routes is whether you designate your Windows server login or use special login settings to gain access to a SQL Server database. Database administrators can generally configure a SQL Server instance to support either or both of these routes. However, a SQL Server instance running on a computer running Windows 98 supports the SQL Server login route only.

The *Button2_Click* procedure interacts with the status of the RadioButton controls to the right of *Button2* in *Form2*. Clicking *Button2* connects a user to the SQL Server version of the Northwind database that installs by default with SQL Server version 7 and later. *Form2* initially opens with the Windows Login radio button selected; the form load event procedure makes this selection by invoking the *Select* method for *RadioButton1*. If a user wants to log in with SQL Server login credentials, she can click the SQL Server Login radio button. Normally, an application such as this will show a pair of text boxes that ask the user to designate a user ID and password. The section "Validating a Password with a TextBox Control" in Chapter 5 presents a sample application that accepts a user ID and a password with an Access database as a back end. You can adapt the user interface from that sample for use with SQL Server.

The sample application for *Button2* in *Form2* of the ADONETSamples project uses a default SQL Server login to connect to the database. If you attempt to run the sample application as is, you will need to update your SQL Server logins so that they include a login with a user ID of *BookAuthor* that has a password of *Rick_Dobson* with access to the SQL Server Northwind database. Alternatively, you can replace the *BookAuthor* user ID setting with any other SQL Server login to which the database administrator has granted access to the Northwind database.

The *Button2_Click* procedure uses the *OleDbConnection* object to connect to a SQL Server database. You can, of course, use the *SqlConnection* class to connect with a SQL Server version 7 or later database. However, if you are an Access developer who uses SQL Server databases only occasionally for basic data access tasks, you might find it convenient to use the OLE DB .NET Data Provider for both Access and SQL Server databases. The click event procedure for *Button2* allows you to contrast the default settings for a connection to a SQL Server database with those for an Access database by displaying the *Connection* properties immediately after connecting to the Northwind database. (Compare these property values with those from the *Button1_Click* procedure.)

The sample code starts by instantiating an *OleDbConnection* object without specifying a connection string. The procedure then sets the *OleDbConnection* object's *ConnectionString* property to one of two settings. If *RadioButton1* is still checked as it was in the form load event procedure, the procedure specifies an integrated security setting that uses the Windows login for identifying the user to the SQL Server instance. If the user clicked the SQL Server Login radio button, *RadioButton1* will no longer be checked, which transfers control to the *Else* clause of the *If...Then...Else* statement for the *Checked* property of *RadioButton1*. This *Else* clause assigns a value to the *ConnectionString* property for the *OleDbConnection* object that shows the syntax for a SQL Server login.

The two connection string settings have the same *Provider, Data Source*, and *Initial Catalog* clauses. The *Provider* clause value of SQLOLEDB designates the type of database server and driver. The *Data Source* clause points at a particular instance of SQL Server. In an environment running multiple instances of SQL Server, you can develop an application against a test server and change the *Data Source* setting to a second server at deployment time. SQL Server names often correspond to the network name for a computer running SQL Server. The designation of *localhost* points to the default instance of SQL Server running on the current computer. Change this setting if you are using a different instance of SQL Server. The *Initial Catalog* clause specifies the name of the database to which you want to connect.

The clauses that are different in the *Then* and *Else* clauses apply to either Windows or SQL Server security. When using the Windows login to connect to a SQL Server instance, include an *Integrated Security* clause in the connection string. Set this clause equal to *SSPI*. For a SQL Server login, replace the *Integrated Security* clause with *User ID* and *Password* clauses. Each SQL Server login has an ID or name and an associated password. Use the name for the *User ID* clause and the password for the *Password* clause.

After the *ConnectionString* property for the *OleDbConnection* object is set in one of two ways, the *Button2_Click* procedure is identical to the *Button1_Click* procedure. Therefore, both procedures output the same array of property values in two message boxes. By contrasting the first message box for the *Button2_Click* procedure (shown in Figure 8-3) with the first one for the *Button1_Click* procedure (shown earlier in Figure 8-2), you can discern differences in the property values associated with *Connection* objects for Access databases from those associated with *Connection* objects for SQL Server databases. As you can see, the *Connection* object's string property values largely duplicate the settings for a connection string. The property corresponding to the *Initial Catalog* clause is the *Database* property. The value for this property shown in Figure 8-3 points at the SQL Server version of the Northwind database. The *ConnectionTimeout* property value is 15, which means the application will wait 15 seconds for a connection attempt to a server to succeed. Although neither connection string setting in the *Button2_Click* procedure explicitly sets this value, 15 seconds is the default assignment for the property.

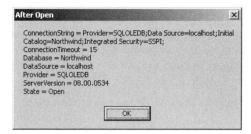

Figure 8-3 Contrast this After Open message box for a connection to a SQL Server database with the After Open message box for an Access database shown in Figure 8-2.

```
Private Sub Button2_Click(ByVal sender As System.Object, _
    ByVal e As System.EventArgs) Handles Button2.Click

    Dim cnn1 As New System.Data.OleDb.OleDbConnection()

    If RadioButton1.Checked = True Then
```

```
        'Assign Windows login to connection string
        'for a SQL Server database
        cnn1.ConnectionString = _
            "Provider=SQLOLEDB;Data Source=localhost;" & _
            "Initial Catalog=Northwind;" & _
            "Integrated Security=SSPI;"
    Else
        'Assign SQL Server login to connection string
        'for a SQL Server database; use valid User ID and
        'Password arguments instead of those here
        cnn1.ConnectionString = _
            "Provider=SQLOLEDB;Data Source=localhost;" & _
            "Initial Catalog=Northwind;" & _
            "User ID=BookAuthor;Password=Rick_Dobson"
    End If

    cnn1.Open()
    Dim str1 As String
    str1 = "ConnectionString = " & _
        cnn1.ConnectionString & vbCr & _
        "ConnectionTimeout = " & _
        cnn1.ConnectionTimeout & vbCr & _
        "Database = " & cnn1.Database() & vbCr & _
        "DataSource = " & cnn1.DataSource & vbCr & _
        "Provider = " & cnn1.Provider & vbCr & _
        "ServerVersion = " & cnn1.ServerVersion & vbCr & _
        "State = " & cnn1.State.ToString()
    MsgBox(str1, , "After Open")

    'Display just state property after closing the
    'OleDbConnection property
    cnn1.Close()
    str1 = "State = " & cnn1.State.ToString()
    MsgBox(str1, , "After Close")

End Sub
```

Connecting to a Database at Your Place or Their Place

One traditional Access database development issue is determining where to connect to the database file from an application file. Often, the developer will build a solution with a test database in one path. Then, deployment of the application will take place with the database in a different path. The path issue specifically addresses where to connect to an Access database file. A couple of approaches exist for dynamically altering the location or path where an application looks for an Access database file. The approach demonstrated in the following listing, which applies to the *Button3_Click* procedure of *Form2*, tries to connect to a database at one location. If that attempt fails, the control passes to a second attempt to connect to a database at a different location. With this strategy, the application will always work at both the developer's test environment and the deployment environment, as long as only one copy of the database file is at the test and deployment environments. You can extend this strategy for use with classic Access ODBC databases because the development and deployment versions of a database will typically have distinct *Data Source* clauses in the connection strings.

The main feature that the *Button3_Click* procedure demonstrates is how to connect with a database in one of two locations. The procedure embeds one *ConnectionString* property assignment and an invocation of the *Open* method in a *Try* clause and embeds a contrasting *ConnectionString* property assignment with an invocation of the *Open* method in a *Catch* clause. If the connection string in the *Try* clause fails, this approach automatically tries to make a connection based on the connection string in the immediately following *Catch* clause for an *OleDbException* object. Place the connection string for the most typical database location in the *Try* clause. Assign the secondary location for the database in the *Catch* location. If the Access database file is not at either location or does not make a connection for some other reason, control passes to a second nested *Catch* clause, which once again traps an *OleDbException* object and gracefully returns control to the application. In the *Finally* clause for the error-trap statement, the *Button3_Click* procedure returns via a message box the state of the connection, which will be open or closed. You can easily amend the sample code to reveal the *DataSource* property or any other property for a *Connection* object.

The closing segment of the *Button3_Click* procedure demonstrates how to conditionally close the *cnn1* object. With a condition expression for an *If...Then...Else* statement based on the *State* property for the *cnn1* object, the sample invokes the *Close* method only if the *Connection* object is open. Because you can invoke the *Close* method for a *Connection* object that is already closed without generating an error, this precise application of the *State* property is not strictly necessary. Nevertheless, your applications might need to conditionally perform some tasks depending on whether a connection is open or closed. The syntax of the *If...Then...Else* statement at the close of the *Button3_Click* procedure demonstrates the syntax for accomplishing that task.

```
Private Sub Button3_Click(ByVal sender As System.Object, _
    ByVal e As System.EventArgs) Handles Button3.Click

    'Instantiate an empty Connection object
    Dim cnn1 As New OleDb.OleDbConnection()
```

```
Dim str1 As String

Try
    'Try to connect with Northwind in the
    'default Access 2000 location
    cnn1.ConnectionString = _
        "Provider=Microsoft.Jet.OLEDB.4.0;" & _
        "Data Source=c:\Program Files\" & _
        "Microsoft Office\Office\Samples\Northwind.mdb"
    cnn1.Open()
Catch exc1 As System.Data.OleDb.OleDbException
    Try
        'Try to connect with Northwind in the
        'default Access 2002 location
        cnn1.ConnectionString = _
            "Provider=Microsoft.Jet.OLEDB.4.0;" & _
            "Data Source=c:\Program Files\" & _
            "Microsoft Office\Office10\Samples\Northwind.mdb"
        cnn1.Open()
    Catch exc2 As System.Data.OleDb.OleDbException
        'If you cannot connect at either Data Source,
        'let user know
        MsgBox("Wasn't able to connect.  Make sure the " & _
            "database file is available and you have a " & _
            "connection string pointing at it.", , _
            "From nested Catch")
        str1 = "State = " & cnn1.State.ToString()
        MsgBox(str1, , "After Close")
    End Try
Finally
    'Display connection state whether connected
    'or not
    str1 = "State = " & cnn1.State.ToString()
    MsgBox(str1, , "From Finally")
End Try

'Cleanup with conditional close; IntelliSense
'offers more options than are available; you can
'only use Open and Close states
If cnn1.State = ConnectionState.Open Then
    cnn1.Close()
Else
    MsgBox("Not able to close at this time.")
End If

End Sub
```

Programming Dynamic Data Access

At least two techniques for programming dynamic data access allow a user to specify the result set at run time. First, you can use a SQL string with a variable as an argument for an *OleDbCommand* command. By letting users control the value of the variable, you can make the result set from the SQL string dynamic at run time. Second, you can add one or more parameters to an *OleDbCommand* object and use the values for these parameters as inputs to SQL strings or even queries in an Access database. The second approach is dynamic because users can set the parameter values at run time. The Access queries can include both data access queries (those that.return a result set) and action queries (such as those for inserts, updates, and deletes).

I have found that most developers consider using parameters less friendly than using variables in SQL strings. Nevertheless, using parameters is a more robust approach. You can use parameters in a wider variety of situations, including data manipulation via data adapters. The final section in this chapter demonstrates this use of parameters with data adapters. This section's coverage of parameters will give you valuable background you need to deal with them later in the chapter.

Figure 8-4 shows the Design view as well as the initial operational view of *Form3* in the ADONETSamples project. The code behind *Form3* demonstrates coding techniques for the two dynamic data access approaches described a moment ago. As with *Form2* in the preceding section, the form load event transforms the Design view of *Form3* into the initial operational view of the form. The click event procedures for *Button1* and *Button2* demonstrate ways of using SQL strings with variables to implement dynamic data access. The click event procedures for *Button3* and *Button4* illustrate techniques of using parameters to achieve dynamic data access. The text boxes on *Form3* allow for user input to the SQL strings and parameters for *OleDbCommand* objects.

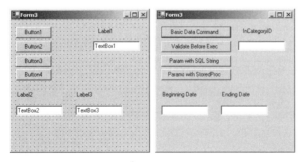

Figure 8-4   The text boxes facilitate the specification of values by users for data access, and the click event procedures for the buttons implement dynamic data access with the values in the text boxes.

Dynamic Data Access with a SQL String and a Variable

The click event procedure for *Button1* reads the *Text* property for *TextBox1* and uses that value for a variable in a SQL string. The *Button1_Click* procedure starts by instantiating the *OleDbConnection* and *OleDbCommand* objects. The procedure uses the connection string to point the *OleDbConnection* object at the Northwind database. Next, the procedure copies the *Text* property value for *TextBox1* to the *str1* string variable and uses this variable in a string expression to specify a SQL statement for a property of the *cmd1* object. The SQL statement counts the number of ProductID values within a CategoryID value. Because the SQL statement returns a scalar value, the procedure uses the *ExecuteScalar* method for *cmd1*. The sample copies the returned scalar value to *int1* and concludes by displaying a message box with the number of products in the specified category and closing the connection.

```
Private Sub Button1_Click(ByVal sender As System.Object, _
    ByVal e As System.EventArgs) Handles Button1.Click

    'Declare and instantiate Connection and Command objects
    Dim cnn1 As New OleDb.OleDbConnection( _
        "Provider=Microsoft.Jet.OLEDB.4.0;" & _
        "Data Source=c:\Program Files\" & _
        "Microsoft Office\Office10\Samples\Northwind.mdb")
    Dim cmd1 As New System.Data.OleDb.OleDbCommand()

    'Save the Text property value of TextBox1 for
    'easy re-use
    Dim str1 = TextBox1.Text

    'Assign Connection and CommandText property values
    'for the cmd1 OleDbCommand object; notice CategoryID
    'value in WHERE clause depends on Text property for
    'TextBox1
    With cmd1
        .Connection = cnn1
        .CommandText = _
            "SELECT Count(CategoryID) FROM Products " & _
            "WHERE CategoryID = " & str1
    End With

    'Save result set from command in int1 memory variable
    cnn1.Open()
    Dim int1 As Integer = cmd1.ExecuteScalar

    'Display result from query
    MsgBox("The number of products in " & _
        "category " & str1 & " is " & _
```

(continued)

```
        int1.ToString & ".")

    'Close connection
    cnn1.Close()

End Sub
```

The sample code demonstrates dynamic data access because a user can input any value from 1 through 8 in *TextBox1* and the procedure will open a message box showing the number of products in the category. Figure 8-5 shows *Form3* with a value of 6 in *TextBox1* just before a click to the Basic Data Command control (*Button1*), along with the message box that the *Button1_Click* procedure returns after the click. The values 1 through 8 are the original CategoryID values from the Northwind database. Entering CategoryID values outside the range of CategoryID values in the Products table into *TextBox1* returns a message box that says the category contains zero products.

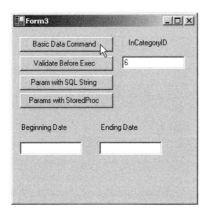

Figure 8-5 A form demonstrating dynamic data access from an Access database with a Windows form in a Visual Basic .NET project

Validating a String Variable Before Using It

If a client has ever accused you of building a system that doesn't work even though it performed all the tasks that you both agreed on, you will appreciate the value of validating user input before using it. Users have a way of entering values that an application does not expect.

Resolving validation issues often has at least a couple of approaches, such as checking data values before a program uses them or catching an *Exception* object after the error happens. This sample performs a couple of checks on the values in *TextBox1* to confirm that it is a valid CategoryID value from the Categories table. The validation occurs in the click event procedure for *Button2*. To help perform data validation, the *Button2_Click* procedure calls a separate

Function procedure (*MaxMinID*) that returns either the minimum or maximum CategoryID value depending on the value of a Boolean variable that the *Button2_Click* event procedure passes it.

The click event procedure for *Button2* is an adaptation of the *Button1_Click* procedure. Therefore, the following listing shows the new code in boldface to make it easy to identify. The listing also shows the *MaxMinID Function* procedure in boldface because it is also new relative to the sample code for *Button1*. The new code in the *Button2_Click* procedure starts by saving the maximum CategoryID value in *MaxCatID* and the minimum CategoryID value in *MinCatID*. Then, the procedure performs as many as two tests on the *str1 String* variable before using the value in the expression for the SQL statement that defines the *CommandText* property for the *OleDbCommand* object defined and manipulated within the *Button2_Click* procedure. The first test uses the *IsNumber* method for the *Char* structure to see whether the value in *str1* represents a number. If *str1*'s value passes this test, the procedure then determines whether *str1*'s value represents a quantity that is less than the minimum CategoryID value or greater than the maximum CategoryID value. Failing either of these tests aborts the normal flow of the procedure and presents a message box with a reminder about entering legitimate values. Aside from these extra lines of code in the *Button2_Click* procedure and the *MaxMinID Function* procedure, this sample duplicates the code for *Button1*.

```
Private Sub Button2_Click(ByVal sender As System.Object, _
    ByVal e As System.EventArgs) Handles Button2.Click

    'Declare and instantiate Connection and Command objects
    Dim cnn1 As New OleDb.OleDbConnection( _
        "Provider=Microsoft.Jet.OLEDB.4.0;" & _
        "Data Source=c:\Program Files\" & _
        "Microsoft Office\Office10\Samples\Northwind.mdb")
    Dim cmd1 As New System.Data.OleDb.OleDbCommand()

    'Save the Text property value of TextBox1 for
    'easy re-use
    Dim str1 = TextBox1.Text

    'Save Minimum and Maximum CategoryID values for
    're-use without re-computing function
    Dim MaxCatID As Integer = MaxMinID(True)
    Dim MinCatID As Integer = MaxMinID(False)

    'First test for validity as a number, then test
    'for number in right range
    If Char.IsNumber(str1) = False Then
        MsgBox("Please enter a valid number for " & _
        "CategoryID.", , "Number check")
```

(continued)

```
            Exit Sub
        ElseIf CInt(str1) < MinCatID Or _
            CInt(str1) > MaxCatID Then
            MsgBox("Please enter a number between " & _
            MinCatID.ToString & " and " & MaxCatID.ToString & ".")
            Exit Sub
        End If

        'Assign Connection and CommandText property values
        'for the cmd1 OleDbCommand object; notice CategoryID
        'value in WHERE clause depends on Text property for
        'TextBox1
        With cmd1
            .Connection = cnn1
            .CommandText = _
                "SELECT Count(CategoryID) FROM Products " & _
                "WHERE CategoryID = " & str1
        End With

        'Save result set from command in int1 memory variable
        cnn1.Open()
        Dim int1 As Integer = cmd1.ExecuteScalar

        'Display result from query
        MsgBox("The number of products in " & _
            "category " & str1 & " is " & _
            int1.ToString & ".")

        'Close connection
        cnn1.Close()

    End Sub

    Function MaxMinID(ByVal Max As Boolean) As Integer

        'Declare and instantiate Connection and Command objects
        Dim cnn1 As New OleDb.OleDbConnection( _
            "Provider=Microsoft.Jet.OLEDB.4.0;" & _
            "Data Source=c:\Program Files\" & _
            "Microsoft Office\Office10\Samples\Northwind.mdb")
        Dim cmd1 As New System.Data.OleDb.OleDbCommand()
        cnn1.Open()

        'Assign Connection and CommandText property values
        'for the cmd1 OleDbCommand object
        cmd1.Connection = cnn1

        'Return the highest or lowest CategoryID value from
        'the Categories table
        If Max = True Then
            cmd1.CommandText = _
```

```
                    "SELECT CategoryID FROM Categories " & _
                    "ORDER BY CategoryID DESC"
        Else
            cmd1.CommandText = _
                    "SELECT CategoryID FROM Categories"
        End If

        'Save result set from command in int1 memory variable
        Dim int1 As Integer = cmd1.ExecuteScalar

        'Return result
        Return int1

        'Close connection
        cnn1.Close()

End Function
```

Figure 8-6 contrasts the operation of the *Button1_Click* procedure with that of the *Button2_Click* procedure. The form on the left shows *TextBox1* with a value of 9. This is outside the original range of CategoryID values for the Northwind database. Clicking *Button1* returns a message box that resembles the top one on the right side of Figure 8-6. Clicking *Button2* displays a message box that resembles the bottom one on the right side of the figure. Notice that the bottom message does not return zero as the count for a nonexistent category. Instead, the message reminds the user to enter a valid number. It is good programming practice to validate user input in production applications. The samples in this book infrequently demonstrate data validation because they are tutorial in nature and are intended to demonstrate a concept other than data validation.

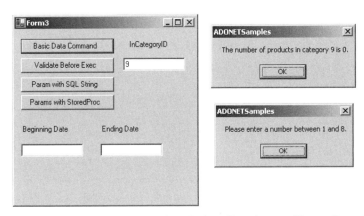

Figure 8-6   Clicking the Validate Before Exec button (*Button2*) reminds you to designate a valid CategoryID value instead of returning a count of the products in a nonexistent category, which happens when you click the top button on the form.

Dynamic Data Access with a SQL String and a Parameter

Instead of using a string variable, you can use a parameter to specify a value for a SQL statement at run time. The parameter can accept input from a text box just as a string variable can. You can use parameters directly with *OleDbCommand* objects or with *Command* objects associated with data adapters. This section describes and demonstrates how to add, specify, and use parameters with *OleDbCommand* objects.

OleDbCommand objects have a collection of *OleDbParameter* objects available through the *OleDbCommand Parameters* property. Your applications can add parameters to this collection with the *Add* method. At a minimum, you must specify a parameter name and data type when adding a parameter to the collection for a command. You can refer to individual parameters within the parameters collection by name or position. This allows you to specify an empty string as the name for a parameter and then refer to an individual parameter by its position in the *Parameters* collection. Whether you reference parameters by name or position, the members of the *OleDbParameterCollection* object align positionally with parameters in the SQL statement for the *CommandText* property of an *OleDbCommand*.

As you specify a parameter that you are adding to the *Parameters* collection for a command, you designate the *System.Data.OleDb* namespace. If you are working in a Windows application, you can specify this namespace by just designating *OleDb* because the *System.Data* namespace is referenced automatically for a Windows application project. Follow the namespace with a period, the enumeration *OleDbType*, and another period, and IntelliSense will come to your aid by displaying a list of available *OleDbType* enumeration values. Select the value that matches the type of data you are specifying for your parameter.

Table 8-1 shows selected *OleDbType* enumeration values that match Visual Basic .NET and common language runtime (CLR) data types. These mappings are not perfect in all cases. For example, the starting date for the *Date* enumeration member in *OleDbType* is December 30, 1899, but the starting date for the Visual Basic .NET *Date* data type is January 1, 0001. Another example of a minor variance is the mapping of the *Char* data type in Visual Basic .NET to the *LongVarWChar* member in *OleDbType*. The *Char* data type represents a single Unicode character, but the *LongVarWChar* enumeration represents a variable-length string of one or more Unicode characters.

Table 8-1   Selected *OleDbType* Enumeration Members Matching Visual Basic .NET Data Types and CLR Data Types

Visual Basic .NET Data Type	CLR DataType	*OleDbType* Enumeration Member
Byte	System.Byte	UnsignedTinyInt
Short	System.Int16	SmallInt
Integer	System.Int32	Integer
Long (long integer)	System.Int64	BigInt
Decimal	System.Decimal	Decimal
Single (single-precision floating point)	System.Single	Single
Double (double-precision floating point)	System.Double	Double
Char	System.Char	LongVarWChar
String (variable length)	System.String (class)	LongVarWChar
Date	System.DateTime	Date
Boolean	System.Boolean	Boolean
Object	System.Object (class)	PropVariant

> **Note**   See the "*OleDbType* Enumeration" topic in the Microsoft Visual Studio .NET Documentation for more *OleDbType* data types and more details on the data types.

The following listing for the *Button3_Click* procedure tackles the same task as the click event procedure for *Button1*. The only differences are in how you specify a variable value for a SQL statement assigned to the *CommandText* property for an *OleDbCommand* object and how you add, specify, and assign a value to the parameter for a command. The lines of code performing these tasks appear in boldface. The SQL statement assignment for the *CommandText* property uses a question mark (?) to denote parameters. You can optionally assign a name, such as *@InCategoryID*. Visual Basic .NET refers to the parameters in the SQL statement for the *CommandText* property by position. Therefore, any name you assign to a parameter in a SQL statement is for your own convenience. Within the *Parameters* collection for a command, Visual Basic .NET can distinguish between parameters by name or position. The *Button3_Click* procedure demonstrates how to use a name to refer to a parameter. The *Add* method for the *Parameters* collection assigns a name (*@InCategoryID*) to the new parameter, and the *Value* property applies to a member in the *Parameters* collection indexed by its name (*@InCategoryID*). Aside from these minor adjustments for using parameters, the code and underlying operation of the *Button3_Click* procedure directly match that for the *Button1_Click* procedure.

```
Private Sub Button3_Click(ByVal sender As System.Object, _
    ByVal e As System.EventArgs) Handles Button3.Click

    'Declare and instantiate Connection and Command objects
    Dim cnn1 As New OleDb.OleDbConnection( _
        "Provider=Microsoft.Jet.OLEDB.4.0;" & _
        "Data Source=c:\Program Files\" & _
        "Microsoft Office\Office10\Samples\Northwind.mdb")
    Dim cmd1 As New System.Data.OleDb.OleDbCommand()

    'Save the Text property value of TextBox1 for
    'easy re-use
    Dim str1 = TextBox1.Text

    With cmd1
        'Assign Connection and CommandText property values
        'for the cmd1 OleDbCommand object; notice CategoryID
        'value in WHERE clause depends on Text property for
        'TextBox1
        .Connection = cnn1
        .CommandText = _
            "SELECT Count(CategoryID) FROM Products " & _
            "WHERE CategoryID = ?"

        'Assign parameter value based on TextBox1; you must assign
        'a name, data type and value for your parameter (other
        'OleDb parameter property value assignments are optional)
        .Parameters.Add("@InCategoryID", OleDb.OleDbType.Integer)
        .Parameters("@InCategoryID").Value = TextBox1.Text
    End With
```

```
'Save result set from command in int1 memory variable
cnn1.Open()
Dim int1 As Integer = cmd1.ExecuteScalar

'Display result from query
MsgBox("The number of products in " & _
    "category " & str1 & " is " & _
    int1.ToString & ".")

'Close connection
cnn1.Close()

End Sub
```

Dynamic Data Access with an Access Query and Parameters

Using strings to specify SQL statements for the *CommandText* property of an *OleDbCommand* object creates code that is easy to read and understand. However, you can achieve superior performance by using a previously compiled query in an Access database file. When Access has a query that takes parameters (known as a *parameter query*), you can specify it with two *OleDbCommand* properties. Assign the query's name to the *CommandText* property value. Use the *StoredProcedure* enumeration member for a *CommandType* property assignment. Then, assign parameters to the *OleDbCommand* object. This approach saves compilation time for a query, lets you take advantage of the built-in query designer in Access, builds on familiar techniques, and transfers fewer bytes between the Visual Basic .NET application file and the Access database file.

The Sales By Year query in the Northwind database was initially designed to be called by the form named Sales By Year Dialog. The form includes a couple of text boxes that allow users to specify beginning and ending dates for the orders in a year (or any date range). The SQL view for the Sales By Year query shows the following representation of the query statement. Notice that the statement declares two parameters in its *Parameters* clause and then uses those parameters in the WHERE clause of the SQL SELECT statement. The parameters point to controls for inputting the beginning and ending dates on the Sales By Year Dialog form. The query returns four fields for each order that falls between the beginning and ending dates. The first of these fields is the shipped date for an order. The first row in the result is the earliest shipped order between the beginning and ending dates. Because the *ExecuteScalar* method returns the first column value from the first row in a result set, the *ExecuteScalar* method for an *OleDbCommand* object based on the Sales By Year query returns the shipped date for the first order in a date range.

```
PARAMETERS [Forms]![Sales by Year Dialog]![BeginningDate] DateTime,
[Forms]![Sales by Year Dialog]![EndingDate] DateTime;
SELECT Orders.ShippedDate, Orders.OrderID, [Order Subtotals].Subtotal,
Format([ShippedDate],"yyyy") AS [Year]
FROM Orders INNER JOIN [Order Subtotals] ON Orders.OrderID =
[Order Subtotals].OrderID
WHERE (((Orders.ShippedDate) Is Not Null And (Orders.ShippedDate)
Between [Forms]![Sales by Year Dialog]![BeginningDate] And
[Forms]![Sales by Year Dialog]![EndingDate]));
```

Notice in Figure 8-7 that *Form3* contains two text boxes for specifying beginning and ending dates. These text boxes allow a user to specify input parameter values for the Sales By Year query. Clicking *Button4* invokes a click event procedure that passes the parameter values in the text boxes to the Northwind database file, invokes the query, saves the first column value from the first row, and displays the saved result in a text box. Because the query name includes blanks, you must enclose the name in square brackets when specifying it as the value for the *cmd1 CommandText* property. Instead of designating parameters by name, the assignment of parameter values uses position indexes. The *Text* property for *TextBox2* is passed to the first parameter, and the *Text* property for *TextBox3* is passed to the second parameter. The first and second parameter positions correspond to the Access form controls referenced in the Jet SQL statement for the query, which you saw a moment ago.

```
Private Sub Button4_Click(ByVal sender As System.Object, _
    ByVal e As System.EventArgs) Handles Button4.Click

    'Declare and instantiate Connection and Command objects
    Dim cnn1 As New OleDb.OleDbConnection( _
        "Provider=Microsoft.Jet.OLEDB.4.0;" & _
        "Data Source=c:\Program Files\" & _
        "Microsoft Office\Office10\Samples\Northwind.mdb")
    Dim cmd1 As New System.Data.OleDb.OleDbCommand()

    With cmd1
        'Assign Connection and CommandText property values
        'for the cmd1 OleDbCommand object
        .Connection = cnn1
        .CommandType = CommandType.StoredProcedure
        .CommandText = "[Sales by Year]"

        'Assign parameter values based on position from
        'TextBox2 and TextBox3; you must assign a name
        '(even a zero-length string), data type and value
```

```
                'for your parameter (other OleDb parameter
                'property value assignments are optional)
                .Parameters.Add("", OleDb.OleDbType.Date)
                .Parameters(0).Value = TextBox2.Text
                .Parameters.Add("", OleDb.OleDbType.Date)
                .Parameters(1).Value = TextBox3.Text
            End With

            'Save result set from command in date1 memory variable
            cnn1.Open()
            Dim date1 As Date = cmd1.ExecuteScalar

            'Display first ShippedDate in result set
            'with Short Date format
            MsgBox(Format(date1, "Short Date"))

            'Close connection
            cnn1.Close()

    End Sub
```

Figure 8-7 shows this sample in operation. The beginning and ending dates are the first and last calendar days in the year 1996. Clicking *Button4* opens a message box that shows the shipped date for the first order in the year. The sample application formats the date as a *Short Date*. If you require the day of the week as well as the month, day, and year, you can specify a *Long Date* format type for the *date1* argument in the *Format* function.

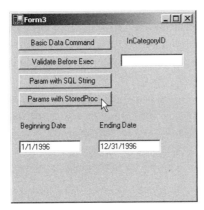

Figure 8-7   Using parameters for an *OleDbCommand* object, your Visual Basic .NET applications can pass values to an Access parameter query.

Programming Dynamic Data Manipulation

This section takes a case study approach to dynamic data manipulation by building a simple version of a typical application. The sample constructs an Access database file and populates the database with a couple of tables while putting some data in one table. This is not the typical part of the application. The two tables have the names Inventory and OrderDetails. The application processes any order for which inventory is on hand. If the inventory for the ordered item is not sufficient to fulfill the order, the order is not processed—it is instead backordered. If another order arrives after a backorder has been made, the order will be processed if its quantity is less than or equal to the number of units in inventory.

The decreasing of inventory units is dynamic in the sense that the reduction depends on whether the number of items ordered is less than or equal to the number of units on hand. This updating of inventory units in response to orders is the typical part of the application. The sample for this section is interesting from another perspective. It demonstrates transaction processing—that is, the marking of an order as processed and the decreasing of the units on hand are tied together in a single transaction. If the units on hand cannot decrease because the number ordered is too great, the order is not marked as processed. (Instead, it is marked as backordered.)

To create the sample database for this section, your project must have a reference to the *ADOX* library. See the "COM Interop" section in Chapter 3 for detailed instructions on adding a reference for a COM library, such as the *ADOX* library. The sample materials for this section depend on *Form4* in the ADONET-Samples project. The project shows a reference to *ADOX* in Solution Explorer. Because I selected the 2.7 version of the *ADOX* library, the *Description* property value for the *ADOX* reference equals Microsoft ADO Ext. 2.7 for DDL and Security; this is the long name for version 2.7 of the *ADOX* library. This version installs with Visual Studio .NET.

Form4 contains just three buttons with respective *Text* property values of *Button1*, *Button2*, and *Button3*. No form load event procedure exists to assign new nondefault *Text* properties. The click event procedure for *Button1* creates an Access database file. The *Button2_Click* procedure adds a couple of tables named Inventory and OrderDetails to the new database and populates the Inventory table with a row of column values. The click event procedure for *Button3* performs the dynamic updating of the two tables in a transaction.

Creating an Access Database Programmatically

Your applications can programmatically create an Access database file with the *Create* method for the *Catalog* class in the *ADOX* library. An empty Microsoft Access database file is different from an empty text file. Specifically, an empty Microsoft Access database file contains a catalog for accepting the structure of a database.

The *Create* method for a *Catalog* object can take a connection string as an argument. The connection string is a standard one for an Access database file that consists of *Provider* and *Data Source* clauses. Not all providers support the *Create* method, but the *Microsoft.Jet.OLEDB.4.0* provider is among those that do. In the listing for the *Button1_Click* procedure, *str1* represents the path and filename for the new database file, which is the value designated in the *Data Source* clause of the connection string argument for the *Create* method. Because the path is the bin subdirectory of the current folder, the procedure doesn't need to include a full path and sets *str1* equal to the filename, db1.mdb. Before attempting to create a new file named db1.mdb, the procedure checks whether one with that name already exists. The listing uses the *Exists* method of the *File* class in the *System.IO* namespace to confirm whether the file exists. If the file exists, the procedure invokes the *Delete* method of the *File* class to remove the previous version of the db1.mdb file from the bin subdirectory.

After ensuring that no database has the name the *Create* method uses to make a new database file, the procedure instantiates a new *Catalog* object, *cat1*. Next, an expression formulates the connection string for the *Create* method based on the value of *str1*. Because the procedure uses an expression, it is easy to substitute a different filename and designate a path without changing the core code for the sample. Invoking the *Create* method adds the db1.mdb file to the bin subdirectory of the ADONETSamples project folder.

The constructor for the *Catalog* class forms a sticky class instance. By *sticky*, I mean that merely setting the *cat1* object to *Nothing* does not remove the object reference from memory after the procedure concludes. Therefore, you need to use a more aggressive means to remove the memory reference. Failing to remove the object reference can cause a second invocation of the procedure to fail. One technique that will succeed is to invoke the *Collect* method of the *GC* class. This class controls the .NET Framework garbage collector. Normally the garbage collector works in the background to remove unreferenced objects, but it does not routinely perform this function for the *cat1* object reference. Invoking the *Collect* method after setting *cat1* equal to *Nothing* forces the garbage collector to immediately remove the *cat1* object from memory. The invocation of the *WaitForPendingFinalizers* method pauses the current thread until the *Collect* method completes.

```
Private Sub Button1_Click(ByVal sender As System.Object, _
    ByVal e As System.EventArgs) Handles Button1.Click

    'Assign database file name to str1
    Dim str1 = "db1.mdb"

    'Delete file if it exists
    If System.IO.File.Exists(str1) Then
        System.IO.File.Delete(str1)
    End If

    'Create cat1 in the file to which str1 points
    Dim cat1 As ADOX.Catalog
    cat1 = New ADOX.Catalog()
    str1 = "Provider=Microsoft.Jet.OLEDB.4.0;" & _
        "Data Source=" & str1
    cat1.Create(str1)

    'Setting to nothing does not cause timely
    'removal from memory

    'Force removal of cat1 from memory by first
    'setting to nothing and second collecting
    'unreferenced objects with the Garbage Collector
    cat1 = Nothing
    GC.Collect()
    GC.WaitForPendingFinalizers()

End Sub
```

Figure 8-8 shows Solution Explorer after running the click event procedure for *Button1*. Notice that db1.mdb appears in the bin subdirectory for the project. To display this directory, you normally have to click the Show All Files icon on Solution Explorer. This icon is located on the toolbar toward the top of Solution Explorer. I also expanded the References folder in Solution Explorer so that you can see the reference to the *ADOX* library.

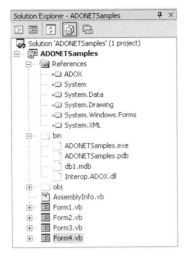

Figure 8-8   The click event procedure for *Button1* in *Form4* of the ADO-NETSamples project adds a new db1.mdb file to the bin subdirectory of the project folder.

Adding Tables to a Database Programmatically

The preceding sample demonstrated how to create a new Access database file programmatically. However, we're only part of the way toward constructing our sample. The next step is to populate the database with tables. In addition, this step inserts a row of column values into one of the new tables.

The two table names are Inventory and OrderDetails. The design for each table illustrates some common features. The Inventory table has just two columns. One column (ProdID) uniquely identifies products; it serves as a primary key for the table. The primary key column has an *Integer* data type, but it is not an autonumber field. The second column (UnitsOnHand) also has an *Integer* data type. In addition, this column has a check constraint requiring its column value to be greater than or equal to 0.

The OrderDetails table is for orders that contain just one item. This isn't a problem because the table in this simple sample contains just one item to order. The column (OrderID) serving as the primary key for the OrderDetails table has an *Integer* data type that is also an autonumber field. The next two columns describe the order. The Quantity column value specifies the number of units ordered for the inventory item identified by the ProdID column value. The final column (BackOrder) can have either of two values. Jet SQL designates this kind of data type as a *BIT* data type; this data type corresponds to a *Boolean* data type in Visual Basic .NET and a *Yes/No* data type in Access.

The *Button2_Click* procedure listing illustrates one approach to creating the Inventory and OrderDetails tables in the db1.mdb file. The implementation uses the *Connection* object in the OLE DB .NET Data Provider to connect the procedure to the db1.mdb file in the bin subdirectory of the ADONETSamples folder. Then, the procedure uses the *ExecuteNonQuery* method for an *OleDb-Command* object to run Jet SQL statements for creating both tables and populating the Inventory table with a single row of column values. The Jet SQL statement operates within the *cmd1* command object as a SQL string assigned to the command object's *CommandText* property.

You launch the specification of a table in a Jet SQL statement with the CREATE TABLE keywords followed by the name of the table. Designate individual columns within a table by specifying their column name, data type, and any special settings, such as settings for an autonumber field, primary key, or a check constraint. The ProdID column specification in the Inventory table illustrates the syntax for designating a primary key without an autonumber field, and the OrderID field specification in the OrderDetails table shows the syntax for specifying an autonumber field for a primary key. The IDENTITY keyword specifies an autonumber field. It takes an ordered pair of values as arguments (*autoincrement seed* followed by *autoincrement step*). The UnitsOnHand column declaration in the Inventory table demonstrates the syntax for a column check constraint requiring column values to be greater than or equal to 0.

Between the two invocations of the *ExecuteNonQuery* methods for creating the Inventory and OrderDetails tables is another invocation of the *ExecuteNon-Query* method. This application of the method illustrates the syntax for adding a row into a table with the INSERT INTO keywords. This is a very basic design. You will typically want to perform some error checks to handle attempts to add a row with a primary value that already exists in the table. For example, you could search for an existing column with the primary key value of the row that you seek to add to a table. In any event, the INSERT INTO statement adds an inventory item with a ProdID column value of 1 and a UnitsOnHand column value of 20.

```
Private Sub Button2_Click(ByVal sender As System.Object, _
    ByVal e As System.EventArgs) Handles Button2.Click

    'Declare and instantiate Connection and Command objects
    Dim cnn1 As New OleDb.OleDbConnection( _
        "Provider=Microsoft.Jet.OLEDB.4.0;" & _
```

```
            "Data Source=db1.mdb")
    Dim cmd1 As New OleDb.OleDbCommand()
    cnn1.Open()

    'Create Inventory and OrderDetails table and
    'initialize Inventory table with column values
    With cmd1
        'Create Inventory table
        .Connection = cnn1
        .CommandText = _
            "CREATE TABLE Inventory(" & _
            "ProdID INTEGER PRIMARY KEY, " & _
            "UnitsOnHand INTEGER, " & _
            "CHECK(UnitsOnHand >=0))"
        .ExecuteNonQuery()

        'Initialize Inventory table
        .CommandText = _
            "INSERT INTO Inventory " & _
                "(ProdID, UnitsOnHand) " & _
                "VALUES(1, 20)"
        .ExecuteNonQuery()

        'Create OrderDetails table
        .CommandText = _
            "CREATE TABLE OrderDetails(" & _
            "OrderID Integer IDENTITY(1,1) " & _
            "PRIMARY KEY, " & _
            "ProdID INTEGER, " & _
            "Quantity INTEGER, " & _
            "BackOrder BIT)"
        .ExecuteNonQuery()
    End With

    'Close connection
    cnn1.Close()

End Sub
```

Dynamic Data Manipulation Within a Transaction

Data manipulation within a transaction is inherently dynamic because a transaction will not necessarily succeed. One common use for a transaction in an application is to wrap together a sequence of action queries. For example, the sample application for this section binds together an attempt to update the UnitsOnHand column value for a row with a specific ProdID column value in the Inventory table with an attempt to add a new row to the OrderDetails table. If the transaction is successful, the transaction reduces the UnitsOnHand for the ordered inventory item and adds a new row to the OrderDetails table with a BackOrder column value of 0 to indicate that the order is processed. If the transaction fails, the UnitsOnHand column value in the Inventory table remains unchanged. The application does enter a new row in the OrderDetails table, but this is a different new row—not the one initially used in the failed transaction. The new row added to the OrderDetails table has a BackOrder column value of -1 to signify a value of *Yes* or *True*.

You can launch a transaction in Visual Basic .NET with two steps. First, you invoke the *BeginTransaction* method for a *Connection* object. This method returns a *Transaction* object. Second, you wrap a *Command* object in a transaction by assigning the returned object from the *BeginTransaction* method to the *Transaction* property of the *Command* object. Any action queries you invoke within the command operate as a single unit—that is, none of the action queries succeed unless they all succeed. If a transaction fails, the .NET Framework throws a *System.Data.OleDb.OleDbException* object. Your applications can catch this object and respond appropriately with any actions suitable for a failed transaction. For example, the sample application in this section resubmits the same order with its BackOrder status set to *True* instead of *False*. In other words, a successful transaction inserts a row in the OrderDetails table and reduces the UnitsOnHand for the corresponding inventory item by the Quantity column value for the new order. When the transaction succeeds, the value of the BackOrder column for the order is 0.

You use two methods when coding any transaction: *Commit* and *Rollback*. Invoke the *Commit* method for a *Transaction* object after all the actions within a transaction succeed. These actions will normally be two or more data manipulation queries (inserts, updates, or deletes). Invoke the *Commit* method for the transaction immediately after the last data manipulation query. If all queries through the last one succeed, your procedure will invoke the *Commit* method and manipulate the data sources in accordance with all action queries within the transaction.

Use the *Rollback* method in the *Catch* clause of a *Try...Catch...Finally* statement. In a *Catch* clause declaration, search for an *OleDbException* object to trap an error with any action query in the transaction. The *Rollback* method can be the first statement in the *Catch* clause. Use this method to dismiss all pending changes to data sources in the transaction. Then, you can make any final commitments that might be necessary, such as saving an order for which you do not have the inventory in stock.

> **Note**   *Transaction* objects have an *IsolationLevel* property that governs the ability of users outside the transaction to interact with the data sources within a transaction. I successfully applied the *ReadCommitted* level, which is the default level for a transaction. This *IsolationLevel* property value locks the values during a read so that no other user can modify the data while a read is in process. However, other users can modify a data source before a transaction commits any changes to the sources that it reads. The *RepeatableRead* value for the *IsolationLevel* property restricts other users from updating the data sources in a transaction until the transaction completes—successfully or otherwise.

The listing for the *Button3_Click* procedure demonstrates the syntax for coding transactions in Visual Basic .NET. Before clicking *Button3*, start with a fresh database file and new Inventory and OrderDetails tables by clicking *Button1* and *Button2*. These two steps initialize the UnitsOnHand column value to 20 for the row with a column value of 1 in the Inventory table. The listing starts by instantiating an *OleDbConnection* object (*cnn1*) that points at the db1.mdb file within the bin subdirectory of the current project's folder. Next, the procedure instantiates an *OleDbCommand* object (*cmd1*).

After instantiating both the *Connection* and *Command* objects, the procedure moves on to wrap the *Command* object in the transaction. This begins with the declaration of a variable (*trn1*) as a transaction. The *Dim* statement for *trn1* does not instantiate a *Transaction* object—it merely reserves a variable of the *OleDbTransaction* type. Before instantiation of the *Transaction* object for the *cnn1* object, you need to open the connection. (The sample opens the *cnn1* object.) Invoking the *BeginTransaction* method instantiates the *Transaction* object, and the sample assigns the *trn1* variable to the method's return value. The next two lines assign the *cnn1* object to the *Connection* property of the *cmd1* object and assign the *Transaction* object pointed at by the *trn1* variable to the *Transaction* property of the *cmd1* object. This completes the wrapping of the *cmd1 Command* object in the *trn1 Transaction* object. At this point, all actions invoked within the transaction must succeed for any of them to succeed.

The *Try…Catch…Finally* statement in the *Button3_Click* procedure puts the transaction to a test. The *Try* clause includes two action queries. The first action query attempts to insert a row into the OrderDetails table. The new row represents an order with a ProdID column value of 1 in a Quantity of 7 units. This action query in the *Try* clause attempts to submit the order with a

BackOrder column value of *False* (0). The value of 0 in the BackOrder column indicates there were enough units on hand to complete the order, and therefore the order was successful. Next, the procedure attempts to execute an update query that reduces the UnitsOnHand column value in the Inventory table for ProdID 1 by 7 units. The update query is the last one in the transaction, so the sample follows it with an invocation of the *Commit* method and finally a *Msg-Box* function providing feedback about a successfully processed order. The transaction can fail at either of the statements in the *Try* clause invoking the *ExecuteNonQuery* method. If a failure occurs at either point, control passes to the *Catch* clause without invoking the *Commit* method or the *MsgBox* function.

Starting with fresh values in the Inventory table (UnitsOnHand column value of 20 and ProdID column value of 1), the procedure can process two orders successfully before the update query generates a failure for the third order by trying to compute a new column value for UnitsOnHand, which is less than 0. In response to a third click to *Button3*, the sample application passes control to the *Catch* clause in the *Button3_Click* procedure. The first statement in this clause clears the transaction by invoking the *Rollback* method for the *trn1* object. Once the transaction is cleared, the application is free to add a new row to the OrderDetails table. This row is nearly the same as the one in the *Try* clause, except that the BackOrder column value is -1 instead of 0. A value of -1 in Access corresponds to a *Yes* or *True* setting for a *Yes/No* variable. The procedure uses an INSERT INTO Jet SQL statement to add the row to the Order-Details table. The *Catch* clause concludes by invoking the *MsgBox* function to alert the user that the order is on backorder instead of being processed.

Another query can select from the OrderDetails table only those rows with a BackOrder column value of -1 to develop a list of orders awaiting processing. After refreshing the Inventory table with new shipments from suppliers, an application can fulfill rows with a BackOrder column value of -1 until the amount of unfilled orders exceeds the inventory.

```
Private Sub Button3_Click(ByVal sender As System.Object, _
    ByVal e As System.EventArgs) Handles Button3.Click

    'Declare and instantiate Connection and Command objects
    Dim cnn1 As New OleDb.OleDbConnection( _
        "Provider=Microsoft.Jet.OLEDB.4.0;" & _
        "Data Source=db1.mdb")
    Dim cmd1 As New OleDb.OleDbCommand()

    'Use BeginTransaction to instantiate
    'an OleDbTransaction object for the
    'OleDbConnection object
```

```
Dim trn1 As OleDb.OleDbTransaction
cnn1.Open()
trn1 = cnn1.BeginTransaction
cmd1.Connection = cnn1
cmd1.Transaction = trn1

'Remove comment marker to confirm default
'IsolationLevel setting
'MsgBox(trn1.IsolationLevel.ToString)

'Insert process orders as long as inventory exists,
'otherwise backorder orders when insufficient units
'are available to process an order
Try
    With cmd1
        .CommandText = _
            "INSERT INTO OrderDetails " & _
                "(ProdID, Quantity, BackOrder) " & _
                "VALUES(1, 7, 0)"
        .ExecuteNonQuery()
        .CommandText = _
            "UPDATE Inventory " & _
                "SET UnitsOnHand = UnitsOnHand - 7 " & _
                "WHERE ProdID = 1"
        .ExecuteNonQuery()
        trn1.Commit()
        MsgBox("Order processed.", , "Order message")
    End With
Catch exc1 As System.Data.OleDb.OleDbException
    trn1.Rollback()
    cmd1.CommandText = _
        "INSERT INTO OrderDetails " & _
            "(ProdID, Quantity, BackOrder) " & _
            "VALUES(1, 7, -1)"
    cmd1.ExecuteNonQuery()
    MsgBox("Order backordered.", , "Backorder message")
End Try

'Clean up when done
cnn1.Close()

End Sub
```

Figure 8-9 displays the output from clicking *Button3* three times after first
clicking *Button1* and *Button2.* On the left, you see three message boxes. The
first two message boxes report successfully processed orders. The bottom message box indicates that the order was saved for subsequent processing. The

Window on the right side of Figure 8-9 shows three rows in the OrderDetails table from db1.mdb. The first two rows have BackOrder column values of 0, but the last row has a column value of -1, which indicates that the order represented by the row awaits processing. The OrderID column values are 1, 2, and 4. Notice that the row with an OrderID value of 3 is missing. This row corresponds to the unsuccessful attempt to process the third order. The attempt to process the third order threw an *Exception* object that made the initial version of the third order with an OrderID of 3 unavailable. The *Catch* clause released the system from the error associated with the exception, and the invocation of the *Rollback* method discarded the consequences of all actions in the third transaction. Then, a new insert query caused Access to issue a new autonumber value (4) for the second attempt to submit the third order with a BackOrder column value of -1.

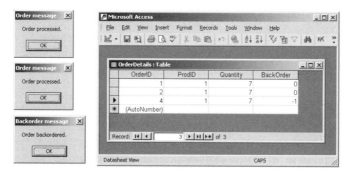

Figure 8-9   Transactions can lead to dynamic data manipulation because their action queries can be rolled back if all actions do not succeed.

Programming *DataAdapter* and *DataSet* Objects

The previous sample illustrated a special way to perform data manipulation that uses *Command* objects and adds the power of transactions to your data manipulation tasks. Although the approach illustrated in the previous sample ensures that no action queries work unless all action queries work, you will not achieve optimum scalability with it. Therefore, you should restrict your use of transactions to cases that absolutely require them. Instead, use a combination of data adapters and datasets for optimum scalability in your data manipulation tasks.

As you have learned, a data adapter acts as a bridge between a data source, such as the Customers table in the Northwind database, and a dataset in a Visual Basic .NET project. A dataset is a disconnected, in-memory copy of all or some of the data from a data source. Users can view and make changes to data in the dataset. When performing a task that requires a connection to a data source, the dataset briefly and automatically connects and disconnects to the data source through the data adapter just long enough to take care of business. Typical tasks that require an open connection include filling or refreshing a local dataset and exchanging updates between a dataset and its corresponding data source. You do not have to program when to open or close the data adapter; the .NET Framework handles that for you. The normally disconnected nature of datasets boosts the scalability of a database. Databases can handle more users because each dataset connects briefly—and only when necessary—to perform a specific task.

Form5 in the ADONETSamples project includes sample code for managing data access and data manipulation through data adapters and datasets. Figure 8-10 shows the form in Design view as well as operational view immediately after the opening of *Form5*. As you can see by the number of buttons, this sample application includes lots of sample code. The module behind *Form5* has a separate procedure for the click event of each button plus a dataset application set up in the form load event.

The amount of sample code is large partly because the application shows how to perform data manipulation based on datasets created with two techniques—one that is code based and another that is graphically based. *Button2* through *Button5* rely on a dataset created via code-based techniques for performing data manipulation. However, *Button6* through *Button9* demonstrate comparable data manipulation tasks with a dataset created graphically. *Button1* shows both metadata and data values from the dataset set up with code in the form load event procedure. The two datasets in the sample application point at the same data source in the Northwind database through a single data adapter. This design permits the sample application presentation to close with a demonstration of a concurrency violation and its workaround. The possibility of concurrency violations is the price that you pay for the scalability advantages that datasets deliver.

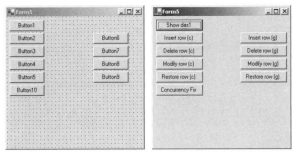

Figure 8-10   The click event procedures for the buttons and the form load event procedure demonstrate coding techniques for data manipulation via data adapters and datasets.

> **Note**   As with several of the preceding forms shown in this chapter, the form load event transforms the form's layout from the Design view to its initial operational view. To keep the focus of this chapter on ADO.NET, the printed sample code does not include the code for the layout tasks. However, the code is available in the ADONETSamples project. The sample for *Form5* is different from all the preceding samples in this project because *Form5* includes ADO.NET programming in its form load event procedure. This important code does appear in the code listing.

Data Manipulation Setup Code

You can set up an *OleDbDataAdapter* for data manipulation by properly configuring four properties: *SelectCommand*, *InsertCommand*, *UpdateCommand*, and *DeleteCommand*. Of course, you need to specify an *OleDbConnection* object for the *Command* objects that you assign to the properties. You can assign stand-alone *OleDbCommand* objects for the four properties, or you can use *Command* constructors in assignment statements that immediately convey an appropriately specified command to a property.

Through the *CommandText* property for a stand-alone *OleDbCommand* object or the SQL string in an *OleDbCommand* constructor, you can specify the operation of an *OleDbDataAdapter* object. The *SelectCommand* property determines the data that the *Fill* method conveys from a data source to a local dataset. For data manipulation tasks such as inserts, updates, and deletes, you need to understand that changes to a dataset are pending until they are accepted or rejected for the dataset. The *Update* method for the *OleDbDataAdapter* class performs several functions:

- Tries to convey pending updates for a local dataset to the underlying data source for the dataset. The *CommandText* property for the objects returned by the *InsertCommand*, *UpdateCommand*, and *DeleteCommand* properties determine which pending changes the *Update* method attempts to transfer to a data source. As Access developers, your underlying data source is likely to be an Access database.

- Accepts the pending changes in the local dataset if no concurrency violations exist. This action can reconcile a local dataset with its underlying data source. However, it is also possible for other users to have changed the data source for a dataset since the last time a data adapter filled it.

■   Can transfer changes from the data source to the dataset to reconcile a dataset with the most recent column values in its data source. The *Update* method will do this provided that the *DataTable* objects in a dataset have primary keys. If no primary keys exist, you can reconcile a dataset with its data source by clearing the dataset and refilling it with the most recent data from a data source.

Because the form load event procedure for *Form5* illustrates issues pertaining to the preceding design principles for *OleDbDataAdapter* objects, this sample's commentary begins with a summary of the ADO.NET code in the *Form5_Load* procedure. This discussion links the data adapter and dataset design issues to a concrete sample and ties the commentary for setting up a data adapter and a dataset to the sample results that you will see later in this section.

The following listing commences with a couple of module-level declarations—one for an *OleDbDataAdapter* object (*dap1*) and a second for a *DataSet* object (*das1*). You need to declare these variables at the module level because multiple procedures within the module reference them. The *Form5_Load* procedure begins by instantiating an *OleDbConnection* object (*cnn1*) that points at the Northwind database. Next, the procedure assigns *OleDbCommand* objects to the *SelectCommand*, *InsertCommand*, *UpdateCommand*, and *DeleteCommand* properties for the *dap1* object. For each property, an *OleDbCommand* constructor designates a SQL statement as a string, and a *Connection* object (*cnn1*).

Notice that the SQL statements for the latter three properties include placeholders (?) for parameters. Therefore, the form load event procedure must add parameters to the *Command* objects defining the corresponding properties. The syntax for the SQL statements defining *Command* objects is standard SQL to whatever database the data adapter connects. The SQL statement for the *SelectCommand* property designates just two columns (CustomerID and CompanyName) from the Customers table in the Northwind database for the *das1* object filled by the data adapter at which the *dap1* variable points. If you are familiar with Jet SQL, you'll recognize that this is basic Jet SQL.

The three blocks of code following the assignment of the data adapter properties illustrate the syntax for adding parameters. These code blocks build on the earlier presentation of parameters, but the blocks also illustrate specialized issues pertaining to data manipulation through data adapters. Because the dataset has just two columns, the data adapter can add rows with just two columns of data from the dataset to the Customers table in the Northwind database. Each column requires a separate parameter, and therefore, the code adds two parameters to the *Parameters* collection for the *InsertCommand* object. The syntax for the invocation of the *Add* method uses positional arguments to designate the properties for each parameter. The first two arguments designate the parameter name and the *OleDbType*. When referencing a string variable of type *LongVarWChar*, you must specify a length for the maximum number of characters in the string. This value is 5 for the incoming CustomerID column value and 40 for the incoming CompanyName column value. You can check your Access database to determine the appropriate maximum length for a string variable. The final argument designates the column name in the data source to which the *dap1* object should add the parameter value.

The syntax used with the *Add* method for adding parameters to the *Parameters* collections for the *UpdateCommand* and *DeleteCommand* objects in the *dap1* object follows the same general format as that of the *InsertCommand* object, with a couple of important exceptions. The *UpdateCommand* object takes three parameters, instead of the two used with the *InsertCommand* object. The first, second, and third parameters for the *UpdateCommand* object designate the revised CustomerID and CompanyName column values in the row for the Customers table specified by a CustomerID value. These parameters must be declared in the same order as that of their placeholders in the SQL statement for the *UpdateCommand* object.

Notice that CustomerID appears twice, each time with a separate name: *@CustomerID* and *@oldCustomerID*. The first instance is the updated CustomerID column value for the row specified by the *@oldCustomerID* parameter value. For the *Update* statement in the *UpdateCommand* object to succeed, the *@oldCustomerID* parameter value—which is the original value supplied to the dataset by the data adapter—must match the current value of the CustomerID of a row in the Customers table. The *SourceVersion* property setting for the *@oldCustomerID* parameter specifies that the *UpdateCommand* should use the original value supplied to the dataset instead of the current value (if the application or a user changed the CustomerID column value in the dataset).

The *DeleteCommand* object requires just one parameter in its *Parameters* collection. Again, this value must be the original value supplied to the dataset by the data adapter. Unless the parameter matches a CustomerID value in the Customers table within the Northwind database, your application should definitely not try to delete a row in the table.

After configuring the parameters for the data manipulation tasks, the form load event procedure moves on to creating the dataset and populating it. The *Fill* method performs these tasks. The method references the *das1* object and designates a *DataTable* object named *CustomerIDsNames* within the *das1* object. The *DataTable* object holds a subset of the column values from the Customers table in the Northwind database. In general, you should give your datasets enough data so that you can avoid repopulating them often. But you should not give them so much data that you cause lengthy delays in filling them and especially in refilling them.

One way to diminish the need to refill a *DataTable* object in a dataset is to specify a primary key for the *DataTable* object. A primary key in a *DataTable* object allows the *Update* method to automatically update a local dataset with only the column values that have been updated since the last population of a *DataTable* object from a data source. The last code block in the form load event procedure's listing shows the syntax for specifying a primary key. The statement assigns an array of columns to the *PrimaryKey* property for the *DataTable* object. Notice that the array has a *DataColumn* type. In this case, the array consists of a single column, namely the *CustomerID* item from the *Columns* collection for the first *DataTable* object in the *das1* dataset. The sample shows a positional index value (0) for representing the sole *DataTable* object within the *das1* dataset. However, you can also use a name index as a string value, such as *CustomerIDsNames*. Using a positional index will usually require less typing.

```
'Instantiate dap1 as an OleDbDataAdapter instance
Dim dap1 As New OleDb.OleDbDataAdapter()

'Instantiate das1 as a DataSet instance
Dim das1 As New System.Data.DataSet()

Private Sub Form5_Load(ByVal sender As System.Object, _
    ByVal e As System.EventArgs) Handles MyBase.Load

    'Declare and instantiate Connection and Command objects
    Dim cnn1 As New OleDb.OleDbConnection( _
        "Provider=Microsoft.Jet.OLEDB.4.0;" & _
        "Data Source=c:\Program Files\" & _
        "Microsoft Office\Office10\Samples\Northwind.mdb")

    'Specify SelectCommand, InsertCommand, UpdateCommand,
    'and DeleteCommand properties
    dap1.SelectCommand = New OleDb.OleDbCommand( _
        "SELECT CustomerID, CompanyName " & _
        "FROM Customers", cnn1)
    dap1.InsertCommand = New OleDb.OleDbCommand( _
        "INSERT INTO Customers " & _
        "(CustomerID, CompanyName) " & _
        "VALUES (?, ?)", cnn1)
    dap1.UpdateCommand = New OleDb.OleDbCommand( _
        "Update Customers SET CustomerID = ?, " & _
        "CompanyName = ? WHERE CustomerID = ?", cnn1)
```

(continued)

```
    dap1.DeleteCommand = New OleDb.OleDbCommand( _
        "DELETE FROM Customers WHERE CustomerID = ?", _
        cnn1)

    'Specify parameters for InsertCommand
    dap1.InsertCommand.Parameters.Add("@CustomerID", _
        OleDb.OleDbType.Char, 5, "CustomerID")
    dap1.InsertCommand.Parameters.Add("@CompanyName", _
        OleDb.OleDbType.VarChar, 40, "CompanyName")

    'Specify parameters for UpdateCommand
    dap1.UpdateCommand.Parameters.Add("@CustomerID", _
        OleDb.OleDbType.Char, 5, "CustomerID")
    dap1.UpdateCommand.Parameters.Add("@CompanyName", _
        OleDb.OleDbType.VarChar, 40, "CompanyName")
    dap1.UpdateCommand.Parameters.Add("@oldCustomerID", _
        OleDb.OleDbType.Char, 5, "CustomerID"). _
        SourceVersion = DataRowVersion.Original

    'Specify parameters for DeleteCommand
    dap1.DeleteCommand.Parameters.Add("@oldCustomerID", _
        OleDb.OleDbType.Char, 5, "CustomerID"). _
        SourceVersion = DataRowVersion.Original

    'Populate das1
    dap1.Fill(das1, "CustomerIDsNames")

    'Define a primary key for the DataTable
    das1.Tables(0).PrimaryKey = _
        New DataColumn() _
        {das1.Tables(0).Columns("CustomerID")}
    ...

End Sub
```

Displaying Metadata and Data from a Dataset

After defining the schema for a dataset and populating a dataset with values from a data source, your application can display metadata describing a dataset and the data inside a dataset. A few basic principles can help you understand how to accomplish these tasks. First, use the *DataSet* object model to tap the levels of structure within a dataset. Chapter 7 provides an overview of the dataset object model. (See Figure 7-6 on page 345 in particular.) Second, within any given *DataTable* object in a dataset, the .NET Framework stores schema information in *DataColumn* objects and stores data values in *DataRow* objects. The click event procedure for *Button1* in *Form5* and a related procedure (*DisplayIDsandNames*) demonstrate approaches to displaying metadata and data based on the *das1* dataset instantiated and populated in the *Form5_Load* procedure.

The *Button1_Click* procedure presents three sets of message boxes. Two of these message box sets present metadata about the *das1* dataset; each of the first two sets contains just one message box. The third message box set allows users to page through the actual values in the dataset. You'll find this paging capability convenient for confirming the effect of data manipulation tasks. The number of message boxes in the third set is a variable depending on the number of rows shown per page and the number of rows of data in the *DataTable* object. For the *CustomerIDsNames DataTable* object, the number of message boxes in the third set is three.

A dataset consists of a collection of *DataTable* objects. Because the *das1* dataset has just one *DataTable* object, its first table is its only table. The *Form5_Load* procedure illustrates the syntax for referring to a table in a dataset by a positional index, but you can also use a name index. The code for presenting the first message box in the *Button1_Click* procedure demonstrates the syntax for using a name index—simply delimit the table name in double quotes. The name that you delimit is the *TableName* property of a *DataTable* object, which the message box displays.

Within any *DataTable* object in a dataset, additional metadata describes the structure of the contents. For example, the columns in a table have names and data types. The overall *DataTable* object can have a primary key. The primary key relies on one or more columns, each of which has a data type. The code leading up to and through the presentation of the second message box in the *Button1_Click* procedure demonstrates how to construct and display this kind of metadata. Each *DataTable* object within a dataset has a *Columns* collection. Metadata about individual columns within a *DataTable* object resides in *DataColumn* objects comprising the *Columns* collection for a *DataTable* object. The sample code illustrates how to use a *For…Each…Next* loop to iterate through the *DataColumn* objects within the *Columns* collection of a *DataTable* object. Any *DataTable* object within a dataset can have a primary key. The primary key can be defined by one or more columns from the *DataTable* object. The *PrimaryKey* property for a *DataTable* object returns an array of *DataColumn* objects that define the primary key for a *DataTable* object. Even if a single *DataColumn* object defines a primary key, you must iterate through the array elements to view the column defining an array. The sample code declares a column array with the *cls1* variable. Using a *For…Each…Next* loop, the sample application loops through the *cls1* array to display the name and data type for the columns defining the primary key.

One of the most common tasks that you will want to perform with a dataset is to view the data values in its *DataTableCollection* collection. The .NET Framework stores the data values for a *DataTable* object in the *Rows* collection property. Use a *DataRow* object in a *For…Each…Next* loop to iterate through the individual rows within the *Rows* collection for a *DataTable* object. You can refer to the column values within a *DataRow* object by positional or name indexes. The listing for *Button1_Click* shows the syntax for using name indexes.

Because a *DataTable* object can contain many rows, it is possible for the characters in the *Rows* collection to exceed the amount of characters that a message box can display. That's the case for the *CustomerIDsNames DataTable* object. The listing demonstrates a solution to this issue by grouping rows into units of 35. The *Button1_Click* procedure therefore displays *DataRow* column values as a succession of 35-row sets. If an odd number of rows are left over after the last full page of 35 rows, the procedure displays the remaining rows after the last full page. The code presenting the message box is actually in a *Sub* procedure (*DisplayIDsandNames*) that the *Button1_Click* procedure calls. Isolating the code in a *Sub* procedure makes it easy to call the procedure for displaying the message box from inside the loop through the rows as well as after the loop.

```
Private Sub Button1_Click(ByVal sender As System.Object, _
    ByVal e As System.EventArgs) Handles Button1.Click

    'Display table metadata for tables in das1
    MsgBox("First table in the dataset " & _
        "has the name " & _
        das1.Tables("CustomerIDsNames").TableName & _
        ".", , "Dataset metadata")

    'Display column metadata for the first table
    'in das1
    Dim str1 As String = "DataTable columns " & _
        "and data types" & vbCr
    Dim dcol As DataColumn
    For Each dcol In das1.Tables(0).Columns
        str1 &= dcol.ColumnName & ", " & _
```

```
                    dco1.DataType.ToString & vbCr
Next

'Display primary keys for the first table
'in das1
Dim cls1() As DataColumn
cls1 = das1.Tables(0).PrimaryKey
str1 &= vbCr & "Primary key columns " & _
    "and data types" & vbCr
For Each dco1 In cls1
    str1 &= dco1.ColumnName & ", " & _
        dco1.DataType.ToString & vbCr
Next

'Display DataTable metadata
MsgBox(str1, , "DataTable metadata")

'Page through row values with up to intPageSize
'rows per page
Dim drw1 As DataRow
Dim int1 As Integer
Dim intPageSize As Integer = 35
str1 = ""
For Each drw1 In _
    das1.Tables("CustomerIDsNames").Rows
    str1 &= drw1("CustomerID") & ", " & _
        drw1("CompanyName") & vbCr
    int1 += 1
    If (int1 - intPageSize) = 0 Then
        DisplayIDsandNames(str1, intPageSize)
        str1 = ""
        int1 = 0
    End If
Next

'Display last page if there are less than
'intPageSize rows to the page
If int1 <> 0 Then
    DisplayIDsandNames(str1, intPageSize)
End If

End Sub
```

(continued)

```
Sub DisplayIDsandNames(ByVal str1 As String, _
    ByVal intPageSize As Integer)

    'Dipslay row values
    MsgBox(str1, , "Column values in groups of " & _
        intPageSize.ToString & " rows or less")

End Sub
```

Figure 8-11 shows the two message boxes displaying metadata for the *CustomerIDsNames DataTable* in the *das1* dataset. The top message box shows the *TableName* property of the *DataTable* object inside the *das1* dataset. The property value appears as part of a string expression to compose a sentence. The second text box in Figure 8-11 displays two sets of metadata about the *CustomerIDsNames DataTable* object in the *das1* dataset. The top part of the second text box shows the column name delimited by a comma from the column data type for each column in the *CustomerIDsNames Data-Table* object. As you can see, the column name values correspond to the SQL statement for the *dap1* data adapter that populates the *DataTable* object. The second set of data in the bottom text box shows the column name and data type for the column defining the primary key in the *CustomerIDsNames Data-Table* object.

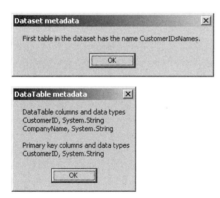

Figure 8-11   You can display metadata about the *DataTable* objects in a dataset.

Figure 8-12 shows the three message boxes with data values for the *CustomerIDsNames DataTable* object. This *DataTable* object, which is based on the Customers table in the Northwind database, contains a total of 91 rows. The first two message boxes each contain 35 rows. This leaves a balance of 21 rows for the third message box to display.

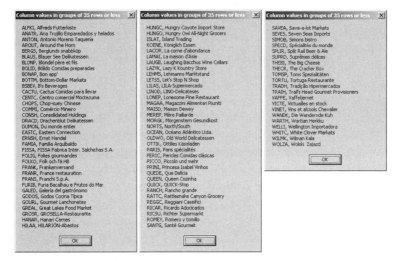

Figure 8-12   You can let users page through the rows of a *DataTable* object in a dataset with a message box.

Manipulating Rows in a Code-Based Dataset

Manipulating data with a data source through a dataset is a two-step process. First, you make a change to the local dataset. Second, you convey the change from the local dataset to the data source. You are likely to make three types of changes: inserting a new row, deleting a row, and changing the value in an existing row. The click event procedures for *Button2* through *Button5* in *Form5* demonstrate how to handle these tasks for the *CustomerIDsNames DataTable* object in the *das1* dataset that the *Form5_Load* procedure populates.

Inserting a Row

Adding a row to a local dataset requires three steps. First, you define a new empty row with the same columns as the original *DataTable* object. Second, you assign values to the columns of the new row. Third, you add the new row of column values to the *DataTable* object. The .NET Framework appends the new row to the end of the *DataTable* object. After appending one or more rows, you can update the data source in a corresponding way by invoking the *Update* method for the data adapter that manages the *DataTable* object in a dataset.

The listing for the *Button2_Click* procedure shows the syntax for adding a new row to the *CustomerIDsNames DataTable* object and then synchronizing the *das1* dataset with the Customers table in the Northwind database. Invoke the *NewRow* method for the *CustomerIDsNames DataTable* object to instantiate a new empty row (*drw1*). The newly created row will have the same format as the existing rows in the *CustomerIDsNames DataTable* object. The new row will be empty, and it will not belong to the *CustomerIDsNames DataTable* object. After instantiating a *DataRow* object with the *NewRow* method, the procedure populates the CustomerID column with a value of *MYCOM* and the CompanyName column with a value of *ProgrammingMSAccess.com*. With the *Add* method for the *Rows* collection, the procedure appends the *drw1 DataRow* object to the end of the *CustomerIDsNames DataTable* object. The *Button2_Click* procedure concludes by invoking the *Update* method for the *dap1* object. This propagates the new row from the *das1* dataset to the Customers table in the Northwind database.

The design of the *Button2_Click* procedure highlights the core steps for inserting a new row into a table—both locally and in the data source for a local *DataTable* object. The procedure does not feature other desirable elements that can distract your attention from the core focus for the sample. For example, clicking *Button2* twice in a row will generate an error because the second click tries to add a row to the local data table that already exists. In a production system, you will probably want to add traps that respond to this and other actions that a user might make.

```
Private Sub Button2_Click(ByVal sender As System.Object, _
    ByVal e As System.EventArgs) Handles Button2.Click

    'Add the row locally
    Dim drw1 As DataRow = _
        das1.Tables("CustomerIDsNames").NewRow()
    drw1("CustomerID") = "MYCOM"
    drw1("CompanyName") = "ProgrammingMSAccess.com"
    das1.Tables("CustomerIDsNames").Rows.Add(drw1)

    'Update the Access database file
    dap1.Update(das1, "CustomerIDsNames")

End Sub
```

Figure 8-13 shows the outcome of clicking *Button2_Click* in the local dataset and in the Northwind database. The window on the left is the last page that the *Button1_Click* procedure generates. The last row in this window shows the new column values of *MYCOM* and *ProgrammingMSAccess.com*. The window on the right side of Figure 8-13 shows the same row of column values in the Customers table for the Northwind database.

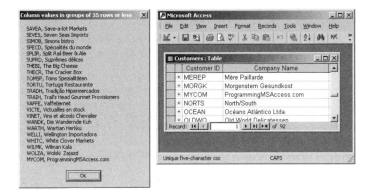

Figure 8-13   With the *Update* method, you can propagate a new row in a local *DataTable* object to its corresponding data source in an Access database.

Deleting a Row

Deleting a row from a local *DataTable* object is an activity that benefits from a primary key for the *DataTable* object. This is because the *Find* method can immediately move to any row corresponding to a primary key value. Without a primary key, you need an alternate means of navigating to a row that you want to delete. For example, you can use a *For...Next* loop or a *For...Each...Next* loop and pass through the rows in a *DataTable* object until you find one or more column values identifying a row to delete.

The listing for the *Button3_Click* procedure shows the code to delete the row added by the click event procedure for *Button2*. The procedure to delete a row starts by applying the *Find* method to the *Rows* collection of the first (and only) *DataTable* object in the *das1* dataset. This is the familiar *CustomerIDs-Names DataTable* object. Because the argument for the *Find* method is *MYCOM*, the method returns a *DataRow* object (*drw1*) whose CustomerID column value equals *MYCOM*. If the row with that CustomerID column value was deleted previously (or never inserted), the method does not populate the row and the *drw1* object remains equal to *Nothing*. Because attempting to delete a row that does not exist throws an *Exception* object at run time, the procedure tests with an *If...Then* statement if the row equals *Nothing* before applying the *Delete* method. After modifying the local dataset with the *Delete* method, the *Button3_Click* procedure invokes the *Update* method for the *dap1* object. This synchronizes the change in the local dataset with the Northwind database.

> **Note**   Invoking the *Delete* method does not physically remove a row from a *DataTable* object in a dataset. The method merely marks the row for deletion. Although your application cannot access a deleted row with the normal methods used to access other rows, special methods that allow you to manipulate deleted rows exist. The concluding sample in this chapter demonstrates the use of one of these methods.

You can confirm the removal of the local row by clicking *Button1* and examining the last page of data. Because the procedure for populating the message box does not depend on the primary key, the new row will fail to appear at the end unless the *Delete* method fails. To confirm the change in the Northwind database, open a fresh Datasheet view of the Customers table and see whether you can find a row with a CustomerID value of *MYCOM*. Because the Datasheet view displays rows by primary key value, look for the row among the CustomerID column values starting with *M*.

```
Private Sub Button3_Click(ByVal sender As System.Object, _
    ByVal e As System.EventArgs) Handles Button3.Click

    'Find row to delete; if present delete it
    Dim drw1 As DataRow = das1.Tables(0).Rows.Find("MYCOM")
    If Not (drw1 Is Nothing) Then
        das1.Tables(0).Rows.Find("MYCOM").Delete()
    End If

    'Update Access database file and local dataset
    'rowstate for found DataRow
    dap1.Update(das1, "CustomerIDsNames")

End Sub
```

Updating a Row

This section contains two samples demonstrating how to update a column value in a row. The first sample makes the update both locally and in the Northwind database, and the second sample restores the row to its original value in both locations. The change is merely to append an *x* to the CompanyName column value in the row with a CustomerID column value of *ALFKI*.

The following listing includes the click event procedures for *Button4* and *Button5*. A click to *Button4* makes the change, and a click to *Button5* restores the column value to its former state. The click event procedure for *Button4* uses the *Find* method to point the *drw1* variable at the row with a value of *ALFKI* for its CustomerID column. Then, the procedure appends an *x* with the &= operator to the end of the string in the CompanyName column for the row at which the *drw1* variable points. By invoking the *Update* method for the *dap1* object, the procedure makes a corresponding revision to the same row in the Customers table within the Northwind database.

The code for the *Button5_Click* procedure starts by pointing the *drw1* variable at the row in the *CustomerIDsNames DataTable* object with a CustomerID column value of *ALFKI*. Two Visual Basic .NET string functions (*Len* and *Mid*) work together to strip the *x* from the end of the CompanyName field in the *drw1 DataRow* object. Then, the *Update* method causes the corresponding change to occur within the Customers table of the Northwind database.

You can verify the operation of the updates with the same techniques used earlier in the sample in the "Inserting a Row" section. Instead of looking on the last data page, you should look on the first page of data because that is where the row with a CustomerID of *ALFKI* appears.

```
Private Sub Button4_Click(ByVal sender As System.Object, _
    ByVal e As System.EventArgs) Handles Button4.Click

    'Select row to modify
    Dim drw1 As DataRow = _
        das1.Tables(0).Rows.Find("ALFKI")

    'Perform row modification by appending an x
    drw1(1) &= "x"

    'Update Access database file and local dataset
    'row state for found DataRow
    dap1.Update(das1, "CustomerIDsNames")

End Sub

Private Sub Button5_Click(ByVal sender As System.Object, _
    ByVal e As System.EventArgs) Handles Button5.Click

    'Select row to restore
    Dim drw1 As DataRow = _
        das1.Tables(0).Rows.Find("ALFKI")

    'Restore by removing last character
    Dim int1 As Integer = Len(drw1(1)) - 1
    drw1(1) = Mid(drw1(1), 1, int1)
```

(continued)

```
'Update Access database file and local dataset
'row state for found DataRow
dap1.Update(das1, "CustomerIDsNames")
```

End Sub

Working with Graphically Based Datasets

The module behind *Form5* creates the *das1* dataset at run time. No trace of the *das1* dataset or its *CustomerIDsNames DataTable* object exists at design time. Using code to specify objects has some distinct advantages, including precise repeatability. No matter how many times you run the code under the same conditions, you will get the same result. When you leave objects for manual creation at design time, your solution is only as repeatable as its documentation and the ability of an analyst to precisely follow any steps in the documentation for creating objects. After building a basic model, you can try variations with a code-based model for creating objects more easily than with a graphically based model. On the other hand, many developers find graphically based approaches faster and easier. Graphical techniques speed development for most developers, and they are therefore great for building prototypes.

Because graphically based approaches offer distinct benefits to both experienced and inexperienced developers, this section shows the graphical steps for creating a dataset based on the Customers table in the Northwind database. To help relate graphical approaches to code-based approaches, the remaining insert, delete, and update samples use the *dap1* data adapter created earlier in the section for the *das1* dataset pointing at the Customers table in the Northwind database. Recall that the sample demonstrates the use of code to create the *das1* dataset. By having graphical and code-based datasets pointing at the same data source, this sample will generate the items needed to demonstrate concurrency conflicts.

Creating a Dataset Graphically

You learned in Chapter 2 (in the section "Building the Jump Start Example") how to create a dataset graphically by dragging tables and views from Server Explorer to a form. This approach facilitates the creation of the *Connection*, *DataAdapter*, and *DataSet* objects without manually coding them. Each dataset created with this approach can accommodate just one *DataTable* object. However, one of the key advantages of a dataset is that it allows the specification of a hierarchical relation between two or more tables. Chapter 7 demonstrated a graphical approach to specifying a hierarchical relation between two *DataTable* objects in a dataset schema. This approach relied on the Dataset Designer. This

section builds on that introduction to the Dataset Designer by specifically showing how to use a dataset schema created with the Dataset Designer for insert,
delete, and update tasks.

You can start to graphically create a dataset that points at the Customers
table in the Northwind database by choosing Project, Add New Item. In the Add
New Item dialog box, select the DataSet template and click Open. If Solution
Explorer is open, you will see a new Dataset entry such as Dataset1.xsd, and
you will see the Dataset Designer window with a link for opening Server
Explorer. Click that link, and open the connection to the database that you want
to use. As stated earlier, this sample uses the Northwind database. Within the
Tables folder for the Northwind database in Server Explorer, drag the Custom-
ers table to the Dataset Designer window.

The steps in the preceding paragraph can generate a set of windows similar to those shown in Figure 8-14. This figure depicts the Visual Studio .NET
IDE immediately after dragging the Customers table to the Dataset Designer
window, which creates a file named Dataset1.xsd. Within the Dataset Designer
window, you will see in the *Dataset1* dataset a graphical depiction of the local
DataTable object, which is named *Customers*. Notice that the graphical solution
automatically creates a local table with a primary key. (See the key next to CustomerID.) Additional column names appear down the side.

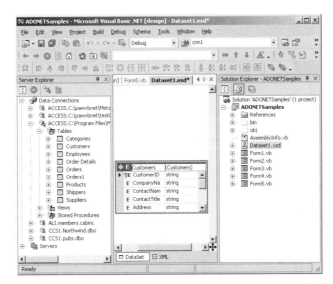

Figure 8-14   Dragging a table to the Dataset Designer window creates a
dataset schema that you can use as the basis for a typed dataset that
appears in the tray below a form.

The Solution Explorer window to the right of the Dataset Designer window shows a Dataset1.xsd object. This dataset is a schema for data. To complete the graphical design of a dataset, you need to open *Form5* in Design view and drag a DataSet icon from the Data tab of the Toolbox to the form. This act opens the Add Dataset dialog box. The default selection is for a typed dataset. If only one dataset exists in Solution Explorer, the Name box shows that dataset. If Solution Explorer contains more than one dataset, the Name box shows the first dataset. You can click the drop-down box next to the name and select any dataset schema on which you want to base a typed dataset. Clicking OK adds an icon for your typed dataset to a tray below your form. (See Figure 8-15.) You can use this dataset with the *dap1* data adapter created earlier in the *Form5* discussion for the ADONETSamples project. You do not need to add *Connection* and *Data-Adapter* objects to the tray below *Form5*. The *Dataset11* dataset works with the *Connection* object for the *dap1* data adapter.

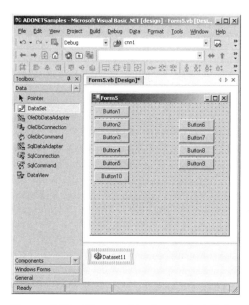

Figure 8-15   The graphically created *Dataset11* object in the tray below *Form5* points at the Dataset1.xsd schema created graphically in the Dataset Designer window appearing in Figure 8-14.

Inserting, Deleting, and Updating with a Graphically Created Dataset

The *Dataset11* and *das1* datasets correspond to the Customers table in the Northwind database, but they have different designs and were created differently. Despite the different techniques for originating the two datasets, you can use the *dap1* object as a data adapter for populating them and for performing data manipulation tasks with them. The code samples for *Button2* through *Button5* demonstrate techniques for programming insert, delete, and update tasks with the *das1* dataset. This section briefly reviews the sample code for *Button6* through *Button9* to demonstrate how to perform the same tasks with the *Dataset11* dataset.

The *Button6_Click* procedure inserts a new row into the *Customers DataTable* object within the *Dataset11* dataset and into the Customers table within the Northwind database. This procedure is analogous to the *Button2_Click* procedure. The main difference between the two procedures is that the *Button2_Click* procedure works with the *das1* dataset while the *Button6_Click* procedure processes the data in the *Dataset11* dataset. The *das1* dataset fills automatically when *Form5* loads because of code in the *Form5_Load* event procedure, but this is not the case for the *Dataset11* dataset. Therefore, the *Button6_Click* procedure starts by invoking the *Fill* method for the *dap1* object. The arguments for the *Fill* method are the *Customers Data-Table* object in the *Dataset11* dataset. After this step, the *Button6_Click* procedure is the same as the *Button2_Click* procedure except for the names of the dataset and the *DataTable* object.

Both the *Button2_Click* and *Button6_Click* procedures achieve the same goal, which is to add a new row to the Customers table in the Northwind database if a row with a CustomerID column value of *MYCOM* does not exist already. However, some subtle differences exist in the operation of the two procedures. The *Form5_Load* procedure populates the *das1* dataset, which is declared at the module level. Therefore, the *das1* dataset persists its initial values—except for edits during a session—from the time that *Form5* opens. On the other hand, the *Button6_Click* procedure repopulates the *Dataset11* dataset each time a user clicks the button. Therefore, the *Dataset11* dataset can reflect more recent data from the Northwind database than the *das1* dataset can.

```
Private Sub Button6_Click(ByVal sender As System.Object, _
    ByVal e As System.EventArgs) Handles Button6.Click

    'Fill Dataset1 via Dataset11
    dap1.Fill(Dataset11, "Customers")

    'Add the row locally
    Dim drw1 As DataRow = _
        Dataset11.Tables("Customers").NewRow()
    drw1("CustomerID") = "MYCOM"
    drw1("CompanyName") = "ProgrammingMSAccess.com"
```

(continued)

```
Dataset11.Tables("Customers").Rows.Add(drw1)

'Update Access database file and local dataset
'row state
dap1.Update(Dataset11, "Customers")
```

End Sub

The click event procedures for *Button7*, *Button8*, and *Button9* appear without detailed comment. The *Button7_Click* procedure deletes the row with a CustomerID column value of *MYCOM* in the *Customers DataTable* object and in the Customers table in the Northwind database. The *Button8_Click* and *Button9_Click* procedures respectively append and remove a string value of *y* from the CompanyName column value for the row with a CustomerID value of *ALFKI*.

```
Private Sub Button7_Click(ByVal sender As System.Object, _
    ByVal e As System.EventArgs) Handles Button7.Click

    'Fill Dataset1 via Dataset11
    dap1.Fill(Dataset11, "Customers")

    'Find row to delete; if present delete it
    Dim drw1 As DataRow = _
        Dataset11.Tables(0).Rows.Find("MYCOM")
    If Not (drw1 Is Nothing) Then
        Dataset11.Tables(0).Rows.Find("MYCOM").Delete()
    End If

    'Update Access database file and local dataset
    'row state for found DataRow
    dap1.Update(Dataset11, "Customers")

End Sub

Private Sub Button8_Click(ByVal sender As System.Object, _
    ByVal e As System.EventArgs) Handles Button8.Click

    'Fill Dataset1 via Dataset11
    dap1.Fill(Dataset11, "Customers")

    'Select row to modify
    Dim drw1 As DataRow = _
        Dataset11.Tables(0).Rows.Find("ALFKI")

    'Perform row modification by appending a y
    drw1(1) &= "y"
```

```
            'Update Access database file and local dataset
            'row state for found DataRow
            dap1.Update(Dataset11, "Customers")

    End Sub

    Private Sub Button9_Click(ByVal sender As System.Object, _
        ByVal e As System.EventArgs) Handles Button9.Click

            'Fill Dataset1 via Dataset11
            dap1.Fill(Dataset11, "Customers")

            'Select row to modify
            Dim drw1 As DataRow = _
                Dataset11.Tables(0).Rows.Find("ALFKI")

            'Restore by removing last character
            Dim int1 As Integer = Len(drw1(1)) - 1
            drw1(1) = Mid(drw1(1), 1, int1)

            'Update Access database file and local dataset
            'row state for found DataRow
            dap1.Update(Dataset11, "Customers")

    End Sub
```

Concurrency Violations

If you have been developing *Form5* along with its discussion in this chapter, your copy of *Form5* will have two different datasets (*das1* and *Dataset11*) connected to the same data source (the Northwind database). Furthermore, the *CustomerIDsNames DataTable* object in *das1* and the *Customers DataTable* object in *Dataset11* both point at the same table (Customers) in the Northwind database. These two datasets allow the simulation of a multiuser application because each dataset can represent a different user. The ability to simulate a multiuser application is helpful for demonstrating a concurrency violation when two users update the same row in an incompatible way.

A concurrency violation is serious because the .NET Framework throws a *DBConcurrencyException* object. If your code does not handle the exception, your code will terminate abruptly. When you catch a *DBConcurrencyException* object, you will often need to perform some action to synchronize your local dataset with the data source to which it corresponds. The exact action to take can depend on the circumstances causing the concurrency violation. A good general approach is to clear an object, such as a dataset or table, and then repopulate it from the data source. This gets the synchronization job done, but it can be expensive in network traffic because you must transfer all the data for a *DataTable* object or dataset even when only one row caused the problem. Another approach is to perform remedial action on a local dataset. The closing concurrency violation sample demonstrates this approach.

Before considering the code, let's examine a set of circumstances that can reliably generate a concurrency violation. Follow these four steps to generate a concurrency violation:

1. Open a fresh copy of *Form5*. (You will need *Button10* and its click event procedure to work around the concurrency violation.) Opening the form populates the *CustomerIDsNames DataTable* object in the *das1* dataset.

2. Click *Button2*. This inserts a new row in the *CustomerIDsNames DataTable* object and propagates the new row to the Customers table in the Northwind database.

3. Click *Button7*. This populates the *Customers DataTable* object in *Dataset11* with the contents of the Customers table in the Northwind database. Then, the click event procedure for *Button7* removes the row added by clicking *Button2* from both the *Customers DataTable* object in *Dataset11* and the Customers table in the Northwind database.

4. Click *Button3* or *Button10*. A click to *Button3* throws an unhandled *DBConcurrencyException* object that aborts the application. The exception occurs because the click event for *Button3* attempts to delete a row from the Customers table in the Northwind database based on the row in the *das1* dataset that the previous step deleted via the *Dataset11* dataset. The click event procedure for *Button10* has a *Try…Catch…Finally* statement for catching the *DBConcurrencyException* object. The *Catch* clause performs a remedial action that reconciles the *CustomerIDsNames DataTable* object with the Customers table in the Northwind database.

The listing for the *Button10_Click* procedure starts by deleting the row with a CustomerID value of *MYCOM* in the *das1* dataset. This row exists in the *CustomerIDsNames DataTable* object because the row was added to the *das1* dataset in the second step and no subsequent action removed the row. Therefore, the attempt to invoke the *Delete* method for the *DataRow* object pointing at the row with a CustomerID of *MYCOM* succeeds. Next, the procedure tries to update the Customers table in the Northwind database to remove the row with a CustomerID value of *MYCOM*. However, this attempt throws a concurrency violation because the third step previously removed the row from the Customers table within the Northwind database. The *Catch* clause traps the *DBConcurrencyException* object and performs a remedial action.

As you have learned, updates to a *DataTable* object are pending until they are finalized. A successful invocation of the *Update* method can finalize pending updates, but the *DBConcurrencyException* object from an unsuccessful *Update* method leaves the pending deletion at the beginning of the *Button10_Click* procedure unfinalized. The application needs to finalize the deleted row for the local *DataTable* object. Invoking the *AcceptChanges* method for the local *DataTable* object achieves the desired result.

Note   You can invoke the *RejectChanges* method for a *DataTable* object in a dataset to restore an original result if an update to a database is rejected for some reason.

```
Private Sub Button10_Click(ByVal sender As System.Object, _
    ByVal e As System.EventArgs) Handles Button10.Click

    'Find row to delete; if present delete it
    Dim drw1 As DataRow = das1.Tables(0).Rows.Find("MYCOM")
    If Not (drw1 Is Nothing) Then
        das1.Tables(0).Rows.Find("MYCOM").Delete()
    End If

    'Attempt to update Access database file and
    'local dataset row state for found DataRow; if
    '.NET Framework throws DBConcurrencyException object
    'accept changes to local table (clearing and re-
    'populating is another valid strategy)
    Try
        dap1.Update(das1, "CustomerIDsNames")
    Catch exc1 As System.Data.DBConcurrencyException
        das1.Tables(0).AcceptChanges()
    End Try

End Sub
```

Summary

This chapter presents coding techniques for typical tasks you might perform with ADO.NET. It starts by drilling down on *OleDbConnection* objects. In particular, the chapter contrasts connection strings in Access databases with those in SQL Server. Then, we discuss *OleDbCommand* objects for dynamic data access. In addition, you learn how to wrap data manipulation queries in transactions. The chapter closes with an in-depth look at performing data manipulation with data adapters and datasets. You see how to set up a data adapter for filling a dataset and handling inserts, deletes, and updates. The chapter also contrasts code-based datasets with graphically generated ones. The final sample illustrates how to handle concurrency conflicts that can occur when two datasets make conflicting changes to an Access database.

9

ADO.NET: Datasets and Data Manipulation on Windows Forms

This chapter wraps up the discussion of ADO.NET by drilling down on two topics: datasets and programming data manipulation on a Windows form. The material in this chapter expands on earlier treatments of these topics. Specifically, Chapter 7 presented ADO.NET from the architectural and conceptual perspectives, and Chapter 8 highlighted a broad range of ADO.NET coding techniques. While this chapter concludes the set of chapters focusing on Windows Forms, it also demonstrates how to use ADO.NET techniques without going into much detail about coding issues.

There are three sections in this chapter. The first section carefully contrasts techniques for creating and using datasets. You learn exactly how various graphical techniques contrast with one another and how graphically created datasets can differ from datasets that you develop with your own code. In particular, the chapter contrasts *typed datasets* with *untyped datasets* and discusses how to create datasets containing multiple *DataTable* objects. The second section focuses on parent-child relationships between *DataTable* objects within a dataset. This section demonstrates how to instantiate and use these relationships to select a subset of child rows matching a parent row. In addition, the sample reveals how to process the rows in the parent and child *DataTable* object dynamically—that is, based on inputs specified at run time. The third section is a case study application enabling the browsing, inserting, deleting, and updating of data in a Microsoft Access database from a Microsoft Windows application project. The case study systematically reviews all the elements of the application, including the Design view for the form, its operation, and the code behind all the events.

Creating and Using Datasets

You know from Chapter 7 that *DataSet* objects lie at the core of many ADO.NET applications. Datasets are one important factor underlying the improved scalability of Access databases via Microsoft Visual Basic .NET. As far back as Chapter 2, you learned how to create a dataset. Since that early introduction to the topic, this book has expanded its coverage of datasets in two significant ways. First, you learned more about the basic technique for creating a dataset in Chapter 2. Second, you learned other techniques for creating datasets (for example, in Chapter 7). This section takes a step back and contrasts three techniques for creating datasets and two varieties of datasets that you can use in your applications. In addition, the section closes by demonstrating one approach for instantiating multiple *DataTable* objects within a single dataset.

Three Ways to Make a Dataset

As you've learned, a dataset is a collection of one or more *DataTable* objects. Each *DataTable* object can have one or more rows of data in its collection of *DataRow* objects, available through the *DataTable* object's *Rows* property. Many possible sources for the *DataTable* objects in a dataset exist, but Access developers will often use a table or query from an Access database. There are at least three approaches to creating a dataset with a *DataTable* object that relies on an Access database as its source.

> **Note** All the samples for this chapter reside in the DatasetForms Windows project available with this book's sample files.

Dragging a Table or Query to a Windows Form

The first technique this book demonstrated for instantiating a *DataSet* object based on an Access database is dragging an Access table or view from Server Explorer to a Windows form. An Access view is a SELECT query with no parameters. Built-in code within Microsoft Visual Studio .NET automatically generates *OleDbConnection* and *OleDbDataAdapter* objects when you drag an Access table or view onto a Windows form. These objects appear in a tray below the form. If you right-click the *OleDbDataAdapter* object, you can choose Generate Dataset to create a new dataset or you can designate a previously existing dataset for the *OleDbDataAdapter* to reference. As you have learned, a data adapter can initially fill a *DataTable* object in a dataset as well as coordinate the contents of a *DataTable* object with an Access data source.

After you generate a dataset for a data adapter with the right-click menu, Visual Studio .NET adds an icon for the dataset to the tray below the form and to Solution Explorer. If you accept the default names for the first dataset in a Windows application project, the dataset in Solution Explorer will have the name DataSet1.xsd and the dataset in the tray will have the name *DataSet11*. The dataset in Solution Explorer is an XML schema file that represents the contents of the dataset and the *DataTable* object corresponding to the Access table or query that you dragged to a Windows form. The *DataSet11* icon in the tray below the form represents a variable pointing at the XML schema file. Your Visual Basic .NET custom application code should reference the *DataSet11* variable. For example, you should reference the *DataSet11* variable when invoking the *Fill* method for an *OleDbDataAdapter* object to populate a *DataTable* object in the dataset based on an Access data source.

If you double-click the DataSet1.xsd file in Solution Explorer, Visual Studio .NET opens a Design view of the *DataSet1* dataset. Figure 9-1 depicts the schema for a *DataTable* object in *DataSet1* based on the Order Details table from the Northwind database. The Visual Studio .NET builder that creates the *DataTable* object in the dataset orders the columns alphabetically by their name. By switching to XML view (see the button on the lower left of the DataSet1.xsd window), you can examine the XML schema code defining the dataset. Even without knowing XML schema language, you will readily recognize the code defining each column. You can rearrange the code to make the column names in Figure 9-1 appear in the same order as in the Design view for the Order Details table in the Northwind database.

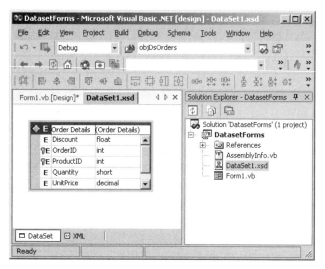

Figure 9-1 A Design view of the schema for the Order Details *DataTable* object in the *DataSet1* dataset of the DatasetForms project

The following listing shows two excerpts from the XML view of the *DataSet1* dataset in Figure 9-1. The top set of XML lines shows the order of the column designations as they initially appear. The bottom set of XML lines presents the order of the columns after minor editing for rearranging the order of column names in the DataSet view. You can reorder the lines with cut-and-paste operations. Simple editing like this can control the order in which columns appear in a DataGrid control based on a dataset.

```
Initial column order:
<xs:sequence>
    <xs:element name="Discount" type="xs:float" minOccurs="0" />
    <xs:element name="OrderID" type="xs:int" />
    <xs:element name="ProductID" type="xs:int" />
    <xs:element name="Quantity" type="xs:short" minOccurs="0" />
    <xs:element name="UnitPrice" type="xs:decimal" minOccurs="0" />
</xs:sequence>


Adjusted column order:

<xs:sequence>
    <xs:element name="OrderID" type="xs:int" />
    <xs:element name="ProductID" type="xs:int" />
    <xs:element name="UnitPrice" type="xs:decimal" minOccurs="0" />
    <xs:element name="Quantity" type="xs:short" minOccurs="0" />
    <xs:element name="Discount" type="xs:float" minOccurs="0" />
</xs:sequence>
```

Dragging a Table or Query to the Dataset Designer

The preceding technique for generating a dataset automatically creates a one-to-one relationship for a dataset and *DataTable* object. If you drag over another Access table or query, you generate a new dataset with its own *DataTable* object. However, as you know, a single dataset can contain multiple *DataTable* objects. A second graphical technique for generating datasets facilitates creating multiple *DataTable* objects within a single dataset.

You can open the Dataset Designer by choosing Project, Add New Item, selecting the DataSet template, and clicking Open. If you accept the default name for the dataset and this dataset is the second one created in a project, Visual Studio .NET names the new dataset *Dataset2* after the Dataset2.xsd file added to Solution Explorer. To add a *DataTable* object to the Dataset Designer, click the Server Explorer link if Server Explorer does not already appear. Then, drag one or more tables from Server Explorer to the Dataset Designer. To maintain comparability with the first dataset, I dragged the Order Details table to the Dataset Designer. If you then switch back to a Windows form and open the Toolbox, you can drag a DataSet icon from the Data tab in the Toolbox. This opens the Add Dataset dialog box. You will normally want to create a typed dataset based on the dataset that you created with the Project, Add New Item command. Use the drop-down box below the Typed Dataset radio button to select the dataset you are using. Figure 9-2 shows the dialog box with a selection of *Dataset2* in the DatasetForms project. Clicking OK creates a new icon in the tray below the form, such as one named *Dataset21*. The icon in the tray denotes a variable that points at a dataset created in the Dataset Designer.

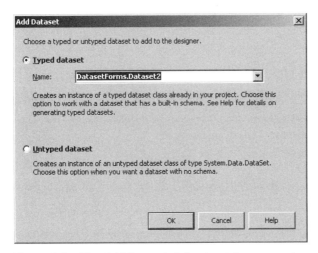

Figure 9-2   The Add Dataset dialog box lets you create a variable pointing at a dataset schema.

The preceding instructions create a typed dataset. A typed dataset is based on a specific dataset schema, such as Dataset2.xsd, and based on the *System.Data.DataSet* class. Notice that the Add Dataset dialog box allows you to create an untyped dataset. An untyped dataset is based on the *System.Data.DataSet* class, but it does not designate a specific schema. For example, an untyped dataset can have no assigned schema, or it can have a schema that you can change. If you select the Untyped Dataset radio button in Figure 9-2 and click OK, Visual Studio .NET declares a variable at a new instance of the *System.Data.DataSet* class. If this is the first untyped dataset in a project, the variable's default name is *Dataset1,* and it appears as an icon in the tray below the Windows form.

Programmatically Creating a Dataset

You can declare a dataset programmatically with a *Dim* statement or with an access modifier term, such as *Friend*. A dataset that you create in this way can be an untyped dataset. To instantiate a new empty untyped dataset, declare a variable based on the *DataSet* class from the *System.Data* namespace. This dataset will have an empty shell for an XML schema. You can populate the dataset with a *DataTable* object based on an Access table or query by using the *Fill* method for an *OleDbDataAdapter* object. After you populate the dataset, the schema for the dataset takes the form of the added *DataTable* object. You can add more tables to the dataset, and the dataset schema will automatically adjust. This behavior is characteristic of an untyped dataset.

The dataset that you create with the *Dim* statement will not have an .xsd file in Solution Explorer. Only typed datasets have a corresponding .xsd file in Solution Explorer. Instead, the dataset that you create programmatically with the *Dim* statement has a schema that you can change dynamically.

Understanding Datasets from the Forms Designer

Any dataset that you create graphically has code for it written by the Windows Form Designer. You can view this code by expanding the *Windows Form Designer generated code* region in the module behind a form. By examining this code, you can gain valuable insights about the datasets created by the Windows Form Designer and tips for your custom code creating datasets.

If you followed along as I created datasets in the previous section, you created three dataset variables graphically: *DataSet11*, *Dataset21*, and *DataSet1*. The first two variables point at .xsd files. That is, these datasets point at the specific XML schema files. The third variable, *DataSet1*, does not point at an .xsd file. Instead, *DataSet1* points at the *DataSet* class in the *System.Data* namespace. The declarations in the DatasetForms project for the three dataset variables highlight these dependencies. For example, the following three lines in the DatasetForms project for *Form1* appear in the *Windows Form Designer generated code* region. The lines are in the declaration area of the *Initialize-Component* procedure. Notice that *DataSet11* is an instance of *DataSet1*. Likewise, *Dataset21* is an instance of *Dataset2*. The DataSet1.xsd and Dataset2.xsd schema files act as class definitions. Both *DataSet11* and *Dataset21* are typed datasets. The following lines of code explicitly indicate the type for each dataset. These types, in turn, depend on the *DataSet* type in the *System.Data* namespace. *DataSet1* is based on the generic *DataSet* class in the *System.Data* namespace.

```
Me.DataSet11 = New DatasetForms.DataSet1()Me.Dataset21 = _
New DatasetForms.Dataset2()
Me.DataSet1 = New System.Data.DataSet()
```

The *InitializeComponent* procedure in the *Windows Form Designer generated code* region is a rich source of code samples for all the objects that you create and edit graphically for a form. The following lines from the procedure define properties for the objects denoted by the *DataSet11*, *Dataset21*, and *DataSet1* variables. The *Namespace* property settings for the *DataSet11* and *Dataset21* objects point at .xsd files. The URLs specifically reference locations in the current project for the .xsd files. (As you have learned, the .xsd files reside within the root folder of the current project.) The *DataSetName* property settings for *DataSet11* and *Dataset 21* point at the schema names associated with the .xsd files. The *DataSetName* property for the *DataSet1* variable points at *NewDataSet* within the *DataSet* type.

```
'DataSet11
'
Me.DataSet11.DataSetName = "DataSet1"
Me.DataSet11.Locale = New System.Globalization.CultureInfo("en-US")
Me.DataSet11.Namespace = "http://www.tempuri.org/DataSet1.xsd"
'
'Dataset21
'
Me.Dataset21.DataSetName = "Dataset2"
Me.Dataset21.Locale = New System.Globalization.CultureInfo("en-US")
Me.Dataset21.Namespace = "http://tempuri.org/Dataset2.xsd"
'
'DataSet1
'Me.DataSet1.DataSetName = "NewDataSet"
Me.DataSet1.Locale = New System.Globalization.CultureInfo("en-US")
```

Custom Initialization Code for a Dataset

Custom ADO.NET initialization code will often appear in the module-level declaration area of the module behind a form and in the form load event. By defining ADO.NET variables in the module-level area, you make the variables available to multiple procedures within a declaration area. The form load procedure is a convenient place to run code (such as for populating a dataset) that might need to run just once during a session. Even if an operation must occur multiple times within a form session, running ADO.NET code in a form load event procedure can make data available when a form opens without any action—such as clicking a button—on the part of a user.

The following listing from the module behind *Form1* in the DatasetForms project includes a couple of module-level variables and a form load event procedure. This listing demonstrates the typical kinds of ADO.NET tasks you can perform for these variables and the form load event procedure. The *dap1* and *das1* variable declarations instantiate two ADO.NET objects used throughout the application. The *Form1_Load* procedure assigns to the *dap1* variable an *OleDbDataAdapter* object pointing at the Order Details table in the Northwind database. The second line in the procedure fills the Order Details *DataTable* object in the *DataSet11* dataset. The *DataTable* object already exists before the *Form1_Load* procedure runs, but there is no data from the Northwind database in the object. The *Fill* method for the *OleDbDataAdapter1* object populates the Order Details *DataTable* object with data. The Windows Form Designer automatically generates the *OleDbDataAdapter1* object when a developer drags the Order Details table from Server Explorer to *Form1*.

```
'Declare and instantiate data adapter (dap1)
'and dataset (das1)
Dim dap1 As New OleDb.OleDbDataAdapter()
Dim das1 As New System.Data.DataSet()

Private Sub Form1_Load(ByVal sender As System.Object, _
    ByVal e As System.EventArgs) Handles MyBase.Load

    'Point data adapter at Order Details table
    'in the Northwind database
    dap1 = _
        New OleDb.OleDbDataAdapter( _
        "Select * FROM [Order Details]", _
        "Provider=Microsoft.Jet.OLEDB.4.0;" & _
        "Data Source=C:\Program Files\Microsoft Office\" & _
        "Office10\Samples\Northwind.mdb")

    'Fill DataSet11 with local data table named
    'Order Details
```

```
OleDbDataAdapter1.Fill(DataSet11, "Order Details")

End Sub
```

Schemas for Typed and Untyped Datasets

Although a dataset is an object for holding data, it is also an XML document. Just as a table in Access can have a Design view and a Datasheet view, an XML document has two views. The schema for an XML document describes the contents, and the matching file of data holds the rows of column values in a dataset. Some XML documents consolidate the schema and data in a single file, but in other cases, the schema and data reside in different files. By viewing the schema for a dataset, you can learn a lot about the structure of the data in a dataset. The discussion of schemas in this section does not deeply examine XML schema syntax conventions. The focus is on contrasting typed datasets with untyped ones. See the book's Chapter Appendix for material that focuses on XML schemas from the perspective of an Access developer building Visual Basic .NET solutions.

> **Note**   ADO.NET is especially attractive because it takes advantage of XML without forcing developers to know about XML syntax. Still, a working knowledge of XML will improve your ability to understand and use select features, such as typed datasets and the *GetXmlSchema* method.

Contrasting Schemas for Typed and Untyped Datasets

The click event procedure for *Button1* in *Form1* of the DatasetForms project contrasts the initial schemas for the *DataSet11* and *das1* datasets. As mentioned earlier, *DataSet11* is a typed schema. Therefore, the schema for this dataset is the only one possible because the *DataSet1* dataset, which is based on the DataSet1.xsd file, is the type for the dataset. In contrast, the *das1* dataset is an untyped dataset. Its type is the generic *DataSet* type in the *System.Data* namespace. Therefore, its schema is not an integral part of its definition. The *Button1_Click* procedure shows the syntax for the *GetXmlSchema* method for a *DataSet* object. The method returns a text stream with the schema for a dataset that you can display in a message box.

```
Private Sub Button1_Click(ByVal sender As System.Object, _
    ByVal e As System.EventArgs) Handles Button1.Click
```

(continued)

```
'Display schema for DataSet11 dataset
MsgBox(DataSet11.DataSetName() & vbCr & _
    DataSet11.GetXmlSchema(), , _
    "Typed Dataset Schema")

'Display schema for das1 dataset
MsgBox(das1.DataSetName() & vbCr & _
    das1.GetXmlSchema(), , _
    "Initial Untyped Dataset Schema")

End Sub
```

Figure 9-3 shows the first of two message boxes displayed by the *Button1_Click* procedure. This message box presents the schema for the *DataSet11* dataset. My purpose in presenting the schema is not to get into a lengthy discussion of schema syntax conventions. However, the average database developer background should be enough for you to recognize the column definitions for the Order Details *DataTable* object in the dataset. These definitions occur between an opening and closing pair of sequence tags, namely *<xs:sequence>* and *</xs:sequence>*. The column names within these tags do not appear in alphabetical order because they were manipulated, as described previously. Below the column definitions, another code block in the XML schema defines the primary key for the Order Details *DataTable* object. The primary key depends on two columns: OrderID and ProductID. This definition appears within a *unique* block with an attribute setting of *PrimaryKey* equal to *true*.

Figure 9-3   The initial schema for the *DataSet11* dataset in *Form1* of the DatasetForms project

Figure 9-4 shows the second message box displayed by the *Button1_Click* procedure. This message box displays the default schema for a dataset that contains no *DataTable* objects. For the purpose of this discussion, the most important point is that no column definitions exist. The schema that appears in this message box corresponds to the schema for the *NewDataSet* dataset in the *DataSet* class definition within the *System.Data* namespace.

Figure 9-4   The initial schema for the *das1* dataset in *Form1* of the DatasetForms project

Creating a Schema for an Untyped Dataset

You can indirectly design a schema for an untyped dataset, such as *das1*, by filling the dataset with the contents of an Access table or query. Specifying a schema for an untyped dataset does not transform the dataset into a typed dataset. The type for a dataset depends on its type when you instantiate it—not whether it has a schema. One important difference between schemas for typed datasets and those for untyped datasets is that you can change the schema for untyped datasets after instantiating a *DataSet* object. This is not possible for typed datasets because the dataset is an instance of the type used to declare it.

The *Button2_Click* procedure displays the schema for the *das1* untyped dataset at two points in its evolution. The initial message box presents the schema immediately after filling the dataset with data from the Order Details table in the Northwind database. The procedure names the *DataTable* object in the *das1* dataset *OrderDetails*. (Remember, you simplify many coding tasks by not using spaces in object names.) When you create a schema for a dataset with the *Fill* method, the .NET Framework does not create a primary key for the *DataTable* object in the dataset. Therefore, the procedure subsequently adds a primary key for the *OrderDetails DataTable* object. Then, the procedure displays the revised schema for the *DataSet* object. The *PrimaryKey* property for a *DataTable* object is a one-dimensional array of *DataColumn* objects. The length of the array increases by 1 for each column in a primary key.

```
Private Sub Button2_Click(ByVal sender As System.Object, _
    ByVal e As System.EventArgs) Handles Button2.Click

    'Fill das1 with Order Details table from the
    'Northwind database; name the DataTable object
    'OrderDetails
    dap1.Fill(das1, "OrderDetails")

    'Display schema for das1 dataset after
    'populating the dataset with a DataTable object
    MsgBox(das1.DataSetName() & vbCr & _
        das1.GetXmlSchema(), , _
        "Untyped Dataset Schema After Filling")

    'Assign a primary key to the OrderDetails
    'DataTable object based on the OrderID and
    'ProductID columns
    das1.Tables("OrderDetails").PrimaryKey = _
        New DataColumn() _
        {das1.Tables(0).Columns("OrderID"), _
        das1.Tables(0).Columns("ProductID")}

    'Display schema for das1 dataset after adding
    'a primary key
    MsgBox(das1.DataSetName() & vbCr & _
        das1.GetXmlSchema(), , _
        "Untyped Dataset Schema " & _
        "After Addition of Primary Key")

End Sub
```

Figures 9-5 and 9-6 show the two schemas displayed by the *Button2_Click* event procedure. The message box in Figure 9-5 includes the column definitions for the *OrderDetails DataTable* object. Notice that the *minOccurs* attribute setting for all columns is 0. A *minOccurs* value of 0 indicates that the designation of a column value for a row is optional. This absence of any required column values is one indication that the schema includes no primary key. A missing *unique* block is another indication that no primary key exists for the *DataTable* object. As mentioned earlier, a *unique* block with an attribute setting of *PrimaryKey* equal to *true* designates a collection of columns specifying a primary key.

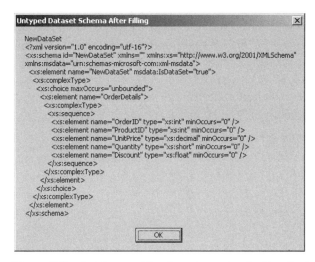

Figure 9-5   A schema without a primary key for the *das1* dataset generated by the code behind *Form1* of the DatasetForms project

The message box in Figure 9-6 is displayed after adding the definition of a primary key to the *OrderDetails DataTable* object. Notice the appearance of the *unique* block and the dropping of the *minOccurs* settings for the OrderID and ProductID columns.

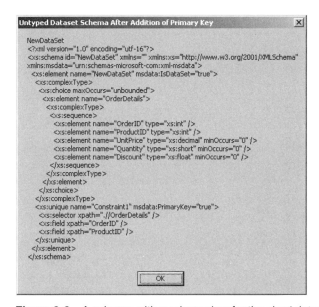

Figure 9-6   A schema with a primary key for the *das1* dataset generated by the code behind *Form1* of the DatasetForms project

Using IntelliSense for Typed Schemas

One advantage of typed datasets that some developers will appreciate is the availability of IntelliSense. Because the .NET Framework knows about the type for a typed dataset and the type is fixed, the .NET Framework can automatically display the appropriate members as you write expressions for the elements within a dataset. With an untyped dataset, you must use the *Rows* collection and explicitly use indexes to reference specific rows and columns in a *DataTable* object. The same goes for referencing the *DataTable* objects within a dataset. The .NET Framework uses IntelliSense to show the *DataTable* objects within a typed dataset, but with an untyped dataset, you have to designate an index for selecting a member from the *Tables* collection for a *DataSet* object.

The *Button3_Click* procedure contrasts the syntax for designating the OrderID column value in the first row of the first *DataTable* object in the *DataSet11* and *das1* datasets. The *DataTable* object has a slightly different name in each dataset, but in both cases, the Order Details table from the Northwind database populates the *DataTable* object. The procedure displays two message boxes to confirm that the value is the same for both expressions with different datasets. Because the *DataSet11* dataset is a typed dataset, you can use dot notation to specify the table and column names within the *DataSet11* dataset. Furthermore, Visual Basic .NET automatically presents a list of candidate items for selection after you type a period. The value in parentheses before the column name (OrderID) is a zero-based numeric index for the row number. The expression for the same column value appears in the *das1* dataset next. Because this expression is for an untyped dataset, you must designate the table name as an index within the dataset's *Tables* collection; you can use either a numeric index value or a named index value. You specify the column within a row by the index value within the second set of parentheses after the designation of the *Rows* collection for a *DataTable* object. As in the syntax for the typed dataset, the first set of parentheses after the *Rows* collection is to designate a specific row in the *DataTable* object. You can use the syntax for the untyped dataset with a typed dataset, but the typed dataset syntax is not available for an untyped dataset.

> **Note** I find using the untyped data syntax for datasets convenient because I have a common syntax that I can use for both typed and untyped datasets, which means I do not have to recall which kind of dataset I'm using before figuring out which syntax to use. In addition, I find untyped datasets easier to develop and apply.

```
Private Sub Button3_Click(ByVal sender As System.Object, _
    ByVal e As System.EventArgs) Handles Button3.Click

    'Contrast the syntax for data access of OrderID column
    'value for first row with a typed dataset (DataSet11)
    'versus an untyped dataset (das1); IntelliSense
    'prompts for table and column names with a typed dataset
    MsgBox(DataSet11.Order_Details(0).OrderID.ToString)
    MsgBox(das1.Tables("OrderDetails"). _
        Rows(0)("OrderID").ToString)

End Sub
```

Creating a Single Dataset with Two *DataTable* Objects

Nearly all the dataset samples in this book contain just one *DataTable* object per dataset. However, database developers can also design datasets with multiple *DataTable* objects. Multiple–*DataTable* designs are often convenient because they permit your applications to logically require an interrelated set of two or more *DataTable* objects, such as objects based on the Orders and Order Details tables in the Northwind database.

This section demonstrates an approach to creating one dataset with two *DataTable* objects. The novel element when working with multiple *DataTable* objects in a dataset is programming a separate *OleDbDataAdapter* object for each *DataTable* object. Therefore, if you have a dataset with *DataTable* objects based on the Orders and Order Details tables from the Northwind database, you can program a separate data adapter to connect each *DataTable* object with its matching table in the database. You can readily point an *OleDbData-Adapter* object at a database object such as a table with a constructor that takes two string arguments: a SQL string expression that specifies a selection, and a connection string to a database from which the SQL string makes the selection. Either before or after defining your data adapters, you can specify a dataset based on the *DataSet* class in the *System.Data* namespace. Then, just invoke the *Fill* method for each *OleDbDataAdapter* object while specifying your dataset as the container for your *DataTable* object based on a separate Access table or query.

The *Button4_Click* procedure for *Form1* demonstrates the syntax for populating a single dataset with two *DataTable* objects. The procedure begins by instantiating a pair of *OleDbDataAdapter* objects pointing at the Orders and Order Details tables from the Northwind database. Next, the procedure instantiates a single *DataSet* object, *das1*; this dataset overrides within the *Button4_Click* procedure the module-level *das1* declaration at the top of the *Form1* module. Then, the procedure invokes the *Fill* method for each data adapter. Each invocation of the *Fill* method designates the *das1* dataset as the container for the *DataTable* object. The procedure concludes by displaying in a message box the count of rows for the *Orders* and *OrderDetails DataTable* objects. The string expression for the *Prompt* argument in the *MsgBox* function demonstrates how to return information about both *DataTable* objects within a single expression. See Figure 9-7 for the message generated by the procedure.

```
Private Sub Button4_Click(ByVal sender As System.Object, _
    ByVal e As System.EventArgs) Handles Button4.Click

    'Instantiate a pair of data adapters
    Dim dap1 As New OleDb.OleDbDataAdapter( _
        "Select * FROM Orders", _
        "Provider=Microsoft.Jet.OLEDB.4.0;" & _
        "Data Source=C:\Program Files\Microsoft Office\" & _
        "Office10\Samples\Northwind.mdb")

    Dim dap2 As New OleDb.OleDbDataAdapter( _
        "Select * FROM [Order Details]", _
        "Provider=Microsoft.Jet.OLEDB.4.0;" & _
        "Data Source=C:\Program Files\Microsoft Office\" & _
        "Office10\Samples\Northwind.mdb")

    'Instantiate a dataset
    Dim das1 As New System.Data.DataSet()

    'Use the data adapters to fill the dataset
    dap1.Fill(das1, "Orders")
    dap2.Fill(das1, "OrderDetails")

    'Return row count from each DataTable object
    MsgBox("Rows in " & _
        das1.Tables(0).TableName & " is " & _
        das1.Tables(0).Rows.Count.ToString & "." & _
        vbCr & "Rows in " & _
        das1.Tables(1).TableName & " is " & _
        das1.Tables(1).Rows.Count.ToString & ".")

End Sub
```

Figure 9-7   A message box from the *Button4_Click* procedure in *Form1* that displays information about two *DataTable* objects in the same dataset

Processing Parent-Child Relationships

Parent-child relationships are very popular in database applications. With this kind of relationship, you can dynamically specify a set of child rows that match a parent row. For example, choosing any row in a *DataTable* object based on the Orders table can lead to the return of a matching set of child rows from another *DataTable* object based on the Order Details table. You can use this type of relationship to dynamically populate a sub form based on the currently selected row in a main form. Alternatively, you can use the parent-child relationship to compute the sum of a field across individual child rows based on a parent row specified at run time. The samples for this section demonstrate two approaches to this second task with ADO.NET. The first approach uses an untyped dataset. The second approach uses a typed dataset.

Computing Child Values with an Untyped Dataset

The sample described in this section computes the total extended price for a range of up to 10 orders starting with an OrderID that the user specifies. The procedure looks up the parent row in one *DataTable* object for the OrderID that a user specifies and then computes the total extended price for the matching rows in a second *DataTable* object based on the Order Details table. Then, the procedure repeats this computation for up to the next nine rows in the Orders table. If the user inputs an out-of-bounds OrderID for the initial order, the application reminds the user to input an order that falls under the correct range. If the user inputs an OrderID that does not have nine rows behind it, the application computes the total extended price for as many parent rows as are available.

The Application's Form and Message Box

Figure 9-8 shows the Design view and initial operational view of *Form2* in the DatasetForms project, which implements the application. The form has three controls—a couple of buttons and a text box. A click to *Button1* uses an untyped dataset to compute the total extended prices for a range of orders. A click to *Button2* performs the same set of calculations with a typed dataset. This contrast's implications about the robustness of untyped datasets vs. typed ones are interesting. The text box on the form provides an easy mechanism for a user specifying the initial OrderID in a set of orders.

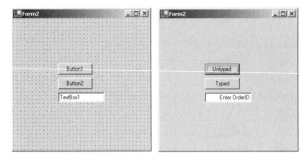

Figure 9-8 Design view and an initial operational view of a form to compute total extended price for a range of orders

The load event procedure for *Form2* transforms the Design view into the initial operation view. This procedure formats the buttons and the text box. Because both buttons perform the same calculation but with different kinds of datasets, the button *Text* property assignments designate the type of dataset used for a calculation. Instead of using a Label control to designate what type of value to enter into *TextBox1*, the form enters an initial value, *Enter OrderID*. The *Form2_Load* procedure also demonstrates how to specify the horizontal alignment for the value in a text box through an assignment of the *TextAlign* property of *TextBox1*. IntelliSense offers a menu of three items for left, right, or center horizontal alignment.

```
Private Sub Form2_Load(ByVal sender As System.Object, _
    ByVal e As System.EventArgs) Handles MyBase.Load

    'Format button captions
    Button1.Text = "Untyped"
    Button2.Text = "Typed"

    'Format text box caption
    TextBox1.Text = "Enter OrderID"
    TextBox1.TextAlign = HorizontalAlignment.Right

End Sub
```

If a user inputs a value of 10248, the application returns a message box similar to the one shown in Figure 9-9. In this instance, the text box contains 10 sentences—one for each of the orders from 10248 through 10257. Each sentence specifies the total extended price for an order. You can confirm the values by opening the Order Subtotals query in the Northwind database, which computes the total extended price for all orders in the database. The application computes the total extended price for no more than 10 orders at a time. In addition, it does so without putting any load on the database file because the computation applies to the application's two *DataTable* objects rather than being made against the original database. The ability to compute parent-child relationships dynamically further enhances the value of datasets.

Figure 9-9   A message box showing total extended price for a range of orders based on a parent-child relationship

Architecture of the Solution

The best view of the application's architecture is available from the module-level declarations behind *Form2* and the *Button1_Click* procedure. The application has three module-level declarations. Two of these are for data adapters pointing at the Orders and Order Details tables in the Northwind database. As you know, the Northwind database relates these tables by their OrderID column values. Similarly, the two *DataTable* objects in the *das1* dataset link to one another via their OrderID column values. All three of the objects declared at the module level get referenced by multiple procedures, which is why the application declares them at the module level.

Users launch the application with two steps. First, they input a value to *TextBox1*. Second, they click one of the two buttons. For example, clicking *Button1* causes the application to present a message box with up to 10 sentences reporting the total extended price for successive orders, including the order designated by the OrderID value in *TextBox1*. The *Button1_Click* procedure performs two kinds of tasks. First, it sets up the main task. However, the most important role for the *Button1_Click* procedure is to invoke a pair of procedures that perform the most significant parts of the application. These called procedures perform the application's main task.

The *Button1_Click* procedure starts by clearing and then filling the *Orders* and *OrderDetails DataTable* objects in the *das1* dataset. You might want to put steps such as these in a load event procedure for a form—especially if the data does not change frequently. However, placing these steps in the *Button1_Click* procedure has the merit of consolidating all the actions for a single task. Next, the procedure specifies the *PrimaryKey* property values for the *Orders* and *OrderDetails DataTable* objects. Many tasks work better in ADO.NET when *DataTable* objects have primary keys. The last task performed directly by the *Button1_Click* procedure is to remove a *DataRelation* item in the *Relations* collection for the *das1* dataset (if one exists). The application needs some way of recognizing an existing *Relation* item to freely create a new *DataRelation* object between *Orders* and *OrderDetails DataTable* objects. Automatically removing an existing *Relation* item between the *DataTable* objects is one way to accomplish this. You can build smarter approaches to this task, but this approach gets the job done without distracting attention from the main objective of the application.

So what is the main purpose of the application? Clearly, the intent is to compute total extended price for a range of up to 10 orders. In the context of this sample, how the application does this is as important as the fact that the application does it. The sample computes the extended prices based on a dynamically formed relation between a row in the *Orders DataTable* object and any matching rows in the *OrderDetails DataTable* object. By calling the *AddParentChildRelation* procedure, the *Button1_Click* procedure specifies a *DataRelation* object between the two *DataTable* objects in the *das1* dataset. Next, the *Button1_Click* procedure calls the *ExtendedPriceReport* procedure. This procedure takes advantage of the *DataRelation* object created by the *AddParentChildRelation* procedure to compute a set of total extended prices. The word *total* is the most important one in the preceding sentence because *total* clarifies that the total extended price for all or most orders will be a sum across the multiple line items within an order. The *Relation* object specified in the *AddParentChildRelation* procedure designates which line items to use for computing the total extended price for a particular order.

> **Note**   One important reason for isolating the logic contained in the *AddParentChildRelation* and *ExtendedPriceReport* procedures is to facilitate the reuse of the code in a parallel version of this sample that uses a typed dataset.

```
'Declare and instantiate two data adapters and a
'dataset; point the data adapters at the Orders
'and Order Details tables in the Northwind database
Dim dap1 As New OleDb.OleDbDataAdapter( _
    "Select * FROM Orders", _
```

```
        "Provider=Microsoft.Jet.OLEDB.4.0;" & _
        "Data Source=C:\Program Files\Microsoft " & _
        "Office\Office10\Samples\Northwind.mdb")
    Dim dap2 As New OleDb.OleDbDataAdapter( _
        "Select * FROM [Order Details]", _
        "Provider=Microsoft.Jet.OLEDB.4.0;" & _
        "Data Source=C:\Program Files\Microsoft " & _
        "Office\Office10\Samples\Northwind.mdb")
    Dim das1 As New System.Data.DataSet()

Private Sub Button1_Click(ByVal sender As System.Object, _
    ByVal e As System.EventArgs) Handles Button1.Click

    'Fill Orders and OrderDetails DataTable objects
    'in the das1 dataset
    das1.Clear()
    dap1.Fill(das1, "Orders")
    dap2.Fill(das1, "OrderDetails")

    'Assign primary keys to the Orders and
    'OrderDetails DataTable objects based on
    'the OrderID and ProductID columns
    das1.Tables("Orders").PrimaryKey = _
        New DataColumn() _
        {das1.Tables(0).Columns("OrderID")}
    das1.Tables("OrderDetails").PrimaryKey = _
        New DataColumn() _
        {das1.Tables(1).Columns("OrderID"), _
        das1.Tables("OrderDetails").Columns("ProductID")}

    'Remove any prior Relation; add Relation between
    'Orders and OrderDetails DataTable objects based
    'on OrderID columns in both DataTable objects
    If das1.Relations.Count > 0 Then
        das1.Relations.Remove(das1.Relations(0))
    End If
    AddParentChildRelation(das1, "Orders", _
        "OrderID", "OrderDetails", "OrderID")

    'Pass dataset and data relation name
    ExtendedPriceReport(das1, _
        "OrdersOrderDetails")

End Sub
```

Adding a Relation Between Two *DataTable* Objects

The *AddParentChildRelation* procedure is beautiful in its simplicity. The procedure performs just one function—it adds a parent-child *DataRelation* object between a pair of *DataTable* objects within a dataset. Because of its simplicity, this is the kind of procedure that you can readily adapt for inclusion in your own custom applications. You must pass five arguments to the procedure when calling it. These arguments specify the elements for creating a parent-child *DataRelation* object between a pair of *DataTable* objects in a dataset. The first argument is the dataset. The procedure accepts this argument with a type of *System.Data.DataSet*. The remaining four arguments are string variables naming the parent and child *DataTable* objects as well as the *DataColumn* object within each *DataTable* object that links to the other *DataTable* object.

The *AddParentChildRelation* procedure has just three short code blocks. First, it defines the *DataColumn* objects for both the parent and child *DataTable* objects to participate in the relation. Second, the procedure instantiates a *DataRelation* object between the parent and child *DataTable* objects. Third, the procedure adds the *DataRelation* object to the dataset that was passed into the procedure as an argument.

```
Sub AddParentChildRelation( _
    ByVal mydas As System.Data.DataSet, _
    ByVal ParentTableName As String, _
    ByVal ParentMatchColumnName As String, _
    ByVal ChildTableName As String, _
    ByVal ChildMatchColumnName As String)

    'Define parent and child columns for
    'a DataRelation object
    Dim parentcol As DataColumn = _
        mydas.Tables(ParentTableName). _
        Columns(ParentMatchColumnName)
    Dim childcol As DataColumn = _
        mydas.Tables(ChildTableName). _
        Columns(ChildMatchColumnName)

    'Instantiate a new DataRelation object
    Dim drl1 As DataRelation
    Dim str1 As String = _
        ParentTableName & ChildTableName
    drl1 = New _
        DataRelation(str1, parentcol, _
        childcol)

    'Add the DataRelation object to the Relations
    'collection for mydas
    mydas.Relations.Add(drl1)

End Sub
```

Computing Extended Price for a Range of Orders

The *ExtendedPriceReport* procedure is mostly responsible for computing the extended price for a range of orders. The procedure computes the extended price for up to 10 orders from some starting point in the *Orders DataTable*. However, the procedure needs some help discovering what the right starting point is. The need arises from the fact the *OrderID* a user inputs to *TextBox1* does not indicate which row number in the *Orders DataTable* object to use as starting point. Visual Basic .NET requires a transformation of the *OrderID* that points at a specific row in the *DataTable* object. Multiple approaches exist for performing this kind of task. The *FirstRowIndex Function* procedure implements one of these approaches. The *ExtendedPriceReport* invokes the *FirstRow-Index Function* procedure to find a starting row in the *Orders DataTable* object for computing a range of total extended prices.

The *ExtendedPriceReport* procedure starts by using the *ParentTable* and *ChildTable* methods to return the parent and child *DataTable* objects in the *DataRelation* object created for the *das1* dataset by the *AddParentChildRelation* procedure. Next, after declaring some variables, the *ExtendedPriceReport* procedure invokes the *FirstRowIndex* procedure to return the row index value for the *Orders DataTable* object that matches the *OrderID* value in *TextBox1*. The return value from the *FirstRowIndex* procedure indicates either an offset from the first row in the Orders *DataTable* object or an error. A value of -1 indicates the row is out of bounds, in which case the procedure displays an error message. If the return value from the *FirstRowIndex* procedure is an *Integer* greater than or equal to 0, a *For...Next* loop uses the value as a starting point for up to 10 iterations (the initial pass through the loop, plus up to nine more). In each pass, the first action is to extract a row from the *Orders DataTable* object (*tbl1*). If the attempt to extract the row fails (for any reason, including no more rows being available), the procedure exits the loop.

After verifying a valid row for an index value in a *Try...Catch...Finally* statement, the sample code calls the *GetChildRows* method. This method takes the *DataRelation* object specifying the relation created in the *AddParentChild-Relation* procedure as an argument. The method returns an array of *DataRow* objects (*ary_Rows*) with the subset of rows in the *OrderDetails DataTable* object matching the OrderID value in the designated *Orders DataTable* row (*drw1*). A nested *For...Next* loop for the rows in the *ary_Rows* array computes extended price for each line in an order and accumulates the result in a *Decimal* variable (*dec1*). As you learned in Chapter 2, the *Decimal* data type in Visual Basic .NET replaces the old *Currency* data type from classic Visual Basic. For brevity, the extended price expression uses a numeric index value instead of a named index value for the columns. However, you can use named indexes; the column index values of 2, 3, and 4 represent UnitPrice, Quantity, and Discount, respectively. The last statement in the outer *For...Next* loop adds the OrderID and extended price as a sentence with a carriage return to the *str1* string variable. After exiting the outer *For...Next* loop, a *MsgBox* function displays the string variable updated on each pass through the loop.

The *FirstRowIndex* function takes a *DataTable* object as an argument and returns either a -1 value or an *Integer* value pointing at a row in the *DataTable* object. By using the *Find* method, the procedure verifies whether the OrderID value in *TextBox1* exists within the *DataTable*. The *Find* method requires a primary index for a *DataTable* object. If the *Find* method returns *Nothing*, the procedure sets its return value to -1 and exits. Otherwise, the procedure enters into a loop and searches for the row with a column value matching the numeric value denoted in *TextBox1*. A *For...Next* loop tracks each row search starting with a value of 0. The last value searched is the offset that the *ExtendedPriceReport* procedure needs as a starting row for computing the extended prices of orders. The procedure returns this value.

```
Sub ExtendedPriceReport( _
    ByVal mydas As DataSet, _
    ByVal drlname As String)

    'Point DataTable variable at the parent
    'table (Orders)
    Dim tbl1 As DataTable
    Dim drl1 As DataRelation = _
        mydas.Relations(drlname)
    tbl1 = drl1.ParentTable

    'Point another DataTable variable at
    'the child table (OrderDetails)
    Dim tbl2 As DataTable = drl1.ChildTable

    'Declare variables for looping through parent
    'and child rows
    Dim drw1 As DataRow
    Dim ary_Rows() As DataRow
    Dim int1, int2 As Integer
    Dim dec1 As Decimal
    Dim str1 As String
    Dim i, j As Integer

    'Save first row index for TextBox1,
    'but ignore value if it is out of bounds
    i = FirstRowIndex(tbl1)
    If i = -1 Then
        MsgBox("OrderID too high or too " & _
```

```
                    "low.   Please enter another " & _
                    "OrderID.", MsgBoxStyle.Exclamation, _
                    "Out-of-bounds message")
            Exit Sub
        End If

        'Attempt to loop through 10 rows starting
        'with the first row
        For j = i To i + 9
            Try
                'Select a parent row
                drw1 = tbl1.Rows(j)
            Catch exc1 As System.Exception
                'Exit if less than 10 rows
                'follow the first row
                Exit For
            End Try

            'Return array of child rows matching selected parent row
            ary_Rows = drw1.GetChildRows(mydas.Relations(0))

            'Loop through child rows to accumulate extended
            'price for child rows matching parent row
            For int1 = 0 To ary_Rows.GetUpperBound(0)
                dec1 += ary_Rows(int1)(2) * _
                    ary_Rows(int1)(3) * (1 - ary_Rows(int1)(4))
            Next

            'Compute string to display computation across child
            'rows for parent rows
            int2 = drw1(0)
            str1 &= "Extended Price = " & _
                Format(dec1.ToString, "Currency") & _
                " for Order ID " & int2.ToString & _
                "." & vbCr
            dec1 = 0
        Next

        'Display string with computations
        MsgBox(str1)

    End Sub

    Function FirstRowIndex( _
        ByVal tbl1 As DataTable) As Integer

        'Variable declarations
```

(continued)

```
        Dim drw1 As DataRow
        Dim int1 As Integer

        'Invoke Find method for first row
        drw1 = tbl1.Rows.Find(TextBox1.Text)

        'Find first row index
        If drw1 Is Nothing Then
            'Return for row not found
            Return -1
        Else
            For int1 = 0 To tbl1.Rows.Count - 1
                If tbl1.Rows(int1)(0) = _
                    CInt(TextBox1.Text) Then
                    'Return index for found row
                    Return int1
                End If
            Next
        End If

End Function
```

Computing Child Values with a Typed Dataset

You can build the preceding solution with a typed dataset instead of an untyped dataset. One advantage of using a typed dataset is that you can create the dataset graphically. The graphical creation of a dataset such as the one in the preceding sample can be accomplished in just two steps. First, drag the Orders and Order Details tables from Server Explorer to the Dataset Designer. Second, drag a DataSet icon from the Data tab of the Toolbox to the Windows form (*Form2*) that needs to reference the typed dataset. When you build the dataset graphically, you gain the benefit of having automatically created primary keys for your *DataTable* objects in the dataset. Therefore, you need to modify your setup code for the solution so that you do not attempt to re-create them with your code.

Graphically Creating a Dataset with Two *DataTables*

To create a dataset graphically with two *DataTable* objects, you need to use the Dataset Designer. Start to open the designer by choosing Project, Add New Item. Then, select DataSet in the Templates pane in the Add New Item dialog box and click Open. This opens the Dataset Designer. If you have already created the datasets described so far in this chapter, Visual Studio .NET will automatically suggest Dataset3.xsd as the filename for your dataset schema. However, you can use any name you choose with an .xsd extension. Simply revise the suggested filename for the schema file in the Name box on the Add New Item dialog box. The sample code does not refer to the dataset schema directly, but rather to a variable pointing at the schema. Therefore, you must coordinate the variable's name with the sample code.

After the Dataset Designer opens, click the Server Explorer link on the designer to show Server Explorer (if it is not already available). Then, drag over separately the Orders and Order Details tables from the Northwind connection to the Dataset Designer. That's all there is to it! The dataset is done. Figure 9-10 shows the Dataset Designer window between Server Explorer on the left and Solution Explorer on the right. Server Explorer appears with the Tables folder for the Northwind connection open. The Dataset Designer appears with the Orders table display stacked above the Order Details table display. Solution Explorer shows Dataset3.xsd selected because that object was used most recently.

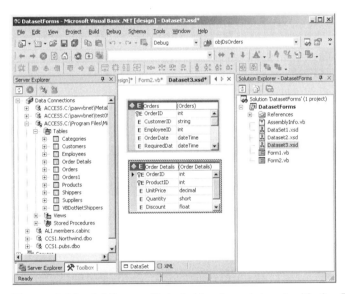

Figure 9-10   Adding multiple tables to a dataset with the Dataset Designer

Because of your experience with the graphical Query Designer in Access (or other databases), you might be tempted to add a foreign key constraint between the tables by dragging from the OrderID column in the Order Details *DataTable* to the OrderID column in the Orders *DataTable*. This opens the Edit Relation dialog box in Visual Studio .NET. The dialog box in Figure 9-11 shows the Orders *DataTable* object as the parent table for the Order Details *DataTable* object. The OrderID columns in both *DataTable* objects apparently link the two

DataTable objects. The settings in Figure 9-11 show a foreign key constraint named OrdersOrder_x0020_Details. (See the Name box in the figure.) *Do not graphically add a foreign key constraint this way.* Doing so can generate an error in the sample code; see the next section for the details and the workaround to the error. The Chapter Appendix describes the correct process for specifying a *Relation* object between two *DataTable* objects with the Dataset Designer in Visual Studio .NET.

> **Note** Because some developers are likely to graphically add a foreign key constraint by dragging the OrderID column from the child *DataTable* to the parent *DataTable*, I purposely added it to the Dataset3.xsd file with the settings shown in Figure 9-11. My code sample removes the faulty specification if it exists. If the constraint does not exist, the sample code works properly.

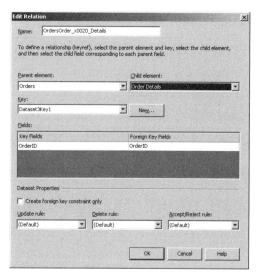

Figure 9-11   If you specify a foreign key constraint by dragging a column from the child *DataTable* to a parent *DataTable*, the Edit Relation dialog box might look like this.

As you have learned, a dataset schema can act as a class for the definition of an object instance based on it. You can create an instance of the *Dataset3* class by dragging a DataSet icon from the Data tab of the Toolbox and referencing *DatasetForms.Dataset3* as the source for a typed dataset object. (See Figure 9-12.) This adds an icon named *Dataset31* to the tray below *Form2* in the DatasetForms project. Your code for the solution can refer to a variable named *Dataset31*, just as the preceding sample referred to a variable named *das1* to designate an untyped dataset instance.

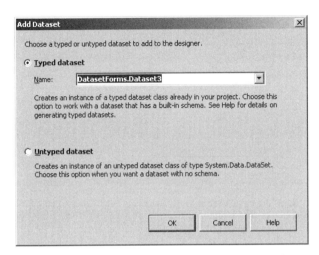

Figure 9-12   To create a typed dataset, you can reference a *DataSet* in the current project.

Processing a Typed Dataset with a Foreign Key Constraint

If you perform the preceding steps for creating a typed dataset, you will have a dataset variable named *Dataset31* pointing at a dataset defined by the selections in Figure 9-10 and Figure 9-11. To process this dataset and compute extended prices for a range of orders, you need a slightly different setup procedure than the one for the untyped dataset. On the other hand, the supporting procedures (*AddParentChildRelation*, *ExtendedPriceReport*, and *FirstRowIndex*) are used and remain completely unchanged. Therefore, by reviewing the *Button2_Click* procedure, you can appreciate all the special factors associated with processing the typed dataset.

The *Button2_Click* procedure for processing the typed dataset has two major design differences and one major operational difference from the *Button1_Click* procedure previously discussed for computing extended prices with an untyped dataset. The first design difference appears around the code for filling a *DataTable* object with rows from the Order Details table in the Northwind database. If you specify a foreign key constraint incorrectly (as many developers will be naturally inclined to do), an attempt to fill the child *DataTable* object, which is the Order Details *DataTable* in this sample, fails because of the throwing of a *System.Data.ConstraintException* object. Therefore, the procedure wraps the attempt to fill the Order Details *DataTable* object within a *Try...Catch...Finally* statement. If the procedure catches the *System.Data.ConstraintException* object, it attempts to recover by removing the default name for the foreign key constraint (see Figure 9-11) and attempting to refill the Order Details *DataTable*.

A second design distinction between the click event procedure for *Button2* and the one for *Button1* is that the *Button2_Click* procedure has no need to add a primary key. This is because the built-in code for generating the typed dataset automatically adds primary keys that match those in the original data source. When creating your own untyped dataset, it is necessary to explicitly add primary key constraints.

The third difference between the *Button1_Click* procedure and the *Button2_Click* procedure is an operational one. This distinction pertains strictly to the first pass through the click event procedure, and it applies only if an application designer graphically creates a foreign key constraint in the Order Details *DataTable* object. This foreign key constraint creates a *DataRelation* object that exists side by side with the constraint for the parent-child relationship. Removing the foreign key constraint does not remove the parallel *DataRelation* object for the parent-child relationship. Therefore, on the first pass through the click event procedure for *Button2*, the procedure detects the *DataRelation* object for the foreign key and removes it. I call this an operational distinction because the same code exists in the *Button1_Click* procedure, but there is no *DataRelation* object to remove on the first pass through that click event procedure. Conditionally testing for a *DataRelation* object is relevant to either procedure after the first pass through the click event procedure. This is because the first pass through either procedure will always add a valid *DataRelation* object. If the code blindly added another object, it could fail because of an attempt to create a duplicate *DataRelation* object.

```
Private Sub Button2_Click(ByVal sender As System.Object, _
    ByVal e As System.EventArgs) Handles Button2.Click

    Dim das3 As DataSet = Dataset31

    'Clear dataset and fill Orders
    'DataTable object in the dataset
    das3.Clear()
    dap1.Fill(das3, "Orders")

    'Demonstrates problem with link between two
    'DataTable objects in the Dataset Designer;
```

```
'cannot fill child DataTable object
Try
    dap2.Fill(das3, "Order Details")
Catch exc1 As System.Data.ConstraintException
    'Fix and recover from error; optionally,
    'uncomment MsgBox function to document
    'error
    'MsgBox(exc1.GetType.ToString & vbCr & _
    '    exc1.Message)
    das3.Tables(1).Constraints. _
        Remove(das3.Tables(1). _
        Constraints( _
        "OrdersOrder_x0020_Details"))
    dap2.Fill(das3, "Order Details")
Catch exc1 As System.Exception
    MsgBox("Get help from your consultant." _
        , , "Help")
End Try

'Remove any prior Relation; add Relation between
'Orders and Order Details DataTable objects based
'on OrderID columns in both DataTable objects
If das3.Relations.Count > 0 Then
    das3.Relations.Remove(das3.Relations(0))
End If
AddParentChildRelation(das3, "Orders", _
    "OrderID", "Order Details", "OrderID")

'Pass dataset and data relation name
ExtendedPriceReport(das3, _
    das3.Relations(0).RelationName)

End Sub
```

Browsing and Manipulating Data with a Form

This section presents a sample that demonstrates how to manage browsing, inserts, deletes, and updates through a Windows form. You have already seen bits and pieces of this code, but no prior sample brought all the elements together in one simple application. You can use this sample as is or as a starting point for more highly customized applications. The sample's presentation starts with the form design and operation. Then, the discussion of the sample moves to the form load event procedure, which prepares for the browsing and data manipulation functions. The focus then shifts to procedures managing browsing, inserts, deletes, and updates.

The sample works with a version of the Shippers table in the Northwind database. Because this sample explicitly enables data manipulation, the sample application actually works with a copy of the Shippers table named VBDotNet-Shippers. This approach enables you to restore the table at any time by simply deleting the current version of the VBDotNetShippers table and making a new copy of the original Shippers table in the Northwind database. You can create the VBDotNetShippers table from the Database window in the Northwind database with the following steps:

1. Select the Shippers table and choose Edit, Copy.

2. Next, choose Edit, Paste.

3. Click the Structure And Data radio button if it is not already selected in the Paste Table As dialog box. Type **VBDotNetShippers** in the Table Name box.

4. Click OK.

> **Note**   Although the application works with the VBDotNetShippers table in the Northwind database, the local *DataTable* object coordinated with the VBDotNetShippers table has the name Shippers. This makes for less typing. The distinction also helps to clarify when the discussion refers to an Access database table and when it refers to a local *DataTable* object in a dataset.

Design and Operational Views of *Form3*

Figure 9-13 presents design and operational views of *Form3* in the Dataset-Forms project. Three text boxes enable the viewing of column values, and two of those text boxes permit the editing of the values that appear within them. The text box for the ShipperID column values has its *ReadOnly* property set to *True*; this permits viewing but not editing of the text box's contents. Because ShipperID is an autonumber field, the Access database manages its value. Users can view and modify the contents of the other two text boxes.

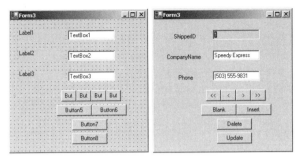

Figure 9-13   Design and operational views of a Windows form for data browsing and manipulation

The form offers four buttons for browsing that appear above four more buttons for data manipulation. The browsing buttons from left to right enable moves to the first, previous, next, and last row in the *DataTable* object (*Shippers*) serving as the source for the form. The button *Name* properties are *Button1* through *Button4* from left to right.

A pair of buttons directly below the browsing buttons enables inserts. By clicking *Button5*, a user clears the form and disables the connection between the form's text boxes and the *Shippers DataTable* to permit the input of column values for a new row. After data entry is complete, a click of *Button6* launches an update of the VBDotNetShippers table in the Northwind database and the matching *DataTable* object in the local dataset. The application updates the Northwind database before finalizing any changes to the local *DataTable* object. A couple of factors underlie this order of operation, including the need to confirm entry in the database before finalizing a change in the local *DataTable* object. In the case of an insert into a table with an autonumber primary key, another consideration is recovering the database autonumber field value before finalizing the insert in a local *DataTable* object. After the insert, the *Button6_Click* procedure restores browsing functionality so that text boxes show the currently selected row from the *Shippers DataTable* object.

The operation of the Delete and Update buttons (*Button7* and *Button8*) is more straightforward than that for inserting new rows. Simply use the browsing buttons to navigate to a record. To delete an item, just click the Delete button to delete the row showing on the form. To update an item, change a column value showing in a text box and then click Update.

What the Application Does

Figure 9-14 shows the application in operation. When the application opens, the form shows the first row in the *Shippers DataTable* object. Clicking *Button4* (>>) displays the last row in the *Shippers DataTable* object. The top left window in Figure 9-14 shows *Form3* just after a click to *Button4*.

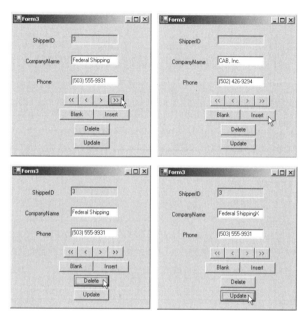

Figure 9-14   A Windows form in a Visual Basic .NET application can enable browsing and manipulating of data in an Access database.

Clicking *Button5* (Blank) clears the form so that you can enter a new row in the Northwind database's VBDotNetShippers table and the corresponding local *DataTable* object. The top right window in Figure 9-14 shows the form just before the entry of the data for a new shipper. Notice that the ShipperID text box is blank. This is because the ShipperID autonumber field value is not determined from within the Visual Basic .NET application. Instead, the ShipperID column gets its value from the Northwind database. Clicking the Insert button in the top right window sends the proposed row from the local *DataTable* object to the database, retrieves an autonumber field value, and finalizes the proposed value in the local *DataTable* object while assigning the correct ShipperID value. Therefore, after clicking Insert, the ShipperID value shows a 4 if that is the next autonumber field value for the VBDotNetShippers table.

The bottom left window in Figure 9-14 shows the form immediately after a click to the Delete button with the CAB, Inc. shipper showing. The click removes the row for CAB, Inc. in both the VBDotNetShippers table within the Northwind database and its matching local *DataTable* object. Therefore, the window shows the last row before the entry of the CAB, Inc. shipper—namely the row for Federal Shipping.

The bottom right window in Figure 9-14 reveals the row for Federal Shipping immediately after an update of its name. (Notice the *X* appended to it.) You can make a change by navigating to a row and performing an edit, such as the one shown in the bottom right window. The edit registers in the local *DataTable* as a proposed row as soon as a user navigates to a new row or clicks the Update button. Clicking the Update button (*Button8*) can propagate the proposed change from the local *DataTable* object to the corresponding table in the Northwind database.

Whenever you modify a *DataTable* object in a disconnected dataset connecting to a database table, the possibility of a concurrency conflict exists if more than one user can modify the database. Therefore, you should either restrict changes to just one user such as a database administrator or code your application so that it can handle concurrency conflicts between a local *Data-Table* object and a database table. To keep the focus on basic data manipulation techniques in Windows Forms, this sample assumes changes will be made by a single user. See Chapter 8 for a more in-depth discussion of concurrency violation issues along with a sample demonstrating how to handle concurrency violations.

The Form Load Event Procedure

The following listing shows the form load event procedure along with the module-level variables for the code behind *Form3*. The three variables declared at the module level are *dap1*, *das1*, and *cnn1*. The *dap1* variable points at a data adapter that serves to coordinate the contents of the local *Shippers DataTable* object with the VBDotNetShippers table in the Northwind database. The major function of the form load event procedure is to configure the *OleDbData-Adapter* object at which *dap1* points. The *das1* variable refers to the dataset that contains the local *Shippers DataTable* object. The *das1* variable plays a role in every data function, from initially populating the local *DataTable* object to deleting rows. The *cnn1* variable points at the connection to the Northwind database from the Visual Basic .NET application. The configuration of the *dap1* variable in the form load event procedure relies on references to the *cnn1* variable, and the event procedure that populates the local *DataTable* with the auto-number field value for new rows also uses the *cnn1* variable.

The *Form3_Load* procedure accomplishes four data management goals:

■ Configuring the *OleDbDataAdapter* for browsing and data manipulation

■ Initially filling the *Shippers DataTable* object with values from the VBDotNetShippers table in the Northwind database

■ Adding a primary key constraint to the *Shippers DataTable* object

■ Binding the form's text boxes to *DataColumn* objects in the *Shippers DataTable* object

Beyond these data-related goals, the load event procedure formats the controls on *Form3* by performing actions such as assigning *Text* property values, making *TextAlign* property settings, and setting the *ReadOnly* property of *TextBox1* to *True*. To conserve space and keep the focus on ADO.NET tasks, the listing in the book does not show the formatting code. See the *Form3_Load* procedure in the DatasetForms project for the complete procedure listing.

The most sophisticated task for the load event procedure is configuring the *OleDbDataAdapter* for browsing and data manipulation. The procedure configures the data adapter represented by the *dap1* variable with a series of four main property assignments. These properties are named *SelectCommand*, *InsertCommand*, *DeleteCommand*, and *UpdateCommand*. You can use each property to get or set an *OleDbCommand* object associated with the *dap1 OleDbDataAdapter*. The *OleDbCommand* constructor used in the sample to make property assignments takes two arguments. One argument specifies a Jet SQL string designating a data command, such as a SELECT, an INSERT, a DELETE, or an UPDATE statement.

Configuring the *InsertCommand*, *DeleteCommand*, or *UpdateCommand* properties for a data adapter requires parameters for the passing of values between a local *DataTable* object and a database object. The code behind the data manipulation buttons updates the local *DataTable* object to establish proposed changes, coordinates these changes to the *DataTable* object with the corresponding Northwind database object (the VBDotNetShippers table), and finalizes the changes to the local *DataTable* object. For the DELETE and UPDATE data commands in the current sample, it is necessary to coordinate one or more column values in a *DataTable* object with the same column values in an Access database table or query. For example, you can't update a column value in a row that another user removed from an Access database table. Attempting to perform this task generates a concurrency violation. Similarly, trying to delete a row previously deleted by another user generates a concurrency violation. The INSERT data command is not subject to a concurrency violation because the Access database assigns a unique autonumber field value to each row just before committing the row to a database object.

The *SelectCommand* property specifies the data available to fill a local *DataTable* object. In the sample code, the procedure designates all columns for all rows. However, you can designate a subset of both the columns and the rows in an Access data source. If you are not comfortable writing Jet SQL, use the graphical query designer in Access to formulate a query, and then copy the code in the SQL view to the constructor statement for the *OleDbCommand* object specifying the *SelectCommand* property. The second argument for the *OleDbCommand* constructor specifying the *SelectCommand*, *InsertCommand*, *DeleteCommand*, and *UpdateCommand* properties for the *dap1 OleDbData-Adapter* is the *cnn1* variable that points at the Northwind database. (See the module-level declarations.)

> **Note** The Visual Studio .NET Data Adapter Configuration Wizard exists to help define queries for an *OleDbDataAdapter* object. However, it fails for selected Access queries, such as joins for three tables. Therefore, a good practice is to systematically use the query designer in Access for assistance in developing queries.

The *OleDbCommand* object for the *InsertCommand* property of *dap1* uses the INSERT INTO keywords to specify a row of values from a local *Data-Table* for insertion into an Access database through a table or query. In the context of this sample, the values are for the CompanyName and Phone columns in the VBDotNetShippers table of the Northwind database. You need a parameter for each value that you intend to transfer from a *DataTable* object in a Visual Basic .NET application to a table or a query in an Access database file. Use the *Add* method for the *Parameters* collection of an *OleDbDataAdapter*'s *Insert-Command* object to specify a parameter for a column value. The *Form3_Load* procedure shows the syntax for this method in the current application. The *Add* method arguments designate, in order, the parameter name, the data type, the length of the parameter, and the name of the column in a database to receive the parameter value.

After specifying the *InsertCommand* property for *dap1*, the procedure shows the syntax for designating a *DeleteCommand* property. If you are deleting just one row at a time, you will want to specify a DELETE statement with a WHERE clause designating via a primary key the current row showing on the form. When the primary key is an autonumber field, as in the VBDotNetShippers table, you can specify just one column as the argument for the WHERE clause.

Specifying an *UpdateCommand* property for an *OleDbDataAdapter* object requires parameters for each column value for which you permit an update. In the sample application, these are the CompanyName and Phone columns. Users cannot update the ShipperID column values because these are autonumber fields that Access manages. In the sample application, the *UpdateCommand* object permits the update to succeed as long as the primary key in a local *DataTable* object matches a corresponding primary key value in an Access table. At your option, you can specify more rigid criteria for an update to succeed. The *UpdateCommand* object specifies a *SourceVersion* property for the parameter designating the ShipperID in the WHERE clause of its *CommandText* property. The *SourceVersion* property is set to *Original*. This setting designates a match on the original value from the local *DataTable* object with the Northwind table. The setting is not strictly necessary in the context of this problem because users cannot change the ShipperID value. (The ShipperID text box has a *ReadOnly* property setting of *True*.) When a user can change the primary key (for example, when you are not using autonumber field values for a primary key), assigning the *SourceVersion* property is critical. The *SourceVersion* property for a parameter allows your application to have a new primary key value but to match on the original primary key value.

The remaining three blocks of code shown in the listing for this procedure are straightforward (or at least relatively familiar). First, a *Fill* method populates the *Shippers DataTable* object in the *das1* dataset based on the current values in the VBDotNetShippers table in the Northwind database. At this point, the procedure designates the name for the *DataTable* in the *das1* dataset. Second, the *Form3_Load* procedure assigns a primary key to the Shippers *DataTable* object. Third, the listing closes with three additional statements that bind the *Text* property setting for *TextBox1* through *TextBox3* to a *DataColumn* in the *Shippers DataTable* object. You add a *DataBinding* object to a control by specifying three arguments: the name of the control's property, the name of the dataset holding the data source, and the name of a *DataColumn* object within the *DataTable* object.

> **Note** Form controls have a collection of *DataBinding* objects because the .NET Framework enables the binding of various data sources to multiple form control properties.

```
Dim dap1 As New System.Data.OleDb.OleDbDataAdapter()
Dim das1 As New System.Data.DataSet()
Dim cnn1 As New OleDb.OleDbConnection( _
    "Provider=Microsoft.Jet.OLEDB.4.0;" & _
    "Data Source=c:\Program Files\" & _
    "Microsoft Office\Office10\Samples\Northwind.mdb")

Private Sub Form3_Load(ByVal sender As System.Object, _
    ByVal e As System.EventArgs) Handles MyBase.Load

    'Specify SelectCommand property
    dap1.SelectCommand = New OleDb.OleDbCommand( _
        "SELECT * FROM VBDotNetShippers", cnn1)

    'Specify InsertCommand property and parameters
    dap1.InsertCommand = New OleDb.OleDbCommand( _
        "INSERT INTO VBDotNetShippers " & _
        "(CompanyName, Phone) " & _
        "VALUES (?, ?)", cnn1)
    Dim prm1 As OleDb.OleDbParameter = _
        dap1.InsertCommand.Parameters.Add("@CompanyName", _
        OleDb.OleDbType.VarChar, 40, "CompanyName")
    Dim prm2 As OleDb.OleDbParameter = _
        dap1.InsertCommand.Parameters.Add("@Phone", _
        OleDb.OleDbType.VarChar, 24, "Phone")

    'Specify DeleteCommand property and parameters
    dap1.DeleteCommand = New OleDb.OleDbCommand( _
        "DELETE FROM VBDotNetShippers " & _
        "WHERE ShipperID = ?", cnn1)
    Dim prm3 As OleDb.OleDbParameter = _
        dap1.DeleteCommand.Parameters.Add("@ShipperID", _
        OleDb.OleDbType.Integer)
    prm3.SourceColumn = "ShipperID"

    'Specify UpdateCommand property and parameters
    dap1.UpdateCommand = _
        New OleDb.OleDbCommand("UPDATE VBDotNetShippers " & _
        "SET CompanyName = ?, Phone = ? " & _
        "WHERE ShipperID = ?", cnn1)
    Dim prm4 As OleDb.OleDbParameter = _
        dap1.UpdateCommand.Parameters.Add("@CompanyName", _
        System.Data.OleDb.OleDbType.VarWChar, 40, "CompanyName")
    Dim prm5 As OleDb.OleDbParameter = _
        dap1.UpdateCommand.Parameters.Add("@Phone", _
```

(continued)

```
                    System.Data.OleDb.OleDbType.VarWChar, 24, "Phone")
           Dim prm6 As OleDb.OleDbParameter = _
               dap1.UpdateCommand.Parameters.Add( _
               New System.Data.OleDb.OleDbParameter("@oldShipperID", _
               OleDb.OleDbType.Integer))
           prm6.SourceColumn = "ShipperID"
           prm6.SourceVersion = DataRowVersion.Original

           'Fill the Shippers table
           dap1.Fill(das1, "Shippers")

           'Define a primary key for the DataTable object
           das1.Tables(0).PrimaryKey = _
               New DataColumn() {das1.Tables(0).Columns("ShipperID")}

           'Bind the text boxes
           TextBox1.DataBindings.Add("Text", das1, _
               "Shippers.ShipperID")
           TextBox2.DataBindings.Add("Text", das1, _
               "Shippers.CompanyName")
           TextBox3.DataBindings.Add("Text", das1, _
               "Shippers.Phone")
           ...

       End Sub
```

Browsing Through Rows

To delete or update a row, this application requires you to browse to that row. The click event procedures for *Button1* through *Button4* enable browsing. (See Figure 9-13 for the positions of these buttons on *Form3*.) Adding a *DataBinding* object to a TextBox control enables you to browse column values in a *DataTable* object for the bound control. In this case, the bound objects are the *DataColumn* objects in the Shippers *DataTable* object. As mentioned, the *Form3_Load* procedure links *TextBox1* with the ShipperID *DataColumn* object, *TextBox2* with the CompanyName *DataColumn* object, and *TextBox3* with the Phone *DataColumn* object.

Your application can change the row shown from a *DataTable* object by modifying the *Position* property for the *BindingContext* object associated with a dataset and a *DataTable* object. Any one form can have multiple *BindingContext* objects associated with various *DataTable* objects. When a form opens, all bound controls show the first position, or row, in the data source to which those controls bind. This corresponds to *Position* property value of 0. You can move bound controls to the first position in a *DataTable* at any time during a session by setting the *Position* property to 0. The *Button1_Click* procedure implements this approach for navigating to the first row in the *Shippers Data-Table* object. Increase the *Position* property value for a *BindingContext* object by 1 to move to the next row or decrease the *Position* property value by 1 to move to the preceding row. The click event procedures for *Button2* and *Button3* move backward and forward through the *Shippers DataTable* by subtracting and adding 1 to the current *Position* property value. The *Count* property reflects the total number of rows in the *DataTable* to which a control binds through the *DataBinding* property. By subtracting 1 from the *Count* property value for a *BindingContext* object, you can specify the *Position* value for the last row in a *DataTable*. The *Button4_Click* event procedure uses this feature to navigate to the last row in the *Shippers DataTable* object.

```
Private Sub Button1_Click(ByVal sender As Object, _
    ByVal e As EventArgs) Handles Button1.Click

    'Move to first position
    Me.BindingContext(das1, "Shippers").Position _
        = 0

End Sub

Private Sub Button2_Click(ByVal sender As Object, _
    ByVal e As EventArgs) Handles Button2.Click

    'Move to previous position
    Me.BindingContext(das1, "Shippers").Position _
        -= 1

End Sub

Private Sub Button3_Click(ByVal sender As System.Object, _
    ByVal e As System.EventArgs) Handles Button3.Click

    'Move to next position
    Me.BindingContext(das1, "Shippers").Position _
        += 1

End Sub

Private Sub Button4_Click(ByVal sender As System.Object, _
    ByVal e As System.EventArgs) Handles Button4.Click

    'Move to last position
    Me.BindingContext(das1, "Shippers").Position = _
        Me.BindingContext(das1, "Shippers").Count - 1

End Sub
```

Inserting a New Row

Three event procedures handle the insertion of a new row into the local *Shippers DataTable* object and the corresponding insertion into the VBDotNetShippers table in the Northwind database. Two of these event procedures apply to the *Button5* and *Button6* click events. The third event procedure applies to the *RowUpdated* event. The .NET Framework raises this event after it executes a data command against a data source, such as the VBDotNetShippers table in the Northwind database. The *Button5_Click* procedure prepares the form for the entry of a new row of data. The *Button6_Click* procedure invokes the *Update* method to transfer a new row from the *Shippers DataTable* object to the VBDotNetShippers table in the Northwind database. The *OnRowUpdated* procedure handles the *RowUpdated* event to populate the local *DataTable* object with the primary key autonumber field value assigned by the Access database. This step is necessary to keep the primary key in the *DataTable* object synchronized with the primary key in the Northwind VBDotNetShippers table.

To use *Form3* for data entry, be sure its text box controls are unbound from the *DataColumn* objects in the *Shippers DataTable* object. You can achieve this result by invoking the *Clear* method for the *DataBindings* collection associated with each text box. Typically, you will want to enter a new row of column values. Therefore, the sample application clears the *Text* property settings of each text box with the object's *Clear* method. The *Button5_Click* procedure demonstrates the syntax for both actions.

After the *Button5_Click* procedure readies the form for data entry, a user can input a new set of column values. However, the application needs to enable users to transfer values from the form to the local *DataTable* object, and the application needs to pass the values from the local *DataTable* object to the database associated with the *DataTable* object through the *dap1 OleDbDataAdapter*. The *InsertCommand* object for the *dap1* data adapter moderates the transfer of information from the *Shippers DataTable* object to the VBDotNetShippers table in the Northwind database. The *Button6_Click* procedure invokes the *Update* method for the *dap1* data adapter to launch the exchange of information between the local *DataTable* object and the database table.

After the exchange completes, the .NET Framework raises the *RowUpdated* event. Through an *AddHandler* statement, the *Button6_Click* procedure designates the *OnRowUpdated* procedure as the delegate for handling the event. After the launching of the *Update* method and the handling of the *RowUpdated* event, the *Button6_Click* procedure closes by reestablishing the

DataBinding settings for the text boxes and moving to the last row in the local *DataTable*. These final steps enable *Form3* to show the most recently added row.

When the application invokes the *OnRowUpdated* procedure, it receives the current row of column values in its *args* argument. The objective for the procedure in this application is to retrieve the autonumber field for the most recently inserted row in the Access database. Starting with Access 2000, Jet SQL acquired the @@IDENTITY statement for achieving this very task within a SELECT statement. Therefore, the *OnRowUpdated* procedure creates an *OleDbCommand* object with the SELECT statement as its *CommandText* property and the *cnn1* connection object specified at the module level. Invoking the *ExecuteScalar* method for the *OleDbCommand* object returns the last autonumber field value. Before closing, the procedure assigns the returned autonumber field value to the ShipperID column in the local *Shippers DataTable* object. This assignment synchronizes the primary key values for the new row in the Northwind database table and its corresponding local *DataTable* object.

```
Private Sub Button5_Click(ByVal sender As System.Object, _
    ByVal e As System.EventArgs) Handles Button5.Click

    'Remove bindings for text boxes
    TextBox1.DataBindings.Clear()
    TextBox2.DataBindings.Clear()
    TextBox3.DataBindings.Clear()

    'Clear text boxes for entry of new row
    TextBox1.Clear()
    TextBox2.Clear()
    TextBox3.Clear()

End Sub

Private Sub Button6_Click(ByVal sender As System.Object, _
    ByVal e As System.EventArgs) Handles Button6.Click

    'Add the row locally with any arbitrary value for
    'its ShipperID column value; the sample specifies
    'a ShipperID value of the maximum Integer data
    'value
    Dim drw1 As DataRow = _
        das1.Tables("Shippers").NewRow()
```

(continued)

```
        drw1("CompanyName") = TextBox2.Text
        drw1("Phone") = TextBox3.Text
        drw1("ShipperID") = Integer.MaxValue
        das1.Tables("Shippers").Rows.Add(drw1)

        'Include an event to fill in the autonumber value
        AddHandler dap1.RowUpdated, _
            New OleDb.OleDbRowUpdatedEventHandler( _
            AddressOf OnRowUpdated)

        'Update the Access database file
        dap1.Update(das1, "Shippers")

        'Re-bind text boxes to columns in Shippers DataTable object
        TextBox1.DataBindings.Add("Text", das1, _
            "Shippers.ShipperID")
        TextBox2.DataBindings.Add("Text", das1, _
            "Shippers.CompanyName")
        TextBox3.DataBindings.Add("Text", das1, _
            "Shippers.Phone")

        'Move to last row in Shippers DataTable object
        Me.BindingContext(das1, "Shippers").Position = _
            Me.BindingContext(das1, "Shippers").Position.MaxValue

    End Sub

    Private Sub OnRowUpdated(ByVal sender As Object, _
        ByVal args As OleDb.OleDbRowUpdatedEventArgs)

        'Include a variable and a command to retrieve the
        'identity value from the Access database
        Dim int1 As Integer = 0
        Dim cmd1 As OleDb.OleDbCommand = _
            New OleDb.OleDbCommand("SELECT @@IDENTITY", cnn1)

        If args.StatementType = StatementType.Insert Then
            'Retrieve the identity value and
            'store it in the ShipperID column
            int1 = CInt(cmd1.ExecuteScalar())
            args.Row("ShipperID") = int1
        End If

    End Sub
```

Deleting the Currently Selected Row

The *Delete* method allows you to mark a row for deletion from a *DataTable* object. The next invocation of the *Update* method removes the matching row from a table in an Access database file and finalizes the proposed change to the local *DataTable* object. In Chapter 8, you learned that the *Delete* method applies to a *Rows* collection member. That chapter showed you how to use the *Delete* method with the *Find* method. However, you need a primary key constraint in a *DataTable* object to invoke the *Find* method. A more robust implementation that does not require a primary key is to use the *Find* method associated with a *DataView* object.

Using this method gives me an opportunity to introduce you to the *Data-View* object, which roughly parallels a view or query in Access. For the *Data-View* object's *Find* method to work, the *DataView* object must be sorted by the column values for the field on which you want to perform a find. The *Button7_Click* procedure shows the syntax for achieving these tasks in the context of the current sample application. After invoking the *Delete* method for the row index discovered with the *DataView* object, the *Button7_Click* procedure invokes the *Update* method for the *dap1 OleDbDataAdapter*. This removes the corresponding row from the VBDotNetShippers table in the Northwind database and finalizes, or accepts, the proposed change to the local *Data-Table* object.

```
Private Sub Button7_Click(ByVal sender As System.Object, _
    ByVal e As System.EventArgs) Handles Button7.Click

    'Create sorted DataView object
    Dim dav1 As DataView = New DataView(das1.Tables("Shippers"))
    dav1.Sort = "ShipperID"

    'Use DataView object to return row index for currently
    'selected row and delete row from DataTable object that is
    'the source for the DataView object
    Dim int1 As Integer = dav1.Find(CInt(TextBox1.Text))
    das1.Tables("Shippers").Rows(int1).Delete()

    'Invoke Update method to finalize deleted row in database
    'file and DataTable object
    dap1.Update(das1, "Shippers")

End Sub
```

Updating a Row

The final procedure in the sample, *Button8_Click*, processes the updating of a row both in the local *DataTable* object and the matching table in the Northwind database. The processing of an update is straightforward. First, you have to commit the proposed change. Second, you invoke the *Update* method to transfer the change through the *UpdateCommand* property for an *OleDbDataAdapter* to the database that the data adapter connects to. To commit the edited value in the form as a proposed change, you can move off and return to the current row in the *DataTable* object. The *DataBinding* objects automatically transfer the form text box values to the local *DataTable* object pointed at by the *DataBinding* objects. If you happen to be on the first row (*Position* property equals 0), you can just attempt to move forward one row.

Although the .NET Framework does not actually revise the value showing in the text boxes, it does update the local *DataTable* object with the form text box values. After revising the local *DataTable* object, the next step is to transfer the change to the table in the Northwind database file. This can be as easy as invoking the *Update* method. You can resolve any possible concurrency violations by adapting the techniques described at the end of Chapter 8. Perhaps the easiest way to avoid concurrency violations is to allow updates only by a designated database administrator.

```
Private Sub Button8_Click(ByVal sender As System.Object, _
    ByVal e As System.EventArgs) Handles Button8.Click

    'Move off current row to propose update
    If Me.BindingContext(das1, "Shippers").Position = 0 _
        Then
        Me.BindingContext(das1, "Shippers").Position -= 1
    Else
        Me.BindingContext(das1, "Shippers").Position -= 1
        Me.BindingContext(das1, "Shippers").Position += 1
    End If

    'Invoke Update method to commit change in database file
    'and DataTable object
    dap1.Update(das1, "Shippers")

End Sub
```

Summary

This chapter presents concepts and samples to enhance your proficiency in three ADO.NET topics. The chapter initially drills down on datasets in ways not covered previously in the book. In particular, the first section highlights the differences between a typed dataset and an untyped dataset while showing you techniques for creating and managing each of these two kinds of datasets. Next, the chapter describes how to manage parent-child relations dynamically between two *DataTable* objects. The presentation reinforces the chapter's earlier material on typed vs. untyped datasets by demonstrating how to handle parent-child relations in each kind of dataset. The chapter concludes with a prototype design for a very common database application—browsing and manipulating data with a series of text boxes on a form. The presentation of this topic follows a case study summary that starts with the form design issues and then systematically leads you through the code underlying each step to implement the overall task.

10

Programming ASP.NET Pages

This is the first of two chapters addressing Microsoft ASP.NET Web applications. ASP.NET is the name for the .NET Framework subset of Web development capabilities. This chapter has two primary objectives. First, the chapter aims to introduce Web development concepts, particularly those implemented through ASP.NET. Second, the chapter aims to give you an operational feel for how to create ASP.NET solutions with Microsoft Visual Basic .NET. The chapter reviews the design and construction of three ASP.NET Web sample applications to illustrate how you build Web solutions with Visual Basic .NET. Creating database solutions with ASP.NET is specifically excluded from this chapter to keep the focus on ASP.NET and clearly present Web applications from a tutorial perspective. Chapter 11 focuses on creating ASP.NET solutions for Microsoft Access databases.

This chapter contains three sections. The first section describes ASP.NET platform requirements and contrasts ASP.NET Web applications with Windows applications and Active Server Pages (ASP) applications. The discussion of platform requirements conveys what you need to build ASP.NET solutions and contrasts these requirements with those for running ASP.NET solutions. For example, this section explains that you can run an ASP.NET solution from a workstation that does not have the .NET Framework installed on it. You will also learn about the important topic of Web pages making round-trips between a browser and a server and its implication for Web page processing.

The chapter's second section drills down further into ASP.NET by presenting important ASP.NET programming concepts, such as the Web Forms *Page* class and controls for this class. Although you can use Visual Basic .NET to build Web applications and Microsoft Windows applications on forms, the forms and the controls on those forms differ for each type of application. This section highlights special issues pertaining to forms and controls for Web applications.

The third section in the chapter demonstrates how to create ASP.NET solutions by presenting the steps for building and evaluating three sample ASP.NET Web applications. The first sample introduces you to the basics of adding a Web form to a solution and using that solution. The second sample builds on the initial sample in a couple of ways. First, it shows how to move controls around a Web page programmatically. The process is different than that for moving controls around a Windows form. Second, the application demonstrates how to refresh a Web solution programmatically. The solution demonstrates a workaround to a problem with the Refresh tool on browsers for ASP.NET solutions. The third sample demonstrates how to use *Session* variables to track the values of variables across multiple forms in a Web application. The sample illustrates a simple approach to authenticating users with a Web form.

Introduction to ASP.NET

This section aims to introduce ASP.NET by describing the platform development and usage issues. In brief, running an ASP.NET page requires far less resources than creating one. Next, the section compares ASP.NET with alternative technologies. First, we will contrast Web applications based on Web Forms with Windows applications based on Windows Forms. Second, you will learn how ASP.NET and ASP contrast with one another.

Platform Requirements and Browser Considerations

ASP.NET Web applications are for Web browsers. You view a Web form in a browser. In ASP.NET, a one-to-one correspondence exists between a Web form and a Web page. A Web form in an ASP.NET Web application project is analogous to a Windows form in a Windows application project. To create a Web form, you need an ASP.NET Web application project. To create a Web application project, you need access to Microsoft Internet Information Services (IIS) version 5 or later, which is the Web server that serves the ASP.NET Web page to a browser. Any operating system that can host IIS, such as Windows 2000 Server or Windows XP Professional, is suitable as a development platform for ASP.NET Web applications. Because ASP.NET applications depend on the .NET Framework, you of course need the .NET Framework on the Web server.

> **Note**   Although not absolutely necessary, many developers will find it convenient to build Web application projects with Web Forms from within Microsoft Visual Studio .NET. This book describes that approach. Visual Studio .NET provides an IDE for Web application projects that runs similarly to the one for Windows application projects.

As Access developers, the Web applications that you build are likely to have data access functionality. When performing data access in ASP.NET Web applications, you need Microsoft Data Access Components (MDAC) 2.7 or later. This requirement, as well as the requirements for the Web server, are development workstation requirements. Because ASP.NET applications run from any browser, you do not need MDAC 2.7 on a client workstation. The Web server performs the data access on behalf of an ASP.NET Web page. Then, any client can consume data on a Web form. The client does not require IIS, MDAC 2.7, or the .NET Framework. The client workstation requires only a browser that can read HTML. However, not all browsers lay out HTML the same way. In addition, selected Web form capabilities, such as data validation, can optionally take advantage of client-side scripting. Script interpreters represent another element that can vary between browsers. Even if a browser has the capacity to correctly interpret a client-side script, users can shut down their browser's script interpreter for security reasons.

> **Note**   A best practice guideline is to standardize on a browser for any Web application, including ASP.NET Web applications. The Visual Studio .NET documentation specifies a minimum of a Microsoft Internet Explorer 5.0 browser to enable client-side scripts. I evaluated the samples in this chapter and Chapter 11 with Internet Explorer 6.0.

Comparing Web Applications with Windows Applications

With the widespread deployment of browsers in organizations, Web solutions are growing in popularity as an alternative to Windows applications. Web applications can be accessed in an identical manner whether a user is at work or at home. All the time that users spend browsing builds their skills for navigating through your custom applications. One especially attractive advantage of a Web application over a Windows application is that the client workstation for a Web application does not require the .NET Framework. When running a Windows application, however, the client workstation must have the .NET Framework installed.

You can deploy a Windows application by distributing a project folder to a computer. It might also be necessary to copy related files that are not situated inside the project folder. For example, numerous samples throughout this book refer to the Northwind database, which is not inside a project folder. In the case of a Web application, the project folder resides on a Web server. Users do not need to load a project folder onto their computer. With Web applications, users merely browse the Web pages on the Web server.

Windows applications work with instances of objects that reside on a workstation. These object instances can provide rich interactivity and other kinds of functionality directly from a workstation. With the exception of client-side scripts, Web applications do not run on a client's workstation. Web servers typically manage user interactivity through an HTTP connection between a client workstation and a Web server. Each user interaction in a Web application requires a round-trip of a Web page from a browser to a Web server and back again to the client workstation. Client-side scripts can provide more responsive user interactivity that does not depend on a Web server. However, this limits the availability of your applications to browsers that can correctly interpret the scripts, and it requires clients to leave their script interpreter running.

Windows Forms makes the layout of controls easy. For example, you can use drag-and-drop techniques to populate a Windows *Form* class instance with controls. This kind of layout makes it easy to arrange controls by their vertical and horizontal displacements from the form borders. Web Forms can offer this kind of design convenience if you use the *GridLayout* setting for the *pageLayout* property. However, doing so restricts the range of browsers that can interpret the layout of controls on a page. Web Forms also offers a layout style for controls that works similarly to the text in a word processor. The *pageLayout* setting name for this style is *FlowLayout*. In this page layout mode, controls and text appear from left to right and from top to bottom. With the *FlowLayout* setting, you cannot drag controls to an absolute position on a Web page. *FlowLayout* mode is the classic HTML formatting style that is widely interpreted by many browsers.

A Web page is stateless in round-trips between a browser and a server. That is, the Web server does not recall anything about the state of a page from one round-trip to the next. The stateless nature of Web pages helps Web servers scale to large numbers of sessions. However, Web applications often benefit from persisting some information about the state of a page. ASP.NET introduces a couple of innovations and takes advantage of prior ASP features to facilitate tracking the state of a page. The new *ViewState* property for a page enables a server to restore control property settings for a page automatically. With ASP, it is necessary to programmatically restore control property settings. You can use the *Session* state variables to store values within a user session so that a page from a user can access the variable values between round-trips to a user. Application state variables enable you to persist values that can be shared across all the users of an application. Because Windows applications run on a workstation, they do not require state management tools between round-trips to a server.

Contrasting ASP.NET with ASP

ASP.NET builds on the great success of ASP as a Web development tool. As you might know, ASP is the object model for programming IIS. ASP developers typically program the server using either VBScript or JScript. VBScript is somewhat similar to classic Visual Basic or Visual Basic for Applications (VBA). In addition, ASP permits—and sometimes requires—the intermixing of script code such as VBScript with HTML content and page layout code. As a result, the script code could be difficult to design and debug because it is not isolated in an environment of its own. Finally, IIS interprets VBScript. This need to interpret the script code for each page slows down the process of presenting a page in a browser.

ASP.NET introduces innovations to address each of the three topics mentioned in the preceding paragraph. First, you can program ASP.NET Web applications with Visual Basic .NET. Notice that I did not say JScript, or even VBScript. By allowing developers to use the same language for Web applications as for Windows applications, ASP.NET lowers the barriers to creating Web applications. Second, ASP.NET introduces a code-behind Web page development paradigm. This model is the same one used in Windows applications that support a code-behind Windows form. This feature is particularly important because it separates the Visual Basic .NET code for a Web page from the HTML layout code for the page. Third, and most important for performance, ASP.NET Web pages run from compiled versions. As with Windows applications, the code implementing a feature is compiled by default only when a user first invokes the feature. Although this can lead to a slightly longer pause when some code is initially compiled (as opposed to interpreted), the compiled code runs substantially faster than the interpreted code on its second use and subsequent uses.

Two more noteworthy points about ASP.NET and ASP relate to the file type each uses for a Web page and your ability to run ASP and ASP.NET pages concurrently. ASP.NET pages have an .aspx file extension as opposed to the familiar .asp extension for ASP pages. This distinction makes it easy to identify which type of page your application uses. The other important consideration is that you can run ASP and ASP.NET Web pages concurrently on a single IIS version 5 or later server. This means that you do not have to re-architect old solutions to start benefiting immediately from the adoption of ASP.NET technology. You can mix and match ASP.NET pages with legacy ASP pages in the same application. Just start adding new functionality with ASP.NET to an application originally created with ASP.

Selected ASP.NET Programming Topics

This section builds on the preceding one and adds more details that highlight Web programming issues conceptually. In particular, you will learn about the Design and HTML views for managing the layout of controls on a form. This section also examines the *Page* class and discusses selected properties and methods that can help you manage the behavior of your forms on a Web page. The section concludes with a brief summary of the types of controls available for populating a form as well as a contrasting of techniques for adding controls to a page.

Web Forms and Their Views

When you create an ASP.NET Web application, it opens to a blank Web form with the name WebForm1.aspx. (See Figure 10-1.) The "Starting the WebPage-Samples Project" section in this chapter demonstrates step-by-step instructions for opening an ASP.NET Web application. This Web form shows the Design view of the page. You can add controls and text to the page from the Design view. In Solution Explorer, you can see that the Web page has the name WebForm1.aspx. You can rename the page by right-clicking it in Solution Explorer, choosing Rename, and entering a new name with an .aspx extension.

Figure 10-1   The default Web form that appears when you create an
ASP.NET Web application

The default settings for *WebForm1* are the *GridLayout pageLayout* property setting with a *showGrid* property setting of *True*. This *pageLayout* property
setting is convenient for laying out controls on a form in the same style that you
use with a Windows form. By right-clicking inside the WebForm1.aspx document and choosing Properties, you can open the DOCUMENT Property Pages
dialog box. This dialog box permits you to set the *pageLayout* property for the
document in WebForm1.aspx. Instead of using the default *GridLayout* setting,
you can choose a *FlowLayout* setting.

With a *FlowLayout* setting, you can add text without controls to a Web
page as you would by using a word processor, and Visual Studio .NET manages
the layout of controls in a document by using traditional HTML flow control layout rules that resemble those for a word processor. You can also set the target
schema for a Web page so that it is compatible with various styles of browsers
from the DOCUMENT Property Pages dialog box. The DOCUMENT Property
Pages dialog box conveniently groups a set of related page properties, but you
can access these properties along with other page properties directly from the
Properties window after clicking any blank area in the page to select the HTML
Document object.

> **Note** Use the DOCUMENT Property Pages dialog box to optimize an ASP.NET Web page for varied scenarios. The *Internet Explorer 5.0* setting for Target Schema with a *GridLayout* setting for Page Layout is convenient when you are writing an application that mandates access via Internet Explorer version 5 or later and you want to take advantage of Windows Forms–style layout features for controls. The *Navigator 4.0* Target Schema with a *FlowLayout* Page Layout setting is appropriate when you have an application in which you cannot dictate the browser for an application and your page has a lot of text that needs editing.

The two tabs to the lower left of the page in Figure 10-1 permit you to toggle the view of a page between Design view and HTML view. A Web page is a collection of HTML elements (or tags). You can add controls to a Web page and edit their properties graphically in Design view or directly with HTML elements in HTML view. If you have a working knowledge of HTML, you might find it instructive to view Web pages in HTML view to see how Visual Studio .NET interprets your graphical layout operations into HTML elements. The following excerpt from the HTML view for the Web page in Figure 10-1 shows that the body of the document consists of an empty HTML form tag. The tag has an *id* attribute setting equal to *Form1*. The *id* attribute corresponds to the *ID* property for a *Control* object. You can use the *ID* property to identify a control programmatically. As you add content to the page, the Web Forms Designer will populate the body block with additional HTML tags. The HTML and Design views of a Web page are flip sides of the content on a Web page.

```
<body MS_POSITIONING="GridLayout">
    <form id="Form1" method="post" runat="server">
    </form>
</body>
```

Another view of a Web page is the Code view. You can expose this view of a Web page by right-clicking a blank area in either the Design or HTML views and choosing View Code. Choosing this menu item opens a new tab in the Web Forms Designer named WebForm1.aspx.vb. This view enables you to add Visual Basic .NET code to control the behavior of a Web page. The code in this view runs on the server. Choosing View Code for the blank page in Figure 10-1 opens the Code view window to the shell for a *Page_Load* event procedure. The WebForm1.aspx.vb and WebForm1.aspx files are separate files that work together to enable one page class. Although you can intersperse server scripts in the HTML for a Web page, that practice defeats one of the major advantages of ASP.NET—isolating the Visual Basic .NET code controlling the behavior of a page from the HTML elements controlling the page's design and content.

The Web Forms *Page* Class

The *Page* class in the *System.Web.UI* namespace can represent a Web page in a project. The Web page corresponding to a *Page* class instance appears in a browser. A *Page* class contains properties and methods that manage the HTML elements and Visual Basic .NET code that controls the form in an .aspx file. The ASP.NET processing model reconstructs a *Page* class instance on each round-trip of a page between a browser and a server. During this process, the page reacts to user input to form controls. One especially helpful feature of a Web page is that it automatically populates the controls on the forms with field values from the last browser session. Developers familiar with ASP coding practice will recall the need to manually populate values for controls on an HTML form in application code.

The *Page_Load* event for a *Page* class instance roughly corresponds to the *Form_Load* event for a Windows *Form* class. As mentioned earlier, the Code view window for a Web page opens automatically to the shell for a *Page_Load* event procedure. This event fires on each round-trip of an .aspx file. Your application might need to process the initial opening of a *Page* class instance differently from one in which a user is posting back information for a page that is already opened. The *IsPostBack* property of the *Page* class returns a value of *False* when the page initially opens; otherwise, it returns *True*. All events for controls on a Web page, such as the *Click* event for a Button, cause a Web page to send information about the event to the server via the HTTP *post* method. Notice the *post* method for the form tag in the preceding code listing; this method setting specifies the HTTP *post* technique for transferring information between a form in a browser and a Web server.

You can refer to individual controls on a Web page through a *Page* class instance. Use the *Me* keyword to refer to *WebForm1* or another page name, denoting a *Page* class instance. For example, designate a Button control with an *ID* property equal to *Button1* as *Me.Button1*. A Web Forms instance corresponds to the HTML *form* tag for a Web page. (See the preceding HTML excerpt.) You can refer to a Web Forms control in an ASP.NET page through the *ControlCollection* class for *Me*. The member of the collection with a *Get-Type.ToString* return value equal to *System.Web.UI.HtmlControls.HtmlForm* is the control for the current Web Forms instance. For example, the control's *ID* property equals the *id* attribute setting for the *form* tag on the current Web page.

Controls on a Web Forms Page

To add controls to a Web page, you can drag controls from the Toolbox to the Web page. As you have learned, you have two modes for laying out controls on a Web page. The default *GridLayout pageLayout* setting is easiest and fastest for formatting forms. Also, the process of adding controls to a Web page has the look and feel of arranging controls on a Windows form. The optional *FlowLayout pageLayout* setting is compatible with a broader range of browsers that do not support Dynamic HTML (DHTML) absolute positioning syntax, such as Netscape Navigator 4.0. If you are familiar with formatting controls on a Windows form, the formatting conventions for a page with a *FlowLayout pageLayout* property might feel awkward and force you to align controls by positioning them within the cells of an HTML Table control on a Web page.

This section mentions three types of controls that you can add to a Web page: Web server controls, HTML server controls, and HTML controls. Add Web server controls from the Web Forms tab of the Toolbox. Add HTML server controls and HTML controls from the HTML tab of the Toolbox. Both HTML server controls and HTML controls use standard HTML tags to define controls—especially for the most commonly used controls, such as text boxes or buttons. One key difference is the use of the *runat* attribute setting for the HTML server controls with a value of *server*. This setting lets Visual Basic .NET code manipulate the control programmatically at the server. You can add controls that will act as HTML server controls without manually adding the *runat* attribute. Simply add the control from the HTML tab in the Toolbox. Then, to convert the control from an HTML control to an HTML server control, right-click the HTML control on the Web form in Design view and select Run As Server Control. Web server controls automatically have their *runat* attribute set to *server*.

You can mix and match any of the three control types concurrently on the same Web page. The Web server controls have the greatest diversity, but they also depart the most from traditional HTML controls. If you have limited experience developing Web applications, the wider selection of Web server controls should more than offset any departures from traditional HTML controls. In addition, Web server controls have a richer set of properties than you can manipulate programmatically. For example, you can use the *Page_Load* event to set the tab order for Web server controls via their *TabIndex* property. HTML server controls do not offer a *TabIndex* property for programmatic manipulation, although you can manipulate the tab order for controls manually through the

Properties window. The Web server controls include many more controls, such as Calendar and AdRotator, than the HTML server controls.

Programming Web Forms

This section features a collection of three sample applications that illustrate the basics of building ASP.NET Web applications with Visual Basic .NET. The purpose of the samples is to reinforce and extend the key concepts of Web development presented in the prior two sections.

Hello and Goodbye Sample

The standard "Hello World" sample is an exercise in how to get a computer program to interact with a user. The user performs a task, such as starting the application or clicking a button, and the program responds by sending some variation of the "Hello World" message. Web applications implemented with Visual Basic .NET do not support a *MsgBox* function for displaying a reply. However, a Web page can include controls with variable text messages. These text messages can refresh on each round-trip of a page between a browser and a server.

The Hello and Goodbye sample illustrates several standard Web features that you are likely to include in many of your applications. First, the review of the layout procedure for the controls on a page illustrates basic design issues while introducing you to a special Web application control. Second, the sample demonstrates how similar a *Page_Load* event procedure in a Web application can be to a *Form_Load* event procedure in a Windows application. This similarity of control layout and programming environments eases the transition process for Access developers who have limited Web development experience. Third, the sample illustrates how to say goodbye to the current Web page (or at least move to another Web page). A Web server Hyperlink control achieves this purpose, and using the HyperLink control demonstrates how to manage this kind of functionality with Visual Basic .NET on a Web page.

Starting the WebPageSamples Project

To start a Web application, you can use the ASP.NET Web Application template. Click New Project from the Start Page in the IDE (or select File, New, Project from the Visual Studio .NET menu). With Visual Basic Projects selected, highlight ASP.NET Web Application in the Templates pane. Specify a Web server name and a Web site location for your new project. Figure 10-2 shows the designation of the WebPageSamples Web site on the localhost Web server.

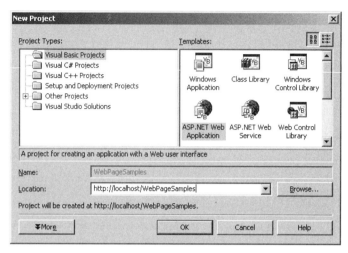

Figure 10-2 Start a new ASP.NET Web application project with the ASP.NET Web Application template.

After you click OK, Visual Studio .NET starts creating folders for the project in two places. First, you might be prompted to authenticate yourself on your chosen server. Enter a valid Windows user ID and password with sufficient permissions to perform project authoring. A Web application's main project folder is within the wwwroot folder of the Web server that you specify when creating the Web application. The project folder on the Web server has your Web pages and other support project files for working with IIS and serving pages to browsers. Visual Studio .NET creates a second project folder for Web application projects in its default location for Visual Studio projects. On my test computer for this book, that project folder is the Visual Studio Projects folder in the c:\\Documents and Settings\Administrator\My Documents\ path. This secondary project folder holds the .sln file that Visual Studio can use to open a project and modify it. The name for the .sln file matches the name for your ASP.NET Web application project.

Laying Out the HelloGoodbye.aspx Web Page
As mentioned previously, a Web application project opens to a blank form. The default name for a new page with the blank form in a new project will be WebForm1.aspx. You can rename the file for the Web page by right-clicking it in Solution Explorer, choosing Rename from the menu, and assigning a new name for the project. I assigned the name HelloGoodbye.aspx to replace WebForm1.aspx.

After you optionally change the page's filename to something meaningful, your next task will likely be adding controls to the page's form. As you can see from the HTML view for your Web page, the whole body of the document consists of a Web form tag. This form is an ASP.NET Web Forms control. You can drag additional controls from the Toolbox onto the form's surface, and the Web Forms Designer will nest those controls within the opening and closing *form* tags.

Figure 10-3 shows three Web server controls in the HelloGoodbye.aspx Web page. I dragged the controls from the Web Forms tab of the Toolbox onto the form. The Button control appears in its default configuration, but the other two controls appear with minor editing. Programmatically formatting Web controls does not rigidly follow Windows Forms conventions, but many similarities exist. As you start to develop ASP.NET solutions, you might find it more productive to adjust selected control properties manually. For example, the Label control is dragged to a longer length. You can see the control's white background blocking the visibility of the grid behind it. Figure 10-3 shows the *HyperLink1* control selected. You can see two of its custom property settings in the Properties window. Clicking in the *NavigateURL* property in the *HyperLink1* property column, and then clicking the button that appears opens the Select URL dialog box to assist you in specifying a destination URL for the HyperLink control. By the way, the URL in this example is the Web site for my favorite seminar tour.

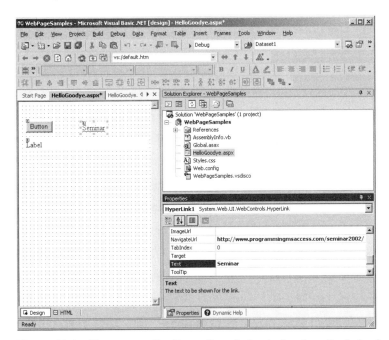

Figure 10-3   You can use the Properties window to fine-tune the behavior of controls on Web pages as you get used to the programmatic interface.

Adding Code Behind the Page

The code behind the page for this sample requires a couple of event procedures. A *Page_Load* event procedure assigns the *Text* property values to the Button and Label controls on the form. By embedding the assignments within an *If...Then* statement, the procedure can make the specifications just once. The condition for the *If...Then* statement is *Not IsPostBack*. This condition is true just once in any Web session: the first time that a user opens the page. Therefore, the code within the *If...Then* statement executes only on the first view that a user gets of the page. After that, the built-in ASP.NET page logic automatically populates the Button and Label controls with the initial values set from within the *If...Then* statement. Custom logic for a page's *IsPostBack* property offers a convenient way of isolating code that needs to run just once. This, in turn, speeds the performance of your applications and reduces the load on your Web server.

Notice that the *Page_Load* event automatically inserts a greeting in the Label control: "This is my initial hello." However, a user can change the greeting by clicking the Button control on the Web page. In a fashion similar to that of the *Page_Load* procedure, the *Button1_Click* procedure adds the new greeting ("Hi, again.") only if it does not already appear. Conditional execution is less important outside the *Page_Load* event procedure. This is because the *Page_Load* event procedure operates on each round-trip for a Web page between a browser and a server, but event procedures for other controls fire only when those specific events get raised based on user actions. It's good practice to keep all event procedures lean, but this is especially so for the *Page_Load* procedure.

```
Private Sub Page_Load(ByVal sender As System.Object, _
    ByVal e As System.EventArgs) Handles MyBase.Load

    'If not posted back, set initial conditions
    If Not IsPostBack Then
        Button1.Text = "Hello again"
        Me.Label1.Text = "This is my initial hello."
    End If

End Sub

Private Sub Button1_Click(ByVal sender As System.Object, _
    ByVal e As System.EventArgs) Handles Button1.Click
```

```
'If not updated message, then update message
If Me.Label1.Text <> "Hi, again." Then
    Me.Label1.Text = "Hi, again."
End If

End Sub
```

Demonstrating the Sample

To test the application from Visual Studio .NET, right-click the HelloGoodbye.aspx file in Solution Explorer and choose Build And Browse. Choosing this option compiles your code and opens a browser session from within Visual Studio .NET. Figure 10-4 shows the built-in browser session after the HelloGoodbye.aspx page initially opens. Notice that the Button and Label controls have nondefault *Text* property settings that differ from those shown in Figure 10-3. The HelloGoodbye.aspx file appears selected in Solution Explorer because the file was last selected to open the page.

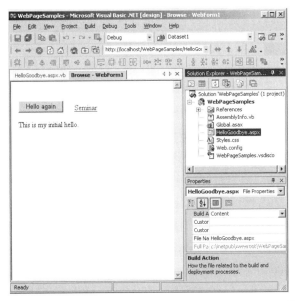

Figure 10-4   The built-in browser makes it easy to verify the operation of ASP.NET Web applications in Visual Studio .NET.

Clicking *Button1* or *HyperLink1* revises the contents of the browser session on the Browse—WebForm1 tab in Figure 10-4. In the case of a click to

Button1, the contents of the Label control on the Web page change. Clicking *HyperLink1* changes the whole page to the home page for my favorite seminar tour. For the hyperlink to operate, you need an open connection to the Internet. In this day of "always-on" broadband connections, the availability of such a connection is growing. If you do even a moderate amount of Web development work, such a connection is likely to prove useful.

Hello and Refresh Sample

As simple as the HelloGoodbye.aspx Web page was, it suffered from a flaw typical of many ASP.NET Web applications. Clicking a browser's Refresh control might or might not refresh the Web page, but it almost always brings up a dialog box similar to the one shown in Figure 10-5. The user must choose between two options. This is probably not what you would prefer. An alternative is to create your own Refresh button inside the application. The next sample revises the previous one to include a custom Refresh button. In addition, the sample disables and hides the Hello Again button after a click to the button alters the Label control display from its initial message to a revised one. When the sample disables the Hello Again button, it moves the *HyperLink1* control to occupy the button's location. A manipulation such as this can have a definite impact on the performance of an application because it removes the possibility of unnecessary round-trips back to the server while concurrently reducing network traffic.

Figure 10-5   Clicking the Refresh button in the browser for an ASP.NET Web application will often bring up this dialog box.

Laying Out the HelloRefresh.aspx Web Page

This new sample can exist within a Web page of its own in the WebPageSamples project folder on the localhost Web server. Therefore, within the current project, choose Project, Add Web Form. If you are progressing along with the sample, this will create a new Web page named WebForm2.aspx. You can right-click the page in Solution Explorer, select Rename, and give the file a more relevant name, such as HelloRefresh.aspx.

Add controls to the form in the arrangement that Figure 10-6 shows. Use the same settings for the HyperLink control as in the previous sample. The major design change for the new sample is the addition of a second Button control. A click to the new button handles the function that you expect from a Refresh control on the browser's toolbar. When a user clicks the new button, our application will refresh the application exactly as we've instructed it to in our program. For example, this revised refresh capability does not show the dialog box appearing in Figure 10-5.

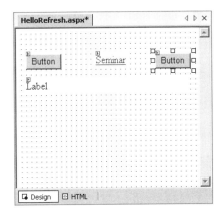

Figure 10-6   The highlighted button shows the new control added to the previous application sample.

Demonstrating the Sample

The operation of this application will help you understand the code review. Therefore, I demonstrate the code before discussing the syntax and organization of the code behind the Web page. The application opens to the window shown in the top left corner of Figure 10-7. This window shows the initial greeting in *Label1* along with the other controls, featuring their custom text property settings. The top right window displays the Web page after the first click to *Button1* (Hello Again). A second click to *Button1* causes the application to resemble the lower left window in Figure 10-7. The window shows that the HyperLink control moves from its initial position to the right of *Button1* to the same position as *Button1*. In addition, *Button1* disappears from the page's form.

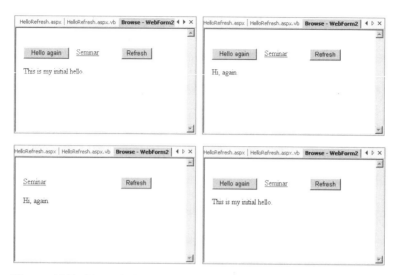

Figure 10-7   Four windows from the Hello and Refresh sample

Clicking *Button2* (Refresh) within the lower left window in Figure 10-7 restores the Web page to its initial appearance. The bottom right window in Figure 10-7 shows the restored page. You can confirm the operation by comparing the lower right and top left windows in Figure 10-7.

Adding Code for the HelloRefresh Page

In addition to the refresh code, this sample demonstrates code for changing the position of, disabling, and hiding a control. By applying logic such as that developed for this sample, you can readily give your Web pages a dynamic and highly interactive feel.

Managing the location of controls on a Web page is more challenging than doing so with a Windows form for a couple of reasons. First, the position for a control on a Web page is not a *Structure* (two ordered *Integer* values comprising a *Point* structure). Instead, displacements from the top and left of the Web page appear within the *style* attribute setting for a control when you are using absolute coordinate positioning as this sample does. This *style* attribute includes other formatting specifications for the control as well. You can switch to the HTML view for the form shown in Figure 10-6 to confirm the design of the *style* attributes for the *Button1* and *HyperLink1* controls. The sample application moves the HyperLink control twice: once from its initial location to the location occupied by the *Button1* control, and a second time from the initial location for *Button1* back to the initial position for *HyperLink1*. Clicking the Refresh button moves the HyperLink control back to its initial position on the page's form.

The second challenge to moving controls around a Web page stems from the fact that Web pages have no memory in transit from a browser to a server (unless special measures are taken). Therefore, simply copying the DHTML *style* attribute settings for the control tags on a Web page to a memory variable in the code behind the page does not solve the problem—even if you define the variable at the module level—because the values of the memory variable are normally lost in transit from a browser to a server. Numerous techniques can help you work around this issue.

This sample demonstrates a simple and relatively familiar technique for Visual Basic developers. It uses the *Shared* access keyword to declare the memory variables for storing *style* attribute settings for the *Button1* and *HyperLink1* controls. This approach has the advantage of using a technique that emerges from your Windows (and even classic Visual Basic) programming experience. The *Shared* access modifier in Visual Basic .NET behaves similarly to the *Static* keyword in classic Visual Basic in that both ways of declaring a variable enable the variable to maintain values over the lifetime of an application.

The sample application stores the original *style* attribute settings for the *Button1* and *HyperLink1* controls in the *str1* and *str2* memory variables, respectively. This enables the writing over of the original *HyperLink1 style* attribute setting with the original attribute setting for *Button1*. The saved memory variables also enable the restoring of the original *style* attribute setting for the *HyperLink1* control.

After the module-level declaration of the *str1* and *str2* memory variables with *Shared* access modifiers, the sample listing shows the code for the *Page_Load* event procedure. This event procedure is identical to the *Page_Load* event for the preceding sample, except for the setting of the *Text* property for the new Button control with a value of *Refresh*. This button refreshes the page's form without displaying the dialog box that appears in Figure 10-5.

The *Button1_Click* procedure is almost entirely new. The *If...Then...Else* statement that comprises the core of this procedure saves the *style* attributes for the *Button1* and *HyperLink1* controls and saves the original *style* attribute for the *Button1* control over the original attribute setting for the *HyperLink1* control. The copying of the *style* attribute for *Button1* to the style attribute for *HyperLink1* is what causes the *HyperLink1* control to move to the position occupied by the *Button1* control. To avoid distracting users with *Button1* in the background behind *HyperLink1* and to ensure that clicks do not activate *Button1*, the application disables *Button1* and makes it invisible.

The *Button2_Click* procedure handles the refresh operation for the application. If the initial message for the *Label1* control is visible, the application simply exits. Otherwise, the procedure performs a sequence of restore operations to refresh the application. In the end, the *Button1* control is visible again and works as it did initially.

```
Shared str1 As StringShared str2 As String

Private Sub Page_Load(ByVal sender As System.Object, _
    ByVal e As System.EventArgs) Handles MyBase.Load

    'If not posted back, set initial conditions
    If Not IsPostBack Then
        Button1.Text = "Hello again"
        Button2.Text = "Refresh"
        Me.Label1.Text = "This is my initial hello."
    End If

End Sub

Private Sub Button1_Click(ByVal sender As System.Object, _
    ByVal e As System.EventArgs) Handles Button1.Click

    'If showing updated message and attribute store
    'is empty, disable/hide Hello again button and
    'move hyperlink in place of button; otherwise
    'assign updated message to Label1
    If Me.Label1.Text = "Hi, again." And _
        str1 = "" Then
        Button1.Visible = False
        Button1.Enabled = False
        str1 = Me.Button1.Attributes("style")
        str2 = Me.HyperLink1.Attributes("style")
        Me.HyperLink1.Attributes("style") = str1
    Else
        Me.Label1.Text = "Hi, again."
    End If

End Sub

Private Sub Button2_Click(ByVal sender As System.Object, _
    ByVal e As System.EventArgs) Handles Button2.Click

    'If initial message showing, ignore click;
    'otherwise, restore controls on and behind
    'HelloRefresh web form
    If Me.Label1.Text = _
```

```
            "This is my initial hello." Then
            Exit Sub
    Else
        'Restore attribute with position settings
        Me.HyperLink1.Attributes("style") = str2

        'Restore other conventional button
        'and label properties
        Me.Button1.Visible = True
        Me.Button1.Enabled = True
        Me.Label1.Text = "This is my initial hello."

        'Restore attribute stores
        str1 = ""
        str2 = ""
    End If

End Sub
```

Logging In to a Protected Page Sample

The final sample in this chapter demonstrates a simple version of a security-by-form sample. The purpose of the sample is to demonstrate how to use *Session* variables to manage state—that is, variables associated with some aspect of an application, such as the whole application, a user's session, or even values for an individual form outside the control values that ASP.NET automatically persists for your applications. This particular application remembers whether a user input *MemberID* and *Password* values. If the user did set these *Session* variables, the application checks their values to authenticate the user. *Session* variables are ideal for this kind of an application because their lifetime is the duration of a session. Furthermore, a user can have values for his *MemberID* and *Password* variables that differ from another user's values. A user logs out by closing the browser session or after a fixed period of inactivity (typically 20 minutes).

Figure 10-8 shows an overview of the sample's design. The design spans four Web pages. Two likely pages from which users can enter the application are the ASPNETMenu.aspx page and the LoginPage.aspx page. If a browser session opens on the ASPNETMenu.aspx page without first setting *MemberID* and *Password Session* variables, the application reminds the user of the missing values and offers a link to the LoginPage.aspx page. The LoginPage.aspx page contains two text box controls for accepting the login information and some code behind the page's form for saving the contents of the text boxes as *Session* variables. If the user inputs invalid *MemberID* or *Password* values, the application sends her to a page describing the problem with a link to the LoginPage.aspx page so that she can correct the problem. Users can exit the application at any page, but the pages informing users about missing *Session* variable values or invalid *Session* variable values are particularly appropriate. For example, a message on each page can contain a telephone number for requesting further assistance, such as help for remembering a forgotten password.

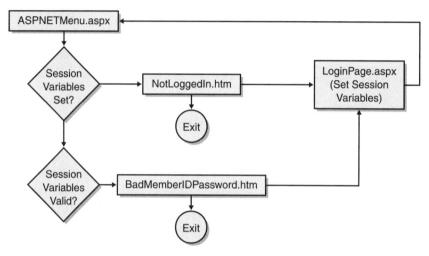

Figure 10-8   A flowchart indicating the logic for the sample demonstrating the use of *Session* variables

Two pages serve as the foundation of the sample application. The LoginPage.aspx page lets a user designate *Session* variables. The ASPNET-Menu.aspx page uses the *Session* variables in two tests. The code behind both of these pages is critical to the application. The NotLoggedIn.htm and Bad-MemberIDPassword.htm pages are basic Web pages with text messages containing a hyperlink.

The LoginPage.aspx Web Page

Figure 10-9 shows a Browse window view of the form for the LoginPage.aspx file. The two TextBox controls accept values for the two *Session* variables that authenticate the user in the current browser session. Clicking the Login button saves the *Text* property value of each TextBox control in a *Session* variable and transfers control to the ASPNETMenu.aspx page.

> **Note**   The purpose of this sample is to introduce you to *Session* vari-
> ables—not to demonstrate best practices for a login application. In a
> practical application, you will want to encrypt at least the *Password*
> value that you pass from a browser client to a Web server.

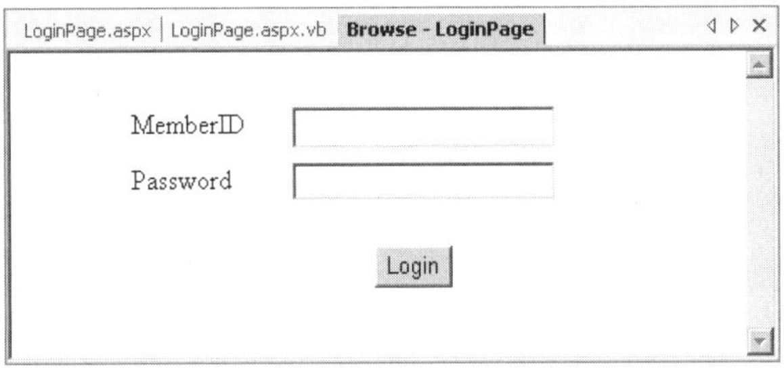

Figure 10-9   A basic custom login page for an ASP.NET Web application

Two short event procedures exist behind the form in Figure 10-9. The *Page_Load* procedure merely assigns *Text* property values for controls on the form. You might be wondering why these assignments are conditional on the *IsPostBack* property of the current *Page* instance being *False*. After all, you might think that a user should log in just once during a session. No matter how reasonable this assumption, nothing in the application requires only one user per session. If a user knows multiple valid *MemberID* and *Password* values, he can successively log in with these values in a single session.

The application invokes the *Button1_Click* procedure when a user clicks the Login button on the form shown in Figure 10-9. The first two lines of the procedure assign the *Text* property values for *TextBox1* and *TextBox2* to *MemberID* and *Password Session* variables. As you can see, the syntax is straightforward. The procedure's third and final line transfers control to the ASPNETMenu.aspx page in the current application. The line uses the *Redirect* method of the *Response* object. The *Redirect* method transfers control to a new URL. The method acts similarly to a hyperlink that a user does not have to click. Because ASPNETMenu.aspx resides in the current folder, you do not need to designate a path. A more general format for the string argument of the *Redirect* method is *http://path/pageinpath.xxx*, in which *xxx* denotes the extension type, such as aspx or htm.

```
Private Sub Page_Load(ByVal sender As System.Object, _
    ByVal e As System.EventArgs) Handles MyBase.Load

    'Set text property values for labels
    'and button
    If Not IsPostBack Then
        Label1.Text = "MemberID"
        Label2.Text = "Password"
        Button1.Text = "Login"
    End If

End Sub

Private Sub Button1_Click(ByVal sender As System.Object, _
    ByVal e As System.EventArgs) Handles Button1.Click

    'Assign text box contents to two
    'Session variables
    Session("MemberID") = TextBox1.Text
    Session("Password") = TextBox2.Text
    Response.Redirect("ASPNetMenu.aspx")

End Sub
```

The ASPNETMenu.aspx Web Page

The ASPNETMenu.aspx page is a simple menu implemented with hyperlinks. Figure 10-10 shows the page in Design view from within Visual Studio .NET. To add a hyperlink to a Web page, select the text for the hyperlink and choose Insert, Hyperlink. The Hyperlink dialog box lets you type the destination URL for the hyperlink or browse to the desired page. The Properties window in Figure 10-10 shows that the third hyperlink is selected because it points at the LoginPage.aspx file on the ccs1 Web server, which is an intranet server in my office. Because the page includes just text, including a header for the menu and the hyperlink text, this page is a likely candidate for using a *FlowLayout* setting for the *pageLayout* property and a *ShowGrid* property value of *False*. When you select a *FlowLayout* setting, the Web Forms Designer automatically sets the *ShowGrid* property to *False*. The *FlowLayout* property setting permits you to add text to a page without embedding it in controls and to manage the text as you would any text in a word processor.

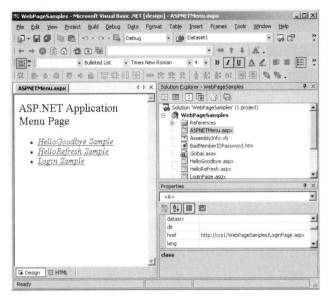

Figure 10-10   A basic menu page implemented with hyperlinks but with
ASP.NET code behind it

What makes the ASPNETMenu.aspx page special is the code behind it. As the flowchart in Figure 10-8 indicates, the page poses two questions about the *MemberID* and *Password Session* variables. First, the page asks whether the variables have assigned values. Second, the page assesses whether the *MemberID* and *Password Session* variables are valid. The *Page_Load* procedure in ASPNETMenu.aspx has two code blocks. The first block shows one approach to handling the first question. If either *Session* variable is an empty string, the default value, the procedure transfers control to the NotLoggedIn.htm page. The second code block authenticates the values in the two *Session* variables. The code accepts just two sets of *MemberID/Password* pairs as valid. These are *Rick/123* and *Virginia/456*. Either of these value pairs entered in *TextBox1* and *TextBox2* on the LoginPage.aspx page prompts the menu of hyperlinks in the ASPNETMenu.aspx page to appear. Any other value pairs transfer control to the BadMemberIDPassword.htm page.

> **Note** A user can specify either a *MemberID* or a *Password Session* variable without designating the other *Session* variable. The application identifies this result as a not-logged-in condition instead of a bad-memberid-password one. This choice of functionality is not important in the current context because the discovery of either condition offers a chance to log in again.

```
Private Sub Page_Load(ByVal sender As System.Object, _
    ByVal e As System.EventArgs) Handles MyBase.Load

    'If no Session variables for MemberID or Password,
    'redirect to NotLoggedIn.htm page
    If Session("MemberID") = "" Or Session("Password") = "" Then
        Response.Redirect("NotLoggedIn.htm")
    End If

    'Authenticate login credentials
    If Session("MemberID") = _
        "Rick" And Session("Password") = "123" Then
        'ok
    ElseIf Session("MemberID") = _
        "Virginia" And Session("Password") = "456" Then
        'ok
    Else
        Response.Redirect("BadMemberIDPassword.htm")
    End If

End Sub
```

Figure 10-11 shows the two information Web pages in the sample application. Each page includes a statement about the problem and a link that points at the LoginPage.aspx where you can remedy the problem. Both pages in Figure 10-11 are standard HTML pages. You can create them in Visual Studio .NET by choosing Project, Add HTML Page. Then, change the *pageLayout* property setting to *FlowLayout*. After making that setting, you can edit text on the pages just as you would with any word processing document. Alternatively, you can create and manage the pages within a program that can create text messages with hyperlinks.

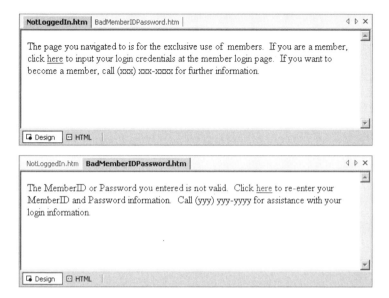

Figure 10-11   A pair of informational pages in the login sample application

Summary

This chapter introduced ASP.NET programming techniques. First, the chapter presented a conceptual review of important ASP.NET programming notions. This background gave you the foundation needed to develop and deploy ASP.NET Web solutions. In addition, you learned about special issues relating to Web development, including properties for the *Page* class and controls on Web Forms. Three samples reinforced and extended the basic Web programming issues presented at the beginning of the chapter. The chapter's concluding sample demonstrated one approach to authenticating users for a Web application with ASP.NET.

11

Implementing ADO.NET on ASP.NET Pages

This chapter builds on the introduction to ASP.NET given in Chapter 10. Chapter 10 provided general background information on ASP.NET without considering ADO.NET issues. This chapter completes the picture for Microsoft Access developers by adding ADO.NET to the mix. The aim of this chapter is to show you how to apply what you already know about the .NET Framework to creating Web applications for your Access databases. Extending Access beyond the confines of Microsoft Windows applications makes your Access databases available to a wider audience of users on a flexible basis. (For example, you can connect via an intranet, an extranet, or the Internet.)

After a brief overview that highlights special issues associated with data processing on Web pages, this chapter presents a series of four samples. These samples take a progressive approach to implementing Web-based data processing tasks. The first sample demonstrates how to create data access solutions with the Data Form Wizard. This is an important technology for those who want to build a solution without writing code or who need a quick and dirty way of prototyping a solution. The next sample demonstrates how to build data access solutions with graphically created ADO.NET objects. Using graphically created ADO.NET objects reduces—but does not eliminate—the coding requirements for a solution. You will have more flexibility in designing page layouts with this approach than with the Data Form Wizard. The third sample illustrates how to use programmatically created ADO.NET objects for data access while illustrating a flexible way of specifying search criteria. The final sample in the chapter presents a Web-based approach to the three classic data manipulation tasks: inserts, updates, and deletes.

Overview of Data Processing with ASP.NET

This section introduces several considerations that can improve your design of Web applications that use data. By this point in the book, you should already have a grasp of the tools that you need for creating data-based solutions on Web pages. In particular, Chapter 10 introduced the elements of ASP.NET application design. Chapters 7 through 9 drilled down on creating data-based solutions with the .NET Framework. Although Chapters 7 through 9 targeted Windows applications, the basic understanding of ADO.NET developed in these chapters applies equally well to Web applications.

At a conceptual level, this section describes special issues that can arise when creating Web applications that use databases. The section concludes with a brief introduction to validation controls that can improve the performance of your Web applications by improving the quality of data that browsers send to a Web server.

Three-Tiered Architecture

Using ASP.NET to manage databases via ADO.NET automatically creates a three-tiered solution, which consists of the following:

- The ASP.NET page in the Web browser
- The Web server
- A database file

The first tier, the ASP.NET page in the Web browser, provides a mechanism for displaying data deposited on a Web page created by the operation of the other two tiers. In addition, the first tier enables users to pass commands along to the Web server through control event procedures that generate a roundtrip of the ASP.NET page between the browser and the Web server.

The second tier, the Web server, processes a page during a roundtrip between itself and a browser. Note that the Web server is not a database or a database manager. Therefore, the Web server does not contain or process data. Typically, the Web server passes commands for data processing to the ADO.NET component of the .NET Framework. For example, the Web server can use ADO.NET connection, command, and data adapter objects to populate a dataset on a Web page. By designing SQL strings with variables based on control property values, you can create dynamic systems.

SQL strings representing data commands operate in the third tier—the database. When working with Access databases, the third tier will be an Access database file. You should locate your Access database files on the Web server for processing via ASP.NET and ADO.NET. This location guideline for an Access database file also applies to Active Server Pages (ASP) and ActiveX Data Objects (ADO). The samples in this chapter use an OLE DB .NET Data Provider for the explicit purpose of working with Access database files. However, you can also adapt the samples to work with client/server database managers, such as Microsoft SQL Server. When working with client/server databases, the database can reside on a computer other than the Web server. In any event, you use the connection string argument for an ADO.NET *Connection* object to connect to a database.

ADO.NET and ASP.NET

The fact that a Web server connects to data via ADO.NET means that all the knowledge that you acquired for use with ADO.NET and Windows applications applies to Web applications. (See Chapters 7 through 9 for more on this topic.) You can drag and drop ADO.NET objects from the Toolbox onto a Web page just as you can with a form in a Windows application. In addition, you can use standard Microsoft Visual Basic .NET to program ASP.NET database solutions. Therefore, you have the flexibility to instantiate ADO.NET database objects at run time. Beyond that, you can use wizards such as the Data Form Wizard to expedite the creation of Web solutions that require data access.

Despite all these similarities between Windows applications and Web applications, some important differences exist. For example, the Data Form Wizard automatically senses when it is running in a Web application and adjusts its functionality. In particular, the wizard enables data access only via a Data-Grid control. Beyond that, the wizard does not enable any kind of data manipulation. Therefore, if your Web application requires inserts, updates, or deletes, you must programmatically add this functionality.

When creating ADO.NET solutions for Web pages, you must consider the impact of roundtrips and control event procedures. During each roundtrip a Web page makes between a browser and a Web server, the Web server reconstructs the page and all objects on it, including any datasets. As a result, the number of datasets on a Web page and their size impact the responsiveness of the page. In addition, the number of roundtrips that an application engenders affects the overall responsiveness of an application. Minimizing roundtrips makes an application feel faster. For these reasons, you should use small datasets and Web controls that maximize the display of data without requiring roundtrips to view more data.

For example, a DataGrid control shows multiple rows without having to return to the server to show another row. Therefore, you can improve the performance of your Web applications by using a DataGrid control instead of using a collection of text boxes with Button controls that enable scrolling through data. Although you can use a DataGrid control for data manipulation, many developers will find using text boxes a more familiar approach. When using TextBox controls to facilitate data manipulation, consider using unbound controls. Using unbound controls speeds the performance of your application by eliminating the processing of a dataset for each update, insert, or delete task.

Built-In Data Validation Tools

The toolbar for Web applications features a collection of tools that help to validate data on a Web page. You can use these tools with or without programming. In addition, the programming can take place on the Web server or on the client. Five types of built-in data validation controls exist. These controls are built into .NET applications just like a text box. Therefore, the data validation controls can deliver some functionality without requiring a roundtrip to the Web server. A data validation control can block the uploading of a page until a user meets a certain requirement. The validation controls generate error messages that either appear next to a control they validate or in a central area for the whole Web page.

The five types of validation controls for Web pages enable you to specify a required field, a range, or a format for the value in another control on a Web page. If your needs are specialized, you can even build your own custom validation controls. For a validation control, you must specify a value for the *ControlToValidate* property. This property specifies the control to which a validation control applies. For example, you can use a RequiredFieldValidator control to necessitate the input of an e-mail address before permitting the roundtrip of a Web page between a browser and a Web server. These validation controls enable you to save roundtrips for incorrectly completed Web pages. Table 11-1 summarizes the five types of validation controls.

Table 11-1   Validation Controls for Web Pages

Validation Control Class Name	Description
RequiredFieldValidator	Detects a missing value for a validated control.
CompareValidator	Enables the comparison of a validated property via an operator (for example, a greater-than or less-than operator). This control also permits you to verify the data type of an entry in a validated control.
RangeValidator	Confirms whether a value for a validated control falls in a specified range.

Table 11-1   Validation Controls for Web Pages

Validation Control Class Name	Description
RegularExpressionValidator	Permits you to specify the rejection of values that are not in a specified format, including pre-built format specifications for items such as telephone numbers as well as your own custom specifications.
CustomValidator	Allows you to develop custom validity specifications not handled by any of the preceding built-in controls.

Validation controls are not an ADO.NET topic because they are controls for a Web page. Therefore, this chapter does not address them further because its aim is to focus on using ADO.NET with Web pages. You can find additional information on validation controls in the Microsoft Visual Studio .NET documentation under the "Developing a Validator Control" topic. In addition, my prior .NET book, *Programming Microsoft SQL Server 2000 with Microsoft Visual Basic .NET* (Microsoft Press, 2002), demonstrates graphical and programmatic ways of using validation controls. Because validation controls apply to the other controls on a Web page, the samples in that book apply equally well to Access and SQL Server databases.

Creating Solutions with the Data Form Wizard

The Data Form Wizard offers you a fast and easy way to build ADO.NET solutions. This speed and efficiency is even more pronounced with Web applications than with Windows applications because the wizard offers fewer options for Web applications. This section walks you through the steps for creating a data-based Web page with the Data Form Wizard. Then, the section demonstrates a couple of programmatic strategies for customizing the code generated by the Data Form Wizard. Follow these samples to stimulate your imagination for ways to customize and extend the data-based Web pages created by the Data Form Wizard.

Building a Solution with the Wizard

Using the Data Form Wizard is one way to prove how easy it is to get started building data-based Web applications. It is common in Web applications to let users display a table or datasheet and browse it. With the Data Form Wizard, creating this kind of application is as easy as making a handful of selections from a succession of dialog boxes. Making these selections creates a dataset and adds Button and DataGrid controls to a Web page. This sample uses the VBDotNetShippers table originally added to the Northwind database in Chapter 9. See the "Browsing and Manipulating Data with a Form" section in Chapter 9 for step-by-step instructions on adding (or reinitializing) the table to the Northwind database.

Note   All the samples from this chapter are available in the Web-DataSamples project included with this book's sample files. Web projects have two project folders: one resides on the Web server in its Inetpub folder's wwwroot directory, and the other typically is located at the local default directory for storing Visual Studio .NET projects. This second folder contains the .sln file for loading the application into Visual Studio .NET for editing.

After creating a new ASP.NET Web Application in Visual Studio .NET, you can start the Data Form Wizard by choosing Project, Add New Item. Then, highlight the Data Form Wizard icon in the Templates pane, and click Open. If this is your first use of the wizard in a Web application, the wizard specifies a default name of DataWebForm1.aspx for the Web page. Clicking Open accepts the default name and presents the wizard's Welcome screen. Click Next to arrive at the screen that allows you to designate a dataset for the Web page. Enter **DatasetDFW** as the name of the dataset in the text box below the radio button with a label of Create A New Dataset Named. The selections from the wizard screens will create a typed dataset with this name and add the dataset to the project folder on the Web server. Clicking Next presents a screen from which you can select from the list of preconfigured database connections in Server Explorer. If the connection that your Web page needs does not appear in the drop-down list on the wizard's second screen, click the New Connection button. This opens the Data Link Properties dialog box. Adapt the instructions in the "Adding a Data Connection to Server Explorer" sidebar in Chapter 2 to specify your new connection.

After specifying the connection for your dataset, click Next. This lets you pick one or more tables and views to provide data for a member in the dataset. (A *member* is another name for a *DataTable* object in a dataset.) For this sample, select the VBDotNetShippers table in the Northwind database. If the table does not already exist (it is a custom table), follow the instructions for creating it in the "Adding a Data Connection to Server Explorer" sidebar in Chapter 2.

The last screen for this sample lets you pick a subset of columns from the table. This sample uses all the columns in the table. Click Finish to complete the creation of the DataWebForm1.aspx Web page and add it to the project folder on the Web server. Solution Explorer shows the Web page file. Visual Studio .NET also presents the Design view of the page. Figure 11-1 shows this view, which includes a button in a table above a DataGrid control. The tray below the Web page shows the ADO.NET objects created by the Data Form Wizard. The *objDatasetDFW* variable in the tray points at the *DatasetDFW* dataset created by the Data Form Wizard selections. In addition, the DataGrid control appears with custom formatting. Notice the formatting for the column headers.

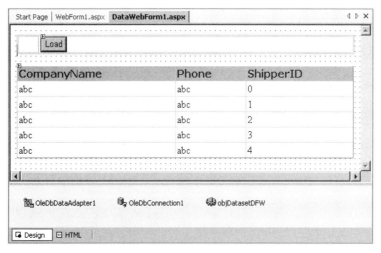

Figure 11-1   The Design view of a Web page automatically created with a few clicks in the Data Form Wizard

Right-clicking DataWebForm1.aspx in Solution Explorer and choosing Build And Browse compiles the page and opens a fresh copy of the page in a Browse window in Visual Studio .NET. This Browse window enables you to preview the operation of the page in a browser. Initially, only the Load button appears. The DataGrid control does not appear because it has no link to a data source. In essence, the control has no data to show. Clicking the Load button fills the *objDatasetDFW* dataset and binds it to the DataGrid control. This displays the current copy of the VBDotNetShippers table from the Northwind database in the DataGrid control on the page. I reinitialized the VBDotNetShippers table as described in "Browsing and Manipulating Data with a Form" section of Chapter 9 so that the table resembles Figure 11-2.

Figure 11-2 The VBDotNetShippers table from the Northwind database showing in the Web page from Figure 11-1

The Load button in DataWebForm1 is good for more than just initially populating the DataGrid control on the page. In a multiuser application (which is what Web applications typically are) users can click Load to refresh the contents of the DataGrid control to reflect the most recent updates to a database application. Therefore, remote users connecting to the database via the Web page can get the latest revisions made by an in-house staff connecting to the same database with both data access and data manipulation capabilities.

Note If you receive an error message when you attempt to run DataWebForm1 that indicates either you don't have permission to access the database file or the file cannot be locked, you need to adjust your security settings on the folder that contains the database file. In Windows Explorer, right click on the folder that contains the Northwind.mdb file. By default this is the Samples folder under C:\Program Files\Microsoft Office\Office10 for Access 2002 and C:\Program Files\Microsoft Office\Office for earlier versions of Access. Select Properties from the context menu. In the Samples Properties dialog box, select the Security tab. Click Add to add a group. In the Select Users, Computers, Or Groups dialog box, select the server on which the Northwind.mdb file is located as the location. Enter **ASPNET** in the Enter The Object Names To Select box and click Check Names. Click OK. Give the new group read and write permissions.

Editing the HTML Behind a Wizard Page

Notice in Figure 11-1 that the Web page has both Design and HTML views. In fact, the HTML view precisely formats the Web page. Even without an in-depth grasp of HTML, adventurous Visual Basic .NET developers can make minor changes to the HTML behind a Web page to reformat the page in subtle ways. For example, Figure 11-2 shows the column header CompanyName without a space between the two words because the Data Form Wizard creates a column header that matches the data field name for the column in a data grid. However, you can modify the *HeaderText* property settings for one or more columns after the Data Form Wizard creates the HTML code for the DataWebForm1.aspx page. This approach enables you to benefit from the automatic design interface provided by the Data Form Wizard but still perform some customization beyond the standard page layout.

You can expose the HTML behind a Web page by clicking the HTML button shown in Figure 11-1. The following excerpt shows a segment of the code generated by the Data Form Wizard for the page shown in Figure 11-2. The general format of HTML is to use an opening and closing tag with other tags optionally embedded between them. Within any tag, you can have zero or more attributes. In HTML, tags correspond roughly to Visual Basic .NET objects, and attributes function similarly to properties. Most of the tags in the following excerpt wrap across multiple lines. For example, the opening *asp:DataGrid* tag extends across four lines.

Within the *asp:DataGrid* opening and closing tags are *Columns* tags. Three *asp:BoundColumn* tags reside within the *Columns* tags. Each *asp:BoundColumn* tag has a couple of attributes. One of these attributes has the name *HeaderText*. For the *asp:BoundColumn* tag with a *DataField* attribute of *CompanyName*, introduce a space between *Company* and *Name* in the corresponding *HeaderText* attribute. After inserting the space, save the page. Then, right-click the page in Solution Explorer, and choose Build And Browse. This opens the page with the new *HeaderText* attribute setting with the CompanyName column from the VBDotNetShippers table.

```
<asp:DataGrid runat="server" DataKeyField="ShipperID" PageSize="5"
 AutoGenerateColumns="False" Height="50px" Width="100%"
 DataMember="Shippers" ID="masterDataGrid" CellPadding="2"
 DataSource='<%# objDatasetDFW %>'>
    <Columns>
        <asp:BoundColumn DataField="CompanyName"
         HeaderText="CompanyName">
```

(continued)

```
        </asp:BoundColumn>
        <asp:BoundColumn DataField="Phone" HeaderText="Phone">
        </asp:BoundColumn>
        <asp:BoundColumn DataField="ShipperID" HeaderText="ShipperID">
        </asp:BoundColumn>
    </Columns>
    <HeaderStyle Font-Names="Verdana" Font-Bold="True" Height="10px"
     ForeColor="Black" BackColor="Silver">
    </HeaderStyle>
</asp:DataGrid>
```

Editing the Visual Basic Code Behind a Wizard Page

Another way of leveraging the code generated by the Data Form Wizard is to edit the Visual Basic .NET code behind the form. DataWebForm1.aspx does not initially show the DataGrid control until a user clicks the Load button. In many applications, you want the data to be available when the form opens—especially with a page such as DataWebForm1.aspx, whose sole purpose is to show data. To achieve this functionality, simply move the code behind the click event for the Load button to the load event for the Web page.

If you select the Load button in Design view, you can determine from the Properties window that its *ID* property is *buttonLoad*. Therefore, the button click event procedure has the name *buttonLoad_Click*. Double-clicking the Load button in Design view opens the Code window for DataWebForm1 to the *buttonLoad_Click* procedure. This window also shows that the *Page_Load* procedure is empty (except for a default comment). To cause the DataWebForm1.aspx page to open with data showing in its DataGrid control, move the code from the *buttonLoad_Click* event procedure shell to the *Page_Load* event procedure shell. The following listing shows how the *Page_Load* event procedure looks after the move. The *buttonLoad_Click* procedure is, of course, empty after the move.

```
Private Sub Page_Load(ByVal sender As System.Object, _
    ByVal e As System.EventArgs) Handles MyBase.Load

    Try
        Me.LoadDataSet()
        Me.masterDataGrid.SelectedIndex = -1
        Me.masterDataGrid.DataBind()
    Catch eLoad As System.Exception
        Me.Response.Write(eLoad.Message)
    End Try

End Sub
```

After the preceding edit, the page opens with data showing in its DataGrid control. However, there is no code behind the Load button. You have a couple of options at this point. First, you can select the button in Design view and either delete it or set its *Visible* property to *False* in the Properties window. Alternatively, you can copy the code in the *Page_Load* procedure into the click event procedure shell for the *buttonLoad_Click* procedure, which restores the *buttonLoad_Click* procedure to its initial state. At this point, it probably makes sense to revise the *Text* property setting for the Load button to *Refresh*.

Using Graphically Created ADO.NET Objects

Web users demand Web pages that are pleasing to the eye and feature interesting content. Because good looks are in the eye of the beholder, you need to be able to format the appearance of your Web controls programmatically based on user input. With run-time control over the formatting of a Web page, users can customize a page until it looks right to them. Allowing users to customize the appearance of controls is one way of engaging visitors so that they stay at a site longer or visit more site pages.

The sample in this section, which appears in the WebForm1.aspx page, has a couple of objectives. First, it shows how to use graphical ADO.NET tools to manage the content appearing on a Web page. By tying the content of a page to a database, you enable the content to automatically adjust whenever the underlying data changes. This approach minimizes transcription errors and reduces the labor needed to keep pages current. Second, the sample code in this section enables users to dynamically format a Web page. In addition, you will see ways of formatting a page that do not require user interaction.

Design and Operation Page Views

Figure 11-3 shows the Design view of the Web page. Notice that the page consists of three Button controls over a DataGrid control. Below the Web page is a tray that holds three ADO.NET objects. The *OleDbConnection1* and *OleDbDataAdapter1* icons were generated by dragging the VBDotNetShippers table from Server Explorer to the Web page in Design view. After selecting only the *OleDbDataAdapter1* icon, you can generate a dataset by right-clicking the variable for the data adapter (*OleDbDataAdapter1*) and choosing Generate Dataset. If this is your first dataset on the Web page, Visual Studio .NET automatically suggests a New name of *DataSet1*. When you click OK, Visual Studio .NET inserts the dataset named *DataSet1* in Solution Explorer and the *DataSet11* icon appears in the tray below the Web page. The

DataSet11 icon represents a variable pointing at the *DataSet1* dataset. Your Visual Basic .NET code behind the Web page can refer to any of the objects in the tray below the page.

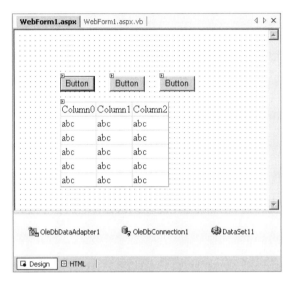

Figure 11-3   A Web page enabling programmatic control over the formatting of a DataGrid control in the *Page_Load* and click event procedures for three buttons

Figure 11-4 shows a pair of windows demonstrating the formatting after the page initially opens (top window) and after a click to the button on the far left (bottom window). Carefully contrasting the top window in Figure 11-4 with the form's Design view shown in Figure 11-3 reveals several formatting touches. First, the column headers appear in bold. Beyond that, the column headers are right aligned. This is particularly evident in the second column, which has a heading of Phone. The item values in the body of the DataGrid control are also right aligned. The buttons permit two ways of formatting. It is obvious that the *Text* property was distinctly assigned to each Button control because the controls have different captions, but the *Width* property of each Button control was set to 75 pixels. Without this assignment of the *Width* property, the width of buttons would vary depending on the *Text* property assignment. By assigning the same value to the *Width* property of each Button control, the application creates a more uniform appearance for the buttons on the Web page.

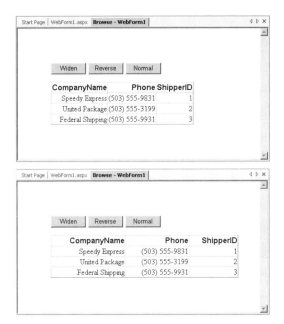

Figure 11-4   Two operational views with different settings for the Data-Grid control's *Width* property

The bottom window in Figure 11-4 reveals one transformation of the page's appearance. This format for the window appears after a click to the Widen button. Clicking the button (*Button1*) widens the overall DataGrid control to a width of 400 pixels, which is about one-third greater than its initial width. This transformation has the effect of more sharply visually defining the first and second columns in the DataGrid control. In addition, the bottom window makes it evident that all three columns are right aligned.

The second and third buttons on the page's form apply a format and restore a base format. By default, the DataGrid control appears with a black foreground on a white background; this is the base format. Clicking *Button2*, which has a *Text* property of *Reverse*, flips these settings so that the foreground is white and the background is black. A click of *Button3*, which has a *Text* property of *Normal*, restores the base format of a black foreground on a white background. The top window in Figure 11-5 shows the DataGrid control on the page after a click to *Button2*, revising the foreground and background colors from their appearance in the bottom window of Figure 11-4.

Because I clicked *Button 2* after clicking *Button1*, the DataGrid control is relatively wide. However, the reversal of background and foreground colors occurs independently of the change in the *Width* property setting for the DataGrid control. Therefore, you can reverse the background and foreground colors with the DataGrid control at its default width or at its expanded width. The bottom window in Figure 11-5 shows the restored black-on-white display of the DataGrid control.

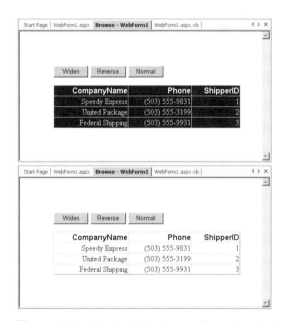

Figure 11-5 A pair of windows with contrasting background and foreground colors for a DataGrid control

The Code Behind the Web Page

The code listing for the module behind the WebForm1 Web page starts with a module-level variable declaration and includes four procedures—a *Page_Load* procedure and three click event procedures for *Button1* through *Button3*. The module-level variable declaration is for a *Style* object named *stl1*, which gets used for different styles in each of the click event procedures. A *Style* object holds a collection of property settings that can impact the appearance of a Web server control, such as a DataGrid control. As you have learned, you drag a Web server control to a Web page from the Web Forms tab on the Toolbox. To use a *Style* object, you first define the cluster of property settings in a style. Then, you apply the *Style* object to the item that you want to reflect the property settings in the *Style* object.

The *Page_Load* Procedure

The *Page_Load* procedure starts with three lines that specify the data for the Web page. These lines draw on the graphically generated ADO.NET objects that appear in the tray at the bottom of Figure 11-3. The first line defines and fills the VBDotNetShippers *DataTable* object in the *Dataset11* dataset. As you can see, the line relies explicitly on the *OleDbDataAdapter1* object. This object was added to the tray at the bottom of Figure 11-3 by dragging the VBDotNetShippers table icon from Server Explorer to the Web page. The *OleDbDataAdapter1* object depends on the *OleDbConnection1* object to collect data from the Northwind database. Filling the VBDotNetShippers *DataTable* object does not require any control on the Web page to show one or more values from the *DataTable* object. The second two lines of code enable the *DataGrid1* control to display the values in the VBDotNetShippers table. The first of these lines assigns the VBDotNetShippers *DataTable* object to the *DataSource* property for the *DataGrid1* control. The second line invokes the *DataBind* method for the control so that the *DataTable* object appears in the control.

The balance of the *Page_Load* procedure addresses formatting issues. The first code block following the code handling the data for the page demonstrates the syntax for manipulating the *HeaderStyle* object for a DataGrid control. The *HeaderStyle* object acts as a *Style* object for a segment of the DataGrid control—namely, the row of column headers defining the control's first row. The code block assigns three settings to the row. First, the code block right-aligns the text within each column. Second, the code assigns an Arial font to the row. This distinguishes the row from those containing the default font, Times New Roman, for the body of the DataGrid control. The code block concludes by setting the font to bold to further distinguish the column headers from the values in the body of the DataGrid control.

The next code block contains just one line. This line applies a single style setting to the body of the DataGrid control. The setting right-aligns the text in the control's body. The line's syntax illustrates how you can use the *ItemStyle* object for a DataGrid control to accomplish this task. The DataGrid control's *ItemStyle* object applies to the body of the values in the control just as the *HeaderStyle* object applies to the row of column headers.

The last two code blocks in the *Page_Load* procedure apply to the Button controls on the Web page. The first code block simply applies the *Text* property values for the buttons. The second block demonstrates a new syntax for assigning a width of 75 pixels to each of the buttons. This code block creates a uniform appearance across the buttons regardless of the length of the *Text* property setting for a button. The Button control exposes its own *Width* property. Therefore, you do not need a *Style* object to set a button's *Width* property. The most important point to note is the syntax for designating a length. The syntax starts with the *Unit* structure followed by the *Pixel* method. You set the *Value* property for the *Unit* structure by specifying a number in parentheses following the method name expressing the unit of measurement. This number designates the number of units of the specified length to set a property.

```
'Instantiate a style
Dim stl1 As Style = New Style()

Private Sub Page_Load(ByVal sender As System.Object, _
    ByVal e As System.EventArgs) Handles MyBase.Load

    'Fill DataSet11
    OleDbDataAdapter1.Fill(DataSet11, "VBDotNetShippers")

    'Set DataSource property for data grid control
    'and bind data grid control to data for viewing
    DataGrid1.DataSource = DataSet11.VBDotNetShippers
    DataGrid1.DataBind()

    'Format column headers
    DataGrid1.HeaderStyle.HorizontalAlign = _
        HorizontalAlign.Right
    DataGrid1.HeaderStyle.Font.Name = "Arial"
    DataGrid1.HeaderStyle.Font.Bold = True

    'Format grid items
    DataGrid1.ItemStyle.HorizontalAlign = _
        HorizontalAlign.Right

    'Assign Text property values
    Button1.Text = "Widen"
    Button2.Text = "Reverse"
    Button3.Text = "Normal"

    'Assign constant Width value so buttons
    'have same width regardless of Text
    'property value
    Dim int1 As Integer = 75
    Button1.Width = Unit.Pixel(int1)
    Button2.Width = Unit.Pixel(int1)
    Button3.Width = Unit.Pixel(int1)

End Sub
```

Button Click Event Procedures

Three click event procedures enable application users to dynamically modify the appearance of the Web page with the DataGrid control. It is no secret that users find interactivity an engaging feature. The trick is to make it a no-brainer for developers so that it costs little to nothing to provide the benefit. The *Style* object might be part of this solution. The click event procedures for *Button1*, *Button2*, and *Button3* illustrate how easy it is to let users change the appearance of a Web page at run time.

The *Button1_Click* procedure lets users widen the DataGrid control from its default width. The procedure achieves this result with just two lines of code. The first line defines a style that specifies a *Width* property setting for the *Style* object. You'll recognize the syntax for specifying the *Width* property because the *Page_Load* procedure demonstrated it to specify a width for the buttons on the page's form. Unfortunately, the DataGrid control does not have a *Width* property, but you can assign a *Width* property for a *Style* object and then apply that *Style* object to the DataGrid control with the *ApplyStyle* method. In addition to the *Width* property, you can set the *BackColor*, *BorderColor*, *BorderStyle*, *BorderWidth*, *ForeColor*, and *Height* for a *Style* object. You can also designate a *FontInfo* object through the *Font* property that nests within a *Style* object and then assign properties for the *FontInfo* object, such as *Name*, *Size*, *Italic*, *Bold*, and *Underline*.

The *Button2_Click* and *Button3_Click* procedures show you how to toggle the background and foreground colors for displaying a DataGrid control. Visual Basic .NET offers a wide selection of colors through the *Color* structure of the *System.Drawing* namespace. You can assign any of these colors to the *ForeColor* and *BackColor* properties of a *Style* object. After making an assignment for the *Style* object properties, your application can show its effect by invoking the *ApplyStyle* method for a control, which is *DataGrid1* in this sample. The top and bottom windows in Figure 11-5 hint at the dramatic effects you can achieve by manipulating color in your applications.

```
Private Sub Button1_Click(ByVal sender As System.Object, _
    ByVal e As System.EventArgs) Handles Button1.Click

    'Set to fixed width of 400 pixels
    stl1.Width = Unit.Pixel(400)

    'Apply a style to the control
    DataGrid1.ApplyStyle(stl1)

End Sub
```

(continued)

```
Private Sub Button2_Click(ByVal sender As System.Object, _
    ByVal e As System.EventArgs) Handles Button2.Click

    'Designate reverse contrast for fonts
    stl1.ForeColor = System.Drawing.Color.White
    stl1.BackColor = System.Drawing.Color.Black

    'Apply a style to the control
    DataGrid1.ApplyStyle(stl1)

End Sub

Private Sub Button3_Click(ByVal sender As System.Object, _
    ByVal e As System.EventArgs) Handles Button3.Click

    'Designate black-on-white appearance
    stl1.ForeColor = System.Drawing.Color.Black
    stl1.BackColor = System.Drawing.Color.White

    'Apply a style to the control
    DataGrid1.ApplyStyle(stl1)

End Sub
```

Using Programmatically Created ADO.NET Objects

One of the most common types of Web applications is one that lets users specify one or more search arguments that determine a result set from a database. This section illustrates an approach to handling this type of application requirement. From a .NET development perspective, the sample in this section differs in an important way from the one in the preceding section. Instead of using graphical tools to specify ADO.NET objects such as *Connection*, *DataAdapter*, and *DataSet*, this sample specifies these objects programmatically. Specifying the objects programmatically rather than graphically requires only a little more code, but the payoff is big if you plan to reuse the approach elsewhere (for example, in another project). Simply copy the code, and your application will work in another context.

When you use graphically created ADO.NET objects, you have to re-create the steps for instantiating ADO.NET objects manually. This, of course, introduces the possibility of variations between contexts. In addition, I find it tedious to follow the graphical steps. If you are of the same mindset, you will find creating ADO.NET objects programmatically an attractive alternative. Chapters 7 through 9 illustrate multiple techniques for programmatically specifying ADO.NET objects.

Design and Operational Page Views

The sample application in this section works with the Customers table in the Northwind database. Users can generate a result set of customers by specifying a country, city, or both for the customers that they want to examine. In fact, users can type only the first letter or any number of letters at the beginning of the name of a country or city, and the application will return all matching rows from the Customers table. The application populates a DataGrid control with a result set after a user clicks the Search button. The DataGrid control shows CustomerID, CompanyName, ContactName, Phone, City, and Country column values for each row in the result set. Figure 11-6 displays a result set based on first letter arguments for both the country and city arguments.

> **Note**   The column headers in the result set do not appear in alphabetical order, which is the default for graphically created ADO.NET objects. Instead, the columns appear in the order that you specify in the SELECT statement for the result set.

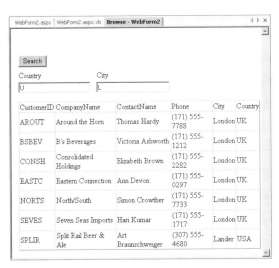

Figure 11-6   A result set on a Web page based on partial inputs for the country and city arguments

Figure 11-7 shows a Design view of the Web page, which is available as WebForm2.aspx in the WebDataSamples project. The DataGrid control appears below the two TextBox controls for gathering search arguments. Notice that no tray appears below the Web page because the application does not use any graphically specified ADO.NET objects. The Button control allows a user to launch a search after inputting characters in the first or second text box.

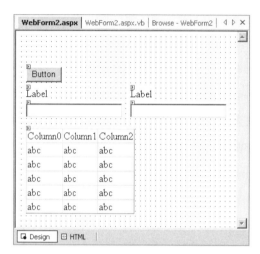

Figure 11-7   The Design view for a Web page enabling lookups based on user inputs to either text box

The Code Behind the Web Page

The code behind the Web page for the sample application consists of three module-level declarations and a pair of event procedures—one for the *Page_Load* event and the other for the click event of the Search button (*Button1*). The three module-level statements declare and instantiate *Connection*, *DataAdapter*, and *DataSet* ADO.NET objects. Actually, only one of these objects (*cnn1*) strictly requires a module-level declaration because it gets used in two or more procedures. However, it is good practice when developing applications with ADO.NET objects to declare them at the module level (unless you are sure that the ADO.NET objects have limited scope). This precaution makes it simple to use the objects in as many procedures as necessary.

The *Page_Load* procedure has two code blocks. One is inside the *If...Then* statement that executes once when the *Page* object initially loads. This block assigns *Text* property values to the *Button1* control and the two Label controls for the text boxes on the Web page. This code needs to run only once because the .NET Framework automatically restores the initial *Text* property settings on subsequent roundtrips of the Web page between the browser and the server. The *cnn1 OleDbConnection* object does not automatically persist between roundtrips. Therefore, the code for managing the *cnn1* connection string runs each time the *Page_Load* event fires.

> **Note**   You can use *Session* variables to persist objects such as ADO.NET objects between roundtrips of a Web page from a browser to a server and back. See Chapter 10 for more in-depth coverage of *Session* variables and a code sample demonstrating their use. This section's sample does not use *Session* variables so that we stay focused on simple declaration techniques for ADO.NET objects.

All the major work for this sample takes place in the *Button1_Click* procedure, and even that code is remarkably straightforward. The most devious task is to get the *CommandText* property for the *cmd1 OleDbCommand* object specified correctly, based on the input to the text box for country (*TextBox1*) and the text box for city (*TextBox2*). An *If…Then…ElseIf…Else* statement handles the assignment. With two text boxes, four possible input states exist. Three of these include having a value in one or both text boxes; the fourth state occurs when neither text box contains a value.

The *Then* and two *ElseIf* clauses handle cases in which a user makes an entry in either or both text boxes. The syntax for the *CommandText* property assignments shows how to use the LIKE operator. This operator permits a user to input any number of characters at the beginning of a name for a country or a city. The *Else* clause of the *If…Then…ElseIf…Else* statement handles the case in which a user clicks the Search button without inputting anything in either text box. This clause writes a message to the Web page by invoking the *Write* method for the *Response* object. The message reminds the user to input something in one or both text boxes. After displaying the message in the *Else* clause, the procedure clears the data source for the DataGrid control and binds the control to the data source. These steps clear any prior result set values showing in the DataGrid for validly entered country or city arguments.

> **Note**   The LIKE operator in the *CommandText* SQL statement uses a percent sign (%) wildcard symbol to designate the asterisk (*) wildcard symbol that Access developers regularly use. ADO uses the % wildcard symbol in a similar fashion.

If a user makes a valid entry in either text box, the procedure then applies the *cmd1* object in code following the *If...Then...ElseIf...Else* statement. Putting the *cmd1* object to use involves two tasks. First, the procedure fills the local *Customers DataTable* object in the *das1* dataset with a subset of the rows selected by the *CommandText* property for the *cmd1* object. Next, the procedure binds the *DataGrid1* control to the *DataTable* object in the *das1* dataset. Because this sample uses an untyped dataset declared at run time, it features a different syntax than the preceding sample for designating a *DataTable* object within a dataset. The prior sample used a dot notation (*datasetname.datatablename*) because it relied on a typed dataset declared at run time. The correct syntax for this sample references the *Tables* collection for the *das1* dataset with an index designating the name of the *DataTable* object (*Customers*).

```
Dim cnn1 As New OleDb.OleDbConnection()
Dim dap1 As New OleDb.OleDbDataAdapter()
Dim das1 As New System.Data.DataSet()

Private Sub Page_Load(ByVal sender As System.Object, _
    ByVal e As System.EventArgs) Handles MyBase.Load

    'When page first opens
    If Not IsPostBack Then

        Button1.Text = "Search"
        Label1.Text = "Country"
        Label2.Text = "City"

    End If

    'Re-assign connection string for current opening
    'of the page
    Dim str1 As String = _
```

```
        "Provider = Microsoft.Jet.OLEDB.4.0;"
    str1 &= _
        "Data Source = c:\Program Files\" & _
        "Microsoft Office\Office10\Samples\Northwind.mdb"
    cnn1.ConnectionString = str1

End Sub

Private Sub Button1_Click(ByVal sender As System.Object, _
    ByVal e As System.EventArgs) Handles Button1.Click

    'Assign CommandText property value based on Text
    'property values for TextBox1 and/or TextBox2; if
    'Text property is missing for both controls, display message
    'to user asking to specify at least one Text property
    Dim cmd1 As New OleDb.OleDbCommand()
    With cmd1
        .Connection = cnn1
        If TextBox1.Text <> "" And TextBox2.Text = "" Then
            .CommandText = _
                "SELECT CustomerID, CompanyName, " & _
                "ContactName, Phone, City, Country " & _
                "FROM Customers " & _
                "WHERE Country LIKE '" & TextBox1.Text & "%'"
        ElseIf TextBox1.Text = "" And TextBox2.Text <> "" Then
            .CommandText = _
                "SELECT CustomerID, CompanyName, " & _
                "ContactName, Phone, City, Country " & _
                "FROM Customers " & _
                "WHERE City LIKE '" & TextBox2.Text & "%'"
        ElseIf TextBox1.Text <> "" And TextBox2.Text <> "" Then
            .CommandText = _
                "SELECT CustomerID, CompanyName, " & _
                "ContactName, Phone, City, Country " & _
                "FROM Customers " & _
                "WHERE Country LIKE '" & TextBox1.Text & _
                "%' AND " & _
                "City LIKE '" & TextBox2.Text & "%'"
        Else
            Response.Write( _
                "Please input the beginning of a city or " & _
                "a country.")
```

(continued)

```
            das1.Clear()
            DataGrid1.DataBind()
            Exit Sub
        End If
    End With

    'Fill Customers DataTable object in dap1
    'DataAdapter object
    dap1.SelectCommand = cmd1
    dap1.Fill(das1, "Customers")

    'Bind DataGrid1 control to Customers DataTable object
    DataGrid1.DataSource = (das1.Tables("Customers"))
    DataGrid1.DataBind()

End Sub
```

Insert, Update, or Delete from a Web Page

The last sample in this chapter demonstrates an approach to performing data manipulation from a Web page by using ADO.NET objects and a DataGrid control. The sample enables a user to insert, update, and delete rows from the VBDotNetShippers table in the Northwind database. This table, initially used in the section "Browsing and Manipulating Data with a Form" in Chapter 9, is a copy of the Shippers table that lets your application manipulate a table without modifying the original Shippers table in the Northwind database.

Design and Operational Page Views

One especially easy way to grasp the substance of this application is to see it in action. The application enables the three basic data manipulation tasks while listing the most recent data from the VBDotNetShippers table.

Inserting a Row

Figure 11-8 shows the insert function in operation. In the top window, you can see the CompanyName and Phone column values for a new row in the VBDot-NetShippers table. The new column values appear in the second and third text boxes on the left side of the Web page. In addition, the cursor rests on the Insert button. After a user clicks the Insert button, the application updates the page, as shown in the bottom window in Figure 11-8. The values in the text boxes move to the DataGrid control, which is bound to the VBDotNetShippers table in the Northwind database.

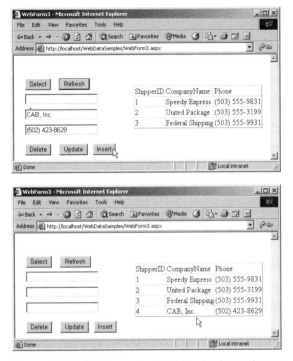

Figure 11-8   The impact of clicking the Insert button

The sample application does not move the column values from the text boxes directly to the DataGrid control. Instead, the click event procedure for the Insert button first adds a new row to the VBDotNetShippers table in the Northwind database with the column values showing in the text boxes. The database creates a new autonumber field value (which supplies the ShipperID value) for the new row. Then, the application refreshes the local VBDotNet-Shippers *DataTable* object to reflect the new version of the VBDotNetShippers table in the Northwind database. Finally, the application rebinds the DataGrid control to the updated local *DataTable* object. In the process of refreshing the local *DataTable* object, the application clears the TextBox controls in the form on the Web page.

Updating a Row

Updating a row is a two-step process. First, you have to select a row by entering its ShipperID column value in the first text box and clicking Select. This populates the remaining two text boxes with the corresponding CompanyName and Phone column values. The top window in Figure 11-9 shows this result—actually, the CompanyName column value appears after updating. Using the column values in the text boxes, you can modify the column values for the selected row. For example, the second text box shows the removal of ", Inc." from the CompanyName column value for the row with a ShipperID value of 4. Clicking the Update button in the top window of Figure 11-9 transforms the Web page to the one in the figure's bottom window. Notice that the row for ShipperID 4 appears without an *Inc.* within the CompanyName column value.

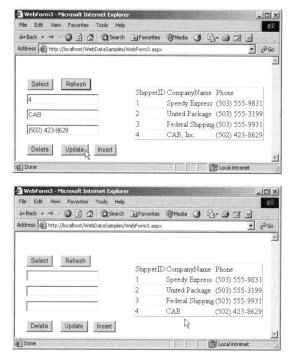

Figure 11-9   The impact of clicking the Update button

As with the Insert button, the impact of clicking the Update button is the result of a multistep process. First, clicking the Update button revises the VBDotNetShippers table in the Northwind database. Second, the application refreshes the local *DataTable* object based on the new version of the table in the database. Finally, the sample rebinds the DataGrid control to the updated *DataTable* object and clears the text boxes.

Deleting a Row

Removing a row from the DataGrid control is straightforward. The user merely enters the ShipperID column value for the row to be removed and then clicks the Delete button. These actions update the background table in the database, the local *DataTable* object, and ultimately the appearance of the DataGrid control. Figure 11-10 shows the deletion of a row in process. The top window shows the entry of the ShipperID for the row with a ShipperID column value of 4. After a click to the Delete button, the Web page transforms as shown in the bottom window.

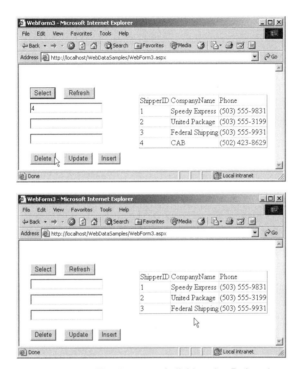

Figure 11-10   The impact of clicking the Delete button

Design View of the Web Page

Figure 11-11 presents the Design view for the Web page shown in various operational views in Figures 11-8, 11-9, and 11-10. The main reason for presenting the Design view is to identify the elements on the Web page so that you can follow the code behind the Web page. As you can see, the page features three TextBox controls with two Button controls above them and three more Button controls below them. A DataGrid control appears to the right of the text boxes.

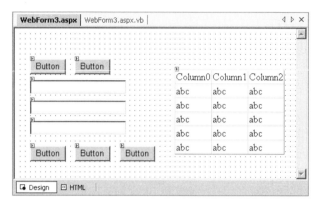

Figure 11-11   A Design view of a Web page for inserts, updates, and deletes

You refer to a control on a Web page programmatically by its *ID* property value. The DataGrid control has the *ID* property value of *DataGrid1*. The three TextBox controls on the page (from top to bottom) have *ID* property settings of *TextBox1*, *TextBox2*, and *TextBox3*. The two *Button* controls above the text boxes have *ID* property values of *Button1* and *Button5*, from left to right. The three *Button* controls below the text boxes have *ID* settings of *Button2*, *Button3*, and *Button4*, from left to right.

The Code Behind the Web Page

The code behind this Web page is intentionally easy to understand. The code integrates a collection of basic ADO.NET and Visual Basic .NET design techniques to perform a set of a common database tasks via a Web connection. By enabling these tasks over a Web connection, the code vastly expands the potential base of users. This is because Web applications do not require the .NET Framework on client workstations, and client computers need not be on a physical LAN. You should, of course, authenticate users before granting them access to a system that lets users manipulate a database. The "Logging In to a Protected Page Sample" section in Chapter 10 presents a basic sample demonstrating how to control access to a Web session via a login process In addition, Chapter 13 focuses on security issues for Access databases in .NET applications.

The code behind the Web page consists of module-level declarations for the ADO.NET objects (*cnn1*, *dap1*, and *das1*), a *Page_Load* procedure, event procedures for each Button control, and a collection of supporting *Sub* and *Function* procedures called by the event procedures. The *Page_Load* procedure features two main code blocks. Within an *If...Then* statement that has *Not IsPostBack* as a condition, you can find the page setup code that needs to execute just once. This code assigns *Text* and *TabIndex* property settings for controls on the Web page. You can use the *TabIndex* property to specify the tab order of controls on a Web page (and a Windows Forms instance). Outside the *If...Then* statement is code for a *Connection* object and a call to the *Refresh Sub* procedure. This *Sub* procedure populates the *DataGrid1* control with the most recent data on the VBDotNetShippers table in the Northwind database.

The *Button1_Click* procedure populates *TextBox2* and *TextBox3* with CompanyName and Phone column values for the row with a ShipperID column value matching the value in *TextBox1*. This capability supports the editing of CompanyName and Phone column values. The application does not support edits to ShipperID column values because the Access database controls this column with an autonumber setting. The *Button1_Click* procedure works with the local *DataTable* object to which the *DataGrid1* control binds. One modification you could make to this procedure would be to add a primary key for the ShipperID column. By making this change, you can use the *Find* method instead of a loop. However, when working with a *DataTable* object that has only a few rows (as in the current sample), you are not likely to gain much advantage by using a primary key.

The click event procedures for *Button2*, *Button3*, and *Button4* have a parallel design, although they support substantially different functions. All the procedures execute a SQL statement to update the VBDotNetShippers table in the Northwind database. In addition, each procedure refreshes the Web page to reflect these changes. Two *Sub* procedures support these capabilities. The *RunSQLString* procedure executes the SQL statement represented by a *String* value. The code for the *RunSQLString* procedure invokes the *ExecuteNonQuery* method to execute the SQL statement, and it manages the opening and closing of the *cnn1 Connection* object around the use of the method. You should leave *Connection* objects open only when they are necessary for a task. The *ClearAllAndRefresh* procedure begins by clearing the dataset (*das1*) to which the *DataGrid1* control binds. Then, the procedure invokes the *Refresh* procedure to repopulate the *DataGrid1* control based on the modification implemented by the SQL statement. The *ClearAllAndRefresh* procedure closes by clearing any values appearing in the TextBox controls. This prepares the Web page for any additional data manipulation.

The uniqueness of the event procedures for each of these three Button controls (*Button2*, *Button3*, and *Button4*) resides primarily in the SQL statement specifying the type of change to make in the VBDotNetShippers table. All three procedures assign a different SQL string to the *str1* variable. The *Button2_Click* procedure demonstrates the syntax for deleting a row based on the ShipperID value in *TextBox1*. The *Button3_Click* procedure shows a syntax for changing the CompanyName and Phone column values of a row specified by the ShipperID value in the *TextBox1* control. The *Text* property values for the *TextBox2* and the *TextBox3* controls specify the revised column values. The *Button4_Click* procedure illustrates the syntax for adding a new row to the VBDotNetShippers table with CompanyName and Phone column values equal to those in the *TextBox2* and *TextBox3* controls. Because the ShipperID column is an autonumber field, you should not designate a value for it.

Within any multiuser application, you need to account for the actions of other users. Other users can affect how or whether a SQL statement should execute. In the current application, you have no need to worry about other users for inserts because the Access database automatically assigns a unique ShipperID value for each new row. However, it is possible for another user to remove the row with a ShipperID value that a user then tries to change or delete. This is because the application relies on optimistic concurrency, which is common for .NET applications and good practice for Web applications that need to support many users.

Accounting for the actions of other users is often highly specific to the needs of a particular application. The sample application in this section checks for the existence of a row by calling the *IsThere Function* procedure. If the procedure returns a value of *True*, the *Button2_Click* and *Button3_Click* procedures proceed to implement either a delete or an update. This level of checking is sufficient for low to moderate levels of data manipulation. If you have a high volume of delete and update transactions that can potentially conflict with one another, you should apply another strategy to ensure that a row is not deleted after you check for its presence but before you operate on it. This is an issue for updates because you cannot modify a row that does not exist. If you try to delete a row that is missing, the application proceeds without an error and updates the *DataGrid1* control to show the row as missing.

At least two strategies for handling concurrency issues with updates are available. First, you can wrap the *IsThere* function call and the *RunSQLString* call in a transaction. This will guarantee a lock on a row from the point at which you check whether it exists until you implement your update. However, this benefit can generate other concurrency issues, such as a row being unavailable to other users while the lock is in effect. A second approach for handling concurrency issues is to write updates with additional information about the identity of the user and the time of the change to a special table. Then, the application can update the main table from the special table during a time of lower transaction volume.

The *Button5_Click* procedure is the least complicated of any of the button click event procedures. This procedure merely calls the *ClearAllAndRefresh*

procedure. In a multiuser application, this process gives any user a chance to
see changes made to the database by other users since the last time that a page
was refreshed. If you plan to update or delete a row, it is a good idea to click
the Refresh button (*Button5*) before attempting to change the database.

```
Dim cnn1 As New OleDb.OleDbConnection()
Dim dap1 As New OleDb.OleDbDataAdapter()
Dim das1 As New System.Data.DataSet()

Private Sub Page_Load(ByVal sender As System.Object, _
    ByVal e As System.EventArgs) Handles MyBase.Load

    'Initialize page
    If Not IsPostBack Then

        'Assign Text property values for buttons
        Button1.Text = "Select"
        Button2.Text = "Delete"
        Button3.Text = "Update"
        Button4.Text = "Insert"
        Button5.Text = "Refresh"

        'Assign TabIndex property for controls
        Button1.TabIndex = 2
        TextBox1.TabIndex = 1
        TextBox2.TabIndex = 3
        TextBox3.TabIndex = 4
        Button2.TabIndex = 5
        Button3.TabIndex = 6
        Button4.TabIndex = 7
        Button5.TabIndex = 8

    End If

    'Re-assign connection string for current opening
    'of the page
    Dim str1 As String = _
        "Provider = Microsoft.Jet.OLEDB.4.0;"
    str1 &= _
        "Data Source = c:\Program Files\" & _
        "Microsoft Office\Office10\Samples\Northwind.mdb"
    cnn1.ConnectionString = str1

    'Invoke Refresh to populate grid control
    Refresh()

End Sub
```

(continued)

```
Sub Refresh()

    'Instantiate connection string
    Dim cmd1 As New OleDb.OleDbCommand()

    'Return all rows from the VBDotNetShippers
    'table from the Northwind database
    With cmd1
        .Connection = cnn1
        .CommandText = _
            "SELECT * FROM VBDotNetShippers"
    End With

    'Fill VBDotNetShippers DataTable object in dap1
    'DataAdapter object
    Dim dap1 As New OleDb.OleDbDataAdapter(cmd1)
    dap1.Fill(das1, "VBDotNetShippers")

    'Bind DataGrid1 control to VBDotNetShippers DataTable object
    DataGrid1.DataSource = (das1.Tables("VBDotNetShippers"))
    DataGrid1.DataBind()

End Sub

Private Sub Button1_Click(ByVal sender As System.Object, _
    ByVal e As System.EventArgs) Handles Button1.Click

    'Populate TextBox2 and TextBox3 with CompanyName
    'and Phone column values for designated
    'ShipperID in TextBox1
    Dim int1 As Integer
    For int1 = 0 To das1.Tables(0).Rows.Count - 1
        If das1.Tables(0).Rows(int1)(0) = _
            CInt(TextBox1.Text) Then
            TextBox2.Text = das1.Tables(0).Rows(int1)(1)
            TextBox3.Text = das1.Tables(0).Rows(int1)(2)
        End If
    Next

End Sub

Private Sub Button2_Click(ByVal sender As System.Object, _
    ByVal e As System.EventArgs) Handles Button2.Click

    'Trap for missing row in database table
    If IsThere(TextBox1.Text) = False Then
        Response.Write("DELETE exit trap")
        Exit Sub
    End If
```

```
    'Specify update SQL string
    Dim str1 As String = _
        "DELETE FROM VBDotNetShippers " & _
        "WHERE ShipperID=" & TextBox1.Text

    'Run SQL String
    RunSQLString(str1)

    'Clear controls and refresh from Northwind
    ClearAllAndRefresh()

End Sub

Private Sub Button3_Click(ByVal sender As System.Object, _
    ByVal e As System.EventArgs) Handles Button3.Click

    'Trap for missing row in database table
    If IsThere(TextBox1.Text) = False Then
        Response.Write("UPDATE exit trap")
        Exit Sub
    End If

    'Specify update SQL string
    Dim str1 As String = _
        "UPDATE VBDotNetShippers " & _
        "SET CompanyName='" & TextBox2.Text & "', " & _
        "Phone='" & TextBox3.Text & _
        "' WHERE ShipperID=" & TextBox1.Text

    'Run SQL String
    RunSQLString(str1)

    'Clear controls and refresh from Northwind
    ClearAllAndRefresh()

End Sub

Private Sub Button4_Click(ByVal sender As System.Object, _
    ByVal e As System.EventArgs) Handles Button4.Click

    'Specify insert SQL string
    Dim str1 As String = _
        "INSERT INTO VBDotNetShippers " & _
        "(CompanyName, Phone) VALUES('" & _
        TextBox2.Text & "', '" & TextBox3.Text & _
        "')"
```

(continued)

```
    'Run SQL String
    RunSQLString(str1)

    'Clear controls and refresh from Northwind
    ClearAllAndRefresh()

End Sub

Private Sub Button5_Click(ByVal sender As System.Object, _
    ByVal e As System.EventArgs) Handles Button5.Click

    'Clear controls and refresh from Northwind
    ClearAllAndRefresh()

End Sub

Function IsThere(ByVal str1) As Boolean

    Dim cmd1 As New OleDb.OleDbCommand()
    Dim int1 As Integer

    'Run SQL statement to determine if ShipperID
    'column value exists
    With cmd1
        .Connection = cnn1
        .CommandText = _
            "SELECT * FROM VBDotNetShippers " & _
            "WHERE ShipperID=" & str1
        cnn1.Open()
        int1 = .ExecuteScalar
        cnn1.Close()
    End With

    'Return True if int1 is greater than 0
    If int1 > 0 Then Return True

End Function

Sub RunSQLString(ByVal str1 As String)

    'Instantiate OleDbCommand object
    Dim cmd1 As New OleDb.OleDbCommand()

    'Assign Connection and CommandText property
    'values before invoking the command
    With cmd1
```

```
            .Connection = cnn1
            .CommandText = str1
            cnn1.Open()
            .ExecuteNonQuery()
            cnn1.Close()
        End With

End Sub

Sub ClearAllAndRefresh()

    'Clear local DataTable object and
    'repopulate from Northwind database
    das1.Clear()
    Refresh()

    'Clear text boxes
    TextBox1.Text = ""
    TextBox2.Text = ""
    TextBox3.Text = ""

End Sub
```

Summary

This chapter introduced you to the basics of data access and data manipulation in Web applications. It began with an overview of what is special about Web applications for data processing. Then, it presented a series of four samples that depicted progressively more sophisticated techniques for processing data in Web applications. The chapter concluded with a sample that demonstrated how to perform inserts, updates, and deletes and monitor the impact of changes by others through a DataGrid control.

12

Programming XML Web Services

Microsoft Visual Basic .NET takes advantage of XML Web services technology to multiply the impact of your Microsoft Access databases. In essence, this technology allows you to expose your Access databases over the Web. However, the client application project for an Access database exposed via XML Web services can be either a Microsoft Windows application or a Web application. The Web connection serves strictly as a channel for passing arguments and returning data. XML Web services enable the transformation of Access databases to client/server applications from file server applications. This can occur because the XML Web services technology always works with two applications—an XML Web service application and a client application. The client application invokes remote procedures in the XML Web service application, and the XML Web service application optionally passes back data to the client application. When XML Web services work with Access databases, it is natural to retrieve data and perform processing in the XML Web service component. This approach can dramatically simplify client programming needs and offer you all the other benefits of .NET development, such as vastly improved scalability.

This chapter offers a practical guide to XML Web services that builds on the basic understanding of the .NET Framework you gained in earlier chapters. The initial section offers a quick overview of the underlying technologies for XML Web services. It is amazing how much the Microsoft Visual Studio .NET IDE dramatically simplifies the use of these technologies so that you can focus on creating your solution. The next section demonstrates how to build a client application for an existing Web service. This section illustrates how to create a

Web client and a Windows client. In the process, you will see how a Web reference represents a Web service in a client application and how a proxy variable points at a Web service through a Web reference. The next section demonstrates how to build your own Web service and create client applications for it. In addition to learning how to code your Web service, you will see how to easily test it.

The next to the last section addresses the topic of deploying a Web service from a development computer to a production computer. The approach outlined in this section is particularly appropriate for large to mid-sized organizations that have staging computers for development purposes only. The chapter concludes with a sample application for using an Access database in a Web service. The Web service performs a lookup for a single column value in a row, for a collection of rows, and for a computed value across multiple rows from a join of two tables. You will learn how to isolate these functions via Web methods and put them to use in a client application.

Underlying Technologies

This section introduces the topic of XML Web services at two levels. The section begins with a brief statement explaining the functionality that XML Web services bring to your applications. Next, the section examines four key underlying technologies. Most of you will not use these technologies directly. Instead, you will create and use XML Web services through Visual Studio .NET. Visual Studio .NET will manipulate these underlying technologies for your XML Web services. Nevertheless, a basic grasp of these technologies will round out your understanding of XML Web services and using them to create solutions for clients with Visual Studio .NET.

Quick Synopsis of XML Web Services

As mentioned, XML Web services comprises a new collection of capabilities for developers that facilitate interoperability between computers via a Web connection. A specific XML Web service can allow one computer to remotely invoke a method—or more precisely, a Web method—on another computer. The technology promises to interface applications built with heterogeneous development environments (for example, Visual Basic .NET on Windows and Java on UNIX). In fact, leading industry firms such as IBM and Microsoft have embraced XML Web services. However, even if XML Web services cannot completely interface applications built with heterogeneous development environments, it will deliver important benefits to both large and small development organizations because XML Web services technologies offer a simple model to implement distributed computing. Therefore, even small organizations can easily share data among computers, even when those computers do not reside on a LAN. In addition, small development organizations can offer value-added services to larger organizations at lower prices that attract more clients.

> **Note**   XML Web services is commonly referred to as *Web services*. I will follow this convention for the balance of the chapter.

At its core, Web services employs a peer-to-peer computing model. One computer provides a service such as a computation, and another computer consumes a service—for example, by providing input for the computation or using the result of a computation. In essence, a Web service is a class that you can run on another computer via a Web connection. The two computers commonly will connect to one another via HTTP, but the Web services model is abstracted so that other connection types can serve this role. A Web service exposes Web methods that enable a client application to manipulate the class running on the computer hosting the Web service. The computers hosting a Web service and its clients have no special requirements other than needing Microsoft Internet Information Services (IIS) installed and running, and needing the .NET Framework installed. For example, in a pair of computers, each can host a Web service for the other computer; a primary domain Web services computer is not needed. In this model, a computer can be both a Web service provider and a Web service client.

XML

XML is rapidly becoming the lingua franca of Web services and many other computing technologies. In the context of XML Web services, XML is the syntax for exchanging data between the hosting and client computers. Although it is not strictly necessary for a host computer to accept data from or return data to a client computer, it is likely that the host computer participates in one or both of these activities (receiving data and returning data). For example, a client computer can pass information—such as an authentication code and a monetary amount to transfer from one account to another—to a host computer of a financial institution. The host computer can validate the authentication code, perform the account transaction, and return a confirmation of the transfer.

Actually, Web services do not exchange data in stand-alone XML documents. The XML containing the data that a host and client computer exchange resides within Simple Object Access Protocol (SOAP) messages that the two computers exchange. Before computers can exchange information, the client computer needs to know about the Web service's input and output arguments. Another XML syntax, known as the Web Services Description Language (WSDL), describes the Web service, including the SOAP message format for exchanging content between the hosting computer and the client computer. I will briefly describe SOAP and WSDL in a moment.

UDDI

Given that you have a Web service available for use on a host computer, client computers need a way of discovering its availability. UDDI, which stands for Universal Description, Discovery, and Integration, is one technology for addressing this need. The UDDI technology enables the registration of Web services in directories that users can search. The directories allow users to discover your Web services, along with Web services provided by other companies, that provide the kind of functionality they seek for applications they create. Through UDDI, a user not only can discover a Web service but can get the WSDL document describing the Web service. You can learn more about UDDI from the Web site that support its standards, *http://www.uddi.org*.

Exactly how clients will discover and select Web services remains to be determined. One way is through directories such as UDDI. You can also discover a Web service by word of mouth or by internal communications within an organization. Departments within a large organization can disseminate information about Web services that they create. For example, a shipping department could publish a Web service for validating postal codes based on street addresses, cities, and states. The marketing department could provide a comparable service for validating e-mail addresses. By leveraging the computing talent within individual departments, Web services offer organizations a way to enjoy the benefits of decentralized organization while providing valuable corporate-wide resources.

WSDL

Web Services Description Language, or WSDL, is an XML grammar for describing a Web service. Every computer hosting a Web service must have a WSDL document for describing the Web service. When a client computer adds a reference to a Web service, it gets a copy of the WSDL document for the Web service. The WSDL document describes the Web methods exposed by a Web service. The WSDL document also contains a specification of the SOAP message for passing arguments to and returning arguments from a Web service. The World Wide Web Consortium (W3C) manages the evolution of the WSDL grammar. At the time of this writing, you can use the following URL to tap into the Web services activities of the W3C: *http://www.w3.org/2002/ws/.*

SOAP

SOAP is a computer protocol for exchanging information in a distributed computing environment. This is the major Web services technology enabling interaction among applications developed with heterogeneous computing systems or even among computers running disparate operating systems, such as Windows and UNIX.

The SOAP specification for exchanging information between computers has three main elements. First, the SOAP processing model defines the rules for exchanging information between a SOAP sender and a SOAP receiver. The SOAP message can pass through one or more intermediaries between the sender and the ultimate receiver. The processing model handles multiple types of exchanges, such as those transmitted from a sender to a receiver without a return response or those passed from sender to receiver with a return response. The second major element of the SOAP specification is the model for a SOAP document. This element defines the types of XML elements and attributes that compose a SOAP document, such as the SOAP message. The third element of the SOAP specification is the manner in which the SOAP documents are bound to an underlying protocol for transmitting messages between sender and receiver computers. At the time of this writing, the W3C is finalizing SOAP version 1.2. You will find the latest document specifying this set of SOAP standards at *http://www.w3.org/TR/soap12-part1/.*

Using a Web Service

A large number of Web services projects will involve the construction of a client application. At least a couple of reasons for this exist. First, the use of a Web service requires a client application. You do not execute a Web service without a client application, except in test mode. A Web service typically has no user interface. Furthermore, one Web service can have multiple client applications. These multiple client applications can expose various Web methods within a Web service or can offer the full set of Web methods available from a Web service in various environments. As an example, this section shows two clients that apply to a single Web service. The first client is a Web application. The second client is a Windows application. You use the same general approach to the construction of each client application.

Building a Web Application Client for a Web Service

To start the construction of the Web application, create a new ASP.NET Web Application project named WebZipCodeClient. Before you can build a client for a Web service, the client application needs a reference to the Web service. Several variations for building this reference exist. When the reference exists in a UDDI registry, you can select it from the registry. This sample draws on a Web service to resolve zip codes based on a street address, city, and state, along with an access code. At the writing of this chapter, the Web service we're using in this example resides in the Test Microsoft UDDI Directory. Microsoft makes this UDDI directory available as a test registry for Web service demonstration projects. The Web services in the registry are provided by third-party organizations.

Adding a Web Reference to a Project

Choose Project, Add Web Reference to show the Add Web Reference dialog box. The left pane contains a link to the Test Microsoft UDDI Directory. Click the link. Next, you need to enter the name of a third-party organization supplying the Web service. EraServer.Net is the name of the third-party organization supplying the zip code resolver for the current application. Therefore, type **EraServer.Net** in the Business Name text box, and click Search. Scroll down the resulting list in the left pane until you see EraServer.Net:ZipCodeResolver. Click the expand button (+) to expose the tModel for the Web service. A tModel uniquely identifies a Web service within a UDDI registry.

Figure 12-1 shows the cursor pointing at the description of the Zip-CodeResolver Web service. A small box opens to display the URL or port for accessing the Web service, *http://webservices.eraserver.net/zipcoderesolver/zip-coderesolver.asmx*. The .asmx file is the access point for the Web service. Clicking the name of the tModel opens in the left pane of the Add Web Reference dialog box the WSDL script that describes the Web service. One important role of the WSDL script is to define a contract for the Web service. For example, the contract states that if a client application invokes one Web method with a list of arguments, the Web service will return a result in a specific format, but if a user invokes another Web method within the Web service, the client will return a different result in another format. Therefore, the WSDL script serves as a contract between a Web service and its client applications.

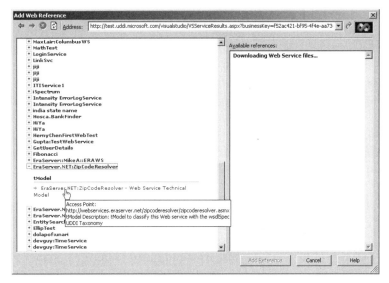

Figure 12-1 The Add Web Reference dialog box exposing the tModel for a Web service that resolves zip codes

Clicking the Add Reference button in the dialog box adds a reference named net.eraserver.webservices to the WebZipCodeClient project. This reference appears in Solution Explorer as a subfolder within the Web References folder. The net.eraserver.webservices reference contains two entries pointing at files: Reference.map and zipcoderesolver.wsdl. The Reference.map file designates the entry point for the Web service on the host computer. As mentioned, this point is an .asmx file. The zipcoderesolver.wsdl file contains the WSDL script that describes the Web service. Visual Studio .NET uses the contents of the Reference.map and zipcoderesolver.wsdl files when your application invokes Web methods through a proxy object that points at the Web service. The proxy object exposes in a client application the Web methods for a remote Web service hosted on another computer.

> **Note** Web services do not require that the host computer and client computer be two separate computers. However, you do not need Web services for a one-computer scenario because you can simply reference a class that is already on a computer. The significant benefit of Web services is to enable you to reference a class (the Web service) on one computer (the host) from a second computer (the client).

Learning About a Web Service

The .wsdl file does not contain the code implementing the Web methods, but the file identifies how to communicate with those methods. For example, the .wsdl file names the Web methods as types, and it specifies the inputs and outputs from the Web methods. This is the minimum that you need to invoke a Web method from a Web service on a remote computer. When developing a client to invoke a Web service, you need to perform due diligence so that you grasp the role of each Web method that you want to use within a Web service. This includes having a thorough understanding of the input and output requirements. The input and output definitions in the .wsdl file do not eliminate the requirement for due diligence. The .wsdl file contents in the client application are for use by Visual Studio .NET in sending a SOAP message to the host computer and in interpreting a SOAP message from the host computer.

Although you need to know more about a Web service than its .wsdl file tells you, the .wsdl file contains valuable clues about it. The following excerpt from the zipcoderesolver.wsdl file identifies the inputs and outputs for the *FullZipCode* and *ShortZipCode* methods in the ZipCodeResolver Web service. (A few especially long, logical lines in the listing from the .wsdl file wrap onto a second line in order to fit on the book page.) As you can see, WSDL script is verbose, but this characteristic helps to make it relatively easy to read and understand, even if you do not have a firm grasp of XML syntax.

Notice that the format for the excerpt includes tags, such as *s:element*, that sometimes contain attribute settings. Furthermore, some tags are hierarchically organized. For example, the *FullZipCode* element contains four other elements: *accessCode*, *address*, *city*, and *state*. These nested elements define the arguments for the *FullZipCode* Web method within the Web service. The attribute settings for the nested arguments are all strings, and they can occur in the call statement no more than once (*maxOccurs*="1"). But these arguments do not have to appear (*minOccurs*="0") for the Web method to return a response. The *FullZipCodeResponse* and *ShortZipCodeResponse* elements define return values from the methods.

```
<s:element name="FullZipCode">  <s:complexType>
    <s:sequence>
      <s:element minOccurs="0" maxOccurs="1" name="accessCode"
      type="s:string" />
      <s:element minOccurs="0" maxOccurs="1" name="address"
      type="s:string" />
      <s:element minOccurs="0" maxOccurs="1" name="city"
      type="s:string" />
```

```
          <s:element minOccurs="0" maxOccurs="1" name="state"
          type="s:string" />
        </s:sequence>
      </s:complexType>
  </s:element>
  <s:element name="FullZipCodeResponse">
    <s:complexType>
      <s:sequence>
        <s:element minOccurs="0" maxOccurs="1" name="FullZipCodeResult"
        type="s:string" />
      </s:sequence>
    </s:complexType>
  </s:element>
  <s:element name="ShortZipCode">
    <s:complexType>
      <s:sequence>
        <s:element minOccurs="0" maxOccurs="1" name="accessCode"
        type="s:string" />
        <s:element minOccurs="0" maxOccurs="1" name="address"
        type="s:string" />
        <s:element minOccurs="0" maxOccurs="1" name="city"
        type="s:string" />
        <s:element minOccurs="0" maxOccurs="1" name="state"
        type="s:string" />
      </s:sequence>
    </s:complexType>
  </s:element>
  <s:element name="ShortZipCodeResponse">
    <s:complexType>
      <s:sequence>
        <s:element minOccurs="0" maxOccurs="1"
        name="ShortZipCodeResult" type="s:string" />
      </s:sequence>
    </s:complexType>
  </s:element>
```

Showing Design and Operational Views

Figure 12-2 shows a Design view and an operational view of the client application. The top window in the figure contains three text boxes with corresponding labels separated from a fourth text box and its label by a Button control.
The top three buttons are for the *street*, *city*, and *state* arguments to the *Full-
ZipCode* Web method. Clicking the Button control (*Button1*) invokes the Web
method and assigns the return value to the *Text* property of the last TextBox
(*TextBox4*) on the Web page.

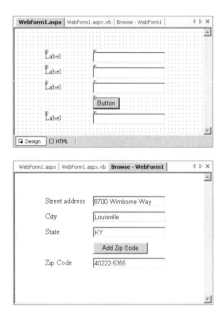

Figure 12-2 Design and operational views of a Web application client for the ZipCodeResolver Web service

The bottom window shows the page with my address in the top three text boxes after I clicked the Button control. A little experimentation with the client application indicated that the Web service does not always return a zip code. For example, when I input an address known to be bogus, the return zip code was 00000-0000. In addition, I input selected addresses of my seminar registrants. Some of these addresses worked, but others failed. Try the Web service for your address and see whether it works. This kind of experimentation is part of the due diligence that you need to perform when evaluating a Web service for use in your applications. As stated earlier, this Web service is merely a test service to illustrate general application issues. It is not meant for use in production environments.

The Code Behind the Web Page

The code behind the Web page in Figure 12-2 consists of a *Page_Load* procedure and a *Button1_Click* procedure. The *Page_Load* procedure makes the initial assignments of the *Text* and *TabIndex* property values for the controls on the Web page. After the initial assignments, the Web page automatically restores the values from the last round-trip of a page or assigns any new values made by a user to the controls on the page.

The most significant part of this application is in the code for the *Button1_Click* procedure. The *Dim* statement for *wsc1* shows the syntax for declaring and instantiating a proxy variable. IntelliSense helps you write out the reference to the ZipCodeResolver Web service from the net.eraserver.webservices Web reference. As mentioned, the Web reference name appears in the Web References folder of Solution Explorer for the WebZipCodeClient project. After the *New* keyword, all you need to specify is *net*. Then, IntelliSense offers a menu for selecting each additional element name for the proxy class. The assignment statement in the *Button1_Click* procedure demonstrates the syntax for invoking a Web method with the proxy variable. Again, IntelliSense offers a menu of items to select after you specify the proxy variable name.

```
Private Sub Page_Load(ByVal sender As System.Object, _
    ByVal e As System.EventArgs) Handles MyBase.Load

    'Make initial control assignments
    If Not IsPostBack Then

        'Assign Text property values
        Label1.Text = "Street address"
        Label2.Text = "City"
        Label3.Text = "State"
        Label4.Text = "Zip Code"
        Button1.Text = "Add Zip Code"

        'Assign tab order for controls
        TextBox1.TabIndex = 1
        TextBox2.TabIndex = 2
        TextBox3.TabIndex = 3
        Button1.TabIndex = 4

    End If

End Sub


Private Sub Button1_Click(ByVal sender As System.Object, _
    ByVal e As System.EventArgs) Handles Button1.Click

    'Designate wsc1 as a proxy variable for the
    'ZipCodeResolver Web service
    Dim wsc1 As New net.eraserver.webservices.ZipCodeResolver()

    'Pass four arguments to the FullZipCode Web method
    TextBox4.Text = wsc1.FullZipCode("9", _
        TextBox1.Text, TextBox2.Text, TextBox3.Text)

End Sub
```

As you can see, Visual Studio .NET trivializes invoking a Web service on another computer in a remote location from the client application. The combination of the powerful technology that Web services exposes and its ease of use make Web services an exciting way to build that draws on the resources of multiple computers and organizations with varied skills. A subsequent sample in this chapter will illustrate how to extend the reach of Access databases via Web services.

Building a Windows Application Client for a Web Service

One of my favorite Web services features in Visual Studio .NET is that you can both create and consume a Web service from a Windows application. This means that everything you already know about creating Windows solutions and ADO.NET solutions applies transparently to Web services. For example, a Windows *Form* object can serve as a client for the ZipCodeResolver Web service just as the Web page in the preceding sample did. Many Access developers find Windows Forms a more natural environment, so this capability is good for us. The key is that you must have an open connection to the Web through which you connect to your Web service. If the Web service is located at an Internet site, you need an open Internet connection from the computer running the Windows application. On the other hand, you can connect to a Web service via your local intranet, which does not require Internet connectivity.

Building the Windows Application Client

Open a new Windows application project. You can name it WindowsZipCode-Client to correspond to the convention for the previous Web application client. Then, add a Web reference to the ZipCodeResolver Web service. You can follow the same steps described in the previous sample. Whether you are adding a Web reference to a Web application or to a Windows application, the process is the same.

After adding the Web reference, you can add controls to *Form1* in the WindowsZipCodeClient project for collecting address information and displaying the resolved zip code. Figure 12-3 shows Design and operational views of the Windows form. The Design view in the left window shows an arrangement of controls that mimics those for the Web page in the preceding sample. Of course, some minor differences exist between the way controls behave in a Windows Forms instance and the way they behave in a Web page. Two salient issues are the contents of the text boxes and the sizing of the Button control.

The TextBox controls in *Form1* are not blank by default (as they are in a Web page). Instead, the TextBox controls have unique *Name* property assignments that appear as their *Text* properties. It is normal practice in Windows Forms programming to clear the *Text* property settings for text boxes. In addition, Button controls on a Windows Forms instance do not automatically expand to accommodate the size of the *Text* property setting (as a Button control on a Web page does). Because the *Text* property assignment is longer than the default *Width* property setting for *Button1*, the client application needs to assign a new *Width* property to *Button1*.

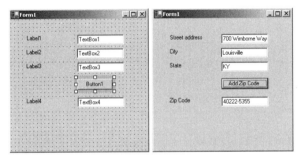

Figure 12-3   Design and operational views of a Windows application client for the ZipCodeResolver Web service

The window on the right in Figure 12-3 shows the operational view of the Windows client. I entered my address and clicked the Add Zip Code button (*Button1*). After its click event procedure executed, the application populated the Zip Code text box (*TextBox4*). The computer running the sample had an open Internet connection so that it could invoke the ZipCodeResolver Web service at *EraServer.net* within the *Button1_Click* procedure.

The Code Behind *Form1*

The code behind *Form1* in the Windows application client is similar to that behind the WebForm1 page in the Web application client. The *Form1_Load* procedure in the Windows application corresponds roughly to the *Page_Load* procedure in the Web application. In addition, the *Button1_Click* procedure is identical in both the Windows application and the Web application. Therefore, the only differences between the two clients are cosmetic ones related to how Windows and Web applications process form controls.

The *Form1_Load* procedure starts with the same code that appears in the *Page_Load* procedure for assigning the *Text* and *TabIndex* properties of selected controls on the form. However, the *Form1_Load* procedure has additional code for formatting the TextBox and Button controls. A loop passes through all the controls on *Form1* and assigns a zero-length string to the *Text* property of any TextBox control. In addition, a *Size* structure assignment revises the default *Width* property of *Button1* to 100 pixels. This widens the control from its default *Width* property value of 75 pixels so that *Button1* does not crop its *Text* property value when *Form1* displays.

```
Private Sub Form1_Load(ByVal sender As System.Object, _
    ByVal e As System.EventArgs) Handles MyBase.Load

    'Assign Label Text property values
    Label1.Text = "Street address"
    Label2.Text = "City"
    Label3.Text = "State"
    Label4.Text = "Zip Code"

    'Assign tab order for controls
    TextBox1.TabIndex = 1
    TextBox2.TabIndex = 2
    TextBox3.TabIndex = 3
    Button1.TabIndex = 4

    'Assign zero-length strings to all text boxes
    'on the form
    Dim ctl1 As Control
    Dim str1 As String
    For Each ctl1 In Me.Controls
        If ctl1.GetType.ToString = _
            "System.Windows.Forms.TextBox" Then
            ctl1.Text = ""
        End If
    Next

    'Format button control
    Button1.Text = "Add Zip Code"
    Button1.Size = _
        New System.Drawing.Size(100, Button1.Height)

End Sub
```

```
Private Sub Button1_Click(ByVal sender As System.Object, _
    ByVal e As System.EventArgs) Handles Button1.Click

    'Designate wsc1 as a proxy variable for the
    'ZipCodeResolver Web service
    Dim wsc1 As New net.eraserver.webservices.ZipCodeResolver()

    'Pass four arguments to the FullZipCode Web method
    TextBox4.Text = wsc1.FullZipCode("9", _
        TextBox1.Text, TextBox2.Text, TextBox3.Text)

End Sub
```

Case Study for a Computational Web Service

One of the real advantages of Visual Studio .NET is the ease with which you can create your custom Web services and then write clients for those services so that others can use them. This section presents a case study that illustrates the steps for creating a Web service to compute the number of days until the end of the month from an input date. Then, the case study shows you how to build a Windows client from the same workstation as well as how to revise that client for use on other workstations.

Building the DaysTilEOM Web Service

To start building a Web service, you need access to an IIS server, just as you do when you build a Web application with the ASP.NET Web Application project template. However, choose the ASP.NET Web Service project template (instead of the one for an ASP.NET Web Application project). This creates an empty project folder on the IIS server that you select, which can be your local IIS server (localhost), as you develop and test your Web service. The project folder resides in the wwwroot subdirectory of the Inetpub directory of the Web server, which is the Inetpub directory of your workstation when you designate localhost as your IIS. For this demonstration, I assigned the name DaysTilEOM to the project folder to convey that the Web service computes the number of days until the end of the month from an input date. As with an ASP.NET Web application, this process creates two folders: one on the Web server and a second folder in the default location for your Visual Studio .NET projects. This second folder contains the .sln file so that you can open the project in Visual Studio .NET for editing.

Web Service Names

A Web service has a variety of handles to which you can apply names. This sidebar reviews several of the names that you need to manage as you assign names to your Web service.

First, you have the name for the project folder on the Web server. By default, Visual Studio .NET assigns WebService1 as the project folder name for the first Web service. Subsequent Web services will have project folders named WebService2, WebService3, and so on. You can override any default name by designating an alternate name when creating a new ASP.NET Web Service project with Visual Studio .NET. Just type over the default name, such as WebService1, with your new name, such as Days-TilEOM. This same name applies to the second folder for the project that holds the .sln file, which Visual Studio .NET uses to edit the project.

Second, when a Web service project initially opens, it opens in Design view. This Design view represents the *WebService* class for the Web service. The class's default name is *Service1*. You can assign a more meaningful name by selecting Design view and then updating the *Name* property for the *WebService* class in the Properties window. For example, I assigned the name *DaysTilEOM* to the class for the Web service in the DaysTilEOM project folder.

Third, the start page for a Web service project has an .asmx extension instead of the .aspx extension found in a Web application project. By the way, in a typical Web service project, the start page is the only page in the project. This start page does not appear as it does in a Web application. Instead, the start page runs code to implement the Web methods for the Web service. The default name for a Web service start page file is Service1.asmx. You can assign a new name for the Web service's start page file in Solution Explorer by right-clicking the file and choosing Rename.

Finally, every Web service has a namespace associated with it. The name for this namespace identifies the Web service much as the .NET Framework namespaces identify groups of classes. By default, Visual Studio .NET assigns the same name (*http://tempuri.org*) to the namespace for all Web services. You should change this default name before attempting to consume the Web service. Each Web service should have a unique name for its namespace. You assign the name for a Web service's namespace in the *Namespace* setting of the *WebService* attribute of the class implementing the Web service.

When a Web service project initially opens in Visual Studio .NET, the project's Design view appears. You can click a link in the view to switch to the Code view for the project. In general, you should not design a user interface inside a Web service because there will be no user to respond to the interface. A Web service should typically accept one or more arguments from a client application and perform an operation. The client application for the Web service manages all interactions with users.

When you open the Code view for a new Web service, you will see a class with the name of the *WebService* class from the Design view. The class declaration in the Code view has the same name as the one you assigned to the *WebService* class in Design view. The class declaration starts with a *WebService* attribute declaration. This attribute takes two settings, one of which is designated by default. This is the *Namespace* setting. You should always change this setting to a unique name before consuming the Web service with a client application. The *Description* setting for a *WebService* attribute does not appear by default, but it is good practice to designate a description anyway. Both the *Namespace* and *Description* property assignments are *String* values.

Below the class declaration is a commented sample for a "Hello world" Web service. This section illustrates the basic syntax for the *WebMethod* attribute, which you must assign to all procedures that you expose from the class implementing the Web service. Procedures without this attribute are available exclusively from within the Web service.

The Code for the DaysTilEOM Web Service

The following listing presents the code for the DaysTilEOM Web service. The automatically generated code from the Web Services Designer is not shown, but a marker indicates where this code appears within the class listing. You can see from the *WebService* attribute declaration that the attribute class belongs to the *System.Web.Services* namespace. The attribute shows the syntax for assigning the *Namespace* and *Description* settings.

The DaysTilEOM Web service has a single Web method named *DaysTilEOM*. The procedure implementing the Web method has a *WebMethod* attribute tag. The tag applies to a *Function* procedure that returns an *Integer* value and takes two *String* arguments. The first argument is the input date. This is the start date from which the Web service computes the number of days to the end of the month. The second argument is a *String* value denoting a valid UserID for authorizing use of the Web service. The UserID must have a length of four digits representing a numeric value greater than 100 and less than 500. Therefore, the leading digit must be 0. If the UserID fails either or both of its tests, *DaysTilEOM* exits without computing the number of days until the end of the month and passes back a value of -1. This is a simple demonstration of how to validate a user. You can use any code-processing techniques to more extensively identify and authenticate a user.

After validating that a user has authority to use the Web method, the procedure converts the *String* value representing a date to a serial *DateTime* value and stores it in the *startdate* variable. Then, the procedure computes in three steps the last day of the month for the date in the *startdate* variable. The first step uses the *DateAdd* function to compute the same day of the next month (*samedaynextmonth*). The second step uses the *DateSerial* function to compute the first day of the next month (*firstdaynextmonth*). In the third step, a *DateAdd* function subtracts one day from the first day of the last month to return the last day of this month (*lastdaythismonth*). Finally, the *DateDiff* function computes the difference in days between the *startdate* and *lastdaythismonth* variable values. A *Return* statement passes back the number of days to the application invoking the *DaysTilEOM* Web method in the Web service with the same name.

```
<System.Web.Services.WebService(Namespace:= _
    "http://www.databasedevelopersgroup.com/DaysTilEOM", _
    Description:="Days 'til end of month.")> _
    Public Class DaysTilEOM
    Inherits System.Web.Services.WebService

#Region " Web Services Designer Generated Code "
...

    'Web service to compute the days to the end
    'of the month
    <WebMethod()> Function DaysTilEOM(ByVal indate As String, _
        ByVal userid As String) As Integer

        'Authenticate user; Userid must be four
        'digits long, greater than 0100 and less
        'than 0500
        If Not (Len(Userid) = 4 _
            And CInt(Userid) > 100 And _
            CInt(Userid) < 500) Then
            Return -1
            Exit Function
        End If

        'Compute datetime value based on indate string
        Dim startdate As DateTime = DateValue(indate)

        'Compute same day next month as indate
        Dim samedaynextmonth As DateTime = _
```

```
        DateAdd(DateInterval.Month, 1, startdate)

    'Compute first day next month
    Dim firstdaynextmonth As DateTime = _
        DateSerial(Year(samedaynextmonth), _
            Month(samedaynextmonth), 1)

    'Computer last day this month
    Dim lastdaythismonth As DateTime = _
        DateAdd(DateInterval.Day, -1, firstdaynextmonth)

    'Return days until end of month
    Return DateDiff(DateInterval.Day, startdate, _
        lastdaythismonth)

End Function

End Class
```

Testing the Web Service

Visual Studio .NET supports built-in testing of a Web service without building a client application. You can invoke the built-in testing capability by right-clicking in Solution Explorer the .asmx file for the project, which has the name Days-TilEOM.asmx in the current Web service, and then choosing Build And Browse. This opens a Browse tab that displays the name of the Web service (for example, Service1 or DaysTilEOM), followed by the *Description* setting for the *Web-Service* attribute. The preceding listing shows this setting to be *Days 'til end of month*. Finally, the Web methods appear. In this case, just a single method named *DaysTilEOM* exists. However, a single Web service can have multiple Web methods.

Click the name for a Web method to open a second window that replaces the initial one on the Browse tab. The new Browse window contains a test page. The excerpt of the Browse window shown in Figure 12-4 displays two text boxes and an Invoke button. The test page contains a text box for each input value to the Web method being tested. Clicking the Invoke button after entering values in the text boxes causes the Web service to execute its Web method and return a value as an XML document to another Browse tab. The tab caption for the new Browse window specifies the values for the text box entries. The contents of the new Browse window show the return value in XML format corresponding to the input values in the tab caption. If you return to the test page, you can input a new set of input values and click Invoke to generate another new Browse window with its input values on the tab caption and a return value in the window.

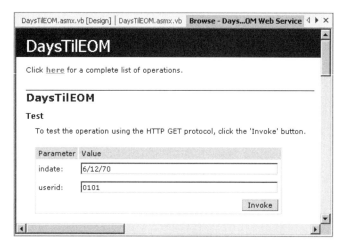

Figure 12-4 The built-in testing dialog box for the *DaysTilEOM* Web method in the DaysTilEOM Web service

Figure 12-5 shows the Browse window with the return value for the input values that appear in Figure 12-4. The month of June has 30 days, so 18 days separate June 12 and the end of the month. The XML document with the return value shows the number 18 between opening and closing *int* tags. The opening *int* tag shows the *Namespace* name for the Web service that appears in the *Web-Service* attribute from the preceding listing.

Figure 12-5 A return value window from the *DaysTilEOM* Web method for the test values shown in Figure 12-4

Building a Client Application on the Localhost

Building a client for a Web service involves the integration of three distinct elements. First, you must add a Web reference to a proxy that points at the Web service for which you are building a client application. Second, you must design a user interface for gathering input and displaying return values (if any exist). This step populates the controls of a Windows *Form* class instance. Third, you need to write code behind the form to invoke the Web service and process any return values from the Web service. This section drills down on each of these steps.

Adding a Web Reference

You can start to add a Web reference by choosing Project, Add Web Reference from within your Windows application project. In the Add Web Reference dialog box, enter the name and path to the Web service in the Address box. For this example, you type in **http://localhost/DaysTilEOM/DaysTilEOM.asmx**. Remember that we created a folder on the local Web server named DaysTilEOM. This name accounts for the first occurrence of DaysTilEOM. The .asmx file in the folder with the name DaysTilEOM refers to the Web service name.

> **Note**   As you know, a one-to-one relationship exists between a Web service and an .asmx file in the Web server hosting one or more Web services. Therefore, you can discover the Web services hosted on a localhost by performing a search for all the .asmx files in the wwwroot subdirectory of the Inetpub folder.

After entering the address and clicking Enter, Visual Studio .NET revises the Available References pane of the Add Web Reference dialog box to show two links labeled View Contract and View Documentation. The pane to the left of Available References initially opens so that you can test the Web service. This view of the Web service corresponds to the View Documentation link in the Available References pane because clicking the View Documentation link retains the view. This is also the same screen as the one presented in response to right-clicking the .asmx file in Solution Explorer for the Web service project and choosing Build And Browse. Clicking the View Contract link causes the left pane to display the .wsdl file for the Web service. As discussed earlier, the .wsdl file defines the input and output arguments for the Web methods in a Web service.

By clicking the Add Reference button below the Available References pane in the Add Web Reference dialog box, you can add a reference for the selected Web service. This is a necessary precursor for declaring and instantiating a proxy variable that enables the use of Web methods from a Web service. Clicking the Add Reference button creates a Web References folder if one did not exist before and populates the folder with a reference to the DaysTilEOM Web service. If this is the first reference in a Web service on the local Web server, the reference appears under a heading of localhost. By expanding the Web reference labeled localhost in Solution Explorer, you see individual references pointing at the .wsdl and .disco files for DaysTilEOM as well as a Reference.map file for the Web service. When you declare and instantiate a proxy variable pointing at the DaysTilEOM Web service, Visual Studio .NET takes advantage of the content in these files in the Web reference to implement an instance of the proxy class. The proxy class instance enables your application to send values to and retrieve them from a Web method in the Web service pointed at by the proxy variable.

The Client User Interface

Figure 12-6 shows *Form1* from the WindowsDaysTilEOMClient project both in Design view and after processing a date. The left window reveals that *Form1* consists of a pair of TextBox controls, three Label controls, and a Button control. The operational view of *Form1* in the right window shows the processing of an input date. The top text box contains a date (January 6, 1950), and the bottom text box contains a valid *UserID* value (0123). The label below the bottom text box shows the number of days between the date in *TextBox1* and the end of the month. The *Text* property for the Label control is a *String* expression that combines the return value from the *DaysTilEOM* Web method with a *String* constant.

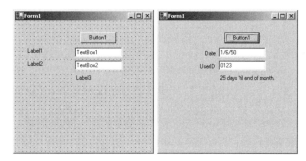

Figure 12-6 Design and operational view of a Windows client for the DaysTilEOM Web service

Form1 shows a little control formatting—especially for the labels. For example, the two labels for the text boxes have their content right-justified. In addition, *Label3*, which is below *TextBox2*, automatically expands its width to fit the length of its *Text* property setting. This is not the default behavior for a Label control on a Windows form.

The Code Behind *Form1*

The code behind *Form1* consists of just two procedures: *Form1_Load* and *Button1_Click*. The *Form1_Load* procedure handles the layout and formatting of the controls on the form. For example, this procedure right-aligns the *Text* property values for *Label1* and *Label2*. In the addition, the procedure sets the *AutoSize* property for *Label3* to *True*. This setting for the property permits *Label3* to expand as necessary to accommodate the width of its *Text* property setting. The first two lines in the *Form1_Load* procedure assign nondefault values to the *Text* property for *TextBox1* and *TextBox2*. The assignment for *TextBox1* is a reminder of the format for inputting a date. *TextBox2* does not receive an assignment, but invoking the *Clear* method is similar to assigning a zero-length string to the *Text* property for the TextBox control.

The *Button1_Click* procedure is the procedure that puts the Web service to work. The *Dim* statement declares *wsc1* as a proxy variable for the Days-TilEOM Web service. For this statement to compile properly, you need a Web reference for the Web service in the project. The second line in the procedure invokes the *DaysTilEOM* Web method within the Web service by using the *Text* property values for *TextBox1* and *TextBox2* as arguments. The statement saves the return value from the method in the *int1* variable. Finally, the procedure processes the return value by exiting with an error message if the return value is -1 or assigning a *String* expression for the number of days from the date in *TextBox1* through the end of the month to the *Text* property for *Label3*.

```
Private Sub Form1_Load(ByVal sender As System.Object, _
    ByVal e As System.EventArgs) Handles MyBase.Load

    'Prompt with date format for date text box
    'and clear userid text box
    TextBox1.Text = "mm/dd/yy"
    TextBox2.Clear()

    'Assign Text property values for labels
    Label1.Text = "Date"
    Label2.Text = "UserID"

    'Align Text property settings
    Label1.TextAlign = ContentAlignment.MiddleRight
    Label2.TextAlign = ContentAlignment.MiddleRight

    'Set Label3 to grow with contents
    Label3.AutoSize = True

End Sub

Private Sub Button1_Click(ByVal sender As System.Object, _
    ByVal e As System.EventArgs) Handles Button1.Click

    'Instantiate DaysTilEOM on localhost
    Dim wsc1 As New localhost.DaysTilEOM()

    'Save the return value from the DaysTilEOM Web method
    'in the int1 variable
```

(continued)

```
Dim int1 As Integer = _
    wsc1.DaysTilEOM(TextBox1.Text, TextBox2.Text)

'Process the return value from the Web method
If int1 = -1 Then
    MsgBox("Invalid UserID; denied access to Web Service.")
Else
    Label3.Text = int1.ToString & " days 'til end of month."
End If

End Sub
```

Building a Client Application on Another Workstation

The same application will work from another workstation with a couple of modifications. You can demonstrate this by starting a new Windows application on a second computer that has the .NET Framework installed. Then, add a new Web reference to the Web service. Next, change the *Dim* statement for the proxy variable pointing at your new Web reference.

When adding a Web reference to a Web service on another computer, you will not be able to discover it on your local Web server unless you have permission to search for .asmx files on the host computer. If you are not trusted with this information, my advice is to manually discover the Web server name, project folder name, and Web service name. Do this by asking the author of the service. In any event, you will not typically try to use a Web service unless you have some information about the Web service from an author. When connecting to a Web service on a local intranet, you can add a Web reference by typing the following URL in the Address box of the Add Web Reference dialog box:

http://servername/projectfoldername/webservicename.asmx

For example, if the Web server with the Web service has the name ccs1 and the Web service has the name DaysTilEOM and is located in a project folder with the same name, you can enter the following:

http://ccs1/DaysTilEOM/DaysTilEOM.asmx

This shows the initial screen for testing the Web service. Click the Add Reference button to add a reference for the Web service to your Windows application. This adds a new Web reference with the name ccs1 to Solution Explorer. Inside the Web reference, you will notice the same three filenames from the preceding sample: DaysTilEOM.disco, DaysTilEOM.wsdl, and Reference.map. However, the content of these files shows that this project links to a Web service on a remote Web server, ccs1.

> **Note**   You might need to reference a proxy server for your browser to discover a Web service on a LAN. You can do this by choosing Tools, Internet Options in Microsoft Internet Explorer. Select the Connections tab in the Internet Options dialog box. Then, click LAN Settings. In the Proxy Server group, select the check box with a label that begins with Use A Proxy Server For Your LAN. Populate the Address box with *http://servername* and the Port box with 80. Replace *servername* with the name of the Web server hosting the Web service that you want to discover. These steps are necessary only for discovering a Web service on a LAN. I recommend you remove them by clearing the Use A Proxy Server For Your LAN check box after discovering the Web service.

After creating the Web reference for the Web service on another computer, you need to update the *Dim* statement for the proxy variable so that it points at the new Web reference. In particular, you must update the statement from

```
Dim wsc1 As New localhost.DaysTilEOM()
```

to

```
Dim wsc1 As New ccs1.DaysTilEOM()
```

Once you make the modification, you can run the revised application. For example, choose Debug, Start to launch the application. Input a date and a *UserID*. Then, click the Button control on the form (*Button1*). The application links to the Web service on the remote Web server and returns the number of days until the end of the month.

Deploying a Web Service

Deploying a solution is a common requirement for many business applications. With Web services, the need arises when you want to make a Web service available from a different Web server than the one that you used to develop the Web service. Typically, the deployed Web service will reside on a Web server that is more widely available or can handle more users than the development Web server. This section demonstrates the deployment of the DaysTilEOM Web service to a local intranet Web server as well as to a Web site on the Internet.

Overview

Deploying a Web service entails two steps. First, you need to copy the relevant files from a folder on the development Web server to a folder on the deployed Web server or Web site. You will typically use a Web site as the target if your Web site is provided by an ISP that shares a Web server across multiple Web site owners. Second, you need a client that connects to the deployed Web service. How you specify the proxy variable for a deployed Web service varies slightly depending on whether the Web service resides on an intranet Web server or the Internet at a Web site.

> **Note** When deploying a Web service to a target Web server or Web site, make sure that the target has the .NET Framework installed. A Web service will function only on a Web server with the .NET Framework installed.

Before deploying a solution, make sure your solution compiles and operates correctly. Use the Build And Browse command to verify proper performance. After verifying valid operation, compile your Web service by choosing Build, Rebuild Solution. This yields a freshly compiled solution. I recommend you deploy to Web servers running the Microsoft FrontPage 2002 Server Extensions because they are easy to use. When your target Web server has these extensions, you can invoke the Project, Copy Project command and automatically copy relevant files from your development Web server to your deployment Web server or Web site. You can even specify a new folder at the target to hold your deployed Web service.

Deploying the DaysTilEOM Web Service

To deploy to a Web server on your intranet, invoke the Project, Copy Project command. In the Destination Project Folder text box, follow the *http://* prefix with the name of your target Web server and the project folder to which you want to copy your application. For example, if your destination server has the name cablat and you want to create a folder named DeployedDaysTilEOM, enter the following URL in the text box:

http://cablat/DeployedDaysTilEOM/

This process copies from the development Web server selected files necessary to run the Web service from the target Web server. It does not copy over all the files, such as the .vsdisco file. When you create a client that points at the target Web service or you already know the URL for the target Web service, discovery files are not strictly necessary in the Web service folder.

When deploying to a Web site on the Internet, the deployment process is almost the same. Replace the server name with the URL for the Internet Web site, such as *http://www.databasedevelopersgroup.com*. You can follow the URL with the name of any destination folder you want to use, such as DeployedDaysTilEOM.

> **Note**   Although you can specify a new Web server and a new folder when you deploy a Web service, the Web service name and startup file remain the same. Therefore, the deployment folder in these examples is DeployedDaysTilEOM, but the Web service name remains DaysTilEOM and the startup file is DaysTilEOM.asmx.

Invoking a Deployed Web Service

The process for invoking a deployed Web service on an intranet was described in the previous section. Essentially, this process is the same as the process for building a client on a workstation other than the one on which the Web service is deployed. See the "Building a Client Application on Another Workstation" section for detailed instructions on how to construct a client application on a Web service deployed to an intranet Web server.

Intranet applications have the potential to deliver significant business value by providing extra security because they can reside behind firewalls. At the same time, this advantage restricts their availability—especially for learning purposes. For example, you cannot connect to the DaysTilEOM Web service deployed to the cablat Web server in my office. On the other hand, you can connect to the same Web service deployed to the *http://www.databasedevelopers-group.com* Web site. Start with any client that you already have for the DaysTilEOM Web service, or build a new one as described in the "Building a Client Application on Another Workstation" section. Then, add a new Web reference to the project. Start by choosing Project, Add Web Reference. Next, type the URL for the target .asmx file in the Address text box. In the current example, this URL would appear as follows:

http://www.databasedevelopersgroup.com/DeployedDaysTilEOM/
DaysTilEOM.asmx

Then, press Enter. Finish adding the Web reference by clicking the Add Reference button.

The preceding steps add a new Web reference named com.databasedevelopersgroup.www to the Web References folder in Solution Explorer for your client application. You can optionally rename the Web reference so that you have a single-part name such as mysinglepartname rather than a multi.part.name. However, no requirement to convert the name format for the Web reference exists: when you build a proxy variable for the Web reference, the variable will normally be a single-part name. You can specify a proxy variable for the Web reference with a *Dim* statement such as this:

```
Dim wsc1 As New com.databasedevelopersgroup.www.DaysTilEOM()
```

Replace any other *Dim* statement declaring the *wsc1* proxy variable with this one. Then, your Windows client application will connect to the Web service at the *http://www.databasedevelopersgroup.com* Web site.

Building an Intranet-Based Client for a Web Service

Most of the Web service clients described in this chapter are Windows applications. However, having a Web application as a client gives you a distinct advantage. A Web application does not require the installation of the .NET Framework on the client computer, but a Windows application does. Therefore, using a Web client rather than a Windows client extends the reach of a Web service.

Figure 12-7 shows a Design view and an operational view of WebForm2.aspx in the WebZipCodeClient project discussed in the "Building a Web Application Client for a Web Service" section. The project resides on the intranet in my office. WebForm2.aspx is the second Web page added to the project. However, this Web page points at a different Web service than that initially used in the earlier discussion of the project. Webform2.aspx points at the DaysTilEOM Web service in the DeployedDaysTilEOM folder at the *http://www.databasedevelopersgroup.com* Web site. The Design and operational views for the Web application client generally parallel those for the Windows application. In fact, much of the code behind the form is the same. You can see the distinct design and operational similarities of Web clients and Windows clients by comparing the forms in Figure 12-7 with those in Figure 12-6.

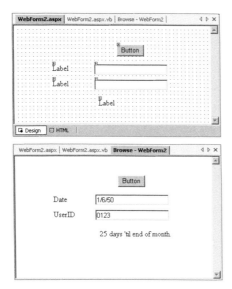

Figure 12-7   Design and operational view of an intranet-based Web client for the DaysTilEOM Web service

The following listing shows the two event procedures in the code behind the Web page. The *Page_Load* event procedure merely performs initial formatting of the controls on the Web page. The *Button1_Click* procedure invokes the DaysTilEOM Web service and processes its return value via the *wsc1* proxy variable. A *Dim* statement points this proxy variable at the DaysTilEOM Web service in the com.databasedevelopersgroup.www Web reference. You can manually create this Web reference as described earlier in this section. As you can see, except for the Web reference, the *Button1_Click* procedure for the Web client is identical to that of the Windows client.

```
Private Sub Page_Load(ByVal sender As System.Object, _
    ByVal e As System.EventArgs) Handles MyBase.Load

    'Initialize controls
    If Not IsPostBack Then
        'Prompt with date format for date text box
        'and clear userid text box
        TextBox1.Text = "mm/dd/yy"
        TextBox2.Text = ""

        'Assign Text property values for labels
        Label1.Text = "Date"
```

(continued)

```
                    Label2.Text = "UserID"
                    Label3.Text = ""
            End If

    End Sub

    Private Sub Button1_Click(ByVal sender As System.Object, _
        ByVal e As System.EventArgs) Handles Button1.Click

            'Instantiate DaysTilEOM on localhost
            Dim wsc1 As New _
                com.databasedevelopersgroup.www.DaysTilEOM()

            'Save the return value from the DaysTilEOM Web method
            'in the int1 variable
            Dim int1 As Integer = _
                wsc1.DaysTilEOM(TextBox1.Text, TextBox2.Text)

            'Process the return value from the Web method
            If int1 = -1 Then
                MsgBox("Invalid UserID; denied access to Web Service.")
            Else
                Label3.Text = int1.ToString & " days 'til end of month."
            End If

    End Sub
```

Building an Internet-Based Client

As mentioned, the preceding sample extends the reach of a Web service because it does not require the .NET Framework on the computer running the client. However, that sample does not extend the reach sufficiently to enable you to browse to a page on the Internet and see the Web service in action. The sample in this section does. In fact, this sample is identical to the preceding one, except that it resides on the Internet. This simple adjustment dramatically extends the reach.

I created a new Web page, WebForm1.aspx, in the WebDaysTilEOMClient project folder of the *http://www.databasedevelopersgroup.com* Web site. As you might have surmised, this Web page has the same design and Web reference as those in the preceding sample, except that this Web page is available on the Internet. Therefore, you can browse to it. Figure 12-8 shows the page in a browser yielding the same result as shown in Figure 12-7. The Address box in the figure shows you the URL to use for running the DaysTilEOM Web service from your browser.

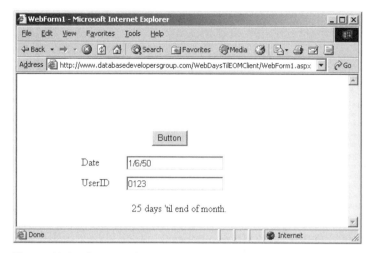

Figure 12-8   An operational view of an Internet-based Web client for the DaysTilEOM Web service

A Web Service for the Northwind Database

This section demonstrates how to build a Web service for an Access database. Running a Web service for an Access database turns it into a client/server system because the user never gets the database file, she merely submits commands to a Web service that manipulates the database file. You can dramatically decrease your network traffic with this use of Web services because the Access database file stays put on the Web service client. Only individual values or datasets pass back to clients from the Web service.

Overview of the Application

This chapter focuses on Web service design and deployment techniques. These techniques are essentially the same whether your Web service returns values from a database, does a computation, or performs some combination of the two. In addition, a majority of the book explained how to program these tasks. The point of this chapter is to show you how to package the code in a Web service and apply what you already learned in this book. This chapter concludes with the presentation of a Web service that focuses on the manipulation of an Access database—the Northwind database.

The Web service we will examine in this section has the name OrderID-Service. It provides three main functions. First, the Web service returns a value.

A user inputs an OrderID, and the Web service looks up the Freight charge for the corresponding order. Second, the Web service returns a dataset. Specifically, the second function returns rows from the Order Details table that match a designated OrderID. This second function is very similar to the first one in that it is essentially a lookup task. The distinction is that the second function returns a collection of values instead of returning a single value. Because Access developers often work with a collection of values, this distinction is important. Third, the Web service computes a value: the sum of the extended price for the line items in an order.

As with many Web service applications, the sample application for this section consists of two projects. The OrderIDService project is a project built from an ASP.NET Web Service template. It consists of three function procedures—one for each Web method—and some related code, such as a module-level declaration and the *ComputeDas1 Function* procedure, which returns a *DataSet* object. The OrderIDServiceClient project is built on the Windows Application template. This project includes a Web reference that points at the OrderIDService project. A proxy variable pointing at the Web reference enables the client application to invoke the Web methods in the OrderIDService project. In addition, the OrderIDServiceClient project features a user interface through a Windows Forms instance, *Form1*, which assists with the collection of input from users and the display of data to users.

The Web Service Project

The code for the Web service appears in the following listing. The attribute settings for the *OrderIDService* class assign a description and a name to override the default namespace for a Web service. Assigning a name helps to ensure the uniqueness of the namespace name, which is guaranteed not to be unique unless you change the default name of *http://tempuri.org/*. The description helps to identify the functions of the Web service in the Web service's Test page. The Web Services Designer–generated code is not shown in this listing. Instead, a region marker signifies where this code goes in the listing. After the marker for the Web Services Designer–generated code, a module-level statement declares and instantiates an *OleDbConnection* object that points at the Northwind database. This *Connection* object appears in a couple of procedures for the Web service.

The three function procedures that appear first in the *OrderIDService* class implement a Web method. Two of the functions rely on a fourth function, *ComputeDas1*, to implement their Web method.

The *Freight Function* procedure looks up the Freight column value for an order with an OrderID column value designated by a string passed to the function. The procedure begins by declaring and instantiating a new *OleDb-Command* object and then assigning its *CommandText* and *Connection* properties in a *With...End With* statement. The assignment for the *Connection* property refers to the module-level *Connection* object. The *CommandText* property is assigned a SQL string that depends on a *String* expression that combines a *String* constant for part of the SQL string with a variable based on the *str1* variable passed to the procedure. By invoking the *ExecuteScalar* method for the *OleDbCommand* object, the procedure stores in the *dec1* variable the Freight column value for the order with the OrderID column value in *str1*. A *Return* statement at the end of the procedure passes the value that has been looked up to the client application for the Web method.

The *Items* procedure returns a dataset with three column values for each line item from the Order Details table with an OrderID value matching the string passed to the *Function* procedure. The *Items* procedure does not compute the dataset that it returns. Instead, the *Items* procedure invokes the *ComputeDas1* procedure, which supports both the *Items* procedure and the *TotalPrice* procedure (discussed in the next paragraph). The *ComputeDas1* procedure starts with a SQL string assignment that selects the Quantity, the ProductName, and a computed term—the ExtendedPrice for each line item matching an OrderID value specified by the *str1* variable value. The procedure uses the SQL string along with the *OleDbConnection* object declared at the module level to construct a data adapter that the procedure in turn uses to populate the *das1* dataset. The *ComputeDas1* procedure passes the *das1* dataset to the *Items* procedure, which passes the dataset to the client project for the Web service.

The *TotalPrice* procedure starts by computing a new instance of the *das1* dataset based on the current value of the *str1 String* variable. Then, the *TotalPrice* procedure loops through the rows of the *das1* dataset and aggregates the ExtendedPrice values in the *dec1* variable that it returns.

```
<System.Web.Services.WebService( _
    Namespace:="http://CABXmlServices/OrderIDService", _
    Description:="Freight, Items, and Total Price.")> _
    Public Class OrderIDService
    Inherits System.Web.Services.WebService

#Region " Web Services Designer Generated Code "

    Dim cnn1 As New OleDb.OleDbConnection( _
        "Provider=Microsoft.Jet.OLEDB.4.0;" & _
        "Data Source = c:\Program Files\Microsoft " & _
        "Office\Office10\Samples\Northwind.mdb")
```

(continued)

```
'OrderIDService
<WebMethod()> Public Function Freight( _
    ByVal str1 As String) As Decimal

    'Declare and instantiate a command object
    Dim cmd1 As New OleDb.OleDbCommand()

    'Assign Connection and CommandText properties
    With cmd1
        .Connection = cnn1
        .CommandText = _
            "SELECT Freight FROM Orders " & _
            "WHERE OrderID = " & str1
    End With

    'Retrieve command
    cnn1.Open()
    Dim dec1 = cmd1.ExecuteScalar
    cnn1.Close()

    'Return command result
    Return dec1

End Function

<WebMethod()> Public Function Items( _
    ByVal str1 As String) As Dataset

    'Compute the dataset for an OrderID
    Dim das1 As Dataset = ComputeDas1(str1)

    'Return dataset
    Return das1

End Function

<WebMethod()> Public Function TotalPrice( _
    ByVal str1 As String) As Decimal

    'Compute the dataset for an OrderID
    Dim das1 As Dataset = ComputeDas1(str1)

    'Loop through rows in dataset to compute
    'total extended price
    Dim drw1 As DataRow
    Dim dec1 As Decimal
    For Each drw1 In das1.Tables(0).Rows
```

```
        dec1 += drw1(2)
    Next

    'Return total price
    Return dec1

End Function

Function ComputeDas1(ByVal str1 As String) As Dataset

    'Define a SQL string to return Quantity, ProductName, and
    'ExtendedPrice by line item for an order with a designated
    'OrderID
    Dim str2 = _
        "SELECT [Order Details].Quantity, ProductName, " & _
        "[Order Details].UnitPrice*" & _
        "[Order Details].Quantity*" & _
        "(1-[Order Details].Discount) " & _
        "AS ExtendedPrice " & _
        "FROM [Order Details] INNER JOIN Products " & _
        "ON [Order Details].ProductID = Products.ProductID " & _
        "WHERE [Order Details].OrderID= " & str1

    'Fill das1 dataset with data adapter
    Dim dap1 As New OleDb.OleDbDataAdapter(str2, cnn1)
    Dim das1 As New Dataset()
    dap1.Fill(das1, "OrderDetails")

    'Return dataset
    Return das1

End Function

End Class
```

Testing and Demonstrating the Web Service

After designing any Web service, it is a good idea to test-drive its operation with the built-in test page capabilities. This enables you to see how your code is operating. You might discover opportunities for fine-tuning your code or fixing logical errors. Beyond that, you can gain experience that helps you to design a client application for the Web service.

Figure 12-9 presents the initial test page for the OrderIDService Web service from within a Browse window in Visual Studio .NET. You can generate this dialog box by right-clicking the .asmx file for the Web service in Solution Explorer and choosing Build And Browse. The tab for the Browse window in Figure 12-9 shows the name for the Web service (or, more precisely, an abbreviation for it that fits on the tab). Just below the Web service name, the *Description* setting for the *WebService* attribute appears. Four hyperlinks appear in the initial test page. The Service Description link opens a window showing the .wsdl file describing the Web service. If you want to dig deeper into the XML describing the Web service, this is a great resource. Next, a separate link appears for each Web method. The links have names that correspond to the *Function* procedure implementing each Web method. Clicking the link for a Web method opens another dialog box containing text boxes for any input arguments to the Web method as well as an Invoke button for launching the Web method.

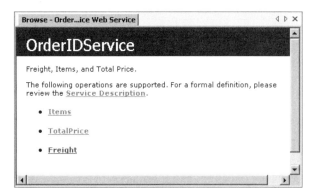

Figure 12-9   The initial Test page for the OrderIDService Web service

As mentioned, the test page for all three Web methods is the same (unless they have different input arguments). The difference between the Web methods is in the response window that appears after a user clicks the Invoke button to launch a Web method. The response window shows the value or values returned by a Web method. For the OrderIDService Web service, both the *Freight* and *TotalPrice* Web methods have the same type of return: a single value with a *Decimal* data type. The difference is that the *Freight* Web method returns a looked-up value, but the *TotalPrice* Web method returns a computed value.

Figures 12-10 and 12-11 show the input and response windows for the *Freight* and *TotalPrice* Web methods, respectively. In both cases, the OrderID value is the same—10248. The bottom window in each figure displays the return value. For example, if you open the Orders table in the Northwind database and look up the Freight column value for the row with an OrderID column value of 10248, the value is 32.38. The *Freight* Web method performs this operation for you. The bottom window in Figure 12-11 shows a value of 440. This is the sum of the extended price for each of the three line items in the Order Details table with an OrderID column value of 10248. The extended price value for a line item is itself the result of a computation based on the Quantity, Unit-Price, and Discount column values for a row in the Order Details table. The bottom windows in Figures 12-10 and 12-11 show the return value as an element in an XML document. Notice that the *Namespace* setting for the Web service appears as an attribute for the *decimal* tag denoting a return value. The *Namespace* name designates the Web service returning the value, and the *decimal* tag specifies the type for the data value. This XML markup is an inherent feature of a Web service.

Figure 12-10   The input and response windows for the *Freight* Web method

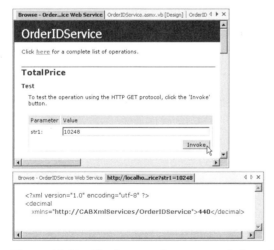

Figure 12-11   The input and response windows for the *TotalPrice* Web method

The *Items* Web method returns a dataset—that is, a set of rows, each containing column values for Quantity, ProductName, and the computed result for the extended price of a line item. The number of rows in the dataset depends on the number of line items in an order. Because ADO.NET represents a dataset as an XML document, the return from the *Items* Web method is an XML document. Figure 12-12 shows an excerpt from the document for an input OrderID value of 10248. Notice that the document has two parts. The top part specifies the structure for the dataset, which includes elements for Quantity, Product-Name, and ExtendedPrice. These elements designate the data type (*short*, *string*, and *double*) with an attribute from the *xs* namespace. The values for the first row in the dataset appear toward the bottom of Figure 12-12. Each row appears between opening and closing *OrderDetails* tags. Within these tags are more tags denoting the individual column values within a row. While the Test page returns the values in this format, you can program access to the dataset values just as you would any other dataset discussed in this book. The client application will illustrate how to control the display of the values in a ListBox control on a Windows Forms instance.

Figure 12-12 An excerpt from the response window for the *Items* Web method with a OrderID value of 10248

Building a Client Application

Building a client application for a Web service such as the OrderIDService involves three steps. First, you create a Windows application or a Web application and add a Web reference pointing at the Web service that you want to invoke. Second, you create a user interface (for example, a Windows or Web form with controls) for collecting values, invoking one or more Web methods, and displaying any return values from the Web methods. Third, you develop code behind the form to invoke the Web methods and process and return values.

Creating a Windows Project with a Web Reference

In developing the client for this demonstration, I started by creating a new Windows application on a different computer than the one used to create the Web service. The client application is available in the sample material for this chapter as the OrderIDServiceClient project with its associated project folder. When you follow this strategy for creating a client, make sure that the client application runs from a computer with the .NET Framework installed. If you do not have a second computer with the .NET Framework installed for evaluation purposes, you have at least a couple of alternatives. First, build the Windows client application on the same computer as the Web service. Second, create an ASP.NET Web page on the same Web server as the Web service. Then, open the Web page from a second computer. The second computer does not need to have the .NET Framework installed to open and invoke the Web service through the Web page because the Web page runs on the Web server but displays in the browser on the second computer.

After creating a client application, add a Web reference to the OrderID-Service Web service. Invoke the Project, Add Web Reference command to open the Add Web Reference dialog box. In my office, this Web service resides in the OrderIDService folder of the ccs1 Web server. Therefore, specify the startup file for the Web service in the Address box of the Add Web Reference dialog box and press Enter. I changed the name of the startup file from its default name of Service1.asmx to OrderIDService.asmx. In my office, the URL for this file is *http://ccs1/OrderIDService/OrderIDService.asmx*. After pressing Enter on the keyboard to input your designated address for the startup file in the Address box, click the Add Reference button when Visual Studio .NET enables it. If this is the first Web reference from the ccs1 Web server, Visual Studio .NET adds a Web service named ccs1 to Solution Explorer for the client application.

Design and Operational Views of the Web Service

The window on the left in Figure 12-13 displays the Design view of the Web service client, and the window on the right is an operational view of the client. *TextBox1* is for specifying an OrderID. *Button1*, *Button2*, and *Button3* invoke the *Freight*, *Items*, and *TotalPrice* Web methods, respectively. *Label2* shows the return value in a sentence for either the *Freight* or *TotalPrice* Web methods, depending on whether *Button1* or *Button3* was clicked last. A click to *Button2*, the Line Items button, populates *ListBox1* with the Quantity, ProductName, and ExtendedPrice for each line item in the order. These line items are the subset of rows from the Order Details table that has OrderID values matching the entry in *TextBox1*.

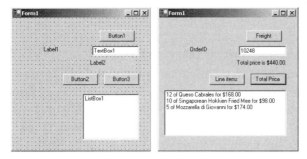

Figure 12-13 Design and operational views of the client application for the OrderIDService Web service

The window on the right in Figure 12-13 shows *Form1* from the Order-IDServiceClient Windows application. I entered **10248** in *TextBox1* for an OrderID value, and I clicked the Line Items and Total Price buttons. Therefore, the line items in *ListBox1* apply to the order with an OrderID value of 10248, and the label below *TextBox1*—*Label2*—displays the sum of the extended prices for the line items in the order. Clicking *Button1* will change the contents of *Label2* to show the freight charge for an order instead of the sum of the extended prices for the line items in an order.

The Code Behind *Form1*

The code behind *Form1* for the client application consists of a module-level declaration that instantiates the proxy variable (*wsc1*) for the Web service, a form load event procedure, and three short click event procedures for the buttons on the form. The *Form1_Load* procedure handles formatting issues. For example, this procedure assigns *Text* property values to the Button controls and *Label1*. The *Form1_Load* procedure also specifies the *Size* and *Location* coordinates for *ListBox1*. In addition, the *Form1_Load* procedure sets the *Visible* property for *ListBox1* to *False*. Later, when a user clicks *Button2* and invokes the *Items* Web method, the client application shows *ListBox1* at the size and location designated in the *Form1_Load* procedure.

The *Button1_Click* and *Button3_Click* procedures have the same format. The *Button1_Click* procedure passes the *Text* property value of *TextBox1* to the Web service pointed at by the *wsc1* proxy variable. *Button1_Click* saves the return value from the *Freight* Web method in *dec1*. Then, the procedure assigns a value to the *Text* property of the *Label2* control. Similarly, the *Button3_Click* procedure invokes a Web method, in this case *TotalPrice* instead of *Freight*. Like *Button1_Click*, *Button3_Click* saves the return value in a *Decimal* data type (*dec1*) and displays the return value from a Web method as the *Text* property value of the *Label2* control.

The *Button2_Click* procedure passes the *Text* property of *TextBox1* to the *Items* Web method of the Web service. The *Items* method returns a dataset. Therefore, the procedure saves the return object from the Web method in the *das1* variable with a *DataSet* type. Then, the *Button2_Click* procedure invokes the *Clear* method for the *Items* collection of the *ListBox1* control. The *Items* collection of a ListBox control reflects the items that display in the control. Next, the procedure declares a variable, *drw1*, with a *DataRow* type. The sample code uses this variable to loop through the rows in the *DataTable* within the *das1* dataset. For each row, the loop formats a line for the ListBox control and invokes the *Add* method for the *Items* collection of *ListBox1* to add the line to the ListBox control.

```
Dim wsc1 As New ccs1.OrderIDService()

Private Sub Form1_Load(ByVal sender As System.Object, _
    ByVal e As System.EventArgs) Handles MyBase.Load

    'Assign Text property values for buttons
    Button1.Text = "Freight"
    Button2.Text = "Line items"
    Button3.Text = "Total Price"

    'Clear TextBox1
    TextBox1.Clear()

    'Format labels
    Label1.Text = "OrderID"
    Label2.Text = ""
    Label2.AutoSize = True
```

(continued)

```vb
            'Size and position ListBox1 relative to TextBox1
            Dim int1 As Integer = TextBox1.Left + TextBox1.Width
            Dim int2 As Integer = int1 - 10
            Dim int3 As Integer = TextBox1.Top + 100
            ListBox1.Size = New System.Drawing.Size(int2, 100)
            ListBox1.Location = New System.Drawing.Point(10, 150)

            'Format ListBox1
            ListBox1.HorizontalScrollbar = True
            ListBox1.Visible = False

        End Sub

        Private Sub Button1_Click(ByVal sender As System.Object, _
            ByVal e As System.EventArgs) Handles Button1.Click

            'Pass Freight Web method in OrderIDService the contents
            'of TextBox1 and save return value in dec1
            Dim dec1 As Decimal = wsc1.Freight(TextBox1.Text)

            'Display returned Freight column value
            Label2.Text = "Freight is " & Format(dec1, "C") & "."

        End Sub

        Private Sub Button2_Click(ByVal sender As System.Object, _
            ByVal e As System.EventArgs) Handles Button2.Click

            Dim das1 As DataSet = wsc1.Items(TextBox1.Text)

            ListBox1.Items.Clear()

            Dim drw1 As DataRow
            For Each drw1 In das1.Tables(0).Rows
                ListBox1.Items.Add(drw1(0).ToString & " of " & _
                    drw1(1) & " for " & Format(drw1(2), "c"))
            Next

            ListBox1.Visible = True

        End Sub

        Private Sub Button3_Click(ByVal sender As System.Object, _
            ByVal e As System.EventArgs) Handles Button3.Click

            'Compute Total Price for OrderID showing in TextBox1
            Dim dec1 As Decimal = wsc1.TotalPrice(TextBox1.Text)
```

```
'Display summed Extended Price for line items in
'OrderID showing in TextBox1
Label2.Text = "Total price is " & Format(decl, "C") & "."

End Sub
```

Summary

After acquainting you briefly with underlying XML Web services technologies, this chapter provides a firm foundation in creating and using Web services. The chapter attacks the topic on three fronts. First, it tackles building clients for an existing Web service. This will be a common development task because one Web service can have various types of clients that selectively expose Web methods or process the return values from Web methods differently. Second, the chapter shows you how to build a Web service and various clients for it. The Web service sample is a basic one that performs a calculation with dates. However, offering some kind of computation is one likely reason for building a Web service. In addition, the discussion of the sample shows how to deploy the Web service solution and build clients for the deployed solution. The chapter concludes with another Web service sample that illustrates how to perform three common tasks for an Access database via a Web service.

13

Securing .NET Applications with Access Databases

Writing secure applications is always an important topic, but its urgency heightens whenever databases are part of a solution. As a Microsoft Access database developer, you can take comfort in knowing that the .NET Framework offers new security features while preserving one of the best ways to lock down applications so that only legitimate users have permissions to access the databases that comprise your solutions. In addition, some of the new .NET security features are particularly easy to implement.

This chapter equips you to start securing your Access database applications in three ways. First, it systematically reviews the core features of the new security offered by the .NET Framework. This review introduces and highlights distinguishing features of .NET security elements, such as code access security, role-based security, and cryptography. Second, the chapter demonstrates how to apply traditional user-level security to a .NET Windows application for an Access database. This section includes a quick review of user-level security as an introduction to tightly securing a sample Access database. Then, the section presents code showing how to use ADO.NET in concert with user-level security to manage secure data access and data manipulation. The chapter's closing section presents forms authentication for .NET Web applications. This easy-to-implement technology can lock down the Web forms at a Web site until users authenticate themselves. Forms authentication offers several strategies for authenticating users, but this presentation illustrates how to use a table in an Access database to validate the credentials of entrants to a Web site.

Overview of .NET Security

.NET Framework security focuses heavily on built-in policies for administering the security of applications. In addition, the .NET Framework offers tools and policies for customizing built-in security policies. Many .NET Framework security features cater to the skills of system and machine administrators. Database developers need to gain a familiarity of .NET Framework security policies so that they can work with administrators to ensure database applications have a proper set of policies that enable those applications to run without interference from security settings. Database developers also must learn that using inappropriate security settings could jeopardize the integrity of the systems on which their applications run.

Database developers need to understand that .NET security techniques do not replace database security practices. Instead, .NET security complements database security. It is critical that database developers master techniques for securely administering their databases. By having a thorough understanding of database security techniques, a developer can understand how to mix and match database security practices with .NET Framework system security policies.

Code Access Security

Code access security policies determine what resources a .NET Framework assembly can reference. The assembly is the basic security unit in the .NET Framework security model. In the examples presented throughout this book, an assembly maps to a project folder. In order to take advantage of code access security, your assemblies must be type safe. This requirement restricts the data types that the methods in an assembly can accept as well as the memory locations that an assembly can reference. Type-safe code helps prevent buffer overruns, which is one common way errant code can break through traditional security safeguards or inappropriately take over resources such as Microsoft SQL Server. The Microsoft Visual Basic .NET compiler returns type-safe code, but not all compilers for .NET languages necessarily do this.

> **Note**   The .NET Framework enforces rules that control how code operates through code *grants*. The grants for an assembly specify the permissions available to the code in the assembly. For example, code that is not type safe cannot run on another computer unless an administrator explicitly permits code to bypass verification for type safety.

From the conceptual level at which this presentation addresses code access security, you need a grasp of evidence, permissions, and security policies. These concepts interact with one another to determine how code operates. For example, the common language runtime (CLR) examines the evidence for an assembly relative to default or customized security policy settings for a computer. Evidence can include where an assembly came from or who its author is. For example, code from the Internet will typically not enjoy the same permissions as code from a local computer. However, code published by a trusted author such as a contractor doing custom work for your organization might override restrictions that normally apply to code derived from the Internet.

Code access permissions are gateways to the resources and functions on a computer. Selected classes that provide code access permissions have names that reflect their uses, such as the following:

- *OleDbPermission* for OLE DB .NET Data Provider permissions

- *SqlClientPermission* for SQL Server .NET Data Provider permissions

- *FileIOPermission* for permissions to read, write, or append files

- *WebPermission* for permissions to connect to Web addresses

- *SecurityPermission* for permissions to manage .NET Framework security

See the "Code Access Permissions" topic in the Microsoft Visual Studio .NET documentation for additional permission class names. Permissions are two-sided tools. On one side, an assembly can present, or demand, the permissions that it needs to run successfully. On the other side, a machine can assign a set of permissions to an assembly based on the evidence for an assembly. If the permission that an assembly needs to run is not available from a machine, the code in the assembly throws an *Exception* object. Assemblies can optionally contain code to gracefully handle exceptions. For example, if an assembly requires the *Microsoft.Jet.OLEDB.4.0* provider but the machine restricts access to this provider, the assembly will fail to load successfully.

Security policy is the set of permissions that apply to the operation of code on a machine. Machine and enterprise administrators can configure security policy permissions for specific requirements. An enterprise administrator can restrict access from individual software publishers (based on their strong name or cryptographic signature) as well as block the downloading of applications from specific Web sites. The .NET Framework simplifies the administration of permissions by assigning assemblies to code groups based on evidence about an assembly. Administrators assign permissions to code groups and inherit permissions based on their membership in a code group. Two tools are available for helping administrators to administer security policy: the .NET Framework Configuration tool (Mscorcfg.msc) and the Code Access Security Policy tool (Caspol.exe).

The .NET Framework permits the administration of security policy at any of four levels, including an enterprise, a machine, an individual user, and an application domain. Application domains define secure, isolated boundaries between two or more processes that can run concurrently on the same computer. The security policy levels appear in hierarchical order with the enterprise level being the highest and the application domain level being the lowest. Typically, different individuals will administer security policy at different levels. A lower level cannot repeal a restriction set at a higher level, but an administrator of a lower level can tighten a restriction so that code meant to run at a higher level throws an *Exception* object instead of successfully operating. For this reason, a higher level can specify that lower levels cannot alter a security policy setting.

The elaborate .NET Framework security architecture enables administrators and developers to work together to protect organizations against typical kinds of security problems. For example, this section described earlier how type-safe code guards against buffer overruns. The call stack is another construct that works in combination with assembly permissions. The call stack can guard against lurking attacks—for example, one in which code without permission to perform a task invokes trusted code to perform that task. The CLR examines the hierarchy of assembly calls in the call stack before enabling a method. Therefore, an Internet application cannot invoke another application to read or write to a machine's hard drive by invoking another trusted assembly to perform the task for the Internet application.

Role-Based Security

Code access security is about managing permissions for code—namely, assemblies—to access resources or perform actions. Role-based security applies the same notions to users and groups of users. As an Access developer, you have experience with role-based security for user-level security with Access database files. We will examine Access user-level security more closely in the next section when demonstrating how to use it with ADO.NET objects. For now, focus on the fact that user-level security makes use of users and groups to control the kind of permissions that users have to the objects in an Access database file. With role-based security, you can define similar kinds of identities as users and groups. Then you can specify permissions for these identities, or you can enable functionality in your application based on individual identities or group memberships.

Access user-level security is an example of a security model for a database. Role-based security in the .NET Framework is for your custom applications. The Access user-level security model applies exclusively to the Access database files. The role-based security model in the .NET Framework is flexible because it allows you to apply a single model to multiple databases. For example, although the details of the Access and SQL Server security models differ, you can expose the same kind of security for both Access and SQL Server databases with the .NET Framework's role-based security. When you need a common application security model for multiple types of databases, the .NET Framework's role-based security model offers an interesting option. If you know that your application will always work exclusively with one type of database (which might be true for some Access developers), using the native security model for a database can simplify your development. This is especially true if you are already familiar with a security model for the type of database that your application references.

Implementing role-based security in the .NET Framework requires up to three steps. First, you define the *Principal* and *Identity* objects. The *Principal* object contains an *Identity* object. The *Identity* object holds information identifying a user, and the *Principal* object specifies roles to which its *Identity* object can belong. You can use the *Principal* object and its associated *Identity* object to authenticate and authorize a user. Authentication is the process for verifying that a user is who she says she is. Authorization is the process of assigning rights to a *Principal* object so that it can perform actions. The .NET Framework provides two types of *Principal* objects. The *WindowsPrincipal* object enables your application to check the Windows group membership of a Windows user. This relieves your application from managing the authentication process because Windows does this when a user logs on to a Windows server. The *GenericPrincipal* object is a generic principal for which you programmatically manage authentication as part of your application.

> **Note**   *Principal* objects are associated with threads within a process. Any one process controlled by a procedure can have multiple threads. For example, you can associate a separate thread with each instance of a class in an application.

The second and third steps for implementing role-based security can work together to enable permissions for *Principal* objects. The second step creates a *PrincipalPermission* object. This object designates an *Identity* object and a role. The third step can demand the *PrincipalPermission* object. If the *Principal* object for the current thread does not match the *Identity* and role demanded via the *PrincipalPermission* object, the .NET Framework throws an *Exception* object. Otherwise, the code in the third step operates normally. Instantiating and demanding a *PrincipalPermission* object is optional because you can directly check the *Identity* and/or role of the *Principal* for the current thread.

Cryptographic Services

Cryptographic services represent another major security element within the .NET Framework. You can achieve three primary security objectives with cryptography in the .NET Framework. First, you can protect your data or your identity. For example, you can encrypt/decrypt user logon credentials as part of a custom logon application. Second, you can verify that data was not altered during transmission. Third, you can learn the publisher of an encrypted document. The "Cryptographic Services" topic in the Visual Studio .NET documentation provides links for drilling down further into .NET Framework implementations of cryptography.

Note   If you're running Microsoft Windows 2000 or Microsoft Internet Explorer version 5.01 or earlier, you need to download and install the High Encryption Pack to ensure the highest level of encryption (128 bits). This is available via Microsoft's Web site at *http://www.microsoft.com/windows/ie/downloads/recommended/128bit/*.

For encrypting and decrypting documents, including datasets as *XmlDataDocument* objects, you can use *private key encryption*. This style of encryption is commonly referred to as *symmetric encryption* because the same key encrypts as well as decrypts documents. The .NET Framework offers several styles of symmetric encryption as separate classes. All symmetric encryption styles can process documents as a series of blocks, such as a series of bytes. To disguise the encryption process, the encrypted value for each block uses some information from the prior block to designate the encrypted value for the current block. An initialization vector plays this role for a document's first block. With symmetric encryption schemes, you can specify the encryption style with three elements: the name for the encryption class, the encryption key, and the initialization vector.

Public key encryption is suitable for encrypting small amounts of data. This style of encryption is referred to as *asymmetric encryption* because it relies on two different yet linked keys. Data encrypted by one key can be decrypted by the other key. The two keys for this style of encryption are known as the *public key* and the *private key*. You can distribute the public key widely without security. A recipient can use the public key to decrypt a document encrypted by the private key. Another use for public key encryption is the transfer of the encryption key for a symmetric encryption style. By using public key encryption to pass the symmetric encryption key, you can securely share a symmetric encryption key between two users. This technique allows public key encryption to support the application of private key encryption. In addition to encrypting documents, public key encryption is useful for making digital signatures to identify a publisher. Therefore, releasing a private key will allow others to impersonate a publisher.

The .NET Framework implements both private key encryption and public key encryption. Creating a cryptographic scheme and even implementing its code is an advanced topic. See the ".NET Framework Cryptography Model" and "Creating a Cryptographic Scheme" topics in the Visual Studio .NET documentation for more details. You can find some illustrative sample code in the selection of topics within the "Cryptographic Tasks" topic in the Visual Studio .NET documentation. Furthermore, Richard Mansfield's DevX Web site article about Visual Basic .NET cryptography, "Keeping Secrets: A Guide to VB .NET Cryptography," contains some instructive sample code: *http://www.devx.com/security/articles/rm0802/rm0802.asp*.

Access User-Level Security and ADO.NET

Access user-level security interoperates well with ADO.NET. With user-level security, you can create .NET solutions that authenticate and authorize data access and data manipulation tasks for Access database files. Those building solutions for Access databases with Visual Basic .NET likely will have good working knowledge of user-level security because it has been so closely associated with Access databases since its early releases. When invoking user-level security, you must understand that security does not impact your code until the code makes a request of the Jet engine. This functionality is common in database solutions, and if it is acceptable for your application, you can rely on user-level security to provide a useful and familiar alternative to the specialized .NET Framework security techniques.

This section examines user-level security from several perspectives. First, the section begins with a quick review of user-level security design and operation issues. This is mostly to refresh your memory and highlight key issues. You should consult Access Help if you want a more in-depth review of user-level security. Second, the section reviews the setup of a database with user-level security. All the instructions are for the Access 2002 user interface, which is similar to earlier versions of Access. Using the Access user interface makes the sample setup easy to follow. I did this to save the sample code for the discussion of management of user-level security. The third and fourth parts of this section present the sample code. The first sample focuses on data access. The second sample demonstrates how to manage security as a gateway for manipulating a database.

> **Note**   One unique benefit of the Access 2002 user interface is the direct access it offers to the Workgroup Administrator on the Tools, Security menu. Users of earlier versions of Access can search for this administrator (for example, by using the Search or Find utility available by right-clicking the Windows Start button).

Review of User-Level Security Design Issues

User-level security is the most robust form of built-in security for Access database files. This form of security requires the existence of a workgroup information file. This file is actually an Access database file, but it has an .mdw extension and plays a special role in user-level security. The .mdw file for a workgroup stores information about the users and groups in a workgroup. These users and groups enjoy permissions, such as the ability to read or update a table in an Access database. One .mdw file can apply to one or more .mdb files. In the user-level security model, the .mdb file contains the database objects, such as tables and queries, as well as permissions to use those objects. User-level security manages security through the intersection of an .mdw file with an .mdb file.

> **Note**   The .mdw file is sometimes referred to as the system database file. This designation is particularly relevant to creating connection strings for Access databases with user-level security.

In a sense, user-level security is always on, but it is not activated until you assign a password to the built-in Admin account. The Admin account initially has a *Null* password. Before assigning a password to the Admin user, anyone can open an Access database file without specifying a password. All the Access database samples shown so far in the book demonstrate how to open database files without user-level security. Once the Admin account has a password, you must specify an .mdw file, a user account, and optionally a user password to open an Access database file. The user account (and its optional password) permit user-level security to authenticate a user. The intersection of the user and group account specifications in the .mdw file with the permissions and database objects in the .mdb file authorize users to perform actions, such as reading and updating database objects. When using Visual Studio .NET to programmatically open a database in which the Admin account has a password, you must update your connection string to designate an .mdw file as well as a user account and the password for the account (if one exists).

All Access databases initially have an Admin user account as well as Admins and Users group accounts. You can create additional user and group accounts to designate the individuals and roles of workgroup members in a user-level security model for an Access database file. The Admin account is initially a member of the Admins group account. Any user account in the Admins group account is an administrator in a workgroup. Users opening an Access database file (.mdb) with an administrator account have unrestricted permissions for the objects in the database. Because the Admin account exists in all Access database files, it is good security practice to remove it from the Admins group after adding another custom-defined user to that group. This practice strengthens your database security because the name of an administrator account is not automatically known.

You will also typically want to remove any permissions for the Users group. This is because any new users you add to a workgroup automatically inherit these permissions. Therefore, individual user accounts have whatever permissions you explicitly assign them plus the permissions they inherit from the Users group. By removing all permissions from the Users group, you maintain stricter control over the permissions to individual user accounts and any group accounts that you create.

Setting Up for the User-Level Security Samples

To set up for the user-level security samples, we will need an .mdw file with designated user and group accounts and an .mdb file with database objects and coordinated permissions for the user and group accounts in the .mdw file. The security samples demonstrate a simple data access task that is restricted to users with permission to read a table and an update task that selectively grants update permission to some but not all users. The .mdb file for the security samples has the name MyNWTables.mdb. This file contains copies of the Categories and Customers tables from the Northwind database. The .mdw file for the security samples has the name MyNWTables.mdw, and it contains users with selective permissions for data access as well as data manipulation.

To begin the setup, open a new session of Access 2002. Choose Tools, Security, Workgroup Administrator. Then, click Create on the Workgroup Administrator dialog box. Access automatically populates the Name and Organization text boxes on the Workgroup Owner Information dialog box with the name and organization of the registered Access licensee. Enter a text string of up to 20 characters into the Workgroup ID text box and click OK. The Workgroup ID value is case sensitive. For the sample workgroup information file, I entered MyNWTables. You should securely store the Workgroup ID value (along with the Name and Organization values on the dialog box) in case you have to reconstruct the workgroup information file. You can save the .mdw file anywhere that your Visual Studio .NET project can access it. The following two security samples use the bin folder within the project folder for a Windows application project named MyNWTables. Browse to the folder in which you want to store your .mdw file, assign a filename such as MyNWTables in the File Name box in the Select Workgroup Information File dialog box, and click Open.

After clicking Open, you are ready to work your way out of the dialog boxes. Start by clicking OK twice. Figure 13-1 shows the dialog box in which you click OK the second time. This dialog box confirms the workgroup information file settings. You might want to take a screen shot of this dialog box to document your workgroup information file settings. Clicking OK here displays yet another message, confirming the successful creation of the workgroup file. Clicking OK in this display and OK in the Workgroup Information File dialog box puts you in a position to use the workgroup information file.

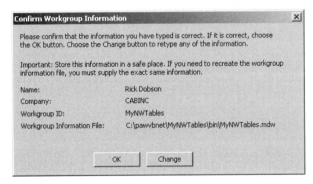

Figure 13-1   The confirmation dialog box for setting up the sample workgroup information file (.mdw)

You can start using the .mdw file by closing and reopening Access. Access automatically uses the last .mdw file created as the workgroup information file. Start by creating three new user accounts: MyAdmin, ReadOnlyUser, and Read-WriteUser. All user accounts will have blank passwords until we change them later in the process. To create a new user, choose Tools, Security, User And Group Accounts. In the resulting dialog box, click New on the Users tab. Enter a user account name and a personal ID for the first user account, such as **MyAdmin** and **MyNWTables**. Just as you saved the workgroup ID along with the name and organization needed to re-create the workgroup information file, you should store the name and personal ID settings for all users. Saving this information permits you to re-create the account if necessary. Figure 13-2 shows the setup settings for the MyAdmin user account. Click OK to finalize the settings. Then, create the other two user accounts, ReadOnlyUser and Read-WriteUser. You can use any legitimate personal ID setting that you prefer—namely, any alphanumeric string 4–20 characters in length.

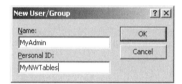

Figure 13-2   Setup settings for the MyAdmin user account

After creating the user accounts, you can manipulate these newly created user accounts as well as the built-in Admin user account. For these samples, you'll need to make changes to the MyAdmin and Admin user accounts. Select MyAdmin from the drop-down box on the Users tab in the User And Group Accounts dialog box. Notice that this user account is a member of the Users group but not the Admins group. Because the security samples depend on the MyAdmin account being a security administrator, select Admins in the Available Groups box and click Add>>. The next step is to remove the Admin account from the Admins group. Start by selecting the Admin user in the drop-down box. With Admins selected in the Member Of box, click <<Remove. This removes Admin as a security administrator. Next, assign a password to the Admin account to require user authentication when opening Access. Click the Change Logon Password tab. Leave the old password box blank, and enter the string "password" into the New Password and Verify text boxes. Click OK to confirm your settings. Assigning a password to the Admin account pops up a Logon dialog box the next time you use Access interactively to perform a task that involves user-level security.

Close and reopen Access to launch a session with MyAdmin as the default security administrator account. Click the Blank Database link on the Task pane. Then, save a new database file (.mdb) named MyNWTables in the bin subdirectory of the MyNWTables Windows application project folder. After clicking Create in the File New Database dialog box, Access pops up a Logon dialog box with MyAdmin as the user account and no password. Click OK. This step makes MyAdmin the owner of the MyNWTables database. Import the Customers and Categories tables from the Northwind database with the File, Get External Data, Import command.

> **Note**   If the Logon dialog box does not default to designating MyAdmin before you create the database file, override the entry and insert MyAdmin as the user account.

After importing the tables, adjust the permissions for the users and groups so that they match our requirements. Choose Tools, Security, User And Group Permissions to open a dialog box. Select the Categories table. Notice that only the MyAdmin user has any permissions for the table. In fact, the MyAdmin user has all the permissions for the Categories table. The same pattern of user permissions applies to the Customers table as well as for new tables and queries. Select the Groups radio button below the User/Group Name box. In this case, both the Admins and the Users groups have all permissions for both tables as well as new tables and queries. Select the Users group in the User/Group Name box with the Categories table selected, and clear all permission check boxes on the dialog box. (Clicking the Read Design check box can accomplish this.) Then, click Apply. Use the same process to clear Users group permissions for the Customers table as well as new tables and queries. You can now set permissions for individual user accounts without having membership in the Users group convey extra permissions.

Start to set permissions for the ReadOnlyUser and ReadWriteUser accounts by clicking the Users radio button. Then, select the ReadOnlyUser account name and the Categories table. Select the Read Data permission check box. Access additionally selects the Read Design check box because Access links these two permissions. (See Figure 13-3.) Clicking Apply assigns the ReadOnly-User account permission to read data from the Categories table. Apply the Read Data permission for the Customers table to the ReadOnlyUser account as well. In the case of the ReadWriteUser account, assign Read Data and Update Data permissions for both the Categories and Customers tables; this process automatically includes Read Design permission as well. After making the permission assignments just described, the Admin user still has no permissions for either the Categories or Customers tables.

Figure 13-3   Permission settings for the ReadOnlyUser account with the Categories table

To complete the security settings, we can add passwords to the three new users added to the MyNWTables.mdw file. We already specified a string value of "password" for the Admin user. At this point, each new user still has a *Null* password value. (That is, these user accounts have no password value.) You can change the password for the MyAdmin user, who is the current user, by choosing Tools, Security, User And Group Accounts. Next, select the Change Logon Password tab. Then, follow the previously described process for adding a password to the Admin user. To assign passwords to the ReadOnlyUser and ReadWriteUser accounts, close and reopen Access with each user account. During the session for each user account, choose Tools, Security, User And Group Accounts and follow the process for assigning a password to the MyAdmin account. In the sample for this chapter, I assigned the string "password" as the password for all three new user accounts.

Note   See my book *Programming Microsoft Access Version 2002* (Microsoft Press, 2001) for VBA code samples that manage and report on user-level security with the *ADOX* object model or Jet SQL.

Selecting from a Secure Access Database with ADO.NET

The first user-level security sample demonstrates how to specify the arguments for a secure connection as well as an approach to managing the connection. The sample's discussion begins with a demonstration of how user-level security works for a simple selection task in a Windows application project. Then, the presentation describes how the code behind the Windows form controls the operation of the application.

Demonstration

Figure 13-4 shows the selection sample application in action with the ReadOnly-User account. The top window shows the Windows form for the application. The top text box (*TextBox1*) displays the user account name. The second text box (*TextBox2*) displays asterisks instead of the password that I typed into the text box. Clicking the top button (*Button1*) with the *Text* property value of Show Scalar opens the second window in Figure 13-4. This window is a message box that merely echoes the connection string that the application uses to connect to the MyNWTables.mdb file. I will discuss the syntax of the connection string when I review the code for the sample. Showing this message box reinforces the value of displaying intermediate values such as connection strings when you debug an application. In a production version of an application, you typically comment out the lines of code that display this type of message box. The bottom window in Figure 13-4 shows the result of the selection statement (a *Count* aggregate function) in a string expression. The function returns the number of CategoryID values in the Categories table.

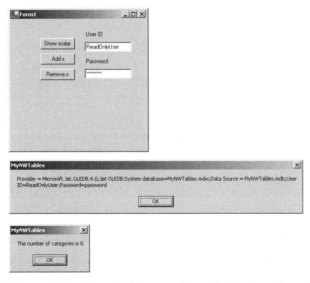

Figure 13-4   The selection sample application in action, with an account that can read from the Categories table

The sequence of windows in Figure 13-4 concludes with a display of the number of categories in the Categories table because the ReadOnlyUser account has permission to read the data in the Categories table. However, what happens if a user inputs a user account that doesn't have Read Data permission for the Categories table? Figure 13-5 shows the sequence of windows for the Admin user. This user is in the MyNWTables.mdw file, so it is a valid user account. However, the account does not have Read Data permission for the Categories table. The top window shows the input values, and the middle window shows the resulting connection string. This type of display can be useful if input values are no longer easily visible elsewhere. The bottom window displays a native error message from the Jet engine. The application uses a *Try...Catch...End Try* statement to return the error message. If the user inputs an invalid user account such as Adminx, the bottom window would confirm that either the user account or password is not valid. Again, this would be a message from the Jet engine displayed inside the Windows application.

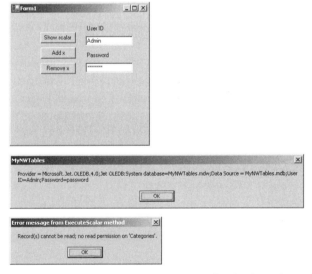

Figure 13-5   The selection sample application in action, with an account that cannot read from the Categories table

Code Behind the Form

The code behind *Button1* takes advantage of four code blocks behind the form: the module-level declaration area, the *Form1_Load* procedure, the *Button1_Click* procedure, and the *ConnectToMyNWTables* procedure. The module-level declaration area that follows includes declarations for the next sample as well. However, this sample relies on the declaration and the instantiation of *cnn1* as an

OleDbConnection object. The other elements of the code use this object reference and invoke methods for it. This *cnn1* variable serves double duty in this code sample as well as the next one.

The *Form1_Load* procedure formats the controls on the form. This procedure groups its code into three units. The first unit formats the labels by assigning *Text* property values as well as setting the alignment so that the text appears close to the text box on the left edge. The second code unit formats the text box controls on *Form1*. This code clears both text boxes of their default assignments and assigns an asterisk as the symbol for representing password characters in *TextBox2*. The closing unit of code in the *Form1_Load* procedure assigns *Text* property values to the three button controls on the form.

The *Button1_Click* procedure works in concert with the *ConnectToMyNWTables Function* procedure to process and report on data from the MyNWTables.mdb file. The *Button1_Click* procedure starts by invoking the *ConnectToMyNWTables* function. While the *Button1_Click* procedure invokes the function, it passes *Text* property values for *TextBox1* and *TextBox2* as arguments. The click event procedure saves the return value from the function in the *cnn1* variable. The *ConnectToMyNWTables* function instantiates a new connection object each time it is invoked based on the current procedure's *Text* property values for *TextBox1* and *TextBox2*. With these design features, the procedure does need code to close the connection object (*cnn1* at the module level) to change the connection string if the text box values differ from the last invocation of the procedure. Next, the *Button1_Click* procedure displays the connection string value computed by the function procedure in a message box.

As mentioned previously, you will probably want to add a comment marker in a production application before the line displaying the connection string, but displays such as this are convenient while you are debugging an application. Next, the *Button1_Click* procedure tries to open the *OleDbConnection* object at which the *cnn1* variable points. If the user inputs a valid user account and password and the database is available, the *Open* method should succeed. The procedure embeds the invocation of the *Open* method in a *Try...Catch...End Try* statement. By printing the *Message* property for *Exception* objects thrown by the *Open* method, the procedure displays native error messages from the Jet engine.

After opening a connection to the MyNWTables Access database, the *Button1_Click* procedure moves on to using the connection. It does this by instantiating *cmd1* as an *OleDbCommand* object. Then, it uses the *cnn1* variable and a SELECT statement to assign property values to the object. Next, the procedure embeds the invocation of the *ExecuteScalar* method for the *OleDb-Command* object in another *Try...Catch...End Try* statement. This statement catches the use of the Admin account, which does not have Read Data permission for the Categories table. The use of the Admin account does not throw an *Exception* in the first *Try...Catch...End Try* statement because the account is valid for making a connection to the MyNWTables database. The next to last statement in the *Button1_Click* procedure displays a count of the rows in the Categories table, and the last statement in the procedure closes the *cnn1* object.

The *ConnectToMyNWTables Function* procedure starts by checking to see whether the user ID or password arguments passed to it are empty strings. If so, the connection will not succeed. The first *Try...Catch...End Try* statement in the *Button1_Click* procedure catches the *Exception* that the .NET Framework throws for either missing value, but the two *If...Then* statements that start the function procedure offer more precise feedback to the user about the cause of the problem and how to fix it. After testing the user ID and password values that serve as inputs to a connection string, the procedure computes the string in four separate parts with semicolons as delimiters between parts. The procedure starts the specification of the connection string by designating the Jet provider.

Next, the procedure adds a pointer for the workgroup information file. Then, the procedure references the data source for the connection object. Both the workgroup information file and the Access database file reside in the bin subdirectory of the project folder. Therefore, you can reference the files without designating any explicit path. The expressions for computing a connection string conclude by appending the user ID and password arguments. The user ID is the user account name in *TextBox1*, and the password argument is the password associated with the user account. The second and fourth parts of the connection string are mandated because the application relies on user-level security. This reliance permits the rejection of user account names that are not in the workgroup information file and the rejection of attempts to perform actions by a user account for which it does not have permission.

```
'Declare and instantiate an OleDbConnection object
Dim cnn1 As New System.Data.OleDb.OleDbConnection()

'Instantiate dap1 as an OleDbDataAdapter object
Dim dap1 As New OleDb.OleDbDataAdapter()

'Instantiate das1 as a DataSet object
Dim das1 As New System.Data.DataSet()

Private Sub Form1_Load(ByVal sender As System.Object, _
    ByVal e As System.EventArgs) Handles MyBase.Load

    'Format label controls
    Label1.Text = "User ID"
```

(continued)

```
        Label2.Text = "Password"
        Label1.TextAlign = ContentAlignment.BottomLeft
        Label2.TextAlign = ContentAlignment.BottomLeft

        'Format text box controls
        TextBox1.Text = ""
        TextBox2.Text = ""
        TextBox2.PasswordChar = "*"

        'Format button controls
        Button1.Text = "Show scalar"
        Button2.Text = "Add x"
        Button3.Text = "Remove x"

End Sub

Private Sub Button1_Click(ByVal sender As System.Object, _
    ByVal e As System.EventArgs) Handles Button1.Click

    'Specify a connection to MyNWTables database
    'with User ID and Password specified in
    'text box controls
    cnn1 = ConnectToMyNWTables(TextBox1.Text, _
        TextBox2.Text)

    'Display connection string for diagnostic purposes;
    'comment this line out in production version
    MsgBox(cnn1.ConnectionString)

    'Connect or exit procedure after displaying
    'diagnostic message if attempt to connect fails
    Try
        cnn1.Open()
    Catch exc1 As System.Exception
        MsgBox(exc1.Message, , _
            "Error message from Open method")
        Exit Sub
    End Try

    'Declare and instantiate an OleDbCommand object
    Dim cmd1 As New System.Data.OleDb.OleDbCommand()

    'Assign Connection and CommandText property values
    'for the cmd1 OleDbCommand object
    cmd1.Connection = cnn1
    cmd1.CommandText = _
        "SELECT Count(CategoryID) FROM Categories"
```

```
'Save result set from command in int1 memory variable
'if ExecuteScalar method succeeds; otherwise, display
'diagnostic message
Dim int1 As Integer
Try
    int1 = cmd1.ExecuteScalar
Catch exc1 As System.Exception
    MsgBox(exc1.Message, , _
        "Error message from ExecuteScalar method")
    Exit Sub
End Try

'Display result from query
MsgBox("The number of categories is " & _
    int1.ToString & ".")

'Close connection
cnn1.Close()

End Sub

Function ConnectToMyNWTables(ByVal inID As String, _
    ByVal inPW As String) As OleDb.OleDbConnection

    'Check for missing User ID or Password
    If inID = "" Then
        MsgBox("Input a UserID please.", _
            MsgBoxStyle.Exclamation, _
            "Input error message")
    End If
    If inPW = "" Then
        MsgBox("Input a Password please.", _
            MsgBoxStyle.Exclamation, _
            "Input error message")
    End If

    'Designate string for connection to MyNWTables database
    '    first, specify provider
    '    second, specify workgroup information file
    '    third, specify target database
    '    fourth, designate a user id and password
    Dim str1 As String = _
        "Provider = Microsoft.Jet.OLEDB.4.0;"
    str1 &= _
        "Jet OLEDB:System database=MyNWTables.mdw;"
    str1 &= _
```

(continued)

```
                  "Data Source = MyNWTables.mdb;"
             str1 &= _
                "User ID=" & inID & ";Password=" & inPW

             'Instantiate an OleDbConnection object and
             'assign a connection string to the object
             Dim cnn1 As New System.Data.OleDb.OleDbConnection()
             cnn1.ConnectionString = str1

             'Return the Connection object
             Return cnn1

        End Function
```

Updating a Secure Access Database with ADO.NET

The second user-level security sample illustrates how to manage data manipulation with a secure Access database. The presentation of the sample starts with a demonstration of how the code operates. Then, the presentation shifts to a review of the code elements.

Demonstration

This user-level security sample demonstrates the impact of the Read Update permission. This permission enables a user account to update a column value in a table or a query. The ReadWriteUser account has this permission for the Customers table, but the ReadOnlyUser account does not. Therefore, an attempt to update the Customers table succeeds for the ReadWriteUser account but fails for the ReadOnlyUser account. As you saw, the ReadOnlyUser account was successful in the prior sample. This distinction confirms your ability to manage permissions for various kinds of database tasks.

This user-level security sample relies on event procedures associated with two buttons. The first button (*Button2*) has a *Text* property value of *Add x*. This is because the button adds an *x* to the end of the CompanyName column value for the customer with a CustomerID column value of *ALFKI* in the *DataTable* object of a local dataset. The application synchronizes the *DataTable* object in the local dataset with the Customers table in the MyNWTables database. After adding the *x* to the local dataset, the procedure updates the database through an *OleDbDataAdapter* object. The second button (*Button3*) has a *Text* property value of *Remove x*. This button simply removes the last character from the same row and column referenced by *Button2* in the *DataTable* object for the local dataset before updating the database to reflect the change.

Figure 13-6 shows a series of three windows that illustrates the operation of *Button2*. The top window shows *Form1* with the ReadWriteUser account specified as the user ID. Because this account has the Read Update permission for the Customers table, the account has the authority to add an *x* to the CompanyName column value for the row with a CustomerID column value of *ALFKI*. The second window shows an Access Datasheet view of the Customers table with the appended *x* that results from clicking *Button2*. Clicking *Button3* displays an intermediate message before removing the last character from the CompanyName column value from the row with *ALFKI* as a CustomerID column value. This message reminds the user that the removal of the last character is based on the connection for the Add X button. That is, *Button3* does not make a fresh connection to the database; instead, it uses the existing connection for the last time the local dataset was populated. The sample code takes advantage of the disconnected dataset object in ADO.NET. Therefore, it operates on the local dataset created when the user last clicked *Button2*. You can confirm that the *x* is removed by going to the Access database and refreshing the second window shown in Figure 13-6.

Figure 13-6   The operation of the second user-level security sample, with a valid account for updating the Access database

Figure 13-7 shows the operation of the second user-level security sample with a user account that is invalid for updating the Customers table in the MyNWTables database. The ReadOnlyUser account has Read Data permission for the Customers table but does not have Update Data permission. The change to the local dataset will succeed because Access user-level permissions do not apply to that table. However, when the application invokes the *Update* method to synchronize the changed local dataset with the Customers table in the Access database, the application throws an *Exception* object. A *Try…Catch…End Try* statement traps the *Exception* object and displays the message returned by the Jet engine in the second window shown in Figure 13-7.

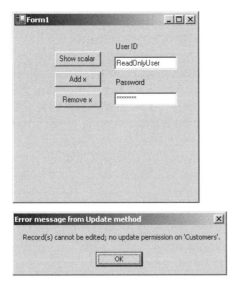

Figure 13-7   The operation of the second user-level security sample, with an invalid account for updating the Access database

Code Behind the Form

The code behind *Form1* for the update of the Customers table in the Northwind database relies on elements in the listing from the prior sample, including data adapter (*dap1*) and dataset (*das1*) declarations at the module level and the *ConnectToMyNWTables Function* procedure. Of course, specialized code that targets the unique needs of this user-level security sample also exists. The following listing includes click event procedures for *Button2* and *Button3* as well as a function procedure, *ConnectForUpdate*, that builds on the function procedure from the prior sample to enable updating a secure Access database over an *OleDbConnection* object.

The *Button2_Click* procedure has three primary objectives. First, the procedure readies the application to update the Customers table in the MyNW-Tables.mdb database file. The procedure meets this goal by testing the return value from the *ConnectForUpdate Function* procedure. A return value of

<;$MI>1 signals a failed attempt to connect. In response to this return value, the code halts by exiting the *Button2_Click* procedure. Second, the procedure updates a local *DataTable* object by appending an *x* to the value in the second column of a row whose first column value equals *ALFKI*. The first step in this update initializes the local *DataTable* object based on the values in the Customers table of the MyNWTables.mdb database file. Third, the procedure invokes the *Update* method for the *dap1* variable instantiated in the *ConnectForUpdate Function* procedure. By invoking the *Update* method in a *Try...Catch...End Try* statement, the procedure can detect an attempt by an unauthorized user to update the Customers table. If the *Update* method succeeds, the procedure ends normally. If a user causes the application to invoke the *Update* method with a user account that does not have Update Data permission, the procedure traps the resulting *Exception* object and displays the associated message from the Jet engine.

The *Button3_Click* procedure generally follows the design of the click event procedure for *Button2*, except that the first step is decidedly different. As you have learned, the role of this procedure is to undo the change implemented by the *Button2_Click* procedure. The first step in the *Button3_Click* procedure does not create a connection to the MyNWTables.mdb file. Instead, it checks to see whether the *das1* dataset, initially populated by the invocation of the *ConnectForUpdate Function* procedure in the *Button2_Click* procedure, has any *DataTable* objects. If the dataset has no *DataTable* objects, the code will have nothing to undo and halts by exiting the *Button3_Click* procedure. If at least one *DataTable* object exists in the *das1* dataset, the procedure prints a message reminding the user it will work with the *Connection* object created by the click to the Add X button (*Button2*).

The second step in the *Button3_Click* procedure differs only slightly from the same step in the *Button2_Click* procedure. The *Button3_Click* procedure removes the last character from the second column value from the *DataTable* object's row, whose first column value is *ALFKI*. This process allows the *Button3_Click* procedure to remove the *x* added by the *Button2_Click* procedure. The third step in the *Button3_Click* procedure is identical to the third step in the *Button2_Click* procedure. Its goal is to synchronize the change to the local *DataTable* with the Customers table in the MyNWTables.mdb file.

The *ConnectForUpdate Function* procedure provides two services. First, it makes a connection to the MyNWTables.mdb file. It does this by calling the *ConnectToMyNWTables Function* procedure while passing the user account name and password value in *TextBox1* and *TextBox2*, respectively. The review of the code for the preceding sample describes the operation of the *ConnectToMyNWTables Function* procedure. The second step involves using the connection created in the first step to assist in the definition of an *OleDb-DataAdapter* object that facilitates updating a database table. You learned in Chapter 8 that this task requires the use of parameters in the specification of properties for an *OleDbDataAdapter* object. In fact, the code in this procedure specifying the ability of the data adapter to populate and update a dataset is an excerpt from the code listed in the "Data Manipulation Setup Code" section of Chapter 8.

```
Private Sub Button2_Click(ByVal sender As System.Object, _
        ByVal e As System.EventArgs) Handles Button2.Click

    'If did not fill dataset, exit procedure
    If ConnectForUpdate() = -1 Then
        Exit Sub
    End If

    'Select row to modify
    Dim drw1 As DataRow = _
        das1.Tables(0).Rows.Find("ALFKI")

    'Perform row modification by appending an x
    drw1(1) &= "x"

    'Update Access database file and local dataset
    'row state for found DataRow
    Try
        dap1.Update(das1, "CustomerIDsNames")
    Catch exc1 As System.Exception
        MsgBox(exc1.Message, , _
            "Error message from Update method")
    End Try

End Sub

Private Sub Button3_Click(ByVal sender As System.Object, _
    ByVal e As System.EventArgs) Handles Button3.Click

    'If no DataTable object in das1, exit procedure
    If Not (das1.Tables.Count > 0) Then
        MsgBox("No DataTable to update.", _
            MsgBoxStyle.Exclamation, _
            "Missing DataTable message")
        Exit Sub
    Else
        MsgBox("Preparing to remove x with " & _
            "Connection from Add x", _
            MsgBoxStyle.Information, _
```

```
            "Message from Remove x")
    End If

    'Select row from DataTable in das1 to restore
    Dim drw1 As DataRow = _
        das1.Tables(0).Rows.Find("ALFKI")

    'Restore by removing last character
    Dim int1 As Integer = Len(drw1(1)) - 1
    drw1(1) = Mid(drw1(1), 1, int1)

    'Update Access database file and local dataset
    'row state for found DataRow
    Try
        dap1.Update(das1, "CustomerIDsNames")
    Catch exc1 As System.Exception
        MsgBox(exc1.Message, , _
            "Error message from Update method")
    End Try

End Sub

Function ConnectForUpdate() as Integer

    'Specify a connection to MyNWTables database
    'with User ID and Password specified in
    'text box controls
    cnn1 = ConnectToMyNWTables(TextBox1.Text, _
        TextBox2.Text)

    'Specify SelectCommand and UpdateCommand properties
    dap1.SelectCommand = New OleDb.OleDbCommand( _
        "SELECT CustomerID, CompanyName " & _
        "FROM Customers", cnn1)
    dap1.UpdateCommand = New OleDb.OleDbCommand( _
        "Update Customers SET CustomerID = ?, " & _
        "CompanyName = ? WHERE CustomerID = ?", cnn1)

    'Specify parameters for UpdateCommand
    dap1.UpdateCommand.Parameters.Add("@CustomerID", _
        OleDb.OleDbType.Char, 5, "CustomerID")
    dap1.UpdateCommand.Parameters.Add("@CompanyName", _
        OleDb.OleDbType.VarChar, 40, "CompanyName")
    dap1.UpdateCommand.Parameters.Add("@oldCustomerID", _
        OleDb.OleDbType.Char, 5, "CustomerID"). _
        SourceVersion = DataRowVersion.Original
```

(continued)

```
                'Populate das1 if you have Read permission for
                'database table behind local DataTable object
                Try
                    dap1.Fill(das1, "CustomerIDsNames")
                Catch exc1 As System.Exception
                    MsgBox(exc1.Message, , _
                        "Error message from Fill method")
                    Return -1
                End Try

                'Define a primary key for the DataTable
                das1.Tables(0).PrimaryKey = _
                    New DataColumn() _
                    {das1.Tables(0).Columns("CustomerID")}

            End Function
```

ASP.NET Application Forms Authentication

Forms authentication is a way of requiring a login to a designated Web form before any of the other Web forms at a Web site become available for browsing. The basic idea behind this model is that users cannot view any Web form pages within a site until the login Web form validates the credentials for a user. Forms authentication offers many ways of authenticating a user, including checking credentials in an Access database. Once a user is authenticated via forms authentication, the user can view any Web form page in the Web site for the duration of the session. In other words, after logging into a session at one site, a user can go to another site and return to the site with forms authentication and still view pages without having to log in again—as long as the login session has not expired.

An implementation of forms authentication will typically involve a minimum of three files at a Web site, but it can involve many more files. First, you need a login form. This form should accept login credentials and execute some code to validate the credentials. In validating the credentials, you can reference a table in an Access database. Second, you need to edit the Web.config file within your Web site. ASP.NET automatically creates a version of the Web.config file with default settings when you initially create a Web application with the ASP.NET Web Application template. You need to change the default Web.config file to enable forms authentication. In particular, you need to specify a page to which unauthenticated users will be redirected. If a user initially attempts to enter a site at any Web form other than the login page, they will be automatically redirected to the login page. Another change you need to make to the Web.config file is to deny anonymous login, which is the default login mode. Third, you need one or more additional Web forms. These other Web forms are secured by the login page. If a user attempts to open any of these other Web forms, he is redirected back to the login page.

> **Note** Redirection via forms authentication applies only to Web pages that are Web forms. If you have an HTML page at a site, a user can browse the Web page without redirection to a login page, even if the login form has not authenticated the user's credentials yet.

Editing the Default Web.config File

To start creating an ASP.NET Web project that uses forms authentication, create a new ASP.NET Web application. I named my sample application Secure-PhoneList because it secures a page containing a list of phone numbers. Open the Web.config file from Solution Explorer. In the Code window showing the contents of the file, scroll down until you see the Authentication section. Immediately below that section will be the Authorization section. Edit the contents of these two sections so that they resemble Figure 13-8.

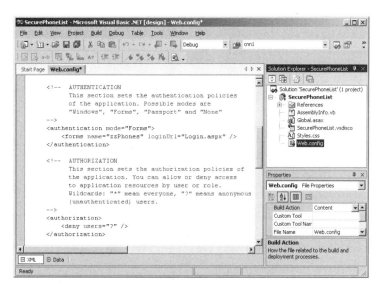

Figure 13-8 The edited Web.config file for the SecurePhoneList Web application project

The opening and closing *authentication* tags in Figure 13-8 bound a *forms* tag within them. An attribute setting within the opening authentication tag specifies *Forms* as the *mode* attribute value. This setting denotes the authentication mode. Note from the comment preceding the opening authentication tag that *Windows*, *Passport*, and *None* are alternative authentication *mode* settings. Within the authentication tags is a *forms* tag that closes itself (/). The *name* attribute designates the name for a cookie that forms authentication uses to track the authenticated status of a user. The *loginUrl* attribute designates the name of the login page within the Web site. This can be any Web Forms page. However, the attribute name is of course fixed, and the attribute is case sensitive.

The edit for the Authorization section has the effect of denying *anonymous login*. Anonymous login is the default way of connecting to Web pages. Enclose a self-closing *deny* tag within the *authorization* tags. By setting the *users* attribute for the *deny* tag to ?, you deny anonymous login. The Authentication and Authorization sections work together to force users to authenticate themselves. The Authentication section specifies the login page, and the Authorization section prevents users from logging into the Web site anonymously.

Creating the Login.aspx Page

Figure 13-9 shows the Design view of the Login.aspx page. The page's design consists of a couple of text boxes, a button, and three labels. The page validates data entered into the text boxes against the Employees table in the Northwind database. The top and bottom text boxes have *ID* property values of *TextBox1* and *TextBox2*. The labels to the left have *ID* property values of *Label1* and *Label2*. *Label3* is the *ID* property value for the label above the text boxes. The button below the text boxes has an *ID* property value of *Button1*.

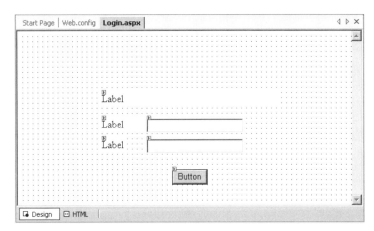

Figure 13-9 The Login.aspx page design for the SecurePhoneList Web application project

The layout of the authentication page should be familiar by now. It has a similar design to several other pages presented throughout this book. However, the code behind the page includes a novel feature because it conditionally invokes the *RedirectFromLoginPage* method of the *FormsAuthentication* class in the *System.Web.Security* namespace. This method redirects the flow to another page. As you will see in the completed solution, the other page and its path are arguments passed to Login.aspx. The role of the login page is to authenticate a user and return control to the page that invoked it. The authentication process creates a cookie to keep track of the authenticated user. As a developer, you can control whether this cookie exists for only the current session or is saved to the user's hard drive. Because users can block their machine from accepting cookies and tamper with cookies if their machine does accept them, there is some merit in not persisting cookies to a user's hard drive.

The code behind the Web form in Figure 13-9 consists of a *Page_Load* procedure and a *Button1_Click* procedure. The *Page_Load* procedure performs formatting tasks for the controls on the page. Because the procedure needs to perform these formatting tasks only for the initial opening of the page, the instructions appear within an *If...Then* statement with *Not IsPostBack* as the condition.

The *Button1_Click* procedure starts by declaring and instantiating *cnn1* as an *OleDbConnection* object pointing at the Northwind database. Next, the procedure declares and instantiates *cmd1* as an *OleDbCommand* object with a SELECT statement that returns the EmployeeID column value(s) matching the LastName and HireDate column values. The WHERE clause in the SELECT statement accepts its criteria from the *Text* property values for *TextBox1* and *TextBox2*. The invocation of the *ExecuteScalar* method for the *cmd1* variable returns the EmployeeID column value that corresponds to the LastName and HireDate column values in *TextBox1* and *TextBox2*. The *int1* variable stores this return value. If no return value exists, *int1* retains its default value of 0.

> **Note**   For the Employees table in the Northwind database, rows are unique by their LastName and HireDate column values. For another table with more employee rows from another database, you might want to redesign the application to use criteria assuring the return of a unique row for any valid pair of criteria values.

The final *If...Then...Else* statement authenticates the credentials input to *TextBox1* and *TextBox2*. The credentials are valid whenever *int1* is greater than

0, the default value for *int1*. When *int1* is greater than 0, the procedure invokes the *RedirectFromLoginPage* method for the *FormsAuthentication* class. You can specify the current user account value (*TextBox1.Text*) as the first argument for the method. The designation of *False* as the second argument directs ASP.NET to leave the cookie in memory instead of persisting it to the user's hard drive. The execution of the method transfers control back to the page that gave up control to Login.aspx to authenticate the user. If the LastName and HireDate column values do not match a row in the Employees table, control passes to the *Else* clause of the *If...Then...Else* statement. In this clause, the *Write* method for the *Response* object indicates that the values in *TextBox1* and *TextBox2* do not specify a valid user. In response to this feedback, a user can try a new pair of values or browse to another page to perform another task that does not require authentication.

```
Private Sub Page_Load(ByVal sender As System.Object, _
    ByVal e As System.EventArgs) Handles MyBase.Load

    If Not IsPostBack Then

        'Assign Text property values to
        'label and button controls
        Label1.Text = "Last name"
        Label2.Text = "Secret"
        Label3.Text = "Enter both a " & _
            "valid last name and secret."
        Button1.Text = "Login"

        'Assign tab order for controls
        TextBox1.TabIndex = 1
        TextBox2.TabIndex = 2
        Button1.TabIndex = 3

    End If

End Sub

Private Sub Button1_Click(ByVal sender As System.Object, _
    ByVal e As System.EventArgs) Handles Button1.Click

    'Declare and instantiate an OleDbConnection
    'object and assign a connection string
    Dim cnn1 As New OleDb.OleDbConnection()
    Dim str1 As String = "Provider=Microsoft.Jet.OLEDB.4.0;"
    str1 &= "Data Source=c:\Program Files\Microsoft "
    str1 &= "Office/Office10/Samples/Northwind.mdb"
    cnn1.ConnectionString = str1
```

```
'Declare and instantiate an OledDbCommand
'object to validate user
Dim cmd1 As New OleDb.OleDbCommand()
cmd1.CommandText = "SELECT EmployeeID " & _
    "FROM Employees " & _
    "WHERE LastName = '" & TextBox1.Text & _
    "' AND HireDate=#" & TextBox2.Text & "#"
cmd1.Connection = cnn1

'Execute OleDbCommand object to validate user
cnn1.Open()
Dim int1 As Integer = cmd1.ExecuteScalar
cnn1.Close()

'If user valid, return control to Phones.aspx;
'otherwise, return a message to the form
If int1 > 0 Then
    System.Web.Security.FormsAuthentication. _
        RedirectFromLoginPage(TextBox1.Text, False)
Else
    Response.Write("Not a valid user.")
End If

End Sub
```

Creating a Secure Web Page

The point of this sample is to make one or more pages that will not open unless a user inputs valid credentials to Login.aspx. This section presents an example of such a page. It does not matter what the page contains—only that the page is a Web form (.aspx). Forms authentication does not secure .htm or .html pages.

The secured page in this sample contains a DataGrid control that the application populates with the FirstName, LastName, and HomePhone column values from the Employees table in the Northwind database. I have, however, tested this sample with simple pages that contain a simple text message. For example, you could use the application to store your passwords for various services. Then, you could access the list from any computer—even while on the road and not directly connected to your LAN in the office. In addition, individuals without the proper credentials would not be able to view the page.

The code for the Phones.aspx page follows. It commences by connecting to the Northwind database and representing the connection with the *cnn1* variable. Next, it uses the *cnn1* variable along with a SELECT statement to specify an *OleDbCommand* object (*cmd1*) that returns the FirstName, LastName, and

HomePhone column values for all rows in the Employees table. Then, the code behind the Phones.aspx page uses an *OleDbDataAdapter* object (*dap1*) to fill a local *DataTable* in a dataset (*das1*) based on the values returned by the SELECT statement for the *OleDbCommand* object at which *cmd1* points. Finally, the code behind the form concludes by assigning the *DataTable* as the *DataSource* property for the DataGrid control on the page. Throughout this process, this page provides a current list of employee home phone numbers from the Employees table. If you had a long list of employees for a company in the Employees table, you could specify some criterion in a WHERE clause for the SELECT statement that narrows the search and reduces the number of return values from the *cmd1* object. For example, you could filter by department, country, or the first letter of the last name.

The point of this sample is not what's on the page. The point is that if a user attempts to open Phones.aspx without first authenticating user credentials for the current session, control passes immediately to the Login.aspx page. The Web.config file specifies this transfer of control by the settings in its Authentication and Authorization sections. If you had more than one Web page other than Login.aspx in the application, as soon as a user validated herself for any other page, she could access all the remaining pages without any need for validation within a session. The authentication of a user extends for the duration of the current session. If the session times out because a user steps away from the computer for a period exceeding the duration of a session (typically 20 minutes), the application requires the revalidation of user credentials if a user tries to reopen Phones.aspx.

```
Private Sub Page_Load(ByVal sender As System.Object, _
    ByVal e As System.EventArgs) Handles MyBase.Load

    'Declare and instantiate an OleDbConnection object
    'with a connection string for the Northwind database
    Dim cnn1 As New OleDb.OleDbConnection()
    Dim str1 As String = "Provider=Microsoft.Jet.OLEDB.4.0;"
    str1 &= "Data Source=c:\Program Files\Microsoft "
    str1 &= "Office/Office10/Samples/Northwind.mdb"
    cnn1.ConnectionString = str1

    'Declare and instantiate an OleDbCommand object
    'that returns the contact info
    Dim cmd1 As New OleDb.OleDbCommand()
    cmd1.CommandText = "SELECT FirstName, LastName, " & _
        "HomePhone As Phone " & _
```

```
      "FROM Employees"
cmd1.Connection = cnn1

'Declare and instantiate a data adapter that
'uses cmd1 to Fill a local DataTable object
Dim dap1 As New OleDb.OleDbDataAdapter()
dap1.SelectCommand = cmd1
Dim das1 As New DataSet()
dap1.Fill(das1, "Contacts")

'Bind the DataTable object to the DataGrid
'control on the page
DataGrid1.DataSource = (das1.Tables(0))
DataGrid1.DataBind()

End Sub
```

Demonstrating the SecurePhoneList Web Application

Initially inputting **http://localhost/SecurePhoneList/Phones.aspx** within a session transfers control to the Login.aspx page in the SecurePhoneList folder on the localhost Web server. Figure 13-10 shows the browser after transfer of control to Login.aspx. Notice particularly the Address box. Appended to the URL for Login.aspx is a question mark and the return URL to which Login.aspx transfers control after a user validates himself successfully. As you can see, the Login.aspx page should return control to Phones.aspx in the SecurePhoneList folder on the localhost Web server.

Figure 13-10   The Login.aspx operational page for the SecurePhoneList Web application project that the Phones.aspx page transfers control to

Entering valid LastName and HireDate column values, such as **Davolio** and **5/1/1992**, transfers control back to the Phones.aspx page. (See Figure 13-11.) Any subsequent attempts to open the Phones.aspx page in the current session succeed without requiring the transfer of control to the Login.aspx page.

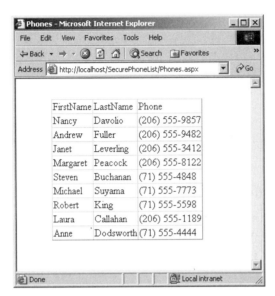

Figure 13-11   The Phones.aspx page for the SecurePhoneList Web application after a user authenticates herself

Summary

This chapter presents three aspects of .NET security. First, it provides a broad overview of major .NET security features. This review exposes you to important concepts and illustrates how the elements of .NET security differ from one another. Second, you learn how to perform secure data access and data manipulation by using ADO.NET and Access user-level security together in Windows applications. The third aspect of .NET security examined in this chapter focuses on Web applications. In a step-by-step fashion, you learn how to use forms authentication to secure the Web forms at a Web site with an Access database.

Appendix

XML for Visual Studio .NET Access Developers

As a Microsoft Access or Microsoft Visual Basic developer, you might be wondering, "Why is there so much excitement surrounding XML?" The answer to that question has more to do with XML's adoption and endorsement by so many industry forces than its features. Nevertheless, XML's features are interesting, and they probably enticed many computing industry forces to develop solutions built with and around XML technologies.

In spite of all the enthusiasm tool developers have for XML, many application developers have little to no XML background. These application developers are not lazy. They are just busy performing the practical, everyday tasks that make computers an essential part of the world's economy. If you are an application developer with limited XML experience, this appendix is for you. Although the presentation starts with the basics, the content includes coverage of how to accomplish meaningful tasks with XML.

This appendix has four sections. First, it introduces you to XML design features. The two primary goals of this section are to acquaint you with the Microsoft Visual Studio .NET XML Designer and familiarize you with the difference between elements and attributes. Next, the focus shifts to schemas. This section shows you how to create, edit, and use schemas for simple tables. You will be pleasantly surprised by how easy and valuable these techniques are. Third, we will examine using XML documents and schemas with Visual Basic .NET. This section closes with a sample that populates an ADO.NET dataset from an XML document. The fourth and final section shows you how to graphically create a *Relation* object indicating a parent-child link in a schema for two *DataTable* objects. Then, the sample demonstrates how to use the graphically created *Relation* object programmatically.

XML Document Design

This section has two primary goals. First, you will learn about the XML Designer in Visual Studio .NET, including how to create a new XML document and populate that document with tags. Second, the section shows you how to create and read XML documents with both element-centric and attribute-centric designs.

XML Document Features

XML documents are merely text with tags to delimit strings. The fact that XML documents are comprised of text means that you can read and understand them without any special interpreter. The tags in XML documents make them easier to interpret than other kinds of text documents because the XML tags highlight particular kinds of values in a text document. If you have ever tried to read a text file that contains information for many columns with few or no delimiters and no meaningful delimiters, you will understand the value of using tags to highlight various kinds of text data. In the same way that tags make it easy for humans to read XML documents, they make it easy for computers to parse the data from an XML document into a database. In addition, industry forces such as the World Wide Web Consortium (*http://www.w3.org*) have promulgated standards to make processing data in XML documents even easier. These standards define and support XML. Furthermore, many of these standards are implemented in XML syntax, which makes understanding them easier once you learn the basics of XML.

When using XML documents to represent table data, it is normal to use tags to mark column values. Developers commonly refer to tags as *elements*. The element names can denote the column names in a table. The values that reside within elements can have types, just as the column values in a table can have data types. XML standards define a large set of built-in primitive types. The XML standards also define built-in derived types. Derived types are derived from primitive types or other derived types. For example, *nonPositiveInteger* and *nonNegativeInteger* both derive from the *integer* type. The *integer* type, in turn, derives from the *decimal* type, which is a primitive type that can designate arbitrary precision numbers. See the "XML Data Types Reference" section in the Visual Studio .NET documentation for more detail on XML types.

In addition to representing values with elements, you can denote them with *attributes*. Attributes specify properties for elements. An attribute is a matching name and value pair. The name designates the property name, and the value specifies the property value. In the context of representing database tables, attributes can represent column names and their corresponding values for an element designating a row in a table. Although standard practices are moving away from representing data values with attributes, it is still common to find attributes in XML documents. Attributes are particularly convenient for denoting properties of an element. Although elements can contain child elements, attributes do not have this capability. Instead, attributes relate to a single tag or element that they modify.

Creating an Element-Centric XML Document

You can start to create an XML document within a Visual Studio .NET project by choosing Project, Add New Item. Then, select XML File from the Templates collection in the dialog box. You can optionally assign a custom name. Otherwise, names in a project folder have default names, such as XMLFile1.xml and XMLFile2.xml. All the files for this appendix reside in a Microsoft Windows application project named XMLSamples.

If you accept the default name and click Open, Visual Studio .NET presents the shell for an XML document (XMLFile1.xml) in a designer containing XML and Data tabs in its lower left corner. Clicking the Data tab for an empty document presents a message stating that the document is not well formed because it is missing a root element. To correct this problem, switch back to the XML tab. Then, type any uniquely named tag within angle brackets (<>). The XML Designer responds by entering a matching closing tag (one with a leading slash, or /). XML documents require a unique element within which all other elements reside. You can name this element anything you want. I chose *Root*. Within your root element, you can enter other elements, such as those for rows and those for columns within rows.

The following XML document represents the values from the Shippers table in the Northwind database. Notice that the document starts with a declaration that it is an XML document. In fact, it is a version 1.0 XML document, and it uses the utf-8 coding convention for converting characters to byte streams. Visual Studio .NET inserted this declaration as a result of selecting the XML File template. Beginning (<?) and ending (?>) delimiters mark the start and end of the declaration.

Notice that the remainder of the document appears in a hierarchical arrangement. The unique *Root* element appears at the top level. The document contains three pairs of *Shippers* elements—one for each row. Within each pair of *Shippers* elements are three more pairs of tags. These tags mark the values for individual columns. Although common, it is not mandatory to represent XML tags hierarchically. In any event, nearly all starting tags have an ending tag, unless a single tag denotes both a start and an end for an element (in which case, the element ends with />). When a single tag denotes an element, the tag can represent values through its attribute settings.

```
<?xml version="1.0" encoding="utf-8" ?>
<Root>
    <Shippers>
        <ShipperID>1</ShipperID>
        <CompanyName>Speedy Express</CompanyName>
        <Phone>(503) 555-9831</Phone>
    </Shippers>
    <Shippers>
```

(continued)

```
        <ShipperID>2</ShipperID>
        <CompanyName>United Package</CompanyName>
        <Phone>(503) 555-3199</Phone>
    </Shippers>
    <Shippers>
        <ShipperID>3</ShipperID>
        <CompanyName>Federal Shipping</CompanyName>
        <Phone>(503) 555-9931</Phone>
    </Shippers>
</Root>
```

I will return to this document later in this appendix to show you how to do more with it than enter data. For now, close the document and choose to save the changes to the file. One of the main purposes of constructing this document is to introduce you to the XML Designer and to familiarize you with an element-centric layout for an XML document.

Creating an Attribute-Centric XML Document

Create the shell for a new XML document named XMLFile2. Arrange this XML document with the column values appearing as attributes instead of as elements. Although you will not commonly represent data values as attributes, you will find it useful to become comfortable with attribute-centric documents. The attribute assignments are typical in many kinds of XML documents—particularly schema documents, which the next section introduces.

Start by specifying a unique root tag for the XML document. You can use the same *Root* element specified in the element-centric XML document. You can also designate each row element with a *Shippers* tag, as Figure A-1 shows. Because the column values for a row appear within an element as attribute values, you can close an element with a trailing slash (/). As with the element names, the attribute names are case sensitive. Because no validation exists on this XML document, there is no built-in check for the correct case when entering new rows. However, it is possible to specify that an XML document match a schema. The schema can catch variation data values that do not match the schema for an XML document. The next section demonstrates how to use a schema for this purpose. All column values for attributes appear within quotes. This is mandatory. The quotes requirement does not follow from a schema. Instead, quotes for attributes help to make an XML document well formed. All XML documents must be well formed.

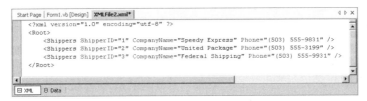

Figure A-1   XML view of an attribute-centric XML document with values based on the Shippers table

XML Schema Design

This section introduces you to XML schemas from two perspectives. First, the section delivers an overview of selected schema design issues, particularly those pertaining to the specification of *DataTable* objects for holding the contents of tables and queries from an Access database. As you learned in the "Schemas for Typed and Untyped Datasets" section in Chapter 9, schemas can define datasets. Next, this section shows you how to create, edit, and use a schema with an XML document, such as one created in the previous section.

Schema Design Issues

XML schemas are to XML documents as database schemas are to databases. A schema is data about data. Programmers typically refer to this kind of data as *metadata*. The metadata defining any given XML schema defines the structure of an XML document. For example, a schema specifies the case for the name of elements and attributes. You can also use a schema to define primary and foreign keys for an XML document representing the contents of a collection of *DataTable* objects in a dataset.

An XML schema is an XML document. Therefore, the syntax conventions that you learned earlier in the discussion of XML documents apply to XML schemas. An XML document that is an XML schema must reference the *http://www.w3.org/2001/XMLSchema* namespace. This namespace defines the XML Schema Definition (XSD) elements, attributes, and types that you can use in an XML schema. The XML schema, in turn, can define the elements, attributes, and types for an XML document. Element definitions within an XML schema can be simple or complex. Within a schema, you can specify simple and complex elements with the *simpleType* or *complexType* tags. A *simpleType* element has neither a child element nor an attribute. In addition, a *simpleType* element always relies on one of the built-in XSD types. Simple types allow you to set attribute values. For example, a simple type can be a variation based on a built-in *string* type. You can use your custom simple type to make a value setting for the string's maximum length by using its *maxlength* setting. A *complexType* element has at least one child element or at least one attribute. A complex type defines a custom (not built-in) type specification for an XML schema. A complex type can contain one or more simple type elements along with one or more attributes.

> **Note** An element in an XML document can have child, sibling, or parent relations to one or more elements in an XML document.

Visual Studio .NET includes tools for automating the creation of an XML schema. Two Visual Studio .NET resources can help you start a schema graphically: you can use a form or the Dataset Designer. The "Jump Start: A DataGrid Sample for the Northwind Shippers Table" section in Chapter 2 illustrates the creation of an XML schema (known as a *dataset*) from a form, and the "Graphically Creating a Dataset with Two *DataTables*" section in Chapter 9 introduces the Dataset Designer. One of the most common uses for the Dataset Designer is to construct a new schema or edit an existing one for a dataset derived from one or more tables and queries in an Access database.

> **Note** Because a typed dataset is an XML schema, the Dataset Designer also facilitates the design of XML schemas. For this reason, you can think of the Dataset Designer as an XML schema designer.

Learning about XML schemas for XML documents that you create in the XML Designer gives you hands-on experience with schema design issues. This experience can help you understand how to read and edit an automatically generated schema based on Access database objects. When using an XML schema with an XML document that you entered yourself, the schema is useful for validating the data in the XML document. In order to validate an XML document against an XML schema, the XML document must reference the XML schema. You can launch validation by choosing the XML, Validate XML Data command within the XML Designer.

Creating, Editing, and Using an XML Schema

To create an XML schema for the XMLFile1.xml document, double-click the document in Solution Explorer. This opens the XML document in the XML Designer. From the XML Designer menu, choose XML, Create Schema. This adds a new file, XMLFile1.xsd, to Solution Explorer. Double-click the .xsd file to open the automatically generated XML schema in the Dataset Designer window. Two tabs in the window's lower left corner enable you to toggle between the Dataset view and the XML view of the XML schema document named XMLFile1.xsd. The Dataset view is graphical, and the XML view is text based.

Choosing View, Toolbox opens a collection of controls that you can use to edit your schema design. Because the XMLFile1.xml document is just a text file, the wizard for creating the schema has no information about special data types or keys that you might want for an XML document. Because XMLFile1.xml is based on the Shippers table, we know that ShipperID should be an *integer* type that is a primary key. However, the *ShipperID* element initially appears with a *string* type, and the element does not serve as a primary key for the document. (See Figure A-2.) Drag the Key tool from the Toolbox to the ShipperID field in the Dataset view of the XML document. This opens the Edit Key dialog box with a suggested name for the key (*RootKey1*) and with ShipperID as the selected field for building the primary key index. Select the Dataset Primary Key check box to designate *ShipperID* as the element on which the document builds a primary key. Leave *Nullable* unselected because primary keys must be unique. Then, click OK. Once Visual Studio .NET returns control to the Dataset Designer, successively click the right side of the cell with the string to the right of the *ShipperID* element name until a list box opens. Use the list box to select another type. Choose *integer* as the type from the box. This completes two settings that you can make in the Dataset view.

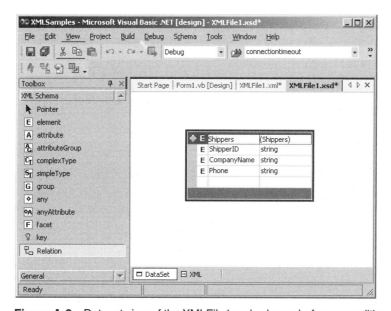

Figure A-2   Dataset view of the XMLFile1.xsd schema before any editing

Click the XML tab to continue viewing and editing the schema. The initial XML schema appears next with wrapping to make it easier to view. This view shows the XML schema for defining the XMLFile1.xml document. Notice that the target namespace for the schema is *http://tempuri.org/XMLFile1.xsd*. XML documents using this schema must refer to that namespace. Also, notice the references to the *xmlns:xs* and *xmlns:msdata* namespaces. These namespaces are the building blocks for the structure of the XMLFile1.xsd schema, much as the XMLFile1.xsd schema is the language for specifying the structure of the XMLFile1.xml document.

```
<?xml version="1.0" ?>
<xs:schema id="Root" targetNamespace="http://tempuri.org/XMLFile1.xsd"
    xmlns:mstns="http://tempuri.org/XMLFile1.xsd"
    xmlns="http://tempuri.org/XMLFile1.xsd"
    xmlns:xs="http://www.w3.org/2001/XMLSchema"
    xmlns:msdata="urn:schemas-microsoft-com:xml-msdata"
    attributeFormDefault="qualified" elementFormDefault="qualified">
    <xs:element name="Root" msdata:IsDataSet="true"
    msdata:EnforceConstraints="False">
        <xs:complexType>
            <xs:choice maxOccurs="unbounded">
                <xs:element name="Shippers">
                    <xs:complexType>
                        <xs:sequence>
                            <xs:element name="ShipperID"
                              type="xs:integer"
                             minOccurs="0" />
                            <xs:element name="CompanyName"
                              type="xs:string"
                             minOccurs="0" />
                            <xs:element name="Phone" type="xs:string"
                             minOccurs="0" />
                        </xs:sequence>
                    </xs:complexType>
                </xs:element>
            </xs:choice>
        </xs:complexType>
        <xs:key name="RootKey1" msdata:PrimaryKey="true">
            <xs:selector xpath=".//mstns:Shippers" />
            <xs:field xpath="mstns:ShipperID" />
        </xs:key>
    </xs:element>
</xs:schema>
```

In the Shippers table, the CompanyName field is required. In addition, the column serving as the index column for the primary key cannot include nulls. Therefore, the elements corresponding to both of these fields can have their *minOccurs* setting changed from 0 to 1. Only the Phone column value is optional in the original Northwind database version of the Shippers table. The *Phone* element consequently can retain its *minOccurs* setting of 0. However, the maximum length settings (in number of characters) for the CompanyName and Phone fields are 40 and 24, respectively. XML schema syntax permits you to designate this kind of maximum length constraint for a *string* type with a *restriction* element nested within a *simpleType* element nested within the original built-in element. Within the *restriction* element, you can specify a *max-Length* constraint or facet for the number of characters. The following excerpt shows the revised formatting for the *ShipperID*, *CompanyName*, and *Phone* elements. The Dataset Designer offers IntelliSense to help with syntax construction, and you can choose Schema, Validate Schema to validate your schema syntax after redesigning it.

```
<xs:element name="ShipperID" type="xs:integer" minOccurs="1" />
<xs:element name="CompanyName" minOccurs="1">
    <xs:simpleType>
        <xs:restriction base="xs:string">
            <xs:maxLength value="40" />
        </xs:restriction>
    </xs:simpleType>
    </xs:element>
<xs:element name="Phone" minOccurs="0">
    <xs:simpleType>
        <xs:restriction base="xs:string">
            <xs:maxLength value="24" />
        </xs:restriction>
    </xs:simpleType>
</xs:element>
```

After verifying your redesigned XML schema, you can close it. Then, open the document that the schema describes. Double-click XMLFile1.xml in Solution Explorer to open the XML document in the XML Designer. Notice that a new attribute appears in the *Root* tag. This attribute designates the namespace for the XMLFile1.xsd schema. The namespace reference indicates that all elements and values in the XML document must conform to the definitions in the schema. Choose XML, Validate XML Data to validate the XML structure relative to the specifications in the schema. If the data you initially entered is valid, you will see a message in the status bar saying that no validation errors were found. Next, change the opening and closing *Phone* tags for the last shipper from *Phone* to *phone*. Because elements are case sensitive, doing so is an error in the specification of the document. If the Task List window is open, an error message (shown in Figure A-3) will appear in it immediately after you change the first tag. The default location for the Task List window is below the XML Designer window. By choosing XML, Validate XML Data, you can generate additional diagnostic information in the window. Without the reference to the XMLFile1.xsd schema, this faulty modification would not raise any error signals. Fix the *Phone* tags for the last shipper and close the XMLFile1.xml document.

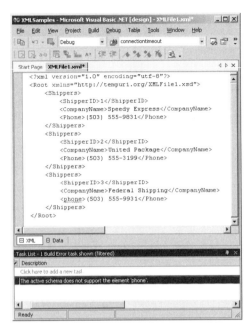

Figure A-3 XML view of the XMLFile1.xml document, with a reference to the XMLFile1.xsd schema, after making an edit to generate an error

Saving, Showing, and Reading XML

This section gives you a hands-on opportunity to process XML documents that you create yourself, have Visual Studio .NET generate, or obtain from a third party. Initially, the section shows how to persist data as XML. Then, you learn how to examine a saved XML document file. The section closes with a sample that populates a dataset based on an XML document.

Saving XML

Start the setup for the XML processing samples by creating a typed dataset named *dsShippers*. As you have learned, a typed dataset is an XML schema that works jointly with the .NET Framework to offer capabilities through class instances based on the *DataSet* class and the XML schema. With Server Explorer open and the Design view of *Form1* for your XMLSamples project showing, drag the Shippers table from the Northwind database connection to *Form1*. After Visual Studio .NET creates the *OleDbDataAdapter1* object pointing at the Shippers table, separately select the object, right-click it, and choose Generate Dataset. In the Generate Dataset dialog box, type **dsShippers** as the name of the new dataset and click OK. These steps add a new file named dsShippers.xsd to Solution Explorer and a variable named *DsShippers1* to the tray below *Form1* that points at the XML schema in dsShippers.xsd. The dsShippers.xsd file is a typed dataset based on an XML schema for a local copy of the Shippers table from the Northwind database. The local copy is a *DataTable* object.

One common application requirement is to persist the contents of one or more tables from a database file locally. This requirement can exist because a connection to a data source is unreliable or because a user is traveling to a location where access to the data source is not available. By saving the contents of a dataset pointing at the Northwind database to a local file in the current project, you make a snapshot of that database available even when you cannot connect to a remote data source (in this case, the Northwind database). The *Form1_Load* and *Button1_Click* procedures work together to persist the contents of a dataset pointing at the Northwind database to a local XML document. The *Form1_Load* procedure fills the *DsShippers1* dataset with contents from the Northwind database as soon as *Form1* opens. Then, when a user clicks *Button1*, the *Button1_Click* procedure transfers the contents of the dataset via the dataset's *WriteXml* method to a local XML document named FromDsShippers1.xml in the root folder of the current project.

> **Note** The *Form1_Load* procedure assigns values to the *Text* property for all three buttons on *Form1*. These assignments help to clarify the role of each button.

```
Private Sub Form1_Load(ByVal sender As System.Object, _
    ByVal e As System.EventArgs) Handles MyBase.Load

    'Fill local dataset from source database
    OleDbDataAdapter1.Fill(DsShippers1, "Shippers")

    'Format buttons
    Button1.Text = "Save XML"
    Button2.Text = "Show XML"
    Button3.Text = "Read XML"

End Sub

Private Sub Button1_Click(ByVal sender As System.Object, _
    ByVal e As System.EventArgs) Handles Button1.Click

    'Write XML representation of dataset contents
    'to a file
    DsShippers1.WriteXml("..\FromDsShippers1.xml")

End Sub
```

You might have to click the Show All Files control on the toolbar in Solution Explorer (once or twice) to make the FromDsShippers1.xml file visible. Double-clicking the file in Solution Explorer opens it in the XML Designer. The XML document's root tag has the name *dsShippers*, and this tag has an *xmlns* attribute pointing at the namespace for the *dsShippers* dataset. The .xsd file for the dataset defines the structure of the XML document in the FromDsShippers1.xml file.

> **Note** The code sample for the *Button3_Click* procedure demonstrates how to assign an XML document, such as the one persisted in the *Button1_Click* procedure, as the source for a dataset.

Showing XML

Clicking *Button2* shows as an XML document in a message box containing the contents for the data source at which the *DsShippers1* dataset points. The *Button2_Click* procedure will fail if the *Button1_Click* procedure isn't invoked first because the *Button2_Click* procedure uses the FromDsShippers1.xml file in the project's root folder as the source for the message box it displays. However, you can generally apply the syntax in the *Button2_Click* procedure to any XML document file. The procedure instantiates an *XmlTextReader* object to make the contents of the XML document available in the *xtr1* variable. Then, a *Do* loop iterates through the XML document nodes to find the first node that has XML markup (for example, a tag). The *ReadOuterXml* method detects this kind of content. In fact, the method returns the markup for the current node and all its children. This is typically the first node after the XML document declaration— the node for the root tag. The document declaration line starts with *<?xml version="1.0"*. Figure A-4 shows the return value from the *ReadOuterXML* method in a message box. If you are working with long XML document files, you might need to show a document in a series of message boxes or use another approach to displaying the XML document contents. Before the *Button2_Click* procedure closes, it closes the *XmlTextReader* object at which the *xtr1* variable points. This frees the object for subsequent use in another process.

```
Private Sub Button2_Click(ByVal sender As System.Object, _
    ByVal e As System.EventArgs) Handles Button2.Click

    'Declare String and XmlTextReader
    Dim str1 As String
    Dim xtr1 As New _
        System.Xml.XmlTextReader("..\FromDsShippers1.xml")
```

```
'Loop to first element that contains XML
Do While (xtr1.Read())
    str1 = xtr1.ReadOuterXml
    If str1 <> "" Then
        MsgBox(str1)
    End If
Loop

'Close XmlTextReader for re-use later
xtr1.Close()

End Sub
```

Figure A-4   A message box showing the contents of a previously saved XML document

Reading XML

The *Button3_Click* procedure populates a dataset based on the contents of an XML document file. The *Button3_Click* procedure creates a *FileStream* object, *fls1*, for an *xtr1 XmlTextReader* object to consume. This technique avoids passing a string directly as the argument to the *XmlTextReader* constructor. A dataset object can directly consume an *XmlTextReader* argument with its *ReadXml* method. The sequence of instructions from the instantiation of the *FileStream* object to the invocation of the *ReadXml* method populates the *das1* dataset with the contents of the XML document at which the *fls1* object points. In this case, the XML document is the XMLFile1.xml file from the "Creating an Element-Centric XML Document" section earlier in this appendix.

After populating the *das1* dataset, the *Button3_Click* procedure calls the *PrintValues* procedure, passing the *das1* dataset and a string for the name of the dataset. This called procedure displays the contents of the dataset, which reflects the contents of the XML document that serves as the source for the dataset. Essentially, the *PrintValues* procedure iterates through the *Tables* collection of the *das1* dataset. Within each *DataTable* object, the procedure iterates through the rows and then the columns within successive rows. Figure A-5 displays the message box presented by the *PrintValues* procedure to confirm the transfer of the XML contents to the dataset. Notice that values appear without XML tags from the dataset.

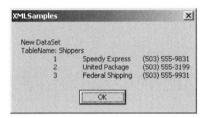

Figure A-5 A message box showing the contents of a dataset populated from an XML document (XMLFile1.xml)

```
Private Sub Button3_Click(ByVal sender As System.Object, _
    ByVal e As System.EventArgs) Handles Button3.Click

    'Open XML document contents into a FileStream object,
    'read the FileStream object into an XmlTextReader
    'object for consumption by a DataSet object
    Dim fls1 As New System.IO.FileStream _
        ("..\XMLFile1.xml", System.IO.FileMode.Open)
    Dim xtr1 As New System.Xml.XmlTextReader(fls1)
    Dim das1 As New DataSet()
    das1.ReadXml(xtr1)

    'Close XmlTextReader
    xtr1.Close()

    'Print out values of each table in the DataSet
    'using the PrintValues function
    PrintValues(das1, "New DataSet")

End Sub

Private Sub PrintValues(ByVal das1 As DataSet, _
    ByVal label As String)

    'Declare variables for looping
    Dim dtb1 As DataTable
    Dim drw1 As DataRow
    Dim dcl1 As DataColumn
    Dim str1 As String

    'Name dataset in message box
```

```
    str1 = vbCr & label & vbCr

    'Loop through tables, and then
    'rows within tables
    For Each dtb1 In das1.Tables
        str1 &= "TableName: " & _
            dtb1.TableName + vbCr
        For Each drw1 In dtb1.Rows
            For Each dcl1 In dtb1.Columns
                str1 &= vbTab & _
                    " " & drw1(dcl1).ToString()
            Next dcl1
            str1 &= vbCr
        Next drw1
    Next dtb1

    'Display message computed in the loop
    MsgBox(str1)

End Sub
```

Relations Between Tables in an XML Document

Creating a parent-child relation between a pair of tables is common in database applications. This section describes how to construct such a relation graphically with the Dataset Designer. As confirmation that the relation exists, the section concludes with a simple Visual Basic .NET piece of sample code. The logic in the sample applies the relation to generate an order history for a customer that pulls rows from an Orders *DataTable* based on a currently selected row in the Customers *DataTable*.

Graphically Creating a Relation Between Two Tables

Graphically linking two tables is a somewhat different process with Visual Studio .NET than with the Access Query Designer. If you try to graphically link two tables in Visual Studio .NET as you would with Access, the process will not work. This section carefully describes an approach to graphically linking tables in Visual Studio .NET. This approach automatically creates an XML schema because the dataset created by the process is a typed dataset.

The sample links local versions of the Customers table to the Orders table. As you will see, this kind of link is convenient for generating an order history for any given customer. Start by creating a new Windows form, *Form2*, in the XMLSamples project and make *Form2* the new startup object for the project. Using a separate form makes it easier to keep track of the projects in the tray below the form.

> **Note**   You can assign a form as the startup object for a project by right-clicking the project in Solution Explorer and choosing Properties. Select the General item below Common Properties in the project's Property Pages dialog box. Click the drop-down box below the Startup Object label, and select an object such as *Form2* to invoke automatically when the project launches. Click OK to confirm your selection and close the dialog box.

Populate *Form2* with its first dataset based on the Customers table in the Northwind database. Instead of naming the dataset *dsCustomers*, name it *dsCustomersOrders*. If you use the drag-and-drop techniques described in the preceding sample with the Shippers table from the Northwind database, Visual Studio .NET creates objects named *OleDbConnection1*, *OleDbDataAdapter1*, and *DsCustomersOrders1*. The *DsCustomersOrders1* variable in the tray points at the dsCustomersOrders.xsd dataset listed in Solution Explorer.

Despite the name for the *DsCustomersOrders1* dataset object, the object represents data from only the Customers table at this point. To add data from the Orders table, we need an *OleDbDataAdapter* object pointing at that table. Dragging the Orders table from the Northwind database connection in Server Explorer to *Form2* adds a second data adapter, *OleDbDataAdapter2*, to the tray below the form. This second data adapter uses the *OleDbConnection1* object initially created with the *OleDbDataAdapter1* object.

Now, the application needs to set up the *OleDbDataAdapter2* object as an interface between the Orders table and the *dsCustomersOrders* dataset. Right-click the *OleDbDataAdapter2* object, and choose Generate Dataset. Instead of clicking the New radio button, click the Existing button to reference an existing dataset. Designate the *dsCustomersOrders* dataset in the current project, which is XMLSamples. In the Choose Which Table(s) To Add To The Dataset box, make sure that the Orders table is selected. Figure A-6 shows *OleDbDataAdapter2* in parentheses after the Orders table to indicate that this data adapter acts as a conduit for the data source to the dataset. Click OK to close the Generate Dataset dialog box.

After specifying a dataset for the *OleDbDataAdapter2* object, the dsCustomersOrders.xsd file has two tables, Customers and Orders. You can view these tables graphically in the schema by double-clicking dsCustomersOrders.xsd in Solution Explorer. Now open or select the Toolbox. Select the *Relation* object from the Toolbox, and drag it to the Orders table. In general, you will add the *Relation* object to the child table in a relation. Visual Studio .NET responds by opening the Edit Relation dialog box. (See Figure A-7.) This dialog box automatically designates CustomerID as the key field from the *Customers* element and CustomerID as the foreign key field from the *Orders* element. Notice that I said *Customers* element and not Customers table. That's because the schema uses an XML element to represent the Customers table from the Northwind database in the dsCustomers-Orders.xsd dataset. For this application, you can accept the other default settings as well. In fact, these settings are robust, so you can accept them in most situations. Click OK to form the relation between the *Customers* and *Orders* elements.

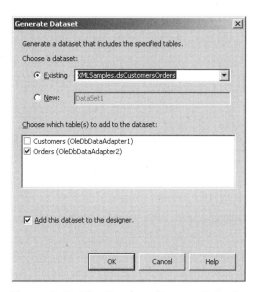

Figure A-6   The Generate Dataset dialog box for adding the Orders table as a data source to the *dsCustomersOrders* dataset in the XMLSamples project

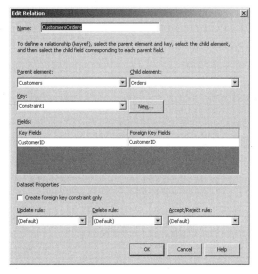

Figure A-7   The Edit Relation dialog box for designating a parent-child relation between the *Customers* and *Orders* elements in the *dsCustomersOrders* typed dataset

> **Note**   The Default selection for the Update Rule, Delete Rule, and Accept/Reject Rule on the Edit Relation dialog box pertains to referential integrity settings. See the "Creating *DataRelation* Objects with the XML Designer" topic in the Visual Studio .NET documentation for additional detail on the settings.

After clicking OK in the Edit Relation dialog box, Visual Studio .NET updates the Dataset view of the *dsCustomersOrders* dataset by adding a connection to depict a one-to-many relationship between the *Customers* element and the *Orders* element. In addition, the XML schema code updates to reflect the relation between the two tables. Closing the dsCustomersOrders.xsd file and saving the changes completes the process of graphically relating the two tables.

Using a Graphically Created Relation

Form2 has a single button (*Button1*) on it. The sample application for using the relation uses the *Form2_Load* and *Button1_Click* procedures. This application generates the history of orders for the first customer in the Customers *DataTable*. With the default primary key index, this customer has a CustomerID value of *ALFKI*.

The *Form2_Load* procedure performs two kinds of tasks. First, it fills the two *DataTable* objects in the *DsCustomersOrders1* dataset from the Northwind database. Even though I have reached the end of the book, I still find it easy to code as though *DataTable* objects magically fill themselves. Of course, this is not the case. Therefore, you will *always* need to fill *DataTable* objects before you can report on their contents. Second, the form load event procedure formats *Button1* by assigning a *Text* property value and increasing the value of the control's *Width* property so that it does not clip the *Text* property value when the form displays.

```
Private Sub Form2_Load(ByVal sender As System.Object, _
    ByVal e As System.EventArgs) Handles MyBase.Load

    'Fill local dataset from source database
    OleDbDataAdapter1.Fill(DsCustomersOrders1, "Customers")
    OleDbDataAdapter2.Fill(DsCustomersOrders1, "Orders")

    'Format Button1
    Button1.Text = "ALFKI Order History"
    Button1.Width += 50

End Sub
```

The trick to using the relation is to understand how the *GetChildRows* method works. This method returns an array of *DataRow* objects based on a row in the parent table. The array of returned rows contains the matching child rows for the selected row in the parent table. In order to complete the specification of the method, you must designate the name of the *Relation* object. The following listing demonstrates how this procedure works. The "Computing Extended Price for a Range of Orders" section in Chapter 9 gives this method additional coverage.

The following listing is simple, but it demonstrates the basics of using a graphically specified *Relation* object. In the declaration area at the top of the procedure listing, the code assigns a value of 0 to the *int1* variable to designate the first row in the parent data source (the first row from the Customers *DataTable*). Next, the *GetChildRows* method populates the *ary_Rows* array with rows from the Orders *DataTable* that have a CustomerID value of *ALFKI* (or whatever the CustomerID value corresponds to in the currently designated row in the Customers *DataTable*). Then, an assignment statement creates a header for a string that populates a message box with the order history. The statement computing the header must appear after populating the *ary_Rows* array because the header refers to the array. A *For* loop iterates through the array and populates the *str1* string with the OrderID and OrderDate column values for each order from the currently selected parent row in the Customers *DataTable*. Finally, a message box presents the results. (See Figure A-8.) By changing the assignment for *int1*, you can generate order histories for other customers.

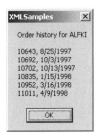

Figure A-8   A message box based on a graphically defined relation that shows the order history for a customer whose CustomerID is *ALFKI*

```
Private Sub Button1_Click(ByVal sender As System.Object, _
    ByVal e As System.EventArgs) Handles Button1.Click

    'Use int1 for target row from parent table (Customers),
    'int2 for enumerator of child rows (Orders), and
    'ary_Rows to hold collection of child rows; str1 stores
    'selected column values from child row collection
    Dim int1 As Integer = 0
    Dim int2 As Integer
```

(continued)

```
Dim ary_Rows() As DataRow
Dim str1 As String

'Compute child rows for int1 value
ary_Rows = _
    DsCustomersOrders1.Customers(int1). _
    GetChildRows("CustomersOrders")

'Define header for MsgBox
str1 = "Order history for " & _
    ary_Rows(0)("CustomerID") & vbCr & vbCr

'Loop through child rows and store selected
'column values in str1
For int2 = 0 To ary_Rows.GetUpperBound(0)
    str1 &= ary_Rows(int2)("OrderID") & ", " & _
        ary_Rows(int2)("OrderDate") & vbCr
Next

'Display selected column values
MsgBox(str1)

End Sub
```

Summary

This appendix introduces you to the basics of working with XML documents and their schemas. Visual Studio .NET has a broad range of tools, including the XML Designer and the Dataset Designer, for managing XML documents. These tools make it relatively easy to perform typical kinds of tasks with XML that leverage your Visual Basic .NET and Access database design skills.

Index

Rick Dobson

Rick Dobson is the author of the Microsoft Press titles *Programming Microsoft Access Version 2002* and *Programming Microsoft SQL Server 2000 with Microsoft Visual Basic .NET*. He is the founder and chief technologist of CAB. He has more than a dozen years' experience delivering professional computer services and is an accomplished author, speaker, and developer. His work has appeared in many publications, including *Byte, Microsoft Office & Visual Basic for Applications Developer, DBMS, Visual Basic Developer, Microsoft Web Developer, Visual Developer,* and *Smart Computing*. He has led training classes in the United States and abroad, teaching developers from companies including Proctor & Gamble, Bell Laboratories, and Cincinnati Gas & Electric.

Since 1999, Rick's company has sponsored its own national tour. Over the years, the content of the tours changed to reflect Rick's books as well as the most recent releases from Microsoft. His 2002 tour was entitled "The Access/SQL Server/VB.NET Development Seminar." The seminar tour attracts independent as well as corporate developers. Among the corporate developers, attendees came from organizations such as Bank of America, Ford, DaimlerChrysler, State Farm Insurance, Prudential, EDS, the U.S. Navy, the Michigan Department of Natural Resources, PACCAR Corporation, and Panasonic. These annual seminars provide Access developers, SQL Server developers, and database administrators the information they require to deliver better solutions to their clients, as well as helping Visual Basic developers put Visual Basic .NET to use for database applications. For specific locations and registration for the next seminar tour, visit *http://www.programmingmsaccess.com/*.

Piston Ring Installer

It's easy to install and remove piston rings with the amazing *piston ring installer*. Tapered jaws support the piston ring, allowing you to remove and install most rings ranging in size from 3/64 inch to 1/4 inch for passenger cars and light trucks. The installer includes a special mechanism to hold it in a locked position. This tool saves you time and money by preventing breakage—just like programming Microsoft Access with Microsoft Visual Basic .NET.

At Microsoft Press, we use tools to illustrate our books for software developers and IT professionals. Tools very simply and powerfully symbolize human inventiveness. They're a metaphor for people extending their capabilities, precision, and reach. From simple calipers and pliers to digital micrometers and lasers, these stylized illustrations give each book a visual identity and add personalty to the series. With tools and knowledge, there's no limit to creativity and innovation. Our tagline says it all: *the tools you need to put technology to work*.

The manuscript for this book was prepared and galleyed using Microsoft Word. Pages were composed by Microsoft Press using Adobe FrameMaker+SGML for Windows, with text in Garamond and display type in Helvetica Condensed. Composed pages were delivered to the printer as electronic prepress files.

Cover Designer:	Methodologie, Inc.
Interior Graphic Designer:	James D. Kramer
Principal Compositor:	Gina Cassill
Electronic Artist:	Michael Kloepfer
Principal Copyeditor:	Michelle Goodman
Indexer:	Seth Maislin

Get a **Free**
*e-mail newsletter, updates,
special offers, links to related books,
and more when you*

register on line!

Register your Microsoft Press® title on our Web site and you'll get
a FREE subscription to our e-mail newsletter, *Microsoft Press Book
Connections.* You'll find out about newly released and upcoming books
and learning tools, online events, software downloads, special offers
and coupons for Microsoft Press customers, and information about
major Microsoft® product releases. You can also read useful additional
information about all the titles we publish, such as detailed book
descriptions, tables of contents and indexes, sample chapters, links to
related books and book series, author biographies, and reviews by other
customers.

Registration is easy. Just visit this Web page and fill in your information:

http://www.microsoft.com/mspress/register

Microsoft

Proof of Purchase

Use this page as proof of purchase if participating in a promotion or rebate offer on
this title. Proof of purchase must be used in conjunction with other proof(s) of
payment such as your dated sales receipt—see offer details.

Programming Microsoft® Visual Basic® .NET for Microsoft Access Databases

0-7356-1819-4

CUSTOMER NAME

Microsoft Press, PO Box 97017, Redmond, WA 98073-9830